Travel in the
United States

GEOGRAPHY AND TRAVEL INFORMATION GUIDE SERIES

Series Editors: Alberta Auringer Wood, Head, Information Services Division, Library, Memorial University of Newfoundland, St. Johns and Clifford H. Wood, Assistant Professor, Department of Geography, Memorial University of Newfoundland, St. Johns

Also in this series:

HISTORICAL GEOGRAPHY OF THE UNITED STATES AND CANADA—*Edited by Ronald E. Grim**

REMOTE SENSING OF EARTH RESOURCES—*Edited by M. Leonard Bryan*

TRAVEL IN ASIA—*Edited by Neal Edgar and Wendy Ma**

TRAVEL IN CANADA—*Edited by Nora Corley Murchison**

TRAVEL IN OCEANIA, AUSTRALIA, AND NEW ZEALAND—*Edited by Robert E. Burton*

*in preparation

The above series is part of the

GALE INFORMATION GUIDE LIBRARY

The Library consists of a number of separate series of guides covering major areas in the social sciences, humanities, and current affairs.

General Editor: Paul Wasserman, Professor and former Dean, School of Library and Information Services, University of Maryland

Managing Editor: Denise Allard Adzigian, Gale Research Company

Travel in the United States

A GUIDE TO INFORMATION SOURCES

Volume 3 in the Geography and Travel Information Guide Series

Joyce A. Post

Index Supervisor
Aretê Publishing Company

Jeremiah B. Post

Map Librarian
Free Library of Philadelphia

Gale Research Company
Book Tower, Detroit, Michigan 48226

Library of Congress Cataloging in Publication Data

Post, Joyce A.
　　Travel in the United States.

　　(Geography and travel information guide
series ; v. 3)
　　Includes indexes.
　　1. United States—Description and travel--1960-
--Bibliography.　2. Tourist trade—United States—
Bibliography.　I. Post, Jeremiah Benjamin, 1937-
II. Title.　III. Series.
Z1245.P67　[E169.02]　016.9173′04927　　81-4375
ISBN 0-8103-1423-1　　　　　　　　　　AACR2

VITAE

Joyce A. Post is the Index Supervisor for Areté Publishing Company and is in charge of the indexing of the ACADEMIC AMERICAN ENCYCLOPEDIA. She is directly responsible for all the geographic entries and many of the map entries in that index. She received her A.B. from Susquehanna University in 1960 and her M.S. from Drexel University, Graduate School of Library and Information Science in 1961. She was the Research Associate for two studies of information needs and information seeking behavior conducted by the Drexel Library School for the Office of Education. She is also a free-lance information broker and indexer. She has been the librarian at the Philadelphia Foreign Trade Library, the Pennsylvania State Law Library, and the Free Library of Philadelphia's Reader Development Program. She is the compiler of the TV GUIDE 25 YEAR INDEX, BY AUTHOR AND SUBJECT (Triangle Publications), the index to THE PRIVATE LIBRARY for 1957-77 (Private Libraries Association), is a joint author of THE INFORMATION-POOR IN AMERICA (Scarecrow Press), and has contributed articles to SPECIAL LIBRARIES and THE INDEXER. She is presently serving on the Board of Directors of the American Society of Indexers and is on the committee to choose the H.W. Wilson Award for the Best Index of the Year.

Jeremiah B. Post is the Map Librarian at the Free Library of Philadelphia. In addition to administering the Map Collection, he is responsible for the selection of materials in the areas of map librarianship, cartography, and travel. He received his A.B. from the University, Graduate School of Library Service in 1961. Some of his publications include AN ATLAS OF FANTASY, rev. ed. (N.Y.: Ballantine Books, 1979); "Historical Map Research" in LIBRARY TRENDS, Winter 1981; "Cities of Wonder: Mythological and Fantasy Cities" (to be published in a catalogue issued by the Cooper-Hewitt Musuem); "Maps and Related Materials on South Asia at the Free Library of Philadelphia" in the Special Libraries Association, Geography and Map Division BULLETIN, December 1980; the introduction to the Dover reprint of Nordenskiold's FACSIMILE-ATLAS (New York: Dover Publications, 1973); and he was the Issue Editor for a special issue on map librarianship of the DREXEL LIBRARY QUARTERLY, October 1973. He has conducted seminars on map librarianship for the Drexel University School of Library and Information Science, has spoken at numerous map workshops, and has presented papers at the annual meetings of the Special Libraries Association, Geography and Map Division. He has served as the Chairman of the Special

Libraries Association, Geography and Map Division and has recently been appointed the Official Liaison between that organization and the newly established Map and Geography Round Table of the American Library Association.

CONTENTS

HOW TO USE THIS INFORMATION GUIDE

The overall arrangement of this information guide is from the large geographic areas to the small. Within the format, the arrangement is from the traditional printed guide materials to the more untraditional sources a traveler might utilize. The opening section on source materials describes bibliographies, directories, encyclopedias, indexes, book stores and services, etc. of use in locating US travel materials.

The US section includes those guidebooks that cover the entire country in either a single title or, as with the Fodor and Mobil guides, a multivolume set or series. Also included here are those magazines devoting all or some of their coverage to US travel, general publishers with a strong travel output, and general organizations providing information of use to the traveler in this country. Data on all the major airlines, automobile clubs and touring services, bus companies, campground chains, car rental firms, hotel/motel chains, and trains are also included.

Regional guidebooks not issued as part of an overall US set are presented in four sections: Northeast, South, Central, and West. We've chosen just four regions to minimize the overlapping of boundaries that inevitably occur when trying to group together such geographic guides, all of which are apt to have defined their areas differently. Even so, some overlaps have still occurred. The Old West Trail Foundation (C-18) for example issues an annual vacation guide to the states of North and South Dakota, Nebraska and Montana. This book will be found in our Central section, since three of the four states are in our Central region. It will not be found in the West section even though that is the key word in the name of the organization.

Individual state sections form the bulk of this information guide and the material for each is presented in a consistent format as follows:

    Books, Atlases, Magazines
    Maps
    Specialized Publishers
    Major Tourist Organization(s)
    Regional Tourism Associations

Other Organizations
Information Centers/Information Phones
Outdoor Recreation Activities
    Bicycling
    Canoeing and Boating
    Fishing and Hunting
    Winter Activities
National/State Parks/Forest, etc.
Individual Cities or Areas
    Printed Guide Materials
    Organizations

General printed guidebooks and other similar materials on the state as a whole are followed by a paragraph describing the general maps for the state. Almost every state has an official map prepared by its department of highways and available either from it directly or through other state agencies. These maps usually have city inset maps, mileage tables, addresses and phone numbers of local state police offices, and interstate strip maps in addition to the regular highway map. In describing these maps we assume the above features and describe only the additional data found on each.

The section on maps is followed by a list of those publishers, if any, with specialized guides to the state. The mailing address, the telephone number, if known, and a brief description of the types of publications issued are provided. A publisher is included if it issues worthwhile material in some quantity dealing with the state. Publishers are also listed in the general US and the four regional sections when they issue a large number of corresponding travel guides. Large, well-known, major publishers whose occasional travel guides are not part of a series or who do not stress travel guides in their output, and who have good bookstore distribution are generally omitted from the publisher lists.

Three parts devoted to organizations promoting travel to the state follow. First is the major tourist organization which is nearly always an official agency of the state. We've attempted to present a rather detailed picture of what literature and services are available from each, but to conserve space we have mentioned each of their publications only once. If they issue a guide to winter sports, for example, it will be mentioned only in the outdoor recreation activities part dealing with winter activities.

Some states have very strong regional tourism associations promoting travel within the state that are independent of both the major state tourism agency and the local chambers of commerce. Others have tourism regions but no separate organizations to which to write. Still others will simply send a list of the local chambers of commerce if you inquire about their regional promotion efforts. A statement regarding this will be found in the part headed "Regional Tourism Associations."

The third part, "Other Organizations," notes hotel/motel organizations issuing directories (these list only those hotels/motels whose owners are members of the organization), local outing groups, and any other organizations that might be potential sources of information for the traveler. We've purposely omitted one category of organization: the state campground owners associations, most of whom also issue an annual campground directory (again only of those whose owners are members). Because the address for obtaining the directory changes frequently, often every year, with the election of new officers, we experienced little success in having our requests forwarded. Often the official state tourist agency can supply the directory.

The "Information Centers/Information Phones" part is a paragraph describing where information on highway information centers may be found. The number of the state toll-free travel information phone, if there is one, is also included. Not all such numbers are listed here though; those available for specific cities, for example, are with the city. Every telephone number is potentially an information phone and most appear with their organization rather than in this part.

The "Outdoor Recreation Activities" part describes mostly nonbook material available on where to go bicycling, canoeing and boating, fishing and hunting, and engage in winter activities. Most books in these categories appear in the beginning part with the other books on the state. However, cross references to these books appear with each discussion in this part. The reader will notice there are no separate categories for hiking and camping. We discovered that this type of information is so directly interrelated to both what is distributed by the individual park and forest agencies and the general outdoors guides listed in the first part that it was redundant to list it separately here. Instead, the next part "National/State Parks/Forests, etc." should be consulted as well as the general hiking and outdoors guides under "Books, Atlases, Magazines."

The "National/State Parks/Forests, etc." part lists first those areas in the state administered by the National Park Service that were considered by us to have enough popular appeal and/or recreation opportunity to justify individual mention. All materials for one national park, monument, etc. are treated together (books are listed first, followed by the principal information-issuing agency, usually the office of the park superintendent) before moving on to a second area. Following these listings of national park areas the reader will find descriptions of information available from the national forests, state parks, state forests agencies, and, in the case of the western states, the Bureau of Land Management state offices.

Important cities and/or areas appear in the last part. They appear in alphabetical order, and all sources (printed information appears first, then the data for organizations) for one city are given before going on to a second. The capital city, regardless of how obscure, has been included for each state because a significant number of travelers are forced to go there on business. Often the only information source for these out the way places is the local chamber of commerce.

The information presented in the final chapter on the US travel industry has, to our knowledge, never before been compiled. The source materials listed here are the ones to consult when studying the industry and include regularly issued statistical surveys of the US travel market, bibliographies of tourism studies, state of the art reviews, surveys of state travel offices, directories, yearbooks, etc. The magazines listed are the ones to read for day-to-day news about the industry. The publishers are those specializing in putting out the daily working tools of the industry. The organizations are those to which persons in the industry belong.

Each individual entry begins with a two-part item number. For the state chapters the letter part is the two-letter state abbreviation created for each state by the U.S. Postal Service and already widely used. We have also used these throughout this information guide both where addresses are given and in the text. For material covering the US as a whole, the two-letter abbreviation US has been chosen; and for each of the four regions the obvious one-letter code is used: N for Northeast, S for South, C for Central, and W for West. For items listed in the two nongeographic chapters on source materials and the travel industry, the respective abbreviations SM and TI are used. A table of these abbreviations follows this section. The second part of the two-part item number is simply a consecutive numbering of the items within that chapter.

The use of this letter-number combination serves to instantly put any reference within its geographic framework or, in the case of the two nongeographic chapters, to indicate the nature of the material. This is especially useful in the subject index where there may be as many as a hundred or more item numbers under any one term. For example, the user interested in canoeing in North Carolina can turn to canoeing in the subject index and quickly locate just those entry numbers beginning with NC. This self-indexing factor will save the user much flipping back and forth between index and text before he uncovers those items that fall within the geographic area of interest.

Not all items or organizations mentioned in the text have been given their own item numbers. These include government agencies that do not issue travel information as their chief function, titles of publications and/or names of organizations mentioned only in the text or in an annotation, and regional tourism associations that are not indexed.

The citation for books is fairly straightforward. The author(s) or editor(s) is (are) given first. If the work is known mostly by its title and/or has different editors over the years, the title is given first. The place of publication, publisher, and publication date follow the title. The complete address of a publisher is included at this point if it is an obscure organization, and we have been able to verify their address. If applicable, the name of the series to which a book belongs, and information about edition and/or frequency of issue is also given.

In describing the various types of illustrative matter in a publication we have noted first what is the most important, either most closely integrated with the text or the most useful in our opinion. In our annotations we have tended to use the terms "quadrangle," "U.S. Geological Survey map," and "topographic map" interchangeably. A topographic map is one which indicates the ups and downs--the hills and valleys--of the countryside depicted. The most commonly available topographic map is the 7 1/2-minute quadrangle issued by the U.S. Geological Survey (SM-25) which covers an area generally of about 6 1/2 miles by 9 miles at a scale of 2 1/2 inches on the map representing about one mile on the ground.

ISBN and LC numbers are included when available. Many of the titles are available both in hardbound and paper editions. This means that there are two different ISBN numbers for each edition. In this case we have given the number of the hardbound edition.

This information guide has six indexes (Author, Title, Subject, Geographic, Organization, and Publisher) and the reader is strongly urged to make use of them. Much of the included material has, of necessity, been arbitrarily placed in one section, but it contains valuable information for the person looking in another only. This is particularly true with the regional material. For example, the Northeast section lists a book on where to go with the kids in New York, Connecticut, and New Jersey. All the individual state guides to hiking the Appalachian Trail are mentioned only once in the entry describing the Appalachian Trail Conference (N-55) that appears in the Northeast section. Yet both of these items will be indexed under all of the states covered in their contents.

TABLE OF ABBREVIATIONS

AK	Alaska	MA	Massachusetts	OR	Oregon
AL	Alabama	MD	Maryland	PA	Pennsylvania
AR	Arkansas	ME	Maine	RI	Rhode Island
AZ	Arizona	MI	Michigan	S	South
C	Central	MN	Minnesota	SC	South Carolina
CA	California	MO	Missouri	SD	South Dakota
CO	Colorado	MS	Mississippi	SM	Source Material
CT	Connecticut	MT	Montana	TI	Travel Industry
DC	District of Columbia	N	Northeast	TN	Tennessee
DE	Delaware	NC	North Carolina	TX	Texas
FL	Florida	ND	North Dakota	US	United States
GA	Georgia	NE	Nebraska	UT	Utah
HI	Hawaii	NH	New Hampshire	VA	Virginia
IA	Iowa	NJ	New Jersey	VT	Vermont
ID	Idaho	NM	New Mexico	W	West
IL	Illinois	NV	Nevada	WA	Washington
IN	Indiana	NY	New York	WI	Wisconsin
KS	Kansas	OH	Ohio	WV	West Virginia
KY	Kentucky	OK	Oklahoma	WY	Wyoming
LA	Louisiana				

ACKNOWLEDGMENTS

In any work of this sort, the compilers owe a debt of gratitude to many people. In the category of "those too numerous to mention by name" are colleagues, authors, publishers, people in the travel industry (both the public and private sectors), and friends whose help and free materials, both solicited and unsolicited, aided us in producing this work. To Dan and Lee Cragg of Arlington, VA for letting us camp in their home while we pursued innumerable guides at the Library of Congress, we owe a debt which can only be erased by reciprocal visits. To that most patient and understanding of children, our son Jonathan, we owe our thanks and love for uncomplainingly letting us visit bookstores to write up guidebooks, make long trips out of town, and hide in our rooms while we worked on this book. While the display racks of many bookstores provided us with examination copies of new guidebooks, the management of the B. Dalton bookstore in Philadelphia deserves our special thanks for allowing us to spend days sitting in their browsing area writing up stacks of guidebooks. At the Library of Congress our debt is both to individuals and to sections: the staff of the Reading Room (particularly James Gilreath) was most helpful; Steve Herman's anonymous deck attendants diligently brought us piles of books from the stacks; a large portion of the staff of the Geography and Map Division helped us at one time or another; and without SCORPIO, the automated on-line catalog, it would have taken us several more months to assemble our data. The Interlibrary Loan Department at the Free Library of Philadelphia (especially Bo) literally searched the country for copies of elusive books for us to examine. Our debt to those good people, and to the cooperative libraries which sent copies, is immense.

INTRODUCTION

The amount of literature and information available to the person wishing to travel in the US is staggering. More and more people are traveling for more and more reasons. One person will fly across the country for a week in a big city; another will pack up the camper for two weeks of boating, fishing, and waterskiing; another will seek solitude in a backcountry trek; and another will go to the mountains for an active week of winter skiing and sports.

We've attempted to include only the information sources that will be of value to most travelers. Even in a book this size we've had to eliminate almost as much as we've included. One writer we came across said that New York City alone "has inspired so many handbooks, directories and guides that a list of them alone would fill a hefty volume."

The reader will not find personal narratives of travel experiences; pictorial guides (all Time-Life books are excluded); guides to flora, fauna, geology, etc.; guides to place names; survival guides for residents (except when they are the only good thing available for an area or when they contain much information a traveler would also find useful); and fishing, canoeing and other guides to individual outdoor recreation activities containing very detailed information for very limited geographical areas.

Guides to cities and areas prepared for special interest groups have usually been excluded. John Fondersmith of the District of Columbia Municipal Planning Office issues a quarterly publication, AMERICAN URBAN GUIDENOTES, which describes current US guidebooks, architectural guidebooks, some foreign guidebooks, and information on guidebook history and collecting, and on writing guidebooks. It may be obtained from American Urban Guides, P.O. Box 186, Washington, DC 20044. Because this publication makes a special effort to include guidebooks dealing with the built environment (architecture, urban planning, historic preservation, etc.), only a few guides of this type have been included in this information guide: those written specifically as a tour guide (a walking or driving tour itinerary, for example) for a well-known area whose architectural and/or historic traditions are its primary travel attraction (Santa Fe, Boston's Beacon Hill, and Williamsburg, VA are three examples).

Introduction

Geographers and geologists are another interest group for whom specialized area guides are frequently prepared. All guides of this nature have been excluded since the American Geological Institute, 5205 Leesburg Pike, Falls Church, VA 22041 recently published their UNION LIST OF GEOLOGIC FIELD TRIP GUIDEBOOKS OF NORTH AMERICA.

Numerous good local guides exist for many other interest groups and we regret that space does not allow listing them. Instead we've included one good overall guide, for example, for the traveler searching for antiques (US-10) and historic places (US-114), the zoo goer (US-76), the stargazer (US-98), the birdwatcher (US-99), the museum goer (US-123), the hall-of-fame (US-154), festival goer (US-183), and the ghost town fan (W-13).

Guides to the US printed in foreign countries and/or in foreign languages have, with few exceptions, been excluded. Most large cities have centers for international visitors that provide language assistance and expedite local arrangements. These have not been individually listed. Instead the umbrella organization for these groups (US-228) from which information on each local center may be obtained has been listed.

Recent studies of the way people seek information show that they usually turn first to a person or organization before they turn to a printed source. Therefore, this information guide has made a special attempt to include, along with the traditional guidebooks, complete information on the convention and visitors bureaus of all major cities; other organizations that specifically promote travel; all major toll-free numbers answering travel requests (a word of caution: these numbers come and go with amazing rapidity); general information about the highway visitor centers network in each state, a phenomenon that accompanied the establishment of the Interstate Highway System; and finally any other unique nonprint travel information sources that we uncovered, such as the CB systems now operating in several states.

We've attempted to include information sources most useful in the vacation planning stage rather than those one would find along the way as one actually travels. Therefore, as in the case of the highway visitor centers mentioned above, exact addresses and phone numbers of such centers have not been given. Instead we've included either that their locations can be found on the official state highway map or have given the address of the state or other agency that will supply a list of addresses.

Nearly all of the guidebooks have been individually examined and the organizations personally contacted for this information guide. Those existing primarily for the travel market and found lacking in quality have been included as a warning. On the other hand, many excellent books have not been included either because they were too specialized or they were not written primarily as travel guides. For those elusive books and organizations that we were not able to track down we've chosen to include, where available, descriptive information quoted from another reputable source rather than no information at all.

By and large, the works listed here are recent publications. The only exception is our inclusion of the Works Progress Administration Federal Writers' Project state guidebooks (the American Guide Series) which are referred to in this information guide as WPA guides. While some of them have been revised, all of them were first compiled around 1940 and, despite their age, are still often the most comprehensive guidebooks available for an area.

Most modern guidebooks have several things in common. They are arranged for quick reference, providing name, address, phone number, season open, hours, admission charges, brief descriptions of points of interest, restaurants, etc. Because of this similarity, many of our annotations may sound repetitious to the person reading this information guide from cover to cover. We're assuming, however, that, like the guides listed in it, it will be used most for quick reference. To relieve some the repetition in the annotations we've sometimes used the phrases "practical information" and "etc." instead of repeating all the who, where, what, when, how much, etc. data. Both in the annotations and in many of the guidebooks themselves, the term "accommodations" means places to eat, places to stay, or both.

A second common feature of many guidebooks is that they are frequently revised. We've made every attempt to examine the latest edition of such titles and have chosen to describe fully the actual copy we had in hand. We indicate "revised annually" or "updated frequently" so the reader will be alerted that there may be a newer editon than the one we have described.

Our sins of omission are infinite, and we've listed only what we've uncovered. For example, an organization contacted in the summer may not have sent us any information about their snow conditions hot line or samples of their skiing guides. It is impossible to keep up with the travel literature. The contents of this information guide will be rather dated by the time it is published, and many of the specific publications listed for the various organizations may no longer be available. However, the general types of material available from them usually does not change much from year to year.

There are many other sources of travel information too numerous to list individually in this information guide. The Sunday editions of most big city newspapers usually have a travel section; the NEW YORK TIMES "Travel Section" is perhaps the best known. These same cities and/or metropolitan regions usually have a monthly magazine containing detailed information on events for that month plus capsule descriptions of all major restaurants. Their titles can be found in ULRICH'S INTERNATIONAL PERIODICALS DIRECTORY (SM-23). Local chambers of commerce are very good sources for information on points of interest, accommodations, and maps. They are all listed in the WORLD WIDE CHAMBER OF COMMERCE DIRECTORY (SM-28). The local centers for international visitors, Travelers Aid Societies, and convention and visitors bureaus will all be listed in the telephone book. If you want to know the best local bike routes and fishing and hunting spots, for example, chances are the area bicycle and sportsmen's shops will stock such guides. The local bookstore will probably have a good selection of maps for the area and most locally produced guidebooks.

Occasionally a syndicated travel series is broadcast on television or radio. In 1978 the radio series "Travel Today" featured up-to-date information on air and sea cruises, walking tours, youth hostel services, etc. Also in that year the Federal Communications Commissions established a new class of noncommercial radio station, the Travelers Information Station. Operating on 530 and 1610 kHz frequencies, they are authorized to transmit information on road hazards, food, gasoline, lodging availability, and other information for motorists.

Nearly every type of outdoor recreation activity has related magazines, and almost all have articles on good places to go to engage in that activity. These magazines are listed in ULRICH'S INTERNATIONAL PERIODICALS DIRECTORY (SM-23). These same activities frequently have local groups that sponsor outings and trips. The ENCYCLOPEDIA OF ASSOCIATIONS (SM-6) lists only the parent body of such groups. They will send you a list of local affiliated chapters, or you can go directly to the local telephone book.

There are several good sources of information available in the local library. The card catalog contains references to guidebooks in a collection under each geographic name with the subdivision "Description and Travel." In large collections this subdivision may be further broken down by the sub-subdivision "Guidebooks" and that in turn, may have a chronological breakdown. The best way to keep up with guidebooks currently being issued by the major publishers is by scanning PUBLISHERS WEEKLY published by R.R. Bowker Co. and the monthly AMERICAN BOOK PUBLISHING RECORD also published by Bowker. The titles listed in the latter publication are arranged numerically by the number assigned to them by the Dewey Decimal Classification System. The range of these numbers for travel in the entire US (except Hawaii) is 917.3 to 917.9; the number for travel guides to Chicago, for example, is always 917.7311, and Washington, DC is 917.53. Once you know the number or numbers for the particular geographic area or areas you are interested in (the librarian can supply these) you can quickly turn to the appropriate pages. For a list of all books of major publishers in print for a given year consult the annual SUBJECT GUIDE TO BOOKS IN PRINT published by R.R. Bowker Co. Look up a geographic area or place with the subheading "Description and Travel," or look up any of the individual outdoor recreation activities under the most commonly used term for that activity.

The compilation of this work was done over a period of several years. The final assembly of most of the material was done during 1978, though, as we had the opportunity, changes and updates were made up until press time.

SOURCE MATERIALS

SM-1   Carlson, Raymond, ed. NATIONAL DIRECTORY OF FREE VACATION AND TRAVEL INFORMATION. New York: Pilot Books, 1978. 48 p. 0-87576-070-8. 78-6456.

Carlson provides a state-by-state listing of names, addresses, and phone numbers of the major state travel/tourism agencies and selected city and local convention and visitors bureaus and/or chambers of commerce. The volume includes the field offices of the U.S. Forest Service, the regional offices of the National Park Service, the regional directors of the U.S. Fish and Wildlife Service, and the district offices of the U.S. Army Corps of Engineers, all of which provide information on their own speciality and locality.

SM-2   CIS INDEX. Washington, DC: Congressional Information Service, 1970-- . Monthly with various cumulations.

This is an index to congressional publications, public laws, and legislative histories which is always published in two sections: a subject index and an abstracts volume. There is a cumulated 1970-74 subject index with individual one volume indexes for subsequent years, and there is an individual abstracts volume for each year beginning with 1970. Monthly subjects and abstracts are issued for the current year. The terms "tourist trade" and "travel" are used regularly in the subject index. This is the best way to find the hearings and other documents issued by each of the subcommittees in the Senate and the House that are concerned with travel: Senate Committee on Commerce, Science, and Transportation, Subcommittee on Merchant Marine and Tourism; House Committee on Interstate and Foreign Commerce, Subcommittee on Transportation and Commerce. For access to documents issued by federal government agencies other than Congress see the MONTHLY CATALOG OF UNITED STATES GOVERNMENT PUBLICATIONS (SM-13).

SM-3   THE COMPLETE TRAVELLER, 199 Madison Avenue, New York, NY 10016 (212/679-4339).

A bookstore specializing in travel materials, The Complete Traveller stocks general and specialized travel guides, foreign language dictionaries, modern and antique travel maps, regional cookbooks, etc.

SM-4 CONSUMERS INDEX TO PRODUCT EVALUATIONS AND INFORMATION SOURCES. Ann Arbor, MI: Pierian Press, 1973-- . Quarterly with annual cumulations. 74-25361.

This indexes those articles from the more popular magazines that provide either some measure of the value of products or services commonly used by consumers or contain much practical information that will enable consumers to make wise choices. It is arranged by these products and services. Section 11 in each bound volume and quarterly issue for the current year covers "Travel and Vacations." How-to and where-to articles are listed, indexed, and arranged by numerous subheadings such as accommodations, river runs, travel and the handicapped, places to visit, and many others. The articles come from such magazines as POPULAR MECHANICS, CHANGING TIMES, BETTER HOMES AND GARDENS, MONEYSWORTH, ESQUIRE, CONSUMERS DIGEST, MADEMOISELLE, TRAILER LIFE, etc.

SM-5 DIRECTORY OF HISTORICAL SOCIETIES & AGENCIES IN THE UNITED STATES & CANADA. 10th ed. Nashville, TN: American Association for State & Local History, 1975. Issued biennially. 434 p. Indexes. 0-910050-15-5. 56-4164.

Arranged by state and community within the state, this book lists the name, address, telephone number, principal officer, size of staff, publications, and programs of each organization; indicates if it is a source of information for the entire state; and notes if it has a historical marker program. Most organizations listed in this directory could possibly supply specific information to the traveler interested in the history of state and local areas.

SM-6 ENCYCLOPEDIA OF ASSOCIATIONS. Edited by Denise Akey. 15th ed. 3 vols. Detroit: Gale Research Co., 1980. Issued annually. 0-8103-0139-3. 76-46129.

This encyclopedia contains a descriptive listing of over 13,000 national trade, professional, and other organizations. The main listing in volume 1 is arranged by 17 large subject categories with an extensive alphabetical and keyword index. A check in this index under the term "travel" will turn up the names of over seventy associations. The secret to using the index is to check out every significant word or term that might be used in describing what it is you are looking for. Remember that this directory includes mostly national organizations and not very many local ones. Volume 2 is in two parts: a geographical index and an executive index. Volume 3 is a periodical supplement of new associations and projects issued in April, July, and November.

SM-7 FORSYTH TRAVEL LIBRARY, Box 2975, 9154 West 57th Street, Shawnee

Mission, KS 66201 (913/384-3440).

This mail-order organization issues 4 catalogs of guidebooks and maps available from them: (1) United States; California; Canada and Alaska; travel games, (2) Hawaii, South Pacific and Australia; Mexico, Central and South America; Orient and Asia; Africa and Middle East; Caribbean; world atlases, (3) Europe; ships and cruises; handicapped travel guides; worldwide travel planners; Berlitz language guides, (4) rail travel guides. The telephone order number is 913/384-0496. They concentrate mostly on the more well-known guidebooks and series such as the Fodors, the Sunset and Mobile guides, and the Rand McNally publications in their US catalog.

SM-8   Goeldner, Charles R. "Where to Find Travel Research Facts." JOURNAL OF TRAVEL RESEARCH 17, no. 1 (Summer 1978): 3-8.

Goeldner lists sources of information available on the tourism, travel, and recreation industries. The article is divided into 8 sections: indexing services; bibliographies and finding guides; periodicals; trade associations; government agencies and publications; yearbooks, annuals, handbooks, etc.; proceedings; and some final suggestions. A summary of the type of information available in each source is provided. This list will also be found in Goeldner's TRAVEL TRENDS IN THE UNITED STATES AND CANADA (TI-4).

SM-9   THE HAPPY WANDERER. Skokie, IL: The Happy Wanderer, (7842 North Lincoln Avenue/60077), Summer 1976-- . Issued quarterly.

Every conceivable world-wide travel destination; type of travel; individual hotels/motels, attractions, etc.; travel products and gear; travel services; etc. appears in this listing of brochures. Each is given a code number, and you can receive any of them free by filling out a postage-paid reader service card. To get on the subscription list call 800/323-1818 toll-free from anywhere in the US except IL. In IL call 312/676-1900 collect.

SM-10 INTERNATIONAL DIRECTORY OF ACCESS GUIDES. New York: Rehabilitation/WORLD, Travel Survey Dept. (20 West 40th Street/10018), 1978. Issued annually. 16 p.

This is an offprint of the first edition of an annual directory of access guides (listing places accessible to persons in wheelchairs) planned to appear in each summer issue of REHABILITATION/WORLD, the quarterly journal of Rehabilitation International U.S.A., a national voluntary agency dedicated to providing services to disabled people throughout the world. This 1978-79 edition appeared in the summer 1978 issue of REHABILITATION/WORLD. It lists a total of 275 currently available access guides; 114 of these are for US cities or states. This offprint also contains an article detailing how the access guide for Dallas was created. Rehabilitation International U.S.A. has a separate "International Travel Program for the Disabled."

SM-11   Jurgen, Jens. 1001 SOURCES FOR FREE TRAVEL INFORMATION: VALUABLE FREEBIES YOU SHOULD KNOW ABOUT. Kings Park, NY: Travel Information Bureau (Box 105/11754), 1978. 144 p. 0-914072-04-8. 78-69811.

A world-wide directory, this volume lists names and addresses of official tourist offices and other organizations from which travel information may be obtained. Telephone numbers are not included although there is a section extolling the convenience of toll-free numbers and describing how they may be obtained. There are other sections giving very practical advice on how to obtain airline and other travel bargains; describing the types of free literature that is available and advice on how to request this literature. A comparison of this book with Carlson's NATIONAL DIRECTORY OF FREE VACATION AND TRAVEL INFORMATION (SM-1) reveals that: (1) Carlson is devoted entirely to the US; (2) Carlson lists phone numbers, including some toll-free numbers; (3) while they both list the official state tourist agency, Carlson lists more local addresses but is limited only to convention and visitors bureaus and chambers of commerce, and Jurgen lists fewer local offices but attempts to seek out those organizations specifically created to provide tourist information in addition to the convention and visitors bureaus and chambers of commerce; and (4) Jurgen supplements the listings with practical advice, Carlson is just a listing.

SM-12   Map Research Co. GUIDE TO FISHING MAPS OF THE U.S.: AN INVENTORY OF FISHING AND STRUCTURE MAPS FOR AMERICA'S LAKES, RESERVOIRS AND OCEANS. Falls Church, VA: Map Research Co. (Box 3113/22043), 1977. 39 p. 77-357299.

This guide is a rather good listing, current as of December 1976, of general fishing brochures and maps plus "fishing structure maps" which indicate depths of bodies of water. A first edition with much room for improvement in later versions, it lists addresses of governmental agencies and private concerns which produce such maps and charts as well as state agencies providing general travel and fishing information. Arranged by state, it notes, with price, which lake and reservoir maps are available and from whom.

SM-13   MONTHLY CATALOG OF UNITED STATES GOVERNMENT PUBLICATIONS. Washington, DC: U.S. Government Printing Office, 1895-- . Monthly with cumulated semiannual and annual indexes. 4-18088.

This is a monthly listing of published government documents arranged by issuing agency. Each issue has an author, title, subject and series/report index. In the subject index you will find references under the headings "travel," "tourist trade," "recreation," "outdoor recreation," and individual geographic names.

SM-14   THE NATIONAL DIRECTORY OF STATE AGENCIES. 2d ed. Compiled by Nancy D. Wright and Gene P. Allen. Washington, DC:

Information Resources Press (2100 M Street NW/20037), 1976. Issued biennially. 646 p. 0-87815-016-1. 76-46708.

Wright and Allen have compiled a two-part directory of the different official state government agencies. The first part is arranged by state and gives the address, phone number, and the name of the chief officer of each of 93 different official government agencies within that state arranged alphabetically and ranging from the Adjutant General's Office to the Workmen's Compensation Board. The second part takes these 93 different categories of agencies and arranges them by each category giving the full information state by state. The categories that would be of possible use to travelers are: "Fish and Game," "Forestry," "Highways," "Historic Preservation," "Parks," and "Tourism."

SM-15   NATIONAL PARK SERVICE MAIL ORDER CATALOG. 2d ed. Washington, DC: Parks & History Association (1100 Ohio Drive SW/20242), 1979. Issued frequently. 81 p. Index.

The catalog is a list of materials, mostly histories, trail guides, guides to native flora and fauna, picture books, and other books in some way related to each of the National Park Service areas. Each title in the catalog may be ordered through the National Bookstore in the National Visitor Center in Washington, DC. Order forms are provided. It is also useful as a bibliography of books about the individual national parks, monuments, seashores, and so forth.

SM-16   Neal, J.A. REFERENCE GUIDE FOR TRAVELLERS. New York: R.R. Bowker Co., 1969. 674 p. Indexes. 0-8352-0227-5. 69-16399.

World wide in scope, this partially annotated bibliography has an extensive US section with state subsections listing major guidebooks, official travel publications, and selected special guides. Its utility is diminished by its age.

SM-17   Nueckel, Susan, ed. SELECTED GUIDE TO TRAVEL BOOKS. New York: Fleet Press Corp., 1974. 117 p. Index. 73-92718.

One third of the 701 entries in this bibliography cover the US but only 25 states and the District of Columbia are represented. It is arranged by 20 large subject topics beginning with "Backpacking" and ending with "Unusual Travel Guides." The format is confusing, the coverage is uneven, and the bibliographic information does not include the publication date. The usefulness of the subject index is limited by the confusing format, and there are no author or title indexes.

SM-18   President's Committee on Employment of the Handicapped. A LIST OF GUIDEBOOKS FOR HANDICAPPED TRAVELLERS. 4th ed. Washington, DC: U.S. Dept. of Labor, 1975. Updated occasionally. 21 p.

This volume primarily lists city guides with price and publishers's address. It is arranged by state (with a foreign section). A revision is being prepared.

SM-19   Schipf, Robert G., ed. OUTDOOR RECREATION. Spare Time Guides, no. 9. Littleton, CO: Libaries Unlimited, 1976. 278 p. Index. 0-87287-123-1. 75-30958.

An excellent bibliography with concise and informative annotations, this volume is concerned with all aspects of outdoor recreation activities with perhaps more stress on how-to than where-to. The arrangement is by activities with separate sections for periodicals and organizations.

SM-20   SEE AMERICA FIRST--ON FILM. Rye, NY: Reymont Associates (29 Reymont Avenue/10580), 1979. [24 p.].

Over 150 16mm color films showing regional, state, and local places of interest are described in this directory. Most of them have been prepared by the various state tourism offices and city visitor bureaus and are available at no charge.

SM-21   TRAILS, Box 94, Collegeville, PA 19426 (215/489-4532).

They publish an extensive catalog (5th ed., 1978. 38 p.) of "guides, maps, books for the backpacker, canoeist and other wayward souls." You can purchase every book in their catalog directly from them, and they will attempt to obtain similiar guides not listed in their catalog.

SM-22   TRAVEL CENTERS OF THE WORLD, 6311 Yucca, Hollywood, CA 90028.

They issue an annual catalog of about 10,000 map and travel items for most parts of the world and seem to have a good coverage of city maps. Travel Centers is a dealer (wholesale and retail) stocking other publishers' material, though one wonders how much is actually in stock and how much must be ordered when your request arrives.

SM-23   ULRICH'S INTERNATIONAL PERIODICALS DIRECTORY: A CLASSIFIED GUIDE TO CURRENT PERIODICALS, FOREIGN AND DOMESTIC. 17th ed. New York: R.R. Bowker Co., 1977. Issued biennially. 2,096 p. Index. 0-8352-0925-3. 32-16320.

Grouped into some 250 subject areas, this is a directory of over 60,000 periodicals of all kinds from all over the world. The main section to use here is "Travel and Tourism." The "Outdoor Life" section includes the hiking, hunting, fishing, backpacking, camping, and skiing periodicals. The "General Interest Periodicals--United States" section cites the names of local and city magazines and periodicals many of which have sections on what to see and do, dining guides, etc. There is an extensive title index in the back.

SM-24   U.S. Bureau of Outdoor Recreation. A CATALOG OF GUIDES TO OUTDOOR RECREATION AREAS AND FACILITIES. 2d ed. Washington, DC: U.S. Government Printing Office, 1977(?). 60 p.

This catalog is a state-by-state listing of outdoor recreation guides published by private, state and federal organizations. The mailing address is given for each guide should the user wish to acquire it. The Bureau of Outdoor Recreation no longer exists. Its functions have been taken over by the Heritage Conservation and Recreation Service.

SM-25   U.S. Geological Survey. INDEX TO TOPOGRAPHIC AND OTHER MAP COVERAGE. Arlington, VA: U.S.G.S., Distribution Branch (1200 South Eads Street/22202). Issued irregularly. 50 plus sheets.

This is actually a series of separate sheets, generally one for each state showing which areas of a state have been mapped by the U.S. Geological Survey. The Geological Survey is the major civilian mapping agency of the US government and produces a variety of different kinds of maps. For the traveler, the most useful are the topographic quadrangle (very detailed maps of small areas showing the terrain with elevations, major buildings, trails, roads, forest cover, bodies of water, and even cemeteries) in 2 sizes (the 7 1/2 minute series at a scale of 1:24,000 or 1 in. represents 2,000 feet or about 2 1/2 in. represents 1 mile, and the 15 minute series at 1 in. represents not quite a mile) and the 1:250,000 scale maps (1 in. represents 4 miles) which shows the terrain in less detail than the topographic quadrangles but still shows small back roads better than road maps. Both are useful for planning trips. The index sheets for each state are revised frequently, but irregularly. The monthly NEW PUBLICATIONS OF THE GEOLOGICAL SURVEY contains a list of new maps and can supplement the index sheets.

SM-26   UNITED STATES GOVERNMENT MANUAL. Washington, DC: U.S. Government Printing Office, 1978. Issued annually. 902 p. Tables. Indexes.

This publication lists government offices and agencies, with addresses of local offices in many cases, giving a description of the function and services of each agency and the address from which to obtain information. Its lists are useful for current officials and addresses of government agencies dealing with travel and/or outdoor recreation.

SM-27   U.S. National Ocean Survey. NAUTICAL CHART CATALOG. Rockville, MD: U.S. National Oceanic & Atmospheric Administration. 5 sheets.

These index maps show which nautical charts depict different areas of the US coastline. Such nautical charts, essential to the boater and useful to the fisherman, indicate the depths of water just off the coast and in rivers and streams emptying into the ocean. The index maps give full ordering information as well as a description of each chart (area covered, scale). Each index is called a "catalog" and they are issued as Catalog 1: Atlantic and Gulf Coasts (including Puerto Rico and the Virgin Islands); Catalog 2: Pacific Coast (including Hawaii, Guam and Samoa Islands); Catalog 3: Alaska (including the Aleutian Islands); Catalog 4: Great Lakes and adjacent waterways; and Catalog 5: Bathymetric Maps and Special Purpose Charts.

SM-28   WORLD WIDE CHAMBER OF COMMERCE DIRECTORY. Loveland, CO: Johnson Publishing Co. (Box 455/80537), 1976. Issued annually. 225 p.

This directory gives name, address, telephone number, chief executive, and population of area served for each individual chamber of commerce. It is arranged alphabetically by state and community (even the smallest), and lists state, regional, and local bodies. Chambers of commerce are often prolific suppliers of good, free information for the traveler.

SM-29   Ziegler, Ronald M. WILDERNESS WATERWAYS: A GUIDE TO INFORMATION SOURCES. Sports, Games, and Pastimes Information Guide Series, vol. 1. Detroit: Gale Research Co., 1979. 317 p. Indexes. 0-8103-1434-7. 78-10410.

This is a very thorough guide to all the reference works, magazines, and other literature (including films); organizations and government agencies; and publishers, book dealers, libraries, and other sources providing information on canoeing, kayaking, and rafting in the US. In addition to sections describing books on technique and accounts of waterways trips (some made as early as 1789), there is a section listing directories of professional outfitters and guides, a 31-page annotated list of waterways guidebooks (arranged by author, with a geographic index), and a 13-page list of map sources.

UNITED STATES

BOOKS AND ATLASES

US-1 ACCESS NATIONAL PARKS: A GUIDE FOR HANDICAPPED VISITORS.
Washington, DC: U.S. Government Printing Office, 1978. 197 p.
Maps. Index. 77-608256.

The guide lists 358 National Park Service administered sites noting
address, telephone number, location and facilities useable by the
handicapped such as width of restroom doors, ramps and elevators,
medical facilities, etc. Periodic updates are planned.

US-2 Airport Operators Council International. ACCESS TRAVEL: AIRPORTS,
A GUIDE TO ACCESSIBILITY OF TERMINALS. 2d ed. Washington,
DC: Federal Aviation Administration, 1977. 19 p.

A tabular presentation, the guide gives "design features, facilities
and services at 220 airport terminals in 27 countries that are important to the handicapped." Airports are listed alphabetically by city
and information given for each includes specifics about parking facilities, getting around outside and inside the airport, elevators, stairs,
interior ramps, doors, boarding, accommodations, rest rooms and
toilets, phones, and other services such as medical and escort.

US-3 AIR TAXI CHARTER AND RENTAL DIRECTORY OF NORTH AMERICA.
River Forest, IL: Air Taxi Charter and Rental Tariff Information Service of North America, (400 Lathrop/60305), 1975. 102 p. 75-
4273.

This directory consists of 2 state-by-state listings: (1) air taxi
operators giving name, address and telephone number and (2) "charter
and rental rates aircraft listings" which give name, address, telephone
number of the operator and the type of aircraft, fees, and services
offered.

US-4 Alegre, Mitchell R. A GUIDE TO MUSEUM VILLAGES: THE AMERI-
CAN HERITAGE BROUGHT TO LIFE. New York: Drake Publishers,

1978. 160 p. Photos. Indexes. 0-8473-1656-4. 77-72399.

The 102 listings, arranged alphabetically by state and community, give the name of the "outdoor museum," location, hours, season, admission fee, and if there are restaurants and/or motels in the area. This is followed by a brief physical description noting background and special features.

US-5   AMERICA: THE DATSUN STUDENT TRAVEL GUIDE. 5th ed. Knoxville, TN: 13-30 Corp. (505 Market Street/37902), 1978. Issued annually. 63 p. Photos.

This looks more like an issue of a magazine than an annual guide, and it is available at student bookstores and/or unions, and at Datsun dealers. It consists of articles on personal travel experiences and descriptions of where to go, all by and for the highly mobile student types.

US-6   AMERICAN EXECUTIVE TRAVEL COMPANION: GUIDE TO TRAVELING ON BUSINESS IN THE 50 STATES. Cambridge, MA: American Executive, 1977. Issued annually. 383 p. Index.

Although this primarily contains business and economic information on the states, 43 "major business cities" are described in greater detail giving, very briefly, weather and transportation information, emergency telephone numbers, brokerage houses, advertising firms, tourist information centers, selected hotels, stores, restaurants, and nightspots. A general US section has a list of major newspapers and periodicals, radio and television stations, and publishers as well as major airlines, principal railways, some shipping lines, and military installations.

US-7   AMERICAN GARDENS: A TRAVELERS GUIDE. New rev. ed. Brooklyn, NY: Brooklyn Botanic Gardens, 1977. 87 p. Photos. Index.

Regionally arranged, the guide gives descriptions of botanical gardens, estate gardens, nature preserves, and commercial enterprises. It also gives hours, admission charges, periods of peak blooms, information about guided tours and educational facilities, and directions. There is a very brief section covering Canada. There is an index by garden name; one by state would also have been useful.

US-8   Angelo, Joseph A., Jr. ENERGY TRAILS: A GUIDEBOOK DESCRIBING ENERGY SITES, POWER PLANTS, SCIENCE MUSEUMS AND OTHER INTERESTING PLACES. Washington, DC: Energy Research & Development Administration, 1976-- . Photos., maps.

Thirteen electrical generating stations (conventional and nuclear), five science museums, two coal mines, and two historic sites connected with energy all open to the public are listed, described (including hours), and located on maps. The first volume covers the northeast US. Other volumes were not yet issued at the time of this writing.

US-9   Annand, Douglass R. THE WHEELCHAIR TRAVELER. Milford, NH:
        the author (Ball Hill Road/03055), 1974. Unpaged.

        Motels, interstate rest areas, restaurants, and tourist attractions are
        rated according to ease of use by a "healthy paraplegic." The
        coverage is uneven, based largely on personal experiences. A 1977
        edition, unexamined by the compilers, has been published.

US-10   ANTIQUE SHOPS & DEALERS, U.S.A.: A COMPREHENSIVE GUIDE
        TO ANTIQUE SHOPS AND DEALERS IN THE UNITED STATES. Edit-
        ed by Evie Doherty and Claire Jarett Roth. New York: Crown,
        1976. 628 p. Photos. Index. 0-517-52721-9. 76-150433.

        This is a handy guide for travelers who like looking for little out-of-
        the-way shops. Shops are arranged by state and then by locality.
        Information given for each includes name, address, phone, date es-
        tablished, hours, types, periods and specialities, and directions.
        There is an index of shops by 17 different specialities from "arms and
        armor" to "toys and automata."

US-11   AOPA'S AIRPORTS U.S.A. 16th ed. Washington, DC: Aircraft
        Owners and Pilots Association (Air Rights Building, 7315 Wisconsin
        Avenue/20014), 1977. Issued annually. 608 p. Maps. Index.

        AOPA provides a descriptive listing of 13,655 landing facilities (air-
        ports, heliports, seaplane bases) both public and private (but not
        military) arranged alphabetically by state giving location (both lati-
        tude and longitude and direction and distance to nearest community),
        field elevation and runway headings, facilities, a chart showing the
        field, and fees. Airport diagrams, rather small, are in a separate
        section.

US-12   Asa, Warren. AMERICAN YOUTH HOSTELS' NORTH AMERICAN
        BICYCLE ATLAS. 3d ed. Delaplane, VA: American Youth Hostels,
        1973. 191 p. Maps.

        Described are 84 regional 1-day or weekend and 88 longer trips
        including mileage, difficulty ratings, and a sketch map. Cycling
        books of small areas and organizations offering tours or their own
        tour maps are added to some of these listings.

US-13   Association for Living Historical Farms and Agricultural Musuems.
        SELECTED LIVING HISTORICAL FARMS, VILLAGES AND AGRICUL-
        TURAL MUSEUMS IN THE UNITED STATES AND CANADA. Washing-
        ton, DC: Smithsonian Institution, 1977(?). 64 p. Photos., map.

        Thirty-two living farms and agricultural musuems are described includ-
        ing hours and admission, special events, directions for locating, and
        an address for further information.

US-14   Atwater, Maxine H. ROLLIN' ON: A WHEELCHAIR GUIDE TO

U.S. CITIES. New York: Dodd, Mead & Co., 1978. 290 p. Bibliography. 0-396-07548-7. 78-15289.

The cities of Chicago, Honolulu, New York, Philadelphia, San Antonio, San Diego, San Francisco, and Washington, DC are discussed at length stressing "accessible" attractions, restaurants, hotels, etc. Very brief mention is made of Boston, Denver, Miami, New Orleans, Phoenix, and Seattle. There is no index, but there is a bibliography called "Travel Information Sources" which lists guides for many places not included in this book. It also has a section arranged by "transportation mode."

US-15   BACK-COUNTRY TRAVEL IN THE NATIONAL PARK SYSTEM. Washington, DC: U.S. Government Printing Office, 1971. 40 p. Photos, map.

Forty-one parks offering "back-country" (not accessible to automobiles) travel are described, briefly noting activities and including a mailing address.

US-16   BAEDEKERS USA. Stuttgart, Germany: Baedekers Autoführer-Verlag GmbH, 1974. 872 p. Maps. Index. 3-87036-280-4.

Although this guide is in German, it is included because of the completeness and reputation of the Baedeker series. The previous US guide was issued in 1909 and was in English; it is hoped there will be another English language edition in the future. The practical information; maps, floor plans and tables; and tour routes for all states, major cities, national parks and other attractions are very concise and thorough.

US-17   Baker, Cozy. A COZY GETAWAY. Washington, DC: Acropolis Books, 1976. 184 p. Index. 0-87491-063-3. 76-15816.

"The traveler with a hunger for the untouristy, unspoiled and unique" will find more than forty getaways in this selection.

US-18   Barish, Jane, and Barish, Mort. MORT'S GUIDE TO LOW COST VACATIONS & LODGINGS ON COLLEGE CAMPUSES: USA & CANADA. Princeton, NJ: CMG Publishing Co. (Box 630/08540), 1978. Updated irregularly. 189 p. 0-9600718-2-2. 74-82872.

The directory lists 180 colleges and universities offering accommodations to nonstudents.

US-19   Baxter, Robert. BAXTER'S USA. Alexandria, VA: Rail-Europe (Box 3255/22302), 1979. 625 p. Maps, drawings. Index. 0-913384-24-0. 77-92700.

This excellent compendium of travel information supercedes the author's previous separate works on travel in the US: BAXTER'S USA BUS TRAVEL GUIDE and BAXTER'S USARAIL PASS GUIDE. The beginning general information is followed by sections on accommodations (YMCA/YWCA, hotel chains, student centers), travel by car, travel by bus, travel by train, travel by plane, and brief US history information. Following this, 45 cities, 23 national parks, 6 resort areas, and 32 "routes through the west" are listed giving accommodations, sights to see, attractions in the area, and other useful information. Addresses and phone numbers for further information are given regularly. We rate this as very useful.

US-20 Birnbaum, Stephen, et al. UNITED STATES: 1979. The Get 'em and Go Travel Guides. Boston: Houghton Mifflin, 1978. 801 p. Index. 0-395-26620-3.

This is an attempt to put practical information in an encyclopedic rather than strict geographic format for the active traveler who wants facts at his fingertips. There are 5 major sections: (1) a guide to vacation planning, (2) a brief almanac of facts and figures for each state, (3) detailed guides to visiting 40 individual US cities (with a section on sources of tourist information for each), (4) a guide to 29 active and/or cerebral vacation themes, and (5) directions for 64 specific driving tours in the country's most spectacular scenic areas.

US-21 Boatner, Mark M. LANDMARKS OF THE AMERICAN REVOLUTION. Harrisburg, PA: Stackpole Books, 1973. 608 p. Maps, photos. Index. 0-8117-0936-1. 73-6964.

Boatner has compiled a comprehensive state-by-state guide to locating and knowing what happened at Revolutionary War sites for scholars, specialists, and sightseers.

US-22 Brandon, Jim. WEIRD AMERICA: A GUIDE TO PLACES OF MYSTERY IN THE UNITED STATES. New York: E.P. Dutton, 1978. 244 p. Photos., drawings, maps. 0-525-47491-9. 77-11641.

Arranged by state and community within each state, this guide attempts to list the major "unusual phenomena" locations. Sometimes the places are natural, sometimes man-made. It tends toward being a guide for the mystically inclined shunpiker, but does offer interesting suggestions of sights and sites not normally noted in guidebooks. The addition of an index would have made this a useful reference book rather than the interesting curiosity it is now; one must know where a weird place is in order to find it in this book.

US-23 Browder, Sue. THE AMERICAN BIKING ATLAS & TOURING GUIDE.

New York: Workman Publishing Co., 1974. 320 p. Maps, photos., drawings. Index. 0-911104-35-6. 75-8816.

This book gives very complete descriptions of 150 regionally arranged bike rides throughout scenic America (including Alaska and Hawaii) giving distance, terrain, traffic, difficulty, best season, places to stay, bicycle repair shops, sources of further information, and a map.

US-24   Brown, Sheldon S. REMADE IN AMERICA: THE GRAND TOUR OF EUROPE & ASIA WITHIN THE U.S.A. Salem, OR: Old Time Bottle Publishing Co., 1972. 384 p. Photos. 0-911068-08-2. 72-79470.

Arranged by state, this book lists, with accompanying photographs, 190 well-known structures in the US copied from or inspired by structures in other parts of the world. Also included are reconstructed rooms in museums. Location, hours, fees, and background information are given for each.

US-25   Butcher, Devereux. EXPLORING OUR NATIONAL PARKS & MONU-MENTS. 7th ed. Boston: Gambit, 1976. 373 p. Photos. 0-87645-094-X. 77-358047.

The descriptions of each park and monument in this classic work are more tributes than guides, giving mostly the history of a park plus its geological, biological, and archaeological highlights.

US-26   Calder, Jean. WALKING: A GUIDE TO BEAUTIFUL WALKS & TRAILS IN AMERICA. Americans Discover America Series. New York: William Morrow & Co., 1977. 340 p. 0-688-03131-5. 77-79232.

This unindexed guide alphabetically lists walks by state and within each state by community. General locations are given along with a rough description, a three-level difficulty rating, hours, and if fees are charged. In spite of the difficult to read typeface, this can be useful if one is in Bemidji, MN, or Ekalaka, MT--but if one wants to look up Itasca State Park or Medicine Rocks State Park, one must know the correct town. Calder's coverage is extensive although superficial, but she does list useful addresses.

US-27   Carlson, Raymond, ed. NATIONAL DIRECTORY OF BUDGET MO-TELS. New York: Pilot Books, 1978. Updated periodically. 56 p. 0-87576-051-1. 75-11992.

This directory lists low-cost chain motel accommodations in 49 states (excludes Hawaii). It also lists headquarters for 30 chains with "800" toll-free reservation numbers where available.

US-28   _____. NATIONAL DIRECTORY OF FREE TOURIST ATTRACTIONS.

New York: Pilot Books, 1978. Revised frequently. 71 p. 0-87576-057-0. 77-3251.

In this volume Carlson provides a state-by-state listing (with addresses, hours, phone numbers) of free museums, gardens, plants, observatories, wildlife and natural history areas, etc. (but mostly museums).

US-29   Cary, Norman M., Jr. GUIDE TO U.S. ARMY MUSEUMS & HISTORIC SITES. Washington, DC: U.S. Army, Center of Military History (distributed by the U.S. Government Printing Office), 1975. 116 p. Photos., maps. 75-619315.

This geographically arranged list of military museums and sites gives travel directions to each location and notes if there is an admission fee. Also indicated is which military service (army, navy, marine, etc.) is highlighted and whether the site is administered by a federal, state, municipal or private agency. Sources of further information are also noted.

US-30   Casewit, Curtis W. GUIDE TO TENNIS RESORTS. New York: Pilot Books, 1978. 31 p. 0-87576-068-6. 78-3402.

A selective state-by-state list of about 250 resorts having tennis courts. Instruction and pro shops have been noted where applicable. The resorts have been graded according to the daily cost of a room plus meals and most of the listing here fall into the "expensive" category.

US-31   Christopher, Bob, and Christopher, Ellen. AMERICA ON $8 TO $16 A NIGHT. 6th ed. A Travel Discoveries Publication. New York: William Morrow & Co., 1978. Issued frequently. 312 p. Sketches, sketch maps. Indexes. 0-688-08321-8. 77-85277.

This title is full of suggestions for economizing. There are 3 main listings: (1) fast food chains listed alphabetically and giving all of their locations, (2) budget motel chains listed alphabetically and giving all of their locations, and (3) a state-by-state listing of budget motels. There are 2 indexes: (1) by state of both motels and restaurants and (2) subject index to the many articles and tips scattered throughout the book.

US-32   CITY MAPS ATLAS & GUIDE. Arlington Heights, IL: Creative Sales Corp. (762 W. Algonquin Road/60005), 1978(?). 246 p. Maps. Indexes.

Creative Sales Corp. makes many of the city area road maps one gets free at rent-a-car agencies. In this volume they compile their state and city maps into an atlas. There are 65 city or metropolitan area maps as well as 20 sectional US maps. There are separate indexes for cities and towns on the sectional maps, suburban communities on the metropolitan maps, car rental agencies (Avis in the copy examined), hotels/motels/restaurants noted on the metropolitan area maps, and major companies' offices located on the metropolitan maps. The index to suburban communities is by metropolitan area and also notes radio and television stations, emergency telephone numbers, major airlines, newspapers, time zone, altitude, and a few points of interest for each area. The maps for the metropolitan areas and the sections of the US are adequate, but the more detailed city maps are better.

US-33   CLOSE-UP, U.S.A. Washington, DC: National Geographic Society, 1978. 16 map sheets and 1 vol. of 208 p. 77-27626.

CLOSE-UP, U.S.A. consists of a boxed set of 15 regional maps of the US and one general map accompanied by a gazetteer. The gazetteer has some weather information (high/low temperatures on a monthly average for selected cities). The regional maps, drawn at varying scales, indicate public lands and general outdoor recreation activities as well as historic sites. The maps also have descriptive text and drawings giving background and history of the regions with travel suggestions.

US-34   Cohen, Marjorie A. WHERE TO STAY U.S.A. FROM 50¢ TO $14 A NIGHT. 4th ed. New York: Council on International Educational Exchange and the Frommer/Pasmantier Publishing Corp. (distributed by Simon & Schuster), 1978. Updated frequently. 312 p. Maps. 0-671-24196-6. 75-8633.

Although it is geared for the student traveler, this work can be of use to anyone. It offers information and suggestions on transportation, books to read, and types of low-cost accommodations ("Y's," dormitories, low-cost motel chains, crashing, etc.). There is a separate section for the foreign visitor as well as a state-by-state listing of cities giving addresses and telephone numbers for accommodations, tourist information, and Travelers Aid and other help agencies. There is no index.

US-35   Colwell, Robert. GUIDE TO BICYCLE TRAILS. Harrisburg, PA: Stackpole Books, 1974. 253 p. Sketch maps, photos. 0-8117-0768-7. 74-4010.

This guide presents 45 suggested itineraries for bike travel rather than a listing of bikeways. Local sources of information, when available, are mentioned. There is a "city-trail" index for sections of the itineraries near 140 cities, but there is no general index.

US-36   _____. GUIDE TO SNOW TRAILS. Harrisburg, PA: Stackpole

Books, 1973. 185 p. Photos. 0-8117-1492-6. 73-11147.
This is a regionally arranged list locating, describing, and evaluating
ski touring and snowshoeing centers in the US.

US-37 _____. INTRODUCTION TO FOOT TRAILS IN AMERICA. Harrisburg, PA: Stackpole Books, 1972. 221 p. Sketch maps, photos.
0-8117-0914-0. 74-179603.

Trail data and maps are given for 81 day or week trails within easy
driving distance of 100 major US cities. Emphasis is on easier
trails and the amount of information given would not satisfy the
serious hiker or backpacker.

US-38 _____. INTRODUCTION TO WATER TRAILS IN AMERICA. Harrisburg, PA: Stackpole Books, 1973. 221 p. Sketch maps, photos.
0-8117-1737-2. 73-1704.

This guide briefly describes flat water and easy white water river
trips within three hours driving time of 125 urban centers. When
available, local sources of information are mentioned as well as 140
active canoe clubs.

US-39 Cromie, Alice H. RESTORED TOWNS AND HISTORIC DISTRICTS
OF AMERICA: A TOUR GUIDE. New York: E.P. Dutton, 1979.
385 p. Maps, drawings, photos. 0-87690-286-7. 78-16392.

Taken as just a listing of restored areas, this is an extensive compilation of historic houses, special musuems, and interesting architecture,
many of which are best seen on walking tours in urban areas. What
is lacking in depth of description is more than made up for in breadth
of coverage. Usually the location description is vague (the maps
don't really help) and, because they change, hours and fees are as a
general rule not noted. Some addresses and phone numbers for further information are given. The continental US is divided into 12
regions and Alaska, Hawaii, and Canada have their own sections at
the end. There is no index. The reader will need to use other
sources for more detailed information.

US-40 _____. A TOUR GUIDE TO THE CIVIL WAR. 2d ed. New York:
E.P. Dutton, 1975. 370 p. Maps. 0-87690-153-4. 64-10926.

Cromie's guide describing museums, monuments, homes, cemeteries,
plantations, and other sites in the 48 connected states and the District of Columbia having a Civil War connection is arranged by state.

US-41 Cure, Karen. MINIVACATIONS, USA. Chicago: Follett, 1976.
216 p. Maps, photos. 0-695-80529-0. 74-29811.

This presents regionally arranged descriptions of 195 short inexpensive get-away destinations throughout the US. Backpacking, bike, canoe and houseboating trips are also suggested, and there is a regional calendar of festivals.

US-42 _____. THE TRAVEL CATALOGUE. New York: Holt, Rinehart & Winston, 1978. 191 p. Drawings, photos. Index. 0-03-020711-8. 77-21276.

This is a magnificent compilation of travel lore including books to read, places to visit, and activities to indulge in. It is arranged by activity and interest making it a bit awkward to use without constant consultation of the index. The lists of official tourist office addresses are quite extensive, and the suggested books for further reading are quite good. This is an excellent beginning book for travel planners.

US-43 D'Alton, Martina. THE RUNNER'S GUIDE TO THE U.S.A. New York: Summit Books (distributed by Simon & Schuster), 1978. 410 p. Maps. Bibliography. 0-671-40070-3. 78-10315.

This is primarily a listing and description of major and many minor marathons and other races with maps of the courses, entry requirements, race details (prizes, sponsors, etc.), suggested places to stay and the like. It also contains a description of where to run in 33 selected US cities with simple maps, but it is not as good as THE TRAVELING RUNNER'S GUIDE (US-149). There is no index, but there are lists of local running clubs and a race calendar along with a list of suggested periodicals.

US-44 Davidson, James D. AN ECCENTRIC GUIDE TO THE UNITED STATES. New York: Berkley Publishing, 1977. 500 p. Photos. Index. 0-425-03455-0.

A mish-mash, but an interesting one, of odd sights to see and unusual sites to venerate. They are lumped together by state, and the states are geographically arranged from Maine to Alaska. The index merely locates the page on which a state section starts. From Miss Nude Teeny Bopper (Indiana) through the original Skid Row (Washington) to the King Crab Festival (Alaska), the places and events share the quality of being different from what most guides suggest.

US-45 Davis, Maxine W., and Tetrault, Gregory J. THE ORGANIC TRAVELER: A GUIDE TO ORGANIC, VEGETARIAN & HEALTH FOOD RESTAURANTS IN THE U.S. & CANADA. Syracuse, NY: Grasshopper Press, 1975. 169 p. Maps. Index. 75-19579.

This state-by-state listing notes by symbols the specialties of each restaurant, and frequently provides a more detailed discussion of the menu. It also gives address, telephone number, hours and seating capacity.

US-46   Deer, Dorothy, ed. BEST HIKING TRAILS IN THE UNITED STATES. Matteson, IL: Greatlakes Living Press, 1977. 230 p. 0-915498-52-9. 77-71553.

The publisher of this book issues several regional hiking guides, and the trails in this book have been selected by the authors of these regional guides to produce this guide to the very best of all trails. Numerous trails in each state are described including location, length, USGS quadrangles to use, and sources of additional information. The geographical coverage is uneven: over half of the book is devoted to trails along the eastern seaboard, while strangely enough, the further west you go the fewer the number of trails described. There is only 1 trail described in all of northern California.

US-47   Dickerman, Pat. ADVENTURE TRAVEL. 4th ed. New York: Thomas Y. Crowell, 1978. Revised frequently. 240 p. Photos. Bibliography. Index. 0-690-01750-2. 77-25745.

This is a comprehensive source book of outfitters, guides, services, and associations offering a variety of guided adventurous excursions in North America by land, water, snow and air. Camping, fishing, downshill skiing, and hunting are excluded. There is a chapter on youth excursions and a bibliography of "how-to" adventure books.

US-48   _____, ed. COUNTRY VACATIONS U.S.A. New York: Farm & Ranch Vacations (distributed by Berkshire Traveler Press), 1976. Issued biennially. 221 p. Photos., maps. 0-913214-01-9.

Listings of working farms, ranches, and other country hosts offering "down-home" opportunities to get back to the land make up this regionally arranged guide. Most listings include comments from previous guests. All necessary "what," "where," and "how much" information is included. This title has been issued since 1949 under the former title of FARM, RANCH & COUNTRYSIDE GUIDE.

US-49   DIRECTORY OF HOTEL & MOTEL SYSTEMS. New York: American Hotel Association Directory Corp. (888 Seventh Avenue/10019), 1976. Published annually. 249 p.

A companion volume to the HOTEL & MOTEL RED BOOK (US-89), this is an alphabetic listing of hotel chains and systems giving officers, address and telephone number of executive offices, toll-free reservation number (if any), and a list of cities which have hotels of that chain (with number of rooms and whether owned by the chain or franchised).

US-50   Drotning, Phillip T. A GUIDE TO NEGRO HISTORY IN AMERICA. Garden City, NY: Doubleday, 1968. 247 p. Index. 68-14168.

Although this book is somewhat dated, the historical information it presents will not have changed that much and it is, therefore, still very useful. It complements the more recent Thum book (US-164) in being arranged by state.

US-51   Dunlop, Richard. BACKPACKING AND OUTDOOR GUIDE. Chicago: Rand McNally, 1978. Revised frequently. 194 p. Photos., maps. Index. 0-528-84170-X. 77-080429.

After an introductory background section suggesting various ways to enjoy the outdoors, there are state-by-state listings of where to camp, backpack, trail ride, hike, canoe, and appreciate conservation and wildlife. The listings provide almost no information other than name (one would have to turn to another source for an address), facilities, and specific information on enjoying a location. The maps are general shaded relief and don't indicate any locations, roads, trails, or contribute any useful information to the user.

US-52   DuPre, Paul. CAMPING AND VACATIONING WITH THE FIRST AMERICANS. Matteson, IL: Greatlakes Living Press, 1977. 218 p. Photos., maps. Bibliography. 0-915498-14-6. 75-41642.

Camping and other recreational facilities on 26 Indian reservations scattered among the states of Arizona, California, Florida, Maine, Michigan, Minnesota, Montana, Nebraska, Nevada, New Mexico, New York, North Dakota, Texas, and Wisconsin are described along with sights to see. There are separate sections on Canada and Alaska. There are two listings of "Indian owned" accommodations: campgrounds and motels/hotels/lodges/cabins. Both give tribe, address, telephone number, and type of facilities.

US-53   Eisenberg, Gerson G. LEARNING VACATIONS: THE GUIDE TO COLLEGE SEMINARS, CONFERENCE CENTERS, AND EDUCATIONAL TOURS IN THE U.S. AND OVERSEAS. Washington, DC: Acropolis Books, 1978. 191 p. Photos. 0-87491-256-3. 78-6791.

US-54   Enzel, Robert G., and Urciolo, John R. THE WHITE BOOK OF U.S. SKI AREAS. 2d ed. Washington, DC: Inter-Ski Services (Box 3635/ 20007) (distributed by Rand McNally), 1977. Issued annually. 311 p. Maps. Index. 77-088510.

This very thorough listing of nearly all ski facilities in the US is arranged both regionally and by state. It lists the name of the ski area; mailing address; telephone number; map location; snow condition telephone number (toll-free frequently); area statistics (elevation, rise, run, difficulty levels, lift information, average weather); season (including hours of operation); rates, equipment rentals, shops and ski schools; other nearby recreational facilities; accommodations; restaurants; "après-ski" (bars/lounges/discotheques); services; and transportation to large cities. It also gives state ski information telephone numbers and contains a glossary.

US-55   Esslen, Ranier. BACK TO NATURE IN CANOES: A GUIDE TO
         AMERICAN WATERS. Frenchtown, NJ: Columbia Publications Co.
         (distributed by Whirlwind Book Co.), 1976. 345 p. Maps.
         0-914366-04-1. 75-39780.

         Regionally arranged, each state has a general introduction followed
         by a brief description of canoeable waterways noting location of
         rental facilities. Further sources of information are listed for each
         state.

US-56   EXXON TRAVEL CLUB VACATION TRAVEL GUIDE. 4 vols. New
         York: Prepared by TravelVision, a division of General Drafting Co.,
         Houston and distributed by Simon & Schuster, 1977. Issued annually.
         Photos., tables, maps.

         Sightseeing and recreation information, a calendar of events, organi-
         zations providing information, lodging information in tables, and
         selected restaurants are listed for many areas in four regional volumes:
         Northeast, Southeast, Central, and West. This guide is probably
         adequate for the general traveler.

US-57   Fehr, Lucy M. SKIING USA: A GUIDE TO THE NATION'S SKI
         AREAS. Americans Discover America Series. New York: William
         Morrow & Co., 1977. 211 p. 0-688-03261-3. 77-90824.

         Arranged alphabetically by state and ski facility name within the state,
         this listing gives the name, mailing address, telephone number, gen-
         eral location, elevation, vertical drop, type and number of lifts,
         availability of instruction, rates and general remarks. State sections
         begin with an indication of the season, a general note on ski lift
         fees and an address for further information.

US-58   Flanagan, William C. THE SMART EXECUTIVE'S GUIDE TO MAJOR
         AMERICAN CITIES. New York: William Morrow & Co., 1975.
         252 p. Maps. 0-688-02944-2. 75-15710.

         Flanagan gives advice on where to stay, eat, drink, enjoy the night-
         life, find airports, etc. as well as giving additional recommended
         reading for 20 American cities.

US-59   FODOR'S BUDGET TRAVEL IN AMERICA 1979. New York: David
         McKay Co., 1979. 626 p. Maps. Index. 0-679-00379-7.

         This book seems to be hastily assembled from the material in the
         eight regional Fodor volumes and not to contain very much on how to
         travel inexpensively. The first 50 pages, devoted to essays on such
         topics as traveling by Amtrak and roughing it, touch on budget travel
         a little. The rest of the book is a state-by-state survey of the usual
         travel material found in any of the eight regional volumes, and there
         is little effort to highlight money-saving ideas. If you're really look-
         ing for a budget travel guide, this book is not recommended. A
         good, useful budget guide to the US as a whole has not yet been written.

US-60   FODOR'S ONLY-IN-AMERICA VACATION GUIDE. Edited by Robert C. Fisher and Leslie Brown. New York: David McKay Co., 1978. 532 p. Map. Index. 0-679-00246-4.

This guide is arranged by 43 types of special interest attractions that a traveler might wish to pursue from "The Airplane" to "Wildlife Sanctuaries." All points of interest within each category are then described state by state. The index is by state, listing all attractions by name.

US-61   FODOR'S FAR WEST. Created by Eugene Fodor. New York: David McKay Co., 1978. Revised frequently. 504 p. Maps. Index. 0-679-00258-8.

US-62   FODOR'S MID-ATLANTIC. Created by Eugene Fodor. New York: David McKay Co., 1978. Revised frequently. 376 p. Maps. Index. 0-679-00261-8.

US-63   FODOR'S MID-WEST. Edited by Eugene Fodor et al. New York: David McKay Co., 1974. Revised frequently. 480 p. Maps. Index. 0-679-00108-5. 74-78826.

US-64   FODOR'S NEW ENGLAND. Edited by Eugene Fodor et al. New York: David McKay Co., 1978. Revised frequently. 400 p. Maps. Index. 0-679-00263-4.

US-65   FODOR'S NEW YORK & NEW JERSEY. Edited by Eugene Fodor et al. New York: David McKay Co., 1974. Revised frequently. 442 p. Maps. Index. 0-679-00105-0. 74-78823.

US-66   FODOR'S ROCKIES & PLAINS. Created by Eugene Fodor. New York: David McKay Co., 1978. Revised frequently. 312 p. Maps. Index. 0-679-00265-0.

US-67   FODOR'S SOUTH-WEST. Edited by Eugene Fodor et al. New York: David McKay Co., 1977. Revised frequently. 431 p. Maps. Index. 0-679-00190-5.

US-68   FODOR'S THE SOUTH. Edited by Eugene Fodor et al. New York: David McKay Co., 1977. Revised frequently. 552 p. Maps. Index. 0-679-00188-3.

Issued in 8 volumes, this set is obviously fuller than the 1-volume version (US-69). There is a regional essay and general essays for each state or state section giving historical background. Each area rating an essay also has several pages of "practical information" listing annual events, special tours, historic sites, museums, general transportation information, sports, nightlife, children's activities, and a list of hotels and restaurants.

US-69   FODOR'S U.S.A. Edited by Robert C. Fisher. New York: David
        McKay Co., 1978. Revised frequently. 955 p. Photos., maps.
        Index. 0-679-00292-8.

Fodor guides are issued frequently but can be maddeningly superficial
and vague as well as being poorly revised (one once recommended a
restaurant in a hotel which had been long demolished). Still, they
can be extremely useful if one is careful. This work has general information (including a section for the foreign traveler) which can be
skipped. "America's Travel Wonders" is basically a section on national parks and major cities. "Distinctly American Vacations" is a
theme or type section (canoeing, caving, birdwatching, ghost towns,
etc.). The state listings are also general giving the usual transportation and sightseeing information and selected hotels and restaurants.

US-70   Folsom, Franklin. AMERICA'S ANCIENT TREASURES: GUIDE TO
        ARCHEOLOGICAL SITES & MUSUEMS. Chicago: Rand McNally,
        1971. 202 p. Photos., drawings. Bibliography. Index. 70-141564.

This regionally arranged directory gives address, hours, fees, and a
brief description of the musuem or site and has a list of state agencies
concerned with American Indian artifacts.

US-71   Ford, Norman D. AMERICA BY CAR. 15th ed. Greenlawn, NY:
        Harian Publications (distributed by Grosset & Dunlap), 1975. 128 p.
        Maps.

Ford gives 30 rather detailed itineraries, with travel time and
worthless route maps, for trips covering the high spots of the US,
Canada, and Mexico.

US-72   _____. OFF THE BEATEN PATH. Greenlawn, NY: Harian Publi-
        cations, 1976. 15th ed. 118 p. Photos.

"Where to vacation or stay-a-while in America's own bargain para-
dises" is the way Ford describes this work. In addition to seeking
out the low cost, Ford also sticks to "undiscovered places where life
remains serene." Information is presented both by type of escapism
and by state.

US-73   _____. TRAVEL WITHOUT YOUR CAR: A GUIDE TO DISCOVER-
        ING AMERICA BY TRAIN, BUS AND SHIP. Greenlawn, NY: Harian
        Publications, 1975. 128 p. Photos. 75-306217.

This regionally arranged guide, with some sightseeing information, to
travel by train, bus, and cruise ship covers all of North America
with 53 routes and tours described.

US-74   Frome, Michael. NATIONAL PARK GUIDE. 12th ed. Chicago:
        Rand McNally, 1978. Revised annually. 224 p. Maps, photos.
        0-528-84172-6. 67-12233.

Brief background, scenic highlights, accommodations and address of the park superintendent are given for all the national parks. Other parklands, archaeological, historical, natural, and recreational areas are described as well as an overview of the National Park Service.

US-75 George, Jean C. THE AMERICAN WALK BOOK: AN ILLUSTRATED GUIDE TO THE COUNTRY'S MAJOR HISTORIC AND NATURAL WALKING TRAILS FROM NEW ENGLAND TO THE PACIFIC COAST. A Sunrise Book. New York: E.P. Dutton, 1978. 301 p. Maps, drawings. Bibliographies. Index. 0-87690-315-4. 78-8567.

There are 14 trails, 9 classed as "nature trails" and 5 classed as "historical trails" described in good general detail, stressing the natural features in the one sort of trail and past events in the other. There is a "bibliography and maps" section for each trail. There is a section on short trails near cities and the final section of the book is on the major biotic communities in the US and where to view them. While better books exist for most of the trails, this is one of the very best overviews that has been published.

US-76 Gersh, Harry. THE ANIMALS NEXT DOOR: A GUIDE TO ZOOS AND AQUARIUMS OF THE AMERICAS. New York: Fleet Academic Editions, 1971. 170 p. 0-8303-0088-0. 71-104745.

Gersh has compiled a state-by-state listing giving all necessary visitor information including parking fees, on-site activities, eating and souvenir facilities, directors name and type of ownership.

US-77 Haas, Irvin. AMERICA'S HISTORIC INNS & TAVERNS. Rev. ed. New York: Arco Publishing Co., 1977. 214 p. Photos. 0-668-02631-6. 76-45410.

One hundred and five US inns and taverns of historical significance are described indicating whether still operating or a museum and giving location and background notes.

US-78 _____. AMERICA'S HISTORIC SHIPS: REPLICAS AND RESTORA-TIONS. New York: Arco Publishing Co., 1975. 128 p. Photos. Index. 0-668-3768-7. 74-30893.

Historical background and some practical finding information is given for 21 berthed ships and eight maritime museums.

US-79 _____. AMERICA'S HISTORIC VILLAGES & RESTORATIONS. New York: Arco Publishing Co., 1974. 150 p. Photos. 0-668-03354-1. 74-77712.

Haas provides a listing of restored areas having archaeological, architectural, historical and social value, giving hours, how to reach, admission charges and historical background.

US-80   ____. CITADELS, RAMPARTS & STOCKADES: AMERICA'S HIS-
TORIC FORTS. Edison, NJ: Everest House, 1979. 127 p. Photos.
0-89696-038-2. 78-74583.

This, most recent, Haas guidebook still has the mediocre quality of
his earlier guides. The selection is arbitrary, the historical data is
superficial and incomplete, and the practical information is limited.

US-81   ____. HISTORIC HOMES OF THE AMERICAN PRESIDENTS: A
TRAVELER'S GUIDE. New York: David McKay Co., 1976. 209 p.
Photos. 0-679-50599-7. 76-26630.

In this guide Haas gives historical and biographical descriptions of
the homes of 31 US presidents open to the public. It is arranged
chronologically by president and brief information is given on how
to get to each and when to visit.

US-82   Hadley, Leila. TRAVELING WITH CHILDREN IN THE USA: A
GUIDE TO PLEASURE, ADVENTURE, DISCOVERY. Americans Discover America Series. New York: William Morrow & Co., 1977.
480 p. 0-688-03132-3. 77-79233.

After a few pages of general travel tips and sources of information,
this work lists places to visit giving name, location, hours/season, and
whether free or fee. The list is by state and city, with state sections
on sports activities and festivals.

US-83   HAMMOND DIESEL STOP DIRECTORY AND ROAD ATLAS. Maplewood, NJ: Hammond, 1976. 95 p. Maps.

"Prepared to assist the diesel car operator in finding fuel stations
easily," this volume shows approximately 8,400 locations in the US
and Canada on several regional and metropolitan area maps. It also
contains a directory of these stations alphabetically by state.

US-84   Hayes, Bob. THE BLACK AMERICAN TRAVEL GUIDE. Rev. ed.
San Francisco: Straight Arrow Books, 1973. 349 p. 0-87932-057-5.
73-88278.

This guide lists hotel, restaurant, and entertainment facilities, and
black history background for 14 US cities. The author has visited
visited each facility and recommends only those with management
sensitivity to the black consumer.

US-85   Highwater, Jamake. FODOR'S INDIAN AMERICA. New York:
David McKay Co., 1975. 431 p. Drawings, maps. Index. 0-679-
00072-0. 74-78821.

This guide gives extensive cultural background and practical information for appreciating and undertaking a visit to the Indian nations all
across the US. It contains many additional sources of local information including tours.

US-86   Hilts, Len. NATIONAL FOREST GUIDE. Chicago: Rand McNally, 1978. 217 p. Photos., maps. 0-528-84174-2. 77-080433.

Each national forest is described noting acreage, address of headquarters, scenic features, both in the forest and nearby. There is also a table of facilities for each forest and "A Catalog of National Recreational Facilities" (a list of other federally administered recreation areas in 30 official categories including national forest visitor centers).

US-87   HISTORIC AMERCA GUIDE. Chicago: Rand McNally, 1978. Revised annually. 281 p. Maps, photos. Index. 0-528-84173-4. 77-080432.

This is a regionally arranged listing of more than 3,000 places of historic interest, giving location, brief description, hours, and admission charges.

US-88   HISTORIC HOUSES OF AMERICA OPEN TO THE PUBLIC. By the editors of American Heritage. An American Heritage Guide. New York: American Heritage Publishing Co., 1971. 320 p. Photos. 0-07-001135-4. 79-149725.

Arranged by state, this book gives brief descriptions, by whom operated, hours, and how to reach historic houses in all 50 states.

US-89   HOTEL & MOTEL RED BOOK. New York: American Hotel Association Directory Corp., 1979. Issued annually. 739 p. Tables.

Arranged by state and city, this is a directory of American Hotel & Motel Association members, giving address, telephone number, toll-free or TWX number, manager, credit cards accepted, number of rooms and rates. Accompanied by the DIRECTORY OF HOTEL & MOTEL SYSTEMS (US-49).

US-90   HOTEL AND TRAVEL INDEX. New York: Ziff-Davis, 1978. Issued quarterly. Photos., maps.

This is an international listing of hotels with a section on hotel/motel systems giving headquarters address, phone, officers, and a section on reservation services. The US section is arranged by state and city listing hotels/motels alphabetically giving manager, rates, address, telephone number, and number of units.

US-91   Hunter, John F. THE GAY INSIDER: USA. New York: Stonehill Publishing Co. (distributed by Dell), 1972. 629 p.

Most guides for the homosexual traveler are underground publications, difficult to obtain, and often not reliable. Even this publication is dated. It borders on a survival manual and life-style guide, but a substantial section is devoted to locating and describing gathering places for "gays" with recommendations for some. There is a state-by-state "legal status" table.

US-92   Hunter, Susan. A FAMILY GUIDE TO AMUSEMENT CENTERS. New York: Walker, 1975. 182 p. Photos. Index. 0-8027-0451-4. 73-90384.

Ranging from the Alabama Space and Rocket Center to the Circus World Museum in Wisconsin Dells, this book lists just over a hundred "amusement centers"--oceanariums, wild animal habitats, reconstructed villages, and other such places. Location, hours, fees, major attractions, and accommodations are noted. There is a city index.

US-93   INTERNATIONAL ADVENTURE TRAVELGUIDE. Seattle: American Adventurers Association (distributed by Timber Press), 1978. Issued annually. 498 p. Photos. Indexes. 0-917304-12-8.

This volume describes "2,000 worldwide adventure trips and expeditions--land, sea, air and underwater--open to public participation." This means that addresses are given with each trip description so the trip organizer can be contacted directly by the reader instead of going through the American Adventurers Association (US-218) which charges a yearly membership fee. The guide is first divided into four major sections: land, water, air, and underwater, then by specific type of trip, and finally by geographic areas down to the state level. There are geographical and trip operator indexes and appendixes listing clubs and associations; schools and camps; and organizational members of the American Adventurers Association. Can be kept up to date with this organization's bimonthly ADVENTURE TRAVEL magazine (US-190). A comparison of the US sections of this guide with Dickerman's ADVENTURE TRAVEL (US-47) shows little overlap; this guide tends to have more listings, but many of those in the Dickerman guide do not appear here. Those searching for possible adventure trips should consult both.

US-94   Jaffe, Miles, and Krieger, Dennis. SKIING THE BEST: A GUIDE TO THE TOP 50 SKI AREAS IN THE U.S. AND CANADA. New York: Random House, 1978. 319 p. Photos., maps. 0-394-72408-9. 78-55720.

Ten ski areas in the far west, 23 in the Rockies, and 17 in the east have been chosen for the quality of their skiing and the character of the area. The information provided for each is quite complete and specific: how accessible is it; descriptions of slopes (with an aerial photograph or diagram showing all the slopes), lifts, and lift lines; and the nature of the area: its accommodations, restaurants, après-ski and night life, diversions, child care, and costs.

US-95   Jordan, Emil L. PICTORIAL TRAVEL GUIDE OF SCENIC AMERICA.

Maplewood, NJ: Hammond, 1976. 256 p. Maps, photos. 0-8437-3665-8. 75-37581.

This guide is regionally arranged, concentrating on the character of major cities and areas rather than their specific scenic attractions. It has been irregularly published since 1955 under varying titles.

US-96   Kenyon, Lee. THE TRAVEL PLANNER'S ELEVATION GUIDE. Soquel, CA: A Sure Thing Publications (Box 616/95073), 1978. 34 p.

The compiler, an AAA touring counselor, has taken over 50 major US routes (mostly in the West), 39 California secondary routes, and 13 Canadian routes and listed the major cities, areas, or high or low points along each route and has given an elevation figure for each. These figures were taken from other reference sources. The use of this guide, in conjunction with a road map, will tell persons with heart or lung problems or those pulling a heavy load where they might encounter difficulties. A revision in 1979 or 1980 is planned which will also include mileages. Such a revision should increase the usefulness of this unique compilation of data.

US-97   Keown, Ian, with Burnham, Linda. VERY SPECIAL PLACES: A LOVERS' GUIDE TO AMERICA. 2d ed. New York: Macmillan, 1978. 360 p. Maps, drawings. 0-02-077230-0. 78-7716.

Keown and Burnham have prepared regionally arranged descriptions of inns and hotels that are "idyllic hideaways" for lovers, not swingers, where one can "enjoy the finer things in life" like "watching sandpipers at sunset. . . ."

US-98   Kirby-Smith, Henry T. U.S. OBSERVATORIES: A DIRECTORY AND TRAVEL GUIDE. New York: Van Nostrand Reinhold, 1976. 173 p. Photos., maps. Index. 0-442-24451-7. 76-4448.

Fifteen major observatories are described in great detail including nearby accommodations. Almost 300 other installations are briefly listed and located.

US-99   Kitching, Jessie. BIRDWATCHERS GUIDE TO WILDLIFE SANCTUARIES. New York: Arco Publishing Co., 1976. 233 p. Photos. Bibliography. Index. 76-5388.

This is a listing of 295 wildlife sanctuaries arranged by state and province located in the US and Canada. It gives name, mailing address and location of sanctuary with number of bird species observed, a brief physical description, and the date of the last checklist of bird sightings. When appropriate, fees are noted and other books and pamphlets on the sanctuary are listed.

US-100 Landi, Val. THE BANTAM GREAT OUTDOORS GUIDE TO THE UNITED STATES AND CANADA: THE COMPLETE TRAVEL ENCY-

CLOPEDIA AND WILDERNESS GUIDE. New York: Bantam Books, 1978. 854 p. Photos., maps. Bibliography. Index. 0-553-01112-X.

This is a mammoth and very thorough guide for those persons who, in particular, like to plan their travel around fishing and hunting, or the national forests. It also covers canoeing and river running, hiking, skiing, and other types of outdoor recreation and adventure travel to a lesser extent. Places to engage in these specific activities in each state (Hawaii and the District of Columbia are excluded) are described in full detail giving natural history background as well as the names and addresses of thousands of fishing and hunting lodges and camps; wilderness outfitters; and maps, guides, and booklets. The index is limited to the specific places, activities, and subjects covered, and does not include the individual lodges, outfitters, organizations, publications, etc. that are mentioned. The bibliography is uneven and lists mostly older books. The author is the editor of OUTDOOR LIFE magazine.

US-100a Lay, Richard. INTERSTATE GUIDE TO GOOD LISTENING. Matteson, IL: Greatlakes Living Press, 1977. 188 p. Maps. Index. 0-915498-47-2. 77-71555.

This guide identifies AM, FM, and FM-stereo broadcast stations located close to eight major interstate systems: I-5, I-25, I-40, I-55, I-75, I-80, I-90, and I-95. Information for each station includes: network affiliation (if any), call number, day and night radius of coverage, hours on air, programming emphasis, and extent of sports coverage. A beginning section of sketch maps, one for each state, shows approximate locations of interstates and communities. The main arrangement is geographic by each interstate route with an alphabetical index of cities and communities.

US-101 LEAHY'S HOTEL-MOTEL GUIDE. 101st ed. Chicago: American Hotel Register Co., 1976. Issued annually. 175 p. Maps.

More inclusive in coverage than the HOTEL & MOTEL RED BOOK (US-89), this guide notes the population of a community and then lists the major hotels and motels giving mailing address, number of rooms, and minimum rates. The current RAND McNALLY ROAD ATLAS (US-139) is bound in at the end.

US-102 Lewis, Gomer. GOMER'S BUDGET TRAVEL DIRECTORY. Maplewood, NJ: Hammond, 1978. 224 p. Maps. 0-8437-3455-8. 78-5091.

This is mainly a listing of over 4,000 hotels and motels in each state offering economical accommodations. It also contains other helpful hints on traveling economically plus discount coupons.

US-103 Lightman, Sidney, ed. THE JEWISH TRAVEL GUIDE. 25th ed. London: Jewish Chronicle Publications, 1977. Revised annually. 304 p. Photos. 0-900498-65-X.

A world listing, this guide has an extensive US section, noting synagogues and some kosher restaurants and museums.

US-104 Logan, Harry B. A TRAVELER'S GUIDE TO NORTH AMERICAN GARDENS. New York: Charles Scribners' Sons, 1974. 253 p. Photos. Index. 0-684-13493-4. 73-1103.

Logan has compiled a very complete state-by-state listing giving brief descriptions with address and season and hours. "Gardens" is loosely defined to include arboretums, parks, homes, other places with garden collections, and some nurseries and experimental gardens. Puerto Rico, the Virgin Islands and Canada are also included. There is a list of plant societies and a name index.

US-105 Lord, Suzanne. AMERICAN TRAVELER'S TREASURY: A GUIDE TO THE NATION'S HEIRLOOMS. Americans Discover America Series. New York: William Morrow & Co., 1977. 588 p. 0-688-03130-7. 77-292.

This is a brief listing, by state, of museums, historic sites, religious shrines, architecturally interesting structures, and the like giving location (usually address), hours, and fees.

US-106 Makens, James C. MAKENS' GUIDE TO U.S. CANOE TRAILS. Irving, TX: Le Voyageur Publishing Co., 1971. 86 p. Bibliography. Index. 70-175111.

Almost 900 canoe trails, arranged by state, are briefly described noting access points, portages, degree of difficulty, drop, length, etc. Unfortunately the bibliography contains quite a few typographical errors which leads one to question the correctness of the other data also. Still, this book is a classic in its field.

US-107 Marquis, Arnold. A GUIDE TO AMERICA'S INDIANS: CEREMONIALS, RESERVATIONS AND MUSEUMS. Norman: University of Oklahoma Press, 1974. 267 p. Photos., maps. Bibliography. Index. 0-8061-1133-X.

While containing primarily historical and sociological information, this book does list, by region, tribes and reservations, campgrounds, and a calendar of annual events. Appendixes list museums with Indian collections, Indian organizations, and "Indian-interest" publications.

US-108 Marx, Robert F. BURIED TREASURE OF THE UNITED STATES: HOW AND WHERE TO LOCATE HIDDEN WEALTH. New York: David McKay Co., 1978. 401 p. Photos. Bibliography. 0-679-50795-7. 77-10966.

At least half of the book is a very complete state-by-state listing of locations on land and in or near water where treasure may be found.

There is a large beginning how-to section. The 10 appendixes include a bibliography of treasure hunting books, a list of periodicals, a list of where gem stones can be found, sources of additional information, local offices of the Bureau of Land Management, locations of known gold deposits, federal rules and regulations, historical societies, a list of US treasure hunting maps and charts, and a list of treasure-hunting clubs. The author is a professional diver and treasure hunter, has written numerous books on the topic, and operates a Florida salvage and diving company. This is a major work.

US-109 May, Judy, and May, Dean. GREAT DIVING-I. Harrisburg, PA: Stackpole Books, 1974. 256 p. Maps, photos. 0-8117-2022-5. 74-14587.

Both coastal and inland (rivers, lakes, ponds) areas are covered and specific wrecks or other features of interest, both natural and manmade, are listed and briefly described. Areas include the Atlantic and Gulf coastal states and the inland states of Ohio, Pennsylvania, West Virginia, Kentucky, and Tennessee. The authors also include local dive shops, which are good sources of information on local diving conditions, and a list of decompression chambers.

US-110 Meves, Eric. GUIDE TO BACKPACKING IN THE UNITED STATES. Rev. ed. New York: Collier Books, a division of Macmillan, 1979. 289 p. Maps. Bibliography. Index. 0-02-029330-5. 76-44352.

This guide gives "state by state descriptions of backpacking conditions [trails, terrain, climate, flora and fauna, wildlife, backpacking facilities, sources of further information] in more than 300 forests, parks and wilderness areas."

US-111 MOBIL CITY VACATION & BUSINESS GUIDE. Chicago: Rand McNally, 1978. Revised frequently. 352 p. Maps, photos. 0-528-84807-0. 76-3107.

Described are 53 cities (including Disney World) in 47 sections (seven "twin cities" listed) giving general description (with map of the central city), convention facilities, entertainments, sightseeing, emergency phone numbers, events, and accommodations.

US-112 MOBIL TRAVEL GUIDE. 7 vols. Chicago: Rand McNally, 1978. Issued annually. Maps.

The 7 volumes cover: (1) Northeastern States, (2) Middle Atlantic States, (3) Great Lakes Area, (4) Southwest and South Central Area, (5) Southeastern States, (6) Northwest and Great Plains States, and (7) California and the West. Each volume is arranged alphabetically by the states included in that volume. Overall state information includes a brief history; brief information on national and/or state parks, forests, and recreation areas; hunting and fishing; the interstate highway system; liquor; and additional sources of information. A directory of towns which lists what to see and do; annual or seasonal events; and rated hotels/motels, etc.; and restaurants follows. Some of the most frequently visited locations have additional descriptive information and a suggested auto tour with a map. Where applicable, listings include information on where languages other than English and where facilities for the handicapped are available.

US-113 NAGEL'S ENCYCLOPEDIA-GUIDE: USA. Geneva: Nagel Publishers, 1973. 880 p. Maps. Index.

A handy, brief, but authoritative guide, providing history and culture as well as outstanding landmarks for all of the states plus 36 major cities. Also, it includes an extensive listing (no descriptions) of hotels and restaurants, and many good fold-out city maps. It would be useful for the foreign traveler to the US, as it is available in English, French and German editions.

US-114 THE NATIONAL REGISTER OF HISTORIC PLACES. Washington, DC: U.S. Government Printing Office, 1976. 3d ed. 961 p. Photos., maps, diagrams. Index. 76-10861.

This volume locates and briefly describes all properties in the National Register of Historic Places as of December 31, 1974. It is noted whether each site is designated a National Historic Landmark, an Historic American Building Survey, or an Historic American Engineering Record. The arrangement is by state, then county, then community with brief historical essays preceeding each state listing.

US-115 NATIONAL SURVEY OF HISTORIC SITES AND BUILDINGS. Washington, DC: U.S. Government Printing Office, 1968-- . Photos., maps.

A multivolume set that is still in progress, each volume deals with a separate area/period of US history giving full historical background and locating and describing sites.

US-116 NAUTICAL MUSEUM DIRECTORY. 3d ed. New York: Quadrant Press, 1973. 80 p. Photos.

"An illustrated directory listing nautical museums and preserved vessels in the United States and Canada," this volume includes season and hours; admission fees; special events; parking, picnic areas, and eating facilities; and gift shops where available.

US-117 NEW FREE CAMPGROUNDS: A LIST OF PLACES, TOWNS AND OTHER LOCATIONS WHERE YOU CAN PARK OVERNIGHT WITHOUT CHARGE, OR FOR A SMALL FEE. Rev. ed. Topeka, KS: American Publishing Co., 1976. 128 p. 76-377795.

This is a directory of useful and extensive listings of free and very inexpensive campgrounds. The entries are very abbreviated.

US-118 Norback, Peter, and Norback, Craig. NEWSWEEK TRAVEL GUIDE
TO THE UNITED STATES. New York: Newsweek Books, 1979.
580 p. 0-88225-267-4. 78-65503.

The authors present basic information in a standardized format of 23
categories for each of the 50 states. They make no attempt to rate,
evaluate, or tell the reader what he/she might enjoy. The information given includes: weather; name, address, and phone number of
the state chamber of commerce, tourism offices of the state and
selected major cities, state highway department, various state highway welcoming centers, and the state police; requirements and fees
for hunting and fishing licenses; and lists of campgrounds, resorts
and beaches, boating areas, bicycle trails, foot trails, ski areas,
amusement parks and attractions, state fairs, national parks and
forests, state parks and forests, historic sites, hostels, and points of
interest.

US-119 NUDIST PARK GUIDE. 7th ed. Orlando, FL: American Sunbathing
Association, 1975. Issued frequently. 145 p. Maps, tables.

A regionally arranged directory of nudist resorts with maps and tables
indicating facilities, and giving addresses, telephone numbers, and
restrictions.

US-120 OAG TRAVEL PLANNER & HOTEL/MOTEL GUIDE: NORTH AMERI-
CAN EDITION. Oak Brook, IL: Reuben H. Donnelley Corp. Issued quarterly. Maps.

The hotel/motel information is selective and minimal (rate range,
telephone number, and address), but this compilation has a hotel/
motel systems executive offices directory, plans of the major air
terminals, a state-by-state calendar of events, a table of airport
facilities for the handicapped and elderly, an 800 toll-free directory,
a "Destination Index" (most of the volume) giving nearest airline and
connecting transportation for most US cities and resort areas, and a
list of military installations with nearest airports. It also has much
information on international travel, and is available in a European
edition.

US-121 OFFICIAL AIRLINE GUIDE: NORTH AMERICAN EDITION. Oak
Brook, IL: Reuben H. Donnelley Corp. Issued twice monthly.

This mammoth compilation--the "Bible" of its field--of airline data
lists direct flights, schedules, fares, and connecting flight information. It can be found on every travel agent's desk and is usually
called "the OAG." Part 2, "Ground Transportation Services" and
also issued twice a month, is arranged by rentor/leasor and is an
international listing--with major stress on the US--of the major
vehicle rental services. Within each listing by firm, the arrangement
is geographic: alphabetical by state then community. Location(s),
telephone number(s), and rates are listed. The firms in the issue checked

were Avis, Budget, Econo-Car, Hertz, and National. It is the most useful single source for car rental information. There is also a worldwide edition of the OAG.

US-122 THE OFFICIAL HOTEL & RESORT GUIDE. 3 vols. New York: Ziff-Davis, 1976. Issued annually. Loose leaf. Maps.

This is an international directory of hotels which is completely revised annually through replacement pages issued at regular intervals throughout the year. Volume 1 is devoted to the US and is arranged by state and city. It lists address, telephone number, manager, representative, rates, number of rooms, credit cards accepted, and facilities for major hotels. There is a classified directory by level of accommodation (deluxe, first class, tourist) and a list of hotel representatives and hotel chain reservation offices.

US-123 THE OFFICIAL MUSEUM DIRECTORY: UNITED STATES, CANADA. Washington, DC: American Association of Museums, 1975. Published biennially. 850 p. 0-87217-005-5. 79-144808.

This directory contains "current, comprehensive information about approximately 5,225 museums in the United States and Canada." It is arranged by state or province with several appendixes, one of which lists the institutions by over 80 different subjects from "arts and crafts" to "woodcarving museums."

US-124 THE OFFICIAL RAILWAY GUIDE: NORTH AMERICAN PASSENGER TRAVEL EDITION. New York: National Railway Publication Co. Issued monthly except January/February and July/August.

This guide lists schedules and fares of passenger rail lines including suburban services, connecting bus/ferry services, and rail tour operators.

US-125 Oglesby, Claire C. DISCOVER USA: THE BICENTENNIAL TRAVEL GUIDE. The Acropolis Americana/Bicentennial Series. Washington, DC: Acropolis Books, 1975. 264 p. Photos., maps. Index. 0-87491-015-3. 75-35579.

A regionally arranged guide, this book gives very brief information on communities and special sights. It lists selected industrial tours; has special sections on national parks, American Indians, annual events, and travel tips; and lists state tourist offices and some centers that serve the foreign visitor.

US-126 O'Keefe, M. Timothy, ed. UNDERWATER SOCIETY OF AMERICA'S INTERNATIONAL DIVERS GUIDE. Orlando, FL: Toss (Box 5756/32805), 1976. 300 p. Photos., maps.

Half of this very thorough volume describes in detail diving sites in in the US arranged by state. There is also a "yellow pages" of diving services by state.

US-127 Onosko, Tim. FUN LAND U.S.A.: THE COMPLETE GUIDEBOOK TO 100 MAJOR AMUSEMENT AND THEME PARKS. New York: Ballantine Books, 1978. 296 p. Photos., maps. Index. 0-345-27438-5. 78-1050.

If you have fond recollections of amusement parks from your youth or are a present-day roller coaster "freak" you'll enjoy just reading this book, with all its photographs and its thirteen beginning essays on such topics as constructing theme parks and individual rides, the ultimate roller coaster, and an amusement park of the future. Two thirds of the book is devoted to state-by-state descriptions of the parks, including location with map, telephone, price policy, parking, hours, number of rides, slowest day of the week, picnicking and camping facilities, availability of nearby accommodations, and guest services.

US-128 Paananen, Wayne, and Paulsen, Reinhart. WHEELER'S HIGHWAY RADIO DIRECTORY. Park Ridge, IL: Print Media Services (222 South Prospect Avenue/60068), 1977. Issued annually. 223 p. 0-671-22767-X.

Arranged alphabetically by state then community, this book lists the radio stations in the "lower 48" states. Given for each station is the format (talk, news, rock and roll, country/western, etc.), frequency, call letters, day and night effective range, news network (if any), and live sports coverage (if any). There is a separate listing for public radio as well as a section on Citizen Band radio that includes a dictionary of terms.

US-129 PAN AM'S USA GUIDE. 2d ed. New York: McGraw-Hill, 1976. 634 p. Photos., maps. Index. 0-07-048423-6. 76-10387.

Written primarily for the first-time visitor to the US from abroad, this guide mentions all the major points of interest in the US and possessions, but it provides little detailed information. It is arranged by state with a name index.

US-130 Perrin, Alwyn T., ed. THE EXPLORERS LTD. SOURCE BOOK. 2d ed. New York: Harper & Row, 1977. 413 p. Photos., drawings. Index. 0-06-011252-2. 75-26224.

This is a basic book for the do-it-yourself explorer who prefers the more unusual travel activities. For 28 exploring activities in 7 broad categories (wilderness, sea, air, emergency, vagabonding, exploring, miscellaneous) this volume lists sources of information (organizations, publications, places to learn) and equipment necessary to engage in the activity. The second edition devotes more space to gear than to information sources.

US-131 Perrin, Rosemarie D. EXPLORERS LTD. GUIDE TO LOST TREA-
SURES IN THE UNITED STATES & CANADA. Harrisburg, PA:
Cameron House (Stackpole Books), 1977. 204 p. Drawings. Bib-
liography. Index. 0-8117-2074-8. 77-5595.

With over 300 treasures described, this list, alphabetically arranged
by state or province, notes the kind of treasure (buried, lost mine,
shipwreck), nature of the treasure (gold, silver, jewelry, etc.),
general location, and has a map or chart showing the area. Appendixes cover bibliographies, maps and charts, treasure law, metal
detectors, and archives and historical societies.

US-132 Postal, Bernard, and Koppman, Lionel. AMERICAN JEWISH LAND-
MARKS: A TRAVEL GUIDE AND HISTORY. Rev. ed. 3 vols.
New York: Fleet Press Corp., 1977-- . Index.

Postal and Koppman have compiled a thorough, comprehensive guide
to landmarks, shrines, public buildings, etc. of Jewish association.
Volume 1 was published in 1977 and covers the Northeastern states
from Maine to West Virginia. Volume 2 published in 1979, covers
the South and Southwest and volume 3, covering the Middle West
and West, is in preparation.

US-133 Powers, Edward, and Witt, James. TRAVELING WEATHERWISE IN
THE U.S.A. New York: Dodd, Mead & Co., 1972. 299 p.
Tables, maps. 0-396-06360-8. 73-153892.

An overview of US weather is presented in this volume with charts
for particular aspects of weather, e.g. tornadoes, hay fever, smog.
The general climate discussions are interesting, but the detailed
charts for 93 selected cities are the most useful feature of this book.

US-134 Price, Steven D. HORSEBACK VACATION GUIDE. Brattleboro,
VT: The Stephen Greene Press, 1975. 183 p. Photos. Bibliography.
Index. 0-8289-0243-7. 73-86035.

International in scope, this is a chatty and discursive guide to leisure
activities involving horses. It lists organizations sponsoring pack
trips, state tourist information agencies, parks with public riding
facilities, hunt clubs, foreign tourist offices, leading horse shows
and rodeos, major racetracks, and endurance rides.

US-135 Pyle, Sara. CANOEING AND RAFTING: THE COMPLETE WHERE-
TO-GO GUIDE TO AMERICA'S BEST TAME AND WILD WATERS.
Americans Discover America Series. New York: William Morrow &
Co., 1979. 363 p. Photos. Index. 0-688-08398-6. 78-26272.

Ms. Pyle offers a detailed view of each state's water route possibilities from guided white water tours to family safe trails.

US-136 Randall, Charles E., and Clepper, Henry. FAMOUS AND HISTORIC

TREES. Washington, DC: American Forestry Association, 1976. 90 p. Photos. Index. 76-39710.

This list of "famous" trees gives location and historical background for each entry. It is arranged by thematic sections such as trees associated with people, with US history, with schools, with religion and each section is subdivided by state. The index is by tree specie.

US-137 RAND McNALLY CAMPGROUND AND TRAILER PARK GUIDE. Chicago: Rand McNally, 1977. Published annually. 619 p. Maps, tables, photos. 0-528-84754-6. 76-24285.

This volume provides "45 points of information for nearly 20,000 public and private parks in North America." It includes locations with map reference, facilities and activities listed in easily read state tables, and campground citizen's band radio listings. The eastern and western US sections are also published separately.

US-138 RAND McNALLY INTERSTATE ROAD ATLAS. Chicago: Rand McNally, 1978. 96 p. Maps. 0-528-89061-1. 76-54616.

This is a smaller, handier size than the RAND McNALLY ROAD ATLAS (US-139). Individual state maps show major roads, and in the back there is a section of 17 city maps showing major bypass roads and interstates. Most states have information centers on these interstate highways wherever they enter a state. The centers are not indicated on these maps, but the traveler should look for them when crossing state lines on major roads. The book includes a 20 page section on several things to do and points of interest in each state. Maps of the Canadian provinces are also included.

US-139 RAND McNALLY ROAD ATLAS: UNITED STATES, CANADA, MEXICO. 54th ed. Chicago: Rand McNally, 1978. Issued annually. 129 p. Maps. Indexes. 75-654428.

Adequate to good road maps for all the states make this the best general road atlas currently available for the US. Time zones are noted, mileage tables are given for distances between major cities, and the maps are indexed.

US-140 RAND McNALLY VACATION AND TRAVEL GUIDE. Chicago: Rand McNally, 1977. 276 p. Maps, photos. Index. 76-44094.

Arranged by region and then by state, this guide describes in detail 150 travel destinations. Each description includes information about other places to visit within easy driving distance. Maps are included for each state.

US-141 Reamy, Lois. TRAVELABILITY: A GUIDE FOR PHYSICALLY DISABLED TRAVELERS IN THE UNITED STATES. New York: Macmillan,

1978. 298 p. Photos., maps. Index. 0-02-601170-0. 78-13569.

A step-by-step guide to trip planning for handicapped Americans, TRAVELABILITY provides answers to questions such as should you go alone or with a group, what problems you can expect to face, and to whom you can go for help, medical questions and answers. Part II describes in detail problems encountered in traveling by car, bus, train, plane, and boat. Part III, "Where to Go and Where to Stay," describes in depth a vacation in Hawaii; includes a state-by-state listing of such items as travel information sources, directories of barrier-free places and appropriate transportation companies; and gives advice on hotel and motel chains with barrier-free design and facilities.

US-142 RESTORED VILLAGE DIRECTORY. 3d ed. New York: Quadrant Press, 1973. 80 p. Photos. Index.

Arranged by state, this work gives location, background and description, hours, fees, special events, and facilities, noting whether the village is restored, recreated, or a replica.

US-143 Rice, William, and Wolf, Burton, eds. WHERE TO EAT IN AMERICA: AN INDISPENSIBLE GUIDE TO FINDING WHAT YOU WANT TO EAT WHEN YOU WANT TO EAT IT IN THE 30 MOST-TRAVELED AMERICAN CITIES. New York: Random House, 1977. 422 p. 0-394-73438-6. 77-5969.

This guide is arranged by the 30 most-traveled American cities and within each by the following categories: (1) "Big Deal" which lists the major first-class restaurant(s) worth eating at and frequently one with a major reputations not worth eating at, (2) "International" which lists ethnic restaurants by type of food prepared, (3) "Specialty" which lists restaurants by type or styles of food or cooking, (4) "For Individual Needs" which lists, for example, where to go if you only have time for one meal, you need all-night service, or you want a Sunday brunch, and (5) "Markets" which lists where to shop for food. Address, phone number, hours, price range, credit cards accepted, and frequently specific menu recommendations are given for each restaurant.

US-144 Riley, Laura, and Riley, William. GUIDE TO THE NATIONAL WILDLIFE REFUGES. Garden City, NY: Doubleday, 1979. 653 p. Maps, photos. Index. 0-385-14014-2. 78-60300.

Listing over 300 wildlife refuges, this work gives short descriptions of each, including both plants and animals for which the refuge is known. Each entry notes "how to get there," hours and season, what to see, what to do, where to stay, weather information, suggested clothing, nearby points of interest, and an address for further information. The maps are inadequate for finding the refuges. The color photographs of wildlife are good.

US-145 Rudner, Ruth. OFF AND WALKING: A HIKER'S GUIDE TO AMERICAN PLACES. New York: Holt, Rinehart & Winston, 1977. 270 p. Photos., maps. Bibliographies. 0-03-015596-7. 76-29913.

A very good, if lopsided, guide to hiking in the US. The first half is how-to advice and the second half is detailed information on 7 hikes in selected national parks and forests. The hike descriptions are personal and factual. Each hike has its own brief bibliography. Appendixes include a bibliography, national park and forest lists, lodgings and entrance fees in parks, various commercial suppliers, and selected stables for pack trips.

US-146 Ruhe-Schoen, Janet. PAN FOR GOLD ON YOUR NEXT VACATION: A GUIDE TO LOW-COST UNIQUE ADVENTURES. New York: Pilot Books, 1978. 31 p. Bibliography. 0-87576-059-7. 77-1378.

A brief guide to possible places to pan in 12 states and including the appropriate state agency to write to for further information. Discusses briefly the necessary equipment, panning technique, and where to sell your gold.

US-147 RUSSELL'S OFFICIAL NATIONAL MOTOR COACH GUIDE. Cedar Rapids, IA: Russell's Guides. Issued monthly. Maps.

In this "Bible" of bus schedules by bus lines, Greyhound and Trailways predominate, but smaller, independent lines are also included. Route maps are included in each monthly issue with a separate map supplement issued semiannually. The separate list of suburbs, bus depots/stations/terminals, hospitals, and military installations is issued irregularly.

US-148 Safran, Rose. VERY SPECIAL RESORTS. Stockbridge, MA: The Berkshire Traveller Press, 1973. 222 p. Drawings. Index. 0-912944-10-2. 73-83796.

This book includes descriptions of 76 "nice places" offering domestic vactions with wide open spaces, gracious hospitality, and self-contained facilities featuring at least two major sports activities. It is regionally arranged with an index of activities.

US-149 Scheerer, R. Penelope, and Schwanbeck, John R. THE TRAVELING RUNNER'S GUIDE: WHERE TO RUN IN 21 CITIES AROUND THE U.S. New York: E.P. Dutton, 1978. 259 p. Maps. 0-525-47530-3. 78-14824.

This guide gives detailed descriptions of two or more routes for runners staying in the downtown area of 21 major US cities. A detailed map, and a description of the terrain, and volume of traffic are given. Also included for each city is a list of downtown hotels, their facilities and hours for breakfast and a chart giving month by month data on sunrise and sunset, average daily temperature, and mean number of days with precipitation.

US-150 Scott, David L., and Scott, Kay W. TRAVELING AND CAMPING IN THE NATIONAL PARK AREAS. 3 vols. Chester, CT: Globe Pequot Press (Old Chester Road/06412), 1979. Maps.

The three volumes cover three separate geographic areas: western states (173 p. 0-87106-099-X), eastern states (185 p. 0-87106-001-9), and mid-America (177 p. 0-87106-000-0). The authors describe "76 parks, telling what each area has in the way of activities, facilities, camping, fishing and so on. At least one map is given for every area." National parks, national seashores, national historic sites, national monuments, and national historic parks are all included.

US-151 Simpson, Norman T. COUNTRY INNS AND BACK ROADS. 12th ed. Stockbridge, MA: The Berkshire Traveller Press, 1978. Issued annually. 364 p. Maps, drawings. 0-912944-47-1. 78-51116.

This is a guide to 160 inns in 25 states and Canada, noting the special appeal and resources of each inn and including directions to each.

US-152 SKI TOURING GUIDE: THE SKI TOURER'S MANUAL. 15th ed. Troy, VT: Ski Touring Council, 1978. Issued annually. 189 p. Maps. Bibliography.

The first part gives general information (a lot of how-to), includes a list of northeast campgrounds which are open in winter and which offer ski touring opportunities, and a list of recommended books, magazines, and films. Part 2 lists numerous ski trails, by state or region, giving, where available, the name, location, telephone number, and a detailed description of the trail. Some addresses of agencies giving further information are noted. Emphasis is mostly on the northeast states.

US-153 Smith, Spencer, et al., eds. FODOR'S SEASIDE AMERICA. New York: David McKay Co., 1977. 536 p. Map. Index. 0-679-00282-0.

Smith describes seaside attractions in the 24 states having coastal borders. The volume includes specific information on tourist information services, seasonal events, maritime museums, seaside national and state parks, seaside camping, coastal cruises, islands, ferries, yachting, beaches, fishing, coastal hunting, and seaside hotels and motels in each state.

US-154 Soderberg, Paul, et al. THE BIG BOOK OF HALLS OF FAME IN THE UNITED STATES AND CANADA. 3 vols. New York: R.R. Bowker, 1977-- . Index. 0-8352-0990-3. 77-82734.

Volume 1 covers sports; volume 2 covers arts and entertainment, business and industry, North American culture, and science and technology; and volume 3 covers collegiate, city and state halls of fame. The very comprehensive listings give location, history, services available and, for the larger ones, biographical information on the honorees. The sports included in volume 1 range from angling to wheelchair sports.

US-155 STANDARD HIGHWAY MILEAGE GUIDE. Chicago: Rand McNally, 1978. 499 p. Tables, maps.

The shortest road miles between 1,100 selected cities in the US and Canada have been computed and are listed in the tables which comprise most of this volume. The state maps at the end of the volume indicate which cities are among the 1,100 and are designed to allow the calculation of distances from these key cities to other cities and towns on the map. In the 1978 edition there were several incorrect listings, and a supplement correcting these errors has been issued but may not be in any given copy. New editions are issued at irregular intervals; the previous edition was in 1973.

US-156 STEAM PASSENGER SERVICE DIRECTORY. Middletown, NY: Empire State Railway Musuem, 1973. Issued annually. 144 p. Photos. Index.

This is "an illustrated directory listing tourist railroad, trolley and museum operations with regularly scheduled or intermittent passenger service."

US-157 Stember, Sol. THE BICENTENNIAL GUIDE TO THE AMERICAN REVOLUTION. 3 vols. New York: E.P. Dutton, 1974. Maps. Indexes. 73-23108.

Although useful for detailed directions to specific sites, this is more a geographically oriented history than a guidebook. Volume 1 covers the North, volume 2 covers the Middle Colonies, and volume 3 covers the South.

US-158 Stern, Jane, and Stern, Michael. AMAZING AMERICA. New York: Random House, 1977. 463 p. Photos. Indexes. 0-394-73410-6. 77-90313.

A potpourri of over 600 places and sights that are a bit out of the ordinary, this book has no thematic focus and rambles from hobo conventions to fire museums. It has a general and subject index. The descriptions give full details about location, hours, and fees.

US-159 _____. ROADFOOD. New York: Random House, 1977. 384 p. Index. 0-394-73508-0. 77-90314.

This is a state-by-state guide to over 400 diners, cafes, truckstops,

roadside stands, and tearooms all within 10 miles of a major highway and where you can usually get a full meal for under $5. Each
establishment has a rating, lengthy description, and the address,
phone number, and hours are given. At the end of each state section there is a list of fairs and festivals that celebrate American
food.

US-160 Taussig, Joseph K., and Taussig, Dorothy P. TRAVEL GUIDE FOR
SERVICEMEN. Chicago: Rand McNally, 1971. 64 p. Maps,
photos. 0-528-843305. 76-145961.

While mostly an atlas of states and cities, this does include a state-
by-state directory of military and naval bases offering accommodations
for service families.

US-161 Terry, Thomas P. UNITED STATES TREASURE MAP ATLAS. La
Crosse, WI: Specialty Products, 1974. 142 p. Maps.

In this guide "more than 5,000 treasure locations are listed on individual state maps." This publisher issues many books on this topic.

US-162 Thomas, Bill, and Thomas, Phyllis. LAKESIDE RECREATION AREAS.
Harrisburg, PA: Stackpole Books, 1977. 160 p. Photos., maps.
0-8117-2104-3. 76-54716.

Arranged alphabetically by both state and by lake within a state,
this work describes over 200 selected U.S. Army Corps of Engineers
lakes noting location, hunting and fishing possibilities, camping
facilities, "other activities," and area attractions. Addresses for
further information are given. At the end of each state section is a
brief listing of additional Corps of Engineers lakes merely giving location. Rather poor state maps accompany the text.

US-163 Thompson, Toby. SALOON: A GUIDE TO AMERICA'S GREAT BARS,
SALOONS, TAVERNS, DRINKING PLACES AND WATERING HOLES.
New York: Viking Press, 1976. 288 p. Index. 0-670-61622-2.
76-26549.

This very personal selection of drinking places gives locations and has
descriptions that read like a novel.

US-164 Thum, Marcella. EXPLORING BLACK AMERICA: A HISTORY AND
GUIDE. New York: Atheneum, 1975. 402 p. 0-689-30462-5.
74-19428.

"A guidebook to museums, monuments and historic sites commemorating
the achievements of Black Americans," this volume is arranged by
specific aspects of the black experience.

US-165 TOLL-FREE DIGEST: A DIRECTORY OF OVER 3600 TOLL-FREE

TELEPHONE NUMBERS. New York: Warner Books, 1977. Issued annually. 368 p. 0-446-89339-4.

Three quarters of this book is a state-by-state listing of hotels, motels, and inns in each community arranged alphabetically by chain (Best Western, Days Inns, etc.). One fourth of the book lists services, from air cargo to Western Union, many of which are related to travel and leisure: local airline offices, car rental firms, charter trips, golf, Amtrak offices, ski resorts, and travel services.

US-166 TOURING WITH TOWSER. White Plains, NY: Gaines Dog Research Center, 1977. 61 p.

This is a state-by-state directory of hotels and motels that accommodate guests with pets.

US-167 TRAILER LIFE RV CAMPGROUND AND SERVICES DIRECTORY: U.S./CANADA/MEXICO. Calabasas, CA: Trailer Life Publishing Co., 1978. 1,266 p. Maps, photos.

This is an alphabetical state-by-state listing of both appropriate campsites, based on inspections, for those traveling with RVs (recreational vehicles), and places to obtain RV services and supplies. An introductory section describes where to go and what to see in every state and gives the official state agency to write to for hunting and fishing information.

US-168 TRAVELAIDE: A VACATION GUIDE: Argo, IL: 3M National Advertising Co. (6850 South Harlem Avenue, Bedford Park/60501).

The travelaide directory and map is a series of 8 regional editions of guides to motels, restaurants, and attractions "distributed to travelers, through selected interstate service stations, state welcome/information centers, car rental agencies, and travel service businesses." Each issue is mostly a hodge-podge of advertisements for local establishments plus a very confusing, limited, and uneven milepost guide to services along each interstate highway keyed to the maps. The listings of motels and restaurants are mostly the chain establishments specializing in budget rooms and fast food. The Exxon (US-56) and Mobil guides (US-112) are more thorough in their listings, but if you do not care about quality travel services, this series has the virtue of being free and actually keyed to pertinent interstate highways. The regional editions are: (1) the Northeast states, published annually in April; (2) the Mid-Atlantic states, published semiannually in October and April; (3) the Southern states, published semiannually in January and July; (4) Florida, published semiannually in April and October; (5) the Eastern Midwest states, published semiannually in November and May; (6) the Mid-Western states, published semiannually in September and March; (7) the Southwest states, published semiannually in December and June; and (8) the Far West states, published semiannually in February and August. Geographical coverage of each edition varies. A Northern Midwest Directory covering Montana, North Dakota, South Dakota, Minnesota and Wisconsin was discontinued, and future plans call for editions based on smaller regions. A Colorado/Utah edition was planned for September 1978.

US-169 THE TRAVELERS GUIDE TO GOLF. By the editors of Golf Digest. Norwalk, CT: Golf Digest, 1976. 192 p. Photos., maps. Index. 0-914178-09-1. 76-25368.

This world-wide guide to golf resorts is devoted largely to those in the US. It gives name, address, phone, description of golf course, fees, other golf facilities, other recreational facilities, lodging, rates, business meeting facilities, and directions. It is regionally arranged with a name index. Each February issue of GOLF DIGEST magazine has a directory of courses called "Places to Play."

US-170 THE TRAVELERS GUIDE TO TENNIS. By Barry Tarshis and the editors of Tennis Magazine. Norwalk, CT: Tennis Magazine, 1976. 142 p. Photos., maps. Index. 0-914178-10-5. 76-25369.

This regionally arranged guide to resorts with a genuine tennis program is devoted largely to resorts in the US. It gives address, phone, tennis facilities, court fees, court assignment system, instructional program, other recreational facilities, accommodations, rates, and how to get there.

US-171 TRAVELER'S TOLL-FREE TELEPHONE DIRECTORY. Burlington, VT: Landmark Publishing, 1977. Revised occasionally. 128 p.

While by far the largest number of entries is for hotels and motels (findable by state/city as well as chain), other services of use to travelers are also listed, e.g. campgrounds, airlines, vehicle rental, insurance, credit card firms, tennis resorts, train and bus lines, and travel and tour agencies. The name of the service, the traveler's location ("if you are here"), and the toll-free number are listed.

US-172 24 HOUR FULL-SERVICE AUTO-TRUCK STOPS. 2d ed. Rye, NY: Reymont Associates (29 Reymont Avenue/10580), 1977. Issued annually. 45 p.

"A nationwide guide," this lists "more than 500 round-the-clock auto-truck stops along or near the Interstate Highway System--offering food, lodging, fuel, repairs, and other services--for long-distance motorists, vacationers, and owners of recreational vehicles."

US-173 U.S. National Park Service. DOORWAY TO ADVENTURE: VISIT A LESSER-USED PARK. Washington, DC: U.S. Government Printing Office, 1975. 42 p. Photos.

A self-defeating publication, this lists, by state, those parks deemed "lesser-used" noting location, accommodations, and facilities.

US-174 _____. INDEX OF THE NATIONAL PARK SYSTEM AND AFFILI-
ATED AREAS AS OF JUNE 30, 1977. Washington, DC: U.S.
Government Printing Office, 1977. Updated frequently. 80 p.
Photos. Index.

The brief text describes the National Park System and its types of
areas (natural, historic, recreational, and affiliated). The main body
of this book is a state-by-state listing of all the areas within it administered by the National Park Service giving location, mailing
address, acreage, and outstanding characteristics of each.

US-175 UNITED STATES TENNIS CLUB REGISTRY. Irvine, CA: Tennis
Club Registry, 1976. 143 p.

This is an alphabetical listing by state of "tennis clubs, resort hotels
featuring tennis, ranches, camps and schools." Most of the listings
merely have a name and address, but a few of the listings are much
fuller, noting staff and facilities.

US-176 U.S. Travel Service. USA PLANT VISITS 1977-1978. Washington,
DC: U.S. Government Printing Office, 1977. Issued frequently.
153 p.

This is arranged by state and city with an industry classification
index. It notes restrictions, gives an address and contact person for
each listed industrial company offering visits of its premises to out-
siders.

US-177 _____. VISIT U.S.A. OUTLETS ABROAD. Washington, DC: U.S.
Government Printing Office, 1976. 32 p.

This is a selected list of retail travel agents and tour products in
other countries promoting travel to the US.

US-178 VISITING OUR PAST: AMERICA'S HISTORYLANDS. The World in
Color Library. Washington, DC: National Geographic Society, 1977.
400 p. Photos., maps. 0-87044-003-9. 77-21828.

This is essentially a heavily illustrated general historical survey of
the US accompanied by a 64-page "Supplemental Guide to Selected
Sites" arranged by state giving locational information on the few
chosen places and very brief background and descriptions.

US-179 VISITOR ACCOMMODATIONS, FACILITIES, AND SERVICES 1978-79.
Washington, DC: U.S. Government Printing Office, 1978. 93 p.

This is an alphabetical listing by park/area/site name of private concerns offering lodgings, facilities, and services on a concession basis
in the National Park System. When rates are given, the year the
rates apply are noted. Services include newsstands, transportation,

food, tours, and trips, firewood, and equipment rentals. Mailing addresses and, sometimes, telephone numbers are given.

US-180 Von Haag, Michael, and Crew, Anna, eds. A MONEYWISE GUIDE TO NORTH AMERICA. 13th ed. A Travelaid Publication. New York: Two Continents Publishing, 1978. 328 p. Maps. 0-902743-13-9.

Designed for the European student traveler, the emphasis is, naturally, on youthful activities and interests and on traveling inexpensively. Somewhat superficial, it is a good general beginning guide covering a lot of territory. Galleries, museums, architectural sights, local information sources, entertainment, and lodgings are stressed.

US-181 Vuilleumier, Marion R. AMERICA'S RELIGIOUS TREASURES. A Spiritual Heritage Travel Guide. New York: Harper & Row, 1976. 286 p. Photos., maps. Index. 0-06-068940-4. 76-9342.

This guide includes regionally arranged descriptions of primary places of religious importance, mostly church buildings. Practical visitor information is not given.

US-182 WALKING TOURS OF AMERICA. New York: Kinney Shoe Corp. (Box 5006, Dept. T/10022), 1979. 4 sets. Maps.

The Kinney Shoe Corp., in cooperation with the President's Council on Physical Fitness and Sports, sponsors a continuing program of "Walking Tours of America." They have prepared guided walks in 60 areas throughout the US. Each walk "is published as a separate brochure, featuring a special walker's map, a roundup of local legend, historic facts, outstanding points of interest, notes on geographic attractions, and tips on recreational, dining and shopping options." The walks are packaged in four sets according to geographical location--East, West, South and Southwest, and Midwest. It has been announced that Collier Books will publish these tours as a complete book with the title WALKING TOURS OF AMERICA, edited by Louise Feinsot.

US-183 Wasserman, Paul, et al., eds. FESTIVALS SOURCEBOOK. Detroit: Gale Research Co., 1977. 656 p. Indexes. 0-8103-0311-6. 76-48852.

FESTIVALS SOURCEBOOK is "a reference guide to fairs, festivals and celebrations in agriculture, antiques, the arts, theater and drama, arts and crafts, community, dance, ethnic events, film, folk, food and drink, history, Indians, marine, music, seasons and wildlife." The main arrangement is by 18 broad categories of festivals with state breakdowns. There are indexes by month, by event name, by state with local community breakdown, and by subject (a more narrow breakdown than the broad categories of the main arrangement).

US-184 WHEELERS RECREATIONAL VEHICLE RESORT AND CAMPGROUND
GUIDE. Park Ridge, IL: Print Media Services (distributed by Simon
& Schuster), 1977. Issued annually. 592 p. Maps. Index.

The main volume (North American edition) begins with an introduction in English, French, and Spanish. This is followed by brief and
often informative articles. The main part is a state-by-state listing
of sites, with distinctions between campgrounds, recreational vehicle
resorts and mobile home parks. The guide gives location, address,
some facilities, season, and a rating. Also issued in three regional
editions: Northeasterner, Southeasterner, and Westerner.

US-185 WINE COUNTRY U.S.A./CANADA. Rye, NY: Reymont Associates
(29 Reymont Avenue/10580), 1975. 28 p.

A state-by-state listing of wineries giving address, phone, visiting
days and hours, this volume also indicates whether a tour is available
and whether wine is sold on the premises.

US-186 Wood, Peter. RUNNING THE RIVERS OF NORTH AMERICA. Barre,
MA: Barre Books (distributed by Crown), 1978. 296 p. Maps.
0-517-53313-8. 77-26833.

The first 100 pages are devoted to technique, equipment and how-to
information. Then follows descriptions of over 50 navigable rivers in the US
which includes locations of put-ins, availability of rentals, sources of
further information, etc. as well as general river details. It is regionally arranged, and there is no index.

US-187 WOODALL'S CAMPGROUND DIRECTORY. Highland Park, IL:
Woodall Publishing Co. (distributed by Grosset & Dunlap), 1978.
Issued annually. 496 p. Maps.

This is a state-by-state directory of campgrounds giving location,
facilities, restrictions, and a rating. Eastern and western regions are
also published separately. Woodall also issues a monthly magazine
WOODALL'S TRAILER AND RV TRAVEL, and several other publications not directly related to travel.

US-188 THE WORLD ATLAS OF GOLF. New York: Random House, 1976.
280 p. Photos., maps. 0-394-40814-4. 76-10297.

The US rates its share of great golf courses in any international guide.
Twenty US courses are in the major section (Great Courses) of this
atlas and 19 are in the supplemental section of the 100 merely outstanding courses. A great course is described thoroughly: history, famous
matches (almost stroke-by-stroke), description of each hole, etc. The
bird's-eye-view course diagrams are most impressive. There are copious
photographs. The merely outstanding have a course diagram and brief
description.

US-189 WORLDWIDE YACHT CHARTER AND BOAT RENTAL GUIDE. 5th ed. Grosse Pointe, MI: Jack & Linda Grenard (18226 Mack/48236), 1977. Issued annually. 54 p. Photos. Bibliography.

This world listing, a bit awkwardly arranged, of companies and individuals offering yacht and boat rentals, gives mailing address and sometimes telephone number. It lists yacht name, length, whether sail and/or power, rigging, number of berths, whether "bareboat" or with captain, and rates. There are brief informative articles on aspects of chartering. Under "companies and services" it lists a few books, mostly cruising guides.

MAGAZINES

US-190 ADVENTURE TRAVEL. Seattle: Adventure Travel Publications (444 NE Ravenna Boulevard, Suite 301/98115).

This bimonthly (first issue: June/July 1978) magazine published by Adventure Travel Publications, a subsidiary of the American Adventures Association (US-218) features articles and high-quality color photographs of adventure travel expeditions, natural history, and conservation and wildlife. It has regular sections on adventure trips, adventure gear, and adventure books.

US-191 BETTER HOMES AND GARDENS. Des Moines, IA: The Meredith Corp. (1716 Locust Street/50336).

Of all the general, mass-market magazines BETTER HOMES AND GARDENS (BHG) has the best and most extensive regular travel section. US destinations are usually featured. These are frequently presented around a theme, and the what-to-see and do information in the articles often corresponds to the geographic region in which that edition is circulated. The magazine is indexed in the READERS GUIDE TO PERIODICAL LITERATURE. The Research Department of BHG issues INDICES OF THE TRAVEL MARKET on a regular basis. This pulls together all the travel industry statistics, tables, and research data from almost 30 different sources. BHG also commissions and publishes its own statistical studies on developing the family travel market, regional travel markets, etc.

US-192 GOING PLACES: THE MAGAZINE FOR ACTIVE TRAVELERS. Radnor, PA: Chilton Co. (Chilton Way/19089).

You'll have to get on the good side of your travel agent and purchase lots of trips from him or her to see this magazine. Agents buy this slick bimonthly consumer travel magazine and then send it to their best clients. It stresses mostly international travel, but there's usually one article per issue on a US destination. It's designed to make you want to visit the places featured, and there are numerous how-to articles and columns as well on such topics as air flights, travel products, tours, etc. It began publication in 1976.

US-193 KEY MAGAZINE. New York: Key Magazines (1 East 42d Street/10017).

These are a series of uniform advertising magazines describing dining, shopping, entertainment, and other events in over 25 individual metropolitan area editions. They are published locally, are usually issued weekly and are distributed free in hotel lobbys and other places with a high tourist turnover. The above address is for the East National Sales Office. The Midwest National Sales Office is located at 105 West Madison Street, Chicago, IL 60602. The West National Sales Office is located at 651 Brannon Street, San Francisco, CA 94107. They are available for the following areas: Atlanta, Carmel/Monterey, Chicago, Cincinnati, Columbus, Dallas, Detroit, Fort Worth, Houston, Kansas City, Los Angeles, Miami, Nashville, New York City, Oklahoma City, Palm Springs, Phoenix, Pittsburgh, St. Louis, San Francisco, and Tulsa.

US-194 NATIONAL GEOGRAPHIC MAGAZINE. Washington, D.C.: The National Geographic Society (17th & M Streets NW/20036).

The society was organized in 1890 "for the increase and diffusion of geographic knowledge." Since its inception, it has sponsored over 1,500 explorations and research projects and it diffuses this knowledge through this, its monthly journal as well as its books; globes; atlases; sheet maps; NATIONAL GEOGRAPHIC WORLD, a magazine for children 8 years and older; television shows; and exhibits in Explorers Hall in its Washington, DC headquarters building. Although most of the articles in the magazine are not written as travel articles, many are about specific areas of the country and provide excellent background reading and photographic coverage for travelers contemplating visits to those areas. The magazine is indexed in the READERS GUIDE TO PERIODICAL LITERATURE. In addition, the Society publishes its own index to the magazine: volume 1 indexes the issues from 1888 to 1946, and volume 2 from 1947 to 1976 with annual supplements beginning with 1977.

US-195 TRAVEL & LEISURE. New York: American Express Publishing Corp. (1350 Avenue of the Americas/10019).

Of the two general travel magazines, see also TRAVEL INCORPORATING HOLIDAY (US-197), this one is more concerned with maintaining its upbeat image, contains less practical information, and has less US coverage. It is issued monthly (since 1938), and sometimes its regular feature "Go" contains US travel newsnotes.

US-196 TRAVELHOST, THE NATIONAL INN-ROOM MAGAZINE FOR TRAVELERS. Dallas, TX: Omni Industries (6116 North Central Expressway, Suite 1020/75206).

This is a weekly magazine produced and published locally in over
40 regional editions. It is placed in hotel rooms and is directed to
the traveling business executive. It contains current information on
points of interest, dining and entertainment, as well as local televi-
sion programming for the week, and has many advertisements. It is
available for the following areas: Albuquerque/Santa Fe, Atlanta,
Atlantic City, Austin, Baton Rouge, Birmingham, Chicago, Dallas,
Denver, Fort Worth, Houston, Jacksonville, Las Vegas, Los Angeles,
Madison, Miami, Milwaukee, Minneapolis/St. Paul, Monterey Bay
Cities, New Orleans, Oklahoma City, Orange County, CA, Phoenix,
Portland, OR, Reno, Sacramento, Salt Lake City, San Antonio, San
Diego, San Francisco, St. Louis, Tampa, and Washington, DC.

US-197 TRAVEL INCORPORATING HOLIDAY: THE MAGAZINE THAT ROAMS
THE GLOBE. Floral Park, NY: Travel/Holiday Magazine (51 Atlantic Avenue/11001).

TRAVEL magazine has been published since 1901, and beginning with
the November 1977 issue, HOLIDAY magazine, which had been published since 1946, was merged with it. This monthly magazine features destinations all over the world, but each issue contains several
articles about the US. A regular feature, "Around the U.S.," contains
many interesting newsnotes. It is indexed in the READERS GUIDE TO
PERIODICAL LITERATURE, and they issue their own subject and author
index periodically. This is the best, most easily obtainable, general
travel magazine for the US.

US-198 WHERE MAGAZINE. Argo, IL: 3M National Advertising Co.
(6850 South Harlem Avenue, Bedford Park, IL 60501).

This weekly guide to dining, shopping, entertainment, and special
events is found in leading hotel and motor inn lobbys. It is pub-
lished locally in over 25 regional editions: Atlanta, Baltimore,
Boston, Chicago, Cincinnati, Cleveland, Dallas, Denver, Detroit,
Fort Lauderdale, Fort Worth, Honolulu, Houston, Los Angeles, Miami,
Minneapolis/St. Paul, New Orleans, New York City, Orange County,
CA, Orlando, Philadelphia, Phoenix, St. Louis, San Diego, San Fran-
cisco, and Washington, D.C.

PUBLISHERS

US-199 ARROW PUBLISHING CO., 1234 Chestnut Street, Newton Upper
Falls, MA 02164.

One of the major producers of city (and occasionally county) maps,
Arrow sells its maps and atlases both directly and through local distributors, usually the largest newsdealer in an area. The maps are
usually quite informative and useful.

US-200 AVIATION BOOK CO., Box 4187, Glendale, CA 91202.

They publish/distribute several useful airport directories and travel guides. The AIRPORT APPROACH PLATE ATLAS includes frequently updated large-scale exact reproductions of instrument flight approaches for all airports in each of three regional editions: west, north, and south. The FLIGHT GUIDE AIRPORT & FREQUENCY MANUAL, edited by Monty Navarre, is a three-ring, frequently updated, directory that can be held in one hand, of runway diagrams and other important data about airports including location, elevation, runway length, radio navigation frequencies, etc. It comes in 2 volumes: volume 1 covers 11 western states and volume 2 covers 37 states east of the Rocky Mountains. The PILOTS GUIDE TO CALIFORNIA AIRPORTS is a frequently revised directory for the visual flight pilot showing airport photos, pattern and runway diagrams, communications data, information about airport businesses, and facilities, etc. Also available is the WESTERN STATES FLY-IN CAMPGROUND DIRECTORY by George Deshler.

US-201 BREVET PRESS, Box 1404, 519 West Tenth, Sioux Falls, SD 57101.

This publisher specializes in books about the heritage of the Dakotas and in a series of state guides to historical markers and sites. These guides to South Dakota, North Dakota, Nebraska, Wisconsin, and Illinois have already been published, and are described separately in this information guide. Additional volumes in the historical markers and sites series are planned for Kansas, Tennessee, Missouri, Florida, and California.

US-202 CHAMPION MAP CORP., Box 17435, Charlotte, NC 28211.

Champion maps, as well as being sold, are often given away by local banks and real estate agents. The quality of the maps range from good to adequate. As of this writing, Champion seems to be expanding its list of areas mapped.

US-203 DOLPH MAP CO., 430 North Federal Highway, Fort Lauderdale, FL 33301.

Good maps for a variety of cities and towns across the US are issued by this publisher.

US-204 EAST WOODS PRESS BOOKS, Fast & McMillan Publishers, 6000 Kingstree Drive, Charlotte, NC 28210.

East Woods Press publishes a number of excellent where-to outdoor recreation guides in the areas of hiking, canoeing, walking, and skiing.

US-205 FROMMER/PASMANTIER PUBLISHING CORP., 70 Fifth Avenue,
New York, NY 10011.

Frommer/Pasmantier are publishers of thorough, inexpensive paperback
guides to Boston, Las Vegas, Los Angeles, New York, San Francisco,
Washington, DC and other popular US cities. Their books are distributed by Simon & Schuster, 630 Fifth Avenue, New York, NY
10020.

US-206 GOUSHA CO., 2001 The Alameda, Box 6227, San Jose, CA 95150.

This subsidiary of the Times-Mirror Corp. publishes adequate road
and city maps, both as sheets (folded) and in atlases (road). Most
of its map output is done for oil companies (notably Chevron), airlines, auto clubs, banks, and other commercial firms which often
give the maps away. It is probably number 3 (after Rand McNally
[US-215] and Hammond [US-208]) among the commercial road map
makers. It also publishes guide books and travel magazines with a
controlled circulation.

US-207 HAGSTROM CO., 450 West 33d Street, New York, NY 10001.

They are a major producer of street maps and atlases for urban areas,
primarily in the northeast around New York City, but ranging fairly
widely around the US. Their maps are readable, if not the best
quality. They are known for their county maps/atlases.

US-208 HAMMOND, Maplewood, NJ 07040.

Popularly thought of as number 2 (after Rand McNally [US-215]) in
the domestic map field, Hammond turns out decent road maps issued
both as individual maps and in atlases. They also publish some travel
guides and often provide the maps found in the guidebooks of other
publishers as well as for use and distribution by the major oil companies and other businesses.

US-209 HASTINGS HOUSE PUBLICATIONS, 10 East 40th Street, New York,
NY 10016.

They are a publisher of several major travel series. The most important of these are their recent revisions of several of the original
WPA American Guides all of which have been included in this information guide. (Somerset Publications, also known as the Scholarly
Press, 19722 East Nine Mile Road, St. Clair Shores, MI 48080,
has been issuing recent reprints of several of the original WPA Guides.
However, these are just reissues of the original guides with their original
text and are not to be confused with the Hastings House editions with
their revised textual material.) Another of their series is the "In Color

series: SAN FRANCISCO IN COLOR, TIDEWATER VIRGINIA IN COLOR, NANTUCKET IN COLOR, TEXAS IN COLOR, CHICAGO IN COLOR, and many others, none of which have been included in this information guide because they provide no factual travel information. Hastings House also publishes a large number of travel books which are not part of any series. Write to them for a complete catalog.

US-210 DAVID McKAY CO., 750 Third Avenue, New York, NY 10017.

This company is the publisher of the far-ranging, internationally known Fodor's guides.

US-211 MEDIA VENTURES, 715 Hulman Bldg., 120 West Second Street, Dayton, OH 45402.

They publish a "50 Great Mini-Trips Book" series. As of this writing, volumes in this series have been issued for Ohio, Kentucky, Michigan, Florida, Indiana, Illinois, and Pennsylvania. They appear individually in this information guide.

US-212 WILLIAM MORROW & CO., 6 Henderson Drive, West Caldwell, NJ 07006.

They are a regular trade publisher with a large line of US travel guides including their "Americans Discover America" series. These titles appear throughout this information guide. They also publish all the Fielding guides to travel in Europe and other foreign countries.

US-213 101 PRODUCTIONS, 834 Mission Street, San Francisco, CA 94103.

Most of their books are natural foods and ethnic cookbooks, and they publish the "Best Restaurants" series. Individual titles in this series appear throughout this information guide. They have also done a few books on country inns.

US-214 PILOT BOOKS, 347 Fifth Avenue, New York, NY 10016.

They publish a number of concise guides to free travel information and attractions as well as a directory of budget motels all by Raymond Carlson.

US-215 RAND McNALLY & CO, Box 7600, Chicago, IL 60680.

Generally rated as number one in the domestic map field, they publish an extensive array of guidebooks, both of a general nature and on specific areas and activities, as well as state and city maps and their well-known road atlases. The company maintains its own retail stores in New York, Chicago, and San Francisco.

US-216 STACKPOLE BOOKS, Cameron & Kelker Streets, Harrisburg, PA 17105.

They publish a number of outdoor guides, including the series by Robert Colwell.

US-217 U.S. GOVERNMENT PRINTING OFFICE, Washington, DC 20402.

This is the U.S. government's primary printer/publisher/bookseller from whom most of the official travel publications listed throughout this information guide may be obtained. For access to these publications use the MONTHLY CATALOG OF UNITED STATES GOVERNMENT PUBLICATIONS (SM-13) and the SELECTED LIST OF GOVERNMENT PUBLICATIONS, the mailing list of which you can get on at no charge by writing to the above address.

ORGANIZATIONS

General

US-218 THE AMERICAN ADVENTURERS ASSOCIATION, 444 NE Ravenna Blvd., Suite 301, Seattle, WA 98115 (206/527-1621).

Membership in this organization entitles you to ADVENTURE TRAVEL magazine (US-190); the INTERNATIONAL ADVENTURE TRAVELGUIDE (US-93); ADVENTURE TRAVEL NEWSLETTER, a monthly listing of specific expeditions, publications, educational trips, etc. available around the world; discounts on literature, photographic equipment and selected adventure trips; and special Association sponsored, members-only adventure trips.

US-219 AMERICAN ASSOCIATION OF RETIRED PERSONS, 1909 K Street NW, Washington, DC 20049 (202/872-4700).

AARP provides many services for its members, among them a Travel Service which creates trips "to meet the needs and tastes of the mature traveler." These trips are planned jointly for AARP and the NRTA (National Retired Teachers Association). The national headquarters' address and phone number of NRTA is the same as that given above for AARP.

US-220 AMERICAN CANOE ASSOCIATION, 4260 East Evans Avenue, Denver, CO 80222 (303/758-8257).

Founded in 1880, this organization provides a myriad of services for its members: it leads many canoe and river trips and develops maps and guides to canoeable areas; it monitors policies affecting access to rivers; it sponsors safety education and racing activities; it publishes CANOE magazine (bimonthly, first published in 1973); and it provides a discount book buying service which offers a very good selection of regional where-to canoe guides. There are numerous affiliated local groups that sponsor river tips. What was originally just canoeing has now expanded to include kayaking, rafting, river running, and several styles of specialized racing and the Association serves all interests.

US-221 AMERICAN INDIAN TRAVEL COMMISSION, 10403 West Colfax Avenue, Suite 550, Westland Bank, Lakewood, CO 80215 (303/234-1707).

This is "an independent, non-profit corporation established in 1972 by Indian leaders. Its purpose is to help Native Americans and Native Alaskans in the development, promotion, and operation of tourism interests in Indian Country, U.S.A." This "Indian Country" consists of 90 million acres, and the Commission promotes travel to more than 300 tribal-built resorts, campgrounds, and trailer parks in these native-owned lands. They supply a brochure describing these resorts and campgrounds and the recreation facilities available at each. They also issue a quarterly newsletter which is a central source of information on Indian tourism activities. In addition, they sponsor seminars and provide marketing assistance for Indians both already in the travel business and those considering such a move.

US-222 AMERICAN YOUTH HOSTELS, National Campus, Delaplane, VA 22025 (703/592-3271).

This is a nonprofit association founded in 1934 as a community service to provide year-round opportunities for outdoor recreation and inexpensive educational travel through hosteling (traveling "under your own steam" and staying at youth hostels which are inexpensive overnight dormitory-like accommodations under adult supervision). It is one of 48 national hosteling associations affiliated with the International Youth Hostel Federation. In this country, in 1977, there were 29 local councils in 18 states operating nearly 200 hostel facilities. Check the local phone book under American Youth Hostels for the names and locations of these local councils and/or hostels. Each of these is also described in the annual AYH pocket-sized handbook (1977 ed., 176 p.) which is free to members. As we go to press, it has been announced that this handbook is now available to the public at large from East Woods Press (US-204). The title is HOSTELING U.S.A. Membership is open to all ages and entitles you to use all AYH hostels and to participate in the small group adventure trips sponsored by AYH. Memberships are obtainable from local councils, hostels or the national headquarters at the above address. In addition to the annual handbook, AYH also issues the NORTH AMERICAN BICYCLE ATLAS (US-12) and several International Hostel Guides. Many of the local councils produce their own guides. For example, the Minnesota Council issues a 76-page bike atlas describing tours throughout the state, the Pittsburgh, PA Council has a HIKING GUIDE TO WESTERN PENNSYLVANIA now in a fourth edition, and the Metropolitan New York Chapter publishes a monthly magazine called HOSTELING.

US-223 BIKECENTENNIAL, Box 8308, Missoula, MT 59807.

They organized the Trans-America Bicycle Trail in 1976, issue several route directories for the Trail, sponsor a number of escorted bicycle tours throughout the country, and publish a RESOURCE DIRECTORY FOR BICYCLE TOURISTS.

US-224 BOAT OWNERS ASSOCIATION OF THE UNITED STATES, Washington National Headquarters, 880 South Pickett Street, Alexandria, VA 22304 (703/823-9550).

This organization, more popularly known as BOAT/US, began in 1965 and provides a great number of services for its members: group rate marine insurance, a lobbying voice and consumer protection bureau, a single source for all federal and state boating forms and regulations, correspondence courses in navigation, and a chart distribution service. In addition, there are 4 major publications available to members: (1) an annual MEMBER SERVICE CATALOG (1978-79 ed., 48 p.) which thoroughly describes all the benefits of membership, (2) an annual BOATING BOOK BUYERS GUIDE (1978 ed., 18 p.), a very comprehensive guide to boating literature (all items in the catalog may be ordered through the Association at discounts), (3) a CONSUMER EQUIPMENT GUIDE which consists of a master reference issue and bimonthly supplements to boating equipment and accessories which can be purchased at highly favorable prices through the organization, and (4) BOAT/U.S. REPORTS, a monthly (May/June and November/December are combined) newsletter with regular sections covering new boating products and books, classified ads for boats and equipment, and a chart update.

US-225 DIABETES TRAVEL SERVICE, 349 East 52d Street, New York, NY 10022 (212/751-1076).

Their primary goal is to provide members with counseling and up-to-date information on all aspects of traveling with diabetes and special tours and cruises designed with the diabetic in mind. The DTS CLUB NEWS is a monthly newspaper and, in addition to the travel articles, includes sports, recipes, and general articles. The organization provides a hotline for assistance in emergency travel situations and the number is given out only upon joining. Membership also includes the above newspaper, diabetic ID cards in foreign languages, associate membership in the International Association for Medical Assistance to Travelers and discounts on books and merchandise.

US-226 GRUMMAN BOATS, Marathon, NY 13803.

In addition to manufacturing their own ever-popular aluminum canoes, this company publishes four very useful booklets for canoeists. Their RENT-A-CANOE DIRECTORY (1976 ed., 38 p.) is a state-by-state listing, with addresses and telephone numbers, of liveries from which canoes may be rented. In the back there is an unannotated listing of where-to canoe guides. The directory is updated regularly. THE GRUMMAN BOOK RACK FOR CANOEISTS is a 12-page annotated listing of 80 basic canoe books, most of which are devoted to how-to rather than where-to. The LEARN-TO-CANOE DIRECTORY is a 12-page state-by-state listing of local canoe clubs which offer training ranging from basic canoeing to white water skills. GROUP-CAMPING BY CANOE is a brief guide on how to organize an expedition of several days duration for a group. Grumman's public relations firm, Rockwell and Newell, 12 East 41st Street, New York, NY 10017 (212/725-0420) maintains a complete file of canoe tripping and canoe activities available across the country.

US-227 NATIONAL ASSOCIATION OF CONSUMERS AND TRAVELERS, 1000 Sunset Ridge Road, Northbrook, IL 60062 (312/498-1500).

This is a discount travel club, founded in 1964, that provides its 100,000 plus members with discounts on hotels and motels, car rentals, prescriptions, and other supplies. It provides trip routing and travel information and publishes BUYWAYS, a quarterly; a NACT HOTEL/MOTEL DIRECTORY, revised annually; and a RESTAURANT AND CAMPGROUND DIRECTORY, revised annually.

US-228 NATIONAL COUNCIL FOR COMMUNITY SERVICE TO INTERNA-TIONAL VISITORS (COSERV), Meridian House, 1630 Crescent Place NW, Washington, DC 20009 (202/332-1028).

Local volunteer-staffed COSERV organizations provide the following arrangements for the short-term foreign visitor to their cities: professional appointments, conferences, and field trips of interest to the visitor; interpretive sightseeing; language assistance; visits or overnight stays in American homes; and other information, maps, and guidance. They prefer to plan the visits of travelers under government or private sponsorship. Many of the local COSERV groups also provide some services to nonsponsored visitors, and those providing services to all are listed in a WHERE TO PHONE directory available from the above address. Only phone numbers are given in this directory, as COSERV has found that visitors tend to be more serious and precise about their needs if a telephone call is involved. It also permits a discussion of specific requests and an opportunity to explain just what services the local COSERV group can and cannot provide.

US-229 THE NATIONAL EASTER SEAL SOCIETY FOR CRIPPLED CHILDREN AND ADULTS, 2023 West Ogden Avenue, Chicago, IL 60612 (312/243-8400).

State and local affiliates of the society have been developing and distributing area guidebooks to accessible facilities for the handicapped for more than 20 years. The parent organization at this address issues a regularly updated DIRECTORY OF EASTER SEAL GUIDEBOOKS TO ACCESSIBLE FACILITIES. It is arranged alphabetically by state and by localities within each state, and includes the local address to write to for each guide, most of which are free.

US-230 SIERRA CLUB, 530 Bush Street, San Francisco, CA 94108 (415/981-8634).

The Sierra Club, founded in 1892 by John Muir, has grown to an internationally known outdoors and conservation organization of over 250 groups, 50 chapters, and 10 regional conservation committees. A list of the chapters may be obtained from the headquarters address above or any of the following 9 US offices: (1) Alaska Office, 545 East 4th Avenue, Anchorage, AK 99501; (2) Los Angeles Office, 2410 Beverly Blvd., Suite 2, Los Angeles, CA 90057; (3) Midwest Office, 444 West Main, Room 10, Madison, WI 53703; (4) New York Office, 800 Second Avenue, New York, NY 10017; (5) Northern Plains Office, Box 1078, 331 Main Street, Lander, WY 82520; (6) Northwest Office, 4534 1/2 University Way NE, Seattle, WA 98105; (7) Sacramento Office, 1107 9th Street, Room 405, Sacramento, CA 95814; (8) Southwest Office, 338 East De Vargas, Santa Fe, NM 87501; (9) Washington, DC Office, 330 Pennsylvania Avenue SE, Washington, DC 20003. Most chapters have regional groups, many of which sponsor their own outings and publications. Consult the local telephone book, your local chapter, the appropriate office listed above, or the headquarters office for the regional group nearest you. As a member, you receive the bimonthly SIERRA: THE SIERRA CLUB BULLETIN, a chapter newsletter, a discount on many Sierra Club Books, and the opportunity to participate in hundreds of outings sponsored by the Outings Department of the Club, its chapters and regional groups. The Sierra Club publishes many books and calendars. Requests for their publications list and orders should be addressed to Sierra Club Books, Box 3886, Rincon Annex, San Francisco, CA 94119. Their "Totebook" series consists of about 20 titles of practical how-to and where-to information in a handy pocket size.

US-231 SKI TOURING COUNCIL, West Hill Road, Troy, VT 05868 (802/744-2472).

This is a noncommercial, nonprofit, all-volunteer committee founded in 1962 for the sole purpose of introducing the then forgotten sport of ski touring. It gives free advice to any person or group wishing to start a ski touring program. It issues two annual publications: the SKI TOURING GUIDE (US-152) and the SKI TOURING SCHEDULE (15th ed., Winter 1978-79, 83 p.). The latter is a chronological listing, with complete information, of workshops, tours, and races, mainly in the East.

US-232 SOCIETY FOR THE ADVANCEMENT OF TRAVEL FOR THE HANDICAPPED, 26 Court Street, Brooklyn, NY 11242 (212/858-5483).

The purposes of the organization are to: (1) create greater awareness among the suppliers of the travel industry about the special problems of the handicapped traveler as well as the potential of the market, (2) serve as a clearinghouse for information about the range of special services and travel programs currently available for the handicapped, and (3) educate travel agents and tour operators to gain greater expertise in seeking out and selling to handicapped travelers.

US-233 TRAVELERS AID ASSOCIATION OF AMERICA, 701 Lee Street, Suite 600, Des Plains, IL 60016 (312/298-9390).

This is the umbrella organization--which provides no services itself-- for the local Travelers Aid societies. These local societies "help travelers in trouble" by providing: (1) emergency funds for stranded travelers, (2) relocation services, and (3) traditional travel information services. Each local society is an independent organization, though they do cooperate. They are usually found in train, plane, and bus stations. Consult the local telephone book for addresses and numbers.

US-234 TRAVELER'S INFORMATION EXCHANGE, 356 Boylston Street, Boston, MA 02116 (617/536-5651).

This organization, formerly known as the Women's Rest Tour Association, was founded in 1891 to provide guidance for "women of cultivated tastes and small means" who wished to travel abroad. One of its first publications was a list of lodging and lodging houses used and vouched for by the founding members. These lodging lists are still published; the FOREIGN LODGING LIST is issued in even numbered years, and the LODGING LIST OF AMERICAS in the odd numbered years. Now, as then, these lists are available only to members who sign a pledge to neither share, lend, nor give away their Lodging Lists. THE PILGRIM SCRIP is the annual magazine of the group in which members write of their travel experience.

US-235 U.S. ARMY, CORPS OF ENGINEERS, Washington, DC 20314.

Many environmentalists do not agree with the land acquisition policy of this department of the government. They build dams and flood large land areas in an effort to provide water control and recreation opportunities for boaters, fishermen and hunters. Regardless of your feelings, you will have to admit that many of the maps issued by the various division offices listed below of these recreation areas are very good and provide a great deal of useful where-to graphic information for the boater, fisherman, and hunter. Each of these divisions also has several district offices under it, each of which also issues good literature. (1) Lower Mississippi Valley Division, Box 80, Vicksburg, MS 39180 (601/636-1311); (2) Missouri River Division, Box 103, Downtown Station, Omaha, NE 68101 (402/221-7208); (3) New England Division, 424 Trapelo Road, Waltham, MA 02154; (4) North Atlantic Division, 90 Church Street, New York, NY 10007; (5) North Central Division, 536 South Clark Street, Chicago, IL 60605; (6) North Pacific Division, Box 2870, Portland, OR 97208 (503/221-3768); (7) Ohio River Division, Box 1159, Cincinnati, OH 45201; (8) Pacific Ocean Division, Building 230, Fort Shafter, Honolulu, HI

96813; (9) South Atlantic Division, 510 Title Bldg., 30 Pryor Street SW, Atlanta, GA 30303 (404/221-6715); (10) South Pacific Division, 630 Sansome Street, Room 1216, San Francisco, CA 94111; (11) Southwestern Division, Main Tower Bldg., 1200 Main Street, Dallas, TX 75202 (214/767-2510). Nearly every dammed lake has been mapped and great numbers of individual lake maps are available from each division and district. There is a series of six regional brochures describing lakeside recreation opportunities at all Army Corps of Engineers projects within that region: New England, Northeast, Southeast, Midwest, Southwest, and West.

US-236 U.S. BUREAU OF INDIAN AFFAIRS, Public Information Office, Washington, DC 20242.

They issue two very useful publications for the traveler planning to visit Indian country. The AMERICAN INDIAN CALENDAR (1978 ed., 85 p.) is an annual state-by-state listing of ceremonials, dances, feasts, and celebrations held throughout the year on or near American Indian reservations. In the back is a list, with addresses and phone numbers, of the twelve Bureau of Indian Affairs area offices that can verify these events and supply additional information. INDIAN LAND AREAS: GENERAL is a large map (24 1/2 in. X 39 in.) of the US on which the land areas owned by the various tribes are shown in color as well as the various Indian-run tourist complexes.

US-237 U.S. FISH AND WILDLIFE SERVICE, Assistant Director for Public Affairs, Washington, DC 20240.

They provide useful, annual lists. The DIRECTORY OF NATIONAL WILDLIFE REFUGES is arranged by state and gives the county, date established, acreage, and primary species found on each individual refuge. The REFUGE MANAGERS' ADDRESS LIST, also arranged by state, gives name of manager, address, and phone number. Individual managers must be contacted about hunting, fishing, boating, and other privileges available on each refuge.

US-238 U.S. FOREST SERVICE. Information Office, Box 2417, Washington, DC 20013 (202/447-3760).

The Forest Service manages over 150 national forests, numerous wilderness and primitive areas, approximately 20 national grasslands, and cooperates in the management of approximately 30 wild and scenic rivers, the National Trail System, and those national recreation areas that are located in national forest lands. Opportunities for outdoor recreation on these areas are practically infinite. Such recreation is provided by trails, streams, woodlands, and the natural forest environment, and as of June 30, 1974 the Forest Service maintained 6,413 developed campground and picnic sites, 322 swimming sites, 857 boating sites, and 216 winter sports sites. NATIONAL FOREST VACATIONS is a very excellent 55-page guide to these opportunities. There are over 20 visitor information centers on Forest Service lands.

Descriptions of these will be found in the 13-page EXPLORE! A VISITOR'S GUIDE TO DISCOVERY IN THE NATIONAL FORESTS. It doesn't include some of the newer centers (NATIONAL FOREST VACATIONS has a more up-to-date listing and a map showing locations), but it describes the programs and opportunities available at the first 20 that were established. Both of these publications are available from the above address. SEARCH FOR SOLITUDE, also available from this address, is a 32-page guide to outdoor recreation in the wilderness and primitive areas of the national forests. There are 9 Forest Service Regional Offices (listed below), and these are the best sources of information for specific areas. They issue excellent large-scale (often at a scale of 2 in. represents 1 mile) maps of individual forests showing roads, trails, hunting and fishing areas, boating areas, camping areas, winter sports areas, etc. (1) Northern Region, Federal Bldg., Missoula, MT 59801; (2) Rocky Mountain Region, 11177 West 8th Avenue, Box 25127, Lakewood, CO 80225 (303/234-4185); (3) Southwestern Region, 517 Gold Avenue SW, Albuquerque, NM 87102 (505/766-2444); (4) Intermountain Region, Federal Bldg., 324 25th Street, Ogden, UT 84401 (The Intermountain Region is one of the most prolific producers and distributors of guides to their area. NATIONAL FORESTS OF THE INTERMOUNTAIN REGION is a very large map/brochure showing all boundaries, recreation sites, and individual forests addresses. CAMP AND PICNIC IN THE NATIONAL FORESTS OF THE INTERMOUNTAIN REGION is an 82-page guide published in 1976 giving a map and recreation site information for each of the 16 national forests in the region); (5) California Region, 630 Sansome Street, San Francisco, CA 94111; (6) Pacific Northwest Region, 319 SW Pine Street, Box 3623, Portland, OR 97208 (503/221-2971); (7) Southern Region, 1720 Peachtree Road NW, Suite 800, Atlanta, GA 30309; (8) Eastern Region, 633 West Wisconsin Avenue, Milwaukee, WI 53203; (9) Alaska Region, Federal Office Bldg., Box 1628, Juneau, AK 99802. A very thorough coverage of the recreation opportunities and available literature for the individual national forests and their associated areas will be found in the book by Landi (US-100).

US-239 U.S. NATIONAL PARK SERVICE, Chief, Office of Communications, Department of the Interior, Washington, DC 20240 (202/343-7394).

The National Park Service (NPS) was established in 1916 and administers about 300 national parks, seashores, lakeshores, monuments, historic sites, historical parks, military parks, memorial parks, battlefield sites, scenic riverways, and recreation areas. At each area it provides interpretive services for visitors through a visitor information center, and it operates campgrounds and other visitor facilities at most other areas. All of the major and most popular NPS areas have been written up individually for this sourcebook. There are 7 books, booklets, or map/guides that describe what to see and do in NPS areas as a whole: (1) ACCESS NATIONAL PARKS: A GUIDE FOR HANDICAPPED VISITORS (US-1); (2) BACK-COUNTRY TRAVEL IN THE NATIONAL PARK SYSTEM (US-15); (3) CAMPING IN THE NA-

TIONAL PARK SYSTEM, 1978 ed., presents, in tabular form, information on services, facilities, fees charged, seasons, etc. at campgrounds in 100 NPS areas; (4) DOORWAY TO ADVENTURE: VISIT A LESSER-KNOWN PARK (US-173); (5) INDEX OF THE NATIONAL PARK SYSTEM AND AFFILIATED AREAS (US-174); (6) NATIONAL PARKS OF THE UNITED STATES: MAP AND GUIDE, 18 1/2 in. X 27 1/2 in., the map side shows the locations of all NPS areas, regions, and regional offices; the other side describes, in tabular form, the activities, facilities, and accommodations available at each NPS area; and (7) NATIONAL PARK SERVICE GUIDE TO THE HISTORIC PLACES OF THE AMERICAN REVOLUTION by James V. Murfin. Listed below are the 9 NPS Regional Offices: (1) North Atlantic Regional Office, 15 State Street, Boston, MA 02109 (617/223-2915); (2) Mid-Atlantic Regional Office, 143 South Third Street, Philadelphia, PA 19106 (215/597-7018); (3) National Capital Regional Office, 1100 Ohio Drive SW, Washington, DC 20242 (202/426-6700); (4) Southeast Regional Office, 1895 Phoenix Blvd., Atlanta GA 30349 (404/996-2520); (5) Midwest Regional Office, 1709 Jackson Street, Omaha, NE 68102 (402/221-3471); (6) Rocky Mountain Regional Office, Box 25287, Denver, CO 80225 (303/234-3095); (7) Southwest Regional Office, Old Santa Fe Trail, Box 728, Santa Fe, NM 87501 (505/988-6375) (W-58); (8) Western Regional Office, 450 Golden Gate Avenue, Box 36063, San Francisco, CA 94102 (415/556-4122); (9) Pacific Northwest Regional Office, 1424 Fourth Avenue, Room 931, 4th and Pike Bldg., Seattle, WA 98101 (206/442-0170). A request to each will bring the official map/brochure of any area administered by the NPS. Most national parks have their own cooperating association that publishes literature, leaflets, maps, and other interpretive literature about the park that would otherwise not be available through the use of federal funds. They also operate the bookshops in the park visitors centers and support individual park libraries and special nature and history reference collections. Many of them issue their own PUBLICATIONS PRICE LIST AND ORDER FORM. The individual associations are usually called the "(name of park) Natural History Association" and usually have the same address as the park.

US-240 U.S. SKI ASSOCIATION, 1726 Champa Street, Suite 300, Denver, CO 80202 (303/825-9183).

Organized in 1904, the USSA (not a government agency) is responsible for promoting skiing on all levels, which includes fielding the Olympic Ski Team. There are nine geographic divisions of USSA (see list below), and many local ski clubs are affiliated with their appropriate division. Most divisions supply ski information to their members and have a selection of local guidebooks for skiing in their region. The Rocky Mountain Division Office, for example, issues the ANNUAL OF ROCKY MOUNTAIN SKIING (1977-78 ed., 136 p.), a very thorough guide to all Rocky Mountain ski areas. (1) USSA/ Alaska, 8140 Cranberry Street, Anchorage, AK 99502; (2) USSA/Central, Box 66014, AMF O'Hare, Chicago, IL 60666; (3) USSA/Eastern, 22 High Street, Brattleboro, VT 05301; (4) USSA/Far West, 3325 Wilshire, Suite 1340, Los Angeles, CA 90010; (5) USSA/Intermountain, 1431 Terry Drive, Idaho Falls, ID 83401; (6) USSA/Northern, 1732 Clark Avenue, Billings, MT 59102; (7) USSA/Pacific Northwest, Box 6228, Seattle, WA 98188; (8) USSA/Rocky Mountain, 1463 Larimer, Denver, CO 80202; (9) USSA/Southern, Box 801, Belmont, NC 28012.

US-241   U.S. TRAVEL SERVICE, U.S. Department of Commerce, Washington, DC 20230.

The U.S. Travel Service (USTS) was established by the International Travel Act of June 29, 1961 (22 U.S.C. 2121-2127; sec. 2124 establishes the USTS), and until the spring of 1976, was concerned only with promoting travel to the US by residents of foreign countries. This continues to be the main focus of its activity. The Domestic Tourism Promotion Program, begun with funding authorized by Congress in November 1975, has suffered since its inception from a lack of defined roles and an inability to agree on appropriate channels through which to operate. In 1978, when Congress appropriated no money for this arm of the USTS, its existance was seriously threatened. A domestic public service advertising campaign was conducted in 1976 to persuade Americans to travel within the US. Also issued in that year was a 40-page TRAVELER'S GUIDE TO INFORMATION SOURCES, out of print at this writing. It lists addresses and phone numbers of state and major city tourism offices; locations of highway welcome centers by state; national park addresses; sources for language and emergency assistance, and currency exchange for international visitors; and a brief bibliography. No other compilation of similar information on even this small a scale has since been issued. In December 1976 a series of 11 pamphlets collectively entitled TRAVELER'S GUIDE TO SPECIAL ATTRACTIONS was introduced and is still available as of this writing, although there are no plans to have them reprinted. Each pamphlet focuses on a variety of US travel attractions related by a common theme: (1) American Culture-Centers for Performing Arts, (2) American Indian-Pow Wows and Festivals, (3) American Industry-Tours and Visits, (4) Skyscrapers, (5) Underwater Recreation, (6) Automobile Museums, (7) Oceanariums, (8) Winter Resorts, (9) Health Resorts, (10) The Supernatural-Haunted Houses and Legendary Ghosts, and (11) Living History Farms. In 1977 a series of 9 pamphlets collectively packaged and entitled CONSUMER'S GUIDE TO TRAVEL INFORMATION was introduced, and these also are still available as of this writing. As opposed to the above series which stressed where-to travel, this series provides how-to information. The individual titles are: "Tips for an Energy-Wise Vacation" (D-1), "Getting the Best Value for your Vacation Dollar" (D-2), "How to Get an Air Fare Deal" (D-3), "Helpful Hints for the Older Traveler" (D-4), "Helpful Information Sources" (D-5) (10 pages mostly of national park and national forest addresses and a few other hints of where to go for information), "Traveling with Pets" (D-6), "The Benefits of Using a Travel Agent" (D-7), "Travel Tips for the Handi-capped" (D-8), and "Your Rights and Responsibilities--Know Before You Go" (D-9). Another brochure issued under the same title as the above series, CONSUMER'S GUIDE TO TRAVEL INFORMATION is the frequently updated (every few months) STATE & TERRITORIAL TOURISM OFFICES. This gives addresses, phone numbers, and, where applicable, toll-free phone numbers. Despite the same overall title, it is not part of the previously mentioned packet of the same name, and must be requested separately. The USTS issues 20 travel planning area guides, each centered on a key US gateway city, and providing detailed information on getting around and what to see. However, these are written primarily for the use of interna-tional visitors. Americans would do better contacting the specific organizations and consulting the books mentioned throughout this in-formation guide. Another of their brochures entitled U.S.A. TRAVEL INFORMATION sounds promising but simply explains how to make traveling easier in the US for the international visitor.

US-242 VACATION EXCHANGE CLUB, 350 Broadway, New York, NY 10013.

Exchanging houses is an economical way to visit an area and get to know it as a native. For a small fee you submit information on your house and whether you are willing to exchange or rent. Your listing will be included in one of two HOME EXCHANGE BOOKS issued every spring; one in February, the other in April. These are world-wide listings, but the US section is extensive and is broken down by state. You arrange actual exchanges through your own correspon-dence; this service just publishes the lists of interested parties. You can also insert a listing if you are interested in providing hospitality while you remain in your home, if you are seeking a subscriber will-ing to rent only, and if you are seeking a youth exchange. This ser-vice first started in 1960.

AIRLINES

The name of the individual airline inflight magazine, most of which contain a map(s) showing the routes traveled by the airline and travel articles about areas and cities flown to by that airline, is given after the telephone number. Most airlines make available a system-wide timetable that frequently includes a city-by-city list of information/reservation/ticket sales/ground service offices and all regional toll-free numbers which may be called for reservations and information.

US-243 ALLEGHENY AIRLINES, Executive Offices, Washington National Air-port, Washington, DC 20001. FLIGHTIME.

As we went to press this airline changed its name to USAir.

US-244 AMERICAN AIRLINES, 633 Third Avenue, New York, NY 10017 (212/557-1234). AMERICAN WAY.

They issue an annual (1978 ed., 80 p.) TRAVEL GUIDE TO BLACK CONVENTIONS & CONFERENCES.

US-245 BRANIFF INTERNATIONAL AIRWAYS, Box 35001, Dallas, TX 75235 (214/358-6011). BRANIFF'S FLYING COLORS.

US-246 DELTA AIR LINES, Hartsfield Atlanta International Airport, Atlanta, GA 30320. SKY.

US-247 EASTERN AIRLINES, Executive Offices, Miami International Airport, Miami, FL 33148. REVIEW.

US-248 FRONTIER AIRLINES, 8250 Smith Road, Denver, CO 80207 (303/398-5151). FRONTIER.

US-249 HUGHES AIRWEST, International Headquarters, San Francisco International Airport, San Francisco, CA 94128 (415/573-4000). SUN-DANCER.

US-250 NATIONAL AIRLINES, General Office, Box 592055, Miami, FL 33159. ALOFT.

US-251 NORTH CENTRAL AIRLINES, 7500 Northliner Drive, Minneapolis, MN 55450 (612/726-7411). NORTHLINER.

As we went to press, this airline and Southern Airlines merged to form Republic Airlines.

US-252 NORTHWEST ORIENT AIRLINES, Minneapolis/St. Paul International Airport, St. Paul, MN 55111 (612/726-2111). PASSAGES.

US-253 PAN AMERICAN WORLD AIRWAYS, General Offices, Pan Am Bldg., New York, NY 10017. CLIPPER.

US-254 TRANS WORLD AIRLINES, 605 Third Avenue, New York, NY 10016. TWA AMBASSADOR.

US-255 UNITED AIR LINES, Box 66100, Chicago, IL 60666 (312/952-4000). MAINLINER MAGAZINE.

US-256 WESTERN AIRLINES, World Way Postal Center, Box 92005, Los Angeles, CA 90009 (213/646-2345). WESTERN'S WORLD.

AUTOMOBILE CLUBS AND TOURING SERVICES

US-257 ALA AUTO AND TRAVEL CLUB, 888 Worcester Street, Wellesley, MA 02181 (617/237-5200).

This New England motor club has offices in Maine, New Hampshire, Vermont, Massachusetts, Connecticut, and Rhode Island. It began as the American Legal Association and provided just legal services for motorists, but now it is a full-fledged auto and travel club. They issue 4 directories: ALA SIGHTS TO SEE BOOK is an annually issued guide (1978 ed., 448 p.) to where to go and what to see in the US, Canada, and Mexico; ALA WHERE TO STAY BOOK is an annually issued guide (1978-79 ed., 240 p.) listing thousands of carefully selected hotels, motels, inns, lodges, and resorts in the US, Canada, and Mexico (copies of this are also printed up for the National Automobile Association (US-264) and are called the NAA WHERE TO STAY BOOK); ALA WHERE TO TAKE THE KIDS BOOK describes places of special interest to families; and ALA TOP TOURS is a series of tour booklets, one for each of the New England states, including maps, directions, and descriptions of interesting places to visit. The club also provides the usual routing services and issues a quarterly magazine called AWAY.

US-258 ALLSTATE MOTOR CLUB, 30 Allstate Plaza, Northbrook, IL 60062.

This club, for members only, is like most other motor clubs in offering automobile services and travel features. The latter includes personalized routings and a quarterly magazine called DISCOVERY that has many articles about travel in the US.

US-259 AMERICAN AUTOMOBILE ASSOCIATION, National Headquarters Organization, 8111 Gatehouse Road, Falls Church, VA 22042 (703/AAA-6000).

The AAA, a nonprofit organization founded in 1902, is a federation of motor clubs with over 900 club offices and branches throughout the US and Canada. AAA offers a wide range of domestic and foreign travel services, has an active cadre of field representatives who inspect and endorse accommodations and restaurants, issues a large number of maps and publications for the use of its members, and offers a wide range of other services for its members and communities. A directory, DUES AND SERVICES OF AFFILIATED CLUBS AND ASSOCIATIONS, of the home offices (over 200), their membership dues and the services they offer members is issued every summer by the Promotion Department of AAA. Many of the larger affiliated clubs publish monthly newspapers that frequently contain articles describing local driving tours and points of interest. AAA issues a wide range of very good to excellent maps, many of which are revised annually. There is an overall US map; 4 regional maps (Eastern States-North, Eastern States-South, Central States, Western States); 27 state maps

(several maps combine two or more states); and numerous city and
area maps. As of 1978, there were 20 TOURBOOKS covering the
US. Alaska is included in another TOURBOOK covering Western
Canada. These TOURBOOKS are revised annually and coverage of
states within the individual volumes of this series frequently changes
as TOURBOOKS are split or merged. Each TOURBOOK is uniformly
arranged. There are 2 main sections: what to see and where to
stay/where to dine. Within each main section the listings are by
state. A state "what to see" section begins with a general section
on history, geography, economy, education, regularly scheduled
events, and factual information such as alcoholic beverage laws,
legal holidays, locations of state information centers, and where to
write for additional information including fishing and hunting regulations. A chart showing recreation facilities in state parks and
other areas, with an orientation map keyed to the chart, follows.
The third and major part of the "what to see" section is an alphabetical directory of towns or areas within each state with descriptions
of nearby points of interest and attractions. Extensive information
on getting around, what to see and do, being informed, tours, where
to dine, nightlife, especially for children, shopping, special events,
etc. and a good map are provided for major cities and are excerpted
to form the 8 CITIBOOKS mentioned below. The "where to stay/
where to dine" section classifies, gives rates, facilities, and a rating
for accommodations and gives brief information but no rating for restaurants. As of 1978, there were 11 campground directories, which, like the
TOURBOOKS, are updated annually and change state coverage due to
splits and mergers of individual volumes. All campgrounds must
meet AAA requirements before they are recommended. The lists of
campgrounds are arranged alphabetically by community nearest a campground, and include rates, facilities, dates open, and number of sites
for tent and RV camping. Eight pocket-sized CITIBOOKS are issued
annually and contain essentially the same information from the TOUR-
BOOKS. They are issued for Chicago, Los Angeles, Miami/Miami
Beach/Fort Lauderdale, New Orleans, New York, St. Petersburg/
Tampa, San Francisco, and Washington, DC. The AAA "Triptik" is
an individually tailored routing service for members. Strip maps show
driving times and, linking communities to the TOURBOOKS, provide
good information and maps for the tourist who likes to stick to major
roads and interstate highways. The traveler who prefers to explore
the quieter, less-traveled byways will get little help from the Triptik
service. All the above publications, plus other services for motorists
and travelers, including several maps and guidebooks for other areas
of the world, make a membership in AAA one of the best travel in-
vestments available.

US-260 CHEVRON TRAVEL CLUB, Box P, Concord, CA 94524.

Chevron no longer has a free travel service for maps and routings,
but they do have a Chevron Travel Club. There is a toll-free number
for information about the club: 800/227-1306. Tour and trip planning services and a quarterly magazine, CHEVRON USA, are two of
the many services offered to members.

US-261 EXXON TOURING SERVICE, Box 307, Florham Park, NJ 07932 (201/474-5919).

The touring service provides free marked routings or maps for motor trips. There are 3 offices from which these free services may be requested by anyone. Requests to the New Jersey office, listed above, may be made by mail and phone. Requests to the Houston office at 800 Bell Street, Box 2180, Houston, TX 77011 (713/656-2312) may be made by mail, phone, or walk-in. The New York City office at 1251 Avenue of the Americas (50th Street and 6th Avenue) is for walk-in requests only. The Exxon Travel Club, Box 52099, Houston, TX 77052 is a members-only service. It offers personalized trip planning services, an EXXON TRAVEL CLUB TRAVEL ATLAS, 7 regional VACATION TRAVEL GUIDES, and a quarterly magazine VISTA USA.

US-262 GULF TOURGIDE INFORMATION SERVICE, Box 93, Versailles, KY 40383.

A free 96-page GULF TOURGIDE atlas is available from this address. Interstate and sectional maps of the US are available free at Gulf service stations. There is also a Gulf Auto Club, Box 946, Houston, TX 77001 that is not related to the free Tourgide Service. Members pay a fee, and one of the benefits is the bimonthly magazine ODYSSEY which always has several articles about travel in the US.

US-263 MOBIL TRAVEL SERVICE, Box 25, Versailles, KY 40383.

Mobil does not have a members-only travel club, but it does offer a routing service to the public free of charge at this address.

US-264 NATIONAL AUTOMOBILE ASSOCIATION, 1730 Northeast Expressway, Box 29037, Atlanta, GA 30359 (404/634-1261).

This is an affiliation of southern state motor clubs that provides its members with individualized route planning, marked maps, accommodations directories, and descriptive literature. Motor clubs and automobile associations from the following states are affiliated with the NAA: Alabama, Arkansas, Georgia, Indiana, Kentucky, Louisiana, Mississippi, North and South Carolina, Tennessee, Texas, Virginia, and West Virginia. See also US-257.

US-265 TEXACO TOURING CENTER, Box 1459, Houston, TX 77001 (713/666-8000).

A request to this address will bring free maps and personalized routings. There is no walk-in center to obtain this service. Texaco does not not have a membership-only motor club.

BUS LINES

US-266 GRAY LINE SIGHT-SEEING ASSOCIATION, 7 West 51st Street,

New York, NY 10019 (212/245-9330).

Since 1910 this company has been providing local, guided sight-seeing tours by bus. In addition, they now also provide multilingual tours; boat and air sightseeing tours; individual charter services; limousine, transfer, and shuttle services; and convention planning services. Local Gray Line member companies provide tours in over 80 US cities or areas as well as numerous foreign locations. Folders describing the tours, itineraries, and rates originating from each city or area may be obtained by writing to the above address or by checking the local yellow pages. An annual OFFICIAL SIGHTSEEING SALES AND TOUR GUIDE (68th ed., 1978., 369 p.) outlines 1,300 tours offered by over 160 Gray Line members and is available from the above address. The Gray Line Companies are a subsidiary of the Grey-hound Corporation.

US-267 GREYHOUND LINES, Greyhound Tower, Phoenix, AZ 85077 (602/248-5000).

In addition to offering connecting routes between nearly all large and middle-size US cities and towns, Greyhound also offers their Ameri-pass, an unlimited travel plan; numerous vacation package tours; bus charters; an Ameri-Lodging plan allowing room savings at Ramada, Sheraton, or Howard Johnson inns; package express service; and special "Helping Hand" assistance for disabled travelers. Consult the local yellow pages for the local Greyhound office which will supply information on all the above services. A bimonthly master system timetable and US map showing all routes may be obtained from the above address. Call 800/528-6055 toll-free for information and reservations and 800/528-0447 for group travel arrangements.

US-268 TRAILWAYS, 1500 Jackson Street, Dallas, TX 75201 (214/655-7711).

The entire Trailways System is made up of 15 regional Trailways motor coach lines. They issue an overall system timetable which includes the addresses and phone numbers of these regional lines plus several route maps. The Trailways "Eaglepass" allows unlimited travel on their coaches for either a 1 or 2 month period. There is no toll-free number available to the public. Consult the telephone book for the name and number of the nearest local office. For information on the various Trailways motorcoach tours, contact Trail-ways Tours, 1512 Commerce, Suite 500, Dallas, TX 75201 (214/655-7711).

CAMPGROUND CHAINS

US-269 JELLYSTONE CAMPGROUNDS, 236 Michigan Street, Sturgeon Bay, WI 54235 (414/743-6588).

They issue an annual directory (1978 ed., 40 p.) of all their Yogi

Bear's Jellystone Park Camp-Resorts and their Yogi Bear's Family Motor-Inns, most of which are located, at this time, east of the Mississippi River. The address and phone number, an inset map showing exact location, nearby points of interest, facilities, and rates are given for each outlet. For year-round, toll-free reservations call 800/558-2954. In Wisconsin, call 800/242-2931 between May 1 and Labor Day. At other times call collect 414/743-6588.

US-270 KAMPGROUNDS OF AMERICA, Box 30558, Billings, MT 59114 (406/248-7444).

They issue two annual publications: (1) KAMPGROUNDS OF AMERICA CAMPERS ATLAS (1978 ed., 144 p.) which has individual state maps on which all KOA's are located and a directory of individual KOA's giving address and phone number, inset map showing exact location, local points of interest, available recreation facilities and services, and 11 pages of discount coupons in the back; and (2) KOA HANDBOOK AND DIRECTORY FOR CAMPERS (1978 ed., 112 p.) which duplicates the directory information from the atlas above (on less durable paper) and contains short how-to articles for campers. The first title must be purchased, the second is distributed free to campers at any KOA Kampground. They have no toll-free reservation number.

US-271 UNITED SAFARI INTERNATIONAL, 1111 Northshore Drive, Drawer 203, Knoxville, TN 37919 (615/584-8536).

This is a campground chain that stretches across the country. They issue an annual directory that describes and locates on an inset map each individual campground. Their year-round toll-free reservation and information number is 800/251-9740. In Tennessee call 615/584-8536.

CAR RENTAL FIRMS

All of the companies listed below issue a bimonthly "Worldwide Directory," which lists each individual rental office with phone number, hours, and the various vehicle rental rates available. In addition, the local offices of each stock free area maps produced for the chain by either the Creative Sales Corp. or the Goushā Co. (US-206). Toll-free reservation telephone numbers are given after the general administrative office phone number.

US-272 AVIS, World Headquarters, 1114 Avenue of the Americas, New York, NY 10036 (212/398-2900). 800/331-1212 in the continental US. In Oklahoma call 800/482-4554.

US-273 BUDGET RENT-A-CAR CORP. 35 East Wacker Drive, Chicago, IL 60601 (312/641-0424). 800/228-9650. For the Sears Rent-A-Car locations operated by Budget Rent-A-Car call 800/228-2800.

US-274 THE HERTZ CORP., 660 Madison Avenue, New York, NY 10021. 800/654-3131 in the continental US. In Oklahoma call 800/522-3711 and in Hawaii call 800/654-8200.

US-275 NATIONAL CAR RENTAL, Executive Office, 5501 Green Valley Drive, Minneapolis, MN 55437 (612/830-2121). 800/328-4567. In Minnesota call 800/862-6064 and in Alaska and Hawaii call 800/328-6321.

HOTEL AND MOTEL CHAINS

Nearly all of these chains issue a directory of their individual motels, inns, etc. These fully describe the range of rooms and rates plus all other facilities and services at each, and they usually show exact locations with individual inset maps. Many of them indicate which of their facilities are accessible to the handicapped. Information about each chain's toll-free number(s) is given after the general administrative telephone number.

US-276 BEST WESTERN, Best Western Way, Box 10203, Phoenix, AZ 85064 (602/957-4200). 800/528-1234 in the continental US. In Arizona call 800/352-1222.

They issue: (1) an annual (1978 ed., 88 p.) ROAD ATLAS & TRAVEL GUIDE which contains individual state maps and 15 metropolitan area maps on which their motels, hotels, and resorts are located, plus a state-by-state listing of individual locations, (2) ROAD MAP & DIRECTORY issued in 4 regional editions (Northeast US and Canada, Southeast US, Central US and Canadian Prairie Provinces, and Western US and Southwest Canada) each of which shows individual locations, and (3) an annual GROUP RATES directory, a state-by-state listing of those motels offering group rates.

US-277 BUDGET MOTELS & HOTELS OF AMERICA, 1115 East Hennepin Avenue, Minneapolis, MN 55414 (612/331-6405). 800/328-5511. In Minnesota call 800/462-5355.

US-278 DAYS INNS OF AMERICA, 2751 Buford Highway NE, Atlanta, GA 30324 (404/325-4000). They have several regional toll-free reservation numbers. Contact them directly or consult their directory for these numbers.

US-279 ECONO-TRAVEL MOTOR HOTEL CORP., Box 12188, Norfolk, VA 23502 (804/461-6111). 800/446-6900. In Virginia call 800/582-5882.

US-280 HILTON HOTELS CORP., 9880 Wilshire Blvd., Beverly Hills, CA 90210 (213/278-4321). They have over 20 regional toll-free reservation and information numbers. Consult their directory or the local yellow pages for these numbers.

US-281 HOLIDAY INNS, Executive Offices, 3742 Lamar Avenue, Memphis, TN 38118 (901/362-4001). 800/238-8000. In Tennessee call 800/ 542-5270.

They also issue HOLIDAY INN ROAD ATLAS (1978 ed., 88 p.) with individual state maps and 22 city maps on which all Holiday Inns and Holiday Inn Trav-L-Parks (campsites with modern facilities and utility hook-ups) are located. To make reservations at a Trav-L-Park call 800/238-5555. In Tennesee, call collect 901/362-4518.

US-282 HOWARD JOHNSON'S, 222 Forbes Road, Braintree, MA 02184 (617/848-2350). 800/654-2000. In Oklahoma call 800/522-9041.

US-283 HYATT INTERNATIONAL HOTELS, 39 South LaSalle Street, Suite 320, Chicago, IL 60603 (312/782-0100). 800/228-9000 in the continental US.

US-284 IMPERIAL "400" MOTELS, 1830 North Nash Street, Arlington, VA 22209. 800/531-5300.

US-285 MARRIOTT HOTELS, 5161 River Road, Washington, DC 20016 (301/ 986-5000). 800/228-9290.

US-286 RAMADA INNS, Box 590, Phoenix, AZ 85001 (602/273-4000). 800/228-2828 in the continental US. In Nebraska call 800/642-9343.

US-287 SCOTTISH INNS FRANCHISE CORP., GateWest, Suite 114, 515 Two Mile Parkway, Goodlettsville, TN 37072 (615/859-6161). 800/251-1962. In Tennessee call 800/342-1819.

US-288 THE SHERATON CORP., 60 State Street, Boston, MA 02109 (617/ 367-3600). 800/325-3535 in the continental US. In Missouri call 800/392-3500.

US-289 SUPER 8 MOTELS, Box 1456, Aberdeen, SD 57401. 800/843-1991. In South Dakota call 800/592-1898.

US-290 TRAVELODGE INTERNATIONAL, 250 TraveLodge Drive, El Cajon, CA 92090. (714/442-0311). 800/255-3050. In Kansas call 800/ 332-4350.

Also available at the general toll-free number is "Travelphone North America," begun in 1971, which provides language assistance to visitors from other countries. French, German, Spanish, and Japanese are the main languages available; sometimes Italian and Portugese are also available. They also issue a series of 8 regional US map/directories of their TraveLodges: Northeast, Southeast, North Central, South Central, Northwest, Southwest, Northern California including Hawaii, and Southern California.

TRAINS

US-291 AMTRAK TRAVEL CENTER, Box 311, Addison, IL 60101.

Amtrak was created by the Rail Passenger Service Act of October 31, 1970 to revitalize US rail passenger service. Numerous individual and escorted tours all across the country have been developed and are described in a large annually produced booklet. (The 1978 tour book, called DESTINATION AMERICA, described 110 different Amtrak tours in a 100-page book). In addition, Amtrak issues informative literature about their ski vacation rail tours; the USA Rail-Pass, which allows unlimited coach travel within a 2-week to 1-month time period; the long distance "name" trains of the past that still remain; and all other routes, tours, and services they provide. They also issue a system-wide national timetable. Write to the above address for all this printed literature. Amtrak has a long list of regional reservation and train schedule information toll-free numbers. They have additional numbers in some cities for arrival and departure information. They have another list of toll-free numbers just to handle reservations on the high-speed Metroliners that run between Boston and Washington, DC, and they have special toll-free numbers for teletypewriter reservation and information service for deaf persons. These numbers will be found in the annual tour book, in the national train timetables, and in the local yellow pages. A guide to Amtrak services for elderly and handicapped travelers, called ACCESS AMTRAK, is available from the national headquaters office: National Railroad Passenger Corp., 400 North Capitol Street NW, Washington, DC 20001.

US-292 AUTO-TRAIN CORP., 1801 K Street NW, Washington, DC 20006. 800/424-1111.

Auto-Train is a private corporation, not connected with Amtrak, that provides "hassle-free" transportation for you and your car between Lorton, VA, just 15 miles south of Washington, DC, and Sanford, FL, near Orlando and Disney World. Occasionally there is talk of establishing other Auto-Train routes, between Chicago and Denver, and between northern and southern California, for example, but none of these intriguing ideas has ever gotten off the ground.

NORTHEAST

BOOKS AND ATLASES

N-1   Alper, M. Victor. AMERICA'S FREEDOM TRAIL: A TOUR GUIDE
        TO HISTORICAL SITES OF THE COLONIAL AND REVOLUTIONARY
        WAR PERIOD. New York: Macmillan, 1976. 562 p. Photos,
        maps. Index. O-02-097150-8. 75-44415.

        This fairly extensive history of the Revolutionary War in Massachu-
        setts, New York, New Jersey, and Pennsylvania is arranged by lo-
        cality and describes sites (with hours and fees), and lists the address
        and telephone number of visitor information centers. Public transpor-
        tation and guided tours are noted. There is a separate list of accom-
        modations.

N-2   AMC RIVER GUIDE. 2 vols. Boston: Appalachian Mountain Club,
        1976-78. Maps.

        Descriptions in this guide are arranged by watersheds, and the scope
        is confined to rivers with only brief comments on the lakes through
        which they flow. Information is given on the difficulty of the river,
        descriptions of the scenery, the appropriate USGS maps to use, and
        campsites along the river. Volume 1 covers Maine and northern New
        Hampshire, and volume 2, covering the rest of New England, was
        published in 1978. Previously, this title was known as the AMC
        NEW ENGLAND CANOEING GUIDE.

N-3   ANGLERS' GUIDE TO THE UNITED STATES ATLANTIC COAST: FISH,
        FISHING GROUNDS & FISHING FACILITIES. 8 vols. Edited by
        Bruce L. Freeman and Lionel A. Walford. Washington, DC: U.S.
        Government Printing Office, 1974-76. Maps, drawings.

        Each volume has a historical background to fishing an area with a de-
        scription of the most commonly caught fish (including a drawing) which
        lists varieties, scientific name, size, habits, season, suggested fishing
        method(s), and bait. Each volume describes part of the Atlantic
        coastline and further subdivides the section on individual map pages

which indicate the areas where specific fish are caught. Each map has an accompanying table of facilities and one for recreational areas keyed to the map. The volumes range in length from 16 to 24 pages and cover the following areas: Passamaquoddy Bay, ME to Cape Cod (1974); Nantucket Shoals to Long Island Sound (1974); Block Island to Cape May, NJ (1974); Delaware Bay to False Cape, VA (1974); Chesapeake Bay (1976); False Cape, VA to Altamaha Sound, GA (1976); Altamaha Sound, GA to Fort Pierce Inlet, FL (1976); and St. Lucie Inlet, FL to the Dry Tortugas (1976).

N-4   Benton, Christine M. COUNTRY ROADS AND SCENIC DRIVES IN THE MIDDLE ATLANTIC STATES. Chicago: Contemporary Books, 1979. 195 p. Photos. Index. 0-8092-7514-7. 78-57453.

Defining "Middle Atlantic States" as Delaware, Maryland, New Jersey, New York, and Pennsylvania, this book describes the pleasures and sights to be found on roads which are neither interstates nor turnpikes. Many of the roads are cross-state and are major routes, but they permit a more leisurely observation of the rural countryside than the high-speed roads. Specific sights are noted and rather exact descriptions for finding them are given, though a few maps would have been helpful. The rather skimpy descriptions of sights are offset by the number of them. This book is part of a series which stresses country and back roads for different sections of the US in opposition to the major high-speed roads.

N-5   Beram, Sandy. BACK BEFORE BEDTIME: A GUIDE TO ONE-DAY ADVENTURES WITH CHILDREN IN NEW YORK, NEW JERSEY AND CONNECTICUT. New York: Quick Fox, 1978. 267 p. Photos., maps. Indexes. 0-8256-3093-2. 77-088727.

Arranged in four basic parts, this guide to one-day adventures for parents with children under 16 contains very complete descriptions plus all the extra practical information those traveling with small children need to have. The first 80 pages are a very extensive month-by-month guide to what to do in all 3 states; the other 3 parts are city-by-city listings in each of the 3 states of what to see and do there. Each state has its own index by category of attraction or activity. There are discount coupons in the back.

N-6   Berman, Steve. THE NORTHEASTERN OUTDOORS. Boston: Stone Wall Press, 1977. 287 p. Photos., drawings, maps. Index. 0-913276-21-9. 76-52519.

A field as well as a travel guide, about half of this book is on natural history. There are brief descriptions, with maps, of 117 hiking trails in New England, New York, and Pennsylvania with lists of "useful" addresses appended.

N-7   _____. SOUTHERN NEW ENGLAND FOR FREE. Chester, CT:

Peqout Press, 1976. 125 p. Photos., maps. 0-87106-067-1. 76-2123.

Divided into nature, historical, architectural, art, and "chop suey" (melange) trips, this guide attempts to indicate interesting places to visit in Massachusetts, Connecticut, and Rhode Island for merely the cost of fuel. Location, hours, telephone numbers, and special features are noted.

N-8   BOATING ALMANAC. 6 vols. Severna Park, MD: Boating Almanac Co. (603 McKinsey Road/21146), 1978. Issued annually. Maps.

Each of the volumes is issued annually and contains complete cruising information, lists of boating services, and many advertisements. Volume 1 covers Massachusetts, New Hampshire, and Maine; volume 2 covers Long Island, Connecticut, and Rhode Island; volume 3 covers New Jersey, Delaware Bay, Hudson River, Lake Champlain, and Erie Canal; volume 4 covers Chesapeake Bay, Delaware, Maryland, District of Columbia, and Virginia; volume 5 covers North and South Carolina and Georgia; and volume 6 covers Florida.

N-9   Brosnahan, Tom. ARTHUR FROMMER'S DOLLAR WISE GUIDE TO NEW ENGLAND. New York: Frommer/Pasmantier Publishing Co. (distributed by Simon & Schuster), 1978. Revised frequently. 365 p. Maps. 0-671-24194-X.

This widely distributed guide describes moderately priced hotels and restaurants and tells how to get there and what to see and do in the states of Massachusetts, Rhode Island, Connecticut, New Hampshire, Maine, and Vermont. It also includes special coverage of ski resorts.

N-10   Bryfonski, Dedria. THE NEW ENGLAND BEACH BOOK. New York: Walker, 1975. 172 p. Photos., maps. 0-8027-0453-0. 73-93682.

Over 170 New England beaches are described listing location, parking, water conditions (seasonal), beach size and condition, and "support" areas (where to find food, lodgings, entertainment).

N-11   Chapin, Suzy, and Squier, Elizabeth. GUIDE TO RECOMMENDED COUNTRY INNS OF NEW ENGLAND. 4th ed. Chester, CT: Pequot Press, 1978. 270 p. Photos. Indexes. 0-87106-070-1. 73-83255.

"Inn" is defined as a year-round establishment offering both food and lodging. The book lists 107 inns, giving location, facilities, number of rooms, telephone number, rates, and personal comments by the authors. The indexes are by region and name.

N-12   Crain, Jim, and Milne, Terry. CAMPING AROUND NEW ENGLAND.

Rev. ed. New York: Random House, 1975. 94 p. Maps, drawings. Indexes. 0-394-70644-7. 73-20589.

This is a geographical guide for the serious camper to facilities, from "Kampgrounds of America" to forest camps, in 18 New England regions. Activity and feature indexes list campgrounds where individual interests may be pursued.

N-13   Dvorah, Charles. HOUSEKEEPING COTTAGES: A GUIDE TO SELECTED COTTAGE RESORTS IN NEW YORK AND NEW ENGLAND . . . . Glen Head, NY: Glen Head Press, 1976. 99 p. Maps. 77-150376.

This good guide for those who want to get away from it all describes quiet housekeeping cottages in New York, Massachusetts, Maine, and New Hampshire.

N-14   Farney, Michael H. NEW ENGLAND OVER THE HANDLEBARS: A CYCLIST'S GUIDE. Boston: Little, Brown & Co., 1975. 174 p. Maps, photos. 0-316-27465-8. 75-19265.

The author gives text narratives of 40 actual trips in coastal, river and mountain areas of Massachusetts, Vermont, New Hampshire, Maine, and Connecticut with mileages and maps.

N-15   Flaste, Richard, et al. THE NEW YORK TIMES GUIDE TO CHILDREN'S ENTERTAINMENT IN NEW YORK, NEW JERSEY AND CONNECTICUT. New York: Quadrangle/The New York Times Book Co., 1976. 226 p. Maps, photos. 0-8129-0654-3. 76-9709.

This guide is thematically arranged by the kinds of adventures enjoyable to children: zoos and safaris, restorations, amusement centers, museums, trains, boats, planes, theater, places of work, restaurants, recreation and state parks, and skyscrapers.

N-16   Flues, Anderson, and Flues, Marilyn. MID ATLANTIC CAMPGROUND DIRECTORY. Herndon, VA: the authors, 1977. 126 p. Maps. 75-7004.

This list of 1,100 state, federal, and private campgrounds in Delaware, Maryland, New Jersey, North Carolina, Pennsylvania, South Carolina, Virginia, and West Virginia briefly notes location, season, telephone number, rates, and facilities. Discount coupons are included.

N-17   Gabler, Ray. NEW ENGLAND WHITE WATER RIVER GUIDE. New Canaan, CT: Tobey Publishing Co., 1975. 236 p. Maps, tables, photos. Bibliography. 75-322481.

The table listing 45 New England rivers with length of trip(s), average times, gradient, difficulty, driving time from Boston and Springfield, scenery, etc. is followed by more detailed descriptions of each trip with a map for each. A glossary of terms and a small list of canoeing organization are included.

N-18   Garvey, Edward B. HIKING TRAILS IN THE MID-ATLANTIC STATES. Matteson, IL: Greatlakes Living Press, 1976. 214 p. Photos., maps. Bibliography. Index. 0-915498-21-9. 75-41634.

The descriptions of trails (distance, location, special features) in Virginia, West Virginia, Maryland, Pennsylvania, Delaware, and New Jersey are supplemented with general hiking tips and a listing of hiking clubs in the area.

N-19   Goodrich, Anne. ENJOYING THE SUMMER THEATRES OF NEW ENGLAND. Chester, CT: Pequot Press, 1974. 147 p. Photos. Indexes. 0-87106-139-2. 73-88252.

Forty-two theatres and playhouses in New England are listed giving location, telephone number, ticket price range, general performance times, and typical offerings. Twenty-seven music and dance festivals are also described with location, ticket price range, season, and telephone number.

N-20   Harting, Emile C. A LITERARY TOUR GUIDE TO THE UNITED STATES: NORTHEAST. Americans Discover America Series. New York: William Morrow & Co., 1978. 218 p. Photos. Index. 0-688-03281-8. 77-18439.

For those interested in visiting places associated with authors--authors' homes; locales of novels, poems, and plays; museums and libraries with literary exhibits, etc.--this guide gives background material as well as addresses, hours, and other practical information.

N-21   Hechtlinger, Adelaide. THE PELICAN GUIDE TO HISTORIC HOMES AND SITES OF REVOLUTIONARY AMERICA. 3 vols. Gretna, LA: Pelican Publishing Co., 1976. Photos.

This guide includes photographs of famous Revolutionary War period homes and landmarks, exact locations, hours open, significant features, notable history, and admission prices. Six New England states (Maine to Connecticut) are covered in volume 1. Volume 2, covering the Middle Atlantic states, and volume 3, covering the South, are also planned.

N-22   Henley, Thomas A., and Sweet, Neesa. HIKING TRAILS IN THE NORTHEAST. Matteson, IL: Greatlakes Living Press, 1976. 212 p. Photos. Index. 0-915498-18-9. 75-41637.

Hiking trails in New England, New York, New Brunswick, and Nova Scotia are located and described.

N-23   Hitchcock, Anthony, and Lindgren, Jean. COUNTRY NEW EN-

GLAND ANTIQUES, CRAFTS AND FACTORY OUTLETS. The Compleat Traveler's Companion. New York: Artemis Books, 1978. 156 p. Maps, photos. Index. 0-89102-141-8. 78-6502.

All antique and craft shops and factory outlets are listed together by community and the communities arranged alphabetically within each state. The address, phone number, and specialty are given for each.

N-24 _____. COUNTRY NEW ENGLAND INNS. The Compleat Traveler's Companion. New York: Artemis Books, 1978. 189 p. Photos., maps, sketches. 0-89102-139-6. 78-6379.

The inns included "were chosen for their inherent charm, based partially on their architectural style, location, furnishings, and history." Arranged by state, the individual inn descriptions appear under the town or village in which they are located. There is no index by inn name. A new edition of this title was announced as we went to press as part of a series of "Inns of America" covering all of the US and Canada.

N-25 _____. COUNTRY NEW ENGLAND SIGHTSEEING AND HISTORICAL GUIDE. The Compleat Traveler's Companion. New York: Artemis Books, 1978. 228 p. Maps, photos. Index. 0-89102-140-X. 78-9093.

Listing mainly historical and other points of interest that are unique to New England, this book is arranged by state; within each state, by region; and within a region, by towns and villages. There is an index of towns.

N-26 _____. COUNTRY NEW ENGLAND SPORTS AND RECREATION. The Compleat Traveler's Companion. New York: Artemis Books, 1978. 185 p. Photos. Index. 0-89102-142-6. 78-7937.

Including a wide range of sport and recreation activities, this title is arranged like the other volumes in this series: by towns within each state. Especially valuable is the beginning essay for each state which lists the many brochures on enjoying specific outdoor activities available from various state agencies. There is an index of towns.

N-27 Jorgenson, Neil. A GUIDE TO NEW ENGLAND'S LANDSCAPE. Chester, CT: Pequot Press, 1977. 256 p. Photos., maps, diagrams. Index. 0-87106-088-4. 77-75660.

"The traveler interested in the natural features will usually find little information in the conventional tourist guides. . . .The intent of this book is to strike a balance between a scientific text on the aspects of the landscape and the conventional organization of a guidebook." Each section first describes bedrock, land surface fea-

tures, or a type of vegetation and then lists the best place to see
that particular feature. There is an index to specific place names,
but none by state. Since the book's main arrangment is topically by
landscape feature, there is no easy way of exploring these features
if you are in a general geographic area and want to know what
there is to see there.

N-28   Kosoy, Ted. A BUDGET GUIDE TO NEW YORK AND NEW EN-
GLAND. New York: St. Martin's Press, 1976. 279 p. Photos.
75-40795.

N-29   _____. A BUDGET GUIDE TO WASHINGTON D.C. AND THE
CENTRAL ATLANTIC STATES. New York: St. Martin's Press, 1976.
265 p. Photos. 75-40794.

All the Kosoy "Budget Guides" are included in this information guide
as a warning and example of a bad travel guide. In the first place,
the values used in the listing of "budget" accommodations are subject
to question: rates at the selections are not what most travelers on a
budget could afford. Secondly, the selection of attractions is limited
to the ones found in almost any guidebook, and no attempt is made
to point out those that might have no or a small admission fee.
Thirdly, the guides contain no additional information or tips on traveling inexpensively. In short, they contain no real "budget" information, and what they do contain is very ordinary, putting them into a
category of "non-essential" guidebooks. There are no indexes.

N-30   Kugelman, Jon, and Kugelman, Nancy, eds. A DIRECTORY OF
TOURIST HOMES IN THE EASTERN UNITED STATES & MARITIME
CANADA. Hartford, CT: McBride & Howe Books (157 Sisson Ave-
nue/06105), 1978. 48 p., plus 1979 supplement. Sketches.

Staying in a community tourist home is an excellent way to meet
local people and obtain information on the really worthwhile things
to see and do. Many times the house itself will be architecturally
fascinating (although the bathroom is usually "down the hall" and
the plumbing somewhat antiquated) and it certainly provides a personalized alternative to the impersonal sterility of the motel chains,
often at less than half their cost. This directory, in spite of its
many inadequacies, is an attempt to list such homes. It is a handy
size and will take up little room in the glove compartment of your
car. The directory is by no means thorough or systematic in its
coverage; just names, addresses, and phone numbers are cited. But
it is a good beginning at covering a little used travelers resource and
deserves all the support it can get. Another booklet GUIDE TO
GUEST HOUSES AND TOURIST HOMES U.S.A. is supposed to be
available from the Tourist House Association of America, Box 355A,
Greentown, PA 18426. They did not respond to our request for information so we cannot recommend this publication.

N-31   Neuer, Kathleen. THE INN BOOK: A FIELD GUIDE TO OLD
        INNS AND GOOD FOOD IN NEW YORK, NEW JERSEY, EASTERN
        PENNSYLVANIA, DELAWARE AND CONNECTICUT. 2d ed. New
        York: Random House, 1976. 222 p. Drawings, maps. 0-394-
        72048-2. 75-29409.

        One hundred and four "inns" (broadly defined to mean interesting
        places to eat) are listed by the author's own unique area classifica-
        tion, giving a fairly thorough description which includes address,
        telephone number, hours, specialities, and whether or not lodgings
        are also available. The appendix lists those with lodgings by state.

N-32   Newberry, Lida. ONE-DAY ADVENTURES BY CAR: WITH FULL
        ROAD DIRECTIONS FOR DRIVES OUT OF NEW YORK CITY.
        3d ed. New York: Hastings House, 1978. 280 p. Maps. Indexes.
        0-8038-5382-3. 77-14532.

        This guide describes points of interest along more than 120 trips into
        New Jersey, the Poconos, along the Hudson River Valley, and into
        Connecticut, Long Island, and Staten Island. Specific information
        about hours, fees, and detailed directions for the driver are included.
        There is a list of performing arts centers.

N-33   THE NEW ENGLAND GUIDE. Concord, NH: The New England
        Guide, 1977. Issued annually. 158 p. Photos., maps.

        This guide to the points of interest and events in Maine, New Hamp-
        shire, Vermont, Massachusetts, Rhode Island, and Connecticut also
        includes many advertisements. The guide has a toll-free number,
        800/258-3624, for information, reservations, weather, etc. that may
        be called during the summer season Monday-Friday, 9A.M.-5P.M. from
        New York, New Jersey, Pennsylvania, Delaware, Maryland, Washington,
        DC and all of New England except New Hampshire. From other
        areas call 603/224-4231.

N-34   Robinson, William F. ABANDONED NEW ENGLAND: ITS HIDDEN
        RUINS AND WHERE TO FIND THEM. Boston: New York Graphic
        Society, 1976. 211 p. Photos., drawings, maps. Index. 0-8212-
        0654-0. 75-24590.

        Primarily, though not exclusively, concerned with industrial archaeol-
        ogy, this heavily illustrated work does briefly list where to find
        abandoned mills, railroads, canals, farms, factories, etc., but the
        bulk of the text is historical.

N-35   Rothafel, Roxy. ROXY'S SKI GUIDE TO NEW ENGLAND. Char-
        lotte, NC: East Woods Press Books/Fast & McMillan Publishers,
        1978. 190 p. Maps, photos. 0-914788-08-6. 78-61682.

        The author's forthright ski reports are carried on 24 northeast radio
        stations, he writes a weekly ski column, and is the former director of

a ski school. In part I of this guide the author sets forth his frank, often irreverent, opinions on the ski industry, snow, ski schools, equipment, and ski reports. This last section gives the phone numbers for 24 local radio stations in Connecticut, Massachusetts, Vermont, New Hampshire, and Maine. He feels that local weather forecasts are the best gauge of ski conditions. Part II is a guide to ski areas in Connecticut, Massachusetts, Vermont, New Hampshire, and Maine. In addition to accurate details about the slopes themselves, the author describes the atmosphere and types of people you will find at each area as well as costs, accommodations, quality of food, etc.

N-36   Settel, Trudy, and Settel, Irv. CLOSE-TO-HOME AUTO TOURS. New York: Hawthorne Books, 1973. 245 p. Maps, drawings. 73-2603.

This compilation of 114 one- and two-day auto tours within 20 east coast states from Maine to Florida includes "tour maps indicating major roadways and mileage and descriptions of historical, cultural, and scenic stops along the route." The individual tours and maps were prepared by and used in an extensive advertising series sponsored by the American Petroleum Institute during the 1973/74 gasoline crisis.

N-37   Shosteck, Robert. CAMPERS' PARK GUIDE: WHERE TO CAMP, WHAT TO DO IN 888 PARKS, FORESTS AND OTHER RECREATION AREAS FROM MAINE TO FLORIDA. McLean, VA: EPM Publications (1003 Turkey Run Road/22101), 1978. 663 p. Maps. Indexes. 0-914440-23-3. 78-6928.

This selective listing, arranged by state from north to south, of recreational areas in the states along the Atlantic Ocean (plus inland New England, West Virginia, Kentucky, and Tennessee) uses symbols to indicate services and facilities. The park numbers in the list are keyed to the state maps. Name, mailing address, telephone number, a brief description, "what to do," nearby attractions, any pertinent literature, and rather crude driving instructions to the camp or park are given. There is a recreational area name index and a special interest index.

N-38   _____. WEEKENDER'S GUIDE: PLACES OF HISTORIC, SCENIC & RECREATIONAL INTEREST WITHIN 200 MILES OF THE WASHINGTON-BALTIMORE AREA. 4th ed. Washington, DC: Potomac Books, 1977. 401 p. Maps, drawings. Bibliography. Indexes. 0-87107-037-5. 77-368152.

Places of interest in Virginia, Maryland, Delaware, southern New Jersey, southeastern Pennsylvania, and the West Virginia eastern panhandle are briefly described (with hours and fees) and located. Accommodations and restaurants are noted. There are separate sections for camping, skiing, and wineries and vineyards. Some information on hunting is included.

N-39   Thollander, Earl. BACK ROADS OF NEW ENGLAND. New York: Clarkson N. Potter (distributed by Crown), 1974. 224 p. Drawings, maps. 73-89086.

Hand lettered and drawn throughout, this is mainly an art book rather than an information source. Of use only as a guide to where the back roads are, there is not much information for enjoying yourself along the way. The author is in the process of doing a whole series of "Back Roads" guides.

N-40   Thomas, Bill. EASTERN TRIPS & TRAILS. Harrisburg, PA: Stackpole Books, 1975. 253 p. Maps, photos. 0-8117-2033-0. 75-2003.

Listed are 56 (or 71 if the Adirondack Forest Preserve counts as 15 rather than 1 area) places for hiking in 16 states (the eastern sea-board states plus West Virginia, Vermont, and New Hampshire), giving descriptions, locations, and where to hike, backpack, camp, and drive. Addresses for further information are also given.

N-41   Tobey, Eric, and Wolkenberg, Richard. NORTHEAST BICYCLE TOURS. New Canaan, CT: Tobey Publishing Co., 1973. 280 p. Maps, photos. 0-440-6233-395.

The authors describe 130 bicycle tours lasting from 3 hours to 3 months in New England and New York. Included with each description is a map, mileage, terrain, exact directions, camping facilities, fun spots, and bicycle repair shops.

N-42   WATERWAY GUIDE: "THE YACHTSMAN'S BIBLE." 29th ed. 3 vols. Annapolis, MD: Marine Annuals, 1976. Issued annually. Maps, tables. 54-3673.

Issued in 3 volumes (Southern: Florida and the Gulf Goast, Northern: the Atlantic coast from New York to Canada and the New York state internal waterways (Hudson River and Erie Canal), and Mid-Atlantic: everything in between) this set gives descriptions of coastal waters, maps, local marinas, and tables indicating facilities. Even the advertisements are informative.

N-43   YANKEE MAGAZINE'S GUIDE TO NEW ENGLAND. Dublin, NH: Yankee. Issued biannually.

The magazine format guide is issued in spring/summer and fall/winter editions by the publishers of YANKEE MAGAZINE and THE NEW ENGLANDER. It is full of articles, suggestions of things to see and do, lists of events, lodging and restaurants, advertisements, etc. for seasonal enjoyment of the 6 states of New England from Maine to

Connecticut. Earlier issues were called THE YANKEE GUIDE TO THE NEW ENGLAND COUNTRYSIDE.

N-44   YANKEE MAGAZINE'S TRAVEL MAPS OF NEW ENGLAND. Dublin, NH: Yankee, 1978. 34 p. Maps.

General, but adequate, road maps of New England and 10 general city street maps all by The National Survey (N-51) comprise this book. Unspectacular, but useful, it notes recreation areas.

N-45   Yeadon, David. HIDDEN CORNERS OF NEW ENGLAND. New York: Funk & Wagnalls, 1976. 182 p. Drawings. 0-308-10240-1. 75-42072.

This is not intended as a practical guide to tourist-oriented facilities, but is rather for the traveler who enjoys the rough, unpaved back roads of true New England. It consists of the author's personal experiences and sketches in 28 areas of the 6 New England states.

N-46   _____. HIDDEN CORNERS OF THE MID-ATLANTIC STATES. New York: Funk & Wagnalls, 1977. 182 p. Drawings. Index. 0-308-10286-X. 76-30417.

You will find it hard to keep to your armchair with this book. It contains captivating descriptions and sketches describing 28 coastal and mountain back-country areas in New Jersey, Delaware, Maryland, Pennsylvania, and Virginia.

N-47   Ziegler, Katey. SKI TOURING GUIDE TO NEW ENGLAND. 3d ed. Boston: Eastern Mountain Sports, 1976. 240 p. Maps. Bibliography. Index.

This guide, jam-packed with where-to suggestions, really makes you want to get up and go. It describes 17 ski-touring areas in Maine, 52 in New Hampshire, 38 in Vermont, 53 in Massachusetts, and 17 in Connecticut. The emphasis is not so much on the trails themselves, but rather on how to get to each area, available accommodations, general information about trails, where to get maps, etc. Tours on 40 abandoned railroad grades are mentioned and the appropriate USGS map(s) to use is given. Numerous sources for further information are included.

N-48   Zook, Nicholas. A GUIDE TO THE GARDENS OF NEW ENGLAND OPEN TO THE PUBLIC. Barre, MA: Barre Publishing Co., 1973. 96 p. Photos. 0-8271-7251-6. 72-92469.

Although the information per se is good, this is a typically badly arranged Zook guide. The first part (most of the book) contains rambling appreciations of the various kinds of gardens, (arboretums, nature trails, house/museum gardens, parks, etc.) mentioning specific places but giving no practical information. The last chapter gives the practical information, but there are no tie-ins for the reader to the discussions in the first part. There is no index.

N-49   _____. HOUSES OF NEW ENGLAND OPEN TO THE PUBLIC. Barre, MA: Barre Publishing Co., 1968. 126 p. Photos. 68-17070.

This is a guide to the history and descriptions of 254 houses notable for their fine architecture, antiques, and landscape gardening in Massachusetts, Connecticut, Rhode Island, New Hampshire, Vermont, and Maine.

MAGAZINES

N-50   NORTHEAST OUTDOORS. Waterbury, CT: Northeast Outdoors (70 Edwin Avenue/66708).

This monthly newspaper for camper and RV owners contains many general articles on how and where to camp, regular columns on events and new books, and many advertisements. They also issue an annual campground directory each spring.

MAPS

AAA (US-259) issues an Eastern States--North map. Exxon (US-261) issues a New England map and an Eastern US map. Rand McNally (US-215) issues an Eastern US map.

PUBLISHERS

N-51   THE NATIONAL SURVEY, Chester, VT 05143.

While this firm produces many excellent maps, heavily laden with advertising, they do not sell directly to the public. The advertisers, or local tourist agencies, give away the maps or sell them at a moderate price. Concentrating mainly on the northeast US, The National Survey has done general touring road maps, ski resort maps, and county maps.

N-52   NEW HAMPSHIRE PUBLISHING CO., Box 70, Somersworth, NH 03878 (603/692-3000).

This is a major publisher of outdoor guidebooks for the northeast. Most of their books fall into one of four series. The titles published so far in their "Fifty Hikes" series are: FIFTY HIKES IN CENTRAL PENNSYLVANIA by Tom Thwaites, FIFTY HIKES IN CONNECTICUT by Gerry and Sue Hardy, FIFTY HIKES IN MAINE by John Gibson,

FIFTY HIKES IN MASSACHUSETTS by Paul and Ruth Sadlier, FIFTY HIKES IN NEW HAMPSHIRE and FIFTY MORE HIKES IN NEW HAMPSHIRE both by Daniel Doan, FIFTY HIKES IN NEW HAMPSHIRE'S WHITE MOUNTAINS by Daniel Doan, and FIFTY HIKES IN VERMONT by Ruth and Paul Sadlier. The titles published so far in their "25 Walks" series are: 25 WALKS IN RHODE ISLAND by Ken Weber, 25 WALKS IN THE DARTMOUTH-LAKE SUNAPEE REGION by Mary L. Kibling, 25 WALKS IN THE FINGER LAKES REGION by Bill Ehling, and 25 WALKS IN THE LAKES REGION by Paul H. Blaisdell. The titles published so far in their "20 Bicycle Tours" series are: 20 BICYCLE TOURS IN NEW HAMPSHIRE by Tom and Susan Heavey, and 20 BICYCLE TOURS IN VERMONT by John S. Freidin. The titles published so far in their "25 Ski Tours" series are: 25 SKI TOURS IN CONNECTICUT by Stan Wass and David Alvord, 25 SKI TOURS IN MAINE by Karl Beiser, 25 SKI TOURS IN THE GREEN MOUNTAINS by Sally and Daniel Ford, 25 SKI TOURS IN THE WHITE MOUNTAINS by Sally and Daniel Ford, and 25 SKI TOURS IN WESTERN MASSACHUSETTS by John Frado, Richard Lawson, and Robert Coy.

N-53   PEQUOT PRESS, Old Chester Road, Chester, CT 06412.

They publish a large number of New England guides, including several walking and biking guides. As we went to press, this publisher changed its name to Globe Pequot Press.

ORGANIZATIONS

N-54   APPALACHIAN MOUNTAIN CLUB, 5 Joy Street, Boston, MA 02108 (617/523-0636).

The Appalachian Mountain Club, the oldest club of its kind, was founded in 1876 and is a member of the Appalachian Trail Conference (N-55). It maintains hundreds of miles of hiking trails; conducts educational workshops in hiking leadership, snowshoeing, canoeing, rock climbing, etc.; conducts a great variety of outings; publishes a number of guidebooks and maps; and maintains one of the largest mountaineering libraries in the country.

N-55   THE APPALACHIAN TRAIL CONFERENCE, Box 236, Harpers Ferry, WV 25425 (304/535-6331).

The Appalachian Trail, extending from Mt. Katahdin in Maine to Springer Mountain in Georgia, was inaugurated in 1937. Much of the credit for establishing the trail and for preserving it today belongs to the Appalachian Trail Conference (ATC) organized in 1925. It is the mother organization to 34 local clubs that are directly responsible for sections of the trail. Listed below are the guidebooks to the Appalachian Trail available from the ATC. Some are published by ATC, some by the individual clubs, but all are available from the ATC. The detailed trail descriptions in these guides give precise locations, to the nearest hundredth of a mile, of springs, shelters, "viewpoints," side trails, sources of supplies, streams, ponds, and trail hazards. All the guides have maps. GUIDE TO THE APPALACHIAN TRAIL IN MAINE, 9th ed., 1978, published by the Maine Appalachian Trail Club. GUIDE TO THE APPALACHIAN TRAIL IN NEW HAMPSHIRE AND VERMONT, 2d ed., 1968, 284 p., published by the ATC. GUIDE TO THE APPALACHIAN TRAIL IN MASSACHUSETTS AND CONNECTICUT, 5th ed., 1978, 212 p., published by the ATC. GUIDE TO THE APPALACHIAN TRAIL IN NEW YORK AND NEW JERSEY, 8th ed., 1977, 127 p., published by the New York-New Jersey Trail Conference. GUIDE TO THE APPALACHIAN TRAIL IN PENNSYLVANIA, 4th ed., 1977, 157 p., published by the Keystone Trails Association. GUIDE TO THE APPALACHIAN TRAIL FROM THE SUSQUEHANNA RIVER TO THE SHENANDOAH NATIONAL PARK, by Dana and Helen Dalrymple, 9th ed., 1974, 194 p., published by the Potomac Appalachian Trail Club (0-915746-06-9, 75-313960). GUIDE TO THE APPALACHIAN TRAIL AND SIDE TRAILS IN THE SHENANDOAH NATIONAL PARK, edited by Molly T. Denton, 8th ed., 1977, 288 p., published by the Potomac Appalachian Trail Club (0-915746-07-7, 76-17452). GUIDE TO THE APPALACHIAN TRAIL IN CENTRAL AND SOUTHWESTERN VIRGINIA, 7th ed., 1974, 318 p., published by the ATC (75-310170). GUIDE TO THE APPALACHIAN TRAIL IN TENNESSEE AND NORTH CAROLINA: CHEROKEE, PISGAH AND GREAT SMOKIES, 5th ed., 1976, 366 p., published by the ATC. GUIDE TO THE APPALACHIAN TRAIL IN THE GREAT SMOKIES, THE NANTAHALAS AND GEORGIA, 5th ed., 1975, 341 p., published by the ATC. Other publications of the ATC are the bimonthly (except July) APPALACHIAN TRAILWAY NEWS begun January 1940 and containing reports on trail conditions and activities of member clubs. The APPALACHIAN TRAIL DATA BOOK (formerly the MILEAGE FACT SHEET) by Raymond F. Hunt published in 1977 (107 p. 77-369452) "lists the peaks, gaps, falls, rivers, etc. and the shelters, access roads, supply sources, and Post Offices in geographical order from Maine to Georgia opposite cumulative distance tables that read in both directions." Maps of the various sections of the trail are available separately from the ATC.

N-56   DISCOVER NEW ENGLAND, 480 Boylston Street, Boston, MA 02116 (617/267-8605).

This organization was established in the fall of 1978 to promote travel to the New England area. As its first task, it has taken over the operation of the New England Vacation Center (N-60).

N-57   EASTERN NATIONAL PARK & MONUMENT ASSOCIATION, 314 Market Street, Philadelphia, PA 19106 (215/597-7129).

Their principal function is to sponsor, publish, and distribute interpretive materials appropriate to each of the 80 eastern national parks, monuments, historic sites, recreation areas, seashores, etc. under their jurisdiction. They issue many road and trail guide booklets and operate the bookstores found in the individual National Park Service visitor centers.

N-58   NEW ENGLAND INNKEEPERS ASSOCIATION, 25 Huntington Avenue, Boston, MA 02116.

They issue a map/guide to inns, motels, and resorts throughout New England.

N-59   NEW ENGLAND TRAIL CONFERENCE, Vera V. Whitney, Secretary, Apt. #24103, 3595 Post Road, Warwick, RI 02886.

A coalition, founded in 1916, of over 50 outdoor and hiking organizations, serving primarily as a clearinghouse for information on footpaths throughout New England. There are no individual memberships, but interested persons are invited to attend the annual conference held each spring at which time the constituent organizations report on the conditions of trails and shelters they maintain. Their address changes from time to time as new officers are elected but past officers seem to be conscientious about forwarding mail. They issue 2 informative publications. HIKING TRAILS OF NEW ENGLAND is a sketch map of the various New England trail systems showing general trail routes and highway access. It is not a detailed map. It also includes a state-by-state bibliography of trail guidebooks and maps. It is revised approximately every 5 years, and the last edition was published in 1975. NEW ENGLAND TRAILS is the printed report of the annual meeting and includes all the detailed information on trail and shelter conditions submitted by the member organizations.

N-60   NEW ENGLAND VACATION CENTER, 1268 Avenue of the Americas, New York, NY 10020 (212/757-4455).

They are a New York City office where information on traveling in the states of Maine, Vermont, New Hampshire, Massachusetts, Connecticut, and Rhode Island may be obtained. They are a walk-in information center, and their hours are Monday-Friday, 9A.M.-5P.M. Our several mailed requests for information brought no response.

N-61   PARKS & HISTORY ASSOCIATION, 1100 Ohio Drive SW, Washington, DC 20242.

Their principal function is to sponsor, publish, and distribute interpretive materials appropriate to each of the 19 greater Washington, DC, areas administered by the National Park Service.

SOUTH

BOOKS AND ATLASES

S-1   Alper, M. Victor. AMERICA'S HERITAGE TRAIL: A TOUR GUIDE
       TO HISTORICAL SITES OF THE COLONIAL AND REVOLUTIONARY
       WAR PERIOD. New York: Macmillan, 1976. 323 p. Photos.,
       maps. Index. 0-02-501690-3. 75-45113.

       Selected sites in North Carolina, South Carolina, and Virginia
       connected with early US history (up to the Revolutionary War) are
       located and described. A fairly full historical background is given,
       and hours and fees are noted. A "Chronology of the American
       Revolution" is included. There are brief hotel/motel listings.

S-2   Blankenship, Samuel M. A BACKPACKING GUIDE TO THE SOUTH-
       ERN MOUNTAINS. New York: Ballantine Books, 1974. 183 p.
       Maps. Bibliography. 0-345-24020-0.

       Thirty-two hikes in the southern Appalachians are described in good
       detail, noting length, difficulty, elevations, map coverage, location,
       campsites, and side trails.

S-3   Burmeister, Walter F. APPALACHIAN WATERS. 2d ed. Oakton,
       VA: Appalachian Books, 1974-- . Multivolume set. Maps.

       The first edition was published in 1962. As of this writing, 5
       volumes of the new edition have appeared: volume 1 covers the
       Delaware and its tributaries, volume 2 covers the Hudson and its
       tributaries, volume 3 covers the Susquehanna and its tributaries,
       volume 4 covers southeastern US rivers, and volume 5 covers the
       Upper Ohio Basin. Coverage of all the major river basins from
       Maine to Florida rising in the Appalachians is planned. General
       data is given (distances, drop, time, difficulty, scenery) for the
       whole river system. Individual streams, creeks, and rivers are then
       described in detail.

S-4   Carter, Randy. CANOEING WHITE WATER: RIVER GUIDE. Rev.

ed. Oakton, VA: Appalachian Outfitters (Box 11, 2930 Chain Bridge Road/22124), 1974. 267 p. Photos, maps.

This is a "standard guide" to 95 white water rivers and streams in Virginia, eastern West Virginia, and the Great Smoky Mountains area.

S-5   Corbett, H. Roger, et al. BLUE RIDGE VOYAGES. 4 vols. Oakton, VA: Appalachian Books, 1972-74. Maps, photos.

This set contains very thorough descriptions, with river ratings, of selected river and creek trips in Maryland, Virginia, West Virginia, and on the Shenandoah River. The work is recommended.

S-6   Crain, Jim, and Milne, Terry. CAMPING AROUND THE APPALACHIAN MOUNTAINS INCLUDING THE BLUE RIDGE AND GREAT SMOKIES. New York: Random House, 1975. 94 p. Maps, sketches. 0-394-70682-X. 73-20588.

The book lists, with brief descriptions, campgrounds located in "Appalachia"--the Appalachian Mountains from southern Pennsylvania to northern Georgia. It is similar in format to the other titles in this series of books by these authors.

S-7   Durrance, Jill, and Shamblin, William, eds. APPALACHIAN WAYS: A GUIDE TO THE HISTORIC MOUNTAIN HEART OF THE EAST. Washington, DC: Appalachian Regional Commission, 1976. 220 p. Bibliography. 76-603180.

This book captures the flavor of the Appalachian region with 30 written sketches about its way of life. It includes map guides to craft fairs, music, theater, national historic sites, parks, forests, and there are descriptions of attractions in 13 states.

S-8   FODOR'S OLD SOUTH. New York: David McKay Co., 1978. 470 p. Sketches, maps. Bibliographies. Index. 0-679-00240-5.

This book describes plantations, mansions, food, battlefields, gardens, and other things to see and do reminiscent of the pre-1900s way of life in 11 southern states. It also includes lists of hotels/motels and restaurants and tells where to write for additional information.

S-9   Kosoy, Ted. KOSOY'S BUDGET-TRAVEL GUIDE TO FLORIDA AND THE SOUTH. New York: St. Martin's Press, 1976. 250 p. 75-9488.

See the annotation with the other Kosoy guides (N-28) for a description of this superficial series.

S-10   Perdue, Lewis. COUNTRY INNS OF MARYLAND, VIRGINIA AND WEST VIRGINIA. Washington, DC: Washingtonian Books, 1977.

178 p. Drawings, photos., map. Index. 0-915168-24-3. 76-58103.

Seventy-nine inns in the 3 states, some offering overnight accommodations, are described and evaluated. The listing is divided into 6 regions.

S-11 Shosteck, Robert. POTOMAC TRAIL AND CYCLING GUIDE. Oakton, VA: Appalachian Books, 1976. 4th ed. 179 p. Maps. Index. 0-87107-030-6. 68-31585.

Fifty-six hikes near the Potomac River are described in detail. Also included are 11 long (over 10 miles) and 17 short bike rides around Washington and into Virginia and Maryland. There is a section on natural history.

S-12 Stein, Rita. A LITERARY TOUR GUIDE TO THE UNITED STATES: SOUTH AND SOUTHWEST. A Morrow QUILL Paperback. West Caldwell, NJ: William Morrow & Co., 1979. Photos. Index. 0-688-08173-8.

"A state-by-state guide to places with literary associations that are open to the public. . . .Addresses, directions and hours are listed. . . ."

S-13 Sullivan, Jerry, and Daniel, Glenda. HIKING TRAILS IN THE SOUTHERN MOUNTAINS. Matteson, IL: Greatlakes Living Press, 1975. 252 p. 0-915498-04-9. 75-9297.

About 220 trail or trail clusters are described in good detail noting location, length, and map coverage.

S-14 Tolf, Robert W. COUNTRY INNS OF THE DEEP SOUTH: A GUIDE TO ROMANTIC HOSTELRIES. San Francisco: 101 Productions, 1978. 200 p. Sketches.

This is a guide to some 60 unusual vacation retreats from Virginia to Florida with individual notes on the history, environs, rates, and credit cards accepted.

S-15 Winokur, Lou, and Winokur, Alice. JOY IN THE MOUNTAINS. Boca Raton, FL: the authors (Box 2532/33432), 1977. 195 p. Photos., maps. Index. 77-365501.

This is a very complete guide to what to see and do in the southern Appalachian Mountains, including the Blue Ridge Parkway. It includes the states of North Carolina, Tennessee, and Virginia. It is arranged by type of activity with a geographical index.

MAPS

AAA (US-259) issues an Eastern States--South map. Both Exxon (US-261) and Rand McNally (US-215) issue an Eastern US map.

PUBLISHERS

S-16 ALEXANDRIA DRAFTING CO., 6440 General Green Way, Alexandria, VA 22312 (703/750-0510).

This firm specializes in producing rather detailed city/county/region street maps of urban areas in Maryland, Virginia, and (just starting) Pennsylvania--with Atlanta thrown in--as well as fishing maps of the mid-Atlantic coast and selected fresh water bodies. The maps are generally of excellent quality.

S-17 APPALACHIAN BOOKS, Box 249, Oakton, VA 22124.

They are a major publisher of water guides and other outdoor guides to the Appalachians.

S-18 PELICAN PUBLISHING CO., 630 Burmaster Street, Gretna, LA 70053.

This company publishes several guides to plantation homes, gardens, and architecture of Louisiana and New Orleans as well as more general guides for Mississippi, Virginia, Texas, and San Diego.

ORGANIZATIONS

S-19 MOTORIST ASSISTANCE PROGRAM (MAP).

This is a radio network designed to help motorists traveling along interstate highways in Virginia, North and South Carolina, Georgia, and and Florida make decisions on where to stay and/or what to do or see. Thirty-nine AM radio stations supply information 12 times a day, every day from 6A.M. to 6P.M. A directory and map are available at local motels, hotels, and gas stations, or from the Coastal Plains Region Commission, 1725 K Street NW, Suite 413, Washington, DC 20006 (202/634-3910).

S-20 POTOMAC APPALACHIAN TRAIL CLUB, 1718 N Street NW, Washington, DC 20036 (202/638-5306).

This member of the Appalachian Trail Conference (N-55) was founded in 1927, and is responsible for the Appalachian Trail from Pine Grove Furnace, PA to Rockfish Gap, VA. They publish 2 of the guides to the trail (N-55), numerous maps, and POTOMAC APPALACHIAN issued 12 times a year as a newsletter and irregularly as a magazine. Magazine no. 3 (Spring 1975) has a 12-page bibliography of US trail guidebooks compiled by Paula Strain on pages 28-39. Supplements to this list appear in subsequent issues of the magazine.

S-21 TENNESSEE VALLEY AUTHORITY, Information Office, Knoxville, TN 37902 (615/637-0101).

The Tennessee Valley Authority (TVA) was established as a means of regulating the Tennessee River system back in the 1930s. Its series of 20 dams (all open for tours) created numerous man-made lakes for boating, fishing, and other recreation activities. The TVA covers seven states: Tennessee, Mississippi, Georgia, Alabama, Kentucky, North Carolina, and Virginia. Information about the TVA as a whole and about visiting the dams and steam plants may be obtained from the above address. There is a toll-free number to obtain information about TVA activities and programs that is available Monday-Friday, 8A.M. to 4:45P.M. Outside Tennessee call 800/251-9242, in Tennessee call 800/362-9250, in the Knoxville area call 632-4100. RECREATION ON TVA LAKES is a very good overall map/guide to all of the 25 lakes and the boat docks, resorts, state parks, US Forest Service camp areas, etc. to be found at each. Also available are good detailed recreation maps (scales vary, ranging between 1 in. represents 1 mile to 1 in. represents 2 miles) of each of the lakes. These are also available from the above address. Navigation charts, maps, and jointly produced TVA-USGS topographic maps, as well as a variety of other maps and atlases are available from: TVA, Map Sales, 400 Commerce Avenue SW, Knoxville, TN 37902. An INDEX TO NAVIGATION CHARTS AND MAPS OF TVA RESERVOIRS and an INDEX TO TVA-USGS TOPOGRAPHIC MAPS, TENNESSEE VALLEY WATERSHED will help to identify just which ones you want. The Division of Forestry, Fisheries and Wildlife Development of the TVA (Norris, TN 37828) issues numerous guides to canoeing and fishing. The Land Between the Lakes is being developed by the TVA as a national demonstration in outdoor recreation, environmental education, and resource management. It is a 170,000 acre peninsula located between 2 lakes in western Kentucky and Tennessee. An overall MAP & GUIDE TO LAND BETWEEN THE LAKES, a quarterly calendar of events, and much information about trails, camping, hunting, wildlife, etc. is available from: Central Information Office, Land Between the Lakes, Tennessee Valley Authority, Golden Pond, KY 42231 (502/924-5602) or (502/362-8367).

S-22   TRAVEL SOUTH, USA, 3400 Peachtree Road NE, Lenox Towers, Atlanta, GA 30326 (404/231-1790).

Primarily an umbrella promotion organization for 11 southern states, this is not a source of information for the general traveling public. They have sponsored special advertising sections in numerous popular mass-market magazines. They also analyze travel market data and present an annual report on what sectors of that market are reaching and influencing the southern economy.

CENTRAL

BOOKS AND ATLASES

C-1   Bagg, Alan. 50 SHORT CLIMBS IN THE MIDWEST. Chicago:
Contemporary Books, 1978. 234 p. Photos., maps. Bibliography.
Index. 0-8092-7668-2. 77-91194.

After a brief introduction on equipment, the climbs in Illinois, Iowa,
Michigan, Minnesota, Ohio, and Wisconsin are described and located,
noting nearby attractions and accommodations. Lists of climbing
schools, midwest climbing clubs, equipment suppliers, and a glossary
of terms are included.

C-2   Brant, Warren E. A LOG TO THE LOWER MISSISSIPPI RIVER.
St. Paul, MN: American Motor Logs (2099 La Crosse Avenue/55119),
1976. 80 p. Maps, photos. Index. 76-354605.

C-3   _____. A LOG TO THE OHIO RIVER. St. Paul, MN: American
Motor Logs, 1978. 80 p. Maps, photos. Index.

C-4   _____. A LOG TO THE UPPER MISSISSIPPI RIVER. 2d ed. St.
Paul, MN: American Motor Logs, 1977. 80 p. Maps, photos.
Index.

These 3 road guides follow each river from end to end giving historical background and describing points of interest along the way. The
Ohio River volume begins with its headwaters in southwestern Pennsylvania and ends with where it empties into the Mississippi. The Upper
Mississippi River volume begins with that river's headwaters in northern
Minnesota and follows it to St. Louis, and the Lower Mississippi River
volume continues to the Gulf of Mexico. Separate sections give information about annual events, house boat rentals, marinas, campgrounds, hotels/motels, and restaurants. There are many maps, and
each volume has an index.

C-5   Cantor, George. THE GREAT LAKES GUIDEBOOK: LAKES ONTARIO

AND ERIE. Ann Arbor: University of Michigan Press, 1978. 225 p. Maps, photos. Bibliography. Index. 0-472-19650-2. 77-13606.

The author describes the best and most significant sights and attractions on the shoreline of the Great Lakes having an appeal that is unique to these lakes. Several of the points of interest are described in great detail. The author includes many easy to read maps and outlines several suggested walks and scenic drives. Two subsequent volumes are planned on Lakes Huron and Michigan and Lakes Michigan and Superior.

C-6　　Junior League of Minneapolis. MISSISSIPPI HIGHWAY: A GUIDE TO THE RIVER FROM THE DAYTON AREA TO HASTINGS. Minneapolis: the author, 1976. Maps.

This out-of-print guide describes over 200 points of interest as well as provides information on hiking, biking, boating, nature appreciation, camping and picnicking. It also includes a guidebook section on the twin cities of Minneapolis/St. Paul.

C-7　　LAKELAND BOATING'S CRUISE PLANNING GUIDE TO THE GREAT LAKES. By the editors of Lakeland Boating. Ann Arbor, MI: Boating Publications, 1974. 284 p. Charts, photos. 74-81257.

This guide to the water conditions and marina facilities on the 5 Great Lakes plus the Georgian Bay, the North Channel, and Lake St. Clair is copiously illustrated with aerial photographs and harbor charts.

C-8　　Malo, John W. MIDWEST CANOE TRAILS. Chicago: Contemporary Books, 1978. 186 p. Photos., maps. Index. 0-8092-7680-1. 77-91182.

About 100 canoeable rivers in Illinois, Indiana, Iowa, Michigan, Minnesota, Wisconsin, and Ontario are described in varying, but generally good detail (including the scenic aspects). Each state chapter has a list of information sources on canoeing in that state. A list of over 300 canoe liveries is appended.

C-9　　Michaelson, Mike. SNOWMOBILE TRAILS. Chicago: Greatlakes Living Press, 1974. 288 p. Maps, sketches. 74-23002.

Descriptions, with maps, of regularly maintained and marked snowmobile trails in Illinois, Indiana, Michigan, Minnesota, New York, Ohio, Wisconsin, and Ontario are given. Also mentioned are other winter activities, local accommodations and dining spots, and highway access to the trails.

C-10　　Palzer, Bob, and Palzer, Judy. WHITEWATER, QUIETWATER: A GUIDE TO THE RIVERS OF WISCONSIN, UPPER MICHIGAN AND NORTHEAST MINNESOTA. Two Rivers, WI: Evergreen Paddleways,

1973. 156 p. Maps, photos.

"Prepared in cooperation with the University of Wisconsin Hoofers Outing Club of the Wisconsin Union," this volume includes complete descriptions, with specially drawn maps, of 65 one-day canoe trips in Wisconsin and surrounding areas. There is a second edition (0-916166-02-3) published in 1976 which was not examined by the compilers.

C-11   QUIMBY'S HARBOR GUIDE TO THE ENTIRE NAVIGABLE MISSISSIPPI RIVER, THE ARKANSAS, AND ILLINOIS WATERWAYS, THE ST. CROIX, MINNESOTA AND BLACK RIVERS. Prairie du Chien, WI: Quimby's Harbor Guide (Box 85/53821), 1976. Issued annually. 65 p. Sketch maps, sketches. Index.

This guide, with its very confusing cut-and-past layout, claims to list all harbors with minimum gas pump service between the upper end of the river system in Minnesota and the Gulf of Mexico. Also included are harbor sketches, navigation tips, and some brief descriptions of towns at some harbors.

C-12   Settel, Trudy, and Settel, Irv. CLOSE-TO-HOME AUTO TOURS (MIDWEST EDITION). New York: Hawthorne Books, 1974. 221 p. Maps. 73-19374.

Arranged alphabetically by state from Arkansas to Wisconsin, this book includes descriptions, with maps, of 110 one- to two-day trips in 18 central states. You may have seen these tours used as promotional pieces by the American Petroleum Institute in your newspaper during the gasoline crisis of 1974.

C-13   Sullivan, Jerry, and Daniel, Glenda. HIKING TRAILS IN THE MID-WEST. Chicago: Greatlakes Living Press, 1974. 224 p. Maps. Index. 0-915498-00-6. 74-173586.

This guid gives descriptions of hiking trails in Illinois, Indiana, Michigan, Minnesota, Missouri, Ohio, Wisconsin, and Ontario, including location with map; length; camping along the trail; public transportation to and from each trail; general description of the terrain; and where to obtain additional information, guides, or maps.

C-14   Thomas, Bill. MID-AMERICA TRIPS AND TRAILS. Harrisburg, PA: Stackpole Books, 1975. 238 p. Photos., maps. 0-8117-2037-3. 74-34053.

Fifty-five wilderness areas in 17 states giving hiking, backpacking, and camping possibilities are described and located.

MAPS

AAA (US-259) issues a Central States map. Rand McNally (US-215) issues a Central/Western US map.

PUBLISHERS

C-15   ROCKFORD MAP PUBLISHERS, 4525 Forest View Avenue, Box 6126,
Rockford, IL 61125 (815/399-4614).

They have issued state atlases for Illinois, Indiana, Michigan, Minnesota, and Wisconsin. In addition to reproducing individual county
maps, each state atlas contains information on state and national
parks, camping, canoeing, boating, fishing, hunting, skiing, etc.

ORGANIZATIONS

C-16   DELTA QUEEN STEAMBOAT COMPANY, Home Port Office, 511
Main Street, Cincinnati, OH 45202

This is the company that provides paddlewheel steamboat tours on the
Mississippi River. There are two boats: the smaller authentic Delta
Queen, and the new larger Mississippi Queen. Unfortunately, all
sailings are sectional round-trip package tours and there is no one
continuous trip of the entire length of the river.

C-17   MIDWEST SKI AREAS ASSOCIATION, Box 418, Afton, MN 55001
(612/436-7292).

They publish a brochure MID-AMERICA SKI GUIDE: A HANDY
LISTING AND MAPS THAT SHOW YOU WHERE TO SKI AND SHOP
IN THE MIDWEST that is available only to members. You may write
to them for information, however, and they have a 24-hour ski conditions report available by calling 612/436-5218.

C-18   OLD WEST TRAIL FOUNDATION, Box 2554, Rapid City, SD 57709.

This regional, nonprofit, umbrella, marketing organization promotes
travel to the states of Montana, North and South Dakota, and
Nebraska. They issue an annual VACATION GUIDE (1978 ed.,
38 p.) which is "your guide to highways, historic trails, city circle
tours, attractions, accommodations, restaurants, campgrounds, gift
and specialty shops, traveler services." All these are located on
maps, and there are many advertisements.

C-19   OZARKS REGIONAL COMMISSION, 1100 North University Avenue,
Suite 109, Evergreen Place, Little Rock, AR 72207 (501/378-5905).

This is a "federal-state-local partnership organized in 1966 to promote
economic growth and development in Arkansas, Kansas, Louisiana,
Missouri, and Oklahoma." It issues one very general booklet describing points of interest in all five states, but the traveler would do
better contacting each individual state tourism office.

WEST

BOOKS AND ATLASES

W-1   Brewster, David. THE BEST PLACES #2: DAVID BREWSTER'S GUIDE
        TO OREGON, WASHINGTON AND BRITISH COLUMBIA. 2d ed.
        Seattle: Madrona Publishers, 1977. 356 p. Maps, drawings. Index.
        0-914842-22-6. 77-11114.

        The author describes what he considers the best restaurants, hotels/
        motels, resorts, tourism opportunities, and shops. Restaurants get the
        most space. Everything is rated on a scale of five and information
        on address, season, price category, credit cards accepted, and bar
        service is also supplied. This would be a very good book to accom-
        pany the AAA TOURGUIDES (US-259).

W-2   Bridge, Raymond. TOURGUIDE TO THE ROCKY MOUNTAIN WILDER-
        NESS. Harrisburg, PA: Stackpole Books, 1975. 160 p. Photos.,
        maps. 0-8117-2036-5. 75-9885.

        The author has sought out those places not getting excessive use,
        and he covers the entire Rocky Mountain chain from Montana to New
        Mexico. He concentrates on 3 areas in Montana, 2 in Idaho, 4 in
        Wyoming, 1 in Utah, 6 in Colorado (none are in Rocky Mountain
        National Park), and 2 in New Mexico. An outline map, area ap-
        proaches, campgrounds, hikes, backpacking trips, and the name of
        the appropriate USGS map to use are given for each. The first 50
        pages are a how-to discussion on enjoying the wilderness.

W-3   Casewit, Curtis W. TENNIS RESORTS: A GUIDE TO SPORTING
        VACATIONS IN THE WEST. San Francisco: Chronicle Books, 1978.
        135 p. Photos. 0-87701-109-5. 78-2772.

        This guide includes resorts, lodges, and tennis ranches that offer at
        least 2 courts and instruction. It describes tennis facilities available
        at each, and gives a brief description of what else there is to see
        and do in the area. It is regionally arranged, focussing mostly on

California, the Pacific Northwest, the Rockies, and the Southwest. It also includes a few outstanding resorts in Hawaii, and the eastern US.

W-4   Cromie, Alice H. TOUR GUIDE TO THE OLD WEST. New York: Quadrangle/The New York Times Book Co., 1977. 464 p. Photos., maps. 0-8129-0641-1. 76-9695.

Towns or sites that played a part in the settling of the west and museums depicting the old west are described. They are alphabetically arranged within each of 19 states, some of which are as far east as Arkansas and Nebraska.

W-5   Evans, Laura, and Belknap, Buzz. DINOSAUR RIVER GUIDE. Boulder City, NV: Westwater Books, 1973. 64 p. Maps, photos. 73-79803.

This guide to the river begins with suggestions for boating in Flaming Gorge National Recreation Area which straddles the Wyoming/Utah border and then goes on to provide a graphic river and shore guide (1 in. represents about 1/2 mile) to the Green River as it continues south into Dinosaur National Monument in Colorado and back into Utah. There's very little written text, but the river graphics more than make up for this by showing locations of rapids, contours, elevations, river-side roads, canyons, campgrounds, etc. The southflowing Green River through Utah is picked up where it leaves off in this guide by the DESOLATION RIVER GUIDE (UT-11).

W-6   EXPLORER'S GUIDE TO THE WEST. 6 vols. San Jose, CA: Goushā Co., 1972. Maps, photos. Indexes. 79-189652.

This handy, pocket-sized boxed set is full of practical information, with maps, about what to see and do. Volume 1 describes 9 major cities; volume 2, the coast; volume 3, the southern mountains; volume 4, the northern mountains; volume 5, the rivers and lakes; and volume 6, the deserts. There are 2 large separate fold-out maps: a wilderness escape map, and a prospectors's treasure map.

W-7   FODOR'S OLD WEST. Edited by Eugene Fodor and Robert C. Fisher. New York: David McKay Co., 1976. 504 p. Photos, maps. Index. 0-679-00181-6. 77-371528.

This complete guide to seeing and reliving the old west describes points of interest and activities in 22 states. A few selected hotels/ motels and restaurants are mentioned. There are 5 background essays.

W-8   Franzwa, Gregory M. THE OREGON TRAIL REVISITED. St. Louis: Patrice Press, 1972. 417 p. Photos., maps. Bibliography. Index. 72-80581.

The author begins with a general history of the trail and then gives exact directions to finding the remains of the trail from present-day highways in Missouri, Kansas, Nebraska, Wyoming, Idaho, and Oregon. A new edition has been announced.

W-9   Freer, Blaine. THE SPORTSMAN'S GUIDE TO THE PACIFIC NORTH-WEST. Garden City, NY: Doubleday, 1975. 290 p. Photos, maps. Bibliography. Index. 0-385-05831-4. 74-18847.

"A where-when-how-and-with-what-equipment guide to individual and family sports," the book is arranged by type of activity and includes fishing (mostly this), hunting, boating, sailing, scuba diving, skiing, camping, hiking, climbing, river running, kayaking and canoeing, bicycle touring, golf, airplaning, and rockhounding. The writing style is "folksy" rather than practical. There are many suggestions on where to go in Oregon, Washington, Idaho, and western Montana to enjoy these activities, and there are many, many more sources of information listed, including both organizations to write to (including guide services) and guidebooks to use. The author is the outdoor writer for the Seattle POST-INTELLIGENCER. This book would be best used as a beginning guide for suggestions.

W-10   Jackson, Earl. YOUR NATIONAL PARK SYSTEM IN THE SOUTH-WEST IN WORDS AND COLOR. 3d ed. Globe, AZ: Southwest Parks and Monuments Association, 1976. 68 p. Photos., maps. 0-911408-37-1. 76-358234.

This guide includes brief descriptions of 66 national parks, monuments, recreation areas, historic sites, memorials, and seashores, as well as practical information for the tourist, including where to write for further information.

W-11   Jenkinson, Michael. LAND OF CLEAR LIGHT: WILD REGIONS OF THE AMERICAN SOUTHWEST AND NORTHWESTERN MEXICO--HOW TO REACH THEM AND WHAT YOU WILL FIND THERE. A Sunrise Book. New York: E.P. Dutton, 1977. 305 p. Photos., maps. Bibliography. Index. 0-87690-203-4. 76-17542.

This is a book for the serious traveler who wishes to explore and appreciate the quiet back roads and natural history of the outdoors areas of Arizona, New Mexico, southcentral Utah, southwestern Colorado, and northwestern Mexico. Full descriptions include history and exploration tips, and a "guide notes" section for each area that gives access roads, the best way to get around, camping, supplies, special features, and sources of information. There are many easy-to-read maps.

W-12   Johnson, Robert N. GOLD DIGGERS ATLAS. 4th ed. Susanville, CA: Cy Johnson & Son (Box 288/96130), 1975. 64 p. Maps.

This work indicates the locations where gold has been found in western US and notes, very generally, the areas for "lost" mines.

W-13   _____. N.W. GEM FIELDS & GHOST TOWN ATLAS. Susanville, CA: Cy Johnson & Son, 1969. 47 p. Maps.

The maps indicate roads, gem fields, Indian artifacts, old mining claims, and ghost towns (including "ghost forts"), giving brief descriptions of the abandoned communities. The states of Washington, Oregon, Idaho, Montana, and Wyoming and parts of the Dakotas and Nebraska are covered.

W-14   Killeen, Jacqueline, et al. COUNTRY INNS OF THE FAR WEST. San Francisco: 101 Productions, 1977. 180 p. Maps, sketches. 0-89286-120-7. 77-10015.

The author gives tales of and tributes to 58 hostelries from Santa Barbara to Vancouver Island. Practical information on getting to and staying at each inn is also included with a sketch.

W-15   Kosoy, Ted. A BUDGET GUIDE TO CALIFORNIA AND THE PACIFIC COAST STATES. New York: St. Martin's Press, 1977. 234 p. Photos. 0-312-10692-0. 76-62778.

See the annotation with the other Kosoy guides (N-28) for a description of this superficial series.

W-16   Lesure, Thomas B. ALL THE SOUTHWEST: ARIZONA, SOUTHERN CALIFORNIA, COLORADO, NEVADA, NEW MEXICO, TEXAS, UTAH. 3d ed. Greenlawn, NY: Harian Publications (distributed by Grosset & Dunlap), 1974. 364 p. Photos., maps. 74-169201.

Information for each state is presented in 3 parts: facts about the state (flora and fauna, climate, housing, traffic and liquor laws, taxes, retirement factors); vacation practicalities (public transportation, hunting and fishing, festivals, sports, special sights for children, etc.); and an alphabetical community directory which describes points of interest and a selected list of places to stay.

W-17   Lowenkopf, Anne N., and Katz, Michael. CAMPING WITH THE INDIANS. Los Angeles: Sherbourne Press, 1974. 320 p. Maps, photos. Index. 0-8202-0164-2. 75-308818.

"A complete guide to the recreational, camping, and outdoor facilities of the Indian reservations of the 4-corner states (Utah, Arizona, Colorado, New Mexico)." This exciting book is arranged by tribe (Hopi, Navajo, Apache, Ute, Hualapai, Havasupai, Papago) with additional chapters on the Pueblo people and Phoenix, Arizona.

W-18   Navarre, Monty. THE AIRGUIDE TRAVELER: SOUTHWESTERN STATES. Long Beach, CA: Airguide Publications (1207 Pine Avenue/ 90813), 1977. 302 p. Photos, maps. Index.

The author gives complete information on resorts, visitor attractions, and parks and forests in Arizona, California, Nevada, and Utah. Information about the nearest airport is always included for the pilot/vacationeer who flies his or her own private plane and who is the target audience for this book.

W-19 PACIFIC BOATING ALMANAC. 3 vols. Edited by William Berssen. Ventura, CA: Western Marine Enterprises (Box Q/93001), 1979. Issued annually. Maps, photos., tables. 65-2700.

This series gives very complete information on water conditions, marinas and harbor facilities, restaurants, and events for all areas along the Pacific coast. Three volumes are available: Pacific Northwest and Alaska; Northern California and Nevada; and Southern California, Arizona and Baja. There are special sections on marine radio, tides, and astronomical data. Also included are many useful aerial photographs and charts showing mooring locations.

W-20 PACIFIC COAST HIGHWAYS: A VISUAL AND FACTUAL GUIDE TO THE MAJOR NORTH-SOUTH ROUTES OF THE PACIFIC STATES AND WESTERN CANADA, WITH MAJOR CONNECTING ROUTES. . . . Los Angeles: Automobile Club of Southern California, 1977. 143 p. Maps, sketches.

This no-nonsense guide describes driving conditions, points of interest, side routes, and gives a reproduction of the AAA strip maps for 3 north-south routes through California, Oregon, and Washington: Route 101 (coastal route) from Los Angeles to the Olympic Peninsula; Route 5 (valley route) from Tijuana to Vancouver; and Routes 395 and 97 (desert/mountain route) from San Diego to Seattle. There is a large section describing connecting routes to most of the more popular places of interest off these 3 main routes.

W-21 Rubenstein, Robert. BEST RESTAURANTS: PACIFIC NORTHWEST. San Francisco: 101 Productions, 1976. 208 p. Sketches. Indexes. 0-912238-85-2. 76-15968.

This is a guide to "unique top-quality restaurants in all price ranges" in Oregon (mostly Portland), Seattle, and Vancouver and Victoria in British Columbia. Descriptions include address, phone, hours, credit cards accepted, parking, type of bar service, price category, and a reproduction of the menu. There are geographical and cuisine indexes.

W-22 Satterfield, Archie. THE LEWIS AND CLARK TRAIL. Harrisburg, PA: Stackpole Books, 1978. 224 p. Drawings, maps. Index. 0-8117-0935-3. 77-17631.

While this book is mostly a popular history of the Lewis and Clark expedition followed by a personal account of a modern trip by motor home over the same route, we include it because it has 25 pages of maps and tables indicating 580 points of interest noting activities and attractions.

W-23   Schafer, Ann. CANOEING WESTERN WATERWAYS: THE COASTAL
        STATES. New York: Harper & Row, 1978. 272 p. Maps. Bib-
        liography. Index. 0-06-013798-3. 76-54410.

W-24   _____. CANOEING WESTERN WATERWAYS: THE MOUNTAIN
        STATES. New York: Harper & Row, 1978. 279 p. Maps. Bib-
        liography. Index. 0-06-013797-5. 74-1851.

        The beginning and ending pages on technique are identical in both
        volumes. So is the last section on "Sources of Canoeing Information"
        which lists films, state travel agencies, maps, books (both how-to and
        where-to), magazines, clubs, and suppliers. The major portion of
        each volume briefly describes places to canoe in 12 western states.
        The coastal states volume includes California, Oregon, Washington,
        and Hawaii; the mountain states volume includes Arizona, Colorado,
        Idaho, Montana, Nevada, New Mexico, Utah, and Wyoming. The
        intent is to list many places rather than to describe few places in
        great detail, therefore these volumes are best used for trip suggestions.

W-25   Schaffer, Jeff P., et al. THE PACIFIC CREST TRAIL. 2d ed. 2
        vols. Wilderness Press Trail Guide Series. Berkeley, CA: Wilderness
        Press, 1976-77. Maps, photos. Bibliography. Index. 76-1354.

        Volume 1 (0-911824-58-8) published in 1977, covers California and
        volume 2 (0-911824-49-9) published in 1976, covers Oregon and Wash-
        ington. Detailed descriptions and reproductions of all topographic
        maps for the entire trail are given. In the California volume the
        maps and text are interspersed, while in the Oregon/Washington volume
        the trail is described first and the map section follows.

W-26   Schwind, Dick. WEST COAST RIVER TOURING: ROGUE RIVER
        CANYON AND SOUTH. Beaverton, OR: Touchstone Press, 1974.
        223 p. Photos., maps. 0-911518-27-4. 74-79542.

        Ten major river systems, each with several trips or "runs" listed, are
        described in good detail. Each run is rated, maps are noted, area
        drained is recorded, and scenery is listed. Good how-to information is
        also included.

W-27   Seymour, Catryna T. ENJOYING THE SOUTHWEST. Philadelphia:
        Lippincott, 1973. 252 p. Maps, sketches. Index. 0-397-00902-X.
        73-4617.

        This is "an interpretive exploration through the culture, history,
        archaeology and natural beauty" of the Indian and canyon areas of
        Utah, Arizona, Colorado, and New Mexico, concentrating on the
        national parks and monuments rather than the cities and omitting
        restaurants and entertainment. It also tells where to write for further
        information and includes practical how-to notes. See W-11 for a
        similar, more recent book.

W-28   SKIER'S GUIDE TO THE WEST. By the editors of "Ski." New York: Times Mirror Magazine, 1975. 144 p. Maps, photos, 0-87955-428-2. 76-358642.

This guide describes 112 western downhill ski areas, including a geographic map, a slope diagram, address, and phone number. There are briefer reports on 80 western cross-country ski touring centers which include address and phone number.

W-29   Spring, Bob. 60 UNBEATEN PATHS: AN UNUSUAL GUIDE TO THE UNUSUAL IN THE NORTHWEST. Seattle: Superior Publishing Co., 1972. 143 p. Photos., maps. 0-87564-611-5. 72-79095.

When you've seen the major attractions of Washington and Oregon and are still unsatiated, this book will give you more suggestions. All are on most maps, and although maps are included in this book, the traveler will need to get his own to actually find his way. In addition, no practical, exact information is provided on trails, campsites, etc. You will find suggestions on such sights as shipwrecks, waterfalls, rhododendrons, and everything in between.

W-30   Spring, Bob, et al. THE NATIONAL PARKS OF THE NORTHWEST. Seattle: Superior Publishing Co., 1976. 184 p. Photos., maps. 0-87564-015-X. 76-6935.

Primarily made up of very stunning photographs, the text briefly gives background, facilities, and special features of each park (including vegetation and wildlife). Acitivities are also noted. The material in this volume on each of the national parks included (Olympic National Park, Mount Rainier National Park, North Cascades National Park, Sawtooth National Recreation Area, Craters of the Moon National Monument, Oregon Caves National Monument, John Day Fossil Beds National Monument, Crater Lake National Park, Klamath Basin National Wildlife Refuge, Lava Beds National Monument, and Redwood National Park) is also available separately.

W-31   Spring, Ira, and Manning, Harvey. WILDERNESS TRAILS NORTHWEST. Beaverton, OR: Touchstone Press, 1974. 190 p. Photos., maps. 0-911518-25-8. 74-76841.

"A hiker's and climber's overview-guide to national parks and wilderness areas in Wyoming, Montana, Idaho, northern California, Oregon, Washington, British Columbia, Canadian Rockies." Fifty-six of the 72 areas described are in the US.

W-32   Squire, James L., and Smith, Susan E. ANGLERS' GUIDE TO THE UNITED STATES PACIFIC COAST: MARINE FISH, FISHING GROUNDS AND FACILITIES. Washington, DC: U.S. Government Printing Office, 1977. 139 p. Maps, drawings.

Covering fishing along the coasts of California, Oregon, Washington,

Alaska, Hawaii, American Samoa, and Guam, this volume is more compact than its Atlantic counterpart (N-3). Fairly small areas (about 150 miles depending on the straightness of the coast) are described giving fish caught, general climate, suggested fishing spots, etc. The map which accompanies each section indicates shorefishing areas, bottomfishing areas, fishing reefs, kelp beds, depth of water, and fishing facilities. A table of facilities is keyed to the map.

W-33   Stein, Rita. A LITERARY TOUR GUIDE TO THE UNITED STATES: WEST AND MIDWEST. A Morrow QUILL Paperback. West Caldwell, NJ: William Morrow & Co., 1979. Photos. Index. 0-688-08174-6.

In this volume, "the author describes literary landmarks in the area, covering many places where pioneer stories and western writings have been identified or used as settings. . . ."

W-34   Sterling, E.M. WESTERN TRIPS AND TRAILS: HIKES, DRIVES, AND CAMPS IN 50 PRIME AREAS. Harrisburg, PA: Stackpole Books, 1974. 351 p. Photos., maps. 0-8117-2035-7. 74-649.

The author describes 50 national, state, and local parks, monuments, and wilderness areas in Montana, Wyoming, Colorado, Idaho, Utah, Arizona, Washington, Oregon, and California. A general map is provided for each place plus information on how to reach the area, where to drive, where to hike, backpacking opportunities, where to camp, and where to get information.

W-35   Stockley, Tom. WINERY TOURS IN OREGON, WASHINGTON, IDAHO AND BRITISH COLUMBIA. Mercer Island, WA: The Writing Works, 1978. 123 p. Maps. 0-916076-22-9. 78-8997.

The author, who writes a weekly wine column for THE SEATTLE TIMES, describes (with address, hours, phone, and illustration of bottle label) 18 wineries in Oregon, 9 in Washington, 1 in Idaho, and 5 in British Columbia.

W-36   SUNSET BEACHCOMBERS' GUIDE TO THE PACIFIC COAST. By the Sunset editorial staff. Menlo Park, CA: Lane Books, 1966. 112 p. Maps, photos. Index. 66-15333.

This old but still useful book gives descriptions of each of the publicly accessible beaches between San Diego and Cape Flattery in the far northwest tip of Washington.

W-37   SUNSET WESTERN CAMPSITES 1978. 17th ed. Menlo Park, CA: Lane Publishing Co., 1978. Issued annually. 400 p. Maps.

This is a guide to "more than 9,000 campgrounds for RVs and tents from the Rockies to the Pacific, Alaska to Mexico."

W-38 SUNSET WESTERN TRAVEL ADVENTURES. Menlo Park, CA: Lane
Publishing Co., 1978. 216 p. Photos., maps. 0-376-07001-3.

A wealth of information will be found in this guide which resembles
a thick magazine and which will probably be issued annually. (The
first edition was published in 1978). Articles on just about every
type of travel adventure are included and each is followed by a listing of where to engage in that activity or the names of groups
sponsoring that activity. The information gives you everything you
need to know, including costs. The advertisements are useful too;
some have been grouped by subject into a "Travel Adventures Directory." Finally, there is a reader service section whereby you can
receive free brochures by circling numbers on a sheet.

W-39 Sykes, George K., Jr., and Sumner, David. GUIDE TO NATURAL
WONDERS OF THE WEST. Harrisburg, PA: Stackpole Books, 1978.
192 p. Photos., maps. Index. 0-8117-2113-2. 77-28586.

Seventy-six natural areas in Washington, Oregon, California, Nevada,
Arizona, Idaho, Utah, Montana, Wyoming, Colorado, and New
Mexico are described briefly and often superficially, giving an address
for further information. The maps are adequate for locating the site
generally, and the photographs are rather nice.

W-40 WESTERN GEM HUNTERS ATLAS: ROCK LOCATIONS FROM CALI-
FORNIA TO THE DAKOTAS AND BRITISH COLUMBIA TO TEXAS.
14th ed. Susanville, CA: Cy Johnson & Son (Box 288/96130), 1973.
80 p. Maps. Bibliography.

These maps indicate the major roads and gem collecting locations,
noting if a fee is charged, if the area is "off limits," and, on the
maps themselves, books dealing with specific areas.

W-41 Wolf, James R. GUIDE TO THE CONTINENTAL DIVIDE TRAIL. 2
vols. Continental Divide Guides Series. Vol. 1: Missoula, MT: Mountain Press Publishing Co. (279 West Front Street/59801), 1976. Vol. 2:
Lynnwood, WA: Signpost Publications, 1977. Photos., maps. Bibliography.

Volume 1 covers northern Montana from the Canadian border to Rogers
Pass, giving detailed hiking instructions and a description of the
countryside. The appendix gives background information and important
addresses. Two folded map sheets accompany the first volume. Volume 2 covers southern Montana and Idaho from Rogers Pass, near
Helena, to Yellowstone National Park.

W-42 Wood, Amos L. HIKING TRAILS IN THE PACIFIC NORTHWEST.
Matteson, IL: Greatlakes Living Press, 1977. 202 p. Photos.,
maps. Bibliography. 0-915498-36-7. 77-71554.

Twenty-eight trails in northern California, Oregon, Washington,
British Columbia, and southeast Alaska are described, briefly noting

type of trail, distance, high/low point, terrain, season, trail surface, trail history, weather, scenic portions, wildlife, and other items of interest. There are lots of photographs and the maps range from fair to good.

W-43   Zwicker, Ted, ed. UNUSUAL VACATIONS FOR PARTICULAR PEOPLE. Los Angeles: Travel News, 1974. 74 p. Maps, sketches. 0-915080-01-X. 74-18994.

"A critical review of [30] selected guest ranches, mountain lodges and unusual resorts in the western United States." The author gives name, address, and phone number of the hosts, a general description, a map, and directions for finding each place.

MAGAZINES

W-44   DESERT: MAGAZINE OF THE SOUTHWEST. Palm Desert, CA: William and Joy Knyvett, publishers (Box 1318/92260).

This monthly began publication in 1937. Almost all of the articles will serve as an inspiration to desert region trip planners. There are regular book review, calendar of events, and recipe columns. They also sponsor the Desert Magazine Book Shop at 74-425 Highway 111 at Deep Canyon Road, Palm Desert, CA 92260 which advertises the availability of maps, prints, cookbooks, local history, etc. throughout the magazine. A number of desert tour operators appear among the advertisers.

W-45   SUNSET: THE MAGAZINE OF WESTERN LIVING. Menlo Park, CA: Lane Publishing Co. (Willow & Middlefield Roads/94025).

This magazine has been published monthly in regional and special editions since 1898 and reflects the western life-style. Each issue contains many articles in 7 regular sections: travel, home management, landscaping and outdoor building, food and entertaining, building and remodeling, workshop and craft projects, and gardening. The magazine is indexed in the READERS GUIDE TO PERIODICAL LITERATURE.

MAPS

Both AAA (US-259) and Exxon (US-261) issue a Western US map. Rand Mc-Nally (US-215) issues a Central/Western US map. See also W-12, W-13, and W-40.

PUBLISHERS

W-46   CAXTON PRINTERS, Box 700, Caldwell, ID 83605.

They have published fine western books for over 60 years, including the numerous Colorado ghost town books of Robert L. Brown (COLORADO GHOST TOWNS: PAST AND PRESENT, GHOST TOWNS OF THE COLORADO ROCKIES and JEEP TRAILS TO COLORADO GHOST TOWNS), SOUTHERN IDAHO GHOST TOWNS by Wayne Sparling, GHOST TOWNS OF THE NORTHWEST by Norman D. Weis, and several others now out of print.

W-47   DEAN PUBLICATIONS, Box 1545, Palm Desert, CA 92260.

In the spring of 1978 they had published 6 "Family Fun Guides" one to each of the following western national parks: Waterton Lakes and Glacier International Peace Park, Joshua Tree National Monument, Sequoia and Kings Canyon National Parks, Yosemite National Park, Grand Teton National Park, and Yellowstone National Park. These are basically childrens activity booklets to which the adult members of the family can contribute to increase the child's appreciation of the uniqueness of each park.

W-48   LANE PUBLISHING CO., Willow and Middlefield Roads, Menlo Park, CA 94025.

This is a well-known publisher of large-format, informative, and heavily illustrated books on gardening and landscaping; building, remodeling, and home design; hobbies and crafts; cooking; and travel and recreation. There are 18 titles (11 cover the 6 states of Alaska, Arizona, California, Hawaii, Oregon, and Washington; 7 cover foreign areas) in the Sunset Travel Guide Series and 11 more that are called "Pictorials," all of which are devoted to western US. The latter series emphasizes spectacular photography while the former series emphasizes useful factual travel information. They also publish SUNSET MAGAZINE (W-45).

W-49   NEVADA PUBLICATIONS, Box 15444, Las Vegas, NV 89114.

They publish ghost town guides for Nevada, Arizona, and Colorado as well as books on Las Vegas and Death Valley.

W-50   SIGNPOST PUBLICATIONS, 16812 36th Avenue West, Lynnwood, WA 98036.

They are publishers of both how-to and where-to books for backpackers, climbers, canoers, campers, bicyclists, and snow travelers of the Pacific Northwest. They also issue SIGNPOST FOR NORTHWEST HIKERS, a newsletter for backpackers and campers in this area.

W-51   SUPERIOR PUBLISHING CO., 708 Sixth Avenue North, Box 1710, Seattle, WA 98111.

Basically, they are a major publisher of pictorial books, preserving the color and flavor of America's western past. They issue a whole series of ghost town books by Lambert Florin; specific titles cover Alaska-British Columbia-Yukon, Arizona, California, Colorado-Utah, Montana-Idaho-Wyoming, Nevada, New Mexico-Texas, Oregon, Washington, and an overall western ghost town guide. They also have extensive lines of books about Indians, Alaska, and the Pacific Northwest.

W-52   THOMAS BROTHERS MAPS, 1326 South Broadway, Los Angeles, CA 90015.

They issue very good street maps, both as sheet maps and as atlases, for several cities and counties, primarily in California but recently expanding into Washington and Arizona. The maps are well-indexed and usually easy to read, and are revised at frequent intervals.

W-53   THE TOUCHSTONE PRESS, Box 81, Beaverton, OR 97005 (503/646-8081).

They are a small press that issues a large number of hiking, bicycling, climbing, river running, skiing, and back country road books for California, Oregon, Washington, Colorado, and Hawaii.

W-54   WESTWATER BOOKS, Box 365, Boulder City, NV 89005 (702/293-1406).

They publish 5 mile-by-mile river runners' guides, included separately in this information guide, to the Green/Colorado River system as it flows through Wyoming, Colorado, Utah, and Arizona. They also have a book buying service featuring other books of interest to western river runners. Their annual catalog is called BOOKS FOR RIVER RUNNERS.

W-55   THE WRITING WORKS, 7438 SE 40th Street, Mercer Island, WA 98040 (206/232-2171).

They publish a number of guidebooks to Washington and Oregon.

ORGANIZATIONS

W-56   DUDE RANCHERS ASSOCIATION, Route South Laramie via Tie Siding, WY 82084 (307/745-7077).

They publish a directory of ranches in Arizona, California, Colorado, Idaho, Kansas, Montana, Oregon, Washington, and Wyoming where you can go for a ranch vacation. The Association's quarterly magazine, published since 1932, THE DUDE RANCHER, also has articles about and listings of dude ranches.

W-57   THE FOREMOST WEST, 4400 Grape Street, Denver, CO 80216.

They promote travel to the states of Arizona, Colorado, Nevada, New Mexico, and Utah and provide package vacations to the most popular destinations in these states. They are a part of the Four Corners Regional Tourism Organization also at the above address.

W-58   NATIONAL PARK SERVICE, SOUTHWEST REGIONAL OFFICE, Box 728, Santa Fe, NM 87501 (505/988-6375).

Of all of the National Park Service regional offices, this one advertises its information services the most aggressively and is the only one that has a series of uniform brochures created especially for them for each of the 33 National Park areas within their jurisdiction. In addition to describing the main attraction of each area, each brochure tell you how to get there, describes nearby attractions, tells where the nearest accommodations and meals may be obtained, describes the prevailing weather, and gives the local address to obtain additional information. They also publish A HOLIDAY & VACATION PLANNING GUIDE TO THE FEDERAL PARKS OF THE SOUTHWEST designed to be used by travel writers and travel agents. It's actually a bound cumulation of the individual area brochures.

W-59   PACIFIC NORTHWEST NATIONAL PARKS ASSOCIATION, 523 Fourth and Pike Bldg., Room 807, Seattle, WA 98101.

Their principal function is to sponsor, publish, and distribute interpretive materials appropriate to each of the 8 far northwest national parks, historic sites, and recreation areas under their jurisdiction. Seven are in the state of Washington, the other is in Idaho. They issue many road and trail guide booklets and operate the bookstores found in the individual National Park Service visitor centers.

W-60   PACIFIC NORTHWEST TRAVEL ASSOCIATION, 1008 James Street, Seattle, WA 98104.

They issue an annual VACATION GUIDE to scenic areas, attractions, accommodations, dining, campgrounds, shops, traveler services, and highways in Idaho, Montana, Washington, and Oregon.

W-61   SOUTHWEST PARKS AND MONUMENTS ASSOCIATION, 339 South Broad Street, Box 1562, Globe, AZ 85501 (602/425-4392).

Their principal function is to sponsor, publish, and distribute interpretive materials appropriate to each of the 40 lesser-known national monuments, historic sites, recreation areas, and seashores under their jurisdiction. (The more widely known western national parks each have their own association, known as "natural history associations," whose addresses are the same as the individual national park address). They issue many road and trail guide booklets and operate the bookstores found in the individual National Park Service visitor centers. The Broad Street address is a walk-in information center.

INDIVIDUAL STATE SECTIONS

ARRANGED ALPHABETICALLY

ALABAMA

BOOKS, ATLASES, MAGAZINES

AL-1   Foshee, John H. ALABAMA CANOE RIDES AND FLOAT TRIPS. . . .
Huntsville, AL: Strode Publishers, 1975. 263 p. Maps, photos.
0-87397-087-X. 75-26074.

"A detailed guide to the Cahaba and 25 other creeks and rivers of
Alabama plus put-ins, take-outs and general information about numerous other streams of the state." Detailed maps accompany the
descriptions plus the name of the appropriate USGS map to use is
also included. The rides, many of which are close to Birmingham,
range from 3 1/2 to 14 miles, and are therefore appropriate for
1-day trips. Many rides are for the novice, although all are rated
according to difficulty and hazards, and several fall into the "whitewater" category.

AL-2   Walker, Alyce B., ed. ALABAMA: A GUIDE TO THE DEEP SOUTH.
Rev. ed. American Guide Series. New York: Hastings House,
1975. 411 p. Photos., maps. Bibliography. Index. 0-8038-0391-
5. 75-16314.

This is a revision of the original WPA guide first published in 1941.
There are opening essays describing the state, followed by descriptions
of 10 cities and 16 highway tours. There is also a chronology of
Alabama history.

MAPS

The official ALABAMA HIGHWAY MAP is prepared by the State Highway Dept.,
but is available from the Bureau of Publicity and Information (AL-3). The
1977-78 ed. describes points of interest and facilities at state parks. AAA
(US-259) and Exxon (US-261) both put out a joint map for Alabama/Georgia.
Goushā (US-206) and Rand McNally (US-215) each put out a single map for
Alabama. The Alabama Power Co., Box 261, Birmingham, AL 35291 makes
available a number of recreational maps for 8 reservoirs within its jurisdiction.

MAJOR TOURIST ORGANIZATION

AL-3   ALABAMA BUREAU OF PUBLICITY AND INFORMATION, Room 403,
        State Highway Bldg., 11 South Union Street, Montgomery, AL 36130
        (205/832-5510).

        Their major piece of literature is ALABAMA HAS IT ALL (1978 ed.,
        58 p.) which is a comprehensive guide to points of interest, with
        maps; hunting and fishing information; and facilities at state parks,
        private campgrounds, and national forests. They also issue a calendar
        of events and INTERSTATE INTERLUDES, which features 23 driving
        tours, with directions and maps, for getting off interstate highways to
        see the real Alabama.

REGIONAL TOURISM ASSOCIATIONS

ALABAMA MOUNTAIN LAKES ASSOCIATION, 1516 Central Parkway SW,
Decatur, AL 35601 (205/350-3500).

        They issue a general brochure to attractions in north Alabama and
        provide maps, directories, and other information on what to see and
        do in Decatur and Huntsville, home of the Alabama Space and Rocket
        Center.

DEKALB COUNTY TOURIST ASSOCIATION, Box 125, Fort Payne, AL 35967
(205/845-2741).

GULF SHORES TOURIST ASSOCIATION, Gulf Shores, AL 36542 (205/968-
7511).

HISTORIC CHATTAHOOCHEE COMMISSION, Box 33, Eufaula, AL 36027
(205/687-9755).

TALLACOOSA HIGHLAND LAKES ASSOCIATION, Box 97, Westover, AL
35186 (205/678-6994).

OTHER ORGANIZATIONS

AL-4   ALABAMA HOTEL AND MOTEL ASSOCIATION, 660 Adams Avenue,
        Suite 254, Montgomery, AL 36104 (205/263-3407).

AL-5   ALABAMA TRAVEL COUNCIL, 660 Adams Avenue, Montgomery, AL
        36104 (205/263-3407).

        They are mainly an organization working with other travel agencies
        within Alabama to promote travel to that state. They no longer

provide a walk-in information center, but they will send some travel brochures issued by other travel establishments.

INFORMATION CENTERS/INFORMATION PHONES

The Bureau of Publicity and Information (AL-3) has a toll-free number: 800/633-5761.

OUTDOOR RECREATIONAL ACTIVITIES

CANOEING AND BOATING. See (AL-1).

FISHING AND HUNTING. ALABAMA HAS IT ALL, available from the Bureau of Publicity and Information (AL-3), lists public lakes and hunting areas. Also contact the Alabama Division of Game and Fish, Dept. of Conservation and Natural Resources, Administrative Bldg., 64 North Union Street, Montgomery, AL 36130.

NATIONAL/STATE PARKS/FORESTS, ETC.

The U.S. Forest Service, National Forests in Alabama, Box 40, Montgomery, AL 36101 issues a visitor/recreation map (1 1/4 in. represents 5 miles) covering all national forests and national forest recreation areas in Alabama and listing facilities available at each.

Contact the Alabama Dept. of Conservation and Natural Resources, Information and Education Dept., 64 North Union Street, Montgomery, AL 36130 (205/832-6323) for information about state parks and available camping and recreational facilities.

INDIVIDUAL CITIES OR AREAS

Montgomery—Printed Materials

AL-6   Junior League of Montgomery. A GUIDE TO THE CITY OF MONT-GOMERY. Montgomery: the author (305 South Lawrence Street/36104), 1969. 119 p. Photos. 71-17063.

Descriptions of buildings of noteworthy architectural style, old homes, houses of worship, historic buildings, state buildings, and colleges are keyed to a difficult-to-read map to provide a tour guide. Five one-day tours out of Montgomery are also briefly described.

Good maps of Montgomery are available from Arrow Publishing Co. (US-199) and Champion Map Corp. (US-202).

Montgomery—Organizations

AL-7   MONTGOMERY AREA CHAMBER OF COMMERCE, Convention and
Visitor Promotion Division, Box 79, Montgomery, AL 36101 (205/834-
5200).

They issue a detailed street map and guide, a monthly calendar of
events, WHERE TO DINE, SHOP, SLEEP IN MONTGOMERY (with
maps) and A DRIVING TOUR OF HISTORIC MONTGOMERY.   They
operate a visitor information center at 220 North Hull Street.   There
is a "Fun Fone" at 265-2783 which is a recorded message of daily
events.

ALASKA

BOOKS, ATLASES, MAGAZINES

AK-1   ALASKA: THE MAGAZINE OF LIFE ON THE LAST FRONTIER. Anchorage: Alaska Northwest Publishing Co.

This monthly magazine features real-life adventure stories, travel articles, history and lore, and many color photographs. It began publication in 1935 as the ALASKA SPORTSMAN. A cumulated index for 1935-1972 is available from the publisher. An offshoot of the magazine is the Alaska Magazine Travel Service, 139 Second Avenue South, Edmonds, WA 98020.

AK-2   ALASKA FISHING GUIDE. Anchorage: Alaska Northwest Publishing Co., 1978. Issued annually. 172 p. Photos., maps. Index. 0-88240-108-4. 75-17664.

A how-to as well as a where-to guide, this work gives rates on ferries, air taxi charges, fishing seasons, limits, fees, and a description of Alaskan game fish. There is a list of 557 selected fishing spots.

AK-3   ALASKA HUNTING GUIDE. Anchorage: Alaska Northwest Publishing Co., 1978. Issued annually. 208 p. Photos., maps. 0-88240-110-6. 74-81787.

More how-to than where-to information is listed in this guide, but it does note the ranges of the game animals.

AK-4   ALASKA TRAVEL GUIDE. 18th ed. Edited by Larry Lake. Salt Lake City: Alaska Travel Guide (Box 21038/84121), 1978. Issued annually. 560 p. Photos., maps. Index.

This guide gives very detailed information on the Alaskan transportation system (including mile-by-mile highway logs), towns, accommodations, national parks, tours, events, hunting, and fishing. There is a community index and a Rand McNally map of Alaska in a pocket in the back.

AK-5   Bush, Hal. ALASKA TRAVEL HANDBOOK. Algonac, MI: Alaska
        Travel Handbook, 1974. 155 p. Map. 74-186941.

        This "itinerary" road guide for RV users contains no good maps. Only
        travelers who are willing to follow Bush's road log and descriptions to
        the letter as they travel will want this.

AK-6   Colby, Merle. A GUIDE TO ALASKA: LAST AMERICAN FRONTIER.
        American Guide Series. New York: Macmillan, 1939. 427 p.
        Photos., maps. Bibliography. Index.

        This original WPA guide for Alaska is out of print and has not been
        revised. The first 104 pages are a general compendium of facts and
        figures about the state's history, peoples, government, natural wealth,
        commerce, transportation, communications, and national defense. The
        remainder of the volume is devoted to detailed descriptions of the
        major regions, towns, and communities.

AK-7   Cross, Cliff. ALASKA. Tucson, AZ: H.P. Books (Box 5367/85703),
        1969. 170 p. Maps, photos. Index. 0-912656-38-7. 78-22107.

        The contents were copyrighted in 1969, but the book was still in
        print in 1978. The author takes you along the Alaska Highway from
        the US border to Fairbanks noting points of interest and travel service
        facilities (campgrounds, gas stations, etc.) at south/north mileposts.
        Many side trips to the major travel destinations of Alaska are also
        described. Over 20 fishing maps are included as well as information
        on getting around by ferry and train. The format is confusing.

AK-8   Johannsen, Neil, and Johannsen, Elizabeth. EXPLORING ALASKA'S
        PRINCE WILLIAM SOUND: ITS FIORDS, ISLANDS, GLACIERS AND
        WILDLIFE. Anchorage: Alaska Travel Publications, 1975. 306 p.
        Photos., maps. Bibliography. Index. 0-914164-03-1. 75-1912.

        This guide includes chapters on gateways (highway access to the
        area); facilities (places to stay); history; geology; climate; wildlife;
        fishing; vegetation; detailed descriptions of 3 state ferry routes across
        the Sound, including points of interest and descriptions of the major
        communities along the way; descriptions of 10 small-boat cruising
        areas; and brief descriptions of 10 hikes.

AK-9   Kerr, Lois. HOW TO GET THE MOST OUT OF YOUR CRUISE TO
        ALASKA. North Vancouver, B.C.: J.J. Douglas, 1976. 119 p.
        Photos., maps. Bibliography. 0-88894-107-2. 76-383736.

        This guide to the Inside Passage from Vancouver to Skagway gives
        only minimal advice on the cruise itself. Instead, this is a book
        to use as you wend your way through the state. It will help you
        explore and appreciate the passing scenery and towns, either by
        water or on land.

AK-10   Knox, Bob, and Knox, Wilma. ALL ABOUT CAMPING IN ALASKA
         AND THE YUKON. Grass Valley, CA: Rajo Publications (Rt. 1,
         Box 877, McCourtney Road/95945), 1973. 196 p. Photos, maps.

         The authors describe points of interest along the various highway
         routes and give extensive specific practical information for the
         camper. The first-time camper in Alaska will find this guide partic-
         ularly useful. There is a 2-page list of "Sources of Further Informa-
         tion."

AK-11   LOU JACOBIN'S GUIDE TO ALASKA, THE YUKON, AND BRITISH
         COLUMBIA. Edited by Lou Jacobin. Anchorage: Far North Pub-
         lishing, 1975. Issued annually. 385 p. Photos., maps. Index.

         General information as well as specific travel information on Alaska
         is included in this publication. Events, transportation, parks and
         monuments, people, living conditions, history, totems, fishing, and
         accommodations are described. The work is arranged by region of
         the state with an index of communities.

AK-12   MILEPOST: ALL-THE-NORTH TRAVEL GUIDE. 30th ed. Anchorage:
         Alaska Northwest Publishing Co., 1978. Issued annually. 500 p.
         Photos., maps. 0-88240-102-5.

         ". . .thousands of facts on every city, town, village, park, wildlife
         area, and scenic attraction. . .in Alaska and northwestern Canada
         . . .contains detailed, mile-by-mile information on every route, and
         includes a large colorful map, 70 area and city maps, and special
         information for fishermen, bicyclists, wild flower fanciers, hikers,
         and rock hounds." The large-scale, color, pull-out map is also
         available separately under the title of PLAN-A-TRIP map. MILEPOST
         is the most complete guide to Alaska.

AK-13   Nienhueser, Helen. 55 WAYS TO THE WILDERNESS IN SOUTH
         CENTRAL ALASKA. Seattle: The Mountaineers, 1972. 160 p.
         Maps, photos. Indexes. 0-916890-30-9. 72-83325.

         All these trips are in the areas surrounding Anchorage. Most are hiking
         trails, but a few are skiing and canoe trails. A USGS map with the
         trail marked in red and detailing length, elevation gain and highest
         point, best season, and the name of the USGS map to use are in-
         cluded with each trip description. There are indexes by trail name,
         trail length, and season.

AK-14   Piggott, Margaret H. DISCOVER SOUTHEAST ALASKA WITH PACK
         AND PADDLE. Seattle: The Mountaineers, 1974. 268 p. Maps,
         photos. Bibliography. Index. 0-916890-35-X. 74-81954.

         This book is geographically arranged with several trips beginning from
         each of the major towns in the Alaska section of the Inside Passage:
         Ketchikan, Sitka, Juneau, Skagway, etc. Most of the trips are on

foot, but the traveler will have to have a boat immediately at hand
to explore fully all the areas described here.

AK-15   Spring, Norma. ALASKA: THE COMPLETE TRAVEL BOOK. 2d ed.
New York: Macmillan, 1975. 274 p. Photos., map. Index.
0-02-613260-5. 75-20228.

This is a good, general, fairly recent guidebook giving ". . .prices,
accommodations, climate, travel arrangements, food and drink,
clothing, ski resorts, shopping and sightseeing. . . .listings of campsites, museums, package tours, park services, travel agencies, and
business recruiters."

AK-16   SUNSET TRAVEL GUIDE TO ALASKA. 3d ed. By the editors of
Sunset Books and Sunset Magazine. Menlo Park, CA: Lane Books,
1978. 112 p. Photos., maps. Index. 0-376-06033-6. 77-90724.

Arranged by section of the state, this heavily illustrated guide gives
places to visit, hints for the traveler, and background on the various
locations.

AK-17   28 TOP FISHING LAKES IN THE MATANUSKA-SUSITNA VALLEY,
ALASKA. Anchorage: Alaska Road and Recreation Maps (Box 2459/
99510), 1977. 36 p. Maps, photos.

This is a compilation of 18 detailed maps of fishing lakes, showing
depth contours, boat launch or public access sites, camping areas,
lodges, roads, trails, and additional information about restaurants
and services (groceries, gas, etc.). The area covered is generally
north of Anchorage in southcentral Alaska. The lakes range in
distance from about 100 miles north along the Parks Highway to
Denali State Park, to about 50 miles east along the Glenn Highway.
Most of them are in the central region centered around the towns of
Wasilla and Palmer.

AK-18   Weber, Sepp. WILD RIVERS OF ALASKA. Anchorage: Alaska
Northwest Publishing Co., 1976. 169 p. Maps, photos. Index.
0-88240-071-1. 76-15272.

Basic information is given for 53 Alaska rivers, including water classifications, distance, and a map.

MAPS

The state does not publish an official road map. Goushā (US-206) and Rand
McNally (US-215) each issue a map of Alaska. AAA (US-259) issues a map
of Alaska and northwestern Canada. The Bureau of Land Management, Alaska
State Office, 555 Cordova Street, Pouch 7-512, Anchorage, AK 99510 issues
brochures on each of the different Alaska highways (Denali Highway, Steese

and Elliott Highways, Taylor Highway, and Richardson Highway) and the visitor services and points of interest to be found along the way. Alaska Road and Recreation Maps, Box 2459, Anchorage, AK 99510 issues 2 maps: (1) the PARKS HIGHWAY map locates motels and lodges, roadside fishing areas, gas stations, and campgrounds along the highway from Anchorage to Fairbanks via Mount McKinley National Park, and (2) THE MATANUSKA VALLEY ROAD AND RECREATION MAP locates hotels and lodges, gas stations, restaurants, campgrounds, churches, roads, and lakes and streams in southcentral Alaska in an area lying roughly between the towns of Willow and Palmer. There is a pull-out map included with MILEPOST (AK-12) and one in the pocket of the ALASKA TRAVEL GUIDE (AK-4). See also AK-17.

PUBLISHERS

AK-19   ALASKABOOKS. Box 1494, Juneau, AK 99801.

This is the publishing outlet for the books of Mike Miller, a prolific Alaska writer specializing in sports and travel. One of his books is titled OFF THE BEATEN PATH IN ALASKA.

AK-20   ALASKA NORTHWEST PUBLISHING CO., Box 4-EEE, Anchorage, AK 99509.

This is the major publisher of Alaska material. They do numerous travel publications; many personal accounts of the Alaska life-style; many art and pictorial works; cookbooks and other how-to volumes; histories; childrens books; sportsmens books; natural history guides; ALASKA GEOGRAPHIC, a quarterly magazine with each issue devoted to monographic, photographic coverage of specific subjects; THE ALASKA JOURNAL, a quarterly featuring history and arts of the north; and FACTS ABOUT ALASKA: THE ALASKA ALMANAC, a thorough compendium of information on all aspects of Alaska.

AK-21   ALASKA TRAVEL PUBLICATIONS, Box 4-2031, Anchorage, AK 99509 (907/274-3912).

They issue several publications on Alaska that are included in this chapter as well as one by their editors entitled EXPLORING KATMAI NATIONAL MONUMENT AND THE VALLEY OF TEN THOUSAND SMOKES.

MAJOR TOURIST ORGANIZATION

AK-22   ALASKA STATE DIVISION OF TOURISM, Pouch E, Juneau, AK 99811 (907/465-2010).

They issue a very comprehensive annual guide DISCOVER. . .THE WORLDS OF ALASKA (1978 ed., 62 p.). The first half describes the regional points of interest throughout the state. The second half is called the "Alaska Travel Index" and is a staggering listing of information sources: tour operators; travel agents; how to get there by air, highway, rail, and sea; camping facilities; hotels/motels/inns; wilderness lodges; entertainment and attractions; annual events; "flightseeing" tours; marine charters; historic places, parks, and museums; photographic safaris; river touring; package tours; sportfishing; trekking/trail rides/dog sledding/mountaineering; car, camper and motor home rentals; fish and game information; hotel reservations; licensed hunting guides; travel counselors; and vehicle shipment by water. This "Information Sources" section lists chambers of commerce, convention and visitors bureaus, selected guidebooks, travel maps and charts, and visitor information centers.

OTHER ORGANIZATIONS

AK-23   ALASKA AIRLINES, Box 68900, Seattle, WA 98188.

They fly between Seattle and all major Alaskan cities. There is a toll-free reservations and information number that can be dialed from anywhere in the US except Alaska, Hawaii, and Washington: 800/426-0333. In Washington call 800/552-0670. ALASKAFEST is the monthly inflight magazine.

AK-24   ALASKA HOTEL/MOTEL ASSOCIATION. c/o Alaska Airlines, Seattle-Tacoma International Airport, Seattle, WA 98158 (206/433-3144).

AK-25   ALASKA MARINE HIGHWAY SYSTEM, Pouch R, Juneau, AK 99811.

State of Alaska-operated ferry liners provide scheduled water transportation (passengers and vehicles) between Seattle and Skagway on the Inside Passage (the Southeast System) and the ports on the Kenai Peninsula, Kodiak Island, and Prince William Sound (the Southcentral System). The two systems do not interconnect. They will send a general brochure plus a schedule which includes cost information along with arrival and departure times. For reservations call 907/465-3941 in Juneau; 907/272-7116 in Anchorage; 206/623-1970 in Seattle; and 604/627-1744 in Prince Rupert.

AK-26   ALASKA RAILROAD, Pouch 7-2111, Anchorage, AK 99510. (907/265-2494 in Anchorage; 907/465-7736 in Fairbanks).

This is a federally operated railroad providing year-round passenger and freight service between Anchorage and Fairbanks via Mount McKinley National Park and summer passenger service only between Anchorage and Whittier on Prince William Sound.

INFORMATION CENTERS/INFORMATION PHONES

A list of visitor information centers in Anchorage, Cordova, Haines, Juneau,

Palmer, Portage Glacier, Skagway, and Tok will be found in the "Information Sources" section of the "Alaska Travel Index" in DISCOVER. . .THE WORLDS OF ALASKA issued by the Division of Tourism (AK-22).

OUTDOOR RECREATION ACTIVITIES

BICYCLING. See AK-31.

CANOEING AND BOATING. The Bureau of Land Management, Alaska State Office, 555 Cordova Street, Anchorage, AK 99501 provides 2 brochures on "Alaska's River Trails." One covers the northern region, the other the southern region. See also AK-14 and AK-18.

FISHING AND HUNTING. Contact the Alaska Dept. of Fish and Game at either the main office at Subport Bldg., Juneau, AK 99811 (907/465-4112), or either of the regional offices at 333 Raspberry Road, Anchorage, AK 99502 (907/344-0566), or 1300 College Road, Fairbanks, AK 99701 (907/452-1531). Hunting and fishing is allowed on 9 of the 18 National Wildlife Refuges in Alaska. For information contact: U.S. Fish and Wildlife Service, Alaska Area Office, 1011 East Tudor Road, Anchorage, AK 99503. See also AK-2, AK-3 and AK-17.

WINTER ACTIVITIES. See AK-30.

NATIONAL/STATE PARKS/FORESTS, ETC.

Mount McKinley National Park

AK-27   EXPLORING ALASKA'S MOUNT McKINLEY NATIONAL PARK. 2d
         ed. By the editors of Alaska Travel Publications. Anchorage: Alaska
         Travel Publications, 1976. 312 p. Maps, photos. Bibliography.
         Index. 0-914164-04-X. 76-4404.

         This is a very thorough, easy to use guide. A large section describes
         visitor facilities (including the 2 visitor centers). It includes a
         good mile-by-mile guide, with maps, of Park Road, and there are
         descriptions and maps of 25 hikes in the park.

AK-28   Washburn, Bradford. A TOURIST GUIDE TO MOUNT McKINLEY.
         Rev. ed. Anchorage: Alaska Northwest Publishing Co., 1976.
         79 p. Photos., maps. Bibliography. Index. 0-88240-089-4. 76-
         28403.

         This guide describes "mile-by-mile through the Park over Mount
         McKinley Park Highway. . .the record of McKinley climbs."

AK-29   MOUNT McKINLEY NATIONAL PARK, Box 9, McKinley Park, AK
99755 (907/683-2294 or 683-2295).

A general map/brochure is provided plus a map/brochure on hiking
in the park.   A brochure, HOW TO TRAVEL IN MOUNT McKINLEY,
describes the shuttle bus system that operates beyond the point where
private vehicles are allowed.   There are 2 visitor centers: the Riley
Creek Visitor Center, near the park entrance and open daily from
5:30A.M. to 11P.M.; and the Eielson Visitor Center, located along
Park Road at mile 66 (beyond where private vehicles may go) and
open from 8A.M. to 7:30P.M. daily.   For information about lodging
and other concessioner services write: Mount McKinley National Park
Co., McKinley Park, AK 99755.

There is a National Park Service Information Office at 540 West 5th Avenue,
Room 202, Anchorage, AK 99501 (907/276-8166) which provides information
on facilities at all the lands in Alaska administered by the National Park
Service. It is open Monday–Friday, except holidays, throughout the year.
Hours are 7A.M.-5P.M. in the summer and 7:30A.M.-4:30P.M. the remainder
of the year.

There are 2 national forests in Alaska. Write to: Forest Supervisor, Chugach
National Forest, Pouch 6606, Anchorage, AK 99502 (907/272-4485) for a
detailed map of the forest and for reservations at recreation cabins within the
Forest.   The Visitor Information Center at the Portage Glacier Recreation Area
within the Forest is open 7 days a week from 9A.M.-6P.M. in the summer;
hours are reduced in the winter.   The other national forest, Tongass National
Forest, is divided into 3 regions, and each region must be contacted individ-
ually for information and reservations in the primitive backcountry cabins:
Forest Supervisor, Chatham Area, Tongass National Forest, Box 1980, Sitka,
AK 99835 (907/747-6671); Forest Supervisor, Ketchikan Area, Tongass National
Forest, Federal Bldg., Ketchikan, AK 99901 (907/225-3101); and Forest Supervisor, Stikine Area, Tongass National Forest, Box 309, Petersburg, AK 99833
(907/772-4266).   The Visitor Information Center at the Mendenhall Glacier
Recreation Area within the Forest is open 7 days a week from 7A.M.-8P.M.
in the summer; hours are reduced in the winter.   The maps of the individual
forests show locations of roads, trails, airfields, campgrounds, winter sports
areas, and state ferry routes.   The backcountry recreation cabins are used
mostly by hunters and fishermen.   The Alaska Region of the U.S. Forest Service, Office of Information, Box 1628, Juneau, AK 99802 (907/586-7416)
may be contacted also.   They operate an information center in the Federal
Bldg., 709 West 9th Avenue, Juneau, that is open 8A.M.-5P.M. during
weekdays.

The Bureau of Land Management, Alaska State Office, 555 Cordova Street,
Anchorage, AK 99501 (907/277-1561) maintains many campgrounds and trails
throughout the state and should be contacted directly for further information.

The Alaska Dept. of Natural Resources, Division of Parks, 619 Warehouse
Avenue, Suite 210, Anchorage, AK 99501 (907/274-4676 provides information
on state parks, recreation areas, waysides, and historic sites.

INDIVIDUAL CITIES OR AREAS

Anchorage—Printed Materials

AK-30 Hannan, Leo. SKI TOURING IN THE ANCHORAGE AREA. N.p.: Nordic Ski Club of Anchorage, 1970. 31 p. Maps. 75-29449.

This guide is photo-offset from typewritten copy and describes, with maps, 10 tours.

A map of Anchorage is available from Arrow Publishing Co. (US-199).

Anchorage—Organizations

AK-31 ANCHORAGE CHAMBER OF COMMERCE, 612 F Street, Anchorage, AK 99501 (907/272-2401).

They operate a Log Cabin Visitor Information Center located adjacent to City Hall at Fourth and F Streets (907/279-3632). Since they are operated by the Municipality of Anchorage, the free Anchorage bikeways map issued by the City Parks and Recreation Dept. should be available here.

AK-32 ANCHORAGE CONVENTION/VISITOR BUREAU, Plaza 201, East Third Avenue, Anchorage, AK 99501 (907/278-1549).

They issue an annual STREET MAP AND GUIDE, SHOPPING AND DINING DIRECTORY and WHAT TO WEAR AND BUY IN ALASKA.

Fairbanks—Printed Materials

AK-33 INTERIOR AND ARCTIC ALASKA VISITORS GUIDE. 5th ed. Fairbanks: Fairbanks Daily News-Minor, 1978. Issued annually. 32 p. Photos., maps.

This is a tabloid-style newspaper supplement describing outdoors things to see and do in both the southeastern and Arctic Ocean sections of the state.

Maps of the Fairbanks area are available from Arrow Publishing Co. (US-199) and annually (1978, 14th ed.) from Alaskan Arctic Publications, Box 438, Fairbanks, AK 99707.

Fairbanks—Organizations

AK-34 GREATER FAIRBANKS CHAMBER OF COMMERCE AND CONVENTION AND VISITOR BUREAU, 550 1st Avenue, Fairbanks, AK 99701 (907/

452-1105 for the Chamber of Commerce; 907/456-5774 for the Convention and Visitor Bureau).

The Chamber of Commerce is the Visitors Information Bureau for the Fairbanks area and is open Monday-Friday from 8A.M.-5P.M. They provide mimeographed guides to what to see and do; hotels and motels; restaurants, camping, climate, and statewide sources of information.

Juneau

Maps of Juneau are available from Rudy J. Ripley, 313 Coleman Drive, Juneau, AK 99801 and the Alaska Dept. of Highways, 101 Highway Office Bldg., Box 1467, Juneau, AK 99802.

AK-35   JUNEAU CHAMBER OF COMMERCE, 200 North Franklin Street, Juneau, AK 99801 (907/586-2201).

They issue a general brochure and a map/leaflet which includes both a map of the overall Juneau area and a map of a walking tour of Juneau. Brief descriptions of points of interest are included. This address is also a walk-in information center.

ARIZONA

BOOKS, ATLASES, MAGAZINES

AZ-1   ARIZONA HIGHWAYS. Phoenix: Arizona Highways.

Begun in 1925 and now published monthly by the Arizona Dept. of Transportation, this is probably the most stunning and best known of all the state magazines. The issue examined had articles about the Navajo, CJ. "Buffalo" Jones, the Arizona Historical Society Musuem, and a lavish centerfold group of Arizona photographs. There is a regular book review column.

AZ-2   Bunker, Gerald. ARIZONA'S NORTHLAND TRAILS. Glendale, CA: La Siesta Press (Box 406/91209), 1972. 36 p. Maps, photos. Index. 0-910858-49-4.

The author describes hiking trails in 7 areas of northern Arizona within a 20-mile radius of Flagstaff, including the San Francisco Peaks and Oak Creek Canyon.

AZ-3   De Mente, Boye. INSIDERS GUIDE FOR THE NEW ARIZONAN: PHOENIX, SCOTTSDALE, TEMPE, MESA, TUCSON, AND OTHER COMMUNITIES. Phoenix: Phoenix Books, 1977. 174 p. Maps.

While some of the information included will be of interest only to would-be residents (house hunting, finding a job, etc.), the sections on participant and spectator sports, recreational and cultural facilities, where to take the children, and dining will also interest the traveler. Tucson receives the most thorough coverage with additional information on sights to see.

AZ-4   _____. VISITOR'S GUIDE TO ARIZONA'S INDIAN RESERVATIONS. Phoenix: Phoenix Books, 1978. 115 p. Maps. 0-914778-14-5.

The author describes visitor attractions, annual festivals and dances, hunting and fishing opportunities, camping and other overnight accommodations, and rules and regulations useful for visiting the various

Navajo, Hopi, Hualapai, Havasupai, Kaibab Paiutes, Apache, Pima, Maricopa, Mohave, Papago, and Chemehuevi Indian Reservations in Arizona.

AZ-5   Dutton, Davis, and Pilgre[e]n, Tedi. THE GREAT FAMILY FUN GUIDE TO ARIZONA. New York: Ballantine Books, 1974. 165 p. Photos., maps. Index. 0-345-24271-8. 75-306298.

This is a regional guide to parks, museums, and natural and manmade wonders where families can have a good time. It includes hours, phone numbers, admission costs, and a calendar of annual events.

AZ-6   Golden, Robert E. INSIDER'S GUIDE TO OUTDOOR RECREATION IN ARIZONA. Phoenix: Phoenix Books, 1973. 187 p. Maps, photos. Index.

This thorough guide to outdoors Arizona includes practical information on everything from national to city parks, camping to skiing, ghost towns to gardens, and everything in between. There is a list of local chambers of commerce.

AZ-7   McDannel, Wally. A GUIDE TO ARIZONA'S WATERWAYS. Tucson: Arizona Waterways, 1977. 160 p. Photos., maps. Index. 77-353156.

This very complete guide describes the setting, how to get there, the waterway itself, the facilities, the fish, and where to go for further information for 89 lake areas. It is geographically arranged with a name index.

AZ-8   Miller, Joseph. ARIZONA: THE GRAND CANYON STATE. 4th ed. American Guide Series. New York: Hastings House, 1966. 532 p. Photos., maps. Bibliography. Index. 66-20364.

This revision of the original 1940 WPA guide begins with a background section covering everything from natural history to folklore. It then goes on to describe tours of 11 cities and towns, 13 highway tours, and 5 park and 4 trail tours of Grand Canyon National Park. There is a chronology of Arizona history.

AZ-9   Nelson, Dick, and Nelson, Sharon. 50 HIKES IN ARIZONA. Glenwood, NM: Telcolote Press (Box 217/88039), 1976. 3d ed. 116 p. Maps, photos. Index.

Length, elevation, season, general description, reproduction of the USGS map with route lined in, and a photograph are included for each hike.

AZ-10 OUTDOOR ARIZONA. Phoenix: Phoenix Publishing Co. (4707 North 12th Street/85104).

This monthly magazine's purpose is to provide ideas for vacation trips and travels in Arizona. In addition, there are always several articles per issue of interest to fishermen or hunters. Very often, each monthly issue will have a separately published and sold "Visitors' Guide" supplement to a specific region in the state. These describe fishing, activities, scenic attractions, campgrounds, and accommodations in each. For example, the December 1977 supplement to OUT-DOOR ARIZONA was a 38-page VISITORS' GUIDE TO YAVAPAI COUNTY (Prescott, Jerome, Sedona), the April 1978 supplement was a 38-page VISITORS' GUIDE TO COCONINO COUNTY (Flagstaff, Page, Sedona), the June 1978 supplement was a 46-page VISITORS' GUIDE TO MARICOPA COUNTY (Phoenix, Scottsdale, etc.), and the July 1978 supplement was a 62-page VISITORS' GUIDE TO THE COLORADO RIVER (Lake Powell, Grand Canyon, Lake Mead, Lake Havasu, Yuma, etc.).

AZ-11   SUNSET TRAVEL GUIDE TO ARIZONA. 4th ed. By the editors of Sunset Books and Sunset Magazine. Menlo Park, CA: Lane Publishing Co., 1973. 128 p. Photos., maps. Index. 0-376-06054-9. 73-75758.

Nearly all the attractions to see in Arizona are described here, but practical information on how to get to each, admission charges, etc. is lacking, although sometimes an address to write to for further information is given. It does not include restaurants or accommodations. A new edition was published in 1978.

AZ-12   Thollander, Earl. BACK ROADS OF ARIZONA. Flagstaff, AZ: Northland Press (Box N/86002), 1978. 168 p. Sketches.

"Thollander's remarks and mostly sepia sketches remind one alternately of scientific field journals and travelers' post cards sent home to family and friends. His funny little area maps are amazingly accurate."

MAPS

The official ARIZONA ROAD MAP is prepared by the Arizona Dept. of Transportation and is distributed by ARIZONA HIGHWAYS magazine (AZ-1). The 1978 ed. has a list of points of interest and uses symbols to show roadside rest areas, campsites, airports, ski areas, public boat access areas, and localities providing 24-hour hospital emergency service. AAA (US-259), Exxon (US-261) and Rand McNally (US-215) each issue a combined Arizona/New Mexico map. Goushā (US-206) issues a separate Arizona map. A series of 7 "Arizona Multi-Purpose and Outdoor Recreational Facilities Maps" on a scale of 1 in. represents 5 miles is available from the Office of Tourism (AZ-15). No. 1 covers the southeastern section of the state; No. 2, the southwestern; No. 3, the west central; No. 4, the mid-central; No. 5, the east central; No. 6, the northeastern; and No. 7, the northwestern.

PUBLISHERS

AZ-13 ARIZONA HIGHWAYS, 2039 West Lewis Avenue, Phoenix, AZ 85009.

In addition to publishing ARIZONA HIGHWAYS magazine (AZ-1), they issue a yearly scenic engagement calendar, many lavish books, and color slides of many of the photographs appearing in ARIZONA HIGHWAYS. There is a 47-page catalog, arranged by subject, of these slides. They also issue a series of very brief leaflets entitled: VACATIONER'S PARADISE (a guide to fishing and campgrounds); MOUNTAINS OF SOUTHERN ARIZONA, SUPERSTITION MOUNTAINS and GHOST TOWNS IN ARIZONA.

AZ-14 PHOENIX BOOKS, 1641 East McLellan Blvd., Phoenix, AZ 85016 (602/274-4608).

In addition to publishing several guidebooks on Arizona, they issue RETIRING IN ARIZONA by Boye De Mente and several maps: an illustrated sighseeing map of Arizona, a sightseeing map of Phoenix-Scottsdale, an Arizona tourist and mileage map, and a sightseeing poster of Arizona.

MAJOR TOURIST ORGANIZATION

AZ-15 ARIZONA OFFICE OF TOURISM, 1700 West Washington, Room 501, Phoenix, AZ 85007 (602/271-3618).

They issue the following brochures: ARIZONA (a general guide to Arizona's attractions, with special sections on ski areas, national parks and monuments, state parks, and water sports); EXPLORE AMAZING ARIZONA'S GOLDEN TRAILS (outlines 4 driving tours of 1/2 to 3 days for family fun excursions); ARIZONA TRAVELERS' GAZETTE (a tabloid newspaper first issued in the summer of 1978 and full of travel suggestions, reprints of newspaper articles from the late 1800s, and a list of sources for additional information, mostly chambers of commerce); ARIZONA: LAND OF ADVENTURE FOR YOUNG AMERICANS (appropriate for youngsters); a yearly calendar of events; ARIZONA CAMPGROUND DIRECTORY; ARIZONA GUEST RANCHES; ARIZONA GHOST TOWNS; ARIZONA ROCK HOUND GUIDE; CACTI, WILDFLOWERS AND DESERT PLANTS OF ARIZONA; a guide to the NATIONAL PARK SYSTEM IN ARIZONA; and the very informative THE GRAND CANYON & NORTHERN ARIZONA.

OTHER ORGANIZATIONS

AZ-16 ARIZONA HOTEL & MOTEL ASSOCIATION, 3033 North Central Avenue, Suite 205, Phoenix, AZ 85012 (602/264-6081).

They issue an ARIZONA ACCOMMODATIONS DIRECTORY.

AZ-17 THE NAVAJO NATION, Parks and Recreation Dept., Window Rock, AZ 86515 (602/871-5561).

Navajoland consists of approximately 25,000 square miles in the northeast corner of Arizona with Window Rock as the tribal headquarters. They provide much information on Monument Valley and other Navajo Tribal Parks; fishing in Navajoland; lists of rest areas and camping facilities, and motels and hotels; festivals and celebrations; and outfitters providing river trips, pack saddle treks, and aircraft excursions. Arizona Highways (AZ-13) issues a small brochure on TRAVEL IN NAVAJOLAND. A NAVAJOLAND U.S.A. MAP is available from KC Publications, Box 14883, Las Vegas, NV 89114.

INFORMATION CENTERS/INFORMATION PHONES

There is one highway information center, the Willcox/Cochise Visitor Center, Interstate 10, Willcox, AZ 85643 (602/384-4271).

OUTDOOR RECREATION ACTIVITIES

CANOEING AND BOATING. An ARIZONA BOATING GUIDE (only 10 of the 48-pages are devoted to where-to boat) is available from the Arizona Game and Fish Dept., 2222 West Greenway Road, Phoenix, AZ 85023 (602/942-3000). See also AZ-7 and AZ-18.

FISHING AND HUNTING. ARIZONA FISHIN' HOLES: A GUIDE TO POPULAR FISHING WATERS AND FACILITIES IN ARIZONA and the hunting regulations, which includes a map of wildlife areas, are available from the Arizona Game and Fish Dept., 2222 West Greenway Road, Phoeniz, AZ 85023 (602/942-3000). For up-to-date fishing information 24-hours a day, call 602/959-FISH. This number is sponsored by OUTDOOR ARIZONA (AZ-10). See also AZ-7 and AZ-10.

NATIONAL/STATE PARKS/FORESTS, ETC.

Grand Canyon National Park

AZ-18 Belknap, Buzz. GRAND CANYON RIVER GUIDE. Boulder City, NV: Westwater Books, 1969. Unpaged. Maps, photos. 70-92769.

This is a detailed guide to 288 miles of the Colorado River from Lees Ferry near the Arizona/Utah border at the southern terminus of Lake Powell to Iceberg Canyon near the Arizona/Nevada border at the eastern terminus of the Lake Mead area. The river is graphically portrayed at a scale of approximately 1 in. represents 1/2 mile with locations of all rapids indicated and many rated on a difficulty scale of 1 to 10. The contours of the shore and side canyons with elevations indicated are drawn in. There are many accompanying photographs whose captions and excerpts from the 1875 Powell REPORT ON EXPLORATION OF THE COLORADO RIVER OF THE WEST AND ITS TRIBUTARIES are the only textual matter in this guide. It is also available in a waterproof edition.

AZ-19   Butchart, Harvey. GRAND CANYON TREKS and GRAND CANYON TREKS II. Rev. ed. 2 vols. Glendale, CA: La Siesta Press (Box 406/91209), 1976. Photos., maps.

The first book in this series describes inner canyon trails and the second describes Marble Canyon and other newly acquired lands in 1975 lying to the west. These are not detailed guides but, rather, are general descriptions of where remote trails for experienced hikers may be found. The author is the expert in this area: Colin Fletcher consulted him when planning his trip that resulted in THE MAN WHO WALKED THROUGH TIME.

AZ-20   A PHOTOGRAPHIC AND COMPREHENSIVE GUIDE TO GRAND CANYON NATIONAL PARK. Casper, WY: World-Wide Research and Publishing Co., National Parks Division, 1977. 118 p. Photos., maps. 77-154053.

This book contains mostly stunning photographs. The largest part of the text is devoted to the history of the Park. There are much smaller sections on its natural history and a motorist's view of the south and north rims.

AZ-21   Scharff, Robert, ed. GRAND CANYON NATIONAL PARK. New York: David McKay Co., 1967. 198 p. Photos., maps. Bibliography. Index. 67-13550.

This guide to seeing the Grand Canyon (the rims as well as the inner canyon), the plant and animal life, the Indians of the region, and the available accommodations and services includes a directory of place names and was produced in cooperation with the National Park Service. Its comprehensive coverage is unsurpassed and needs to be updated.

AZ-22   GRAND CANYON NATIONAL PARK, Box 129, Grand Canyon, AZ 86023 (602/638-2401).

They provide extensive information and brochures on enjoying the south and north rims of the park; visitor activities; visitor facilities; lodges; campgrounds; commercial tours; rim walks and hikes; and inner canyon hikes, camping, mule trips, and river tours. THE GRAND CANYON GUIDE, issued weekly in newspaper format during the summer season by the Grand Canyon Natural History Association, is a complete guide to what to see and do. The South Rim Visitor Center is located in Grand Canyon Village, 3.5 miles north of the south entrance station. It is open every day, but hours vary with the season. Reservations for inner canyon campsites and permits for wilderness trails are available at the Backcountry Reservations Office on the Visitor Center Patio. There are 2 north rim information stations: the main one is the National Park Service Information Desk in Grand Canyon Lodge at Bright Angel Point, the other is the Jacob Lake Information Station located 32 miles north of the north rim entrance station. Recorded up-to-date information about weather, road conditions, and interpretive activities is obtained by calling 602/638-2245, 24 hours a day. As you approach either of the south rim entrance stations you can obtain information by tuning in to 1610 on your A.M. radio dial. The Grand Canyon National History Association, Box 399, Grand Canyon, AZ 86023, operates the Visitor Center bookstore, provides a mail order service for books and maps about the Grand Canyon (write to them for their publications list), and publishes their own GUIDE TO INNER CANYON HIKING. The Office of Tourism (AZ-15) puts out a very informative brochure listing organizations to contact for travel information and services. It's called THE GRAND CANYON & NORTHERN ARIZONA. ARIZONA HIGHWAYS (AZ-13) issues a brief leaflet on what to see and do within the Park. For information about accommodations, bus tours, and services at the south rim (open year-round) contact: Grand Canyon National Park Lodges, Grand Canyon, AZ 86023 (602/638-2401 or 638-2631). For information about accommodations at the north rim (open May to October), contact: Utah Parks Co., Cedar City, UT 84720.

AZ-23   HAVASUPAI TOURIST ENTERPRISE, Supai, AZ 86435 (602/448-2121).

To see another aspect of the Grand Canyon, plan a visit to this Shangri-La, Havasu Canyon, 40 miles northwest of Grand Canyon village. The only way you can get to it is by descending an 8 mile trail by foot or horseback. Write to this address for information on accommodations, camping, hiking, and saddle and pack horses.

A good map of the park is available from the National Geographic Society (US-194). It originally appeared as the map supplement to the July 1978 issue of NATIONAL GEOGRAPHIC MAGAZINE.

Petrified Forest National Park

AZ-24   PETRIFIED FOREST NATIONAL PARK, Holbrook, AZ 86025.

They provide a general map/brochure which includes a detailed road guide, information about nearby campgrounds and motels, and hiking. There is a visitor center at the northern entrance in the Painted Desert area of the park.

A good guide to all the National Park Service areas in Arizona, called
NATIONAL PARK SYSTEM IN ARIZONA is available from the National Park
Service, Western Regional Office, 450 Golden Gate Avenue, San Francisco,
CA 94102 (415/556-4122).

There are 7 national forests in Arizona, each with its own address, but you
can obtain very good detailed maps of each, hiking and backcountry information, etc. from the U.S. Forest Service, Southwestern Region Office, Federal
Bldg., 517 Gold Avenue SW, Albuquerque, NM 87101. The Sabino Canyon
Visitor Information Center is located in the Coronado National Forest in the
Santa Catalina Ranger District, Rt. 15, Box 277-F, Tucson, AZ 85715 (602/
749-3223). It is open year-round from 9A.M.-6P.M.

The Bureau of Land Management, Arizona State Office, 2400 Valley Bank
Center, Phoenix, AZ 85073 operates 26 recreation sites, primitive areas,
campgrounds, rockhound areas, etc. throughout the state. Most of them have
facilities for picnicking, camping, hiking, fishing, hunting, etc. Large, detailed visitors' maps and visitors' guides are available for most of these areas.

An overall state parks brochures, plus individual map/brochures of each park
are available from: Arizona State Parks, 1688 West Adams Street, Phoenix,
AZ 85007 (602/271-4174).

INDIVIDUAL CITIES OR AREAS

Oak Creek Canyon—Printed Materials

AZ-25   Aitchison, Stewart W.   OAK CREEK CANYON AND THE RED ROCK
        COUNTRY OF ARIZONA: A NATURAL HISTORY AND TRAIL GUIDE.
        Flagstaff, AZ: Stillwater Canyon Press (Box 1557/86002), 1977(?).
        144 p.   Photos., maps.

        This is a "guide to the climate, geology, archaeology, history,
        biology, roads, and trails."

Oak Creek Canyon—Organizations

AZ-26   SEDONA-OAK CREEK CANYON CHAMBER OF COMMERCE, Box 478,
        Sedona, AZ 86336 (602/282-7722).

        This is the central information source for the spectacular red rock cliff
        area of Oak Creek Canyon south of Flagstaff. The office is located
        on Route 89A near the downtown shopping area of Sedona and is open
        9A.M.-12P.M. and 1P.M.-5P.M. 6 days a week. They provide in-
        formation on restaurants, galleries, shops, recreation activities, and a
        map/directory. The canyon itself is located in the Coconino Na-
        tional Forest, Sedona Ranger District, Box 300, Sedona, AZ 86336

(602/282-4119). They issue an Oak Creek Canyon map/brochure
listing things to do and recreation sites. ARIZONA HIGHWAYS
(AZ-13) issues a brief Oak Creek Canyon leaflet that lists motels,
trailer parks, and campgrounds.

Phoenix—Printed Materials

AZ-27   Bogert, John, and Bogert, Joan.   100 BEST RESTAURANTS IN THE
VALLEY OF THE SUN. Phoenix: Arizona Desert Minerals Co.,
1977. 159 p. Indexes. 77-79784.

This is "an economy gourmet guide to dining out in the greater
Phoenix area." Descriptions include address, phone, author's rating,
food specialty, hours, parking, credit cards accepted, and cost of an
average dinner for 2. There is a chapter on places serving Sunday
brunch. It is arranged alphabetically by restaurant name with indexes by cuisine, location, and rating.

AZ-28   Junior Women's Club of Phoenix, comp. DIRECTORY OF BARRIER
FREE BUILDINGS. Phoenix: Easter Seal Society of Arizona, 1975.
73 p.

AZ-29   PHOENIX MAGAZINE'S '78 SUPERGUIDE. Phoenix: Phoenix Publishing Co. (4707 North 12th Street/85104), 1978. 46 p. Photos.

"From restaurants to racing, discos to drama, sports to scenic drives,"
this is "your complete guide to things to do in the Valley (and beyond)". "The Valley" refers to the Valley of the Sun which is the
greater Phoenix/Scottsdale area. At least half of this guide, which
is in magazine format, is a restaurant listing in which each restaurant
appears to have paid to be included.

AZ-30   Steckler, Stuart J. THE GUIDE TO DINING OUT: PHOENIX, SCOTTS-
DALE AND TEMPE. Phoenix: Oryx Press, 1977. 143 p. Indexes.
0-912700-47-5. 76-56721.

There are 134 restaurants described, rated, and indexed by type of
food served and geographical area.

AZ-31   Thomas Brothers Maps. PHOENIX AND VICINITY POPULAR STREET
ATLAS. Los Angeles: Thomas Bros., 1976. 160 p. Scales: 1 in.
represents 26,400 ft.; 1 in. represents 2,640 ft. Indexes.

Maps of Phoenix are available from AAA (US-259); Arrow Publishing Co.
(US-199); Champion Map Corp. (US-202); First National Bank of Arizona,
100 West Washington, Phoenix, AZ 85003; Goushā (US-206); and Rand Mc-
Nally (US-215).

Arizona

Phoenix—Organizations

AZ-32   PHOENIX & VALLEY OF THE SUN CONVENTION & VISITORS
BUREAU, 2701 East Camelback, Suite 200H, Phoenix, AZ 85016
(602/957-0070).

They issue a twice yearly VALLEY OF THE SUN VISITORS GUIDE
(Spring & Summer 1978 ed., 50 p.). It is very complete and contains information on driving tours; a map/guide to accommodations,
restaurants, golf, tennis, attractions, and shopping; and local transportation. They also issue a quarterly ACTIVITIES, ATTRACTIONS &
MAP which includes a calendar of events. The address above is a
walk-in information center open Monday-Friday, 8:30A.M.-5P.M.; they
also operate an information booth at the Phoenix Sky Harbor Airport.
There is a "hot-line" at 956-6200 which is a recorded listing of
weekly events. There is a toll-free number at 800/528-0483 for hotel
reservations only. Do not call this number for tourist information.

Tuscon—Printed Materials

AZ-33   Bookmap Corp. PROFILE OF TUCSON: A DRAMATIC NEW PRE-
SENTATION OF FACTS AND INFORMATION FOR TUCSON AND
ADJACENT AREAS. San Antonio, TX: International Aerial Mapping
Co. (8927 International Drive/78216), 1972. 64 p. Photos., maps.
Index. 74-187208.

Brief textual pages in the front describe tourist attractions; annual
events; include a motel, hotel, and resort list; restaurant and night
club list; civic data with map of civic center; recreational facilities;
educational facilities with map of the University of Arizona campus;
hunting and fishing; and transportation facilities with map of major
bus routes.· There is a "tourguide map" which shows the roads out of
Tucson to 12 points of interest (descriptions of these points of interest
are omitted). The remainder of the volume is a city atlas with
street index.

AZ-34   METROPOLITAN TUCSON STREET ATLAS. Phoenix: Phoenix Mapping (1320 North First Street/85004), 1976. 30 p. Scale: 3/4 in.
represents 2 miles. Index.

AZ-35   THE TUCSON VISITOR. Tucson: Kisro Publications (5132 North
Pueblo Villas Drive/85704).

This free guide to events, dining, theater, sports, points of interest, and entertainment is issued weekly September through June
and monthly in July and August. It also contains an area map on
which 6 tours are outlined. Many advertisements are included.

See also AZ-3.

Maps of Tucson are available from Champion Map Corp. (US-202), Gousha̅ (US-206), and Rand McNally (US-215).

Tucson—Organizations

AZ-36   TUCSON CONVENTION & VISITORS BUREAU, La Placita-
Magdalena Bldg., 120 West Broadway, Box 27210, Tucson, AZ 85726
(602/791-4768).

They issue general brochures on Tucson, a combination accommodations (including ranches and campgrounds) and calendar of events
brochure, a map/brochure of golf and tennis facilities, and a climate
brochure.

ARKANSAS

BOOKS, ATLASES, MAGAZINES

AR-1   ARKANSAS: A GUIDE TO THE STATE. American Guide Series.
New York: Hastings House, 1941. 447 p. Photos., maps.

This original WPA guide is arranged in 3 sections: general background, descriptions of 8 major cities and towns, and 17 state-wide
highway tours.

AR-2   ARKANSAS TOUR GUIDE. Little Rock, AR: The Woods Brothers
Agency (809 West 2d Street/72201), 1977. Issued annually. 112 p.
Photos., maps.

This extensive guide to the attractions of Arkansas contains many
addresses to write to for information plus many advertisements of local
establishments. It is available from the Dept. of Parks and Tourism
(AR-3).

MAPS

The official ARKANSAS STATE HIGHWAY MAP is prepared and issued by the
Arkansas State Highway Dept., Map Sales-Room 204, Box 2261, Little Rock,
AR 72203. It is also available from the Dept. of Parks and Tourism (AR-3).
The 1977 edition contains a list of state and national parks and forest recreation areas, historic memorials, Corps of Engineers Projects use areas, and
brief mention (with no addresses or phone numbers) of other sources of information (organizations only). AAA (US-259), Exxon (US-261), Goushā (US-206),
and Rand McNally (US-215) each issue a combined Arkansas/Louisiana/Missis-
sippi map.

MAJOR TOURIST ORGANIZATION

AR-3   ARKANSAS DEPT. OF PARKS AND TOURISM, Tourism Division, 149
State Capitol Bldg., Little Rock, AR 72201 (501/371-1511).

In addition to the comprehensive ARKANSAS TOUR GUIDE (AR-2),
they issue an annual calendar of events, ARKANSAS CAMPER'S
GUIDE (lists only publicly-owned campgrounds, including those in state
and national parks and national forests), and TRAILS OF ARKANSAS
(contains brief descriptions of 15 hiking trails published in cooperation with the Arkansas Trails Council, 1510 Broadway, Little Rock,
AR 72202).

REGIONAL TOURISM ASSOCIATIONS

Most of the associations below issue one in a uniform series of tour guide
books which contain information on attractions; motels, lodges, resorts; campgrounds; fishing; calendar of events; maps; etc. These are largely excerpted
from the ARKANSAS TOUR GUIDE (AR-2).

ARKANSAS GREAT SOUTHWEST RECREATIONAL ASSOCIATION, Saratoga
Landing and Millwood Inn, Saratoga, AR 71859.

ARKANSAS RIVER VALLEY TOURIST ASSOCIATION, Box 822, Russellville,
AR 72801.

BONANZA LAND, 613 Garrison Avenue, Fort Smith, AR 72901 (501/783-
6118).

DELTA HIGHLANDS PROMOTION ASSOCIATION, First National Bank, Box
160, Helena, AR 72342 (501/338-6754).

DIAMOND LAKES TRAVEL ASSOCIATION, Box 1500, Hot Springs National
Park, AR 71901 (501/321-1700).

GREERS FERRY LAKE ASSOCIATION, Box 408, Heber Springs, AR 72543
(501/362-6633).

HEART OF ARKANSAS TRAVEL ASSOCIATION, Box 3232, Little Rock, AR
72203 (501/376-4781).

NORTHEAST ARKANSAS TOURIST ASSOCIATION, Box 525, Pocahontas, AR
72455.

NORTHWEST ARKANSAS RECREATION AREA, Box 308, Rogers, AR 72756
(501/636-5650).

OZARK GATEWAY TOURIST COUNCIL, 409 Vine Street, Batesville, AR
72501 (501/793-2383).

OZARK MOUNTAIN REGION, Box 122, Mountain Home, AR 72653.

SOUTHEAST ARKANSAS REGIONAL TOURIST DEVELOPMENT CORP., Box 29, Warren, AR 71671 (501/226-2601).

OTHER ORGANIZATIONS

AR-4   ARKANSAS INNKEEPERS ASSOCIATION, Box 9426, 8121 Interstate-30, Little Rock, AR 72209 (501/568-1058).

INFORMATION CENTERS/INFORMATION PHONES

The Dept. of Parks and Tourism (AR-3) sponsors 8 tourist information centers at major highway entry points into Arkansas. These are located on the official highway map.

OUTDOOR RECREATION ACTIVITIES

CANOEING AND BOATING. THE FLOAT STREAMS OF ARKANSAS is available from the Dept. of Parks and Tourism (AR-3). BUFFALO RIVER CANOEING GUIDE and MULBERRY RIVER CANOEING GUIDE are available from the Ozark Society Book Service, Box 725, Hot Springs, AR 71901. Several individual river maps showing public boating access sites, boat dock and fishing services, and portage points are available from the Arkansas Game and Fish Commission, Game and Fish Commission Bldg., 2 Capitol Mall, Little Rock, AR 72201.

FISHING AND HUNTING. Information on where to hunt and fish may be obtained from the Arkansas Game and Fish Commission, Game and Fish Commission Bldg., 2 Capitol Mall, Little Rock, AR 72201. A biennial OUTDOOR GUIDE TO ARKANSAS LANDS (maps of International Paper Co.'s Wildlife Management Areas) is available from International Paper Co., Box 758, Camden, AR 71701, Attn.: Wildlife Specialist.

NATIONAL/STATE PARKS/FORESTS, ETC.

Hot Springs National Park

AR-5   A GUIDE TO HOT SPRINGS FOR THE HANDICAPPED. Little Rock: Garland County Easter Seal Society for Crippled Children and Adults, 1967. 16 p.

AR-6   HOT SPRINGS NATIONAL PARK, Box 1860, Hot Spring National
        Park, AR 71901.

        They issue a map/brochure to the park and mimeographed lists of bath
        and physical therapy rates (the 8 bathhouses on Bathhouse Row are
        concessions of the federal government).

AR-7   HOT SPRINGS VISITOR & CONVENTION BUREAU, Box 1500, Hot
        Springs National Park, AR 71901 (501/321-1700).

        They issue an 80-page booklet describing accommodations, attractions,
        and things to do in the city of Hot Springs National Park and the
        nearby mountain areas. They also issue a map of the city of Hot
        Springs National Park and Garland County, AR. They have a toll-
        free number: 800/643-5426.

Information and maps about the national forests in Arkansas may be obtained
from the U.S. Forest Service, Southern Region, Suite 800, 1720 Peachtree
Road NW, Atlanta, GA 30309. There is a visitor information center at
Blanchard Springs Caverns in Ozark National Forest.

The Dept. of Parks and Tourism (AR-3) provides information on campsites in
state and national parks and forests.

INDIVIDUAL CITIES OR AREAS

Little Rock

Good maps of Little Rock are available from the Ashburn Map Co., 4113 Old
Denton Road, Fort Worth, TX 76117; Champion Map Corp. (US-202); and the
Commercial National Bank of Little Rock, 200 Main, Little Rock, AR 72201.

AR-8   LITTLE ROCK BUREAU FOR CONVENTIONS AND VISITORS, Box
        3232, Little Rock, AR 72203 (501/376-4781).

CALIFORNIA

BOOKS, ATLASES, MAGAZINES

CA-1   Abeloe, William N. HISTORIC SPOTS IN CALIFORNIA. Stanford, CA:
        Stanford University Press, 1966. 642 p. Maps, photos. Index.
        66-17562.

        An overwhelmingly thorough listing, by county, of just about any
        spot considered historic, with brief descriptions and background; this
        is more than most people would want.

CA-2   Beck, David. SKI TOURS IN CALIFORNIA. Berkeley, CA: Wilderness
        Press, 1972. 210 p. Maps, photos. 0-911824-21-9. 72-89918.

        This official publication of the Far West Ski Association contains de-
        scriptions, maps, and profiles of 38 tours.

CA-3   Bulkin, Rena. ARTHUR FROMMER'S DOLLAR WISE GUIDE TO CALI-
        FORNIA AND LAS VEGAS. New York: Frommer/Pasmantier Publish-
        ing Corp. (distributed by Simon & Schuster), 1977. Updated fre-
        quently. 297 p. Maps. 0-671-22724-6.

        This concise guide to the traditional tourist sites of San Francisco,
        Los Angeles, San Diego, and coastline areas also contains a 16-page
        section on Las Vegas. Information on hotels and restaurants is given
        also with emphasis on those that are medium priced.

CA-4   CALIFORNIA: A GUIDE TO THE GOLDEN STATE. Rev. ed.
        American Guide Series. New York: Hastings House, 1967. 733 p.
        Photos., maps. Bibliography. Index. 66-28988.

        This is a second revision of the original WPA guide first published
        in 1939. Preliminary pages are devoted to a monthly calendar of
        regular events, a list of places to visit, sporting events, and the
        best places to engage in outdoor recreation, including winter sports.
        The rest of the volume follows the usual WPA guide format: 14 in-
        ductory essays on various aspects of California life and history, guides

to 14 major cities, and road descriptions of 14 highway tours. In addition, there are sections on Death Valley National Monument, Sequoia and Kings Canyon National Parks, and Yosemite National Park. There is a chronology of California history.

CA-5   CALIFORNIA BIKE TOURS. A Goushā Weekend Guide. San Jose, CA: Goushā Publications, 1972. 144 p. Maps, photos. 0-913040-16-9. 72-80662.

This volume describes "64 detailed bike rides, each with its own map showing all traveled roads and key intersections." There are 24 rides in the Los Angeles area, 10 in the San Diego area, 20 in the San Francisco area, and 10 in other areas. Included with each description is information on mileage, terrain, best time for touring, a difficulty rating, pointers on what to expect, and brief mention of a few points of interest.

CA-6   CALIFORNIA HISTORICAL LANDMARKS. Sacramento: California Dept. of Parks and Recreation, 1975. Revised frequently. 146 p. Photos. Index. 76-62068.

This numerical listing of 879 registered historical landmarks gives brief descriptions.

CA-7   Camphouse, Marjorie V. GUIDEBOOKS TO THE MISSIONS OF CALIFORNIA. Pasadena, CA: Ward Ritchie Press, 1974. 126 p. Photos. Bibliography. 0-378-03792-7. 74-78588.

The author describes 21 missions and includes practical information on date constructed, location, and hours. A map showing locations would have been helpful.

CA-8   Coleberd, Frances. ADVENTURES IN CALIFORNIA: A RECREATION GUIDE TO THE GOLDEN STATE. San Francisco: Chronicle Books, 1976. 167 p. Photos. Index. 0-87701-075-7. 75-45435.

This guide has an unusual approach. Arranged by the months of the year, it gives suggestions for jaunts to take appropriate for that time of year and describes festivals and events that take place regularly throughout the state. It includes addresses, hours, and phone numbers.

CA-9   _____. HIDDEN COUNTRY VILLAGES OF CALIFORNIA. San Francisco: Chronicle Books, 1977. 178 p. Photos. 0-87701-101-X. 77-21926.

The author gives written portraits of 18 quaint country villages describing the history, people, and some of the interesting buildings of each.

CA-10   Cooper, Patricia, and Cook, Laurel. HOT SPRINGS AND SPAS OF CALIFORNIA: A GUIDE TO TAKING THE WATERS. San Francisco: 101 Productions, 1978. 156 p. Drawings. Index. 0-89286-145-2. 78-10665.

This guide contains complete information on 39 hot springs and spas ranging from hot tubs to elaborate week-long programs in the state's most luxurious spas.

CA-11   Crain, Jim. HISTORIC COUNTRY INNS OF CALIFORNIA. San Francisco: Chronicle Books, 1977. 205 p. Photos., maps. 0-87701-088-9. 77-727.

Arranged by broad regions, this directory lists selected inns giving history, description, location, address, telephone number, and whether offering meals as well as lodging. There are photographs of each, but there is no index.

CA-12   Crain, Jim, and Milne, Terry. CAMPING AROUND CALIFORNIA. New York: Random House, 1975. 158 p. Sketch maps and sketches. Bibliography. Indexes. 0-394-73051-8. 74-23058.

This book is arranged around 43 sectional, sketched maps. Trails, campgrounds, roads, parks, points of interest, and cities and towns are located on each map, and accompanying each is a directory of camp sites in the map area, the names of the USGS quadrangle maps that cover the same area as the authors' map(s), and brief information on points and activities of interest. In the back there is a calendar of annual events, suggestions for several tours, and lists of organizations supplying information. There are indexes by type of sport or activity, by features or types of points of interest, and of campgrounds suitable for special purposes (boat-in camps, group camps, etc.).

CA-13   DISCOVERING THE CALIFORNIA COAST. By the editors of Sunset Books and Sunset Magazine. A Sunset Pictorial. Menlo Park, CA: Lane Publishing Co., 1975. 238 p. Photos., maps. Index. 0-376-05181-7. 75-6221.

Filled with nice, even beautiful, photographs (typical of this series) of the California coast, the text is only briefly descriptive on a superficial level. While not containing travel information as such, this book, like so many picture books, spurs a desire to visit the places shown, and should be classed as a travel incentive book or a travel inspiration book.

CA-14   FODOR'S CALIFORNIA 1979. New York: David McKay Co., 1979. 215 p. Maps. Index. 0-679-00425-4.

Useful facts are crammed into this rather good guide. General information on planning a trip, weather, and general costs is followed by information on cities, areas, and attractions.

CA-15 THE GREAT RESTAURANTS OF CALIFORNIA. By the Camaro Eating
Teams. . . . An Eating Team Book. Los Angeles: Camaro Publishing
Co., 1975. 213 p. Maps, drawings. Indexes. 0-913290-11-4.
75-40177.

Anonymous eating teams have picked the 100 best California restaurants.
Each is described, noting specialties, and a map accompanies each
writeup. Address, hours, credit cards accepted, and other essential
information is noted. There are indexes by community and by cuisine
style.

CA-16 Herzbrun, Raye, and Herzbrun, Bob. CALIFORNIA'S TOP TEN
RESTAURANTS AND 266 OTHER GREAT PLACES TO EAT THAT
DON'T RIP YOU OFF! Los Angeles: Armstrong Publishing Co.
(5514 Wilshire Blvd./90036), 1977. 128 p. Indexes. 0-915936-
04-6. 77-77904.

There are many lists of top 10 restaurants here: the top 10 in California, the top 10 in Los Angeles, the top 10 oriental restaurants in
Los Angeles and so on. The top 10 restaurants in each of 12 different cuisines or specialties have been selected for both the Los
Angeles and San Francisco areas. There are also top 10 overall
restaurants listed for each of the following areas: San Diego,
Carmel/Monterey, Sacramento, and Palm Springs. There are indexes
by name, area, and cuisine.

CA-17 Hood, Ron. SIERRAS: TOPOGRAPHIC REFERENCE GUIDE TO THE
SIERRA NEVADA MOUNTAIN RANGE AND PORTIONS OF THE MT.
SAN GORGONIO AND MT. SAN JACINTO WILDERNESS AREAS.
Northridge, CA: Wilderness Way Internationale, 1975. 93 p.
Scale: 1 in. represents 3 miles. 75-24252.

Essentially, this is the reproduction of 60 USGS topographic maps
covering the Sierra Nevada Mountains with an added index of major
places. While a little difficult to read at times, it is much more
convenient to carry than the USGS sheets.

CA-18 Houk, Walter. CALIFORNIA'S TOP 10 VACATIONS. Los Angeles:
Armstrong Publishing Co. (5514 Wilshire Blvd./90036), 1978. 143 p.
Photos., maps. Index. 0-915936-08-9. 78-52684.

A chapter is devoted to what to see and do in each of the top 10
vacation destinations of California: San Diego, San Francisco, Los
Angeles, Monterey Peninsula, Santa Barbara, Yosemite National Park,
Palm Springs and the low desert, gold country, Orange County fun
factories, and the wine country. In addition, there are chapters on
the top 10 resorts; the top 10 seaside towns; the top 10 small cities,
towns, and hideaways; and the top 10 ski resorts.

CA-19 Leadabrand, Russ. EXPLORING CALIFORNIA BYWAYS: TRIPS FOR
A DAY OR A WEEKEND. 7 vols. Los Angeles: Ward Ritchie Press,

1967-73. Photos., maps, drawings. Indexes. 67-15078.

Volume 1 covers from Kings Canyon to the Mexican border (1967), volume 2 is entitled IN & AROUND LOS ANGELES (1968), volume 3 covers the desert country (1969), volume 4 covers mountain country (1970), volume 5 covers historic sites of California (1971), volume 6 covers Owens Valley (1972), and volume 7 is entitled AN HISTORICAL SKETCHBOOK (1973). These volumes are based on a series of articles originally published in WESTWAYS. The descriptions of back roads and what to see on them is low-key and personal, but extremely informative.

CA-20　　　　. GUIDEBOOK TO THE SOUTHERN SIERRA NEVADA, INCLUDING SEQUOIA NATIONAL FOREST. Los Angeles: Ward Ritchie Press, 1968. 184 p. Photos., maps. Bibliography. Index. 68-18435.

This is a general guide to the byways of the southern Sierra Nevada where there is a "smaller press of people" than found in the large national parks in the northern area. It includes some historical background, boating and fishing locations, list of trails, etc., but the overall treatment is quite general. The serious traveler would want more detailed information and maps.

CA-21　Reichert, Arthur. TOUR THE COUNTRY ROADS: DISCOVER THE RUSTIC WONDERS OF CALIFORNIA. Fresno, CA: Valley Publishers, 1978. 108 p. Maps, photos. 0-913548-53-7. 78-55734.

The route outlined here for a 13-day round trip on California's country roads looks good. Unfortunately the book's usefulness is greatly reduced by the text which is nothing more than a stupidly insipid dialogue between the author and his wife that strikes new lows for the women's movement. This is a perfect example of how not to write a travel book.

CA-22　Riley, Frank W. TRAVEL ADVENTURES IN CALIFORNIA. Los Angeles: Bill Muster, The Traveler's Almanac, 1976. 64 p. Photos. 76-19165.

This selective guide briefly describes numerous off-the-beaten-track things to do and places to go throughout the state. The author is the travel editor of LOS ANGELES MAGAZINE and writes a regular travel column, "Roamin' With Riley," for several large western newspapers. In addition, LOS ANGELES MAGAZINE (1888 Century Park East, Los Angeles, CA 90067) publishes an annual GUIDE TO 52 GREAT WEEKENDS compiled by this author.

CA-23　Robinson, John, ed. CALIFORNIA STATE PARKS. Menlo Park, CA: Lane Books, 1972. 128 p. Photos., maps. Index. 0-376-06773-X. 79-180519.

This guide covers state parks, state beaches, state recreation areas, wayside camps, scenic or scientific reserves, and state historic parks. "Included in the information given about a park are directions for getting to it; where to write for further information. . .; and where supplies can be obtained nearby." It is arranged geographically with a name index.

CA-24   Thollander, Earl. BACK ROADS OF CALIFORNIA: SKETCHES AND TRIP NOTES. 2d ed. A Sunset Pictorial. Menlo Park, CA: Lane Publishing Co., 1977. 207 p. Sketches, sketch maps. 0-376-05013-6. 76-40552.

This falls more into the "personal recollection" subcategory of travel books with most book space devoted to the author's sketches of back roads views along 42 different routes. It would be most useful as a suggestion book to California byways.

CA-25   Winnett, Thomas. SIERRA NORTH: 100 BACK-COUNTRY TRIPS IN THE HIGH SIERRA. 3d ed. Berkeley, CA: Wilderness Press, 1976. 288 p. Photos., maps. Bibliography. Index. 0-911824-46-4. 75-38175.

CA-26   Winnett, Thomas, and Schwenke, Karl. SIERRA SOUTH: 100 BACK-COUNTRY TRIPS IN CALIFORNIA'S SIERRA. 2d ed. Wilderness Press Trail Guide Series. Berkeley, CA: Wilderness Press, 1975. 280 p. Photos. Index. 0-911824-41-3. 74-27688.

The first volume encompasses the region from Carson Pass to Mono Creek; the second volume, the region from Mono Creek to the southern end of Sequoia National Park. The trips range in length from overnight to 2-week expeditions. Included with each trail description is a trail elevation profile and the name of the topographic maps to use.

CA-27   Wood, Basil C. THE WHAT, WHEN AND WHERE GUIDE TO NORTHERN CALIFORNIA. Garden City, NY: Doubleday, 1977. 150 p. Maps. Index. 0-385-05052-6. 75-2858.

CA-28   _____. THE WHAT, WHEN AND WHERE GUIDE TO SOUTHERN CALIFORNIA. Garden City, NY: Doubleday, 1975. 130 p. Maps. Index. 0-385-05041-0. 73-22797.

These are good, concise, straight-to-the-point guides to amusement parks, zoos, art galleries, museums, missions and places of worship, state and county parks and historic landmarks, homes and buildings of historic interest, national parks and monuments, botanical gardens and nature centers, wineries, scenic chair rides, industrial tours, and other miscellaneous attractions. They are arranged together by general geographic area, and a map, phone number, hours, and admission charges are given for each.

CA-29   Wright, Bank. SURFING CALIFORNIA. Redondo Beach, CA: Mañana Publishing, 1973. 176 p. Maps, photos. 73-78956.

Beginning at the Oregon border and continuing south to the Mexican border, this book briefly describes and locates on maps each area of the California coast suitable for surfing.

CA-30   Yeadon, David. EXPLORING SMALL TOWNS. 2 vols. Los Angeles: Ward Ritchie Press, 1973. Maps, sketches. Indexes. 72-83979.

Volume 1 covers southern California and volume 2 covers northern California. The descriptions only include background information on each town, and the only where-to information is a general regional map which locates each town. These books would best be used as an armchair suggestion guide. Each volume is regionally arranged with a complete index.

Northern California

CA-31   BEST RESTAURANTS: SAN FRANCISCO & NORTHERN CALIFORNIA. Rev. ed. By the editors of California Critic. San Francisco: 101 Productions (distributed by Scribner), 1977. 206 p. Sketches. Indexes. 0-89286-117-7. 77-8516.

This guide is arranged by geographic area and includes Marin County, East Bay, the Monterey area, Napa/Sonoma, Mendocino area, the Mother Lode, Lake Tahoe area, and the central valley area, in addition to San Francisco. Reproductions of menus are frequently included. There are indexes by area, type of cuisine, and specialty (brunch, lunch, late supper).

CA-32   Bleything, Dennis, and Hawkins, Susan. GETTING OFF ON 96 & OTHER LESS TRAVELED ROADS: DRIVES AND HIKES IN THE TRINITY ALPS, REDWOODS AND SISKIYOUS. Beaverton, OR: Touchstone Press, 1975. 79 p. Maps, photos. 0-911518-32-0. 75-9248.

The authors describe 25 drive and hike trips, with outline map, in the Klamath Mountain area (northwestern California and southwestern Oregon) suitable for families with children, the casual hiker, and the family car.

CA-33   Dillon, Richard H. EXPLORING THE MOTHER LODE COUNTRY. Pasadena, CA: Ward Ritchie Press, 1974. 126 p. Photos., map. Index. 0-378-03462-8. 73-77043.

This is a guide to seeing and appreciating the 250-mile area of central California along Highway 49 where the Forty-Niners struck gold.

CA-34   GUIDE TO THE MOTHER LODE COUNTRY. Los Angeles: Automo-

bile Club of Southern California, 1973. 63 p. Maps, drawings.
74-176058.

A driving guide to State Route 49 from Mariposa to Sattley through
the old gold mining country, this work gives a "now and then" vig-
nette of each community along the way plus brief mentions of facilities, services, and activities.

CA-35   Hayden, Mike. EXPLORING THE NORTH COAST FROM THE
GOLDEN GATE TO THE OREGON BORDER. San Francisco:
Chronicle Books, 1976. 160 p. Photos. Bibliography. Index.
0-87701-085-4. 76-45823.

This useful, all-round guide to appreciating and exploring northern
California is arranged by the coastal counties with information on
specific phenomena of the region (abalone, bicycling, gray whales,
etc.) presented in boxed sections throughout the book. There are 8
pages of information sources.

CA-36   Jackson, Joan. 50 BIKING HOLIDAYS: 50 SCENIC ROUTES TO
PEDAL FROM OLD MONTEREY TO THE GOLDEN GATE. Fresno,
CA: Valley Publishers, 1977. 104 p. Photos., maps. 0-913548-
45-6. 77-89786.

Based on a series in the SAN JOSE MERCURY NEWS, the bike tours
give detailed directions and a little background on the scenic sights.
The maps are adequate. There is no index.

CA-37   Jackson, Ruth A. COMBING THE COAST: SAN FRANCISCO THRU
BIG SUR: COASTSIDE BACKROADS AND BACKGROUND. San
Francisco: Chronicle Books, 1972. 144 p. Photos., maps. Index.
0-87701-014-5. 72-183234.

The author's enthusiasm is catching! The book is full of all sorts of
inside tips on where to go, what to see, where to stay and eat on
US coastal Highway 1 from south of San Francisco to south of Big
Sur.

CA-38   Lowe, Don, and Lowe, Roberta. 100 NORTHERN CALIFORNIA
HIKING TRAILS. Portland, OR: Criterion (distributed by Touchstone
Press), 1970. 230 p. Photos., maps. 73-118326.

This guide is divided into 4 geographic sections: Klamath Mountains,
Lassen Peak area, Lake Tahoe area, and Yosemite. Each trail description includes a reproduction of the USGS topographic map with the
trail marked in red, the name of the topographic map to use, trail
length, distance, elevation gain, and best season to hike.

CA-39   Meyers, Carole T. WEEKEND ADVENTURES FOR CITY-WEARY
FAMILIES: A GUIDE TO OVERNIGHT TRIPS IN NORTHERN CALI-

FORNIA. Albany, CA: Carousel Press (Box 6061/94706), 1977. 97 p. Maps. 0-917120-03-5. 77-71550.

This is a good book full of lots of sound advice both for traveling with youngsters and of places to go. The areas covered are: the coastal highway, the wine country, Lake Tahoe, the gold rush country, and Yosemite. Information provided for each includes: organizations that supply information, babysitting services, stops along the way, where to stay, where to eat, and things to do.

CA-40   Murphy, Tom A. 50 NORTHERN CALIFORNIA BICYCLE TRIPS. Beaverton, OR: Touchstone Press, 1972. 126 p. Maps, photos. 0-911518-13-4. 72-89635.

There are 15 trips in the San Francisco area, 12 in the north bay counties, 10 in the Monterey Peninsula/San Jose area, and 13 in the Sacramento Valley/Mother Lode/Sierra area. "The average trip length is slightly more than eighteen miles, with eleven trips under ten miles in distance and five over thirty miles long." In addition to the description, a map, the distance, riding time needed, road/ traffic conditions, locations of facilities, and a difficulty rating are provided for each ride. This is a companion volume to 50 SOUTHERN CALIFORNIA BICYCLE TRIPS (CA-58).

CA-41   NORTH OF SAN FRANCISCO. Santa Rosa, CA: North of San Francisco, 1975. 188 p. Photos., maps. 0-916310-01-9. 75-29782.

Covering Sonoma County and adjacent parts of the Napa Valley and the Points Reyes region in California, this lists restaurants, shops, wineries, and the like for that region with a brief historical background for each town or section. The descriptions of the commercial establishments are quite detailed, noting history, price range, address, hours, credit cards accepted, and the phone number. Fine-- until you read the fine print and discover that these listings, mainly of restaurants, are paid advertisements. There is no index. Use with caution.

CA-42   Pomada, Elizabeth. PLACES TO GO WITH CHILDREN IN NORTHERN CALIFORNIA. Rev. ed. San Francisco: Chronicle Books, 1976. 160 p. Photos. Index. 0-87701-039-0. 73-77335.

The introduction says the author has concentrated on places that are educational, historical, and "entertaintional"; those available year round; those that were free; and on places to go rather than things to do. She has not attempted complete coverage of parks since they are frequently visited anyway. She has included special restaurants with appeal to children. Exact address, phone number, hours, and admission fee are included with each description of the more than 350 attractions. It has an annual events calendar, and is regionally arranged with a name index.

CA-43 SUNSET TRAVEL GUIDE TO NORTHERN CALIFORNIA. Rev. ed.
By the editors of Sunset Books and Sunset Magazine. Menlo Park,
CA: Lane Publishing Co., 1975. 160 p. Photos., maps. Index.
0-376-06555-9. 75-6219.

This guide describes all the major attractions in northern California
from Hearst Castle in San Simeon to the northern border. Practical
information on how to get to each, admission charges, etc. is spotty.
Restaurants and accommodations are not included.

CA-44 Wallach, Paul. GUIDE TO THE RESTAURANTS OF NORTHERN
CALIFORNIA. Los Angeles: Brooke House, 1976. 449 p. Index.
0-912588-11-X. 76-643061.

The author describes and rates approximately 700 restaurants north of
Santa Barbara. There are indexes by location, cuisine, and specialty
(children, late evening, view, etc.).

CA-45 Yeadon, Anne, and Yeadon, David. HIDDEN RESTAURANTS: NORTH-
ERN CALIFORNIA. Los Angeles: Camaro Publishing Co., 1973.
219 p. Maps, sketches. Indexes. 0-913290-04-1. 74-75705.

This guide features "out-of-the-way places serving good food at
inflation-fighting prices." It gives practical information such as address, hours, availability of a bar, credit cards accepted, and locates
each on a map. It is arranged by region with indexes by region,
cuisine, and restaurant name.

Southern California

CA-46 BEST RESTAURANTS: LOS ANGELES & SOUTHERN CALIFORNIA.
Rev. ed. By the editors of California Critic. San Francisco: 101
Productions (distributed by Scribner), 1978. 253 p. Indexes.
0-89286-118-5. 78-18227.

This book describes family-run, low-overhead restaurants serving
quality food in the Los Angeles, San Diego, Santa Barbara, and Palm
Springs areas. There are indexes by geographical area and cuisine.
The authors of this and the similar guide to San Francisco and northern California (CA-31) issue a monthly restaurant review newsletter
called CALIFORNIA CRITIC. It is available from 834 Mission Street,
San Francisco, CA 94103.

CA-47 Kurk, David, and Miller, Robert H. BICYCLE TRAILS OF SOUTHERN
CALIFORNIA: THE DEFINITIVE WORK ON WHERE TO BICYCLE IN
SOUTHERN CALIFORNIA. 2d ed. Los Angeles: Price/Stern/Sloan,
1974. 156 p. Maps. 0-8431-0358-2. 74-196832.

This work covers over 80 routes, with 23 in the Los Angeles area.
Information included for each is limited to a map, very brief road
directions, length, traffic conditions, terrain, where facilities may

be found, brief mention of highlights, comments, and occasionally a suggested side trip. In comparing the trips in this book with those in 50 SOUTHERN CALIFORNIA BICYCLE TRIPS (CA-58) there is not much overlap. The Beverly Hills trip in each volume covers different territory. Generally speaking, the trips in this book stick close to built-up areas, while those in the other head for the open countryside.

CA-48   Leadabrand, Russ. GUIDEBOOK TO RURAL CALIFORNIA. Los Angeles: Ward Ritchie Press, 1972. 128 p. Photos. Index. 0-378-03692-0. 71-180604.

The author describes places to see crops in southern California, places to see animals, wildflowers, fall colors, rural fairs, and a few selected scenic drives.

CA-49   _____. GUIDEBOOK TO THE MOJAVE DESERT OF CALIFORNIA, INCLUDING DEATH VALLEY, JOSHUA TREE NATIONAL MONUMENT, AND THE ANTELOPE VALLEY. Los Angeles: Ward Ritchie Press, 1966. 180 p. Photos. Bibliography. Index. 0-378-10131-5. 66-26520.

This guide is "an informal, casual guidebook to the western portion of the Mojave Desert." Historical background and a general road guide are included for each of the smaller desert areas covered. It includes Death Valley National Monument for which more recent and comprehensive guides than this are available, but it also includes Joshua Tree National Monument for which the chapter in this book is one of the few existing guides.

CA-50   _____. GUIDEBOOK TO THE MOUNTAINS OF SAN DIEGO AND ORANGE COUNTIES. Los Angeles: Ward Ritchie Press, 1971. 126 p. Photos., maps. Bibliography. Index. 75-151195.

"Including the Santa Ana Mountains, the Palomar country, the Julian-Cuyamaca country, the Laguna Mountains, and the mountain area south of Interstate 8 in Orange and San Diego Counties," this is a brief, general guide for getting acquainted with the area and appreciating its historical significance.

CA-51   _____. GUIDEBOOK TO THE SAN BERNARDINO MOUNTAINS OF CALIFORNIA, INCLUDING LAKE ARROWHEAD AND BIG BEAR. Los Angeles: Ward Ritchie Press, 1964. 118 p. Photos., map. Index. 64-17157.

This is a description of a motor tour emphasizing back roads. Historical sites are noted, and there is a short section on trails.

CA-52   _____. GUIDEBOOK TO THE SAN GABRIEL MOUNTAINS OF CALIFORNIA. Rev. ed. Los Angeles: Ward Ritchie Press, 1964. 120 p. Photos, maps. Index. 64-2958.

Essentially this is a back country motoring guide with a few trail listings attached. The major stress is on historical background.

CA-53 Lee, Georgia, et al. AN UNCOMMON GUIDE TO SAN LUIS OBISPO COUNTY, CALIFORNIA. San Luis Obispo, CA: Padre Productions (Box 1275/93406), 1977. 160 p. Sketches. 0-914598-18-X. 75-2794.

San Luis Obispo County is a central California coastal county extending from Pismo Beach in the south to San Simeon in the north, including Morro Bay. Places to go, things to see, facts, figures, history, and directions are presented in a single alphabetical arrangement from abalone to zoo. More "Uncommon Guides" are planned by the publisher.

CA-54 Lowe, Don, and Lowe, Roberta. 100 SOUTHERN CALIFORNIA HIKING TRAILS. Beaverton, OR: Touchstone Press, 1974. 224 p. Maps, photos. 74-189510.

Defining "southern California" as south of a line drawn through San Francisco, this work gives very thorough trail descriptions noting distance, elevation gain/loss, season to hike, average time, high point, and upon which topographic map(s) the trail can be located. There is no index.

CA-55 Lowe, George. "WHERE CAN WE GO THIS WEEKEND?" Rev. ed. Los Angeles: J.P. Tarcher, 1975. 182 p. Indexes. 0-87477-044-0. 75-15011.

The author writes the "Trip of the Week" column for the Sunday LOS ANGELES TIMES. The preface says the material here is freshly re-written. Almost 200 southern California trip suggestions in 27 categories (rockhounding, breath-taking views, industrial, etc.) are described, including road directions. An additional 33 weekend trips are described. A name index uses an asterisk to indicate those places of interest to children. There is also a geographical index.

CA-56 Meyer, Nancy. WHERE TO TAKE YOUR GUESTS IN SOUTHERN CALIFORNIA. Los Angeles: Ward Ritchie Press, 1972. 128 p. Photos. Index. 0-378-03552-5. 72-84096.

The premise behind this book assumes you've moved to California, haven't explored it at all yourself, and haven't the slightest idea of where to direct visiting relatives. Most of the suggestions here will be found in any area guidebook, but this information is good if you don't know where to begin.

CA-57 OCEAN RECREATION: MONTEREY TO SAN DIEGO. Los Angeles: Automobile Club of Southern California, 1978. Revised frequently. 64 p. Photos., maps. Index.

This is "a guide to water sports, fishing, recreation facilities, and tourist attractions along the central and southern coast of California."

CA-58   Schad, Jerry, and Krupp, Don. 50 SOUTHERN CALIFORNIA
         BICYCLE TRIPS. Beaverton, OR: Touchstone Press, 1976. 112 p.
         Maps, photos. 0-911518-38-X. 75-39166.

         The trips are regionally arranged and go as far north as Santa Barbara,
         as far east as Joshua Tree National Monument, and as far south as
         the Mexico border. They range in length from 6 to more than 60
         miles. A map, the distance, required riding time, road/traffic con-
         ditions, where facilities may be found, and a difficulty rating are
         included with each trip description. This is a companion volume
         to 50 NORTHERN CALIFORNIA BICYCLE TRIPS (CA-40).

CA-59   Starry, Roberta M. EXPLORING THE GHOST TOWN DESERT.
         Pasadena, CA: Ward Ritchie Press, 1973. 112 p. Maps, photos.
         Bibliography. Index. 0-378-03782-X. 73-77045.

         The author describes 10 tours to take to ghost or near-ghost towns in
         a triangular section of the Mojave Desert with the towns of Trona at
         the apex and Mojave and Four Corners on Route 58 forming the
         lower base points. Each tour has an easy to read, detailed map.

CA-60   SUNSET TRAVEL GUIDE TO SOUTHERN CALIFORNIA. 4th ed. By
         the editors of Sunset Books and Sunset Magazine. Menlo Park, CA:
         Lane Publishing Co., 1974. 160 p. Photos., maps. Index. 0-376-
         06754-3. 74-76544.

         This rather good guide describes all the major attractions in southern
         California from Tijuana, Mexico to Hearst Castle in San Simeon.
         Practical information on how to get to each, admission charges, etc.
         is spotty, and it does not include restaurants and accommodations.

CA-61   Thomas Brothers Maps. SAN BERNARDINO-RIVERSIDE COUNTIES
         POPULAR STREET ATLAS. Los Angeles: Thomas Bros., 1976. 513 p.
         Scales vary. Index.

CA-62   _____. SANTA BARBARA-VENTURA COUNTIES POPULAR STREET
         ATLAS. Los Angeles: Thomas Bros., 1976. 345 p. Scales vary. Index.

CA-63   Wallach, Paul. GUIDE TO THE RESTAURANTS OF SOUTHERN
         CALIFORNIA. Pasadena: Arroyo Books, 1977. 522 p. Indexes.
         0-378-06765-6. 77-93085.

         The author describes and rates approximately 900 southern California
         restaurants located in a region bounded by Malibu, San Bernardino,
         and San Diego. There are indexes by location, cuisine, and specialty
         (inexpensive, early evening dining, dining out of doors, etc.).

CA-64   Yeadon, Anne, and Yeadon, David. HIDDEN RESTAURANTS:
         SOUTHERN CALIFORNIA. Los Angeles: Camaro Publishing Co.,

1972. 213 p. Maps, sketches. Indexes. 73-174233.

This guide, concentrating on those restaurants offering high quality and low price, gives the usual practical information for each and locates the restaurant on a map. It is arranged by region with indexes by region, town, cuisine, and name.

MAPS

As of this writing there is no official highway map, but the Office of Visitor Services (CA-72) plans to issue an official visitors map in 1979. AAA (US-259) issues a general California map. Exxon (US-261) issues a combined California/Nevada map. Gousha (US-206) and Rand McNally (US-215) each issue a general California map plus maps of Fresno-southern Sierra, Stockton-northern Sierra, San Bernardino-Riverside, San Jose, and Santa Barbara. KYM'S GUIDES, published by Triumph Press, Box 75445, Sanford Station, Los Angeles, CA 90075, is a series of about 75 different regional detailed maps and charts on which are located fishing, boating, hunting, hiking, and camping areas. Recreation Marketing, Box 878, Oakland, CA 94604 issues a RECREATION, TOUR & SERVICE GUIDE MAP to both northern and southern California. They contain information on fishing, boating, campgrounds, hunting, water sports, winter sports, national and state parks, points of interest, missions, wineries, etc. They are especially strong on fishing and boating. Similar maps in this series are also available for the following regions: the San Francisco Bay area, Clear Lake, Lake Tahoe, Lake Alamanor, and the Bodega/Tomales Bay area. See also CA-17, CA-76, CA-79, and all of the Thomas Brothers atlases mentioned throughout this chapter.

PUBLISHERS

CA-65 CAMARO PUBLISHING CO., Worldway Postal Station, Box 90430, Los Angeles, CA 90009.

They publish a number of restaurant guides to California.

CA-66 CHRONICLE BOOKS, 870 Market Street, San Francisco, CA 94102.

Begun as a publisher of California guidebooks, this company has expanded to include popular fine arts and contemporary living. They will continue to expand in the guide book line as well. They publish a series of "Tacklebox Guides" that tell where good fishing may be found and include many maps. Individual titles are CALIFORNIA STEELHEAD FISHING, TRINITY RIVER FISHING, KLAMATH RIVER FISHING, SHASTA LAKE FISHING, CALIFORNIA TROUT FISHING, and SAN DIEGO BASS LAKES FISHING.

CA-67 BOB REEDY, BOX 21-4152, Sacramento, CA 95821

He issues a series (all unexamined by us) of "Family Fun Guidebooks" containing maps and data on lakes; streams; trails; national, state, and local parks; campgrounds; golf courses; museums; historic sites; marinas; etc. Titles with both maps and text are: OUTDOOR TRAILS GUIDEBOOK TO NORTHERN CALIFORNIA, STRIPED BASS/DELTA GUIDEBOOK, MODOC GUIDEBOOK, SHASTA GUIDEBOOK, TAHOE GUIDEBOOK, and ALPINE/EL DORADO GUIDEBOOK. The maps of this series cover EL DORADO/STANISLAUS GUIDE, TAHOE/PLUMAS GUIDE, MENDOCINO GUIDE, SONOMA/MENDOCINO COAST GUIDE, SIERRA GUIDE, and LASSEN GUIDE. U.S. Forest Service maps are used as the base map on which all the additional information mentioned above is overprinted.

CA-68   WARD RITCHIE PRESS, 474 South Arroyo Parkway, Pasadena, CA 91105.

Unfortunately, we must report that this excellent publisher of guide-books has gone out of business. We are including them because of past excellence in the publication of guidebooks which are classics, even if a bit dimmed by time. From the late 1960s through the early 1970s, Ward Ritchie Press issued the guidebooks written by Russ Leadabrand and others which, for their time, were the best for sections of California and the west. Several of these older works are listed in this information guide and are, for descriptions of natural features which have not changed, still among the best. It is to be hoped that other publishers will issue revisions of the major classic guide-books. Even so, many of their books, found in libraries or in second-hand bookstores, will, for the next several years, continue to be of use to the traveler.

CA-69   LA SIESTA PRESS, Box 406, Glendale, CA 91209 (213/244-9305)

They publish quite a number of small, but thorough, outdoor guides to the California deserts and the Sierra Nevadas.

CA-70   VALLEY PUBLISHERS, a division of Book Publishers, 8 East Olive Avenue, Fresno, CA 93728 (209/485-2690).

They are specialists in Californiana, community histories, and tour guides.

CA-71   WILDERNESS PRESS, 2440C Bancroft Way, Berkeley, CA 94704 (415/843-8080).

They publish an extensive selection of maps and guidebooks to outdoor areas and outdoor recreation activities. Nearly all of their titles are for areas in California, but they are beginning to expand geographi-cally and similar guides have been issued for Hawaii, Minnesota, etc. Their topographic maps are considered even better than the USGS maps since they have done their own resurveying, have added more information of interest to hikers, and have included appropriate photo-graphs and a place-name index. They also issue a series of "High

Sierra Hiking Guides." Each of the 21 96-page guides in this series includes information on trail routes, climate, geology, history, trail-heads, flora and fauna, campsites, swimming, and fishing. Each is based on the USGS quads of that area and has an index. Separate areas in the High Sierras are covered by each guide. For example, there is a guide to Tuolumne Meadows, 1 to Mt. Whitney, 1 to Mono Craters, and so on. Wilderness Press also issues a series of 5 "High Sierra Fishing Guides."

MAJOR TOURIST ORGANIZATION

CA-72   CALIFORNIA OFFICE OF VISITOR SERVICES, Box 1499, Sacramento, CA 95805. (916/322-1396).

From 1975 to the summer of 1978, California had no official state travel office. As of this writing they were just starting up again and had only 1 publication available: a list of regional tourism organizations and local chambers of commerce from whom information can be obtained. They are in the process of preparing an official visitors map. Travelers are still urged to contact the local convention and visitors bureaus and chambers of commerce as well as the California Chamber of Commerce (CA-77).

REGIONAL TOURISM ASSOCIATIONS

CA-73   GOLDEN CHAIN COUNCIL OF THE MOTHER LODE, Box 1246, Auburn, CA 95603 (916/885-0416).

They issue a map/guide to the 9 counties (Madera, Mariposa, Tuolumne, Calaveras, Amador, El Dorado, Placer, Nevada, Sierra) along State Route 49 where gold was discovered in 1848-49. The highway here is referred to as the "Golden Chain." Their address is 217 Maple Street in Auburn.

CA-74   REDWOOD EMPIRE ASSOCIATION, 360 Post Street, San Francisco, CA 94108 (415/421-6554).

Established in the 1920s, they provide information on what to see and do along the California coastline from San Francisco north to the Oregon border. They issue a very thorough annual (1978 ed., 47 p.) REDWOOD EMPIRE VISITORS' GUIDE. It contains maps; lists of points of interest and attractions; hotels/motels/resorts/RV parks; restaurants/entertainment; wineries; lists of services (banks, retailers, automobile dealers, real estate offices, etc.); lists of events; local chambers of commerce; transit information; fishing information; and a list of campgrounds. There is also a year-round walk-in information center at this address which is on the north side of Union Square. The Association also sponsors the Rea-Josephine County Visitors Infor-

mation Center at Sunny Valley, OR, just 14 miles north of Grants
Pass, OR on Interstate Highway 5. It is open only in the summer.

CA-75   SHASTA-CASCADE WONDERLAND ASSOCIATION, Box 1988,
Redding, CA 96001 (916/243-2643).

Established in 1931, they promote tourism to the 6 northern California
counties of Lassen, Modoc, Shasta, Siskiyou, Tehama, and Trinity.
They supply a wealth of information and literature. Their information center is located at South Market and Parkview Streets in Redding
and is open year-round 5 days a week from 8A.M. to 5P.M.

The headquarters of the Shasta-Trinity National Forest is located at 2400
Washington Street, Redding, CA 96001 (916/246-5222). They have a 3-
minute recorded phone message (916/246-5338) providing information on lake
levels, boat ramps, campgrounds, and other information of interest to fishermen and boaters. CB Channel 8 provides information on the Shasta Lake area.

OTHER ORGANIZATIONS

CA-76   AUTOMOBILE CLUB OF SOUTHERN CALIFORNIA, 2601 South
Figueroa Street, Los Angeles, CA 90007.

They are a very prolific organization when it comes to publishing
maps and guides to California and southern California in particular.
These are only available to members, but they alone would be worth
the fee to join. In addition to the many items mentioned throughout
this California chapter, they issue guides to NORTHERN CALIFORNIA
AND NEVADA GOLF COURSES, SOUTHERN CALIFORNIA GOLF
COURSES, SOUTHERN CALIFORNIA MOUNTAIN TRAIL HIKING,
SANITARY DISPOSAL STATIONS AND PROPANE OUTLETS (a state-
wide map/guide), RECREATIONAL VEHICLE RENTALS (lists central
and southern California companies that rent), RIVERBOAT TRIPS (an
annual listing of scheduled western riverboat expeditions), ROCK-
HOUNDING (list places in southern California open to rockhounding),
PUBLIC SHOOTING RANGES (a county/city listing of shooting
ranges in southern California open to the public), a map of SANTA
BARBARA COUNTY AND CITY OF SANTA BARBARA, and WESTWAYS,
a monthly magazine which includes lists of events, has historical and
travel articles, photographic essays, books and restaurant review
columns, etc.

CA-77   CALIFORNIA CHAMBER OF COMMERCE, Box 1736, Sacramento, CA
95808 (916/444-6670).

They issue several informative brochures: TRAVEL CALIFORNIA--
SOURCES OF INFORMATION (lists regional associations, touring services, hotel/motel and campground directories, transportation services,
places to go, things to do, and selected books and maps), a quarterly

listing of fairs and fiestas, and a winter sports guide. The chamber may be visited at 455 Capitol Mall in Sacramento.

CA-78 CALIFORNIA HOTEL & MOTEL ASSOCIATION, 520 Capitol Mall, Suite 706, Sacramento, CA 95814 (916/444-5780).

CA-79 CALIFORNIA STATE AUTOMOBILE ASSOCIATION, 150 Van Ness Avenue, San Francisco, CA 94101.

In addition to the numerous maps mentioned throughout this California chapter, they issue good, detailed regional maps covering the entire state.

CA-80 CCINC. AUTO TAPE TOURS, Box 385, Scarsdale, NY 10583 (914/472-5133.

This organization supplies cassettes providing an informative and entertaining narrative timed for normal driving speeds for Gettysburg National Park, Great Smoky Mountains National Park, Rocky Mountain National Park, Glacier National Park, Grand Teton National Park, and Lancaster/Pennsylvania Dutch Country, but their biggest output consists of 14 similar auto tape tours for California: (1) San Francisco to Sacramento; (2) Sacramento to South Lake Tahoe; (3) South Lake Tahoe to Mariposa; (4) Mariposa to Fresno; (5) Monterey to Fresno; (6) Monterey to San Luis Obispo; (7) San Luis Obispo to Los Angeles; (8) Fresno to Los Angeles; (9) San Francisco/Wine Country; (10) San Francisco to Monterey; (11) Sacramento to Mariposa; (12) Monterey to Mariposa; (13) Reno to South Lake Tahoe; (14) Sacramento to Reno. The California tapes are available from Hertz locations at the Fresno, Los Angeles, Monterey, Reno, Sacramento, San Diego, and San Francisco airports. In most cases you have to buy the tapes and furnish your own cassette player; a few rent the tapes and a recorder.

INFORMATION CENTERS/INFORMATION PHONES

The state does not have a "system" of highway information centers, but the Office of Visitor Services (CA-72) was preparing, in the fall of 1978, a general list of information centers. Most local chambers of commerce are valuable walk-in sources of literature and information and the Office of Visitor Services supplies a partial list of these.

OUTDOOR RECREATION ACTIVITIES

BICYCLING. The California Dept. of Transportation (also known as CALTRANS), 1120 N Street, Sacramento, CA 95814 (916/322-4314) issues many good bicycling maps. The BERKELEY TO LAKE TAHOE BICYCLE TOURING GUIDE, the CENTRAL VALLEY BICYCLE TOURING GUIDE, the SAN FRANCISCO BAY AREA TOURING GUIDE, and the PACIFIC COAST BICYCLE TOURING GUIDE are leaflets that give detailed highway directions but barely adequate maps. Better highway maps with bicycle routes colored in may be obtained for each of the 11 district offices of CALTRANS. A list of these offices is available from the above address. They also make available a 100-page map/guide to the Pacific Coast Bicentennial Bicycle Route. The Automobile Club of Southern California (CA-76) issues a good SOUTHERN CALIFORNIA BICYCLING guide. See also CA-5, CA-36, CA-40, CA-47, CA-58, CA-116, and CA-161.

CANOEING AND BOATING. The California Dept. of Navigation and Ocean Development, 1629 S Street, Sacramento, CA 95814 issues a 3-part GUIDE TO CALIFORNIA BOATING FACILITIES which locates each facility (both coastal and inland) on a map and tells whether launching, berths, fuel, and/or supplies are available. The northern area guide covers the Oregon border to Bodega Bay, the central area guide covers Bodega Bay to Point Conception, and the southern area guide covers Point Conception to San Diego Bay. The Automobile Club of Southern California (CA-76) issues 2 guides: CENTRAL AND SOUTHERN CALIFORNIA BOATING which presents descriptions of individual boating areas in a regional arrangement; NORTHERN CALIFORNIA BOATING is a map/guide locating all boating areas and has tables showing available facilities at each See also CA-67 and the "Maps" section of this chapter.

FISHING AND HUNTING. The California Dept. of Fish and Game, The Resources Agency, 1416 Ninth Street, Sacramento, CA 95814 issues 2 series of very detailed fishing guides. The "Anglers' Guide Series" describes inland locations (over 40 have been prepared, but only about 15 are still available) and the "Ocean Fishing Maps" describe coastal locations (6 are available). Map/guides of each individual wildlife area are available. The Automobile Club of Southern California (CA-76) issues a guide to PRIVATELY OPERATED FISHING PONDS in southern California. See also CA-66, CA-67, CA-71, and the "Maps" section of this chapter.

WINTER ACTIVITIES. The Automobile Club of Southern California (CA-76) issues a WINTER SPORTS guide which describes ski and "snow play areas" in California, Colorado, Idaho, Nevada, New Mexico, Utah, and Wyoming. See also CA-2, CA-100, and CA-111.

NATIONAL/STATE PARKS/FORESTS, ETC.

Death Valley National Monument

CA-81   Gebhardt, Chuck. BACKPACKING DEATH VALLEY: A HIKER'S GUIDE. San Jose, CA: Mastergraphics, 1975. 134 p. Maps, photos. Index. 75-27630.

The Death Valley hiker has several unusual obstacles to overcome, so almost half of this handy little book is devoted to desert survival and equipment essentials. Fifteen day hikes, most of which are easy to moderate treks, under 10 miles in length round trip are described with a map for each. The backpacking (i.e., hikes of longer duration) section suggests many trips and refers these hikers to the USGS quadrangles.

CA-82   Kirk, Ruth, and Kirk, Louis. EXPLORING DEATH VALLEY. 3d ed. Stanford, CA: Stanford University Press, 1977. 88 p. Photos., maps. Index. 0-8047-0943-2. 76-48022.

This classic over-all guide, in its third edition, gives suggested automobile trips, jeep trips, and hikes, with background and sights to see. There is a directory of transportation, lodgings, and campgrounds.

CA-83   DEATH VALLEY NATIONAL MONUMENT, Death Valley, CA 92328 (714/786-2331).

They issue an informative general map/guide, a DIRT ROAD TRAVEL AND BACK COUNTRY CAMPING guide, and mimeographed guides to activities, the back country, hiking, temperatures, and services available at Scotty's Castle. The Visitor Center, located in the Furnace Creek area, is open 8A.M.-5P.M. daily from May to October and 8A.M.-9P.M. daily November through April. The Death Valley Natural History Association, Box 188, Death Valley, CA 92328, handles sales of all publications, and a list of these is available from them. Some of these are: DEATH VALLEY: A GUIDE-BOOK AND SUMMARY (a 22-page booklet covering geology, flora and fauna, history, services, and including a bibliography and maps), a camping leaflet, GETTING AROUND DEATH VALLEY BACK-COUNTRY, and BADWATER SELF-GUIDING AUTO TOUR. There are two places within the Monument where lodging is available. (1) Furnace Creek Inn & Ranch Resort, Death Valley, CA 92328 (714/786-2345). The inn is open November 1 to April 30 and the Ranch is open all year. Call 800/227-4700 for toll-free reservations and information. Within California call 800/622-0838. (2) Stove Pipe Wells Village, Death Valley, CA 92328. To call, dial the San Bernardino Toll Operator at area code 714 and ask for Stove Pipe Wells Toll Station #1. It is open year-round.

There is a KYM'S GUIDE for Death Valley. See the "Maps" section of this chapter for further information. The Automobile Club of Southern California (CA-76) issues a GUIDE TO DEATH VALLEY which has a detailed map plus lists of points of interest, campgrounds, and accommodations. The California State Automobile Association (CA-79) issues a map of the DEATH VALLEY AND GRAND CANYON REGION.

California

Golden Gate National Recreation Area

CA-84 Doss, Margot P. PATHS OF GOLD: IN AND AROUND THE
GOLDEN GATE NATIONAL RECREATION AREA. San Francisco:
Chronicle Books, 1974. 176 p. Maps, photos. 0-87701-053-6.
74-175897.

This is a descriptive guide, with maps, to 46 walks within the
Golden Gate National Recreation Area which mostly includes the
headlands area northwest of San Francisco and Marin County.

CA-85 GOLDEN GATE NATIONAL RECREATION AREA, Fort Mason, CA
94123 (415/566-0560).

This recreation area includes 3 separate geographic regions: approximately 10 miles of the coastal area of the San Francisco peninsula,
large areas in the Marin Headlands north of the Golden Gate Bridge,
and Alcatraz, for which reservations are necessary (call 415/546-
2805). There is a visitor center at Fort Mason, Bldg. 201, which is
open Monday-Friday, 8:30A.M.-4:30P.M. They provide a general
map/brochure and an extensive guide to other points of interest in the
area.

Lassen Volcanic National Park

CA-86 LASSEN VOLCANIC NATIONAL PARK, Mineral, CA 96063.

This is a 106,000 acre expanse of forests, lakes, and mountains
dominated by Lassen Peak, a volcano at the southern tip of the Cas-
cade Mountain chain in northern California. There are 2 visitor
information centers open from early June to late September: 1 at
Manzanita Lake at the northwest entrance (open 8A.M.-8P.M.) and
the other at Sulphur Works at the southwest entrance (open 8A.M.-
5.P.M.). They supply a general map/guide and brochures describing
scheduled activities, campgrounds within the park and backcountry
information, and information on campgrounds and lodging in the
nearby vicinity of the park. The Loomis Museum Association, also
at the above address, publishes a 56-page LASSEN TRAILS booklet,
plus ROAD GUIDE TO LASSEN VOLCANIC PARK, and numerous
other guides.

Point Reyes National Seashore

CA-87 Arnot, Phil. A TRAILGUIDE TO POINT REYES NATIONAL SEA-
SHORE. San Carlos, CA: Wide World, 1976. 101 p. Maps, photos.
76-151281.

Ten major and 5 minor hikes are described in rather personal terms.
The guide, with its chapters on technique, is informative and useful.

CA-88   Dalbey, Alice F. THE VISITOR'S GUIDE TO POINT REYES NA-
         TIONAL SEASHORE. Riverside, CT: Chatham Press, 1974. 79 p.
         Photos., maps. 0-85699-098-1. 73-89770.

         The author gives information on history; weather; points of interest;
         trails; nearby accommodations and services; and address, phone, and
         hours of 2 information centers and 1 youth hostel.

CA-89   POINT REYES NATIONAL SEASHORE, Point Reyes, CA 94956 (415/
         663-1092).

         There are 3 visitor centers: the Bear Valley Visitor Center at park
         headquarters is open 8A.M.-4:30P.M. all year; Drakes Beach Visitor
         Center is open Friday-Monday, 8:30A.M.-5P.M. during the summer
         (415/669-1250); and the Lighthouse Visitor Center is open 10A.M.-
         5:30P.M. (415/669-1534). The area is particularly suited for hiking
         and backpacking, and information about permits, etc. (including a
         weekend shuttle bus) is available from the above address.

Redwood National Park

CA-90   Anthrop, Donald F. REDWOOD NATIONAL AND STATE PARKS.
         Healdsburg, CA: Naturegraph, 1977. 70 p. Maps, photos.,
         sketches. 0-87961-059-X. 76-28198.

         The first half is devoted to redwood ecology and the effects of human
         occupancy on the coastal redwood forests. The second describes
         natural features, trails, fishing opportunities, and campgrounds in
         Redwood National Park, Prairie Creek Redwoods State Park, Del
         Norte Coast Redwoods State Park, and Jedediah Smith Redwoods State
         Park. A map is also provided for each.

CA-91   Dolezal, Robert J. EXPLORING REDWOOD NATIONAL PARK.
         Eureka, CA: Interface California Corp. (distributed by Touchstone
         Press), 1974. 231 p. Maps, photos. 0-911518-28-2. 74-76859.

         While much of this book concerns the flora, fauna, geology, weather,
         and history of the area, there is a section on fishing and a detailed
         description of 23 "hiking and watercraft trails." Location of each
         trail, distance, difficulty, average time, special equipment needed,
         maps to use, and general background are given. There is no index.

CA-92   REDWOOD NATIONAL PARK, Drawer N, Crescent City, CA 95531
         (707/464-6101).

         The park is located along the northern California coast and was estab-
         lished in 1968 to preserve the tallest trees in the world. They issue
         a general map/guide and a most informative newspaper format VISITOR
         GUIDE. They operate a year-round information center at park head-
         quarters in Crescent City at the corner of Second and K Streets. In

the summer information is also available at the Orick, Redwood, and Hiouchi Ranger Stations.

See also CA-74.

Sequoia and Kings Canyon National Parks

CA-93   SEQUOIA AND KINGS CANYON NATIONAL PARKS, Three Rivers, CA 93271 (209/565-3341, ext. 15).

Park information may be obtained at the park headquarters office at Ash Mountain, at the Lodgepole Visitor Center, the Grant Grove Visitor Center all in Sequoia National Park, and in Cedar Grove in Kings Canyon National Park. Call the above number, extension 51, for backpacking information. Call 209/565-3351 for a recorded message about weather, road conditions, etc. For lodging and meal service reservations in Sequoia National Park contact the Sequoia & Kings Canyon Hospitality Service, Sequoia National Park, CA 93262 (209/565-3373); in Kings Canyon contact the Sequoia & Kings Canyon Hospitality Service, Kings Canyon National Park, CA 93633 (209/335-2314). The park provides a general map/brochure, information about pack trips, and issues SEQUOIA BARK, a biweekly (in season) park newspaper describing activities and events. The Sequoia Natural History Association at the above address makes available a number of interpretive guidebooks to the area.

There is a KYM'S GUIDE for Sequoia-Kings Canyon. See the "Maps" section of this chapter for further information. The California State Automobile Association (CA-79) issues a map of the Sequoia and Kings Canyon National Parks area.

Yosemite National Park

CA-94   Clark, Lewis W., and Clark, Virginia D. YOSEMITE TRAILS. Escondido, CA: Western Trails Publications, 1976. 112 p. Maps, photos. Index. 76-19361.

Maps, trail profiles (graphs presenting elevation gain/loss), descriptive text, and background information are given for the major trail groups.

CA-95   Jones, William R. TEN TRAIL TRIPS IN YOSEMITE NATIONAL PARK. Olympic Valley, CA: Outbooks (Box 2006/95730), 1977. 78 p. Maps, photos.

The author, former chief naturalist of the park, describes 3 hikes in Yosemite Valley, 1 in the Mariposa Grove of Giant Sequoias, and 6 in the High Sierras region of the Park.

CA-96   Scharff, Robert, ed. YOSEMITE NATIONAL PARK. New York:
        David McKay Co., 1967. 213 p. Photos., maps. Index. 67-
        18002.

        This volume is old and the information in the chapter on accommoda-
        tions and services will need to be verified. However, the bulk of
        the book dealing with geology, trails, plant life, wildlife, seeing
        the park by auto (this may be out of date also), and things to see
        and do is still basically useful.

CA-97   YOSEMITE: A COMPLETE GUIDE TO THE VALLEY AND SURROUND-
        ING UPLANDS. . . . 3d ed. High Sierra Hiking Guides. Berkeley, CA:
        Wilderness Press, 1974. 88 p. Photos., map in pocket. Index.
        0-911824-34-0. 74-95768.

        This detailed guide gives background (flora, fauna, geology, climate)
        and a description of 16 day hikes, 5 backpack trails, and 2 lateral
        trails.

CA-98   YOSEMITE NATIONAL PARK, Box 577, Yosemite National Park, CA
        95389 (209/372-42222).

        They operate a very busy visitor center in Yosemite Valley where
        much information is dispensed and many activities are going on. The
        Yosemite Natural History Association at the above address (209/372-
        4532) publishes the newspaper format YOSEMITE GUIDE which con-
        tains a detailed day-by-day list of visitor activities and indicates
        those which are suitable for visitors in wheelchairs. Other publica-
        tions it issues are a 77-page YOSEMITE ROAD GUIDE, TRAILS OF
        YOSEMITE VALLEY, and a YOSEMITE TRAIL GUIDE PACKET which in-
        cludes 6 individual trail guides to outlying areas of the Park. All
        these and others are listed in their PUBLICATIONS PRICE LIST AND
        ORDER FORM. The Yosemite Park and Curry Co., Yosemite National
        Park, CA 95389 (209/373-4171) is the Park concessionnaire and makes
        available all classes of accommodations, restaurants, grocery stores,
        gas stations, guided tours, horseback trips, bicycles, High Sierra camps
        and trips, ski touring and downhill programs, climbing schools, etc.

There is a KYM'S GUIDE for Yosemite. See the "Maps" section of this chapter for further information. The Automobile Club of Southern California
(CA-76) issues a GUIDE TO YOSEMITE NATIONAL PARK which includes a
detailed map and lists of points of interest, recreation opportunities, accommodations, and campgrounds. Optima Publications, Los Altos, CA 94022 issues
a series of 6 "Where-To-Hike Maps" of Yosemite. These are only suitable for
suggestions. The serious hiker will want more specific information and maps.

A good guide to all the National Park Service areas in California, called the
NATIONAL PARK SYSTEM IN CALIFORNIA is available from the National
Park Service, Western Regional Office, 450 Golden Gate Avenue, San Fran-

cisco, CA 94102 (415/556-4122). Call this number for general information. For a recorded message, called PARKCAST, about road and weather conditions, and for campground information call 415/556-6030. Information is also available from the Los Angeles Field Office, 300 North Los Angeles Street, Los Angeles, CA 90012 (213/688-2852). The PARKCAST number there is 213/688-2902.

There are 17 national forests in California. The U.S. Forest Service, California Regional Forester, 630 Sansome Street, San Francisco, CA 94111 (415/556-0122) issues a 35-page RECREATION GUIDE: NATIONAL FORESTS IN CALIFORNIA which describes the location, character, recreation opportunities, and address and phone number of each one. Information on campgrounds and maps of each individual forest are also available from the above address. In addition, they issue a good map to the California stretch of the Pacific Crest National Scenic Trail.

The Bureau of Land Management, California State Office, 2800 Cottage Way, Room E-2841, Sacramento, CA 95825 maintains 42 campgrounds throughout the state plus 3 major recreation areas. The of these, the largest, is called the California Desert Conservation Area and covers the entire southeast desert corner of the state from El Centro to Bishop. Long-range plans call for the opening of over 70 separate areas (some are already open) for recreational use and off-road recreational vehicles. HIGH DESERT RECREATION RESOURCES GUIDE is a very informative map/guide to this area showing campgrounds, points of interest, roadside rests, rockhound areas, and all roads from freeways to dirt trails. The Barstow Way Station, 831 Barstow Road, 1 block north of Interstate 15 at Central Barstow Exit, Barstow, CA 92311 (714/256-3591), is the central source of desert recreation information for this area. The second major recreation area is the King Range National Conservation Area along the coast, 230 miles north of San Francisco and 70 miles south of Eureka. The third major recreation area is Cow Mountain, also in northern California, between Ukiah and Lakeport in the Mayacmas Mountains. "Recreation Guides," including a detailed map, are available for both of these areas.

The California Dept. of Parks and Recreation, The Resources Agency, Box 2390, Sacramento, CA 95811 (916/445-2358) issues a very detailed annual GUIDE TO THE CALIFORNIA STATE PARK SYSTEM. It locates each park on a map and lists facilities available at the over 220 areas maintained by this agency. Individual map/guides are available for many of the areas. See also CA-23.

The California Dept. of Forestry, The Resources Agency, 1416 Ninth Street, Sacramento, CA 95814 (916/445-9920) issues maps of state forest lands in 2 scales: 1 in. represents 1 mile, and 1/2 in. represents 1 mile. Much smaller map/brochures to individual state forests are available at each forest headquarters office.

The 2 auto clubs of California, the Automobile Club of Southern California

(CA-76) and the California State Automobile Association (CA-79), jointly issue 2 map/guides to campgrounds: NORTHERN CALIFORNIA CAMPING and CENTRAL AND SOUTHERN CALIFORNIA CAMPING. Each campsite is located on a map and there are tables listing facilities at each.

INDIVIDUAL CITIES OR AREAS

Lake Tahoe—Printed Materials

CA-99 Hayden, Mike. GUIDEBOOK TO THE LAKE TAHOE COUNTRY. 2 vols. Los Angeles: Ward Ritchie Press, 1971. Photos. Bibliographies. Indexes. 70-158890.

Volume 1 covers Echo Summit, Squaw Valley and the California shore and volume 2 covers Alpine County, Donner-Truckee and the Nevada shore. This good driving guide stresses history, sights, back roads, trails, and fishing.

The California State Automobile Association (CA-79) issues maps of LAKE TAHOE REGION and LAKE TAHOE COMMUNITIES. There is a KYM'S GUIDE for Lake Tahoe. See the "Maps" section of this chapter for further information.

Lake Tahoe—Organizations

CA-100 GREATER NORTH LAKE TAHOE CAMBER OF COMMERCE, Box 884, Tahoe City, CA 95730 (916/583-2371).

They issue a good mix of literature describing what to see and do, recreation opportunities, campgrounds, beaches, and dining. For information on skiing in this area contact: Ski Lake Tahoe, Box Z, Incline Village, NV 89450 (702/831-4222).

CA-101 SOUTH LAKE TAHOE VISITORS BUREAU, Box 15090, South Lake Tahoe, CA 95702 (916/544-5050).

They supply much useful information including an annual TAHOE TRAVELER'S ALMANAC that describes things to do in both the summer and winter; and lists hotels/motels, theaters, entertainment, and restaurants. In California only you can dial 800/822-5977 toll-free for information.

There is a National Forest Lake Tahoe Visitor Center (916/541-0209) off Route 89 west of South Lake Tahoe on Fallen Leaf Road.

Los Angeles—Printed Materials

CA-102 AROUND THE TOWN WITH EASE: A GUIDE FOR THE PHYSICALLY

LIMITED PERSON. Los Angeles: Junior League of Los Angeles, 1968. 44 p.

A new edition is planned.

CA-103 Clark, David. L.A. ON FOOT: A FREE AFTERNOON. Los Angeles: Camaro Publishing Co., 1972. 205 p. Maps, sketches. 73-174185.

The author describes 12 complete tours in various sections of Los Angeles each with a unifying theme. You must drive to the beginning of each tour, but from there each is walkable within an afternoon, or, even better according to the author, bikeable. Useful maps accompany each tour.

CA-104 Dwan, Lois. 1977 LOS ANGELES RESTAURANT GUIDE. Rev. ed. A Tarcher/Goushā Southern California Guide. Los Angeles: Tarcher/Goushā Guides, 1976. 206 p. Indexes. 0-87477-052-1. 76-24713.

The author, restaurant editor of the LOS ANGELES TIMES, describes over 400 places to dine. The main listing is alphabetical by name of restaurant, and there are indexes by area, price, type of food served, type of restaurant, and rating.

CA-105 Haggart, Stanley, et al. ARTHUR FROMMER'S GUIDE TO LOS ANGELES. New York: Frommer/Pasmantier Publishing Corp. (distributed by Simon & Schuster), 1977. 218 p. Maps.

For the first-time traveler to Los Angeles, this guide briefly mentions the traditional travel sites, accommodations, and eating places of the area including Disneyland and its environs. There is a chapter entitled "Along the Coast from Malibu to San Diego." There is no index.

CA-106 Kegan, Stephanie. IN AND AROUND L.A. FOR KIDS. San Francisco: Chronicle Books, 1977. 144 p. Maps, photos. 0-87701-102-8. 77-22859.

Instead of being arranged by themes of attractions, like so many other children's guidebooks, this one is arranged by region and extends south to San Diego and north to San Luis Obispo. Also, it sticks strictly to things to see and doesn't include sports, clubs, classes, etc. This is not to its discredit, as the selections will be sure to interest children and the practical information (finding directions, phone number, hours, fees) and descriptions are complete. There is an annual events listing. There is no index.

CA-107 Lewis, Roz. THE LITTLE RESTAURANTS OF LOS ANGELES. Los Angeles: Camaro Publishing Co., 1972. 211 p. Maps. Indexes. 73-168307.

Containing "over 100 unusual restaurants serving great food for $1.50 to $3.95," this guide is arranged alphabetically by type of cuisine served. It locates each restaurant on a map and includes the usual practical information, but there is no rating. There are alphabetic and geographic indexes.

CA-108 Lobo, Anthony. OFF THE BEATEN TRACK IN LOS ANGELES. A Nash Travel Guide. Los Angeles: Nash Publishing Corp., 1973. 136 p. 0-8402-8042-04. 72-81858.

This guide is not highly recommended. There are no maps. The places mentioned in the chapters on getting around, where to stay and eat, and points of interest are the very conventional ones and not off-the-beaten track at all. The chapter headed "Insider High-lights," which one might expect would contain the information promised in the title, is strictly a guide for swingers. Use this only if you've never been to Los Angeles and can't find any other guide-book.

CA-109 Pashdag, John, and Woller, Jim. ALL NIGHT L.A. San Francisco: Chronicle Books, 1978. 132 p. Photos. 0-87701-112-5. 78-3557.

While this may seem more of a "survival guide" for the locals, the out-of-town traveler, arriving late at night and suffering from jet-lag, can also find the descriptive listing of all-night services and facilities rather useful. The book is arranged by general type of services (meals, entertainment, emergencies, etc.), and the listings are interspersed with anecdotal tidbits. There is no index.

CA-110 RANGNO'S SOUTHERN CALIFORNIA GUIDE. Los Angeles: Louis Rangno (501 South Fairfax Avenue, Suite 204/90036).

"A monthly magazine-directory for visitor attractions, restaurants, hotels, motels, entertainment, sightseeing, sports," this guide has been published since 1919. It covers mostly the Los Angeles area with very brief sections on Santa Barbara and San Diego.

CA-111 Smith, Bill. SKI LOS ANGELES. Pasadena, CA: Ward Ritchie Press, 1974. 93 p. Photos., maps. 0-378-03873-7. 74-76470.

The author describes where to ski within a 1 1/2 hour drive of Los Angeles in the Angeles and San Bernardino National Forests. He also tells you how to get there.

CA-112 Thomas Brothers Maps. LOS ANGELES-ORANGE COUNTIES POPU-LAR STREET ATLAS. Los Angeles: Thomas Bros., 1976. 497 p. Scale: 1 in. represents 2,800 ft. Index.

CA-113 Tucker, Robin. FEET FIRST: CITYSIDE & COUNTRYSIDE WALKING TOURS IN LOS ANGELES. Los Angeles: Ward Ritchie Press, 1974.

96 p. 0-378-03862-1. 73-90547.

Once you've gotten to 1 of the 5 countryside or 5 cityside tour areas, this book isn't too bad, if you don't mind your guidebooks chatty and folksy. However, using this book alone, you are going to run into difficulty finding the starting place for each tour. The 2 included maps contribute nothing. Each of the countryside tours is through a botanical garden only. The Clark book (CA-103) is better.

CA-114 Weingarten, Lila, and Granz, Thea. WHERE TO GO AND WHAT TO DO WITH THE KIDS IN L.A. Los Angeles: Price/Stern/Sloan, 1971. 125 p. 0-8431-0109-1. 73-125081.

These brief descriptions of where and how to keep children amused in Los Angeles cover such topics as hiking and picnicking, puppet shows and other children's theaters, museums, plant tours, craft and hobby classes, clubs, amusement parks, zoos and animal farms, movie studios, and annual events. There is no index.

CA-115 Welles, Annette. THE LOS ANGELES GUIDE BOOK. Los Angeles: Sherbourne Press, 1972. 531 p. Photos. Bibliography. Index. 0-8202-0074-3. 72-172483.

This sadly out of date book can still be useful with its histories of the neighborhoods and nearby communities, and its general discussion of ethnic foods and wines. The more specific "what to do section" was remarkably thorough, if selective in spots, when compiled, noting address, telephone number, hours, specialties, and any other noteworthy things about restaurants, shops, flea markets, bookstores, musuems and galleries, special attractions, sports activities, libraries, and many more things. A section on transportation noted telephone numbers for airlines, bus lines, car rental agencies, and cabs. Newspapers, broadcasting stations, and annual events are listed. Pray for a revised edition.

CA-116 Weltman, Gershon, and Dubin, Elisha. BICYCLE TOURING IN LOS ANGELES. Los Angeles: Ward Ritchie Press, 1972. 125 p. Maps, photos. Index. 0-378-03512-6. 74-178866.

The 23 tours described cover the city itself, as well as the coastal and foothills areas. The descriptions are informative, and the maps (one for each tour) are excellent.

Rand McNally (US-215) and Gousha (US-206) and each issue maps of Los Angeles, Long Beach, Orange County, the San Fernando Valley, and the San Gabriel Valley. Other maps are available from Exxon (US-261). The U.S. Army Corps of Engineers, Los Angeles District, Box 2711, Los Angeles, CA 90053 issues a LOS ANGELES AREA BICYCLE TRAILS map/brochure. The Automobile Club of Southern California (CA-76) issues a LOS ANGELES &

VICINITY map which covers an area from the Santa Monica Mountains to
Palm Springs, a LOS ANGELES AREA FREEWAY SYSTEM map, GUIDE TO
METROPOLITAN LOS ANGELES and GUIDE TO DOWNTOWN LOS ANGELES
(both of which have good maps and lists of points of interest), a STREET MAP
OF CENTRAL AND WESTERN AREA, METROPOLITAN LOS ANGELES, a
guide to access roads and seating at Dodger Stadium and at the Coliseum/
Sports Arena, a guide to the roads and terminals at Los Angeles International
Airport, a map of SAN BERNARDINO COUNTY AND LAKE MEAD, a GUIDE
TO SAN BERNARDINO MOUNTAINS (good maps and descriptions of points of
interest and things to do), and a STREET MAP OF ORANGE COUNTY CITIES
(a 66-page atlas).

The Los Angeles and southern California weather information telephone number
is 213/554-1212.

Los Angeles—Organizations

CA-117 GREATER LOS ANGELES VISITORS AND CONVENTION BUREAU,
505 South Flower Street, Los Angeles, CA 90071 (213/488-9100 or
213/628-3101).

They issue an annual (1978 ed., 112 p.) OFFICIAL SOUTHERN CALI-
FORNIA TRAVEL GUIDE prepared especially for the use of travel
agents and convention planners, but individual visitors might be able
to obtain copies also. In addition to describing attractions, shopping,
transportation and tours, accommodations, and dining/nightlife in the
greater Los Angeles area, these are also covered in sections devoted
to Orange County, Palm Springs, San Bernardino, San Diego, and
Mexico. The following small brochures are regularly distributed:
maps, a general brochure describing things to do and events, self-
guided tours, a hotel/motel guide, a restaurant guide, a campsites
brochure, and an outdoor recreation guide. The Visitors Information
Center is at the above address which is located in the Atlantic Rich-
field Shopping Plaza. The hours are Monday-Friday, 9A.M.-5P.M.

CA-118 ANAHEIM AREA VISITOR & CONVENTION BUREAU, 800 West
Katella Avenue, Anaheim, CA 92803 (714/533-5536).

They make available an ANAHEIM AREA LODGING GUIDE and an
ANAHEIM AREA RESTAURANT GUIDE plus individual brochures on all
the attractions in the area.

For information about Disneyland contact: Guest Relations, DISNEYLAND,
Box 3232, Anaheim, CA 92803 (714/533-4456 or 213/626-8605, ext. 101).

CA-119 BEVERLY HILLS VISITORS AND CONVENTION BUREAU AND CHAM-
BER OF COMMERCE. 239 South Beverly Drive, Beverly Hills, CA
90212 (213/271-8174).

They issue a BEVERLY HILLS GUIDE which tells where to stay, dine, and shop, and lists other services such as beauty services, employment agencies, orchestras, banks, golf and tennis courts, churches, etc.

CA-120 HOLLYWOOD CHAMBER OF COMMERCE, 6324 Sunset Blvd., Hollywood, CA 90028 (213/469-8311).

They issue an annual VISITORS GUIDE AND MAP which is a detailed street map on which a few attractions have been located and on which places to stay and eat are listed.

Monterey/Carmel/Big Sur—Printed Materials

CA-121 Knox, Maxine. EXPLORING BIG SUR, MONTEREY, CARMEL. Los Angeles: Ward Ritchie Press, 1973. 126 p. Photos. Index. 73-75100.

This is a good description of the physical area and its major attractions. It contains a calendar of annual events.

The California State Automobile Association (CA-79) issues the following maps: MONTEREY PENINSULA CITIES and TOUR MAP OF MONTEREY PENINSULA.

Monterey/Carmel/Big Sur—Organizations

CA-122 MONTEREY PENINSULA CHAMBER OF COMMERCE AND VISITOR AND CONVENTION BUREAU, Box 1770, Monterey, CA 93940 (408/649-3200).

They issue a general map/brochure, information on recreation opportunities, a guide to places to stay, a dining guide, a golf and tennis guide, and a calendar of events. They are located at 380 Alvarado Street in Monterey.

Napa Valley—Printed Materials

CA-123 Morgan, Jefferson. ADVENTURES IN THE WINE COUNTRY. San Francisco: Chronicle Books, 1971. 128 p. Photos., maps. Index. 0-87701-008-0. 77-161030.

This breezily written and now somewhat dated book covers all of California's wine regions, describing the wines and the wineries, briefly noting restaurants and lodgings.

CA-124 Topolos, Michael, et al. NAPA VALLEY WINE TOUR. St. Helena, CA: Vintage Image, 1977. 182 p. Drawings, maps. 0-918666-06-6. 77-76842.

A pleasant book describing the Napa Valley in general, this work lists selected lodgings and restaurants (giving hours, specialties, price ranges, capacity, credit cards accepted, address, and telephone) and special places to visit before describing 48 wineries. Address, telephone, hours (if any), facilities, winemaker, wines produced, vineyard size (if having own vineyard), and volume produced are noted briefly in an appendix while the primary text gives history and any special features. The maps are good.

CA-125 Yeadon, Anne, and Yeadon, David. WINE TASTING IN CALIFORNIA: A FREE WEEKEND. Los Angeles: Camaro Publishing Co., 1973. 187 p. Maps, drawings. Indexes. 0-91329-05-X. 73-85632.

Arranged by the 7 wine producing areas of California, this guide lists 111 wineries offering tours and wine tasting, giving a brief history of each, a drawing, a map, directions, and hours. The indexes of wineries are by region and by name. By all counts, this is an excellent volume. There is a section on wine lore.

The California State Automobile Association (CA-79) issues maps of SONOMA AND NAPA COUNTIES and NAPA AND VICINITY (neither show winery locations).

Napa Valley—Organizations

CA-126 NAPA CHAMBER OF COMMERCE, Box 636, Napa, CA 94558 (707/226-7455).

They issue a map GUIDE TO NAPA VALLEY WINERIES and guides to restaurants, places to stay, picnic facilities, bike routes, golf courses, and antique dealers. Their street address is 1900 Jefferson in Napa.

CA-127 WINE INSTITUTE, 165 Post Street, San Francisco, CA 94108 (415/986-0878).

They issue CALIFORNIA'S WINE WONDERLANDS which is a county-by-county guide to wineries open to the public located in 32 of the state's 58 counties. It contains maps and a name index.

Palm Springs—Printed Materials

CA-128 Delaney, Jack. PALM SPRINGS A LA CARTE: CHOOSE WHAT TO DO AND SEE IN PALM SPRINGS AND THE SURROUNDING AREA. Palm Springs: ETC Publications (distributed by Chicago Review Press), 1978. 138 p. Photos. 0-914090-49-6.

Written in a discursive style rather than arranged for quick reference, this book covers major points of interest, accommodations, restaurants, golf and tennis, desert trips, and other things to do outdoors. The lack of an index, especially in a book written in this manner, is particularly inexcusable.

CA-129 Hartley, Fred, and Hartley, Glory. A GUIDE TO PALM SPRINGS AND THE COACHELLA VALLEY. Rancho Mirage, CA: Hartley Enterprises (Box 701/92270), 1977. 128 p. Photos., maps.

The authors describe what to see and do, restaurants, hotels, shopping, art galleries, theatre, and social events in Palm Springs. They describe what to see and do only in 10 nearby areas. There are additional chapters on what to do with children, tours and excursions, and other day-to-day information for enjoying the area.

The Automobile Club of Southern California (CA-76) issues GUIDE TO PALM SPRINGS-INDIO AREA which contains detailed maps plus lists of points of interest, accommodations, restaurants, and golf courses. The City of Palm Springs, Planning Dept., Box 1786, Palm Springs, CA 92262 issues a city bike map.

Palm Springs—Organizations

CA-130 PALM SPRINGS CONVENTION & VISITORS BUREAU, Municipal Airport Terminal, Palm Springs, CA 92262 (714/327-8411).

Sacramento—Printed Materials

CA-131 Thomas Brothers Maps. SACRAMENTO COUNTY POPULAR STREET ATLAS. Los Angeles: Thomas Bros., 1976. 206 p. Scales: 1 in. represents 4,260 ft; 1 in. represents 2,200 ft. Index. 64-120.

Maps of Sacramento are available from the California State Automobile Association (CA-79), Goushā (US-206), Rand McNally (US-215), and the Sacramento Metropolitan Chamber of Commerce, Box 1017, Sacramento, CA 95805. The Sacramento Dept. of Parks and Recreation, Box 2390, Sacramento, CA 95811, issues BICYCLING THROUGH THE MOTHER LODE.

Sacramento—Organizations

CA-132 SACRAMENTO CONVENTION & VISITORS BUREAU, 1100 14th Street, Sacramento, CA 95814 (916/449-5291).

They make available a map of the metropolitan area, a VISITOR'S GUIDE (briefly covering history, points of interest, outdoor recreation activities, how to get around, and gold rush country), a dining and lodging guide, and a calendar of events. There is an Old Sacramento Visitors Center at Second and K Streets (916/446-4314) that is open 7 days a week, 10A.M.-6P.M.

San Diego—Printed Materials

CA-133 Gray, Anne. THE WONDERFUL WORLD OF SAN DIEGO: CHIL-
DREN'S ADVENTURES IN THIS EXCITING CALIFORNIA CITY. 2d
ed. Pelican Guide Book Series. Gretna, LA: Pelican Publishing
Co., 1975. 79 p. Photos. 0-88289-081-6. 74-76733.

Gray has written "a guide to the historical and recreational points of
interest in San Diego as seen through the eyes of two children."

CA-134 Mendel, Carol. SAN DIEGO ON FOOT. San Diego: the author
(Box 6022/92106), 1973. 94 p. Maps, sketches. 74-160966.

Foot directions, distance, and background for appreciating sights
along the way are given for 20 walking tours in the greater San
Diego area including La Jolla and Torrey Pines State Reserve.

CA-135 SAN DIEGO GUIDE. 10th ed. San Diego: San Diego Guide (Box
81544/92138), 1978. Issued annually. 286 p. Photos., maps.
Index.

This is a comprehensive guide to shopping, restaurants, sports, nightlife, and points of interest in the San Diego area with additional
chapters on La Jolla and Tijuana. It includes a calendar of events
and discount coupons.

CA-136 Shad, Jerry. BACKCOUNTRY ROADS & TRAILS: SAN DIEGO
COUNTY. Beaverton, OR: Touchstone Press, 1977. 96 p. Photos.,
maps. 0-911518-46-0. 76-57336.

Five motor trips, each with connected hiking trails, are described in
fair detail. The hiking trails are described in a bit more detail.
There is no index.

CA-137 A STEP IN TIME: SAN DIEGO FOR THE HANDICAPPED. San
Diego: Junior League of San Diego, 1977. 54 p.

CA-138 Thomas Brothers Maps. SAN DIEGO COUNTY POPULAR STREET
ATLAS. Los Angeles: Thomas Bros., 1976. 148 p. Scale: 1 in. represents 2,900 ft. Index.

Maps of San Diego are available from the Automobile Club of Southern California (CA-76), Goushā (US-206), and Rand McNally (US-215). The City
of San Diego Information Center at City Hall, Second & C Streets, San Diego,
CA 92101 issues a city bike map.

San Diego—Organizations

CA-139 SAN DIEGO CONVENTION AND VISITORS BUREAU, 1200 Third Avenue,

Suite 824, San Diego, CA 92101 (714/232-3101).

They issue a VISITOR'S MAP, a quarterly listing of events, a hotels/ motels guide to San Diego County and Baja Mexico, a dining and entertainment guide to San Diego County and Baja Mexico, a tour services guide, a camping guide, a shopping guide, a tennis guide, a golf guide, a water sports guide, an auto rentals guide, and a VISIT MEXICO! guide. They also issue a 110-page travel and vacation planner for visitors, travel agents, and convention planners and delegates. The latter is sold on newsstands. It includes points of interest and attractions, sight-seeing, transportation and charter services, dining, accommodations, conventions, shopping, and visitor facts. They also issue A STEP IN TIME (CA-137). There are 2 walk-in information centers: the visitor information center in the Mission Bay area at East Mission Bay Drive and Clairemont (714/276-8200) and the Plaza Information Booth in Horton Plaza at Broadway & 3d (714/234-5191). They also have offices in Chicago (333 North Michigan Avenue, Suite 1521, Chicago, IL 60601 [312/263-1388]) and in Washington, DC (910 17th Street NW, Suite 432, Washington, DC 20006 [202/467-5958]). For a recorded message summarizing the day's events, call 714/239-9696. The City Park and Recreation Dept. at 714/236-5740 also provides information.

San Francisco Area—Printed Materials

CA-140 Brant, Michelle. TIMELESS WALKS IN SAN FRANCISCO: A HIS-
TORICAL WALKING GUIDE TO THE CITY. Richmond, CA: Lompa
Press, 1975. 71 p. Maps, photos. 76-353726.

The author describes historic points of interest along 9 one-hour walking tours.

CA-141 Doss, Margot P. THE BAY AREA AT YOUR FEET. San Francisco:
Chronicle Books, 1970. 184 p. Maps, photos. Index. 0-87701-
007-2. 73-21157.

The author, the expert on walks in San Francisco, describes, with a map for each, 43 walks.

CA-142 _____. GOLDEN GATE PARK AT YOUR FEET. San Francisco:
Chronicle Books, 1970. 157 p. Maps, photos. Index. 0-87701-
005-6. 74-13413.

The author describes, with a map for each, 37 walks in Golden Gate Park.

CA-143 _____. SAN FRANCISCO AT YOUR FEET: THE GREAT WALKS IN
A WALKER'S TOWN. Rev. ed. New York: Grove Press, 1974.
200 p. Maps, photos. Index. 0-8021-0054-6. 73-21004.

This is a great guide for exploring the secrets of San Francisco on foot. None of the walks is longer than half a day and some are as short as 20 minutes. The author gives the distance, tells what type clothes to wear, how to get to the area by public transportation, and the availability of nearby parking.

CA-144 _____. THERE, THERE: EAST SAN FRANCISCO BAY AT YOUR FEET. San Francisco: Presidio Press, 1978. 294 p. 0-89141-055-4.

The author describes 76 walking tours "organized around points of natural and historic interest in the East Bay: Oakland, Berkeley, San Jose, Richmond, and the hills beyond."

CA-145 _____. WALKS FOR CHILDREN IN SAN FRANCISCO. New York: Grove Press, 1970. 63 p. 68-29454.

CA-146 Godwin, John, et al. ARTHUR FROMMER'S GUIDE TO SAN FRANCISCO. New York: Frommer/Pasmantier Publishing Corp. (distributed by Simon & Schuster), 1977. 217 p. Maps.

This guide is aimed at the first-time visitor to San Francisco. It briefly mentions the traditional tourist spots, accommodations, and eating places, and there are short sections on what the children would like, and excursions to the Napa Valley and Yosemite. There is no index.

CA-147 A GUIDE TO OAKLAND AND PARTS OF BERKELEY FOR THE PHYSICALLY DISABLED AND AGING. Oakland, CA: Easter Seal Society for Crippled Children and Adults of Alameda County (2757 Telegraph Avenue/94612), n.d. 42 p.

A new edition was planned for mid-1978.

CA-148 GUIDE TO SAN FRANCISCO FOR THE DISABLED. San Francisco: Easter Seal Society of San Francisco (6221 Geary Blvd./94121), 1976. 38 p.

CA-149 Hansell, Franz T. THE GREAT FAMILY FUN GUIDE TO SAN FRANCISCO. A Comstock Edition. New York: Ballantine Books, 1974. 249 p. Photos. Index. 0-345-23976-8. 74-9935.

This is a very complete guide to what to see and do with children in San Francisco and the areas south to Santa Cruz and north to Russian River. In addition to points of interest, shopping with kids, playgrounds, churches for kids, transportation, nature activities, and restaurants are included.

CA-150 _____. AN OPINIONATED GUIDE TO SAN FRANCISCO. A Comstock Edition. New York: Ballantine Books, 1974. 268 p. Maps.

Index. 0-345-23868-0. 74-174337.

An "insiders" guide to the city, the author doesn't force his prefer-
ences on you (for one that does see CA-160), as one might expect
from the title. Instead, he gives you many good tips on seeing the
"real" San Francisco.

CA-151 Lewis, Mary, and Lewis, Richard D. WHERE TO GO AND WHAT
TO DO WITH THE KIDS IN SAN FRANCISCO. Los Angeles: Price/
Stern/Sloan, 1972. 159 p. Index. 0-8431-0189-X. 72-76841.

Descriptions of things to do and places to visit are grouped into
large topics: outdoor adventures; concerts, film, TV, and theater;
free tours; museums; birthday party suggestions; hobby classes; organizations; out-of-town visitors; and miscellany. Descriptions include
address, phone number, hours, admission costs, and finding directions.
It includes a calendar of regularly scheduled events.

CA-152 Lewis, Roz. THE LITTLE RESTAURANTS OF SAN FRANCISCO.
Los Angeles: Camaro Publishing Co., 1973. 223 p. Maps, sketches.
Indexes. 0-913290-06-8. 73-85631.

"Over 100 unusual restaurants serving great food for $1.50 to $4.95"
are alphabetically arranged by type of cuisine served. The author
locates each restaurant on a map and includes the usual practical
information, but with no rating. There are alphabetic and area indexes.

CA-153 Meyers, Carole T. EATING OUT WITH THE KIDS IN SAN FRAN-
CISCO AND THE BAY AREA. Albany, CA: Carousel Press (Box
6061/94706), 1976. 72 p. Index. 0-917120-02-7. 76-28829.

The author eliminates the fast food chains in favor of those "more
reflective of the area's local color." She gives a very good idea of
what to expect at each restaurant and, at times, special advice on
visiting each with children. The usual practical restaurant information (hours, price range, credit cards accepted, etc.) plus information on availability of high chairs and/or booster seats is provided
with each description. It is regionally arranged with a cuisine index.

CA-154 Olmsted, Nancy. TO WALK WITH A QUIET MIND: HIKES IN
THE WOODLANDS, PARKS AND BEACHES OF THE SAN FRANCISCO
BAY AREA. A Sierra Club Totebook. San Francisco: Sierra Club
Books, 1975. 255 p. Maps. Bibliography. 0-87156-125-5. 75-
1053.

This guide devotes as much space to describing the natural history of
an area as it does to the trails themselves. Most hikes tend to be
easy or moderate, allowing for enjoyment of these natural attractions
along the way. Five hikes in the Golden Gate area, and 11 each in
the Mount Tamalpais and Point Reyes areas to the north are described.
Each hike has a general outline map.

CA-155 Read, R.B. SAN FRANCISCO AFFORDABLE FEASTS: 120 RESTAUR-
ANTS NOT REVIEWED ELSEWHERE. A California Living Book. San
Francisco: San Francisco Examiner, 1977. 252 p. 0-89395-001-7.
77-74627.

CA-156 _____. THE SAN FRANCISCO UNDERGROUND GOURMET: AN
IRREVERENT GUIDE TO DINING IN THE BAY AREA. 4th ed. A
Fireside Book. New York: Simon & Schuster, 1977. 300 p. In-
dexes. 0-671-22770-X. 77-2561.

Approximately 275 restaurants are described by type of cuisine served
from Afghani to Scandianavian. There are indexes by price (from $1.50
or less to over $7.00), by location within San Francisco, and by name.

CA-157 SAN FRANCISCO. A Goushā Weekend Guide. San Jose. CA;
Gousha Co., 1972. 96 p. Maps, photos. Index. 72-80660.

This is a different, but good, guidebook. It takes 10 major holidays,
assumes a 3-day weekend for each, and tells how to enjoy each day
of each holiday weekend. (Obviously, the information in the guide
can be used anytime, regardless of this arrangement). There are
supplemental chapters on art, music, and theater, and where to buy,
and what. There are many good maps.

CA-158 SAN FRANCISCO: THE BAY AND ITS CITIES. Rev. ed. American
Guide Series. New York: Hastings House, 1973. 496 p. Photos.,
maps. Bibliography. Index. 0-8038-6692-5. 72-5854.

This is a second revision of the original 1940 WPA guide. It includes
a natural history; human history; calendar of annual events; list of
hotels, restaurants, sports centers, churches; detailed descriptions of
points of interest, including those in Oakland, Berkeley, and other
cities and areas in the Bay area. There is a chronology of the area's
history.

CA-159 THE SAN FRANCISCO BOOK-MAP: A GUIDE AND MAP OF SAN
FRANCISCO IN FIVE LANGUAGES. San Francisco: Hollmann Publishing Co., 1974. 194 p. Maps, drawings. Index. 75-307260.

Published in 5 languages all in 1 volume, this English/German/
Spanish/French/Japanese guidebook is very useful, if a bit dated and
needing revision. It gives a brief history of the city, points of
interest (including views and vistas), climate, transportation information (including a map of the airport), tours, annual events, and
museums. More than just San Francisco is covered with information
included on side trips to the Reno/Tahoe area, the Monterey/Carmel
area, and the wine country. Churches, consulates, hotels, nightclubs, etc. are listed. It is accompanied by a separate birds-eye-
view of San Francisco.

CA-160 Shelton, Jack, et al. HOW TO ENJOY 1 TO 10 PERFECT DAYS IN SAN FRANCISCO. Rev. ed. Sausalito, CA: Shelton Publications, 1977. 191 p. 0-918742-00-5. 77-75392.

This appalling book gives a complete regimen for enjoying San Francisco with no thought. The schedule (no lagging) tells one exactly what to do and when to do it ("11:45 A.M. walk three blocks up Taylor Street. . .") with little leeway. He even tells you at what time of day you are to write your postcards! The information is quite good, but the overbearing manner of presentation nullifies much of its value. Follow it exactly, and you will have a good time. For a nice time, take what you can and do things your way--but don't tell the author.

CA-161 Standing, Tom. BAY AREA BIKEWAYS. Berkeley, CA: Ten Speed Press, 1972. 93 p. Maps, photos.

Easy to follow route directions and a detailed route map are given for each of 11 bike trips in San Francisco and 10 in the Marin peninsula across the bay to the north.

CA-162 Teather, Louise. DISCOVERING MARIN: HISTORIC TOUR BY CITIES AND TOWNS. Fairfax, CA: The Tamal Land Press, 1974. 128 p. Bibliography. Index. 0-912908-02-5. 74-77090.

Despite the subtitle, this book is not a tour in the sense that it takes you from point to point describing things along the way. Instead, it describes some of the parks, museums, and landmarks within the communities located in the Marin peninsula as far north as the Point Reyes area.

CA-163 Thomas Brothers Maps. SAN FRANCISCO COUNTY POPULAR STREET ATLAS. Los Angeles: Thomas Bros., 1976. 100 p. Scale: 1 in. represents 1,320 ft. 77-355632.

CA-164 Witnah, Dorothy L. AN OUTDOOR GUIDE TO THE SAN FRANCISCO BAY AREA: EXPLORING WITH BOOTS, BIKES, BACKPACKS, BUSES, BOATS, BOOKS AND BART. Berkeley, CA: Wilderness Press, 1976. 401 p. Photos., maps. Bibliography. Index. 0-911824-35-9. 74-79833.

Witnah describes ". . .84 walks, hikes, climbs, strolls and bike rides, from 1 to 12 miles long, from easy to strenuous--all within 70 miles of the Golden Gate Bridge." Distance, grade, references to published maps, how to get there, features, facilities, regulations, and a description are given for each hike. In many instances, recommended readings and an actual map are included. There is a list of local organizations sponsoring outdoor activities.

Maps of San Francisco are available from Arrow Publishing Co. (US-199), Exxon (US-261), and the Tourmap Co., East 1104 57th Avenue, Spokane, WA

99203. Goushā (US 206) and Rand McNally (US-215) each issue maps of Conta Costa County, Marin County, Oakland-East Bay cities, and San Francisco. The California State Automobile Association (CA-79) issues a general San Francisco map with a street directory, a SAN FRANCISCO TOUR MAP with a long list of points of interest, a BAY AND [SACRAMENTO] RIVER AREA map, an Oakland/Berkeley/Alameda map, and a map of Marin County.

See also Golden Gate National Recreation Area (CA-84) and (CA-85).

The San Francisco/Oakland area weather information number is 415/936-1212.

San Francisco Area—Organizations

CA-165 BERKELEY CHAMBER OF COMMERCE, 1834 University Avenue, Berkeley, CA 94703 (415/845-1212).

They issue a MAP AND GUEST GUIDE which includes listings of hotels/motels, restaurants, sports, theaters, etc.; a sheet describing things to see and do; and separate hotel/motel and dining guides.

CA-166 OAKLAND CHAMBER OF COMMERCE, 1939 Harrison Street, Suite 400, Oakland, CA 94612 (415/451-7800).

They publish guides to things to see and do, hotels and motels, restaurants, and entertainment; a quarterly calendar of events; and a street map of the greater Oakland area. They sponsor visitor information centers at Jack London Square and at designated fire stations throughout the city.

CA-167 SAN FRANCISCO CONVENTION & VISITORS BUREAU, 1390 Market Street, San Francisco, CA 94102 (415/626-5500).

They issue a VISITORS MAP, a listing of events and sightseeing published every 4 months, a hotel/motel guide, a restaurant and night life guide, and a shopping guide. A general brochure THIS IS SAN FRANCISCO is available in French, German, Spanish, Japanese, and Italian. An annual (1978 ed., 116 p.) SAN FRANCISCO VISITOR & CONVENTION GUIDE for visitors, travel agents, convention planners and delegates is for sale at the visitor information center. They operate the San Francisco Visitor Information Center in the Swig Pavilion, Hallidie Plaza, Powell & Market Streets. It is open Monday-Friday, 9A.M.-5P.M., Saturday, 9A.M.-3P.M., and Sunday, 10A.M.-2P.M., and closed Thanksgiving, Christmas, and New Year's Day. There is a 24-hour recorded telephone message of daily events and activities at 415/391-2000. They also have offices in Chicago (333 North Michigan Avenue, Suite 2122, Chicago, IL 60601 [312/263-1838]), and in Washington, DC (1100 17th Street NW, Suite 312, Washington, DC 20036 [202/331-0215]).

California

The East Bay Regional Park District, 11500 Skyline Blvd., Oakland, CA 94619 (415/531-9300) maintains over 30 parks, shorelines, recreation areas, trails, and wildernesses.

COLORADO

BOOKS, ATLASES, MAGAZINES

CO-1   Agnew, Jeremy. EXPLORING THE COLORADO HIGH COUNTRY.
Colorado Springs: Wildwood Press, 1977. 156 p. Photos., map.
Bibliography. Index. 0-918944-00-7. 77-77959.

In spite of the likely sounding title, this book does nothing more than
whet the appetite of the traveler who doesn't know anything about
getting into the Colorado backcountry. It is written in a rambling
style and includes no suggestions on where to go for further practical
information. The bibliography is to even more general books and is
not a complete general Colorado bibliography. The Grout book
(CO-7) is better.

CO-2   Casewit, Curtis W. SKIING COLORADO: A COMPLETE GUIDE
TO AMERICA'S NUMBER ONE SKI STATE. Old Greenwich, CT:
Chatham Press, 1975. 127 p. Photos. 0-85699-123-6. 75-21060.

This book contains mostly descriptions of amenities, lodging, restaurants, and activities to be found in the major ski areas of Colorado.
Very little on the actual ski trails or slopes themselves is provided.

CO-3   COLORADO RECREATION GUIDE. 6th ed. Commerce City, CO:
Colorado Recreation Guides, 1978. 192 p. Maps, photos. Indexes.

This title contains a wealth of information about recreation opportunities, mostly fishing and hunting, on U.S. Forest Service, Bureau of
Land Management, National Park Service, and Colorado state recreation land areas. The short "sightseeing" and "auto tours" sections
stick to outdoors areas. The 33 separate maps at a scale of 1/2 in.
represents 1 mile are the book's most useful feature. All are keyed
for ghost towns, points of interest, campgrounds, picnic areas, rock
and fossil hunting, state recreation areas, fishing, hunting, and skiing.
There are numerous indexes scattered throughout the book.

CO-4   COLORADO/ROCKY MOUNTAIN WEST. Denver: Colorado Magazine (1139 Delaware/80204).

This is an expanded version of COLORADO MAGAZINE which includes extra pages in an additional edition of the basic magazine prepared for readers living in the Rockies. Greater emphasis is placed on family recreation in the Rockies, and there is an annual bound-in ski guide. General articles appearing in both editions cover such topics as gardening, cooking, life-styles, regional and historical lore, etc. It is issued bimonthly.

CO-5 COLORADO SIGHTSEEING GUIDE. Commerce City, CO: Colorado Recreation Guides, 1977. 96 p. Maps.

Compared with the COLORADO RECREATION GUIDE (CO-3), this title leaves out all the hunting and fishing information and has expanded the information on scenic road tours and driving in the Rockies, the national and state parks, outdoor points of interest, and lists of campgrounds. It's still very much an outdoors guide as the brief section devoted to Denver will show. Once again, the many maps showing campgrounds, picnic areas, points of interest, historic sites, ski areas, rockhounding and fossil areas, and road tours contribute much to the book.

CO-6 COLORADO VISITOR REVIEW. Denver: Clearing House Publications (777 Pearl Street/80203).

This monthly guide to "theatre, music, night life, sports, recreation, art, where to stay, dining out, etc." also features short articles on top Colorado destinations and has many advertisements.

CO-7 Grout, William. COLORADO ADVENTURES: 40 TRIPS IN THE ROCKIES. Denver: Golden Bell Press, 1974. 174 p. Maps, photos. 0-87315-058-9. 74-78850.

The traveler should choose this book over the Agnew (CO-1) or Talmadge (CO-17) books. There may not be quite as many suggestions, but at least the information here is specific, the maps are readable, and the 40 trips will keep you going for a long time.

CO-8 Hansen, Harry, ed. COLORADO: A GUIDE TO THE HIGHEST STATE. Rev. ed. American Guide Series. New York: Hastings House, 1970. 504 p. Photos., maps. Bibliography. Index. 0-8038-1145-4. 75-132150.

This revision of the original 1941 WPA guide begins with a description of the state, from geology to the arts, and then goes on to describe 10 towns and cities, 21 highway tours, 3 park and 4 trail tours in Rocky Mountain National Park, and 3 park tours in Mesa Verde National Park. There is a chronology of Colorado history.

CO-9 Lowe, Don, and Lowe, Roberta. 80 NORTHERN COLORADO HIK-

ING TRAILS. Beaverton, OR: Touchstone Press, 1973. 175 p. Photos., maps. 0-911518-20-7. 73-80047.

The information given for each hike includes: verbal description; photograph; distance; elevation gain; season to hike; elevation at highest point; reproduction of the USGS map with the trail lined in red; the name of the specific USGS map(s) to use; and, in the back, the addresses of the appropriate national forests, parks, or recreation area administering bodies. Most of the hikes are no longer than 1 day and none is over 10 miles one way.

CO-10 _____. 50 WEST CENTRAL COLORADO HIKING TRAILS. Beaverton, OR: Touchstone Press, 1976. 112 p. Maps, photos. 0-911518-39-8. 76-661.

Each trail description covers 1 page with photograph(s) and a map on the facing page. Distance, elevation gain, highest point, approximate 1-way time, season, and which USGS topographic maps show the trail are briefly noted. The text is usually a good description of the trail with some specific directions.

CO-11 Norton, Boyd, and Norton, Barbara. THE BACKROADS OF COLORADO. Chicago: Rand McNally, 1978. 205 p. Photos., maps, Bibliography. 0-528-81046-4. 77-6900.

The 44 mini-tours are divided into 3 sections: high country, western slope, and the great plains. There are several general maps in the book, usually 1 for each subgroup of tours in the same general region. The book is extremely personal, and the Nortons are always telling the reader what they liked. The directions are good and the descriptions of the scenery a bit general. Natural and human history are noted in passing. Scattered among the tours are 11 "Colorado Sketches": a bit more background on selected places and people.

CO-12 Ormes, Robert, with the Colorado Mountain Club. GUIDE TO THE COLORADO MOUNTAINS. 6th ed. Sage Books. Chicago: Swallow Press, 1970. 300 p. Maps, photos. Index. 0-8040-0139-1. 72-115033.

The author describes numerous trails in 46 mountain regions all of which can be hiked by parties without special technical knowledge, providing they have an experienced leader. Summits can be reached by at least 1 route that would be considered no more than steep mountainside hiking, but there is often an alternative route for the true mountaineer with ropes and hardware. There are very brief chapters on ski touring, spelunking, and white water boating.

CO-13 Schoenfeld, Carolyn, et al. 1973 NORTHERN COLORADO VACATION AND WEEKEND GUIDE. Boulder, CO: Gentry Guides, 1973. 174 p. Maps, photos. Index. 73-80739.

Much of the information in this book has been incorporated into the authors' other book covering all of Colorado (CO-14), but not all of it. There are 9 locales which are only covered here. In comparing the information given for Estes Park, for example, this book has additional information on conveniences for the traveler (banks, laundromats, etc.), dude ranches/outfitters, daytime and nighttime entertainment, motels/hotels, and sports and outdoor activities. On the other hand, the coverage for Rocky Mountain National Park was identical in both books. The format is the same in both and use of them both together will give the most comprehensive coverage.

CO-14   . TRAVEL TODAY'S COLORADO. Boulder, CO: Gentry Guides, 1974. 198 p. Maps, photos. Index. 74-82525.

This guide is arranged alphabetically by 39 major Colorado travel destinations. For each, specific information is given about campgrounds, fishing spots, museums, restaurants, shops, hiking, scenic drives, entertainment, special activities, etc. Outlines maps are provided for the scenic drives. A separate section analyzes ski areas.

CO-15 Sudduth, Tom, and Sudduth, Sanse. COLORADO FRONT RANGE SKI TOURS. Beaverton, OR: Touchstone Press, 1975. 128 p. Maps, photos. 0-911518-34-7. 75-27837.

This book was prepared under the direction of the Rocky Mountain Division of the U.S. Ski Association (US-240) and 54 tours are described. Information given for each includes: verbal description; whether half-day, one day, or overnight; whether for the beginning, intermediate, or advanced skier; distance; required time; elevation gain; maximum elevation; season to ski; a reproduction of the USGS map section with the tour lined in; and the name of the appropriate USGS map to use.

CO-16   . NORTHERN COLORADO SKI TOURS. Beaverton, OR: Touchstone Press, 1976. 141 p. Maps, photos. 0-911518-44-4. 76-26311.

Sixty-five tours are described and "divided into half-day trips, one-day trips and overnights according to distance and type of terrain."

CO-17 Talmadge, Marian, and Gilmore, Iris. COLORADO HI-WAYS AND BY-WAYS: A COMPREHENSIVE GUIDE TO PICTURESQUE TRAILS AND TOURS. 3d ed. Boulder, CO: Pruett Publishing Co., 1975. 121 p. Photos., maps. 0-87108-079-6. 75-316146.

This is full of intriguing suggestions on seeing the "by-ways" of Colorado. Twenty-six tours are described (although specific directions, locations, and other practical information are missing) and each has an accompanying general and not too useful map. The traveler who wants to take one of these tours will have to gather

additional maps and information to actually find his way. The traveler who is in a specific place and wants to know what by-ways he
can take out of that area will have trouble zeroing in on the appropriate tour since there is no index. This would be most useful as a
source of ideas.

MAPS

The official highway map (called COLORFUL COLORADO) is available from
the Travel Marketing Section (CO-19). The 1978 edition contained information on colleges; museums; national parks and monuments; state parks, recreation areas and historic sites; ski and winter sports areas; the Denver area;
mountain peaks and passes; and telephone numbers to call for road and weather
information. The Colorado Dept. of Highways, Division of Transportation
Planning, 4201 East Arkansas Avenue, Denver, CO 80222 issues a monthly
map showing locations of road construction projects. It's called the STATE
HIGHWAY CONSTRUCTION BULLETIN. Both AAA (US-259) and Rand Mc-
Nally (US-215) issue a combined Colorado/Wyoming map. Exxon (US-261)
issues a combined Colorado/Utah map. Goushā (US-206) issues a single
Colorado map. See also CO-3, CO-5, and CO-18.

PUBLISHERS

CO-18   COLORADO RECREATION GUIDES, Box 1201, Commerce City, CO
80022. 303/426-1428.

They publish 4 very useful guides with many detailed maps to exploring Colorado. COLORADO RECREATION GUIDE (CO-3) and COLO-
RADO SIGHTSEEING GUIDE (CO-5) are described elsewhere in this
chapter. The COLORADO GHOST TOWN AND MINING CAMP-
GUIDE (1978, 112 p.) contains many detailed maps (1/2 in. represents
1 mile) on which all ghost towns and mining camps, campgrounds,
railroads, and wagon and stage roads are located including all jeep
and hiking trails. The text and picture provide much interesting
historic background. The COLORADO FISHING GUIDE (1977, 112 p.)
contains many detailed river drainage maps showing good fishing locations, and camping and recreation areas as well as useful tables and
much practical how-to information. All of these titles are updated
frequently.

MAJOR TOURIST ORGANIZATION

CO-19   COLORADO TRAVEL MARKETING SECTION, Division of Commerce &
Development, 500 State Centennial Bldg., 1313 Sherman Street, Denver, CO 80203 (303/839-3045).

They issue COLORFUL COLORADO INVITES YOU (a large booklet

that describes points of interest in 9 regions of the state); a calendar of events (which has a 2-page listing of information sources); COLO-RADIO MINI-TOURS (briefly describes 15 tours); and COLORADO AD-VENTURE GUIDE (describes and lists information sources for backpacking, ballooning, bicycling, boating, camping, children's camps, Denver mountain parks, fishing, golfing, hunting, Indian lore, jeeping, rafting, railroading, rock-hounding, tennis, and winter recreation).

OTHER ORGANIZATIONS

CO-20 COLORADO DUDE AND GUEST RANCH ASSOCIATION, Box 6440, Cherry Creek Station, Denver, CO 80206 (303/674-4906).

They issue an annual directory of guest ranches (the 1978 edition listed 42).

CO-21 COLORADO MOUNTAIN CLUB, 2530 West Alameda Avenue, Denver, CO 80219.

They issue a large number of hiking, climbing, and other trail guides, and they have conducted outdoor hikes, walks, snowshoe treks, ski tours, etc. since 1912.

CO-22 COLORADO-WYOMING HOTEL & MOTEL ASSOCIATION, Radisson Denver Hotel, Penthouse #4, 1790 Grant Street, Denver, CO 80203 (303/839-1151).

CO-23 ROCKY MOUNTAIN MOTORISTS, 4100 East Arkansas Avenue, Denver, CO 80222 (303/753-8800).

This association is affiliated with the American Automobile Association (US-259) and issues 2 annual publications. The comprehensive WHERE TO VACATION IN COLORADO (1978 ed., 160 p.) has been published since 1928 and contains city-by-city descriptions of scenic drives, attractions, points of interest, and historic background; general information on national forests, parks, and monuments, state recreation areas, forts, ghost towns, backpacking, camping, fishing, skiing, and boating; and a listing of AAA approved motels, hotels, campgrounds, and restaurants. WINTER VACATION IN COLORADO (1978-79 ed., 128 p.), first published in 1978, briefly describes ski areas throughout the state and nearby points of interest, but it is mostly a listing of AAA approved motels, hotels, and restaurants. Both are free to AAA members, but nonmembers may purchase copies.

INFORMATION CENTERS/INFORMATION PHONES

There is a toll-free number to the Travel Marketing Section (CO-19): 800/525-3083. The Dept. of Highways has recorded road conditions reports at 303/630-

1234 or 630-1515. These are especially valuable if you are doing high altitude driving in the Rockies.

OUTDOOR RECREATION ACTIVITIES

BICYCLING. See CO-32.

CANOEING AND BOATING. Contact the Colorado Division of Parks & Recreation, 618 State Centennial Bldg., 1313 Sherman Street, Denver, CO 80203.

FISHING AND HUNTING. Contact the Colorado Division of Wildlife, 6060 Broadway, Denver, CO 80216. They issue, among other publications, the bimonthly COLORADO OUTDOORS written for the layman and containing year-round information on hunting, fishing, camping, boating, and conservation. Two guides, TIM KELLEY'S COLORADO-WYOMING FISHING AND CAMPING GUIDE and TIM KELLEY'S COLORADO-WYOMING HUNTING AND CAMPING GUIDE, are available from: No. 1 Livestock Exchange Bldg., Denver, CO 80216. See also the COLORADO FISHING GUIDE issued by Colorado Recreation Guides (CO-18).

WINTER ACTIVITIES. Colorado Ski County USA, Brownleigh Court, 1410 Grant Street, Denver, CO 80203 (303/837-0973) issues a very detailed annual guide to all the state's downhill ski areas, ski touring areas, and accommodations at skiing areas. This address is a walk-in information center, and the organization also provides a daily recorded snow report at 303/837-9907. The U.S. Ski Association, Rocky Mountain Division, 1463 Larimer, Denver, CO 80202 issues THE ANNUAL OF ROCKY MOUNTAIN SKIING, a very thorough guide of over 100 pages to all Rocky Mountain ski areas. Information on ski touring and snowmobiling will be found in the COLORADO ADVENTURE GUIDE available from the Travel Marketing Section (CO-19). See also CO-2, CO-15, CO-16, WINTER VACATION IN COLORADO issued by Rocky Mountain Motorists (CO-23), and COLORADO WINTER SPORTS GUIDE issued by the Denver & Colorado Convention & Visitors Bureau (CO-33).

NATIONAL/STATE PARKS/FORESTS, ETC.

Dinosaur National Monument

CO-24 DINOSAUR NATIONAL MONUMENT, Box 210, Dinosaur, CO 81610 (303/374-2216).

They issue a mini map/brochure; provide information on campgrounds, hiking, fishing, river trips, etc.; and operate a major visitor center at Dinosaur Quarry, 7 miles north of Jensen, UT which is open 8A.M.-8P.M. in the summer and 8A.M.-4:30 in the winter. There

Colorado

is also a Headquarters Visitor Center located at Dinosaur, CO. The Dinosaur Nature Association provides interpretive materials and trail guide leaflets for sale at the visitor centers. See also W-5.

Mesa Verde National Park

CO-25   MESA VERDE NATIONAL PARK, Mesa Verde National Park, CO 81330.

They publish a mini map/brochure and information on the various cliff dwellings located within the Park, on accommodations and services, campgrounds, hiking, etc. Far View Visitor Center, the park's major information center, is only open during the summer from 8A.M.-5P.M. The Chapin Mesa Museum (Park Headquarters) is open year-round (8A.M.-6P.M. in the summer; 8A.M.-5P.M. the rest of the year), and you can obtain help here in planning your visit as well as answers to your questions. The Mesa Verde Museum Association, Box 38, Mesa Verde, CO 81330 issues a list of selected reference books they sell to help you better enjoy the Park and the American southwest.

See also CO-27.

Rocky Mountain National Park

CO-26   Dannen, Kent, and Dannen, Donna. ROCKY MOUNTAIN NATIONAL PARK HIKING TRAILS: INCLUDING INDIAN PEAKS. Charlotte, NC: East Woods Press, 1978. 288 p. Maps, sketches. Bibliography. Index. 0-914788-06-X. 77-25701.

Over 45 trail or trail systems are described. The maps are adapted from the "Resource Base Maps" prepared by the U.S. Forest Service (US-238). There is a lengthy destination table which gives, among other things, the starting point, distance, and elevation gain.

CO-27   A PHOTOGRAPHIC AND COMPREHENSIVE GUIDE TO ROCKY MOUNTAIN & MESA VERDE NATIONAL PARKS. Caspar, WY: World-Wide Research and Publishing Co., National Parks Division, 1975. 86 p. Photos., maps. 75-332952.

This book contains mostly stunning photographs. The 2 parks are discussed in separate sections, and there is a road guide and brief mention of recreation opportunities and facilities, including visitor centers, for each. The Rocky Mountain National Park section includes descriptions of trails and the Mesa Verde National Park section has a fairly extensive treatment of the archaeological excavations and the culture of the dwellers. There is no index.

CO-28   ROCKY MOUNTAIN NATIONAL PARK, Estes Park, CO 80517.

They issue a map/brochure which shows the major roads, trails, and visitor facilities throughout the park. There are 4 visitor information centers within the park. The one at Park Headquarters, just west of Estes Park, is open year-round. The Moraine Park Visitor Center located just a little farther west, and in the most concentrated area of the park, is open May to October. Alpine Visitor Center, located on Trail Ridge Road near the western boundary of the Park, is open June to October. The West Unit Office is located at the southwest entrance to the park and is also the source of information for the nearby Shadow Mountain National Recreation Area. The Rocky Mountain Nature Association, also at the above address, issues several trail guides to the park. An auto tape tour (CA-80) to the park is available for rent from the National Park Village in Estes Park or from the Grand Lake Chamber of Commerce near the southwest entrance.

CO-29   ESTES PARK CHAMBER OF COMMERCE, Box 3050, Estes Park, CO 80517 (303/586-4431).

They issue FUN GUIDE (a thorough annual guide to activities, amusements, shops, bicycling, churches, commercial services, restaurants, etc.), LODGING GUIDE, and WINTER FUN GUIDE (an annual guide containing basically the same information as in the above FUN GUIDE and having nothing specifically on winter sports). In Denver you can call them at 303/573-3880. You can call 800/525-5616 for weather, activities, road, and ski information.

Information and detailed visitor and travel maps for each of the 11 national forests in Colorado is best obtained by writing the U.S. Forest Service, Rocky Mountain Region, 11177 West 8th Avenue, Box 25127, Lakewood, CO 80225 (303/234-4185). They will also supply the different addresses and phone numbers of each national forest and its individual ranger districts.

The Bureau of Land Management (BLM), Colorado State Office, Room 700, Colorado State Bank Bldg., 1600 Broadway, Denver, CO 80202 provides several recreation sites in Colorado, but apparently has no maps available to either these or other BLM lands throughout the state, since no information was sent in reply to our request.

The Colorado Division of Parks and Outdoor Recreation, 1313 Sherman Street, Room 618, Denver, CO 80203 (303/892-3437) provides an overall brochure describing state parks and recreation areas and facilities available at each. Individual maps of each park and recreation area are also available.

INDIVIDUAL CITIES OR AREAS

Denver—Printed Materials

CO-30   A GUIDEBOOK TO DENVER FOR THE HANDICAPPED. Denver:

Architectural Barriers Committee, n.d.   60 p.

CO-31   Winter, Margaret A.   EXPLORING DENVER WITH CHILDREN
YOUNG AND OLD.   Boulder, CO: Lexicon Co.   (1025 Fifth
Street, Geneva Park/80302), 1971.   137 p.   72-176101.

This very comprehensive guide is arranged in chapters by general
subjects, the largest of which are those on sports and recreation;
business tours; people, ethnic activities, and restaurants; and theater,
music, and performances.   There is also a calendar of events and a
list of activities, by geographical area, outside Denver.

CO-32   Wolfe, Frederick L.   BICYCLE DENVER: 107 BICYCLE TOURS.
Denver: Graphic Impressions, 1976.   264 p.   Maps.   0-914628-08-9.
76-18591.

After the usual biking tips, telephone numbers, etc., this book reproduces, somewhat faintly, portions of the appropriate USGS topographic maps with the individual bike tours marked, indicating danger-
ous spots and portages.   Opposite each map page is a log page
noting distance, topography, points of interest, and special conditions,
with space for personal notes.   The book is impressive.

Rand McNally (US-215) issues a Denver/Colorado Springs/Pueblo Map.   Exxon
(US-261) issues a Denver/Colorado Springs map.   Other Denver maps are avail-
able from Arrow Publishing Co. (US-199), Champion Map. Corp. (US-202),
Goushā (US-206), and Hotchkiss, 4055 Fox, Denver, CO 80216.   A city
bicycle map is available from the Denver Dept. of Parks & Recreation, Parks
Planning Division, 1805 Bryant Street, Denver, CO 80204.

The weather information number in Denver is 303/639-1212.

Denver—Organizations

CO-33   DENVER & COLORADO CONVENTION & VISITORS BUREAU, 225
West Colfax Avenue, Denver, CO 80202 (303/892-1505).

They issue COLORADO ACCOMMODATIONS GUIDE, COLORADO
DINING GUIDE, COLORADO WINTER SPORTS GUIDE (an alphabetical listing of all areas featuring winter sports, giving specific information for participating in each type of activity), and GUIDE TO
DENVER ATTRACTIONS.

CONNECTICUT

BOOKS, ATLASES, MAGAZINES

CT-1   Bixby, William. CONNECTICUT: A NEW GUIDE. New York: Charles Scribner's Sons, 1974. 386 p. Index. 0-684-13787-9. 73-20261.

This book is in 3 sections: an overall statewide background, descriptions of towns and cities arranged alphabetically and including "see and do" information, and extensive appendixes providing concise information on cultural and recreational activities.

CT-2   CONNECTICUT: A GUIDE TO ITS ROADS, LORE AND PEOPLE. American Guide Series. Boston: Houghton Mifflin, 1938. 593 p. Photos., maps.

This original WPA guide is in 3 sections: general background, descriptions and city tours for 24 towns, and mile-by-mile descriptions of the state's highways.

CT-3   CONNECTICUT OUTDOOR RECREATION GUIDE. Hartford, CT: Connecticut Forest and Park Association, 1976. 109 p. Photos., drawings, map.

This is a guide to parks, forests, and sanctuaries. It includes information about facilities available at each.

CT-4   CONNECTICUT WALK BOOK. 11th ed. Hartford, CT: Connecticut Forest and Park Association, 1975. Revised frequently. 181 p. Maps.

A definitive book on trails for the state, this work gives a description and the location of each trail, noting on which USGS quadrangles the trail appears. The maps are attached to the text and fold out.

CT-5   Cullen, Mae T., and Wolfeck, Dorothy F. CONNECTICUT TRIPS: WHAT, WHEN, WHERE. Waterbury, CT: Heminway Corp., 1971. 130 p. Photos. Index. 77-147410.

Compiled with genteel competence, this thematically arranged guide lists and locates major attractions, giving hours, fees, telephone number, and a little background.

CT-6   Detels, Pamela, and Harris, Janet. CANOEING: TRIPS IN CONNECTICUT, THE LONG AND SHORT OF IT. . . . Madison, CT: Birch Run Press, 1977. 128 p. Maps, photos. 0-87106-087-6. 76-58215.

Twenty selected canoe trips on Connecticut waters (rivers, lakes, marshes, tidelands) are briefly located and described with so-so maps for each. There is a short list of major outfitters.

CT-7   Griffith, Jane, and Mullen, Edwin. SHORT BIKE RIDES IN CONNECTICUT. Chester, CT: Pequot Press, 1976. 71 p. Maps. 0-87106-054-X. 75-1924.

Thirty rides from 8 to 25 miles long and ranging in difficulty from flat to hilly are described, including directions on how to get there and a sketch map. These were planned for the cyclist who likes to take his or her time, savor the countryside, and explore things along the way.

CT-8   Keyarts, Eugene. SHORT WALKS IN CONNECTICUT. Chester, CT: Pequot Press, 1968. 85 p. Maps. 68-24038.

CT-9   _____. 42 MORE SHORT WALKS IN CONNECTICUT. Chester, CT: Pequot Press, 1972. 87 p. Maps. 74-187173.

CT-10   _____. SHORT WALKS IN CONNECTICUT: VOLUME 3. Chester, CT: Pequot Press, 1973. 87 p. Maps. 68-24038.

The first volume describes 41 walks and volume 3 describes 42, most of which are on the Connecticut Blue Trails System. Most of the hikes average about 2 to 3 miles in length and are not difficult. Actual trail directions are minimal (the author uses more space telling you how to reach the trail by car), and each accompanying sketch map only shows relationships of trails to roads and landmarks. This is a series for the beginner.

MAPS

The Connecticut highway map is available from the Division of Tourism (CT-11). The 1977-78 edition lists attractions; public recreation areas; ski areas; railroad stations, ferries, and airports; public boat launching sites; covered bridges; information on fishing and hunting, on state parks and forests, and on off-track betting and pari-mutuel facilities. AAA (US-259), Goushā (US-206), and Rand McNally (US-215) each issue a combined map of Connecticut/Massachusetts/Rhode Island.

MAJOR TOURIST ORGANIZATION

CT-11   CONNECTICUT DEPT. OF COMMERCE, DIVISION OF TOURISM,
210 Washington Street, Hartford, CT 06106 (203/566-3385).

They issue 1 major booklet which lists and describes points of interest,
campgrounds, golf courses, salt water fishing, swimming, theaters,
fall activities, winter activities, list of events, and a hotel/motel/
resort guide.

OTHER ORGANIZATIONS

CT-12   CONNECTICUT HOTEL & MOTEL ASSOCIATION, 10 Ford Street,
Hartford, CT 06103. 203/522-0747.

They issue an annual directory of hotels, motels, inns, and resorts.

INFORMATION CENTERS/INFORMATION PHONES

The state maintains 7 highway information centers. A list of these is available
from the Connecticut Dept. of Transportation, Office of Communications, 24
Wolcott Hill Road, Wethersfield, CT 06109. Call 800/243-1685 for toll-free
Connecticut travel information.

OUTDOOR RECREATION ACTIVITIES

BICYCLING. A CONNECTICUT RIDE BOOK (unexamined by the compilers)
is supposed to describe 30 to 40 rides and be available from the Connecticut
Dept. of Environmental Protection, Information & Education, State Office Bldg.,
Hartford, CT: 06115. See also CT-7.

CANOEING AND BOATING. A GUIDE TO PUBLIC ACCESS TO CONNEC-
TICUT FISHING WATERS (listing boat launching facilities) and a CONNECTI-
CUT CANOEING GUIDE are available from the Connecticut Dept. of Environmental Protection, Information & Education, State Office Bldg., Hartford, CT
06115. See also CT-6.

FISHING AND HUNTING. A HUNTING GUIDE TO WILDLIFE MANAGE-
MENT AREAS (describes each area including map, type of game found, and
name of topographic map to use), A GUIDE TO PUBLIC ACCESS TO CON-
NECTICUT FISHING WATERS (see "Canoeing and Boating" above for description), a list of salt water fishing boats for charter, and hunting and fishing
rules and regulations are available from the Connecticut Dept. of Environmental
Protection, Information & Education, State Office Bldg., Hartford, CT 06115.

WINTER ACTIVITIES. Brief information about facilities at the state's downhill ski areas, and a list of cross-county ski areas are included in an annual flyer describing all winter sports and events that is available from the Division of Tourism (CT-11). A brochure on snowmobile trails and rules and regulations is available from the Connecticut Dept. of Environmental Protection, Information & Education, State Office Bldg., Hartford, CT 06115.

NATIONAL/STATE PARKS/FORESTS, ETC.

There are no national parks or national forests in Connecticut. For information and brochures on camping areas, state parks, and forests, contact the Connecticut Dept. of Environmental Protection, Information & Education, State Office Bldg., Hartford, CT 06115.

INDIVIDUAL CITIES OR AREAS

Hartford—Printed Materials

CT-13   Arrow Publishing Co. OFFICIAL ARROW STREET MAP ATLAS, METRO-POLITAN HARTFORD: INCLUDING 50 CITIES AND TOWNS, CAMPUS MAPS OF CENTRAL CONNECTICUT STATE COLLEGE, TRINITY COLLEGE, WESLEYAN UNIVERSITY. Boston: Arrow, 1974. 91 p. Scales very. Index. 76-354055.

CT-14   GREATER HARTFORD HANDBOOK FOR THE HANDICAPPED. Hartford: Architecture for Everyone Committee, 1968. 48 p.

A good map of Hartford is available from the Champion Map Corp. (US-202).

Hartford—Organizations

CT-15   GREATER HARTFORD CONVENTION AND VISITORS BUREAU, One Civic Center Plaza, Hartford, CT 06103 (203/728-6789).

They issue a GREATER HARTFORD VISITORS GUIDE (descriptions of points of interest, accommodations, and restaurants), a map, and a self-guided walking tour brochure.

Mystic—Printed Materials

CT-16   Colby, Jean P. MYSTIC SEAPORT: THE AGE OF SAIL. The Famous Museum Series. New York: Hastings House, 1970. 96 p. Photos., maps. Bibliography. Index. 0-8038-4652-5. 69-15055.

Although not primarily a guide, this book does provide descriptions and background for all the buildings and points of interest in this reconstructed seaport museum town. There is a glossary.

CT-17   MYSTIC SEAPORT GUIDE. Mystic: Marine Historical Association,
        1972. 64 p. Sketches, maps. Index.

        This is a guide to hold in your hand and read as you walk from
        building to building around Mystic Seaport.

Mystic—Organizations

CT-18   MYSTIC SEAPORT, Mystic, CT 06355 (203/536-2631).

        They provide a guide, a map, a calendar of events, and information
        about youth education programs and adult group visits.

CT-19   NEW ENGLAND TOURIST INFORMATION, Olde Mistick Village,
        Mystic, CT 06355 (203/536-1641).

        This is a nonprofit tourist information facility sponsored by the South-
        eastern Connecticut and Mystic Chambers of Commerce. Open 7 days
        a week, year-round, they provide accommodations assistance; display
        over 35 current local restaurant menus; and provide information on
        attractions, sightseeing tours, vehicle rentals, fishing, public recrea-
        tion areas.

New Haven—Printed Materials

CT-20   Byers, Jane C., and McClure, Ruth E. ENJOYING NEW HAVEN:
        A GUIDE TO THE AREA. 4th ed. Hamden, CT: 'Round-the-Town
        Publications (Box 6191/06517), 1974. 119 p. Photos., maps.
        Index.

        This guide to the city for both visitors and tourists includes every-
        thing from an architectural tour of Yale University to bargain shop-
        ping.

CT-21   NEW HAVEN INFO. New Haven: General Advertising & Publishing
        (53 Orange Street/06510).

        This is a monthly guide to accommodations; dining; cultural, recrea-
        tion, and sporting events; and points of interest. It also includes a
        radio, transportation, and telephone directory.

Good maps of New Haven are available from the Arrow Publishing Co. (US-
199), Champion Map Corp. (US-202), and the local AAA office.

New Haven—Organizations

CT-22   GREATER NEW HAVEN CHAMBER OF COMMERCE, 195 Church Street,
        New Haven, CT 06510 (203/787-6735).

DELAWARE

BOOKS, ATLASES, MAGAZINES

DE-1   DELAWARE TODAY MAGAZINE. Wilmington (2401 Pennyslvania
        Avenue/19806).

        This is a monthly magazine touching on all phases of life in Dela-
        ware. There is a regular travel column which frequently features
        points of interest in the greater Delaware Valley. There is also a
        regular "Going Places" column which lists art, music, theater, sports,
        events, plus a regular "Restaurant Guide."

DE-2   Detchon, Helen A., and Detchon, Elliott R. THE "GO . . . DON'T
        GO" GUIDE TO DELAWARE AND NEARBY PENNSYLVANIA.
        Greenville, DE: the authors (Box 4257/19807), 1976. 160 p.
        Photos., maps. Bibliography.

        Sixty-five museums, historic houses, and famous places in Delaware
        and 18 in nearby Pennsylvania (excluding Philadelphia) are described and
        rated on a scale of "must see" to "limited interest." Additional
        sections list parks, restaurants, a calendar of events, and a glossary.

DE-3   Eckman, Jeannette. DELAWARE: A GUIDE TO THE FIRST STATE.
        Rev. ed. American Guide Series. New York: Hastings House, 1955.
        562 p. Photos., maps.

        This is a revision of the original WPA guide keeping the format of
        the first 1938 edition. General background on the state is provided
        as well as descriptions of 8 major cities and towns, and 16 highway
        tours.

DE-4   A GUIDE TO NORTHERN DELAWARE FOR THE DISABLED. Wilming-
        ton, DE: Easter Seal Society of Del-Mar, 1974. 23 p.

DE-5   Jones, Richard H., and Jones, Louise H. WHEELING AROUND
        DELAWARE. N.p., the authors, 1973. 111 p. Maps.

Eighty-one bicycle rides in northern Delaware and adjacent Maryland, Pennsylvania, and New Jersey are listed, noting distance and some hazards. The maps for each ride are well enough drawn, but some are badly reproduced in the copies examined.

MAPS

The official map is available from the State Visitors Service (DE-6). The 1976 edition (this was the latest edition in 1978) contains insets of Wilmington and Dover and a mileage chart. AAA (US-259), Exxon (US-261), Goushā (US-206), and Rand McNally (US-215) each put out a combined Delaware/Maryland/Virginia/West Virginia map.

MAJOR TOURIST ORGANIZATION

DE-6   DELAWARE STATE VISITORS SERVICE, Division of Economic Development, 630 State College Road, Dover, DE 19901 (302/678-4254).

They issue a semiannual calendar of events, CAMPING IN DELAWARE, BICENTENNIAL HERITAGE TRAIL, DOVER HERITAGE TRAIL, NEW CASTLE HERITAGE TRAIL, LEWES HERITAGE TRAIL (the various "trail" guides describe attractions, including hours and admission fees), and a brochure describing walks in Delaware state parks.

OTHER ORGANIZATIONS

DE-7   DELAWARE HOTEL-MOTEL ASSOCIATION, Box 2192, Wilmington, DE 19899 (302/656-8121).

DE-8   DELAWARE STATE CHAMBER OF COMMERCE, 1102 West Street, Wilmington, DE 19801 (302/655-7221).

This is not a primary source of travel information for Delaware, but it does issue a brochure on Wilmington and a list of places of interest in Delaware.

INFORMATION CENTERS/INFORMATION PHONES

The official highway map locates highway information centers with a symbol.

OUTDOOR RECREATION ACTIVITIES

BICYCLING. See DE-5.

FISHING AND HUNTING. Contact the Delaware Dept. of Natural Resources and Environmental Control, Tatnall Bldg., Box 1401, Dover, DE 19901.

NATIONAL/STATE PARKS/FORESTS, ETC.

There are no national parks or national forests in Delaware.

A brochure, DELAWARE OUTDOORS, describing state parks and wildlife areas, is available from either the State Visitors Service (DE-6) or the Delaware Dept. of Natural Resources and Environmental Control, Tatnall Bldg., Box 1401, Dover, DE 19901.

INDIVIDUAL CITIES OR AREAS

Dover—Printed Materials

Franklin Survey Co., 1201 Race Street, Philadelphia, PA 19107 puts out a good map of Dover.

Dover—Organizations

DE-9   GREATER DOVER CHAMBER OF COMMERCE, Treadway Towers, Suite A, Box 576, Dover, DE 19901.

Wilmington—Printed Materials

Arrow Publishing Co. (US-199), Champion Map Corp. (US-202), and Franklin Survey Co., 1201 Race Street, Philadelphia, PA 19107 all issue maps of Wilmington.

Wilmington—Organizations

See DE-8.

DISTRICT OF COLUMBIA

BOOKS, ATLASES, MAGAZINES

DC-1   Alexandria Drafting Co. WASHINGTON, D.C. & VICINITY STREET
        MAP. Alexandria, VA: 1977. 24 p. Scale: 1 in. represents
        2,000 ft. Indexes.

DC-2   Babb, Laura L., ed. THE WASHINGTON POST GUIDE TO WASH-
        INGTON. New York: McGraw-Hill, 1976. 354 p. Photos.,
        maps. Index. 0-07-068393-X. 75-20191.

        Each chapter is by a staff member of the WASHINGTON POST most
        familiar with the particular aspect of Washington being examined.
        There is quite a bit of political background, and the tourist informa-
        tion is scattered throughout the book. There are separate lists of
        restaurants, accommodations, and emergency telephone numbers. Sub-
        urban Washington is included in the coverage.

DC-3   Berkowitz, Alan, and Gilbert, Dave. GREATER WASHINGTON AREA
        BICYCLE ATLAS WITH MAPS, DESCRIPTIONS AND RESOURCES FOR
        CYCLING IN THE MID-ATLANTIC STATES. 2d ed. Washington:
        Potomac Area Council of the American Youth Hostels & Washington
        Area Bicycle Association, 1977. 127 p. Maps.

        Sixty-three bike trips are briefly described, nothing length, terrain
        and surface, points of interest, and difficult spots. Each trip has a
        map.

DC-4   THE BEST OF WASHINGTON: THE WASHINGTONIAN MAGAZINE'S
        GUIDE TO LIFE IN THE NATION'S CAPITAL. Washington: Wash-
        ingtonian Books, 1977. 204 p. Maps, photos. Index. 0-915168-
        25-1. 77-77003.

        This guide covers Washington, DC's history, practical advice to
        travelers, walking tours, 1-day trips, entertainment and sports, out-
        doors, fun with children, where to eat, and shopping. It was pub-
        lished in 1975 as WASHINGTON: THE OFFICIAL BICENTENNIAL
        GUIDEBOOK.

DC-5   Bryant, Beth. WASHINGTON, D.C. ON $15 A DAY. New York:
        Arthur Frommer (distributed by Simon & Schuster), 1978. 279 p.
        Maps, sketches.

        This is a penny-pinching guide to where to stay, where to eat,
        sights to see, nightlife, shops, outdoor activities, and cultural activi-
        ties. There are chapters for international visitors, children, and one
        outlining 4 do-it-yourself tours. It includes the historic towns in
        Virginia plus Annapolis, MD.

DC-6   CAPITAL: THE INSIDER'S GUIDE TO WASHINGTON. Falls Church,
        VA: Capital Magazine Publishing Co. (Box 223/22046).

        This is the most informative and easily used of the several free guides
        to Washington that can be picked up almost anywhere. It contains
        a fold-out map; a calendar of events; a guide to Washington area
        museums, art galleries, churches, historic landmarks, and other points
        of interest; a restaurant review; information on how to use METRO
        (the subway system); a shopping guide; and a television schedule.
        The April 1978 issue examined for this information guide also de-
        scribed walking tours of Alexandria and Georgetown.

DC-7   CAPITAL BELTWAY GUIDE & ATLAS. Olney, MD: Marjec, 1972.
        135 p. Diagrams, maps. 72-193509.

        Presented here are detailed schematic diagrams for each of the 38
        exits on the Capital Beltway (Interstate 495) indicating traffic patterns
        for entering and leaving the Beltway. There are general area maps
        for each exit with lists of shopping centers, communities, parks,
        schools, etc. near the exit. Included is a good bit of interesting,
        if irrelevant, information on living in the area. An invaluable book
        --we wish there were more for other cities.

DC-8   Dresden, Donald. DONALD DRESDEN'S GUIDE TO DINING OUT
        IN WASHINGTON. Washington: Acropolis Books, 1977. 176 p.
        Photos. Indexes. 0-87491-189-3. 77-84325.

        The author rates each restaurant according to food, ambience, and
        rate value. Individual descriptions include address, phone, and price
        range. There are cuisine and geographic indexes. Almost half of
        the book is devoted to reproductions of individual restaurant advertise-
        ments.

DC-9   GREEN ACRES SCHOOL'S GOING PLACES WITH CHILDREN IN
        WASHINGTON. 8th ed. Edited by Elizabeth P. Mirel. Washing-
        ton: Washingtonian Books, 1976. 170 p. Drawings. Index.
        0-915168-16-2. 75-44627.

        In addition to the main sights to see, the compiler describes museums,
        historic sites, neighborhoods and nearby towns, nature, parks, restaur-

ants, shopping, sports, entertainment, and places where behind the scenes would be of interest to children.

DC-10   Heltzer, Paula W., and Levine, Ferne P.   SPOTS.   Rockville, MD: Penfer (Box 1122/20850), 1974.   139 p.   Diagrams.

Primarily a list of theaters, arenas, and stadiums in and around the District of Columbia, this has seating diagrams for many and descriptions of the general types of presentations along with box office telephone numbers.   There are separate lists for selected dinner theaters, spots for children, and "special" spots.

DC-11   Hodges, Allan A., and Hodges, Carol A., eds.   WASHINGTON ON FOOT: 25 WALKING TOURS OF WASHINGTON, D.C., OLD TOWN ALEXANDRIA, VIRGINIA AND HISTORIC ANNAPOLIS, MARYLAND.   Rev. ed.   Washington: Smithsonian Institution Press, 1977.   209 p.   Maps, drawings.   0-87474-525-X.   77-608098.

The very detailed descriptions of 25 walks concentrate almost exclusively on architectural attractions in the District of Columbia, Alexandria, and Annapolis.   They would be of most interest to those studying city planning.   Restaurants are recommended for each tour.

DC-12   Information Center for Handicapped Individuals.   ACCESS WASHINGTON: A GUIDE TO METROPOLITAN WASHINGTON FOR THE PHYSICALLY DISABLED.   Washington: the author, 1976.   131 p.   Map.

This is an appraisal of parking facilities, ease of entrance, internal access, rest rooms, and lowered phones for a cross section of Washington auditoriums and stadiums, banks, churches, government buildings, hospitals, hotels and motels, libraries, museums and galleries, recreation facilities, restaurants, sites of interest, theaters, and transportation facilities.

DC-13   Lasker, Toy.   FLASHMAPS!   THE 1977-78 INSTANT GUIDE TO WASHINGTON.   Chappaqua, NY: Flashmaps, 1977.   Updated annually.   80 p.   Maps.   75-6206.

Forty-six "flashmaps" indicate transportation, "national treasures," government buildings, hotels and motels, selected restaurants (including cafeterias and coffee shops), embassies, selected churches, outdoor statuary, art galleries, colleges and universities, hospitals, libraries, museums, theaters, sports and parks, and taxi zones.   Each map shows the locations of one of the above themes.   There are some building diagrams.   The book concentrates on Washington, but the suburbs are frequently included.   This is a very handy guide for the traveler.

DC-14   McCurdy, Howard E., et al.   AN INSIDER'S GUIDE TO THE CAPI-

TOL: THE COMPLETE WALKING TOUR. Washington: American University, College of Public Affairs, 1977. 96 p. Sketches. 77-151656.

This is an enticing, irreverent guide to the hallways and rooms of Capitol Hill never seen by tourists, with tips contributed by unnamed American University students, many of whom still worked there when this guide was written. Whether you really can get past the "Closed to Visitors" signs and the Capitol Police by wearing a coat and tie or skirt, assuming a business-like mien, and carrying a few stuffed file folders remains to be seen, but assuming you do, this guide will tell you which directions to take to find the various working and committee rooms in the House and Senate chambers. If you don't actually make it to the sacred corridors, you can use this book as an armchair guide to the daily workings of the puzzling legislative machinery there.

DC-15   Powell, Ron, and Cunningham, Bill. BLACK GUIDE TO WASHING- TON. Washington: Washingtonian Books, 1975. 124 p. Maps, photos. Index. 0-915168-09-X. 75-38201.

The authors include Washington's history from a black perspective; how to get around; points of interest for blacks in the District as well as Annapolis and Baltimore in Maryland, and Richmond, Williams- burg and Jamestown in Virginia; a guide for children; shopping and entertainment (a few restaurants are included); and a black directory (includes the names of the members of the Black Caucus of Congress, and of houses of worship). This guide needs to be updated.

DC-16   Smith, Jane O. THE ONE-DAY TRIP BOOK: 101 OFFBEAT EX- CURSIONS IN AND AROUND WASHINGTON. 2d ed. McLean, VA: EPM Publications, 1978. 182 p. Map. Bibliography. Index. 77-28497.

This book is adequate but doesn't completely live up to its title. All of the suggestions are good, but many of them cannot be enjoyed in 1 day if you also count driving time from Washington and back. There just isn't enough time, after driving (instructions are given from the Beltway, but often with no indication of how long the drive will take), to take the Youghiogheny white water trip, for example,or to see the 3 Mercer buildings in Doylestown, PA, or to explore Tangier Is- land. The suggestions are presented by the seasons of the year, a useful idea, but the writing style is pedestrian and often fails to catch the true flavor and excitement of each place. The excursions are indexed by type (including those suitable for the handicapped) and name.

DC-17   Staihar, Janet, and Barnes, Richard, comps. CAPITAL FEASTS: THE MENU GUIDE TO WASHINGTON AREA RESTAURANTS. 6th ed. Washington: Rock Creek Publishing Co. (Box 19273/20036), 1975. Unpaged.

This consists of reproductions of menus from over 120 selected restaurants in the DC area with added text indicating location, hours, credit cards accepted, and telephone number. The arrangement is by area. There is no index.

DC-18 THIS WEEK IN THE NATION'S CAPITAL. Washington: Aires Publishing Co. (5428 MacArthur Blvd., NW/20016).

This weekly guide to "dining, entertainment, theater, points of interest, shopping. . .distributed every Saturday in hotels, motor hotels, restaurants and clubs" has been published since 1920.

DC-19 Truett, Randall B., ed. WASHINGTON, D.C.: A GUIDE TO THE NATION'S CAPITAL. Rev. ed. American Guide Series. New York: Hastings House, 1968. 528 p. Photos, maps. Bibliography. Index. 67-25608.

This revision of the original 1942 WPA guide begins with a general background and then describes over 100 specific buildings, mostly federal, and a few parks. The Georgetown area and the points of interest along Pennsylvania, Massachusetts, and Connecticut Avenues and in Arlington, Alexandria, and Mount Vernon are also described. A list of statues, monuments, and memorials, and a chronology of Washington, D.C. history are included in appendixes.

DC-20 A WALKING GUIDE TO HISTORIC GEORGETOWN. Washington: Foundation for the Preservation of Historic Georgetown, 1971. 52 p. Photos., map. 76-188109.

This is a foot guide to 2 hours of historic and architectural Georgetown.

DC-21 WASHINGTON, D.C. Bethesda, MD: Aircraft Owners & Pilots Association, 1976.

The general tourist information included in this book (where to eat, where to stay, ground transportation, events) is secondary to the listing of 19 airports near Washington giving a very thorough description of facilities and features.

DC-22 Wrenn, Tony P. WASHINGTON, D.C. WALKING TOURS. Washington: Parks & History Association for the National Trust for Historic Preservation, 1975. 129 p. Maps, drawings. 75-9376.

The author describes walking tours of 2 1/2 to 3 hours duration of 3 major public (White House neighborhood, Mall, and Capitol) and 2 residential (Capitol Hill and Kalorama) areas pointing out the historical and architectural landmarks along the way.

MAPS

The WASHINGTON, D.C. AND METROPOLITAN AREA TRANSPORTATION

District of Columbia

MAP is available from the District of Columbia, Dept. of Transportation, Room 519, 415 12th Street NW, Washington, DC 20004. It is very large (scale: 1 in. represents 3,000 ft.) and complete and may be too extensive for most visitors. One side shows the greater metropolitan area and the other, the central Washington, DC area. The latter shows locations of embassies, points of interest, government offices and agencies, hotels/motels, theaters and clubs, transportation centers, and hospitals. Other good maps are a VISITOR'S GUIDE/MAP TO WASHINGTON, D.C. INCLUDING ANNAPOLIS, ALEXANDRIA AND MOUNT VERNON and a NATIONAL CAPITAL AND CHESAPEAKE BAY AREA map, both issued annually by the AAA office in Falls Church, VA (US-259). A McDONALD's CAPITAL SIGHTSEEING MAP locates both points of interest and McDonald's restaurants in Maryland, Washington, and Virginia. Exxon (US-261), Goushā (US-206), and Rand McNally (US-215) each also issue a map. The Metropolitan Washington Council of Governments issues an extensive map of BICYCLE PATHS IN THE WASHINGTON AREA. See also DC-1, DC-3, DC-13, and DC-33.

PUBLISHERS

DC-23   POTOMAC BOOKS, Box 40604, Washington, DC 20016 (202/338-5774).

They publish several guidebooks to the greater Washington, DC area.

DC-24   WASHINGTONIAN BOOKS, 1828 L Street NW, Washington, DC 20036 (202/296-3600).

They are a subsidiary of Washingtonian Magazine and have issued numerous volumes of interest to the traveler.

MAJOR TOURIST ORGANIZATION

DC-25   WASHINGTON AREA CONVENTION AND VISITORS ASSOCIATION, 1129 20th Street NW, Washington, DC 20036 (202/857-5500).

They issue 3 brochures: WELCOME TO WASHINGTON, D.C. (briefly describes the major points of interest and includes a map of the Mall area), WASHINGTON DINING (a 42-page guide listing over 200 restaurants of every range, style, and price in the Washington area), and EASY D.C. TOURING FOR HANDICAPPED. They have a recorded events message at 737-8866.

OTHER ORGANIZATIONS

DC-26   GATEWAY TOURCENTER, 4th and E Streets SW, Washington, DC 20024 (202/USA-0000).

This is a sort of one-stop "tourist shopping center" for free maps and brochures as well as a central location for purchasing various tour tickets. Several orientation presentations are available for a fee. Parking, shuttle services, and other tourist facilities are also available. The center is open 7 days a week and bilingual staff is on hand. Twenty-four hour tourist information is available by calling 202/554-2604.

DC-27   HOTEL ASSOCIATION OF WASHINGTON, D.C., 910 17th Street NW, Suite 512, Washington, DC 20006 (202/833-3350).

DC-28   INTERNATIONAL VISITORS SERVICE COUNCIL OF GREATER WASHINGTON ORGANIZATIONS, 801 19th Street NW, Washington, DC 20006 (202/872-8747 or 202/USA-TRIP).

They provide sightseeing, accommodations, restaurants, etc. information in foreign languages (they issue the major general Washington, DC brochure WELCOME TO WASHINGTON, D.C. in French, Japanese, German, Spanish, and Italian), and 24-hour emergency assistance in 49 languages. They also have multilingual brochures to many individual attractions. Their services are available Monday-Friday, 9A.M.-5P.M. at the Information and Reception Center at the above address, and at the National Visitor Center (DC-30) and Dulles International Airport 7 days a week.

DC-29   NATIONAL CAPITAL PARKS, National Park Service, 1100 Ohio Drive SW, Washington, DC 20242.

DC-30   NATIONAL VISITOR CENTER, Union Station, Massachusetts & Delaware Avenues, Washington, DC 20002 (202/523-5300).

This is the most complete information center in the area. It provides numerous brochures and visitor information assistance for the metropolitan DC area and surrounding states. It is manned Monday-Saturday, 8A.M.-8P.M. and on Sunday, 10A.M.-8P.M. Hotel/motel hotlines and multilanguage assistance are available. There is a National Book Store adjacent which is a good place to purchase local and other guidebooks.

DC-31   PUBLIC CITIZEN VISITORS CENTER, 1200 15th Street NW, Washington, DC 20005 (202/659-9053).

This organization was begun in the mid-1960s by Ralph Nader to provide information to visitors about sitting in on Congressional hearings, getting appointments with local Congressmen, and, in general, to provide visitors with an opportunity to see how the government really works. They issue INSIDE THE CAPITOL, a biweekly calendar of congressional events. They also provide information on guided tours, transportation, cultural events, etc. They're open Monday-Friday, 9A.M.-5P.M. and Saturday 9A.M.-1P.M.

DC-32   SMITHSONIAN VISITOR INFORMATION AND ASSOCIATES'
RECEPTION CENTER. Great Hall, Smithsonian Institution Building
("The Castle"), Washington, DC 20560 (202/381-6264).

This is the centralized information center for the Smithsonian Institution as a whole. Information desks in the major, individual museums and
galleries are staffed from 10A.M.-4P.M. daily. Dial-A-Museum at
737-8811 provides a daily summary of special events in Smithsonian
buildings.

DC-33   WASHINGTON METROPOLITAN AREA TRANSIT AUTHORITY, Community Service Office, 600 5th Street NW, Washington, DC 20001
(202/637-2437).

The above number is to the Route and Schedule Information Office.
They operate 6 transit information centers throughout Washington, DC.
Call 627-1328 for the location of the nearest information center.
Call 637-1261 if you wish to have a schedule sent. Each schedule
has a route map on it. There is a 79-page METRO RIDE GUIDE
that includes neighborhood maps of all metrorail stations, information
on metrobuses serving each station; and hotels, restaurants, shops,
theaters, and points of interest near each metrorail station. A
METROBUS TOUR GUIDE is a map/brochure to the Mall area showing which bus routes stop at the popular points of interest and also
whether eating facilities and guided tours are available. When it
comes to providing extensive, good, courteous transit information,
this system is one of the best in the US.

FLORIDA

BOOKS, ATLASES, MAGAZINES

FL-1   Firestone, Linda, and Morse, Whit. THE FIRESTONE/MORSE GUIDE TO FLORIDA'S ENCHANTING ISLANDS: SANIBEL & CAPTIVA. 2d ed. Richmond, VA: Good Life Publishers, 1978. 123 p. Photos., map. 0-917374-07-X. 78-56041.

Major emphasis is on wildlife and seashells, but fairly extensive lists of restaurants, shops, fishing facilities, and accommodations are also offered. There is no index.

FL-2   FLORIDA: A GUIDE TO THE SOUTHERNMOST STATE. American Guide Series. New York: Oxford University Press, 1939. 600 p. Photos., maps.

This is the original WPA guide in the usual format followed by most volumes in the American Guide Series: background, descriptions of 12 principal cities, and 22 state-wide highway tours.

FL-3   THE FLORIDA BICENTENNIAL TRAIL: A HERITAGE REVISITED. Tallahassee: Bicentennial Commission of Florida in cooperation with the Florida Dept. of Commerce, 1976. 134 p. Photos., maps. Bibliography. 76-624408.

Fifty-two sites contributing to Florida's heritage are described, accompanied by old photographs, a map, and a brief notation of other local points of interest. It is arranged by chronological periods.

FL-4   FLORIDA GOLF GUIDE. Sarasota, FL: Carey, Inc. for the Florida Golf Association (Drawer 1298/33578), 1978. Issued annually. 80 p. Maps. Indexes.

Published since 1976, this guide lists country clubs, golf clubs, golf courses, etc. in 8 geographic sections. Clubs with tennis only are also listed in the appropriate geographic section. Several articles on golf, an events schedule, and indexes to golf and tennis clubs are scattered throughout the booklet.

FL-5   FLORIDA 1976. The American Guides. Pompano Beach, FL: Philippe de Vosjoli & Sons, 1976. 282 p. Maps. 0-916264-00-9. 75-36315.

A short "yellow pages" section gives general information about living and getting around in Florida. Then follows information on more than 150 cities and towns, arranged alphabetically by name, and giving for each: basic information (transportation, communications, etc.), history, points of interest, sports and recreation facilities, useful addresses, hotels and motels, and restaurants. This guide is also available in a Spanish edition (GUIA DE LA FLORIDA EN ESPAÑOL).

FL-6   FODOR'S FLORIDA 1979. New York: David McKay Co., 1979. 343 p. Maps. Index. 0-679-00429-7.

Numerous useful facts are crammed into this good guide. Information on planning a trip, weather, and general costs is followed by information on cities, areas, and attractions.

FL-7   GUIDE TO FLORIDA. 4th ed. Chicago. Rand McNally, 1977. 154 p. Photos., maps. Index. 0-528-84891-7. 77-080428.

This guide divides Florida into 7 geographic regions and describes points of interest and activities in the cities and towns of each. There are additional chapters on the state parks, what to see on the way to Florida, island hopping in the Bahamas and West Indies, a comprehensive campgrounds listing, and accommodations and restaurants arranged by locality.

FL-8   A GUIDE TO FLORIDA'S HISTORIC MARKERS. Tallahassee: Florida Dept. of State, Division of Archives, 1972. 116 p. Map.

The text of each historical marker is reproduced in this list arranged by county. There is no index.

FL-9   Hill, Jim, and Hill, Miriam. FABULOUS FLORIDA. Rev. ed. An Ambassador Guidebook. Clearwater, FL: Ambassador Publications, 1976. 360 p. Maps. Index.

Descriptions of "over 500 fun things to see and do" are regionally arranged.

FL-10   INTERNATIONAL TRAVEL GUIDE TO FLORIDA. 7th(?) ed. Hollywood, FL: Worth International Communications Corp. (Box 2226/ 33022), 1978. 224 p. Photos. Index.

This is a geographically arranged guide to selected attractions, accommodations, shopping, dining, entertainment, services, consulates, sources of additional information, etc. The information itself is adequate, but the guide suffers from uneven coverage and inconsistent arrangement of material. This is especially unfortunate in a guide whose stated purpose is to help the already supposedly confused international traveler to this country. There is an index, but it doesn't pull together all the scattered information. The volume is also available in Spanish, Portuguese, German, French, and Japanese.

FL-11   Osler, Jack M. 50 GREAT MINI-TRIPS IN FLORIDA. Dayton, OH: Media Ventures, 1977. 52 p. 0-89645-004-X.

Not examined, but this is probably very much like the Pennsylvania volume (PA-3) in this series.

FL-12   Puetz, C.J. GUIDE TO FUN IN FLORIDA. Tallahassee: Florida Bureau of Maps, 1974. 152 p. Maps, photos., drawings. Index.

The official state highway maps of each county are reproduced (at various scales) with an overprinting locating parks and providing information on fish camps and river tours. The brief text gives some county history, sights to see, and other recreational activities. The tables indicate the facilities at campsites, fish camps, and marinas.

FL-13   Stachowicz, Jim. DIVER'S GUIDE TO FLORIDA & THE FLORIDA KEYS. Miami: Windward Publications (Box 371005/33137), 1976. 64 p. Charts, photos. 0-89317-007-0. 76-12928.

Numerous charts show various type of diving sites suitable for every type from beginning snorkeling to advanced scuba. Accompanying descriptions provide much worthwhile practical site information. There is a beginning how-to section.

FL-14   Tolf, Robert W. BEST RESTAURANTS: FLORIDA. San Franciso: 101 Productions (distributed by Scribner), 1977. 207 p. Sketches. Indexes. 0-89286-132-0. 77-16740.

This book is arranged in the following areas: the panhandle, west coast, east coast and central area, Palm Beach area, Fort Lauderdale area, Miami area, and the Keys. Restaurant descriptions include address, phone number, hours, credit cards accepted, parking information, extent of bar service, and sometimes a reproduction of the menu. There are geographic, city, and cuisine indexes.

FL-15   Warnke, James R. SIDE ROADS OF FLORIDA. Boynton Beach, FL: Star Publishing Co. (distributed by Great Outdoors), 1973. 90 p. Photos., maps. 73-76416.

An interesting, but rambling, description of 12 less popular sights to see off the beaten track. Several others are briefly noted. This worthwhile book is designed for browsing.

MAPS

The official transportation map is available from the Division of Tourism (FL-16). The 1978 edition lists attractions found in Florida's 12 vacation regions; has a table of facilities at public recreation areas; lists pari-mutuel facilities; and has an interesting schematic of interchanges, service areas, and mileages along Florida's turnpike. AAA (US-259), Exxon (US-261), Goushā (US-206), and Rand McNally (US-215) each issue a good map of Florida. See also FL-12.

MAJOR TOURIST ORGANIZATION

FL-16   FLORIDA DEPT. OF COMMERCE, DIVISION OF TOURISM. Collins Bldg., Tallahassee, FL 32304 (904/487-1462).

They issue FLORIDA VACATION GUIDE (a very general booklet containing no specific information), an events calendar, a major league spring training schedule, and three guides for handicapped visitors: FLORIDA SIGHTSEEING FOR VISITORS WITH LIMITED MOBILITY, GETTING AROUND AT WALT DISNEY WORLD, and TROUT POND RECREATION AREAS FOR THE HANDICAPPED.

REGIONAL TOURISM ASSOCIATIONS

The state is divided into 12 vacation regions but the Division of Tourism (FL-16) should be contacted for information on each region.

OTHER ORGANIZATIONS

FL-17   FLORIDA ATTRACTIONS ASSOCIATION, Box 10116, Tallahassee, FL 32302 (904/222-5877).

They issue an OFFICIAL GUIDE MAP OF FLORIDA ATTRACTIONS.

FL-18   FLORIDA HOTEL & MOTEL ASSOCIATION, Box 1529, Tallahassee, FL 32302 (904/224-2888).

FLORIDA HOTEL & MOTEL TRAVELERS GUIDE is an annual directory of members of the Florida Hotel & Motel Association. It is arranged alphabetically by city and contains a list of toll-free numbers (to be used in Florida only) of 20 lodging chains.

FL-19   FLORIDA TRAIL ASSOCIATION, Box 13708, Gainesville, FL 32604 (904/378-8823).

The association sponsors the 1,300-mile Florida Trail running the length of Florida. Some portions of the trail are on public lands (national and state forests and state parks) and anyone is free to hike these sections. Others are on private lands and can be hiked by members only. The maps that the association issues to these private lands are available only to members.

FL-20 U.S. HIGHWAY 27 ASSOCIATION OF FLORIDA, Box 282, Babson Park, FL 33827 (813/638-1356 or 904/394-2145, ext. 6).

TRAVEL SCENIC-TOLL FREE 27 is a map/brochure showing State High-way 27 from Tallahassee to Miami and Route 1 from there to Key West. Members belonging to the association have their attractions, motels/hotels, campgrounds, restaurants, home development offices, and welcome centers (local chambers of commerce) described and keyed to the map. It is primarily an advertising piece and is widely available to the traveler already in Florida. The association also issues a travel guide and directory which is sent in response to written requests. They operate an "infocenter" at Cleremont, FL on the north side of the Florida Citrus Tower parking area. Call 904/394-4191.

INFORMATION CENTERS/INFORMATION PHONES

The state operates 7 welcome centers where major highways enter the state and 1 on the Intercoastal Waterway at Fernandina Beach. They are open year-round from 8A.M.-5P.M.

OUTDOOR RECREATION ACTIVITIES

CANOEING AND BOATING. GUIDE TO FLORIDA CANOE TRAILS shows the approximate location, with maps, of 35 official canoe trails, lists recom-mended put-in and take-out points, mileages, and tips on individual trails. The folder is available from the Florida Dept. of Natural Resources, Crown Bldg., Tallahassee, FL 32304. CANOEING. . .YOUR APALACHICOLA, OSCEOLA & OCALA NATIONAL FORESTS, FLORIDA is available from: Forest Supervisor, National Forests in Florida, Box 1050, Tallahassee, FL 32302. The folder describes and gives maps for 10 trails. WEST FLORIDA CANOE TRAIL GUIDE by John O. DeLonge is available through the American Canoe Association (US-220). A directory of marine facilities and lists of coastal and inland launching facilities is available from the Florida Dept. of Natural Resources, Crown Bldg., Tallahassee, FL 32304. See also FL-12, FL-22, FL-31, FL-32, and FL-36.

FISHING AND HUNTING. Two guides to sportfishing are available from the Florida Dept. of Natural Resources, Crown Bldg., Tallahassee, FL 32304. ENJOY FLORIDA SPORTFISHING is mostly how-to, but it does have a chart showing regions and season where different types of fish may be caught. FLORIDA SALTWATER SPORTFISHING is a month-by-month guide to good fishing locations. The Florida Game and Fresh Water Fish Commission, Farris Bryant Bldg., Tallahassee, FL 32304 provides 5 regional guides to FRESH

Florida

WATER FISHING, FISH CAMPS & BOAT LANDINGS. The 5 regions are: northeast, northwest, central, south, and the Everglades. See also FL-12, FL-29, and TROUT POND RECREATION AREAS FOR THE HANDICAPPED issued by the Division of Tourism (FL-16).

NATIONAL/STATE PARKS/FORESTS, ETC.

Canaveral National Seashore

FL-21   CANAVERAL NATIONAL SEASHORE, Box 2583, Titusville, FL 32780 (305/867-4675).

This seashore was created in January 1975 from the northern portions of NASA's John F. Kennedy Space Center and Florida's Apollo State Park. The superintendent maintains a temporary office on State Route 402, 7 miles east of Titusville.

Everglades National Park

FL-22   Truesdell, William G. A GUIDE TO THE WILDERNESS WATERWAY OF THE EVERGLADES NATIONAL PARK. Coral Gables, FL: University of Miami Press in cooperation with the Everglades Natural History Association, 1969. 64 p. Charts, photos. 0-87024-119-2. 71-81621.

This is a compilation of charts (scale: 3.17 in. represents 1 mile) of the Wilderness Waterway, a 100 mile inside water route from Everglades City to Flamingo suitable for small craft. The charts show markers and routes, campsites, vegetation types, and channel depths. Accompanying text gives additional useful information on the route, some historical lore, and nature appreciation. See also the 2 companion volumes FL-31 and FL-36.

FL-23   EVERGLADES NATIONAL PARK, Box 279, Homestead, FL 33030.

They offer an official brochure including a map and a brief milepost road guide. There are 4 visitors centers within the park and they are open daily. They provide information on campgrounds, back country campsites, the Wilderness Waterway, canoe trails, and foot trails. The Everglades Natural History Association, at this same address, operates as a nonprofit, educational and interpretive arm of the park and sells many publications about the park, including their own MOTORISTS GUIDE TO EVERGLADES NATIONAL PARK.

Free maps showing the canal system of Florida from Orlando to Everglades National Park, and RECREATION IN THE EVERGLADES containing the above maps and information on boat launching ramps are available from: Central & Southern Florida Flood Control District, Box V, West Palm Beach, FL 33402.

Information about facilities at state parks, recreation areas, special feature sites (historical, archaeological, geological, botanical), museums, and ornamental gardens will be found in FLORIDA'S STATE PARKS GUIDE available from the Florida Dept. of Natural Resources, Crown Bldg., Tallahassee, FL 32304. This agency also supplies state forest maps.

INDIVIDUAL CITIES OR AREAS

Jacksonville—Printed Materials

FL-24   Bledsoe, Harriett L., and Copeland, Mercedes S. DISCOVER JACK-SONVILLE! A COMPLETE FAMILY GUIDE TO JACKSONVILLE, FLORIDA. Jacksonville: Arlingtown Publishers (8750 Burkhall Street/ 32211), 1976. 128 p. Map. Index.

   The authors describe historical sites, sports and recreation, beaches, camping, culture and the arts, etc. and other major Florida attractions in the Jacksonville area.

FL-25   GUIDE FOR THE HANDICAPPED: JACKSONVILLE - A DESCRIPTION OF PHYSICAL FACILITIES IN PUBLIC BUILDINGS. Jacksonville: Junior League of Jacksonville, 1976. 86 p.

   A new edition is planned.

FL-26   SEE JACKSONVILLE AND THE BEACHES. Sarasota, FL: SEEJAX, (3675 Clark Road/33583).

   This free monthly guide to dining, entertainment, sightseeing, shops, sports, and real estate includes St. Augustine and Fernandina Beach, contains many advertisements, and is available in hotels and motels.

Good maps are available from Arrow Publishing Co. (US-199), Champion Map Corp. (US-202), Gousha (US-206), Rand McNally (US-215), the Jacksonville Transportation Authority, and the Jacksonville Developers Investors Service Corp.

Jacksonville—Organizations

FL-27   CONVENTION AND VISITORS BUREAU OF JACKSONVILLE AND JACKSONVILLE BEACHES, 240 West Monroe Street, Jacksonville, FL 32202 (904/353-9736).

   They issue a JACKSONVILLE VISITOR'S MAP & GUIDE and a guide to points of interest prepared by the city of Jacksonville. They also issue lists of accommodations and restaurants. Their address is a walk-in information center open Monday-Friday, 9A.M.-5P.M.

FL-28 JACKSONVILLE BEACHES AREA CHAMBER OF COMMERCE, Box 50427, Jacksonville Beach, FL 32250 (904/249-3868).

They offer a general area brochure, a brochure on the Jacksonville Beaches campground, and lists of restaurants and what to do and see. They are located at 111 North Third Street and are open Monday-Friday, 8:30A.M.-5P.M. for information queries.

Keys/Key West—Printed Materials

FL-29 Apte, Stu. STU APTE'S FISHING IN THE FLORIDA KEYS AND FLAMINGO. Miami: Windward Publishing Co. (Box 370233/33137), 1976. 80 p. Photos., charts.

A good portion of this booklet is devoted to how to catch the "big ones." In the middle there are 15 charts of the Florida Keys and Flamingo with superimposed fish silhouettes showing where 15 different types of fish are likely to be found. These silhouettes are more alike than different, and to identify them, necessitates careful matching of each outline against the silhouette key.

FL-30 KEYGUIDE TO KEY WEST AND THE FLORIDA KEYS. N.p.: George B. Stevenson, 1970. 64 p. Drawings, sketch maps.

This is a guide to US Route 1 as it passes through the islands of the Keys. It includes descriptions of the history, flora and fauna, and facilities on each island. It should be updated.

FL-31 O'Reilly, John. BOATERS GUIDE TO THE UPPER FLORIDA KEYS: JEWFISH CREEK TO LONG KEY. Coral Gables, FL: University of Miami Press in cooperation with the Everglades Natural History Association, 1970. 64 p. Charts, photos. 0-87024-175-3. 70-125659.

There are 25 charts (1 3/4 in. represents approximately 1 mile) showing exact routes to take when exploring Florida Bay waters west of the Keys. Routes between mangroves and mudflats are carefully plotted and varying depths are indicated. Two charts show routes on the ocean side to John Pennekamp Coral Reef State Park. Written descriptions accompany each map. See also the 2 companion volumes in this series FL-22 and FL-36.

FL-32 Papy, Frank. CRUISING GUIDE TO THE FLORIDA KEYS. Minneapolis: Publication Arts, 1977. 119 p. Maps, photos. 77-361603.

This is a rather good guide for navigating the Florida Keys giving clear textual descriptions and directions. Clear general maps with references to more detailed charts are included, as well as some general tourist information.

FL-33 Sherrill, Chris, and Aiello, Roger. KEY WEST: THE LAST RESORT.

Key West: Key West Book & Card Co. (534-6 Fleming Street/ 33040), 1978. 191 p. Photos., drawings, maps. Bibliography. Index.

A bit each on history, plants and animals, sightseeing, culture, and stores makes this a very useful volume for natives and tourists alike.

See also FL-13.

Good maps are available from Metro Graphic Arts, 900 40th SE, Grand Rapids, MI 49508 and the Monroe County Advertising Commission.

Keys/Key West—Organizations

FL-34   GREATER KEY WEST CHAMBER OF COMMERCE, 402 Wall Street, Key West, FL 33040.

There are actually 7 different chambers of commerce for the Keys area. A request to this one will bring the addresses of the other 6. They issue a booklet describing the way of life in Key West, a guide/map leaflet to Key West, and a good map to all the Keys showing Route 1 and listing attractions, amusements, and services.

Miami/Miami Beach—Printed Materials

FL-35   Ingle, Robert D. MIAMI, MIAMI BEACH IN MAPS. Miami Shores, FL: Pica Press, 1972. 80 p. Maps. 72-85468.

A handy, if somewhat dated, guide to the Miami area, this lists airlines, museums, bus and train lines, taxi and bus companies, parks, shopping areas, broadcasting stations, and much more.

FL-36   Sites, George L. BOATER'S GUIDE TO BISCAYNE BAY: MIAMI TO JEWFISH CREEK. Coral Gables, FL: University of Miami Press in cooperation with the Everglades Natural History Association, 1971. 64 p. Charts, photos. 0-87024-233-4. 75-173322.

There are 27 charts (1.6 in. represents approximately 1 mile) tracing 2 routes south from Miami, 1 on each side (bay and ocean) of the islets that join to form the Florida Keys. Written descriptions supplement each detailed chart. See also the 2 companion volumes in this series FL-22 and FL-31.

FL-37   Steiman, Harvey. GUIDE TO RESTAURANTS OF GREATER MIAMI. Chatsworth, CA: Brooke House, 1977. 274 p. Indexes. 0-912588-38-1. 77-2564.

Over 200 restaurants are described and rated in a refreshingly honest, if intensely personal, manner. Location, parking, telephone number, credit cards accepted, seating capacity, and house specialties are noted. The indexes are by rating, specialty, ethnic type, and area.

FL-38   WHEELCHAIR DIRECTORY OF GREATER MIAMI. South Miami: Florida Paraplegic Association, n.d. 54 p.

AAA (US-259) issues an extensive map of the Miami/Miami Beach/Fort Lauderdale area. Other good maps are available from Arrow Publishing Co. (US-199), Champion Map Corp. (US-202), Exxon (US-261), Goushā (US-206), and Rand McNally (US-215).

Miami/Miami Beach—Organizations

FL-39   MIAMI BEACH TOURIST DEVELOPMENT AUTHORITY, 555 17th Street, Miami Beach, FL 33139 (305/673-7070).

They issue HOW TO FIND THE ACTION AFTER YOU GET HERE which describes local attractions, tennis facilities, golf courses, fishing, pari-mutuel sports, shopping, concerts and cultural events, clubs and organizations, skin and scuba diving, water skiing instruction, the public library, discos, lounges, and supper clubs. They also issue a pocket map/guide and a hotel directory.

FL-40   MIAMI-METRO DEPT. OF PUBLICITY AND TOURISM, 499 Biscayne Blvd., Miami, FL 33132 (305/579-6327).

They issue an official tour map, golf guide, cycling guide, and a calendar of events.

Orlando/Central Florida—Printed Materials

FL-41   Arrow Publishing Co. OFFICIAL ARROW STREET MAP ATLAS, CENTRAL FLORIDA, INCLUDING DETAILED STREET MAPS OF GREATER ORLANDO, LAKE ORANGE, OSCEOLA, AND SEMINOLE COUNTIES, WITH DELAND. Newton Upper Falls, MA: Arrow Publishing, 1976. 125 p. Scale: 3 in. represents 1 mile. Index. 77-367466.

FL-42   Dunn, Bill, and Wilkening, David. KIDDING AROUND: MOM AND DAD'S SURVIVAL GUIDE TO METRO ORLANDO. Orlando: Sentinel Star Co. (Box 3612/32802), 1973. 120 p. Maps.

A lot of good information and suggestions are included in this handy little book, but its arrangement by broad subjects, plus the lack of an index and a table of contents makes it difficult to locate anything quickly. A few extra minutes, though, spent in judicious perusal will be rewarding.

FL-43   Landfried, James E., and Wilson, Lloyd R. SO YOU'RE COMING

TO DISNEY WORLD! HERE IS YOUR GUIDE TO ALL OF CENTRAL FLORIDA. Melbourne, FL: Islands Unlimited, 1972. 280 p. Photos., maps. 72-81320.

The authors provide practical information on what to see and do; where to stay; where to rent cars, campers, sporting equipment; and an occasional restaurant advertising section for central Florida from Daytona Beach to St. Petersburg. It also includes directories of campgrounds, fish camps and marinas, and general aviation airports.

FL-44   National Paraplegic Foundation. Central Florida Chapter. ORLANDO'S GUIDE FOR THE HANDICAPPED. Orlando: Orlando Area Tourist Trade Association (Box 15492/32809), 1977. 25 p.

FL-45   ORLANDO-LAND. Orlando: Orlando-Land Publishing Co. (Box 2207/32802).

This is a monthly magazine mainly for residents, but in the middle of each issue is a 30-page pull-out section called ORLANDO FUN GUIDE which describes several auto tours, restaurants, entertainment, attractions, Walt Disney World, golf, and which contains several maps.

FL-46   Perrero, Laurie, and Perrero, Louis. DISNEY WORLD & THE SUN & FUN BELT. Windward Full Color Travel Guide Series. Miami: Windward Publishing, (Box 371005/33137), 1976. 96 p. Photos. Index. 0-89317-014-5. 76-46896.

Half of this little book describes Walt Disney World and nearby hotels/motels, campgrounds, and restaurants. This is followed by descriptions of 14 other attractions in the central Florida area.

AAA (US-259) issues a good map of Orlando and Orange County. Champion Map Corp. (US-202) issues a map of Orlando.

Orlando/Central Florida—Organizations

FL-47   ORLANDO AREA CHAMBER OF COMMERCE, Box 1913, Orlando, FL 32802 (305/425-5563).

They issue an Orlando/Winter Park street map, a hotel/motel directory, a campground directory, and an attractions and night life brochure.

FL-48   WALT DISNEY WORLD, Box 40, Lake Buena Vista, FL 32830 (305/824-4321).

A single request to them will bring a packet full of useful materials. A large general brochure describes the park, answers most questions people ask, and contains a reservation form for every type of accommodation from the Contemporary Resort Hotel to the Fort Wilderness Campground. Also included in the packet are: YOUR COMPLETE GUIDE TO WALT DISNEY WORLD, WALT DISNEY WORLD RESORT GUIDE, a calendar showing hours open each day, and a copy of the latest issue of the monthly newspaper WALT DISNEY WORLD NEWS.

The Division of Tourism (FL-16) issues a guide for the handicapped GETTING AROUND AT WALT DISNEY WORLD.

St. Petersburg/Tampa—Printed Materials

FL-49   GUIDE TO THE TAMPA AREA FOR THE PHYSICALLY HANDICAPPED. Tampa: Hillsborough Community College, 1976.

A new edition is planned for 1979.

FL-50   SEE TAMPA. Sarasota, FL: Brownell Associates, (3675 Clark Road/ 33583).

This free monthly guide to dining, entertainment, sightseeing, shops, sports, and real estate contains many advertisements and is available at major hotels and motels.

Champion Map Corp. (US-202) issues separate maps of St. Petersburg and Tampa. Goushā (US-206) and Rand McNally (US-215) each issue a combined St. Petersburg/Tampa map.

St. Petersburg/Tampa—Organizations

FL-51   GREATER TAMPA CHAMBER OF COMMERCE, Box 420, Tampa, FL 33601 (813/228-7777).

Our request to them for sample copies of their publications brought only the torn out yellow pages from the local telephone directory listing travel agencies and bureaus. We have references to a general brochure, a hotel/motel guide, a sports brochure, and an 8-day tour brochure, but these have not been examined.

FL-52   ST. PETERSBURG BEACH CHAMBER OF COMMERCE, 6990 Gulf Blvd., St. Petersburg Beach, FL 33706 (813/360-6957).

They issue a general booklet, mostly advertisements of motels/hotels, attractions, restaurants, etc., that describes attractions, annual events, sports and recreation, several 1-day side trips, churches, clubs, and a directory of Chamber of Commerce members. During the season their office is open for information Monday-Friday, 9A.M.-9P.M. and on weekends from 10A.M.-3P.M. Off season they are open regular office hours.

FL-53   ST. PETERSBURG CHAMBER OF COMMERCE, Box 1371, St. Petersburg, FL 33731 (813/821-4715).

They issue a big 66-page booklet, DISCOVER FLORIDA'S SUN-COAST, that describes sports and recreation, attractions, entertainment, tropical living, has a calendar of events, and a list of other chambers of commerce and organizations to write to for information. It does not list accommodations, but does contain many motel/hotel, and other similar advertisements.

Tallahassee—Printed Materials

Good maps are available from Arrow Publishing Co. (US-199) and Champion Map Corp. (US-202).

Tallahassee—Organizations

FL-54   TALLAHASSEE AREA CHAMBER OF COMMERCE, Box 1639, Tallahassee, FL 32302 (904/224-8116).

They issue TALLAHASSEE: THE ELEGANT FLORIDA, SCENIC TOUR, YOUR GUIDE TO RESTAURANTS AND LODGING IN TALAHASSEE, map/brochures on the capitol and capitol center, and YOUR GUIDE TO RENTAL LIVING IN TALLAHASSEE. The Chamber of Commerce is housed in a restored building at 100 North Duval Street which acts as an information center. There is an official Florida Welcome Center located just inside the east entrance to the Capitol building (904/488-6167). Both are open from 8A.M.-5P.M.

GEORGIA

BOOKS, ATLASES, MAGAZINES

GA-1   BROWN'S GUIDE TO GEORGIA. College Park, GA: Alfred Brown
       Publishing Co. (Box 87306/30337).

       Begun in the winter of 1972–73 as a quarterly, this magazine went
       monthly with the September 1978 issue. It is "a guide to hiking and
       shopping, to canoeing and eating out, to fishing, antique hunting,
       craft fairs, to people, current events, and history." Each issue con-
       tains a chronological listing of fairs and festivals, a list of sports
       and outings events, and an extensive restaurant guide. The lead
       article in the issue we examined was a 20–page guide to the town of
       Augusta.

GA-2   Chambers, Wicke, and Asher, Spring. WHAT'S UP FOR KIDS IN
       ATLANTA . . . AND GEORGIA. New York: Ballantine Books, 1973.
       148 p. Map. 0-345-23595-9.

       This is a compilation of the authors' regular "What's Up for Kids in
       Atlanta" column in the Atlanta CONSTITUTION. Chapters are en-
       titled "Atlanta Excursions, Entertainment, and Activities," "Eating
       Out," "Creative Living" (suggestions for special days), and "Stay and
       See Georgia." It contains many addresses and phone numbers for
       further information.

GA-3   GEORGIA LIFE. Decatur, GA: Georgia Life (Drawer 1829/30031).

       This quarterly magazine, begun in the summer of 1974, features
       articles on Georgiana, includes a few on geographical areas within
       the state, sometimes has a restaurant guide, and always has a calen-
       dar of events. A cumulative index to the first 2 volumes is available
       from them.

GA-4   Leckie, George G. GEORGIA: A GUIDE TO ITS TOWNS AND
       COUNTRYSIDE. American Guide Series. Atlanta: Tupper & Love,
       1954. 457 p. Photos., maps. 54-10344.

This revision of the original 1940 WPA guide omits the earlier beginning section in that edition on general state background. It does
contain descriptions of 6 major towns and 17 statewide highway tours.

MAPS

The official highway map is available from the Georgia Dept. of Transportation, Division of Planning & Programming, No. 2 Capitol Square, Atlanta,
GA 30334. The 1978-79 edition contains a small scenic map of Georgia,
locations of and facilities at state parks, locations of National Park Service
areas and state historic sites, and addresses to write for further information on
outdoor activities. Other good maps are the combined Alabama/Georgia maps
issued by AAA (US-259) and Exxon (US-261), and the single Georgia maps
issued by Goushā (US-206) and Rand McNally (US-215).

MAJOR TOURIST ORGANIZATION

GA-5   GEORGIA DEPT. OF INDUSTRY & TRADE, TOURIST DIVISION,
        Box 1776, Atlanta, GA 30301 (404/656-3545).

        They issue a series of 7 regional brochures listing points of interest
        and suggesting a 3- or 6-day tour itinerary, a yearly listing of
        festivals, a brochure describing historic homes open to the public,
        GEORGIA. SO MUCH. SO NEAR (containing maps and guides for
        25 mini-tours), a semiannual special events calendar, a golf guide,
        a fishing guide, a list of radio and TV stations, and NATIONAL
        FORESTS (a guide to picnic, camping, and boating facilities and to
        scenic areas).

OTHER ORGANIZATIONS

GA-6   GEORGIA HOSPITALITY & TRAVEL ASSOCIATION, 201 Harris Tower,
        233 Peachtree Street, Atlanta, GA 30303.

        They issue a traveler's guide listing all the association's hotel/motel,
        restaurant, and attraction members. The listings are divided into the
        same 7 tourist regions used by the Tourist Division (GA-5).

INFORMATION CENTERS/INFORMATION PHONES

There are 8 welcome centers located on major highways at the state borders,
1 at the Atlanta airport, and 1 in the town of Plains. A list of these will
be found on each of the regional brochures issued by the Tourist Division
(GA-5). The division also provides a list of these centers giving addresses

and phone numbers. In addition, the welcome centers are located on the official highway map. The division has a toll-free number for information: 800/241-8444.

OUTDOOR RECREATION ACTIVITIES

CANOEING AND BOATING. CANOE GUIDE TO THE SUWANNEE, WITHA-COOCHEE & ALAPAHA RIVERS is available from the Coastal Plain Area Planning & Development Commission, Box 1223, Valdosta, GA 31601. CANOER'S GUIDE TO GEORGIA RIVERS by the Frederica Academy River Project is available through the American Canoe Association (US-220). See also GA-7.

FISHING AND HUNTING. Contact the Georgia Dept. of Natural Resources, Office of Information & Education, 270 Washington Street SW, Atlanta, GA 30334 (404/656-3530). They don't issue too much where-to information, but they do issue a fold-out map/brochure, A GUIDE TO GEORGIA LAKES, RIVERS & STREAMS, which provides information on locations, phone numbers, and facilities available at reservoirs, rivers, small impoundments (dam sites), and public fishing areas where fresh water game fish may be found. The department's official monthly magazine, OUTDOORS IN GEORGIA, contains articles on fishing, hunting, boating, hiking, and camping. Each summer there is a special travel issue.

NATIONAL/STATE PARKS/FORESTS, ETC.

Okefenokee National Wildlife Refuge

GA-7   OKEFENOKEE NATIONAL WILDLIFE REFUGE, 411 Pendleton Street, Box 117, Waycross, GA 31501 (912/283-2580).

The entire refuge is administered by the U.S. Fish & Wildlife Service of the Dept. of Interior. There are 3 primary entrances to the Refuge, each with its own local administrative unit and address: (1) Suwanee Canal Recreation Area provides access from the east at Folkston, GA, and has an information center, a concession, and several hiking trails and driving tours; (2) Stephen C. Foster State Park provides access from the west; and (3) Okefenokee State Park provides access from the north at Waycross and is administered by the Okefenokee Association, a private nonprofit organization which operates under a refuge permit, and which charges an admission fee. But there's no need to write to each. The best source of information is the Refuge itself at the above address. They also provide maps of canoe trails.

Information and maps about the national forests in Georgia may be obtained from the U.S. Forest Service, Southern Region, 1720 Peachtree Road NW, Suite 800, Atlanta, GA 30309. There is a visitor information center at Brasstown Bald in the Chattahoochee National Forest.

The Georgia Dept. of Natural Resources, Office of Information & Education, 270 Washington Street SW, Atlanta, GA 30334 (404/656-3530) will provide information on state parks and historic sites, facilities, and activities. They also issue separate map/brochures for each individual state park.

The Georgia Dept. of National Resources, Office of Planning and Research, Historic Preservation Section, 270 Washington Street SW, Atlanta, GA 30334 (404/656-3530) issues a guide to GEORGIA MUSEUMS & HISTORIC SITES.

INDIVIDUAL CITIES OR AREAS

Atlanta—Printed Materials

GA-8   ACCESS ATLANTA. Atlanta: Georgia Easter Seal Society (3254 Northside Parkway NW/30327), 1978.

GA-9   Aero Surveys of Georgia. ATLANTA AERO ATLAS. Metropolitan Series. Marietta, GA: Aero Surveys, 1976. Issued annually. 95 p. Scale: 2 3/4 in. represents 1 mile. Index. 76-643941.

GA-10   Alexandria Drafting Co. ATLANTA & VICINITY STREET MAP. Alexandria, VA: Alexandria Drafting, 1976. 42 p. Scale: 1 in. represents 2,225 ft. Index.

GA-11   Siddons, Anne R. GO STRAIGHT ON PEACHTREE: A McDONALD CITY GUIDE TO ATLANTA. Garden City, NY: Doubleday, 1978. 224 p. Maps. Index. 0-385-11144-4. 76-16257.

The author takes you in hand and guides you, with directions, on 8 general tours of Atlanta, 6 tours of interest to kids, 6 shopping tours, 3 arts tours, 1 restoration tour, and 2 walking tours. There are sections on where to go for nighttime entertainment, dining, both participatory and spectator sports, and out of town tours. There is a list of hotels and motels. Many points of interest are described more than once, and hours and admission information are in a separate section at the end. The information provided for any one point of interest is superficial, but the coverage is broad. For an in-depth guide to downtown Atlanta see (GA-12). The "McDonald" in the subtitle refers to the originator of this guidebook series and not to the fast food chain.

GA-12   Woodworth, Karl, and Woodworth, Linda. FIND YOUR OWN WAY IN DOWNTOWN ATLANTA: A WALKING TOUR AND STREET-LEVEL GUIDE TO THE "MAGIC CITY OF THE SOUTH." Atlanta: the authors, 1976. 80 p. Sketches. 76-42095.

Thorough walking directions and historical and architectural background

are given for 3 one- to two-hour strolls of modern Atlanta, Georgia
State and the "Underground Atlanta" area, and the State Capitol and
Georgia Museum area.

See also GA-2.

Good maps of Atlanta are available from Arrow Publishing Co. (US-199),
Champion Map Corp. (US-202), Goushā (US-206), Rand McNally (US-215),
and the local AAA office.

Atlanta—Organizations

GA-13   ATLANTA CHAMBER OF COMMERCE, Box 1740, Atlanta, GA 30301
(404/521-0845).

They issue ATLANTA POINTS OF INTEREST, TOUR OF ATLANTA
(guide and map), and ATLANTA HOTELS & MOTELS. In 1974 they
published a 27-page booklet ATLANTA INFORMATION SOURCES,
a guide to selected Atlanta organizations that provide information
and help. It is arranged alphabetically by type of information provided from "arts" to "transportation." They also publish a monthly
magazine, ATLANTA.

GA-14   ATLANTA CONVENTION & VISITORS BUREAU, 233 Peachtree Street
NE, Suite 200, Atlanta, GA 30303 (404/659-4270).

They issue ATLANTA RESTAURANTS, LOUNGES AND DINNER
THEATRES; ATLANTA, WHERE TO SHOP/WHAT TO SEE/HOW TO
GET THERE; and an ATLANTA VISITOR'S MAP AND GUIDE. They
operate 2 visitor information centers: 1 in Peachtree Center Mall
(404/523-6517) and 1 in Lenox Square Mall (404/233-6767).

There are 2 self-guided tours of Atlanta: (1) Auto Tape Tours of Atlanta,
Box 888041, Atlanta, GA 30338 (404/393-4761), and (2) Find Your Own Way
in Downtown Atlanta, Box 8334, Station F., Atlanta, GA 30306 (404/875-
6103).

HAWAII

BOOKS, ATLASES, MAGAZINES

HI-1   Belknap, Buzz, and Belknap, Jodi. THE ILLUSTRATED OAHU TRIP
        MAP. Norfolk Island, Australia: Island Heritage Limited (distributed
        by W.W. Distributors, Ltd., 1132 Auahi Street, Honolulu, HI 96814),
        1971. 96 p. Maps, photos. Index. 71-145452.

        The detailed maps in this volume (1 in. represents about 1/3 of a
        mile) are based on U.S. Geological Survey maps and show prominent
        features and buildings. The work is divided into major trips (wind-
        ward, leeward, inner island, and Pali) marking the routes to take to
        tour the island of Oahu. Photographs supplement the maps and brief
        descriptive text is keyed to numbered features on the maps. The
        maps are very easy to read and the 1971 publication date does not
        detract from the book's usefulness. We recommend this book enthusi-
        astically.

HI-2   Bone, Robert W. THE MAVERICK GUIDE TO HAWAII. Gretna, LA:
        Pelican Publishing Co., 1977. 436 p. Maps. Index. 0-88289-
        152-9. 77-726.

        After 2 background chapters, each island is described in detail, giving
        very practical information on how and where to sight-see. Hotels,
        reservations, services and rentals, museums, etc. are described (with
        telephone numbers and hours, where appropriate). There are useful,
        if not always detailed, maps.

HI-3   Bryan, Edwin H., Jr. BRYAN'S SECTIONAL MAPS OF O'AHU,
        CITY & COUNTY OF HONOLULU. Rev. ed. Honolulu: EMIC
        Graphics (1427 Dillingham Blvd., Suite 307/96817), 1979. 191 p.
        Scales vary. Index.

        All streets on Oahu are indexed (noting zip code). This is one of
        the best atlases to buy when visiting Honolulu.

HI-4   Chisholm, Craig. HAWAIIAN HIKING TRAILS. Rev. ed. Beaverton,

OR: Touchstone Press, 1976. 127 p. Photos., maps. 0-911518-35-5. 75-13696.

Forty-nine hikes on 6 islands are described in detail, giving distance, time, and high points. Included are reproductions of USGS maps with the trails added.

HI-5   Clark, John R.K. THE BEACHES OF O'AHU. A Kolowalu Book. Honolulu: University Press of Hawaii, 1977. 193 p. Maps, photos. Bibliography. Index. 0-8248-0510-0. 77-8244.

The author, a lifeguard who participated in many rescues, felt there was a need for a water safety guide to Oahu. Every beach, beginning with Kaloko Beach in the Honolulu district, and proceeding clockwise around the island, has been listed, giving facilities, lifeguard service, emergency and pay phone locations, nearest fire station, hospital, service station, water activities, and conditions and extent of public access. A historical description of each beach is also included. The maps are quite good. This is definitely one of the better beach books.

HI-6   Davenport, William W., et al. FODOR'S HAWAII 1978. New York: David McKay Co., 1978. Issued annually. 306 p. Maps, photos. 0-679-00260-X.

Complete guides to exploration and practical information are given for the 6 islands of the Hawaiian group of interest to travelers.

HI-7   Gleasner, Bill, and Gleasner, Diana. KAUAI TRAVELER'S GUIDE. Honolulu: Oriental Publishing Co. (Box 22162/96822; distributed by Pacific Mercantile, Box 22156, Honolulu, HI 96822), n.d. 65 p. Photos., maps.

While mostly stunning photographs, this guide also contains information on car rentals, special places to visit, things to do with kids, safe beaches, tennis, golf, fishing, the Kalalau Trail, the weather, history, hotels, and restaurants. There is a map of the island showing 30 points of interest, and individual generalized maps of the cities of Lihue, Poipu, Hanapepe, and Hanalei.

HI-8   Hammel, Faye, and Levey, Sylvan. HAWAII ON $15 and $20 A DAY. 13th ed. New York: Arthur Frommer (distributed by Simon & Schuster), 1978. 311 p. Maps.

The "aim is to show you how to keep your basic living costs--room and three meals only--down to somewhere around $15 to $20 a day." Chapters on getting there, shopping, sightseeing in Honolulu, Oahu, and the other islands describe other low-cost things to see and do.

HI-9   HAWAII, A GUIDE TO ALL THE ISLANDS. 5th ed. By the editors of Sunset Books and Sunset Magazine. Menlo Park, CA: Lane Publishing Co., 1975. 160 p. Photos., maps. Index. 0-376-06306-8. 74-20023.

Major attractions on the islands of Oahu, Kauai, Maui, Molokai, Lanai, and Hawaii are described. There are additional chapters featuring recreation (camping, boat rentals, fishing, hunting, golf, tennis, hiking, cycling, etc.), festivals, annual events, and sources of information. Restaurants and accommodations are not included.

HI-10   HOLIDAY GUIDE TO HAWAII. By the editors of Holiday Magazine. The Holiday Magazine Travel Guide Series. New York: Random House, 1976. Updated frequently. 127 p. Photos. Index. 75-32500.

"What you need to know, things you should see and do, historical background, where to stay and eat" are covered for each of the islands.

HI-11   Kane, Robert S. HAWAII: A TO Z. Garden City, NY: Doubleday, 1975. 194 p. Map. Index. 0-385-09528-7. 74-18813.

This good general guide to the traditional things to see and do in all the islands describes what to see; where to stay; restaurants; entertainment and nightlife; places to golf, play tennis, go fishing and surfing; and shops. It gives a general history and has a miscellaneous section that describes transportation, tour companies, and climate.

HI-12   Lawrence, Jodi. OFF THE BEATEN TRACK IN HAWAII. A Nash Travel Guide. Los Angeles: Nash Publishing Corp., 1973. 163 p. 0-8402-8039-4. 72-81860.

The information here on transportation, hotels/motels, restaurants, and sights to see is not as untraditional as the title implies, and much of it will no doubt be found in some of the most recent Hawaii guidebooks, but the traveler who truly wants to avoid all of the regular tourist routes should check this guide also.

HI-13   Rathbun, Linda M. BICYCLER'S GUIDE TO HAWAII. Hilo, HI: Petroglyph Press (201 Kinoole Street/96720), 1976. 62 p. Maps, sketches. Bibliography. 0-912180-28-5.

The author begins with such practical information as the cost and requirements of flying your bicycle to Hawaii and bicycle registrations (they are required but are only a little over $1.00). The main part of the book describes cycling itineraries and predominant weather patterns, lists bicycle repair shops, and provides a general guide to public campgrounds on each of the islands of Oahu, Kauai, Maui, and Hawaii. There are many maps, but they only show general routes. There are 3 pages of sources of information. This is not a bad little book.

HI-14   Singletary, Milly. DISCOVER HAWAII MINUTE BY MINUTE. Kailua, HI: Press Pacifica (Box 47/96734), 1978. Folded pamphlet. Maps.

The author describes 4 tours on the island of Oahu. Three of them are bus tours, and a brief minute-by-minute commentary of the passing scene is provided. The fourth is a walking tour of historic downtown Honolulu. Similar guides are planned for each of the islands, but others will be in booklet format instead of the folded format of this guide.

HI-15   _____. SEE OAHU VIA THE BUS. Honolulu: M-F-S (Box 15302/96815), 1978. 25 p. Maps.

The bus guide portion of this little booklet isn't nearly as good as Brein's HONOLULU & OAHU BY THE BUS (HI-28), but it does have 2 additional very brief sections not found in Brein: a list of restaurants and a calendar of weekly events. These, however, don't make the book particularly special and for just getting around, you're better off with Brein.

HI-16   Smith, Robert L. HIKING HAWAII: THE BIG ISLAND. Wilderness Press Trail Guide Series. Berkeley, CA: Wilderness Press, 1977. 100 p. Photos., maps. Index. 0-911824-55-3. 76-56548.

HI-17   _____. HIKING KAUAI: THE GARDEN ISLE. Wilderness Press Trail Guide Series. Berkeley, CA: Wilderness Press, 1977. 100 p. Maps, photos. Index. 0-911824-56-1. 76-57113.

HI-18   _____. HIKING MAUI: THE VALLEY ISLE. Wilderness Press Trail Guide Series. Berkeley, CA: Wilderness Press, 1977. 132 p. Maps, photos. Index. 0-911824-61-8. 77-89522.

Each of these 3 Wilderness Press books describes numerous trails (many with short side trails suitable for individual hikes), including a general sketch map, difficulty rating, distance and time required, and road access.

HI-19   Talbott, George T. CRUISING GUIDE TO THE HAWAIIAN ISLANDS. Ventura, CA: Western Marine Enterprises, (Box Q/93001), 1977(?). 136 p. Charts, photos. 0-930030-09-5.

This book includes "sailing and piloting directions, facility information, weather, local oceanography, pertinent state laws, aids to navigation, radio usage, fishing and hunting information, and a light list" for all the islands.

HI-20   Wright, Bank. SURFING HAWAII. Los Angeles: Mountain & Sea (2961 West Eight Street/90813), 1972. 96 p. 72-81871.

This book has not been examined, but it is probably very much like this author's SURFING CALIFORNIA (CA-29) in describing each area of the Hawaiian Islands suitable for surfing.

HI-21   Younger, Ronald M. ALL THE BEST IN HAWAII. A Sydney Clark
Travel Book. New York: Dodd, Mead, 1972. 333 p. Photos.
0-396-06525-2. 72-2341.

Originally written in 1949, the information here is presumably revised. While the information may be updated, the guidebook style
is not. It is written in a discursive, genteel manner rather than
arranged for quick reference. Oahu and Honolulu are the most
fully covered, describing points of interest, shops, hotels, restaurants,
and entertainment. Only points of interest and hotels are given for
Kauai, Maui, Molokai, Lanai, and Hawaii, and information on shops
and restaurants is added for Kauai, Maui, and Hawaii. The book is
not fully indexed. For example, there are no references to individual restaurants but only to the page on which the restaurant section
for each island begins.

MAPS

There is no official map. The University Press of Hawaii, 2840 Kolowalu
Street, Honolulu, HI 96822, issues a series of maps of the individual islands
showing topography, roads, inset maps of towns, points of historic and scenic
interest, hiking trails, parks, beaches, and waterfalls. The other side of the
Rand McNally (US-215) map of Honolulu shows all the islands with major
roads. The National Geographic Society, 17th and M Streets NW, Washington, DC 20036 issues a good map. C & H Marketing, 1123 Kaumoku, Honolulu, HI 96825, issues a map which shows streets for the major urban areas of
the islands of Maui, Hawaii, and Kauai. See also HI-1 and HI-3.

MAJOR TOURIST ORGANIZATION

HI-22   HAWAII VISITORS BUREAU, 2270 Kalakaua Avenue, Honolulu, HI
96815 (808/923-1811).

The above address is their administrative office. There is an information office at 2285 Kalakaua Avenue. The phone number is the same.
They provide a general information brochure, individual map/brochures
for each of the islands, an annual special events calendar, WHAT TO
WEAR AND BUY IN HAWAII, GOLF AND TENNIS IN HAWAII, and
an annual hotel guide. The latter is very detailed, including rates
and a car rental guide. They sponsor 4 other branch offices on the
islands and 5 in the continental US. Contact them at the following
addresses: 180 Kinoole Street, Suite 104, Hilo Plaza, Hilo, HI
96720 (808/935-5271); Box 367, World Square, Kailua, Kona, HI
96740; 3016 Umi Street, Suite 207, Lihue Plaza Bldg., Lihue, Kauai,
HI 96766 (808/245-3971); 200 High Street, Room 431, County Bldg.,
Wailuku, Maui, HI 96793 (808/244-9141); 410 North Mighigan
Avenue, Room 1060, Wrigley Bldg., Chicago, IL 60611 (312/944-
6694); 3440 Wilshire Blvd., Room 203, Central Plaza, Los Angeles,
CA 90010 (213/385-5313); 50 Rockefeller Plaza, Room 1015, Associated Press Bldg., New York, NY 10020 (212/582-7911); 209 Post

Street, Room 615, Brooks Brothers Bldg., San Francisco, CA 94108 (415/392-8173); and 1101 17th Street NW, Suite 1000, Washington, DC 20036.

OTHER ORGANIZATIONS

HI-23   ALOHA AIRLINES, Honolulu International Airport, Box 30028, Honolulu, HI 96820 (802/842-4101).

This airline provides flights between the 5 major islands of the Hawaiian chain. In the US call 800/367-5250 for toll-free reservation information. Their inflight magazine is the monthly SPIRIT OF ALOHA.

HI-24   HAWAIIAN AIRLINES, Box 30008, Honolulu, HI 96820 (808/525-5511).

They schedule mostly island-hopping flights. Their toll-free number is 800/367-5320. They have a New York office at 6 East 43d Street, 11th floor, New York, NY 10017 (212/355-4843). Their inflight magazine, LATITUDE 20, contains much useful information.

HI-25   HAWAII HOTEL ASSOCIATION, 2270 Kalahaua Avenue, Suite 907, Honolulu, HI 96815 (808/923-0407).

INFORMATION CENTERS/INFORMATION PHONES

See Hawaii Visitors Bureau (HI-22).

OUTDOOR RECREATION ACTIVITIES

BICYCLING. See HI-13.

CANOEING AND BOATING. See HI-19.

FISHING AND HUNTING. The Hawaii Division of Fish and Game, 1151 Punchbowl Street, Honolulu, HI 96813 (808/548-4001) provides more information on hunting than on fishing. They issue individual maps to hunting areas and trails on the islands of Hawaii, Kauai, Lanai, Maui, Molokai, and Oahu. They also maintain branch offices on each of these islands. The addresses and phone numbers of each are available from the above address. The Visitors Bureau (HI-22) issues FISHING AND HUNTING IN HAWAII which contains much useful information on fishing charters and hunting guide services, including addresses, phone numbers, and rates. It also includes a brief guide to 4-wheel drive rentals.

NATIONAL/STATE PARKS/FORESTS, ETC.

Haleakala National Park

HI-26 HALEAKALA NATIONAL PARK, Box 537, Makawao, Maui, HI
96768 (808/572-7749).

This park preserves Haleakala Crater, a once-active volcano, and
supplies information and brochures on activities in the crater area, camping, and hiking trails into the crater. There are 2 visitor centers, and a
call to the above number will give a recorded message about weather,
road conditions, and scheduled visitor programs. The Hawaii Natural
History Association, Hawaii Volcanoes National Park, HI 96718
issues A GUIDE TO THE CRATER AREA OF HALEAKALA NATIONAL
PARK by George C. Ruhle (Rev. ed., 1975, 78 p.). Most of it is
devoted to geology, flora and fauna, historical background, etc.,
but the first 14 pages is a visitors' guide which describes what to see
and do, the campground and cabins, and trails into the crater.

Hawaii Volcanoes National Park

HI-27 HAWAII VOLCANOES NATIONAL PARK, HI 96718 (808/967-7311).

Two volcanoes are preserved in this park: Kilauea, intermittently
active, and Mauna Loa, most recently active. The latter is accessible only by a 36-mile round trip, or a 3- or 4-day hike. You can
drive your car right to the rim of Kilauea. They provide information
and brochures on what to see and do, visitor services, trails, accommodations, etc. 808/967-7988 is the number of the Park Trails
Office. If you call 808/967-7977, you will get current information
about on-going eruptions or potential volcanic activity.

The Hawaii Division of State Parks, Outdoor Recreation and Historic Sites, 1151
Punchbowl Street, Honolulu, HI 96813, in cooperation with the Division of Fish
and Game and the Division of Forestry (both also at this same address), has
issued a very excellent ISLAND OF MAUI RECREATION MAP. It contains information on hiking trails, recreation areas, hunting areas, state and county
parks, 4-wheel drive trails, camping areas and shelters, and boat ramps. Hopefully, similar maps for the other islands are in preparation. The Visitors Bureau
(HI-22) provides a good guide, with addresses and phone numbers, to camping
and hiking in state parks and forests.

INDIVIDUAL CITIES OR AREAS

Honolulu and Waikiki—Printed Materials

HI-28 Brein, Michael. HONOLULU & OAHU BY THE BUS. Honolulu: The

Idea Company of Hawaii (1015 Bishop Street, Mezzanine/96813), 1977. Updated frequently. 27 in. x 39 in. sheet. Scales vary.

This thorough map shows the major bus routes on Oahu with insets (and even insets to the insets) detailing the bus routes in the major urban areas and near each of 79 major tourist attractions. A points of interest index is provided. Walks or hikes, hospitals, post offices, information locations, and, of course, bus route number with direction of travel, as well as the main landmarks, are all noted on the map sections. We are impressed.

HI-29   Bushnell, Oswald A. A WALK THROUGH OLD HONOLULU: AN ILLUSTRATED GUIDE. Honolulu: Kapa Associates, 1975. 93 p. Photos., map. 0-915870-00-2. 75-25519.

This is a walking guide to 26 historic landmarks with full historical and architectural descriptions.

HI-30   Cook, Terri. FAMILY GUIDE TO HONOLULU AND THE ISLAND OF OAHU. Honolulu: Hawaiian Service, (Box 2835/96803), 1977. 80 p. Photos., map. 0-930492-00-5. 77-85698.

The author lists public beaches, swimming pools, several hikes, campgrounds, riding stables, industrial tours and other outings, state parks, etc.

HI-31   HAWAII TOURIST NEWS. Honolulu (Box 32/96810).

Published every Thursday and distributed free in Waikiki hotel rooms, this tabloid newspaper is rather unimaginative in its coverage, with shallow articles stressing shopping centers, after-dark entertainment places, etc. Points of interest are treated very superficially as is the token coverage of regions outside the Waikiki/Honolulu area.

HI-32   Kanahele, George S. A NATIVE'S GUIDE TO HONOLULU AND THE ISLAND OF OAHU. Honolulu: Topgallant Publishing Co., 1976. 193 p. Photos., maps. 0-914916-20-3. 76-21257.

This guide is written by a native Hawaiian and the "focus is on 'Hawaiianness.'" He describes things the visitor can do to capture the Hawaiian spirit, 3 walking (Waikiki and Honolulu) and 3 auto and/or boat (Pearl Harbor and Oahu) tours, and where to buy Hawaiian gift items. A directory of information lists, among other things, golf courses, hotels, night spots, restaurants, sightseeing tour organizations, tourist information offices, transportation (including car rentals), and water activities.

HI-33   Kerr, Jennifer, and Seidenstein, Jay. THE HONOLULU UNDERGROUND GOURMET. A Fireside Book. New York: Simon & Schuster, 1972. 186 p. Indexes. 0-671-21352-0. 72-83918.

This guide to restaurants, arranged by nationality of food served, with alphabetical and geographic indexes, needs to be updated.

HI-34   Michaels, Jill. ARTHUR FROMMER'S GUIDE TO HONOLULU. New York: Frommer/Pasmantier Publishing Corp. (distributed by Simon & Schuster), 1978. Updated frequently. 202 p. 0-671-22734-3.

This concise guide to hotels, dining, sightseeing, after-dark entertainment, and shopping in Honolulu provides similar information for the rest of the island of Oahu and the islands of Hawaii, Maui, and Kauai.

Maps of Honolulu are available from Goushā (US-206), Rand McNally (US-215), and The Tourmap Co., East 1104 57th Avenue, Spokane, WA 99203. A map of hotels in Waikiki is available from the Visitors Bureau (HI-22), as well as a PICTORIAL ALOHA GUIDE TO HONOLULU FOR HANDICAPPED TRAVELERS.

IDAHO

BOOKS, ATLASES, MAGAZINES

ID-1 THE HISTORICAL SIGN PROGRAM IN THE STATE OF IDAHO.
Boise: Idaho Transportation Dept., Public Information Section,
[1978?]. 58 p. Sketches, maps, photos.

The exact legend or text appearing on each of over 100 still standing historical signs is reproduced in this booklet. It is arranged in
3 geographic regions.

ID-2 IDAHO: A GUIDE IN WORD AND PICTURE. 2d ed. American
Guide Series. New York: Oxford University Press, 1950. 300 p.
Photos. Bibliography. Index.

This revision of the original 1937 WPA guide begins with a history
and general background and describes 11 state-wide highway tours.
There is a list of place names with origins.

ID-3 IDAHO RECREATION GUIDE. Boise: U.S. Bureau of Land Management, Idaho State Office, [1978?]. 120 p. Maps, drawings.

A preliminary section gives very general information on outdoor recreation and other outdoor activities in Idaho, with lists (including locations and addresses) of wilderness/primitive/natural/scenic areas, dams,
wildlife refuges, fish hatcheries, etc. The majority of the book consists of tables keyed to 16 good sectional maps of the state that give
the name of the recreation site, its map number, general location,
elevation, season, facilities, activities, and attractions. It also
notes addresses for further information.

ID-4 INCREDIBLE IDAHO. Boise: Idaho Division of Tourism & Industrial
Development.

This is a quarterly magazine describing the joys of outdoor Idaho in
stunning photography and text. The issue we examined contained
articles about a personal backpacking experience in the Sawtooths,

an art gallery, Idaho's poet laureate, Jensen's Grove Park at Black-foot, the Selway River, Springtown, Crystal Ice Cave, painter Archie Teater, Moscow Park, and a fishing trip to Cold Springs Creek.

ID-5   SUNSET TRAVEL GUIDE TO IDAHO. By the editors of Sunset Books and Sunset Magazine. Menlo Park, CA: Lane Books, 1969. 80 p. Photos., maps. Index. 0-376-06371-8. 69-13280.

Descriptions of the major points of interest are regionally arranged with a name index.

MAPS

The official highway map is issued by the Idaho Transportation Dept., Box 7129, Boise, ID 83707 and is available either from them or the Division of Tourism & Industrial Development (ID-6). The 1978-79 edition lists state parks and recreation areas, gives brief fishing and hunting information, maps out 6 scenic routes for seeing the state, and locates routes of historic trails on the map. Both AAA (US-259) and Rand McNally (US-215) issue a combined Idaho/Montana/Wyoming map. Gousha (US-206) issues a separate Idaho map.

MAJOR TOURIST ORGANIZATION

ID-6   IDAHO DIVISION OF TOURISM & INDUSTRIAL DEVELOPMENT, Room 108, Capitol Bldg., Boise, ID 83720 (208/384-2470).

They issue a general color booklet that is mostly pretty pictures, a general state facts and history leaflet, IDAHO GENERAL INFORMA-TION (lists chambers of commerce throughout the state, land and property sources of information, a climate table, etc.), an annual events brochure, IDAHO OUTDOOR RECREATION RESOURCES (lists addresses and phone numbers of hot springs, national forests, ski areas, golf courses, and other general information services), IDAHO INDIANS (includes locations of reservations, museums, and pow wows), and IDAHO GEMSTONE GUIDE (lists locations where gemstones, including fossils, may be found).

OTHER ORGANIZATIONS

ID-7   IDAHO INNKEEPERS ASSOCIATION, Box 8693, Boise, ID 83707 (208/362-4766).

They issue an annual directory of accommodations (including campgrounds) and restaurants.

ID-8   IDAHO OUTFITTERS AND GUIDES ASSOCIATION, Box 95, Boise,
        ID 83701.

        Our repeated requests to them brought no response, but we assume they
        are a group of licensed, expert individuals available to fishermen and
        hunters to arrange expeditions and lead them to the best fish and game
        locations.

INFORMATION CENTERS/INFORMATION PHONES

The state has no official highway information welcome centers. The local
chambers of commerce serve this purpose, and a list of them, including phone
numbers, will be found in the IDAHO GENERAL INFORMATION brochure
available from the Division of Tourism & Industrial Development (ID-6).

OUTDOOR RECREATION ACTIVITIES

CANOEING AND BOATING. Detailed river guide/maps to 2 parts of the
Salmon River: the 79-mile east-west stretch between North Fork and Riggins
and generally known as "The River of No Return," and the Middle Fork, a
southern tributary of the major east-west stream, are available from the Forest
Supervisor, Salmon National Forest, Forest Service Bldg., Box 729, Salmon,
ID 88467 or from the U.S. Forest Service, Intermountain Region, Federal Bldg.,
324 25th Street, Ogden, UT 84401. A LOWER SALMON RIVER GUIDE, which
follows the river onward from Riggins to its confluence with the Snake River at
the Oregon border, is available from the Bureau of Land Management, Cottonwood Resource Area Headquarters, Route 3, Box 181, Cottonwood, ID 83522
(208/962-3245). The Idaho Dept. of Fish and Game, Box 25, Boise, ID 83707
(208/384-3700) issues a guide to canoe waters of Idaho and a MOUNTAIN
LAKES OF IDAHO guide. See also ID-3.

FISHING AND HUNTING. Map/guides to fishing and game locations, seasons,
and regulations are available from the Idaho Dept. of Fish and Game, Box 25,
Boise, ID 83707 (208/384-3700). They also issue an IDAHO LAKES & RESER-
VOIRS GUIDE and IDAHO WILDLIFE, a bimonthly magazine. See also ID-3.

WINTER ACTIVITIES. The Division of Tourism & Industrial Development (ID-6)
issues a brochure on ski areas and ski tour packages and their IDAHO OUT-
DOOR RECREATION RESOURCES has a list of ski areas. The Idaho State Parks
& Recreation Dept., 2177 Warm Springs Avenue, Boise, ID 83720 (208/384-
2154) issues a map/guide to snowmobile trails in 6 regions of the state. See
also ID-3 and ID-11.

NATIONAL/STATE PARKS/FORESTS, ETC.

A large part of Idaho is covered with national forests. Large detailed maps of each of the 12 forests, showing roads, trails, ranger stations, recreation sites, boating areas, ski areas, etc. are available from the U.S. Forest Service, Intermountain Region, Federal Bldg., 324 25th Street, Ogden, UT 84401 which covers the southern, widest part of Idaho, and the U.S. Forest Service, Northern Region, Federal Bldg., Missoula, MT 59801 which covers the northern panhandle part of Idaho. In 1972 Congress set aside a large portion of the northern division of the Sawtooth National Forest as the Sawtooth National Recreation Area and the Sawtooth Wilderness. Detailed maps and many separate brochures describing recreation sites, points of interest, day hikes, backpacking, mountaineering, horseback riding, boating, fishing, cross country skiing, snowmobiling, trailbike riding, flowers, birds, and wildlife in these 2 areas are available at the Redfish Lake Visitor Center, open 9A.M.-7P.M. daily from mid-June to early fall, and at the Sawtooth National Recreation Area Headquarters and Visitor Information Center, Box 438, Ketchum, ID 83340 (208/726-8291), open year-round. In Clearwater National Forest, on Route 12 where it crosses the Idaho/Montana Border, the Lolo Pass National Forest Visitor Center is open from June to October.

The Idaho State Parks & Recreation Dept., 2177 Warm Springs Avenue, Boise, ID 83720 (208/384-2154) provides individual brochures on each of the 21 state parks and facilities plus a single sheet on which they are all briefly described.

INDIVIDUAL CITIES OR AREAS

Boise—Printed Materials

Good maps are available from AAA (US-259) and the Syms-York Co., 2401 Main, Boise, ID 83706.

Boise—Organizations

ID-9   GREATER BOISE CHAMBER OF COMMERCE AND VISITORS AND CONVENTION BUREAU, 709 Idaho Street, Box 2368, Boise, ID 83701 (208/344-5515 (Chamber of Commerce) and 208/344-7777 (Visitors and Convention Bureau)).

They issue a detailed city map with a street index, but it does not include any points of interest.. A leaflet describing a sightseeing tour and the quarterly BOISE MAGAZINE are also issued.

The Division of Tourism & Industrial Development (ID-6) issues a CAPITOL GUIDE.

Sun Valley—Organizations

ID-10   KETCHUM-SUN VALLEY CHAMBER OF COMMERCE, Box 465, Ketchum, ID 83340 (208/726-3241).

They provide information on lodging, restaurants, activities, and
the Sawtooth National Forest and campgrounds. They operate a walk-
in information center on South Main Street on Highway 75 which is
open six days a week from 9A.M.-5P.M. There is a toll-free number,
800/635-4406, for information and reservations. The Sun Valley and
Ketchum Resort Association, Box 1568, Sun Valley, ID 83353 (208/
726-4655) is also located in the same walk-in information center on
Highway 75, and the same toll-free number will also put you in
touch with them.

ID-11   SUN VALLEY CO., Publicity Dept., Sun Valley, ID 83353 (800/635-
8261).

They provide seasonal brochures on what to see and do plus brochures
on ski areas and ski schools. The toll-free number may be used for
information and reservations.

ILLINOIS

BOOKS, ATLASES, MAGAZINES

IL-1   BREVET'S ILLINOIS HISTORICAL MARKERS AND SITES. Sioux Falls, SD: Brevet Press, 1976. 271 p. Photos., maps. Indexes. 0-88498-028-6. 75-253.

The text, the location (including the coordinates on the official state map), and an accompanying illustration are included for each marker. The state has been divided into 3 geographic sections, and the book is arranged alphabetically by the counties in each section. There are county, illustration, and general indexes.

IL-2   HIGHROAD CITY MAPS SHOWING THE SECRETS TO GETTING AROUND IN NORTHERN AND CENTRAL ILLINOIS. Marshall, MI: Highroad Publications (901 East Forest Street/49069), 1974. 18 p. Scale: 1 in. represents 2 miles. 76-375849.

Symbols on the maps show locations of bus and railway stations, airports, municipal and police offices, hospitals, shopping districts, points of interest and tourist attractions, motels/hotels, parks and picnic grounds, golf courses, and boat harbors and marinas. The major cities mapped are: Champaign/Urbana; Springfield; Chicago, including the O'Hare airport area; and Peoria.

IL-3   ILLINOIS: A DESCRIPTIVE AND HISTORICAL GUIDE. American Guide Series. New York: Hastings House, 1974. Rev. ed. 775 p. Photos, maps. Bibliography. Index. 0-8038-3381-4. 74-8910.

This second revision of the original WPA guide has 3 sections: general background; descriptions of 19 cities, regions, or towns; and 22 state-wide highway tours. There is a chronology of Illinois history.

IL-4   ILLINOIS CANOEING GUIDE. Springfield: Illinois Dept. of Conservation, 1975. 67 p. Maps, photos.

Each of 23 rivers is described and mapped. The descriptions contain useful practical information on such things as portages and where (if any) food and supplies may be obtained along the way. The maps show access points, bridges, dams, campsites, points of interest, and state park areas.

IL-5   ILLINOIS GUIDE AND GAZETTEER. Chicago: Rand McNally, 1969. 718 p. Photos., maps. Index. 70-82441.

The first 50 pages give a general background to the state (history, architecture, transportation, etc.). The bulk of the work is an alphabetical listing of cities and towns (over 600), giving a population figure (now out of date), the county, and a description of the community. The descriptions vary in fullness from a brief paragraph to a lengthy description giving history, industry, etc. The last 122 pages are a listing of suggested tours.

IL-6   ILLINOIS MAGAZINE. Benton, IL (320 South Main Street/62812).

This magazine began publication around 1962 and is published monthly except for the June/July and August/September combined issues. It contains mostly articles of historic and cultural interest and has a genealogical information exchange column.

IL-7   ILLINOIS STATE ATLAS. Rev. ed. Rockford, IL: Rockford Map Publishers, 1973. 232 p. Scales vary. 76-362818.

The first half of this atlas contains readable, but small, reproductions of each official county map. The last half contains descriptions, maps, and tables of state parks, camping areas, county fairs, waterways, canoeing areas, lakes, fishing areas, 20 scenic tours, a selected hotel/ motel directory, snowmobiling areas, ski areas, and golf courses.

IL-8   Osler, Jack M.   50 GREAT MINI-TRIPS FOR ILLINOIS. Dayton, OH: Media Ventures, 1978. 52 p. 0-89645-006-6.

This volume was not examined, but it is probably very much like the Pennsylvania volume (PA-3) in this series.

MAPS

The ILLINOIS HIGHWAY MAP is prepared by the Illinois Dept. of Transportation and is available at any of the offices of the Office of Tourism (IL-9). The 1977-78 edition includes a list of state parks, historic sites, conservation areas, state forests and areas in Shawnee National Forest and the facilities available at each; and a list of points of interest. The Illinois Dept. of Transportation, 2300 South Dirksen Parkway, Springfield, IL 62764 issues a unique ILLINOIS PUBLIC TRANSPORTATION MAP/DIRECTORY which shows all the intercity rail passenger and bus service routes, scheduled air routes and stops, and communities with local public transportation. One side is a map showing routes.

The other side is a community-by-community listing of available public transportation options, and it includes complete addresses and phone numbers for obtaining schedules and other information. AAA (US-259), Goushā (US-206), and Rand McNally (US-215) all issue a map of Illinois. Exxon (US-261) issues a combined Illinois/Wisconsin map. See also IL-2 and IL-7.

MAJOR TOURIST ORGANIZATION

IL-9   ILLINOIS ADVENTURE CENTER, 160 North LaSalle Street, Room 100, Chicago, IL 60601 (312/793-2094).

The Illinois Dept. of Business and Economic Development, Office of Tourism has 4 offices. The one above is the one to contact, either by mail, phone, or walk-in for information on where to travel in the state. It is located in downtown Chicago. The administrative offices of the Office of Tourism are at 205 West Wacker Drive, Room 1122, Chicago, IL 60606. There are additional offices at Springfield (222 South College Street, Springfield, IL 62706 217/782-7500]) and at Marion (2209 West Main Street, Marion, IL 62959). Any of the 4 offices may be contacted in a pinch. They issue 3 major brochures: ILLINOIS: PRAIRIE HERITAGE, a guide to places of historic interest prepared for the Bicentennial; a very thorough semiannual calendar of events; and a biennial camping guide which lists all camping areas in the state and the facilities available at each. They also issue 3 other more specialized guides: a guide to bike trails; a golf guide; and a guide to commercial, industrial, and educational tours.

REGIONAL TOURISM ASSOCIATIONS

The state is divided into 5 regional tourism areas: southern, western, central, northern, and metro-Chicago. For information on the southern region, contact the Office of Tourism located in Marion (IL-9). For information on the western and central regions, contact the Office of Tourism in Springfield (IL-9). For information on the northern region, contact the Northern Illinois Tourism Council, Route 2, Box 240, Long Grove, IL 60047. In the metropolitan Chicago area contact either of the 2 offices of the Office of Tourism located there (IL-9).

OTHER ORGANIZATIONS

IL-10   ILLINOIS HOTEL & MOTEL ASSOCIATION, 902 Ridgely Bldg., Springfield, IL 62701 (217/522-1231).

They publish an annual directory of members, the ILLINOIS HOTEL/ MOTEL DIRECTORY. It is regionally arranged with a city index. The address, number of rooms, rates, and phone number are given for each hotel/motel.

INFORMATION CENTERS/INFORMATION PHONES

The state has several interstate highway welcome centers that provide information on routings, attractions, special events, and road and weather conditions.
Their locations are shown on the ILLINOIS HIGHWAY MAP.

OUTDOOR RECREATION ACTIVITIES

BICYCLING. The Office of Tourism (IL-9) issues a 19-page guide to ILLINOIS
BIKE TRAILS. General directions for 18 trails are included, but there are no
detailed maps. Also available from them are 3 map/guides (western, central,
and eastern sectors) to the Southern Illinois Biketrail which is the route of the
crosscountry BIKECENTENNIAL (US-223) as it passes through Illinois. See also
IL-20.

CANOEING AND BOATING. An ILLINOIS RIVERS FACILITIES MAP showing
locations of and facilities available at marinas, parks, canals, locks and dams,
etc. is available from the Illinois Dept. of Conservation, Information and Education, 603 Stratton Bldg., Springfield, IL 62706 (217/782-7454). Brief mention of canoe routes appears in the camping guide issued by the Office of
Tourism (IL-9). See also IL-4.

FISHING AND HUNTING. There are several sections within the Illinois Dept.
of Conservation that may be contacted: (1) Information and Education, 603
Stratton Bldg., Springfield, IL 62706 (217/782-7454); (2) Fisheries Division,
100 East Washington, Springfield, IL 62706 (217/782-6424); and (3) Wildlife
Resources Division, 100 1/2 East Washington, Springfield, IL 62706 (217/782-
6384).

NATIONAL/STATE PARKS/FORESTS, ETC.

A map showing roads, trails, recreation sites, visitor information stops, etc. in
Shawnee National Forest, the only national forest in Illinois, is available from
either Forest Supervisor, Shawnee National Forest, 317 East Poplar Street,
Harrisburg, IL 62946, or from the Office of Tourism (IL-9).

The Illinois Dept. of Conservation, Land and Historic Sites Division, 405 East
Washington, Springfield, IL 62706 (217/782-6752) issues a guide to facilities
and camping at state owned parks, historic sites, conservation areas, and forests.
The ILLINOIS CAMPING GUIDE, issued by the Office of Tourism (IL-9), is a
very thorough listing of both public and privately owned campgrounds, complete
with addresses, phone numbers, and facilities for each.

INDIVIDUAL CITIES OR AREAS

Chicago—Printed Materials

IL-11   ACCESS CHICAGO: A GUIDE TO THE CITY. Chicago: Rehabilitation Institute of Chicago (345 East Superior Street/60611), 1975. 83 p.

Also available from this organization is A GUIDE TO THE CHICAGO LOOP FOR THE HANDICAPPED.

IL-12   Bach, Ira J. CHICAGO ON FOOT: WALKING TOURS OF CHICAGO'S ARCHITECTURE. 3d ed. Chicago: Rand McNally, 1977. 392 p. Photos., maps. Index. 0-528-81793-0. 77-369195.

This is a very thorough foot guide to 32 walking tours, including a map, transportation information to the starting point, and the required walking time for each.

IL-13   Baron, Andrea, and Rivkin, Dyann. WHERE TO GO AND WHAT TO DO WITH THE KIDS IN CHICAGO. Los Angeles: Price/Stern/Sloan, 1972. 160 p. Map. Index. 0-8431-0188-1. 72-76840.

The authors provide comprehensive coverage (including hours, fees, and finding information) of outdoor activities; museums; ways to have a memorable birthday party; educational classes, clubs, and groups; nature activities; tours; and entertainment. A chapter for parents provides "survival information." There is a calendar of events.

IL-14   Benton, Chris. CHICAGOLAND NATURE TRAILS. Chicago: Contemporary Books, 1978. 269 p. Photos., maps. Index. 0-8092-7662-3. 77-91183.

Natural areas--from prairie to forest to dunes--in the Chicago area are described and located. More cities should have such guides.

IL-15   THE CHICAGO GUIDEBOOK. By the editors of Chicago Guide. Chicago: Henry Regnery Co., 1973. 239 p. Maps. 73-162016.

This is a brief, thorough (but now out of date), and handy guide to sightseeing, entertainment, art, sports, restaurants, touring, transportation, hotels/motels, shopping, architecture, education, media, and communities. It is arranged by chapters under each of these topics, and there is no index. The only maps included are 2 showing locations of specific communities.

IL-16   Graham, Jory. CHICAGO: AN EXTRAORDINARY GUIDE. Chicago: Rand McNally, 1969. 499 p. Maps. Index. 71-7085.

This is the most thorough, knowledgeable guide to the city. It describes dining and eating places, museums, performing arts, sports for spectators and participants, shops, points of interest including neighborhoods, and a brief list of hotels. There is a calendar of regularly scheduled events. It is unfortunate that it isn't kept up to date with frequent revisions. There is supposed to be a later edition than 1969, but we have been unable to locate it.

IL-17   Kaplan, Sherman. BEST RESTAURANTS: CHICAGO. San Francisco: 101 Productions (distributed by Scribner), 1977. 208 p. Indexes. 0-89286-119-3. 77-5051.

This book describes, rates, gives practical information, and frequently a reproduction of the menu for a wide range of restaurants in Chicago and its suburbs. The author has been reviewing restaurants on Chicago's radio station WBBM for 6 years. There are indexes by price, cuisine, and geographic area.

IL-18   Kupcinet, Sue, and Fish, Connie. CHICAGO GOURMET. A Fireside Book. New York: Simon & Schuster, 1977. 300 p. Map. Indexes. 0-671-22896-X. 77-11041.

The authors describe (including address, phone, hours, credit cards honored, entertainment, parking, banquet facilities, dress, and availability of liquor and wine) 130 distinctive Chicago restaurants and include a recipe provided by the chef of each. There are recipe, location, cuisine, and price range indexes.

IL-19   Lasker, Toy. FLASHMAPS! THE 1978-79 INSTANT GUIDE TO CHICAGO. Chappaqua, NY: Flashmaps (Box 13/10514), 1977. Issued annually. 80 p. Maps. 77-85321.

Forty-six maps show locations of bus and rapid transit routes, consulates, forest preserves, highways and expressways, hotels and motels, museums, night life, parks, restaurants, shops, sightseeing, sports, theaters, and much, much more.

IL-20   Mark, Norman. NORMAN MARK'S CHICAGO: WALKING, BICYCLING AND DRIVING TOURS OF THE CITY. Chicago: Chicago Review Press, 1977. 230 p. Photos., maps. Bibliography. Index. 0-914090-39-9. 77-84293.

The author includes exact directions and practical information with his descriptions of 14 walks, 1 bike tour (lakefront), 3 drives, and 7 pub crawls. This is the best, recent, all-round Chicago guidebook we have found.

IL-21   Rohde, Jill, and Rohde, Ron. THE NEW GOOD (BUT CHEAP) CHICAGO RESTAURANT BOOK. Rev. ed. Chicago: Swallow Press, 1977. 249 p. Indexes. 0-8040-0698-9. 76-3133.

"Where to find great meals at little neighborhood restaurants from $1.50 to $4.95." It is arranged by type of food served with location and name indexes.

IL-22   Swanson, Warren, with Schmeling, Sue. MUSEUMS OF CHICAGO.
         Chicago: Museum Publications of America (10 South Wabash/60603),
         [1977?]. 38 p. Photos., map.

         This is included because it was the only guide to Chicago museums
         that we uncovered. Twenty-five museums (including several zoos,
         arboretums, gardens, etc.) are described, located on a map, and have
         practical information on hours, admission charges, how to get there by
         car or public transportation, on-site food services, and museum shops.

Maps of Chicago are avilable from AAA (US-259); Arrow Publishing Co. (US-
199); Creative Sales Corp., 762 West Algonquin Road, Arlington Heights, IL
60005; Goushā (US-206); and Rand McNally (US-215). The CHICAGO
TRIBUNE, 435 North Michigan Avenue, Chicago, IL 60611 issues a CHICAGO-
LAND MAP. This very fine map, measuring 41 x 35 in., has a metropolitan
area map, with a downtown inset, that shows places of interest; forest preserves;
airports; railroads; bathing beaches; state parks; golf and country clubs; lakes;
race tracks, ballparks, and stadiums; street names; etc. On the other side is a
general road map covering northern Illinois and parts of adjacent states. See
also IL-19.

The Chicago weather information number is 312/936-1212.

Chicago—Organizations

IL-23   CHICAGO ASSOCIATION OF COMMERCE AND INDUSTRY, 130 South
         Michigan Avenue, Chicago, IL 60603 (312/786-0111).

         The above address is a visitors bureau open 8:30A.M.-5P.M., Monday-
         Friday. They issue 2 major pieces of literature: (1) a small map of
         downtown Chicago showing points of interest, hotels and motor inns,
         theaters, city parking garages, and bus and railroad stations; and (2)
         a bimonthly events listing which also includes lists of places of inter-
         est, museums, restaurants, dancing and entertainment establishments,
         exhibits, zoos, hotels/motels, sightseeing tours, transportation services,
         travel information sources, railroad stations, and airports.

IL-24   CHICAGO CONVENTION & TOURISM BUREAU, 332 South Michigan
         Avenue, 20th floor, Chicago, IL 60604 (312/922-3530).

         They issue an annual CHICAGO CONVENTION & TOURISM GUIDE,
         a "travel and recreation planner for visitors, travel agents, convention
         executives and delegates." It contains extensive information on tourist
         attractions, accommodations, restaurants, transportation, shopping, etc.
         They also issue several smaller separate brochures: VISITOR GUIDE &
         MAP (locates attractions and hotels/motels on 3 separate maps: down-
         town Chicago, metropolitan area, and Chicago lakefront area); a
         CHICAGO GUIDE listing things to do and places to visit; a restaurant
         guide; and a shopping guide. They operate a visitor "eventline" at

922-7000 which provides information on entertainment, theater, special events, and sports. They have an office in Washington, DC at 1725 K Street NW, Suite 1105, Washington, DC 20006 (202/466-6680).

Springfield—Printed Materials

IL-25   BUILDING ACCESS GUIDE FOR THE HANDICAPPED AND AGING. Springfield: Altrusa Club of Springfield, Illinois in cooperation with the Easter Seal Society of Illinois and the Illinois Division of Vocational Rehabilitation, 1972. 26 p.

Maps of Springfield are available from Arrow Publishing Co. (US-199) and Champion Map Corp. (US-202).

Springfield—Organizations

IL-26   SPRINGFIELD CONVENTION AND TOURISM COMMISSION, #1 North Old State Capitol Plaza, INB Center, C-15, Springfield, IL 62701 (217/789-2360).

They issue 2 brochures: a general map/guide showing points of interest, and a guide to WALK/DRIVE TOURS. They also provide information on camping, outdoor recreation opportunities, and transportation services.

INDIANA

BOOKS, ATLASES, MAGAZINES

IN-1   CANOE GUIDE. Indianapolis: Indiana Dept. of Natural Resources,
        1975. 108 p. Maps, photos. 76-620994.

        Twenty-one river or stream canoe trips are described somewhat briefly.
There is a special list of which USGS topographical quadrangles cover
each trip. The work is adequate, but it could be better.

IN-2   EXPLORE INDIANA. Rockford, IL: Rockford Map Publishers, 1966.
        158 p. Maps, photos.

        Ninety-two difficult to read county road maps are supplemented by a
gazetteer, a list of parks (noting facilities and activities), a list of
public fishing areas, the text of the state boating laws, crude maps of
canoe trails, a list of campgrounds, a hotel/motel list, a list of rivers
and lakes, and a golf course directory (with map). Hopefully, there
will soon be a revised edition of this title.

IN-3   Hanna, Elizabeth A., ed. HOOSIER GUIDE. Ray, IN: The Hoosier
        Guide Publishing Co. (198 Clear Lake Drive/46737), 1968. 224 p.
        Photos., map.

        This guide has not been updated, and the dates in the festivals and
events sections are, of course, no longer applicable. But if one has
this book (once the major guide to the state) and no other, the regional sections describing historic sites, points of interest, privately-
owned campsites, fishing and hunting areas, golf courses, and state
parks and forests would still be somewhat useful.

IN-4   INDIANA: A GUIDE TO THE HOOSIER STATE. American Guide
        Series. New York: Oxford University Press, 1941. 548 p. Photos.,
        maps.

        This original WPA guide in 3 sections--general background, descriptions
of 14 cities and towns, and 20 state-wide highways tours--is comprehensive, but out of date.

IN-5   Osler, Jack M. 50 GREAT MINI-TRIPS FOR INDIANA. Dayton, OH:
        Media Ventures, 1978. 52 p. 0-89645-005-8.

        This volume was not examined, but is probably very much like the
        Pennsylvania volume (PA-3) in this series.

MAPS

The INDIANA STATE HIGHWAY SYSTEM MAP is produced by the State Highway
Commission but is available from the Tourism Development Divison (IN-6). The
1978 edition has a brief list of state parks, recreation areas, beaches, state
fish and wildlife areas, and state forests. AAA (US-259), Gousha (US-206),
and Rand McNally (US-215) all issue a map of Indiana. Exxon (US-261) issues
a combined Indiana/Michigan map. See also IN-2 and IN-8.

MAJOR TOURIST ORGANIZATION

IN-6   INDIANA DEPT. OF COMMERCE, TOURISM DEVELOPMENT DIVISION,
        336 State House, Indianapolis, IN 46204 (317/633-5423).

        They issue a semiannual calendar of events, INDIANA SCENICIRCLE
        DRIVES (a 132-page booklet describing points of interest along 17 one-day
        drives), a golf course map/guide, and CAMPING AND OUTDOOR
        RECREATION GUIDE (a 124-page geographical guide to sites in Indiana
        offering recreation activities of all kinds: camping, tennis, water
        activities, fishing, hunting, winter activities, bicycling, hiking, boat-
        ing, picnicking, etc. Each geographic section has an alphabetical
        index by name of site, but there is no index by type of activity. A
        final section lists fishing, hunting, boating and towing regulations).

OTHER ORGANIZATIONS

IN-7   INDIANA HOTEL & MOTEL ASSOCIATION, 2312 North Fisher Avenue,
        Speedway, IN 46224 (317/923-4197).

IN-8   TRAVEL INDIANA, 111 North Capitol Avenue, Indianapolis, IN 46204.

        "Travel Indiana is a not-for-profit association of travel and tourism re-
        lated businesses and organizations throughout the state. . .[it] supports
        and coordinates its activities with the Tourism Development Division of
        the Indiana Dept. of Commerce." It was started in 1974. It issues a
        map on which member attractions and hotels/motels are described and
        keyed. State and national parks, state memorials, and state recreation
        areas and rest areas are also indicated.

INFORMATION CENTERS/INFORMATION PHONES

For state park information, call 800/382-4057 toll-free.

OUTDOOR RECREATION ACTIVITIES

CANOEING AND BOATING. See IN-1.

FISHING AND HUNTING. Contact the Indiana Dept. of Natural Resources, Division of Fish and Wildlife, 607 State Office Bldg., 100 North Senate Avenue, Indianapolis, IN 46204. See also IN-2 and the CAMPING AND OUTDOOR RECREATION GUIDE issued by the Tourism Development Division (IN-6).

NATIONAL/STATE PARKS/FORESTS, ETC.

Indiana Dunes National Lakeshore

IN-9   Daniel, Glenda. DUNE COUNTRY: A GUIDE FOR HIKERS AND NATURALISTS. Chicago: Swallow Press, 1977. 220 p. Drawings, maps. 0-8040-0757-8.

The author describes 30 miles of trails in the national park and nearby state park.

IN-10   Komaiko, Jean, and Schaeffer, Norma. DOING THE DUNES. Beverly Shores, IN: Dunes Enterprises, 1973. 231 p. 74-166471.

The authors include descriptions of towns and sites within an hour's drive of the Lakeshore, located in northern Indiana along Lake Michigan. There is information on enjoying the Lakeshore itself, but half of the book contains descriptions of what to see and do, including restaurants, in 4 Indiana and 1 Michigan counties bordering the Lake. In addition, there is a calendar of events, suggestions for 20 tours and a 38-page categorical guide. This is a very thorough, very good guide for a little known area.

IN-11   INDIANA DUNES NATIONAL LAKESHORE, R.R. 2, Box 139-A, Chesterton, IN 46304.

Hoosier National Forest, 1615 J Street, Bedford, IN 47421 is the only national forest in Indiana. Maps on several scales that show recreation sites are available from them.

The Indiana Dept. of Natural Resources, 616 State Office Bldg., Indianapolis, IN 46204 issues a camping guide and a guide to locations and facilities at state beaches, state parks, state recreation areas, and state memorials. They also issue OUTDOOR INDIANA (available from Room 612, State Office Bldg., Indianapolis, IN 46204) published 10 times a year. Although many of the articles reflect the day-to-day responsibilities of this Department, each issue usually has 1 or 2 articles about camping, fishing, hunting, outdoor areas, etc. Three cumulative indexes are available: 1966-1969, 1970-1972, and 1973-1975. See also the CAMPING AND OUTDOOR RECREATION GUIDE issued by the Tourism Development Division (IN-6).

INDIVIDUAL CITIES OR AREAS

Indianapolis—Printed Materials

IN-12   Kriplen, Nancy, and Winter, Margaret A. EXPLORING INDIANAPO-LIS. Rev. ed. Indianapolis: Lexicon Corp., Publishers (One Indiana Square, Suite 3130/46204), 1977. 161 p. Index. 77-365970.

This is a very complete guide arranged thematically by museums, transportation (bus trips, train museums, etc.), nature, the arts, international activities and foods, businesses to visit, active sports, spectator sports, and restaurants. It also contains a calendar of regularly scheduled events.

IN-13   NAVIGATION UNLIMITED IN INDIANAPOLIS FOR THOSE WHO ARE STOPPED BY STEPS. Indianapolis: Marion County Muscular Dystrophy Foundation (615 North Alabama Street, Room 221/46204), 1972. 85 p.

A new edition is planned.

Good maps of Indianapolis are available from Arrow Publishing Co. (US-199); Champion Map Corp. (US-202); George F. Cram, 301 South LaSalle Street, Box 426, Indianapolis, IN 46206; Gousha (US-206); Hagstrom (US-207); Metro Graphic Arts, 900 40th SE, Grand Rapids, MI 49508; and Rand McNally (US-215).

Indianapolis—Organizations

IN-14   INDIANAPOLIS CHAMBER OF COMMERCE, 320 North Meridian Street, Indianapolis, IN 46204 (317/635-4747).

They issue an INDIANAPOLIS METROGUIDE (2d ed., 1978-79, 64 p.), one of a series of similar Metroguide Publications done for other cities "developed specifically for use by residents, prospective residents, corporate managers, planners and employees needing a comprehensive source of diverse data about the Greater Indianapolis metropolitan area." The sections on dining out, shopping, getting about, and "seeing/doing" could be used by visitors but some would, no doubt, be overwhelmed by this publication. A rather good INDIANAPOLIS

VISITORS GUIDE that they issued several years ago has apparently been discontinued.

Our request to the Indianapolis Convention and Visitors Bureau, 100 South Capitol Avenue, Indianapolis, IN 46225 (317/635-9567) brought the reply that they did "not have any travel publications and we do not plan any in the near future."

IOWA

BOOKS, ATLASES, MAGAZINES

IA-1   IOWA: A GUIDE TO THE HAWKEYE STATE. American Guide Series.
New York: Hastings House, 1938. 583 p. Photos., maps.

This original WPA guide in 3 sections--general background, descriptions
of 17 cities and towns, and 17 state-wide highway tours--is comprehensive, but out of date.

IA-2   Pratt, LeRoy G. DISCOVERING HISTORIC IOWA. Des Moines:
Iowa Dept. of Public Instruction, 1975. 313 p. Drawings, maps.
Index. 76-621739.

This listing, by county, of historical societies, museums, landmarks,
historic sites, and natural areas notes hours and fees for each. A
celebration/festival list is included.

MAPS

The STATE TRANSPORTATION MAP is available from the Travel Development
Division (IA-3). The 1978 edition contained a list of state parks and recreation
areas and the facilities available at each, plus extensive information for motorists including a list of over 12 telephone numbers to call for road conditions
and emergencies. AAA (US-259), Goushā (US-206), and Rand McNally (US-
215) each issue a map of Iowa. See also IA-6.

MAJOR TOURIST ORGANIZATION

IA-3   IOWA DEVELOPMENT COMMISSION, TRAVEL DEVELOPMENT DIVI-
SION, 250 Jewett Bldg., Des Moines, IA 50309 (515/281-3100).

They issue a large, general booklet; an events calendar issued every
4 months; a mini-vacations brochure that outlines 8 2- to 3-day trips

in various regions of the state; and information on campgrounds, skiing, and farm vacations.

REGIONAL TOURISM ASSOCIATIONS

The state is divided into 7 tourism regions and information on each is available from the Travel Development Division (IA-3).

OTHER ORGANIZATIONS

IA-4   AMANA COLONIES TRAVEL COUNCIL, Amana, IA 52203.

They issue a GUIDE MAP AND BUSINESS DIRECTORY to the 7 villages of the Amana Colonies. It describes and gives the hours of all shops, museums, and the refrigeration plant.

IA-5   CRC GOLF ENTERPRISES, Box 445, Ames, IA 50010

They issue an annual WHERE TO PLAY GOLF IN IOWA, a brief listing of all golf areas in the state arranged by individual cities and towns.

IA-6   IOWA HOTEL & MOTEL ASSOCIATION, 515 28th Street, Des Moines, IA 50312 (515/283-2000).

They issue an annual fold-out map/guide, IOWA TRAVEL AND AC-COMMODATIONS GUIDE.

INFORMATION CENTERS/INFORMATION PHONES

Highway information sites are located on the STATE TRANSPORTATION MAP. The Iowa Development Commission (IA-3) has a toll-free number 800/362-2843, ext. 3185, but it is to that organization as a whole, and not specifically to the Travel Development Division.

OUTDOOR RECREATION ACTIVITIES

CANOEING AND BOATING. The Iowa Conservation Commission, Wallace State Office Bldg., Des Moines, IA 50319 issues 2 useful publications: MISSISSIPPI RIVER BOATING FACILITIES GUIDE is a listing of facilities available at each Mississippi River access area in each of Iowa's 10 counties lying on the river, and IOWA CANOE TRIPS describes access sites and general water conditions, points of interest, and provides a map for each of 13 canoeable rivers.

FISHING AND HUNTING. Contact the Iowa Conservation Commission, Wallace State Office Bldg., Des Moines, IA 50319. They seem to be particularly strong on fishing guides and issue an IOWA FISHING GUIDE which describes all public fishing lakes of 10 acres or more, and an IOWA TROUT FISHING GUIDE, a large fold-out map/guide to the trout areas of Iowa. Their IOWA HUNTING GUIDE contains maps and in-depth descriptions of waterfowl flyways and wildlife management areas.

NATIONAL/STATE PARKS/FORESTS, ETC.

There are no major National Park Service areas, and no national forests in Iowa.

The Iowa Conservation Commission, Wallace State Office Bldg., Des Moines, IA 50319 issues a guide to state parks and recreation areas which includes information on use of camping and recreation facilities. They also issue separate guide maps and guides to backpacking trails in each state forest. Also available from them is the magazine IOWA CONSERVATIONIST, which provides information on hunting, fishing, camping, trapping, boating, and conservation in Iowa.

INDIVIDUAL CITIES OR AREAS

Des Moines—Printed Materials

IA-7   A GUIDEBOOK TO DES MOINES FOR THE HANDICAPPED. Des Moines: Alpha Chi Omega, Alpha Omicron Alpha Chapter, 1968. 31 p.

Maps of Des Moines are available from Metro Graphic Arts, 900 40th SE, Grand Rapids, MI 49508 and Rand McNally (US-215).

Des Moines—Organizations

IA-8   GREATER DES MOINES CHAMBER OF COMMERCE AND CONVENTION & VISITORS BUREAU, 800 High Street, Des Moines, IA 50307 (515/283-2161).

They issue a quarterly calendar of events; an annual metropolitan guide to dining, lodging, and cocktail lounges; and information on places to tour and sponsored tours.

KANSAS

BOOKS, ATLASES, MAGAZINES

KS-1   HISTORICAL MARKERS IN KANSAS. Topeka: Kansas State Historical
        Society, n.d. 48 p. Photos., map.

        Readable photographs of 84 historical markers are accompanied by a
        map locating each.

KS-2   KANSAS: A GUIDE TO THE SUNFLOWER STATE. American Guide
        Series. New York: Hastings House, 1939. 538 p. Photos., maps.
        Bibliography. Index.

        This original WPA guide describes the state and its people ranging
        from such topics as archaeology to theater, includes tours of 18 cities
        and towns plus 13 highway tours. There is a chronology of Kansas
        history.

KS-3   Patterson, Jerry. TRAVEL GUIDE KANSAS. Wakefield, KS: the
        author, 1970. 62 p. Photos., maps. Indexes.

        Attractions in 6 regions of Kansas are described and keyed to a map.
        There are indexes to towns and to wildlife areas.

MAPS

The KANSAS TRANSPORTATION MAP is available from either the Kansas Dept.
of Transportation, Public Information Dept., State Office Bldg., Topeka, KS
66612 or the Tourist & Tourism Division (KS-4). The 1978 edition contained a
list of state parks, lakes, and reservoirs; a list of AM/FM radio stations; and a
list of telephone numbers to call for road information or emergencies. The
Public Information Dept. also issues a much smaller map showing highways leading to Kansas recreation areas on one side and a reproduction of a 1918 official
map of Kansas state roads on the other side. Both AAA (US-259) and Rand
McNally (US-215) issue a combined Kansas/Nebraska map. Exxon (US-261) issues a combined Oklahoma/Kansas map. Goushā (US-206) issues a separate
Kansas map.

MAJOR TOURIST ORGANIZATION

KS-4   KANSAS DEPT. OF ECONOMIC DEVELOPMENT, TOURIST & TOURISM
DIVISION, 503 Kansas Avenue, 6th floor, Topeka, KS 66603 (913/296-
3487).

They issue a KANSAS TRAVEL GUIDE (1978 ed., 28 p.) which describes fairs and rodeos, sports, camping, highway rest areas, hunting,
lakes, and points of interest in the 6 travel regions of the state. It
is indexed. In addition, they issue an annual calendar of events and
distribute a directory of private campgrounds in Kansas. They also
issue a quarterly magazine called KANSAS! which features articles on
the economy, recreation, history, and natural history of the state.

REGIONAL TOURISM ASSOCIATIONS

The state is divided into 6 travel regions, but there are no regional travel promotion associations. Contact the Tourist & Tourism Division (KS-4) for information on a specific region.

OTHER ORGANIZATIONS

KS-5   KANSAS HOTEL & MOTEL ASSOCIATION, Box J, Garden City, KS
67846

INFORMATION CENTERS/INFORMATION PHONES

Highway information centers in 1978 existed only on a temporary basis and had
no established addresses or phone numbers.

OUTDOOR RECREATION ACTIVITIES

CANOEING AND BOATING. KANSAS CANOE TRAILS GUIDE is available
from Don Charvat, Box 798, Belle Plaine, KS 67013.

FISHING AND HUNTING. Contact the Kansas Fish and Game Commission,
Rural Route 2, Box 54A, Pratt, KS 67124 (316/672-5911).

NATIONAL/STATE PARKS/FORESTS, ETC.

There are no major National Park Service areas and no national forests in Kansas.

The Kansas State Park and Resources Authority, 503 Kansas, Box 977, Topeka, KS 66601 issues YOUR GUIDE TO KANSAS STATE PARK AREAS, RULES AND REGULATIONS, PERMITS.

INDIVIDUAL CITIES OR AREAS

Topeka—Printed Materials

KS-6   A GUIDE TO BARRIER FREE ESTABLISHMENTS. Prepared by the Topeka Human Relations Commission. Topeka: Division for the Disabled (City Hall, Room 54/66603), 1976. 16 p.

A new edition is planned.

A map of Topeka is available from the Champion Map Corp. (US-202).

Topeka—Organizations

KS-7   GREATER TOPEKA CHAMBER OF COMMERCE AND CONVENTION & VISITORS BUREAU, 722 Kansas, Topeka, KS 66603 (913/234-2644).

They issue a list of places to visit, a hotel/motel guide, and a shopping guide.

KENTUCKY

BOOKS, ATLASES, MAGAZINES

KY-1   GRAPHIC STREET GUIDE OF NORTHERN KENTUCKY, INCLUDING
        ALEXANDRIA. . .AND OTHER OUTLYING AREAS. Grand Rapids,
        MI: Metro Graphic Arts, 1973. 28 p. Maps. Scales vary. 75-
        312186.

        This atlas consists of detailed street maps for downtown Cincinnati
        (Ohio) and for the outlying areas around Covington/Newport and Inde-
        pendence in Kentucky.

KY-2   KENTUCKY: A GUIDE TO THE BLUEGRASS STATE. Rev. ed. Ameri-
        can Guide Series. New York: Hastings House, 1954. 492 p. Photos.,
        maps.

        This revision of the original 1939 WPA guide has 3 sections: general
        background, descriptions of 7 cities and towns, and 20 state-wide high-
        way tours.

KY-3   Kentucky Historical Society. GUIDE TO KENTUCKY HISTORICAL
        HIGHWAY MARKERS. Frankfort: the Society, 1969. 337 p. Photos.,
        map. Index. 74-632141.

        This work, arranged alphabetically by the subject of each marker, gives
        the location and text of 1273 historical markers. In 1973 a 120-page
        supplement was issued covering markers erected between July 1, 1969
        and June 30, 1973.

KY-4   KENTUCKY TRAVEL GUIDE. 12th ed. Louisville: Editorial Services
        (Box 357/40201), 1978. Issued annually. 84 p. Maps, photos. In-
        dexes.

        This is a very thorough guide to attractions and landmarks, visitors
        bureaus or information centers, sightseeing and self-guided tours, special
        events, motels/hotels, restaurants, theaters, parks, and camping and
        fishing information in cities and communities in 36 geographic areas of

Kentucky. There are indexes by community and by type of attraction (i.e., caves, historic houses, etc.). This is the single most comprehensive travel guide to Kentucky, and it is available from either the publisher or the Division of Travel and Tourism (KY-9).

KY-5   Lander, Arthur B., Jr. A GUIDE TO KENTUCKY OUTDOORS. Ann Arbor, MI: Thomas Press, 1978. 265 p. Photos. 0-89732-001-8. 78-71189.

"This is the first book to categorize outdoor recreational opportunities in a single state. Two national and 17 state parks, 25 lakes, 6 state and 1 national forest, and 7 nature and science areas are described as potential recreational sites. Opportunities for skiing, scuba diving, hang-gliding, parachuting, and bicycling in Kentucky are also identified."

KY-6   McDowell, Robert E. RE-DISCOVERING KENTUCKY: A GUIDE FOR MODERN DAY EXPLORERS. Frankfort: Kentucky Dept. of Parks, 1971. 193 p. Photos., maps. Bibliography. Index. 73-172463.

This official publication is no longer issued, but it is very thorough and useful, if it can be found. It describes, with many circle tours, a wealth of natural and scenic areas which don't change that much. It also has a list of information centers that is probably out of date now.

KY-7   Osler, Jack M. 50 BEST MINI-TRIPS FOR KENTUCKY. Dayton, OH: Media Ventures, 1977. 52 p. 0-89645-001-5.

This volume was not examined, but is probably very much like the Pennsylvania volume (PA-3) in this series.

KY-8   TRAVELS THROUGH KENTUCKY HISTORY. Louisville, KY: Data Courier for the Courier-Journal Louisville Times, 1976. 120 p. Photos. Index. 76-9479.

More historical background than true guidebook, this book does offer suggestions on places to visit.

MAPS

The OFFICIAL HIGHWAY AND PARKWAY MAP is available from the Division of Travel and Tourism (KY-9). The 1978 edition contained a list of facilities at the state resort parks and a list of radio stations as well as numerous interstate and parkway maps (the latter giving tolls). AAA (US-259) issues a joint Kentucky/Tennessee map and another map showing the Blue Grass Horse Farms and Lexington. Exxon (US-261), Goushā (US-206), and Rand McNally (US-215) each issue a combined Kentucky/Tennessee map. See also KY-1.

MAJOR TOURIST ORGANIZATION

KY-9   KENTUCKY DEPT. OF PUBLIC INFORMATION, DIVISION OF TRAV-
EL AND TOURISM, Capitol Annex, Frankfort, KY 40601 (502/564-
4930).

They issue the KENTUCKY TRAVEL GUIDE (KY-4), CALL OF KEN-
TUCKY (a 72-page lavishly illustrated guide to Kentucky's state parks,
state resort parks, and state shrines), separate brochures on each of
these facilities and an additional folder giving rates and reservation
information, KENTUCKY SCENIC AND HISTORIC TOURS (outlines 8
weekend tours, 6 of which were originated by the American Petroleum
Institute during the 1974 gasoline crisis), GUIDE TO HIKING TRAILS
OF KENTUCKY, GUIDE TO CANOEING STREAMS OF KENTUCKY
(neither the hiking nor canoeing guides include maps, but they do
give the name of the USGS quadrangles to use), calendar of events,
camping guide (includes both state-owned and privately-owned campgrounds), and a golf course directory.

REGIONAL TOURISM ASSOCIATIONS

ELIZABETHTOWN VISITORS & INFORMATION COMMISSION, Box 51-108
North Main Street, Elizabethtown, KY 42701 (502/756-2175).

LEXINGTON TOURIST AND CONVENTION COMMISSION, 421 North Broadway, Lexington, KY 40508 (606/252-7565).

NORTHERN KENTUCKY TOURIST AND CONVENTION COMMISSION, 129
East 2d Street, Covington, KY 41011 (606/261-4678).

OWENSBORO TOURIST COMMISSION, 327 East 18th Street, Owensboro, KY
42361 (502/926-1100).

PADUCAH-McCRACKEN COUNTY TOURIST AND CONVENTION BUREAU,
Box 90, Paducah, KY 42001 (502/443-8783).

OTHER ORGANIZATIONS

KY-10   KENTUCKY HOTEL & MOTEL ASSOCIATION, 719 South Brook Street,
Louisville, KY 40203 (502/583-7521).

INFORMATION CENTERS/INFORMATION PHONES

A list of the highway information centers is found on the OFFICIAL HIGHWAY
AND PARKWAY MAP, and a list may be obtained from the Division of Travel

and Tourism (KY-9). The centers are open 7 days a week from 8A.M.-
4:30P.M. There is a central reservations service for making reservations at
state parks and state resort parks. From most areas in Kentucky, call 800/
372-2961. In Louisville call 583-9796. In Lexington call 252-4913. In
Covington/Cincinnati (OH) call 261-2643. In Ohio, Indiana, Illinois,
Missouri, Tennessee, Alabama, Georgia, South Carolina, Virginia, and West
Virginia call 800/626-2911. In other areas where toll-free service is not
available and in Frankfort call 502/223-2326. This service is available
Monday-Friday, 8A.M.-4:30P.M.

OUTDOOR RECREATION ACTIVITIES

CANOEING AND BOATING. Boating information and regulations may be ob-
tained from the Kentucky Dept. of Transportation, Division of Boating, State
Office Bldg., Frankfort, KY 40601. See also the GUIDE TO CANOEING
STREAMS OF KENTUCKY available from the Division of Travel and Tourism
(KY-9).

FISHING AND HUNTING. For the best places to fish and hunt contact the
Kentucky Dept. of Fish and Wildlife Resources, Capital Plaza, Frankfort, KY
40601 (502/564-4336).

NATIONAL/STATE PARKS/FORESTS, ETC.

Mammoth Cave National Park

KY-11 MAMMOTH CAVE NATIONAL PARK, Mammoth Cave, KY 42259.

The official map/brochure has 3 maps, one of which shows some of
the underground trails. Additional trail information is available at the
visitor center. The visitor center is open daily (except Christmas)
and all cave tours depart from there. For information about lodging and services contact National Park Concessions, General Offices,
Mammoth Cave, KY 42259 (502/758-2217).

There is only 1 national forest in Kentucky: Daniel Boone National Forest,
100 Vaught Road, Winchester, KY 40391. They supply a large detailed map
of the forest as well as information on canoe trails in the forest. For information on hiking, campgrounds, and the facilities at the state parks and state
resort parks, contact the Division of Travel and Tourism (KY-9). See also the
"Information Centers/Information Phones" section of this chapter.

INDIVIDUAL CITIES OR AREAS

Frankfort—Printed Materials

A good map of Frankfort is issued by Arrow Publishing Co. (US-199).

Kentucky

Frankfort—Organizations

KY-12 FRANKFORT TOURIST AND CONVENTION COMMISSION, Box 654, Frankfort, KY 40602 (502/223-8261).

They issue a detailed city map; a walking tour map/brochure; a general attractions brochure which contains a map of the "Boone Tour" of points of interest in the greater Frankfort area; and IN AND AROUND FRANKFORT, a quarterly guide for newcomers and visitors which includes, among other things, a hotel/motel guide, a list of things to do, a map, and brief descriptions of historical attractions in and around Frankfort.

Louisville—Printed Materials

KY-13 Cullinane, John. WALKING THROUGH LOUISVILLE. Louisville: Data Courier, 1976. 112 p. Maps, sketches. Index. 77-150259.

The author describes landmarks along 9 walking tours. There is a combined index to building name and architectural style.

KY-14 Junior League of Louisville, comp. A GUIDE TO LOUISVILLE FOR THE HANDICAPPED. Louisville: Kentucky Society for Crippled Children, 1967. 67 p.

Maps of Louisville are available from the Champion Map Corp. (US-202); Exxon (US-261); Gousha (US-206); Metro Graphic Arts, 900 40th SE, Grand Rapids, MI 49508; Rand McNally (US-215); and the local Citizen's Fidelity Bank.

Louisville—Organizations

KY-15 LOUISVILLE VISITORS BUREAU, Founders Square, 5th & Walnut Streets, Louisville, KY 40202 (502/583-3732).

They issue a map/guide to Louisville which lists hotels/motels and attractions, a quarterly events calendar, a walking tour brochure of center city, a map/guide to horse farms and race courses, and a SEE 'N DO folder which is available in several languages. They distribute a brochure LOUISVILLE AND NEARBY SIGHTS: 4 ONE-DAY DISCOVERY TOURS prepared by the Brown & Williamson Tobacco Corp.

LOUISIANA

BOOKS, ATLASES, MAGAZINES

LA-1   Calhoun, Nancy H., and Calhoun, James. PLANTATION HOMES
OF LOUISIANA. 4th ed. Gretna, LA: Pelican Publishing Co.,
1977. 128 p. Photos., map. Index. 0-911116-50-8. 77-152859.

The authors provide 19 state-wide highway tours covering 250 homes,
giving a brief historical and architectural description, whether open
to the public, brief finding directions, and sometimes a picture.

LA-2   LeBlanc, Joyce Y. THE PELICAN GUIDE TO GARDENS OF LOUISI-
ANA. Gretna, LA: Pelican Publishing Co., 1974. 64 p. Photos.,
maps. 0-88289-003-4. 74-834.

The author describes over 20 (5 in detail) garden spots, giving location, hours, admission fees, picnic opportunities, flowers and seasons,
and other things to see and do in the area.

LA-3   LOUISIANA: A GUIDE TO THE STATE. Rev. ed. American Guide
Series. New York: Hastings House, 1971. 711 p. Photos., maps.
0-8038-4272-4. 75-158007.

This revision of the original 1941 WPA guide is in 3 parts: "Louisiana: past and present," descriptions of 17 cities and towns, and 19
statewide highway tours.

MAPS

The official highway map is available from the Louisiana Dept. of Transportation & Development, Office of Highways, Baton Rouge, LA 70804. The 1977
edition lists public recreation areas, shows natural and economic regions, and
has numerous strip maps of the interstate highways. AAA (US-259), Exxon
(US-261), Goushā (US-206), and Rand McNally (US-215) each issue a combined Arkansas/Louisiana/Mississippi map. See also LA-6.

MAJOR TOURIST ORGANIZATION

LA-4   LOUISIANA TOURIST DEVELOPMENT COMMISSION, Box 44291,
Capitol Station, Baton Rouge, LA 70804 (504/389-5984).

They issue LOUISIANA (a good concise map/brochure describing and
locating points of interest, state parks and public recreation areas,
and 27 tourist centers), HISTORIC LOUISIANA (describing mansions,
forts, battlegrounds, buildings, churches, cemeteries), and LOUISI-
ANA CAPITOL GUIDE.

REGIONAL TOURISM ASSOCIATIONS

ACADIANA REGIONAL TOURIST INFORMATION CENTER, Rt. 1, Box 675,
New Iberia, LA 70560 (318/365-1540).

They are open Wednesday-Sunday, 9A.M.-5P.M. and issue a general
map/brochure describing points of interest.

ACADIANA TOURIST INFORMATION CENTER, Highway 190, Opelousas, LA
70770 (318/948-6263).

They are open Monday-Friday, 8:30A.M.-4:30P.M.

ALEXANDRIA-PINEVILLE-RAPIDES CONVENTIONS COMMISSION, Box 992,
Alexandria, LA 71301 (318/442-6671).

They have 2 locations, 214 Jackson Street in Alexandria and Mac-
Arthur Drive at Louisiana Route 1 North, both of which are open
Monday-Friday 8:30A.M.-4:30P.M.

HOUMA-TERREBONNE TOURIST INFORMATION CENTER, Box 328, Houma,
LA 70360 (504/876-5600).

They are located on US route 90 at South and Charles Streets and are
open Monday-Friday, 9A.M.-5P.M. They issue a general brochure,
and typed information sheets on history, fishing, camping facilities, tours,
motels, and restaurants. They also issue a map and a calendar of events.

LAFAYETTE PARISH CONVENTION & VISITORS BUREAU, Drawer 52066,
Lafayette, LA 70505 (318/232-3737).

They are located on US route 90 at 16th Street (310 Sixteenth Street) and
are open Monday-Friday, 8:30A.M.-5P.M., and Saturday and Sunday,
9A.M.-5P.M. They issue a large city map that includes suggestions
for driving, bicycling, and walking tours, and a TOUR GUIDE that
describes 4 tours.

LAKE CHARLES/CALCASIEU PARISH CONVENTION & TOURIST COMMISSION,

Box 1912, Lake Charles, LA 70602 (318/436-9588).

They are located on Lakeshore Drive at Interstate-10 and the Lake (1211 North Lakeshore Drive) and are open Monday-Friday, 8A.M.-4:30P.M. They issue a general brochure; lists of things to do and places to see, motels, restaurants, and tours; and a guide to the Creole nature trail.

MONROE CONVENTION & TOURIST BUREAU, Box 1302, Monroe, LA 71203 (318/323-3461).

They have 2 locations. 122 St. John Street (318/322-1792) is open daily from 9A.M.-5P.M. 141 deSiard Street (318/387-5691) is open Monday-Friday, 8A.M.-5P.M.

MORGAN CITY TOURIST CENTER, 725 Myrtle Street, Morgan City, LA 70380 (504/384-3343).

They are open daily 9A.M.-4P.M.

NATCHITOCHES TOURIST CENTER, 781 Front Street, Natchitoches, LA 71457 (318/352-4411).

They are open Monday-Friday, 8A.M.-5P.M.

SHREVEPORT-BOSSIER CONVENTION & TOURIST BUREAU, Box 1761, Shreveport, LA 71166 (318/222-9391).

They are located at 629 Spring Street and are open Monday-Friday, 8A.M.-5P.M. They issue a general attractions brochure, a hotel/motel guide, a dining guide, and a fishing guide.

OTHER ORGANIZATIONS

LA-5   LOUISIANA HOTEL-MOTEL ASSOCIATION, 3973 Sherwood Forest Blvd. S., Baton Rouge, LA 70816 (504/293-4753).

LA-6   LOUISIANA TRAVEL PROMOTION ASSOCIATION, Box 64654, Audubon Station, Baton Rouge, LA 70896.

"The Association is a non-profit organization chartered in 1961 to work for the advancement of Louisiana's travel industry in behalf of the private sector of that industry." They issue 2 publications for use by the traveler. LOUISIANA TOUR GUIDE is an annual (1978, 7th ed., 70 p.), widely distributed booklet describing points of interest and information centers along 38 tours throughout the state. LOUISIANA SELF-GUIDED TOUR MAP is a leaflet that briefly describes and keys to the map the major points of interest and selected hotels/motels and restaurants.

INFORMATION CENTERS/INFORMATION PHONES

The state has almost 30 visitor information centers and actively promotes their use in nearly all their travel publications. A list of them will be found in LOUISIANA, the major brochure issued by the Tourist Development Commission (LA-4). Complete information on them is also provided in the LOUISIANA TOUR GUIDE issued by the Louisiana Travel Promotion Association (LA-6).

OUTDOOR RECREATION ACTIVITIES

CANOEING AND BOATING. CANOEING IN LOUISIANA, a 90-page guide, is available from the Lafayette Natural History Museum and Planetarium, 637 Girard Park Drive, Lafayette, LA 70501.

FISHING AND HUNTING. Where-to information and regulations may be obtained from the Louisiana Dept. of Wildlife and Fisheries, 126 Wildlife & Fisheries Bldg., 400 Royal Street, New Orleans, LA 70130.

NATIONAL/STATE PARKS/FORESTS, ETC.

Information on Louisiana's only national forest, Kisatchie National Forest, is available from the Louisiana Dept. of Natural Resources, Office of Forestry, Box 1628, Baton Rouge, LA 70821.

A request to the Louisiana Dept. of Natural Resources, Office of State Parks for their publications describing state parks, campgrounds, and facilities brought the response that they do not supply this information. Contact the Tourist Development Commission (LA-4).

INDIVIDUAL CITIES OR AREAS

Baton Rouge—Printed Materials

LA-7   BATON ROUGE: A GUIDE FOR THE HANDICAPPED. Baton Rouge: Junior League of Baton Rouge (4950-C Government/70806), 1978.

Maps of Baton Rouge are available from Champion Map Corp. (US-202) and International Aerial Mapping, 8922 International Drive, San Antonio, TX 78216.

Baton Rouge—Organizations

LA-8   BATON ROUGE AREA CONVENTION AND VISITORS BUREAU, Box 3202, Baton Rouge, LA 70821 (504/383-1825).

They issue VISITOR GUIDE & MAP, PLANTATION COUNTRY (a guide to plantation homes open to the public), a hotel/motel guide, a dining/entertainment guide, A HOP, SKIP AND A JUMP. . . (describes nearby points of interest), a camping guide, and an OLD STATE CAPITOL brochure. They operate an information center in the Old Capitol Building, River Road at North Blvd. that is open Monday-Friday, 9:30A.M.-5P.M., on Saturday from 10A.M.-5P.M., and on Sunday from 1-5P.M. After office hours call 504/343-6379 for a recorded events message.

There is a state tourist center in the Old Pentagon Barracks, Capitol Avenue at River Road (504/389-5981). It is open Monday-Friday, 8A.M.-4:30P.M.

New Orleans—Printed Materials

LA-9   Collin, Richard H. THE REVISED NEW ORLEANS UNDERGROUND GOURMET. A Fireside Book. New York: Simon & Schuster, 1973. 248 p. Indexes. 0-671-21444-6. 72-90389.

Over 250 restaurants, arranged by specialty, are rated according to price range (from $1.75 or less to $3.95 or less), quality of food, and dining room setting. Address, telephone number, hours, and whether or not there is a bar are also given for each. Several restaurants elsewhere in Louisiana, along the Alabama and Mississippi Gulf coasts, and in Houston are also included. There are indexes by name and rating.

LA-10   Collin, Richard H., and Collin, Rima. THE NEW ORLEANS RESTAURANT GUIDE. New Orleans: Strether & Swann (distributed by Louisiana News Co.), 1977. 240 p. Maps. Index. 77-350680.

Over 400 restaurants in the New Orleans area are listed by type and rated. Each entry notes address, section of town (and if on one of the maps in the book), hours, credit cards accepted, telephone number, specialties, average price range, a sample meal or two, and a brief description. There is a section entitled "For Traveling New Orleanians" which notes selected restaurants around the country.

.LA-11   DuArte, Jack, and Brennan, Jimmy. DUARTE-BRENNAN GUIDE TO NEW ORLEANS CUISINE & DINING. New Orleans: Cuisine Classiques (1403 Annunciation Street/70130), 1976. 91 p. Photos. 76-380200.

This guide gives address, phone, hours, and credit cards accepted; rates cuisine, creativity, presentation, decor, service, atmosphere, and wines; and recommends several specialties for 140 restaurants. It is arranged alphabetically by name of restaurant, and there are no indexes.

LA-12   Griffin, Thomas K. THE PELICAN GUIDE TO NEW ORLEANS:

TOURING AMERICA'S MOST INTERESTING CITY. Gretna, LA: Pelican Publishing Co., 1974. 160 p. Photos. 0-88289-010-7. 74-182889.

This guide to the sights, eating places, entertainment, and sports to be found in New Orleans is presented in a discursive, rather than enumerative, style. There are separate chapters on the Mississippi River and the Mardi Gras, and suggested 5-day travel itineraries to the area for both the affluent and not-so-affluent visitor.

LA-13   GUIDE TO NEW ORLEANS FOR THE PHYSICALLY DISABLED. Metairie, LA: Easter Seal Society for Crippled Children and Adults of Louisiana, (Box 8425/70011), 1978.

LA-14   Kolb, Carolyn. NEW ORLEANS. Garden City, NY: Doubleday, 1972. 271 p. Photos., maps. 71-160873.

The author provides a complete guide to seeing New Orleans with much useful practical information, including (among others) separate sections on the Mardi Gras, a plantation tour, bicycling, camping, tours, nightlife, sports, activities for children, and an annual calendar of events. This standard work now needs to be updated.

LA-15   SEE NEW ORLEANS. New Orleans: SEE Magazines of Louisiana (International Trade Mart, Suite 1047/70130).

This free monthly guide to sightseeing, shopping, dining, and entertainment contains many advertisements, and is available in most hotels and motels.

AAA (US-259), Arrow Publishing Co. (US-199), Champion Map Corp. (US-202), Gousha (US-206), and Rand McNally (US-215) each issue a map of New Orleans.

New Orleans—Organizations

LA-16   GREATER NEW ORLEANS TOURIST & CONVENTION COMMISSION, 334 Royal Street, New Orleans, LA 70130 (504/522-8772).

They issue a NEW ORLEANS VISITORS' GUIDE (lists things to see and do, tours, dining/entertainment, and services), WALKING AND DRIVING TOUR, and a lodging guide. The office at the above address is open daily from 9A.M.-5P.M. for information.

MAINE

BOOKS, ATLASES, MAGAZINES

ME-1   THE AMC MAINE MOUNTAIN GUIDE: A GUIDE TO TRAILS IN
THE MOUNTAINS OF MAINE. 4th ed. Boston: Appalachian
Mountain Club, 1976. 260 p. Maps. Index.

This guide to more than 100 summits in all sections of the state is
intended for use as a pathfinder; it excludes descriptions of views.

ME-2   Bearse, Ray, ed. MAINE: A GUIDE TO THE VACATION STATE.
2d ed. The New American Guide Series. Boston: Houghton Mifflin,
1969. 460 p. Photos., maps. 69-12741.

This "unofficial" revision of the 1937 Maine WPA guide concentrates
a little less on historical background and a little more on practical
travel information than the Isaacson revision (ME-5).

ME-3   DOWN EAST: THE MAGAZINE OF MAINE: Camden, ME: Down
East Enterprise, (Bayview Street/04843).

This monthly magazine about Maine has been published since 1954.
Regular columns include a calendar of events; "Traveling Down East;"
book reviews; and "Outdoor Maine," about fishing and hunting.
Many books, records, calendars, all featuring Maine, are also available from this publisher.

ME-4   Gibson, John. WALKING THE MAINE COAST. Camden, ME:
Down East Magazine, 1977. 109 p. Maps, photos. 0-89272-028-X.
76-49267.

". . .25 walking tours of the Maine coast from Kittery to Mount
Desert Island," are described. Most tours are under 5 miles and over
easy terrain.

ME-5   Isaacson, Dorris A., ed. MAINE: A GUIDE "DOWN EAST." 2d ed.
American Guide Series. Rockland, ME: Courier-Gazette, 1970.
510 p. Photos.

This comprehensive revision of the 1937 WPA guide provides an authoritative, short narrative of Maine history; detailed tour itineraries to historic and scenic Maine; and an overview of the state's environment, resources, industry, and culture.

ME-6   MAINE GUIDE FOR HANDICAPPED AND ELDERLY TRAVELERS. Augusta, ME: Governor's Committee on Employment of the Handicapped, 1976. 18 p.

ME-7   Sadlier, Ruth, and Sadlier, Paul. SHORT WALKS ALONG THE MAINE COAST. Chester, CT: Pequot Press, 1977. 131 p. Maps, photos. 0-87106-077-9. 76-051125.

The 33 "ocean, marsh, mountain, and island walks from Ogunquit to Quoddy" give location, distance, and sights along the way.

MAPS

The official transportation map is available from the Maine Dept. of Transportation, Division of Special Services, Transportation Bldg., Augusta, ME 04330. The 1977/78 edition contains tables of state parks, historic sites, major ski areas, and a list of golf courses. AAA (US-259), Gousha (US-206), and Rand McNally (US-215) each issue a combined Maine/New Hampshire/Vermont map.

PUBLISHERS

ME-8   COURIER-GAZETTE, One Park Drive, Rockland, ME 04841.

They publish the official revision of the Maine WPA guide (ME-5); the COASTAL COURIER, a tourist newspaper guide to the coast of Maine; and many Maine cookbooks.

See also Down East Enterprise (ME-3).

MAJOR TOURIST ORGANIZATIONS

ME-9   MAINE PUBLICITY BUREAU, 3 St. Johns Street, Gateway Circle, Portland, ME 04102 (207/773-7266).

Although this is not the official state travel office, this is the state organization that issues the most substantial information. Our repeated mail requests for samples of their literature were consistently ignored, but a phone call brought results. They've been providing information services since the early 1920s and sponsor 5 information centers throughout the state: the 1 listed above in Portland, 1 in Bangor, 1 in

Kittery located between Interstate-95 and US Route 1, and 2 that are open in the summer only in Fryeburg and Calais. A visit to one of these centers is the best way to obtain their literature. They publish 7 extensive booklets. MAINE INVITES YOU (1978, 44th ed., 72 p.) is an annual, general guide to the points of interest in Maine with many advertisements for accommodations. MOTORING THROUGH MAINE (1978, 44th ed., 76 p.) is issued annually and contains a description of principal highway routes with a gazetteer and a classified index of advertisers. CAMPING IN MAINE (1978, 18th ed., 60 p.) is a regionally arranged listing of camping and tenting areas. MAINE CAMPS AND COTTAGES FOR RENT (1978, 49 p.) lists summer camps and cottages with housekeeping facilities. FISHING AND HUNTING IN MAINE (1978, 4th ed., 32 p.) is arranged by specific types of fish and game and sticks more to the how-to and the "good times" of hunting and fishing, but there is occasional where-to information included also. There are many advertisements of sporting camps. MAINE FOR WINTER VACATIONS (1978, 29th ed., 32 p.) is a geographic listing of winter recreation areas with indexes to those with ski areas, ski touring centers, and snowmobile trails. MAINE REAL ESTATE (1978, 13th ed., 32 p.) is a regional listing of properties and realtors. The MAINE GUIDE FOR HANDICAPPED AND ELDERLY TRAVELERS (ME-6) is available from the bureau.

ME-10   MAINE STATE DEVELOPMENT OFFICE, State House, Augusta, ME 04330 (207/289-2656).

This is the official state travel office, but they do not issue much for the traveler. They do issue brochures on state parks, historic memorials, and fall foliage.

OTHER ORGANIZATIONS

ME-11   MAINE INNKEEPERS ASSOCIATION, 50 Shepard Street, Bath, ME 04530 (207/442-8402).

They issue an annual "Lodging and Food Guide."

ME-12   NORTH MAINE WOODS, Box 552, Presque Isle, ME 04769.

Their purpose is to blend together the interests of landowners, mostly large paper companies who have developed an extensive semiprimitive road system, with the increased use of the area for outdoor recreation. It governs a 2 1/2 million acre area of northwest Maine that has no developed campsites, gas stations, grocery stores, or restaurants. Recreational users are limited to primitive campers, fishermen, hunters, and canoeists using the Saint John River and the Allagash Wilderness Waterway. There are no developed hiking trails. The organization maintains checkpoints at all major road entrances into the area, and all users must register. Contact them for a sportsman's guide/map to the area, a guide to the Saint John River, and for general rules and regulations.

INFORMATION CENTERS/INFORMATION PHONES

See Maine Publicity Bureau (ME-9).

OUTDOOR RECREATION ACTIVITIES

BICYCLING. A bicycling map is available from the Maine Dept. of Transportation, State Office Bldg., Augusta, ME 04330.

CANOEING AND BOATING. A packet of Maine river guides is available from the Maine Dept. of Conservation, Bureau of Parks & Recreation, Augusta, ME 04333. See also ME-12.

FISHING AND HUNTING. The Maine Dept. of Inland Fisheries and Wildlife, 284 State Street, Augusta, ME 04333 (207/289-2871) issues a PUBLICATIONS CATALOG of their numerous titles. See also FISHING AND HUNTING IN MAINE issued by the Maine Publicity Bureau (ME-9) (they also arrange hunting and fishing guide service) and ME-12.

WINTER ACTIVITIES. The official transportation map has a table of major ski areas, the State Development Office (ME-10) issues a skiing brochure, and the Maine Publicity Bureau (ME-9) issues an annual guide called MAINE FOR WINTER VACATIONS.

NATIONAL/STATE PARKS/FORESTS, ETC.

Acadia National Park

ME-13 AMC TRAIL GUIDE TO MT. DESERT ISLAND AND ACADIA NATIONAL PARK. Boston: Appalachian Mountain Club, 1976. 32 p. Map.

The pages in the AMC MAINE MOUNTAIN GUIDE (ME-1) pertaining to Acadia National Park have been excerpted to form this separate publication.

ME-14 ACADIA NATIONAL PARK, R.F.D. #1, Box 1, Bar Harbor, ME 04609.

They issue a map, an information sheet for visitors, and campground and wintertime activities leaflets.

ME-15 BAR HARBOR CHAMBER OF COMMERCE, Box 158, Bar Harbor, ME 04609 (207/288-5103).

For information and brochures on state parks and forests, campsites, the Allagash Wilderness Waterway, Baxter State Park, and other natural areas in the state, contact either the Maine Dept. of Conservation, Bureau of Parks & Recreation, State Office Bldg., Augusta, ME 04333 (207/289-3821) or the Maine Dept. of Conservation, Forest Service, Augusta, ME 04333. See also CAMPING IN MAINE issued by the Maine Publicity Bureau (ME-9) and ME-12.

INDIVIDUAL CITIES OR AREAS

Augusta—Printed Materials

A map of Augusta is available from the Maine Bureau of Public Improvement, Augusta, ME 04333.

Augusta—Organizations

ME-16   KENNEBEC VALLEY CHAMBER OF COMMERCE, 1 University Drive, Augusta, ME 04330 (207/623-4559).

MARYLAND

BOOKS, ATLASES, MAGAZINES

MD-1   Hahn, Thomas F., and Crowder, Orville W. TOWPATH GUIDE TO
        THE CHESAPEAKE AND OHIO CANAL. Glen Echo, MD: American
        Canal & Transportation Center. 1971-- . 1 vol. in 4 sections.
        Photos., maps.

        Part 1 covers Georgetown (Tidelock) to Seneca and was revised in
        1974 (56 p. 79-26184); part 2 covers Seneca to Harpers Ferry; part
        3 covers Harpers Ferry to Fort Frederick; and part 4 covers Fort
        Frederick to Cumberland. This walkers', bikers', and a canoeists' guide
        to the canal gives quite a bit of history and industrial archaeology
        along with the descriptions of the canal and its towpath. Presumably
        the other parts will be revised also.

MD-2   MARYLAND. Annapolis: Maryland Dept. of Economic & Community
        Development, (2525 Riva Road/21401).

        This handsome magazine devoted to "interesting places, people and
        things that are uniquely identifiable with Maryland" frequently con-
        tains directions for various mini-tours. It has been published quarterly
        since the fall of 1968 by the state department which oversees the
        state tourism industry. A cumulated mimeographed five-year index
        with annual supplements is available from the publisher. The magazine
        also publishes numerous booklets and art prints featuring Maryland
        and serves as a book buying service for selected other books about the
        state.

MD-3   OFFICIAL MARYLAND GUIDE TO LANDMARKS OF THE REVOLU-
        TIONARY ERA IN MARYLAND. Annapolis: Maryland Bicentennial
        Commission, 1975. 4 booklets in a folder. Maps, sketches.

        Volume 1: SOUTHERN MARYLAND: THE FLOWERING OF CHESA-
        PEAKE SOCIETY: A GUIDE FOR BICENTENNIAL VISITORS (34 p.
        76-383192) (includes Annapolis), volume 2: EASTERN SHORE: SMALL
        TOWNS AND DIVIDED LOYALTIES: A GUIDE FOR BICENTENNIAL

VISITORS (33 p. 76-383191), volume 3: CENTRAL MARYLAND: A STRATEGIC SUPPLY CENTER FOR THE CENTENNIAL ARMY: A GUIDE FOR BICENTENNIAL VISITORS (26 p. 76-383190) (includes Baltimore), and volume 4: WESTERN MARYLAND: THE BACK COUNTRY AND THE FRONTIER: A GUIDE FOR BICENTENNIAL VISITORS (21 p. 76-383189). The series was offered as "a sampling of significant types of manors, dwellings, mills, churches, and public buildings of the late 18th century which had direct connections with the course of the Revolution."

MD-4   184 MILES OF ADVENTURE: HIKER'S GUIDE TO THE CHESAPEAKE & OHIO CANAL. Baltimore: Boy Scouts of America, Baltimore Area Council, 1970. 49 p. Maps, photos.

This is a detailed hiking guide to the Chesapeake & Ohio Canal from Washington to Cumberland.

MD-5   Papenfuse, Edward C., et al., comps. MARYLAND: A NEW GUIDE TO THE OLD LINE STATE. Studies in Maryland History & Culture. Baltimore: Johns Hopkins University Press, 1976. 463 p. Maps, photos. Index. 0-8018-1874-5. 76-17224.

This is a revision of the original 1940 WPA guide. Specific directions and descriptions of points along the way are given for 45 statewide tours, including 3 for Baltimore and 1 for Annapolis.

MD-6   Robinson, William M., Jr. MARYLAND-PENNSYLVANIA COUNTRY-SIDE CANOE TRIPS: CENTRAL MARYLAND TRIPS. Oakton, VA: Appalachian Books, 1974. 34 p.

Contains "brief descriptions of 3 central Maryland rivers and a couple of reservoirs."

MD-7   SALT WATER SPORT FISHING AND BOATING IN MARYLAND. Alexandria, VA: Alexandria Drafting Co., 1973. 37 p. Scale: 4 in. represents 5 miles. Index. 75-331974.

Twenty-nine colorful charts indicating fishing grounds are accompanied by a description of marinas.

MD-8   Stone, William T., and Blanchard, Fessenden S. A CRUISING GUIDE TO THE CHESAPEAKE INCLUDING THE PASSAGES FROM LONG ISLAND SOUND ALONG THE NEW JERSEY COAST AND INLAND WATERWAY. 3d ed. New York: Dodd, Mead, 1973. 306 p. Photos., maps. Index. 0-396-06826-X. 73-6038.

This collection of modestly detailed descriptions of where to boat in the Chesapeake Bay includes instructions on getting there from New York City. The appendixes note where to obtain government publications of relevance, selected yacht clubs and marinas, and particularly bad spots in the Chesapeake.

MD-9   Waesche, James F. BALTIMORE, ANNAPOLIS AND CHESAPEAKE
COUNTRY: A GUIDE TO ITS TREASURES, PLEASURES AND PAST.
Baltimore: Bodine & Associates, 1976. 159 p. Photos., sketch
maps. Index. 0-910254-10-9. 75-40656.

Historic sights to see and present-day things to do are described for
Baltimore (pp. 1-102), Annapolis (pp. 105-23), and the Maryland
border areas of the Chesapeake (pp. 124-55). The lack of a table of
contents makes this book somewhat difficult to use.

MAPS

The official highway map published by the Maryland Dept. of Transportation is
available from the Division of Tourist Development (MD-11). The 1978 edition
contains numerous inset maps. AAA (US-259), Exxon (US-261), Goushā (US-
206), and Rand McNally (US-215) each issue a combined Delaware/Maryland/
Virginia/West Virginia map. AAA also issues a NATIONAL CAPITAL AND
CHESAPEAKE BAY AREA map.

PUBLISHERS

MD-10   CORNELL MARITIME PRESS/TIDEWATER PUBLISHERS, Box 456, 306
East Water Street, Centreville, MD 21617.

They are publishers of books about Maryland, the Delmarva Peninsula,
and the Chesapeake Bay. They are particularly strong on lore,
legend, and natural history.

See also MD-2.

MAJOR TOURIST ORGANIZATION

MD-11   MARYLAND DEPT. OF ECONOMIC & COMMUNITY DEVELOPMENT,
DIVISION OF TOURIST DEVELOPMENT, 1748 Forest Drive, Annapolis,
MD 21401 (301/269-3517).

They issue MARYLAND (a 44-page overview to state attractions, including historic sites and museums; entertainment; boat cruises; guide
services; parks and forests; and sources of additional information),
annual and quarterly calendars of events (listings by type of event
supplement the chronological listing), DIRECTORY OF MARYLAND
CAMPGROUNDS, DRIVING TOURS OF MARYLAND, an annual group
tour guide, and MARYLAND TRAVEL SCENE. They cosponsor, with
the Maryland State Police, a unique CB radio program aimed at
travelers.

OTHER ORGANIZATIONS

MD-12 MARYLAND HOTEL & MOTOR INN ASSOCIATION, Box 180,
Severna Park, MD 21146 (301/647-7880).

OUTDOOR RECREATION ACTIVITIES

CANOEING AND BOATING. A GUIDE TO CRUISING MARYLAND WATERS
by William B. Matthews, published since 1961, is now in its tenth edition. It
is available from the Maryland Dept. of Natural Resources, Tawes State Office
Bldg., Annapolis, MD 21401. See also MD-6, MD-7, MD-8, and MD-20.

FISHING AND HUNTING. Information on where to hunt and fish, including
many maps, and copies of all regulations are available from the Maryland
Dept. of Natural Resources, Tawes State Office Bldg., Annapolis, MD 21401.
See also MD-7.

WINTER ACTIVITIES. Information on cross-country ski trails is available from
the Maryland Dept. of Natural Resources, Tawes State Office Bldg., Annapolis,
MD 21401.

NATIONAL/STATE PARK/FORESTS, ETC.

Assateague Island National Seashore

MD-13 ASSATEAGUE ISLAND NATIONAL SEASHORE, Route 2, Box 294,
Berlin, MD 21811 (301/641-1441).

This 37-mile barrier island lies within 2 states (Maryland and Virginia)
and several administrative jurisdictions. The northernmost part at the
road entrance to the Maryland end is operated as Assateague State
Park managed by the Maryland Dept. of Natural Resources. The rest
of the Maryland section is what is usually called Assateague Island National
Seashore and is administered by the National Park Service. Most of
the Virginia portion of the island is the CHINCOTEAGUE NATIONAL
WILDLIFE REFUGE (VA-11) administered by the U.S. Bureau of Sport
Fisheries and Wildlife. However, the southernmost 5 mile area is
again administered by the National Park Service as a National Park
Recreation Area. Each of the 4 sections has its own on-site ranger
station which provides information, but information for the entire area
is best obtained by writing to the above address. They issue general
brochures on the Assateague and Chincoteague sections, information
on hike-in and canoe-in campsites, road use regulations, and hunting
areas and regulations.

General information about Maryland state parks and forests is available from

Maryland

the Maryland Dept. of Natural Resources, Tawes State Office Bldg., Annapolis, MD 21401.

INDIVIDUAL CITIES OR AREAS

Annapolis—Printed Materials

MD-14   Schaun, George. ANNAPOLIS GUIDE BOOK AND TOURS OF THE NAVAL ACADEMY. Annapolis: Greenberry Publications, 1971. 52 p. Drawings, maps.

The author describes walking tours of both Annapolis and the Naval Academy, emphasizing historic buildings and providing some practial "getting-around" information.

See also MD-9.

Maps of Annapolis are available from AAA (US-259), Alexandria Drafting Co. (S-16), and Arrow Publishing Co. (US-199).

Annapolis—Organizations

MD-15   CHAMBER OF COMMERCE OF GREATER ANNAPOLIS, 171 Conduit Street, Annapolis, MD 21401.

Baltimore—Printed Materials

MD-16   Alexandria Drafting Co. BALTIMORE & BALTIMORE COUNTY STREET MAP. Alexandria, VA: Alexandria Drafting, 1975. 46 p. Scale: 1 in. represents 2,000 ft. Indexes.

MD-17   Arrow Publishing Co. OFFICIAL ARROW GREATER BALTIMORE . . . STREET MAP ATLAS. Boston: Arrow Publishing [1974?]. 32 p. Scale: 2 1/2 in. represents 1 mile. Index.

MD-18   BAWLAMER! AN INFORMAL GUIDE TO A LIVELIER BALTIMORE. 4th ed. Baltimore: Citizens Planning & Housing Association, Livelier Baltimore Committee (340 North Charles Street/21201), 1976. 192 p. Maps, photos., sketches.

This volume describes things to see and do, what to do at night, bookstores and cultural events, shopping, sports and hobbies, and Baltimore for children. A fifth edition is planned for late 1978. Bawlamer is the phonetic spelling for Baltimore as the natives say it.

MD-19   Eskivith, Rhoda, and Christiansen, Ellene. READY/SET/GO! BALTI-
         MORE GUIDEBOOK FOR THE PHYSICALLY DISABLED. Baltimore:
         The League for the Handicapped (1111 East Cold Spring Lane/21239),
         1977.

MD-20   Mittenthal, Suzanne M. THE BALTIMORE TRAIL BOOK. Baltimore:
         Sierra Club Southeast Chapter, Greater Baltimore Group, 1970.
         163 p. Maps, photos. 72-135292.

         Forty hikes and 8 canoe trips in the Baltimore area are described,
         noting location and level of difficulty.

See also MD-9.

Maps of Baltimore are available from AAA (US-259), Goushā (US-206), and
Rand McNally (US-215).

The Baltimore weather information number is 301/936-1212.

Baltimore—Organizations

MD-21   BALTIMORE PROMOTION COUNCIL, 22 Light Street, Baltimore, MD
         21202 (301/727-5688).

         They issue a VISITORS GUIDE TO BALTIMORE which includes maps,
         a quarterly calendar of events (arranged thematically), DINING OUT
         IN BALTIMORE, PLANT TOURS, and an HISTORICAL GUIDE.
         Tourist information centers are operated at the above address in Suite
         502 on the fifth floor and in the Pennsylvania Railroad Station. A
         recorded schedule of daily events may be dialed at 301/752-4656.

MASSACHUSETTS

BOOKS, ATLASES, MAGAZINES

MA-1   AMC MASSACHUSETTS-RHODE ISLAND TRAIL GUIDE. 4th ed.
Boston: Appalachian Mountain Club, 1978. 460 p. Maps.

This is an "unusual handbook to the forgotten backcountry of an
intensely urbanized region [which] includes hiking areas, state parks,
wildlife sanctuaries."

MA-2   Bearse, Ray, ed. MASSACHUSETTS: A GUIDE TO THE PILGRIM
STATE. 2d ed. The New American Guide Series. Boston: Houghton Mifflin, 1971. 525 p. Photos., maps. 0-395-12091-8. 68-
16270.

This revision of the first WPA guide substitutes the original mile-by-
mile tours with a gazetteer section describing cities and towns. It is
"a regional geography with occasional historical notes. . .not a guide
to accommodations or restaurants."

MA-3   Ripley, Sheldon N., et al. THE 1776 GUIDE FOR MASSACHUSETTS.
Harper Colophon Books. New York: Harper & Row, 1975. 223 p.
Maps, photos. 0-06-090413-5. 74-25421.

In this list of suggested 1-day trips out of Boston which stresses the
Colonial and Revolutionary periods, and notes hours and fees for many
attractions, the breadth of information (number of sites) makes up for
lack of depth in each entry. There is no index.

MA-4   Rubin, Jerome, and Rubin, Cynthia. A GUIDE TO MASSACHUSETTS
MUSEUMS, HISTORIC HOUSES, POINTS OF INTEREST. Newton,
MA: Emporium Publications, 1972. 126 p. 0-88278-004-2. 72-
81231.

This is a regionally arranged listing of "museums open to the public
throughout Massachusetts, including basic information about location,
hours and the nature of collections, and the special services offered
to individuals and groups."

MAPS

The official transportation map is available from either the Massachusetts Dept. of Public Works, c/o Public Relations Office, Room 526, 100 Nashua Street, Boston, MA 02114 or the Division of Tourism (MA-5). The 1977-78 edition contains an index to points of interest and a table of recreational facilities (state forests, parks, and beaches). Another map is available from the Division of Tourism on which are located points of interest. There are lists of ski areas, beaches, state campgrounds, covered bridges, and state tourist information centers, but none of these are located on the map. It also contains the addresses of the state vacation areas and an events calendar. AAA (US-259), Goushā (US-206), and Rand McNally (US-215) each issue a combined Connecticut/Massachusetts/Rhode Island map.

MAJOR TOURIST ORGANIZATION

MA-5   MASSACHUSETTS DEPT. OF COMMERCE & DEVELOPMENT, DIVISION OF TOURISM, 100 Cambridge Street, Boston, MA 02202 (617/727-3201).

    They issue a camping brochure, a calendar of events, and TOURING MASSACHUSETTS (points of interest along 12 tours are generally described). They may also be written to at the following address: Massachusetts, Box 1775, Boston, MA 02105. They provide minimal information. Regional groups (see next section) supply much better information and in greater quantities.

REGIONAL TOURISM ASSOCIATIONS

BERKSHIRE HILLS CONFERENCE, 205 West Street, Pittsfield, MA 01201 (413/443-9186).

    They issue a general attractions brochure; summer and winter guides describing where to stay, campgrounds, dining out, things to do, where to buy, camps, and recreation; a BERKSHIRE ARTS & LEISURE MAGAZINE issued in summer and winter and listing cultural events; and information on hiking, hunting, camping, fishing, boating, etc. There are 9 information booths in the area and 3 area toll-free phone numbers describing local daily activities. All these are listed in the summer guide. There is a toll-free ski conditions phone (800/628-5030) that may be called from New York, New Jersey, Connecticut, Vermont, Rhode Island, and New Hampshire. In Massachusetts call 413/499-0700.

BRISTOL COUNTY DEVELOPMENT COUNCIL, 154 North Main Street, Box 831, Fall River, MA 02722 (617/676-1026).

CENTRAL MASSACHUSETTS TOURIST COUNCIL, Mechanics Tower-Suite 350,

100 Front Street, Worcester, MA 01608 (617/753-2924).

> They issue brochures on central Massachusetts attractions, historical highlights, and where to stay.

ESSEX COUNTY TOURIST COUNCIL OF MASSACHUSETTS, Box 1011, Peabody, MA 01960 (617/532-1449).

> They issue THE ESSEX ADVENTURE map/brochure of points of interest, THE ESSEX ADVENTURE ACCOMMODATIONS/FACILITIES GUIDE (mostly advertisements), a calendar of events, and ADVENTURE IN RECREATION (a guide to outdoor activities).

MIDDLESEX COUNTY TOURISM & DEVELOPMENT COUNCIL, 615 Concord Street, South Framingham, MA 01701 (617/620-0940).

> They issue a tourist map, a facilities guide and directory, a guide to Concord, DINING AND LODGING IN CAMBRIDGE," and SHOPPING AND ENTERTAINMENT IN AND AROUND HARVARD SQUARE. There is an information center in Lexington on Route 128.

MOHAWK TRAIL ASSOCIATION, Charlemont, MA 01339 (413/339-4962).

NORFOLK COUNTY TOURIST COUNCIL, 1776 Heritage Drive, Quincy, MA 02171 (617/328-1776).

> They issue a PATRIOTS TRAIL MAP BROCHURE to historical attractions and a PATRIOTS TRAIL FACILITIES GUIDE & DIRECTORY.

PIONEER VALLEY ASSOCIATION, 333 Prospect Street, Northampton, MA 01060 (413/586-0321).

> They issue THE ABC'S OF PIONEER VALLEY, a map locating things to do, THINGS TO SEE AND DO, a monthly calendar of events, WHERE TO STAY, WHERE TO DINE, CAMPING AND TRAILERING, MAPLE SUGARING, and the BERKSHIRE TRAIL IN PIONEER VALLEY.

PLYMOUTH COUNTY TOURIST COUNCIL, Box 1620, Pembroke, MA 02359 (617/293-3551).

> They issue MASSACHUSETTS MARITIME TRAIL, a do-it-yourself tour guide to things nautical for landlubbers; a hospitality guide to attractions, golf, fishing, bike trails, camping, beaches, motels, and restaurants; guides to motels, camping, golf, group travel, and marinas; and a waterway guide to the Wampanoag Commemorative Canoe Passage.

OTHER ORGANIZATIONS

MA-6   MASSACHUSETTS COUNCIL ON THE ARTS & HUMANITIES, One

Ashburton Place, Boston, MA 02108 (617/727-3668).

They issue COLLECTIONS OF MASSACHUSETTS, a list of museums and historical societies by specialty; 3 regional driving tour brochures describing, with a map, cultural and historical places to visit (Metropolitan Boston and the North Shore; South Shore, Cape Cod & the Islands; Western & Central); and MANSIONS OF MASSACHUSETTS, featuring 12 historic mansions. A guide to all historic homes open to the public in the state is in preparation.

MA-7 MASSACHUSETTS HOTEL-MOTEL ASSOCIATION, 73 Tremont Street, Boston, MA 02108 (617/227-1616).

INFORMATION CENTERS/INFORMATION PHONES

There is a list of highway information centers on the official transportation map. See also Berkshire Hills Conference under "Regional Tourism Associations" and the section "Boston – Information Centers/Information Phones" in this chapter.

OUTDOOR RECREATION ACTIVITIES

BICYCLING. A loose-leaf bicycle atlas describing 35 tours, mostly in eastern Massachusetts, is available from the Massachusetts Dept. of Environmental Management, Division of Forests & Parks, Leverett Saltonstall State Office Bldg., 100 Cambridge Street, Boston, MA 02202. See also MA-9, MA-13, and MA-33.

CANOEING AND BOATING. A list of boating ramps will be found in THE BOSTON GLOBE GUIDE TO FRESH WATER FISHING available from the Massachusetts Division of Fisheries and Wildlife, Leverett Saltonstall Bldg., 100 Cambridge Street, Government Center, Boston, MA 02202. Also contact the Massachusetts Division of Marine & Recreational Vehicles, 64 Causeway Street, Boston, MA 02114. See also MA-18 and MA-37.

FISHING AND HUNTING. The Massachusetts Division of Fisheries & Wildlife, Leverett Saltonstall Bldg., 100 Cambridge Street, Government Center, Boston, MA 02202 doesn't provide much, but they do distribute THE BOSTON GLOBE GUIDE TO FRESH WATER FISHING, which lists trout-stocked waters and best bets for pond fishing. They also have maps of individual wildlife management areas. See also MA-18.

WINTER ACTIVITIES. The Division of Tourism (MA-5) issues a brochure on skiing. For information on snowmobiling, contact the Massachusetts Division of Marine & Recreational Vehicles, 64 Causeway Street, Boston, MA 02114. See also Berkshire Hills Conference under the "Regional Tourism Associations" section of this chapter.

NATIONAL/STATE PARKS/FORESTS, ETC.

Cape Cod National Seashore

MA-8   Koehler, Margaret H. THE VISITOR'S GUIDE TO CAPE COD NA-
TIONAL SEASHORE. Riverside, CT: Chatham Press, 1973. 80 p.
Photos., maps. 0-85699-066-3. 72-92014.

This older, but still useful, general guide to sights and trails in the
National Seashore area also has brief mentions of nearby places outside the seashore, a list of emergency telephone numbers, and a list
of general regulations.

MA-9   CAPE COD NATIONAL SEASHORE, Seashore Headquarters, South
Wellfleet, MA 02663 (617/349-3785).

They offer a map of the seashore and information on hiking and
bicycle trails, beaches, etc. There are no campgrounds. There are
visitor centers at Eastham and Provincetown.

For information and brochures on state parks and forests, contact the Massachusetts Dept. of Environmental Management, Division of Forests & Parks, Leverett
Saltonstall State Office Bldg., 100 Cambridge Street, Boston, MA 02202.

INDIVIDUAL CITIES OR AREAS

Boston—Printed Materials

MA-10   ACCESS TO BOSTON IN '76. Worcester, MA: Easter Seal Society
of Massachusetts, 1976. 64 p.

This is a guide for the physically handicapped.

MA-11   Arrow Publishing Co. OFFICIAL ARROW STREET MAP ATLAS, METRO-
POLITAN BOSTON. Newton Upper Falls, MA: Arrow Publishing,
1973. 84 p. Scale: 2 1/2 in. represents 1 mile. Index. 77-
367461.

MA-12   BOSTON: THE OFFICIAL BICENTENNIAL GUIDEBOOK. A Sunrise
Book. New York: E.P. Dutton, 1975. 319 p. Maps. Index. 0-
87690-146-1.

This guidebook is closely aligned to the special exhibits and happenings in Boston for the Bicentennial and so large portions of it now
seem dated. But the sections on transportation, information centers,
the Freedom Trail and other neighborhood walks (this section has many maps
identifying specific buildings), museums and attractions, shopping, outdoor activities, restaurants, theater, and nightlife are still useful.

MA-13 THE BOSTON BASIN BICYCLE BOOK. Boston: David R. Godine, 1975. 221 p. Maps, photos. 0-87923-133-5. 74-32579.

"A collection of 30 interlocking bicycle rides. . .of between 8 1/2 and 14 1/2 miles. . ." giving a commentary, written directions, and a tracing of the route on the appropriate USGS topographical quadrangle. The book is very complete.

MA-14 Boston Society of Architects. ARCHITECTURE: BOSTON AND CAMBRIDGE. Barre Books. New York: Clarkson N. Potter, 1976. 182 p. Photos., maps. Index. 0-517-52501-1. 76-12589.

This is a copiously illustrated architectural tour of Boston, including Cambridge.

MA-15 Chesler, Bernice. IN & OUT OF BOSTON WITH (OR WITHOUT) CHILDREN. 3d ("Bicentennial") ed. Barre, MA: Barre Publishing Co. (distributed by Crown), 1975. 320 p. Maps. Index. 0-517-52184-9. 75-19417.

This is a very good, thorough guide to things to see and do in Boston with mentions throughout of special ways of enjoying them with children. It is topically arranged in large categories: animals, the arts, day trips, historic sites and exhibits, looking at the city, museums, open space, recreation, tours and visits, and the world around us. There is a list of information centers and events information telephone numbers in Boston (that may be out of date) and the addresses of the official tourist agencies in the northeastern states and Canada. It also includes a calendar of regularly scheduled events.

MA-16 Fisher, Alan. AMC GUIDE TO COUNTRY WALKS NEAR BOSTON WITHIN REACH BY PUBLIC TRANSPORTATION. Boston: Appalachian Mountain Club, 1977. 163 p. Maps, photos.

Each walk description is accompanied by a map and directions for reaching by public transportation or car.

MA-17 Hammel, Faye, assisted by Pollak, Rita. ARTHUR FROMMER'S GUIDE TO BOSTON. New York: Frommer/Pasmantier Publishing Co. (distributed by Simon & Schuster), 1977. 218 p. Maps. 0-671-22729-7.

This is a basic guide of most use to the first-time visitor to Boston. Practical information is given for attractions, hotels, restaurants (there is a large ethnic section), shopping, Boston after dark, a student's guide to Boston, and areas beyond Boston (Cape Cod, etc.). There is no index.

MA-18 Kales, Emily, and Kales, David. ALL ABOUT THE BOSTON HARBOR ISLANDS. A Marlborough House Book. Boston: Herman Publishing, 1976. 120 p. Photos., maps, sketches. Index. 0-89046-054-X. 75-24955.

The Kales describe "their geography, ecology. . .history and future; their lore and romance. . .how to get to them; what to wear, where to picnic. . .where to moor, rent, or charter a boat; where, when, how and what fish to catch; harbor cruises; [and] swimming."

MA-19 McIntyre, Alex M. BEACON HILL: A WALKING TOUR. Boston: Little, Brown, 1975. 118 p. Photos., drawings, maps. 0-316-55600-9. 75-16449.

The author presents a foot guide to the architectural styles of the houses of the Beacon Hill section of Boston.

MA-20 Polk, Nicki. FAMOUS GUIDE TO BOSTON: CITY OF CONTRASTS. New York: Geographica Map Co., 1976. 96 p. Photos., maps. Index.

This is a quick guide to what to see and do, theaters, nightlife, restaurants, sports, hotels/motels, and transportation in Boston. The Freedom Trail is also included.

MA-21 Rubin, Cynthia, and Rubin, Jerome. 11 WALKING TOURS OF BOSTON & CAMBRIDGE. Charlestown, MA: Emporium Publications, 1974. 64 p. Drawings, maps. 0-88278-031-X.

This is a superficial, but interesting, enumeration of what one sees on the tours that have been selected by the authors.

MA-22 Schofield, William G. FREEDOM BY THE BAY: THE BOSTON FREEDOM TRAIL. Chicago: Rand McNally, 1974. 160 p. Photos. Index. 0-528-81941-0. 74-2006.

The author provides entertaining, factual, arm-chair descriptions of the 16 officially designated sites along the Boston Freedom Trail.

MA-23 Silver, Paul A. et al. THE BOSTON PHOENIX'S GUIDE TO CHEAP EATS: INEXPENSIVE DINING IN GREATER BOSTON. 3d ed. Cambridge: Harvard Student Agencies, 1975. 240 p. Indexes. 75-330233.

Restaurants are arranged by price range: under $3.00, under $5.00, under $7.00, and "the sky's the limit," with additional chapters on fast-food and late-night places. Each restaurant is described and rated, and there are indexes by nationality of food served, location, and name.

MA-24 Zanger, Mark. ROBERT NADEAU'S GUIDE TO BOSTON RESTAURANTS. Jamaica Plain, MA: World Food Press (8 Hubbard Street/ 02130), 1978. 378 p. Index. 0-930922-00-X. 78-50749.

Reviews, of over 200 restaurants, that derive from the author's 3 years' experience as a weekly restaurant critic for the BOSTON LEDGER and THE REAL PAPER are arranged by type of food served with a name index. There is a chapter on wine stores.

Maps of Boston are available from AAA (US-259), Champion Map Corp. (US-202), Goushā (US-206), and Rand McNally (US-215).

Boston—Organizations

MA-25 GREATER BOSTON CONVENTION & TOURIST BUREAU, 900 Boylston Street, Boston, MA 02115 (617/536-4100).

They issue an accommodations directory, a dining and shopping directory, a museums and entertainment directory, a monthly listing of events, an arts map/guide, and a Freedom Trail map/guide.

MA-26 METROPOLITAN DISTRICT COMMISSION, PARKS DIVISION, 20 Somerset Street, Boston, MA 02108 (617/727-5215).

They issue a detailed map to fishing, boating, swimming, skiing, ice skating, tennis, golf, zoos, bandstands, public toilets, children's playgrounds, picnic areas, and trails in the greater Boston area. A brochure is also available on Boston Harbor Islands State Park.

Boston—Information Centers/Information Phones

The Boston Common Visitor and Information Center, Tremont Street on Boston Common (617/426-4948) is open daily except Thanksgiving, Christmas, and New Years Day.

The Boston National Historical Park Visitor Center is located at 15 State Street. It is a walk-in center only and has no phone (the Chief of Interpretations of the Park at the Charlestown Navy Yard, Boston, MA 02129 may be called at 617/242-1913). Information on the Freedom Trail may be obtained here.

The City Hall Visitor Center, Boston City Hall at Government Center is open Monday-Friday. The Mayor's Office of Cultural Affairs also maintains a booth here. Freedom Trail busses leave from here.

The Foreign Visitor Center is located at 15 State Street (617/262-4830). It is open Monday-Saturday, 9A.M.-5P.M.

The Harvard University Information Center at Holyoke Center at Harvard Square is open Monday-Saturday.

The MIT (Massachusetts Institute of Technology) Information Center is located at 77 Massachusetts Avenue, Room 7-111, Cambridge.

Massachusetts

The State Visitor Center, located in the Massachusetts State House on Beacon Street, is open Monday-Friday, 10A.M.-4P.M.

There is a Visitor Information Line at 617/338-1976. Operators are on duty daily from 9A.M.-5P.M. There is a recorded message from 5P.M.-9A.M. Information on events and lodging is available here.

A recreation hotline at 617/725-4976 provides information about events sponsored by the Boston Parks and Recreation Dept.

The Boston weather information number is 617/936-1212.

Cape Cod/Martha's Vineyard/Nantucket—Printed Materials

MA-27 Burroughs, Polly. EXPLORING MARTHA'S VINEYARD. Riverside, CT: Chatham Press, 1973. 40 p. Maps, drawings. 0-85699-064-7. 72-93259.

The maps and drawings by Robert James Pailthorpe illustrate the brief text describing the highlights of the island.

MA-28 _____. NANTUCKET: A GUIDE WITH TOURS. Chester, CT: Pequot Press, 1974. 63 p. Photos., maps. 0-87106-144-9. 74-76535.

This is a handy foot guide to touring both Nantucket town and the outlying areas of the island. A short history, how to get there, and accommodations section are also included.

MA-29 CAPE COD ATLAS. Orange, MA: Butterworth Corp., 1974. Rev. frequently. 104 p. Maps, photos.

The maps of Cape Cod at various scales indicate roads, scenic and historic spots, and selected water depths. Many photographs accompany the text which describes the sites indicated on the maps and gives hours and fees. As we go to press the publisher has a new address: 23 Traders Lane, West Yarmouth, MA 02673.

MA-30 CAPE COD GUIDE. Yarmouthport, MA: Cape Cod Guide (Captains Row, Route 6-A/02675).

This is a guide (23 weekly summer issues, and 6 monthly winter issues) to events, movies, real estate, fishing, art galleries, restaurants, golf, beaches, etc. on Cape Cod. There are additional sections on Martha's Vineyard and Nantucket.

MA-31 Chesler, Bernice, and Kaye, Evelyn. THE FAMILY GUIDE TO CAPE COD: WHAT TO DO WHEN YOU DON'T WANT TO DO WHAT

EVERYONE ELSE IS DOING. Barre, MA: Barre Publishing Co. (distributed by Crown), 1976. 310 p. Maps, drawings. Index. 0-517-52096-6. 76-5459.

This is a very good, comprehensive guide to Cape Cod written specifically with the family in mind. It is arranged by communities with sections on Martha's Vineyard, Nantucket, and Plymouth.

MA-32 Doane, Doris, and Fish, Richard. EXPLORING OLD CAPE COD. 2d ed. Riverside, CT: Chatham Press, 1973. 40 p. Maps, drawings. 0-85699-076-0.

These brief descriptions of highlights are arranged by the 16 major sections of the Cape.

MA-33 Griffith, Jane, and Mullen, Edwin. SHORT BIKE RIDES ON CAPE COD, NANTUCKET AND THE VINEYARD. Chester, CT: Pequot Press, 1977. 131 p. Maps. 0-87106-086-8. 76-58214.

Thirty bike rides are described in good detail giving location, length, terrain and surface, and sights to see. The maps are decent.

MA-34 Mackay, Dick. NANTUCKET WHOLE ISLAND CATALOG. Siasconset, MA: Sankaty Head Press, 1976. 79 p. Drawings. 76-11527.

History, getting there, accommodations, dining, entertainment, shopping, sports, tours, and beaches are all included in this guide.

MA-35 Mitchell, John, and Griswold, Whit. HIKING CAPE COD. Charlotte, NC: East Woods Press, 1978. 187 p. Maps, sketches. Bibliography. 0-914788-04-3. 77-93759.

"Ten carefully detailed excursions along the less travelled byways, beaches, marshes, and meadows of Cape Cod" are described, giving map, distance, time required, terrain, directions for finding the trail, and natural and human history. It comes in a handy pocket size.

MA-36 Sadlier, Paul, and Sadlier, Ruth. SHORT WALKS ON CAPE COD AND THE VINEYARD. Chester, CT: Pequot Press, 1976. 96 p. Photos., maps. 0-87106-006-3. 75-34252.

"Twenty-five seashore, marsh, woods, and sanctuary walks with photographs and maps. . . " are described. The book is quite good.

MA-37 Wilensky, Julius M. CAPE COD: WHERE TO GO, WHAT TO DO, HOW TO DO IT. 2d ed. Edited by Frank G. Valenti. Stamford, CT: Westcott Cove Publishing Co. (Box 130/06901), 1976. 214 p. Charts, photos. Index. 77-356454.

This is a cruising guide to all harbors on Cape Cod in a discursive, but informative, style providing all sorts of useful facts from historic background to laundromat locations. Copious use is made of National Ocean Survey charts, and all sites discussed are keyed to the charts. There are appendixes on radio information, obtaining charts, and boat rentals and launching ramps.

MA-38 Wood, Donald. CAPE COD: A GUIDE. Boston: Little, Brown, 1973. 368 p. Maps. 0-316-95163-3. 73-6959.

The author presents comprehensive, useful information on the natural, historical, and recreational resources of the towns of Cape Cod as well as more useful data on campsites, public golf courses, and swimming beaches. There is no index.

A map of Martha's Vineyard is available from Jeremiah Donovan, Edgartown, MA 02539. A map of Nantucket is available from Mitchell's Book Corner, 54 Main Street, Nantucket, MA 02554.

Cape Cod/Martha's Vineyard/Nantucket—Organizations

MA-39 CAPE COD CHAMBER OF COMMERCE, Junction Routes 6 and 132, Hyannis, MA 02601 (617/362-3225).

They issue the CAPE COD VACATIONER (a directory of activities and attractions), CAPE COD RESORT DIRECTORY, SPORTSMAN'S GUIDE TO CAPE COD, and SIX FASCINATING TOURS ON HISTORIC CAPE COD.

MA-40 MARTHA'S VINEYARD CHAMBER OF COMMERCE, Vineyard Haven, MA 02568 (617/693-0085).

They issue a VISITOR'S GUIDE TO MARTHA'S VINEYARD.

MA-41 NANTUCKET ISLAND CHAMBER OF COMMERCE, Nantucket, MA 02254 (617/228-1700).

They issue a visitor's booklet (1978 ed., 104 p.) listing accommodations, restaurants, arts, recreation, calendar of events, historical exhibits, museums, shopkeepers, and transportation services.

See also the section in this chapter on the "Cape Cod National Seashore."

MICHIGAN

BOOKS, ATLASES, MAGAZINES

MI-1   Bloemendaal, Dirk C. MICHIGAN PICTORIAL CAMPGROUND GUIDE.
5th ed. Holland, MI: Michigan Campground Guide, 1975. 160 p.
Photos., maps. Index. 75-312723.

Seventy-two separate state parks and recreation areas are described,
and nearby campgrounds for each are listed. These parks are arranged
geographically by Upper and Lower Peninsula, and there is no index
to either park or campground name. However, there is an index and
guide map by county, so if you know the name of the county, you can
find the campgrounds there. There are brief additional sections on
where to hike and canoe.

MI-2   BOATING, CANOEING IN MICHIGAN. Saginaw, MI: Oak Leaf
Publishing Co., 1972. 32 p. Maps. 75-311076.

This title and its 3 companion volumes (MI-8, MI-9, and MI-12)
are almost alike in that they each contain 20 easy-to-read regional
maps showing national and state forest areas and use symbols to show
campgrounds, parks, and picnic areas. The additional material added
in each title is what makes each a separate publication. BOATING,
CANOEING IN MICHIGAN adds information on fishing sites, canoe
access sites, and harbors and there are brief descriptions of 64 canoe
trails. MICHIGAN TOURIST GUIDE adds information on historic
attractions, a calendar of events, a table of facilities available at
private campgrounds, and lists of rock hound areas and roadside parks.
MICHIGAN TRAILS adds information on ski areas, snowmobile areas,
motorcycle areas, and horse and hiking trails. THE SPORTSMAN:
HUNTING AND FISHING IN MICHIGAN adds information on boat
launching sites, fishing areas, canoe areas, hunting areas, and types
of fish found in Michigan's various water areas.

MI-3   Hansen, Dennis R. MICHIGAN CROSS-COUNTRY SKIING ATLAS:
A GUIDE TO PUBLIC AND PRIVATE SKI TRAILS. East Lansing, MI:
Hansen Publishing Co., 1977. 134 p. Maps. Index. 0-930098-01-
3. 77-80425.

Two hundred and eighty trails are mapped and described, noting distance, acreage, maintainance, difficulty, terrain, if a fee is charged, facilities, and including remarks that seem appropriate.

MI-4 HIGHROAD MAPS: 25 KEY AREAS IN MICHIGAN. Marshall, MI: Highroad Publications, (901 East Forest Street/49068), 1974. 18 p. Scale: 1 in. represents 2 miles. 74-187253.

Symbols on maps show locations of bus stations; hospitals; points of interest; tourist attractions; city, county, and police offices; motels or hotels; travel trailer courts; marinas; parks, picnic grounds, and recreation facilities; chambers of commerce; shopping districts; airports; and golf courses. The major cities mapped are Ann Arbor, Battle Creek, Detroit, Flint, Grand Rapids, Kalamazoo, Lansing, Saginaw, Sault Ste. Marie, and Ypsilanti.

MI-5 MICHIGAN: A GUIDE TO THE WOLVERINE STATE. American Guide Series. New York: Oxford University Press, 1941. 696 p. Photos., maps. 41-52531.

This original WPA guide in 3 sections--general background, descriptions of 17 cities and 20 state-wide highway tours, plus guides to Beaver Island, Isle Royale, and Mackinac Island--is comprehensive, but out of date.

MI-6 MICHIGAN OUTDOOR GUIDE. Dearborn, MI: Automobile Club of Michigan, Touring Dept. and Motor News (Auto Club Drive/48126), 1977. Issued annually. 68 p.

This is a complete guide to national, state, local, and privately owned parks and campgrounds. There is a brief section on Isle Royale National Park and a list of roadside parks and rest areas maintained by the Highway Dept. It has been issued since 1930.

MI-7 MICHIGAN STATE ATLAS. Rev. ed. Rockford, IL: Rockford Map Publishers, 1973. 230 p. Scales vary. 66-1080.

The first half of this atlas contains descriptions, maps, and tables of historic sites, roadside parks, campgrounds, directory of accommodations and restaurants, hunting, fishing, boat launching sites, canoe trails, golf courses, and winter sports. The second half contains readable, but small, reproductions of each official county map.

MI-8 MICHIGAN TOURIST GUIDE. Saginaw, MI: Oak Leaf Publishing Co., 1972. 31 p. Maps. 75-311077.

See MI-2.

MI-9 MICHIGAN TRAILS. Saginaw, MI: Oak Leaf Publishing Co., 1972. 32 p. Maps.

See MI-2.

MI-10   Osler, Jack. 50 GREAT MINI-TRIPS FOR MICHIGAN. Dayton, OH:
         Media Ventures, 1977. 52 p. 0-89645-002-3.

         This volume was not examined, but it is probably very much like the
         Pennsylvania volume (PA-3) in this series.

MI-11   Puetz, C.J. MICHIGAN COUNTY MAPS AND RECREATION
         GUIDE. Lansing, MI: Michigan United Conservation Clubs, [1977?].
         127 p. Maps, drawings. Index.

         Reproductions (at various scales) of the official state highway maps
         for each county with an overprinting indicating parks, campsites,
         trails, nature areas; a gazetteer; and tables of parks and forests
         indicating facilities comprise this volume. It is especially strong on
         fishing and hunting. The publisher also issues an 80-page booklet
         listing mapped lakes in Michigan.

MI-12   THE SPORTSMAN: HUNTING AND FISHING IN MICHIGAN.
         Saginaw, MI: Oak Leaf Publishing Co., 1972. 33 p. Maps. 75-
         318493.

         See MI-2.

MAPS

The OFFICIAL TRANSPORTATION MAP, prepared by the Michigan Dept. of
State Highways and Transportation, is available from the Travel Bureau (MI-13).
The 1978-79 edition lists facilities at Michigan state parks, includes general
information on Michigan festivals, and additional sources of travel information.
AAA (US-259), Goushā (US-206), and Rand McNally (US-215) each issue a
map of Michigan. Exxon (US-261) issues a combined Indiana/Michigan map.
See also MT-2, MT-4, MT-7, MT-8, MT-9, MT-11, and MT-12.

MAJOR TOURIST ORGANIZATION

MI-13   MICHIGAN DEPT. OF COMMERCE, TRAVEL BUREAU, Box 30226--Law
         Building, Lansing, MI 48909 (517/373-0670).

         They distribute a semiannual CALENDAR OF TRAVEL EVENTS, a 32-
         page booklet COUNTRY CAROUSEL: A GUIDE TO PICK-YOUR-OWN
         FARMS AND ROADSIDE MARKETS prepared by the Information Division
         of the Michigan Dept. of Agriculture, a MICHIGAN AUTUMN COLOR
         TOUR GUIDE, and TRAVEL MICHIGAN. . .HANDICAPPERS MINI-
         GUIDE. The most complete sources of more specific information are
         the 4 regional tourist associations.

REGIONAL TOURISM ASSOCIATIONS

EAST MICHIGAN TOURIST ASSOCIATION, 1 Wenonah Park, Bay City, MI
48706 (517/895-8823).

> They publish an annual EAST MICHIGAN TRAVEL GUIDE of over 100
> pages that describes attractions, recreation, and resort facilities. It
> doesn't list accommodations and restaurants; these are covered in the
> annual EAST MICHIGAN AUTO GUIDE. They also issue a map/guide
> to family attractions, a guide to golf and tennis facilities, a LAKE
> HURON SPORTS FISHING MAP, a fall COLOR TOUR GUIDE, an
> EAST MICHIGAN PATHS OF HISTORY map/brochure, an annual
> EAST MICHIGAN WINTER GUIDE (a very extensive guide to down-
> hill and cross-country skiing, snowmobiling, resorts, motels, restaur-
> ants, and festivals), and an equally extensive annual EAST MICHIGAN
> SPORTSMEN'S GUIDE to fishing, hunting, camping, boating, and
> canoeing. Persons in the 517 area code can call 800/322-4825 toll-
> free for information.

SOUTHEAST MICHIGAN TRAVEL AND TOURIST ASSOCIATION, 350 American
Center, Southfield, MI 48034 (313/357-1663).

> They publish a very thorough quarterly travel guide of varying length
> that describes every possible point of interest and vacation activity
> (including biking, hiking, camping, horse racing, etc.) in the area.
> It does not include accommodations and restaurants. They also issue
> a calendar of events; a 30-page guide to OUTDOORS IN SOUTH-
> EAST MICHIGAN that describes boating, fishing, hunting, camping,
> and canoeing opportunities; a ski guide; a golf course guide; and an
> autumn color tours guide. The association also operates "Traveline"
> at 313/357-2600 which is a 24-hour recorded message featuring infor-
> mation on events, and fishing and hunting conditions.

UPPER PENINSULA TRAVEL AND RECREATION ASSOCIATION, Box 400, Iron
Mountain, MI 49801 (906/774-5480).

> At press time, they had separate brochures on attractions, campgrounds,
> fall color tours, waterfalls, winter activities, and 2 larger pieces of
> literature: WHO'S HOST IN MICHIGAN'S UPPER PENINSULA (a
> directory of hotels, motels, resorts, campgrounds, restaurants, attrac-
> tions, and travel facilities) and a MAP AND GUIDE TO TRAVEL
> AND RECREATION. The association is planning to consolidate all of
> these into 1 large annual booklet sometime in the near future.

WEST MICHIGAN TOURIST ASSOCIATION, 136 Fulton East, Grand Rapids,
MI 49503 (616/456-8557).

> CAREFREE DAYS is the name of each of their quarterly vacation guides.
> The spring issue is devoted to points of interest and is over 200 pages;
> the summer issue, almost 100 pages, lists dining, attractions, shopping,

golf, etc.; the fall issue devotes almost 100 pages to winter activities; and the winter issue devotes almost 70 pages to camping, boating and canoeing, and fishing. They also issue a WEST MICHIGAN HOST DIRECTORY which is a listing of accommodations, dining,· sightseeing, camping, boating, fishing, golfing, shopping, convention facilities, etc. available in each community in the region.

OTHER ORGANIZATIONS

MI-14   MICHIGAN DEPT. OF STATE, HISTORY DIVISION, Lansing, MI 48912.

They issue several good guides to historic areas in Michigan. HISTORIC SITES IN MICHIGAN is a comprehensive compilation of 1-page descriptions of all historic areas within the state. HISTORY MUSEUMS IN MICHIGAN: A GUIDE is a 36-page booklet describing 180 museums. MICHIGAN'S HISTORIC ATTRACTIONS is a 31-page county-by-county listing of the more popular historic points of interest, most of which are open to the public.

MI-15   MICHIGAN LODGING ASSOCIATION, 30161 Southfield Road, Cranbrook Centre, Suite 300, Southfield, MI 48076 (313/645-5850).

MI-16   MICHIGAN TRAIL RIDERS ASSOCIATION, 1179 Gam Road, Traverse City, MI 49684.

This nonprofit corporation was organized for the purpose of promoting the use and development of horseback and hiking trails throughout Michigan. It has developed a shore-to-shore "Michigan Riding and Hiking Trail" from Empire on Lake Michigan to Tawas on Lake Huron, and Cadillac to Cheboygan, in the upper Lower Peninsula. A MICHIGAN RIDING AND HIKING TRAIL GUIDE BOOK, now in a third edition, is available to members. It contains detailed maps of the trail and practical trail and trip planning information.

INFORMATION CENTERS/INFORMATION PHONES

The Michigan Dept. of State Highways and Transportation operates over 20 highway travel information centers throughout the state. Their locations are indicated on the OFFICIAL TRANSPORTATION MAP. There are 2 out-of-state Michigan Travel Information Centers: 55 East Monroe, Chicago, IL 60603 (312/372-0080), and 29 Public Square, Cleveland, OH 44113 (216/771-1956). There are 2 toll-free numbers for travel information: 800/248-5456 for out-of-state calls, and 800/292-2520 for use when calling within Michigan.

OUTDOOR RECREATION ACTIVITIES

CANOEING AND BOATING. A 52-page MICHIGAN BOAT LAUNCHING

DIRECTORY shows locations and lists facilities at all boat ramps in the state. A MICHIGAN HARBORS GUIDE describes harbors and facilities on Lakes Michigan, Huron, Superior, and Erie. CANOING IN MICHIGAN describes briefly all canoeable rivers and streams in the state. All 3 are available from the Michigan Dept. of Natural Resources, Box 30028, Lansing, MI 48909 (517/373-1220). The Recreational Canoeing Association, Box 265, Baldwin, MI 49304 issues a LET'S GO CANOEING guide to 20 Michigan rivers and nearby rental liveries, campgrounds, grocery stores, etc. The Travel Bureau (MI-13) issues a MICHIGAN CHARTER BOAT & INLAND GUIDES DIRECTORY. See also MI-2, MI-7, and the publications of all 4 regional tourism associations.

FISHING AND HUNTING. Contact the Michigan Dept. of Natural Resources, Box 30028, Lansing, MI 48909 (517/373-1220). There is a Michigan Fishing Hotline at 517/373-0908. See also MI-7, MI-11, MI-12, and the publications of all 4 regional tourism associations.

WINTER ACTIVITIES. The Travel Bureau (MI-13) issues a comprehensive MICHIGAN WINTER SPORTS GUIDE, a large fold-out map/guide to ski and snowmobile areas. Use the toll-free numbers from the "Information Centers/ Information Phones" section above for snow conditions. See also MI-7, MI-9 and the publications of all 4 regional tourism associations.

NATIONAL/STATE PARKS/FORESTS, ETC.

Isle Royale National Park

MI-17   ISLE ROYALE NATIONAL PARK, 87 North Ripley Street, Houghton, MI 49931 (906/482-3310).

   This close-to-nature National Park is located in Lake Superior, is accessible only by boat or float plane, and is open from mid-May to mid-October. Contact the above office for information on transportation services, camping, hiking, canoeing, boating, fishing, climate, etc. The Houghton Park Headquarters Office, located on the mainland, is open 8A.M.-6P.M. every day in the summer, and 8A.M.-4:30P.M. the rest of the year. For information on transportation to the island, accommodations (including reservations), and outdoor activities contact: National Park Concessions, Box 405, Houghton, MI 49931 (906/482-2890) between June and September. During the other months write: National Park Concessions, General Offices, Mammoth Cave, KY 42259.

For maps and information on campgrounds and recreation activities in Michigan's 4 national forests contact the U.S. Forest Service, Eastern Region, 633 West Wisconsin Avenue, Milwaukee, WI 53203.

The Michigan Dept. of Natural Resources, Box 30028, Lansing, MI 48909 issues lists of camping and other facilities available at state parks and forests. The Department has a Detroit Information Office at 313/256-2760. Also available from the Department are 64 different maps of pathways throughout the state forest system and a brochure describing Michigan's shore-to-shore riding/hiking trail in the northern Lower Peninsula. See also MI-16. A guide to handicapped facilities at Michigan state parks is available from the Travel Bureau (MI-13). See also the series published by the Oak Leaf Publishing Co. (MI-2), (MI-8), (MI-9), (MI-12), and (MI-6).

INDIVIDUAL CITIES OR AREAS

Detroit—Printed Materials

MI-18   Fischhoff, Martin. DETROIT: A YOUNG GUIDE TO THE CITY. 4th ed. Detroit: Speedball Publications, 1973. 339 p. Photos., drawings, sketch maps. Index.

The chapters are: calendar of annual events, restaurants, bars, gourmet centers, shops, "sites to see," theater, cinema, art, music, sports, recreation, and getting around town. There are additional chapters on Ann Arbor and Windsor.

MI-19   GUIDE TO DETROIT FOR THE HANDICAPPED. Prepared by the Tau Beta Association. Detroit: Rehabilitation Institute (261 Mack Blvd./ 48201), 1973.

MI-20   Keller, Martha V., and Weaver, Joan S. WHERE TO GO AND WHAT TO DO WITH THE KIDS IN DETROIT. Los Angeles: Price/ Stern/Sloan, 1974. 160 p. Index. 0-8431-0272-1. 74-193165.

The types of activities described and the chapters into which they are organized are identical to the other "Where To Go, What To Do with Kids" guides published by Price/Stern/Sloan: outdoor adventures; special birthday parties; museums; tours; concerts, film, and theater; classes to develop talent and hobbies; services; and a calendar of yearly events. The format for each description is even identical! There is a special chapter on trips to Windsor, Ontario.

Maps of Detroit are available from AAA (US-259); Gousha (US-206); Metro Graphic Arts, 900 40th SE, Grand Rapids, MI 49508; and Rand McNally (US-215).

The Detroit weather information number is 313/932-1212.

Detroit—Organizations

MI-21   METROPOLITAN DETROIT CONVENTION & VISITORS BUREAU, 100

Renaissance Center, Suite 1950, Detroit, MI 48243 (313/259-4333).

They issue a VISITORS MAP OF THE GREATER DETROIT which lists and locates attractions, theaters, sports stadiums, and shopping malls. It also contains a map and directions for a downtown Detroit walk tour. Their VISITORS GUIDE TO THE GREATER DETROIT brochure repeats the information on the map above and adds a list, with descriptions of restaurants and nightclubs. They also issue a HOTEL & MOTEL GUIDE TO GREATER DETROIT and several brochures describing package tours of Detroit. They operate a walk-in Visitor Information Center on the corner of Jefferson Avenue and Auditorium Drive in front of Ford Auditorium. It is open 7 days a week from 8:30A.M.-6:30P.M. They also have a "What's Line" at 313/298-6190 which is a daily recorded message about sports, nightlife, theater, and special events.

Lansing—Printed Materials

MI-22   ACCESS LANSING. Lansing: Center for Handicapper Affairs (1026 East Michigan Avenue/48912), 1979.

A map of Lansing is available from the Automobile Club of Michigan, Auto Club Drive, Dearborn, MI 48126.

Lansing—Organizations

MI-23   LANSING REGIONAL CHAMBER OF COMMERCE, 510 West Washtenaw, Box 14030, Lansing, MI 48901 (517/487-6340).

A visitors packet and a large city map are available from them.

Mackinac Island—Printed Materials

A map of Mackinac Island is available from the Automobile Club of Michigan, Auto Club Drive, Dearborn, MI 48126.

Mackinac Island—Organizations

MI-24   MACKINAC ISLAND CHAMBER OF COMMERCE, Box 451, Mackinac Island, MI 49757 (906/847-3783).

They have a single map/brochure that locates points of interest and churches, and lists hotels, tourist homes, restaurants, shops, and all transportation services including ferries, airlines, and bike riding.

MINNESOTA

BOOKS, ATLASES, MAGAZINES

MN-1   Beymer, Robert. BOUNDARY WATERS CANOE AREA. Berkeley, CA: Wilderness Press, 1978. 224 p. Maps, photos.

This volume covers the western region of this watery wilderness of northeastern Minnesota. It describes 24 entry points into the area and recommends about twice that number of trips from these entry points, giving day-by-day descriptions and other necessary information. It is invaluable for trip planning as entry points now have quota limitations.

MN-2   Buchanan, James W. THE MINNESOTA WALK BOOK. VOL. 1: A GUIDE TO HIKING & BACKPACKING IN THE ARROWHEAD AND ISLE ROYALE. Duluth, MN: Sweetwater Press (Box 3083/55803), 1974. 105 p. Maps. Bibliography. Index. 74-186952.

The author's descriptions of what to expect on each trail are good, but the maps are not detailed enough and are hard to read. It includes walks in Duluth.

MN-3   Holmquist, June D., and Brookins, Jean A. MINNESOTA'S MAJOR HISTORIC SITES: A GUIDE. 2d ed. St. Paul: Minnesota Historical Society, 1972. 191 p. Photos., maps. Bibliography. Index. 0-87351-072-0. 73-188490.

Thirty-six areas or sites are described with a very full historical background for each. State monuments are also listed.

MN-4   Holmquist, June D., et al., comps. HISTORY ALONG THE HIGHWAYS: AN OFFICIAL GUIDE TO MINNESOTA STATE MARKERS AND MONUMENTS. Minnesota Historic Sites Pamphlet Series. St. Paul: Minnesota Historical Society, 1967. 61 p. Photos., maps. Index. 0-87351-033-X. 67-63490.

Each of the 3 sections (historical markers, state monuments, geological markers) is arranged by the order of erection and reproduces the text of each marker. In 1973 a supplement was issued covering markers erected during 1967-72. More supplements, or a revised edition, are expected.

MN-5 McGuire, Nina, and Budd, Barbara. AN UNCOMMON GUIDE TO MINNESOTA. A Tailored Tours Publication. Minneapolis: Viking Press, 1971. 156 p. Sketch maps, sketches. Index. 74-156495.

The authors have taken Minnesota's points of interest and built 19 highway tours around them. Individual descriptions include location, hours, and fees. A large separate recreation section tells where to go for canoeing, camping, boating, fishing, hunting, skiing, snow-mobiling, and golf, and has a table of facilities at state parks. There is also a calendar of annual events. The address of Tailored Tours Publications is Box 24222, Minneapolis, MN 55424.

MN-6 MINNESOTA: A STATE GUIDE. American Guide Series. New York: Hastings House, 1938. 545 p. Photos., maps.

The original WPA guide in 3 sections--general background, descriptions of 6 cities and towns, and 20 statewide highway tours--is comprehensive, but out of date. However, the added section describing 15 canoe trips in Superior National Forest might still be useful.

MN-7 MINNESOTA STATE ATLAS. 2d ed. Rockford, IL: Rockford Map Publishers, 1976. 245 p. Maps, photos.

Hopefully, this is the new format for the Rockford state atlases with its 87 county maps large and clear enough to read without eyestrain, unlike the earlier edition. State historical markers are listed and located. Campgrounds, wildlife areas (with hunting and fishing regulations), lakes, boating activities, rivers and streams, 11 "Minnetours," park and recreation areas, plant tours, winter sports, selected motels, resorts, selected farm vacations, and golf courses are listed. There is a gazetteer. This book is a bargain.

MN-8 Peters, Robert E. EASY WHEELIN' IN MINNESOTA: A WHEEL-CHAIR ACCESSIBILITY GUIDEBOOK. Minneapolis: Minneapolis Star and Minneapolis Tribune, Education Services Dept. (available from the author, 1 Timberglade Road, Bloomington, MN 55437), 1976. 52 p.

A new edition was planned for late 1978.

MN-9 Whitman, John. WHITMAN'S RESTAURANT GUIDE TO MINNESOTA. Minneapolis: Nodin Press (519 North Third Street/55401), 1976. 213 p.

The author gives complete information for the 135 most popular restaurants in Minneapolis/St. Paul and for 70 other restaurants in the state.

MN-10 _____. WHITMAN'S TRAVEL GUIDE TO MINNESOTA. Minneapolis: Nodin Press (519 North Third Street/55401), 1977. 256 p.
Maps. Index.

This book begins with general information about historical sites;
state parks; national parks, forests, and wildlife refuges; fishing; and
Hennepin County parks; and then goes on to give detailed descriptions for car and walking tours in all popular areas within the state.
It also contains a list of sources of information.

MAPS

The OFFICIAL TRANSPORTATION MAP is available from the Tourist Information
Center (MN-11). The 1977-78 edition contains information on the 5 highway
information centers, the 6 tourist regions and the Tourist Information Center,
the state parks and wayside parks, and a statewide public transportation map.
AAA (US-259), Goushā (US-206), and Rand McNally (US-215) each issue a
map of Minnesota. Numerous maps of the waters of northern Minnesota, many
specifically designed for the fisherman and canoeist, are available from the
W.A. Fisher Co., Box 1107, Virginian, MN 55792. See also MN-7.

MAJOR TOURIST ORGANIZATION

MN-11 MINNESOTA TOURIST INFORMATION CENTER, 480 Cedar Street,
St. Paul, MN 55101 (612/296-5029).

They issue a large booklet describing the 6 vacation regions of Minnesota and all the outdoor vacation opportunities. It also contains addresses and phone numbers for all related sources of information.
MINNESOTA MINNETOURS is a booklet describing 11 circular routes
appropriate for a weekend trip. They also issue an annual calendar
of events and a MINNESOTA CAMPING GUIDE which describes
both privately and publicly owned campgrounds.

REGIONAL TOURISM ASSOCIATIONS

ARROWHEAD MINNESOTA, 400 Hotel Duluth, Duluth, MN 55802 (218/722-
0874).

They issue a comprehensive 47-page vacation planning directory called
MINNESOTA ARROWHEAD.

HEARTLAND MINNESOTA, Box 443, 411 Laurel Street, Brainerd, MN 56401
(218/829-1615).

They issue an annual (1978 ed., 54 p.) TOUR GUIDE TO MINNE-
SOTA HEARTLAND.

HIAWATHALAND MINNESOTA, 212 1st Avenue Southwest, Rochester, MN 55901 (507/288-8970).

> They issue a comprehensive annual (1978 ed., 47 p.) guide called HIAWATHALAND MINNESOTA.

METROLAND MINNESOTA, 2901 Pleasant Avenue, Minneapolis, MN 55408 (612/827-4035).

> They issue an annual, comprehensive MINNESOTA METROLAND ACTIVITIES DIRECTORY, which is for the greater Minneapolis/St. Paul area.

PIONEERLAND MINNESOTA, Box 999, Mankato, MN 56001 (507/345-4517).

> They issue a comprehensive 52-page TRAVEL & VACATION DIRECTORY.

VIKINGLAND MINNESOTA, Box 545, Battle Lake, MN 56515 (218/864-8181).

> They issue a 19-page VIKINGLAND MINNESOTA guide that is mostly advertisements.

OTHER ORGANIZATIONS

MN-12 MINNESOTA HISORICAL SOCIETY, Building 25, Fort Snelling, St. Paul, MN 55111 (612/726-1171).

> They publish a guide to the historic sites they administer that are open to the public.

MN-13 MINNESOTA HOTEL & MOTEL ASSOCIATION, 2001 University Avenue, St. Paul, MN 55104 (612/647-0107).

INFORMATION CENTERS/INFORMATION PHONES

Locations and hours of the highway centers will be found on the OFFICIAL TRANSPORTATION MAP. A toll-free number 800/328-9161 for travel information may be dialed from the following states: Illinois, Iowa, Kansas, Michigan, Missouri, Nebraska, North Dakota, South Dakota, and Wisconsin.

OUTDOOR RECREATION ACTIVITIES

BICYCLING. The Minnesota Council of the American Youth Hostels, Box 9511, Minneapolis, MN 55440 (612/336-2594) issues a 76-page bike atlas describing tours throughout the state.

CANOEING AND BOATING. Nineteen canoeable rivers in the state have been mapped and described, and separate brochures are available for each one. Contact the Minnesota Dept. of Natural Resources, 320 Centennial Bldg., St. Paul, MN 55155 (612/296-4776). Information on some of these rivers will, in addition, also be found in MINNESOTA VOYAGEURS TRAILS, a 48-page guide also prepared by the Dept. of Natural Resources. It contains maps and descriptions of 16 rivers and the Boundary Waters Canoe Area (BWCA). It is available from the Documents Section, Room 140, Centennial Bldg., St. Paul, MN 55101. Also available from the Documents Section are detailed boating guides with mile-by-mile strip maps for each of the following rivers: Crow, Kettle, Rum, St. Croix (2 vols.), and Snake. For additional information on the BWCA, contact: Forest Supervisor, Superior National Forest, Box 338, Duluth, MN 55801 (218/727-6692). The town of Ely is the gateway to the BWCA, and the Ely Chamber of Commerce, Tour/Travel Center, Ely, MN 55731 issues a 15-page brochure listing accommodations, outfitters, portage services, etc. in the area. See also MN-1, MN-6, MN-7, and MN-14.

FISHING AND HUNTING. Contact the Minnesota Dept. of Natural Resources, Division of Fish and Wildlife, 390 Centennial Bldg., St. Paul, MN 55155 (612/296-2894). Their annual BIG GAME HUNTING REGULATIONS guide contains a large map showing deer hunting areas. They also issue a large map showing MINNESOTA WILDLIFE LANDS. Their where-to fishing information seems to be less extensive. See also MN-7.

WINTER ACTIVITIES. An extensive, annual MINNESOTA WINTER GUIDE, available from either the Tourist Information Center (MN-11) or the Minnesota Dept. of Natural Resources, Parks and Recreation Division, Centennial Office Bldg., St. Paul, MN 55155 (612/296-4776), describes downhill and cross-country ski areas and snowmobile areas in each of the 6 regional tourist areas. Also available from the Parks and Recreation Division is a large fold-out map of "Minnesota Snowmobile Trails."

NATIONAL/STATE PARKS/FORESTS, ETC.

Voyageurs National Park

MN-14 VOYAGEURS NATIONAL PARK, BOX 50, International Falls, MN 56649 (218/283-4492).

Established in 1971 and located along the US-Canadian border, travel within this park is primarily by boat. It has been preserved to look much like it did in the late eighteenth and nineteenth centuries when the fur-trading French-Canadians plied these waters in their bark canoes. A small map/brochure; lists of boat rentals, launching sites, outfitters, etc., and campgrounds; and information on backcountry travel and temperatures are available from the above address. A GUIDE TO VOYAGEURS NATIONAL PARK by Michael E. Duncanson is available from the Lake States National Park Association, Box 672, International Falls, MN 56649.

Information and maps on the 2 national forests in Minnesota are available from the U.S. Forest Service, Eastern Region, 633 West Wisconsin Avenue, Milwaukee, WI 53203.

A GUIDE TO MINNESOTA'S STATE PARK SYSTEM and individual map/brochures of each of the trails comprising the Minnesota Recreational Land Trails System are available from the Minnesota Dept. of Natural Resources, Centennial Office Bldg., St. Paul, MN 55155 (612/296-4776). The Division of Forestry of the Dept. of Natural Resources, also at the above address, 612/296-3336, issues extensive maps of 12 of the 55 state forests. Each shows roads, trails, campgrounds, picnic areas, boat landing sites, points of interest, and signed canoe routes.

INDIVIDUAL CITIES OR AREAS

Minneapolis/St. Paul—Printed Materials

MN-15   Ervin, Jean, and Ervin, John. THE TWIN CITIES EXPLORED. Minneapolis: The Adams Press, 1972. 200 p. Photos.

This is "a guide to restaurants, shops, theaters, museums, and other features" in Minneapolis and St. Paul. The "other features" are dance, music, historic sites, points of artistic and architectural interest, green spaces, and regularly recurring events. Descriptions are thorough, but the overall coverage is limited and seems to be aimed at the "upwardly mobile" interested in pursuing "the good life."

MN-16   French, Elizabeth S. EXPLORING THE TWIN CITIES WITH CHILDREN . 2d ed. Minneapolis: Nodin Press (519 North Third Street/ 55401), 1975. 57 p. Maps. Index.

"A selection of tours, sights, museums, recreational activities, and many other places for children and adults to visit together," are arranged alphabetically with an index by categories.

MN-17   McGuire, Nina, and Budd, Barbara. AN UNCOMMON GUIDE TO THE TWIN CITIES. A Tailored Tours Publication. Minneapolis: Viking Press, 1970. 152 p. Sketches, sketch maps. Index. 73-17322.

The authors have chosen the best of the two most likely arrangement schemes--topical over a separate section for each city. There are chapters on finding your way, things to do for all ages, adult getaways, fine dining, the arts, shopping, recreation, education, tours, and worship. The address of Tailored Tours Publications is Box 24222, Minneapolis, MN 55425.

MN-18 TWIN CITIES GUIDE. Minneapolis: Dorn Communications (7101 York Avenue South/55435), 1978. Issued annually. 202 p. Maps, photos.

This guide is aimed primarily at the businessperson planning to relocate in the area, but the traveler will also find the comprehensive sections on hotels, restaurants, shopping, day trips, arts, sports, nightlife, and transportation useful.

See also Metroland Minnesota in the "Regional Tourism Associations" section of this chapter.

Joint maps of Minneapolis/St. Paul are available from AAA (US-259); Goushā (US-206); Hudson Map Co., 2510 Nicollet Avenue, Minneapolis, MN 55404; and Rand McNally (US-215).

Minneapolis/St. Paul—Organizations

MN-19 MINNEAPOLIS CONVENTION AND TOURISM COMMISSION, 15 South 5th Street, Minneapolis, MN 55402 (612/348-4313).

They issue a general brochure, a quarterly calendar of events, and several walking and driving tour booklets.

MN-20 ST. PAUL AREA CONVENTION AND VISITORS BUREAU, Osborn Bldg., Suite 300, St. Paul, MN 55102 (612/222-5561).

They issue a general map/brochure listing points of interest, hotels/ motels, and services; a RESTAURANT AND ENTERTAINMENT GUIDE; a sheet map listing points of interest, parks, and museums/libraries/ theaters; a TOUR TIPS booklet for locating historical, cultural, and recreational points of interest; and TOUR GUIDE, a list of buildings and/or organizations giving tours.

MISSISSIPPI

BOOKS, ATLASES, MAGAZINES

MS-1　　Kempe, Helen K.　THE PELICAN GUIDE TO OLD HOMES OF MIS-
SISSIPPI.　2 vols.　Gretna, LA:　Pelican Publishing Co., 1977.
Photos., maps.

Volume 1 covers Natchez and the old south (0-88289-134-0.　77-
725).　Volume 2 covers Columbus and the north (0-88289-035-9.　76-
20434).　Descriptions include brief historic background, location, and
whether or not the house is open to the public.

MS-2　　MISSISSIPPI: A GUIDE TO THE MAGNOLIA STATE.　American
Guide Series.　New York:　Hastings House, 1938.　545 p.　Photos.,
maps.

The original WPA guide in 3 sections--general background, descriptions of 12 cities and towns, and 17 statewide highway tours--is
comprehensive, but out of date.

MS-3　　Newton, Carolyn S.　OUTDOOR MISSISSIPPI.　Jackson, MS:　University and College Press of Mississippi, 1974.　200 p.　Photos.,
maps.　Index.　0-87805-023-X.　73-86316.

Hunting, fishing, camping, watersports, and rock and fossil collecting
areas are briefly described.　This is the book for Mississippi recreational facilities.

MS-4　　Newton, Carolyn S., and Coggin, Patricia H.　MEET MISSISSIPPI.
Huntsville, AL:　Strode Publishers, 1976.　228 p.　Photos., maps.
Bibliography.　Index.　0-87397-090-X.　75-32109.

Descriptions of mostly noncommercial, historic places of interest are
arranged by county.　There is a place name chapter and a list of
National Register of Historic Places and National Historic Landmarks
in Mississippi.

MAPS

The official highway map is available from the Travel, Tourism and Public Affairs Dept. (MS-5). The 1978 edition lists facilities at state parks national parks, national forest recreation areas and reservoirs. AAA (US-259), Exxon (US-261), Goushā (US-206), and Rand McNally (US-215) each issue a combined Arkansas/Louisiana/Mississippi map.

MAJOR TOURIST ORGANIZATION

MS-5   MISSISSIPPI AGRICULTURAL & INDUSTRIAL BOARD; TRAVEL, TOUR-
        ISM AND PUBLIC AFFAIRS DEPT., Box 849, Jackson, MS 39205
        (601/354-6715).

They issue an extensive general brochure about Mississippi; separate brochures on golf and tennis, state parks, camping, crafts, cultural events, fish and wildlife, forests, lakes and reservoirs, historic sites, museums and art galleries, rivers and streams; a semiannual calendar of events; an annual pilgrimage guide (complete listing, with sources of additional information, for all the antebellum home and community tours); and a CHILDRENS GUIDE TO MISSISSIPPI.

REGIONAL TOURISM ASSOCIATIONS

Mississippi has 5 official area tourist councils, referred to by number, and each issuing a general brochure describing points of interest, things to see and do, landmarks and museums, recreation opportunities, and the addresses of the local chambers of commerce.

AREA TOURIST COUNCIL I, Batesville-South Panola Area Chamber of Commerce, Box 528, Batesville, MS 38606 (601/563-3126).

AREA TOURIST COUNCIL II, Box 1118, Greenwood, MS 38930 (601/453-
0925).

AREA TOURIST COUNCIL III, Chamber of Commerce, Box 51, Philadelphia,
MS 39350 (601/656-1742).

AREA TOURIST COUNCIL IV, Vicksburg Chamber of Commerce, Box 709,
Vicksburg, MS 39180 (601/636-1012).

AREA TOURIST COUNCIL V, Box 1278, Biloxi, MS 39533 (601/374-1257).

In addition to these, there is a Mississippi Gulf Coast Visitors Bureau at the Biloxi Chamber of Commerce on Highway 90 at the Lighthouse. It is open 5 days a week, 8:30A.M.-5P.M. The mailing address is 1036 Fred Haise Blvd., Drawer CC, Biloxi, MS 39533. The phone number is 601/374-2717.

OTHER ORGANIZATIONS

MS-6 MISSISSIPPI INNKEEPERS ASSOCIATION, 1375 Kimwood Drive, Suite 329, Jackson, MS 39211 (601/981-1160).

They issue an annual directory of hotels and motels.

INFORMATION CENTERS/INFORMATION PHONES

A list of Mississippi highway information centers, all located on Interstate highways near the borders, is available from the Travel, Tourism and Public Affairs Dept. (MS-5). They are also located on the official highway map.

OUTDOOR RECREATION ACTIVITIES

CANOEING AND BOATING. A MISSISSIPPI CHARTER BOAT DIRECTORY is available from Sea Grant Advisory Service, Mississippi Cooperative Extension Service, Box 4557, Biloxi, MS 39531.

FISHING AND HUNTING. The Mississippi Game and Fish Commission, Box 451, Jackson, MS 39205 supplies information on best locations throughout the state, plus copies of regulations. Information on coastal fishing opportunities and 8 coastal fishing water guides are available from Sea Grant Advisory Service, Mississippi Cooperative Extension Service, Box 4557, Biloxi, MS 39531. See also MS-3 and the brochure available from the Travel, Tourism and Public Affairs Dept. (MS-5).

NATIONAL/STATE PARKS/FORESTS, ETC.

Natchez Trace Parkway

MS-7 Brown, Dale C., et al. THE COMPLETE GUIDE TO NATCHEZ. Natchez, MS: Myrtle Bank Publications, 1977. 112 p. Photos., map. Index. 76-56980.

This guide includes chapters on the history of Natchez, getting around (including where to stay, eat, and shop), exploring historic and modern Natchez, and 4 short trips from Natchez.

MS-8 NATCHEZ TRACE PARKWAY, Rural Route 1, NT 143, Tupelo, MS 38801.

They supply an official brochure of the parkway that includes a map and landmarks along the trace; information on campgrounds, bicycling, hiking, and horseback riding; and an annual visitor activity schedule. There is a visitor information center in Tupelo, open daily from 8A.M.-5P.M. (until 6P.M. in the summer months). They also administer the Brices Cross Roads National Battlefield Site and the Tupelo National Battlefield, both sites of Civil War skirmishes.

MS-9   NATCHEZ-ADAMS COUNTY CHAMBER OF COMMERCE, Box 725, Natchez, MS 39120 (601/445-4611).

They issue several brochures on the antebellum mansion pilgrimages, a calendar of events, and a self-guided walking tour brochure.

The National Forest Supervisor, Box 1291, Jackson, MS 39205 supplies information and maps on Mississippi's 6 national forests.

The Mississippi State Park System, 717 Robert E. Lee Bldg., Jackson, MS 39201 supplies information on state parks, camping areas, and historic sites. See also the brochures available from the Travel, Tourism and Public Affairs Dept. (MS-5).

Mississippi has several waterway districts that include water parks with recreational facilities, boat launching ramps, campgrounds, and stocked lakes. The Pat Harrison Waterway District, Drawer 1509, Hattiesburg, MS 39401 has developed 5 water parks in the Pascagoula River Basin in the southeast corner of the state. The Pearl River Basin Development District, 2304 Riverside Drive, Box 5332, Jackson, MS 39216 is in the southcentral part of the state, and the Tennessee-Tombigbee Waterway Development Authority, Drawer 671, Columbus, MS 39701 is in the northeast corner of the state.

INDIVIDUAL CITIES OR AREAS

Jackson—Printed Materials

MS-10   Junior League of Jackson, Mississippi, comp. A KEY TO JACKSON FOR THE PHYSICALLY LIMITED. Jackson, MS: Easter Seal Society of Mississippi (Box 4958/39216), 1976. 69 p.

Champion Map Corp. (US-202); International Aerial Mapping, 8927 International Drive, San Antonio, TX 78216; and the Public Relations Dept. of the City of Jackson all provide maps.

Jackson—Organizations

MS-11   JACKSON CHAMBER OF COMMERCE, Box 22548, Jackson, MS 39205 (601/948-7575).

They issue THINGS TO SEE AND DO IN BEAUTIFUL JACKSON, MISSISSIPPI.

MISSOURI

BOOKS, ATLASES, MAGAZINES

MO-1   Gass, Ramon D. MISSOURI HIKING TRAILS: A DETAILED GUIDE
        TO SELECTED HIKING TRAILS ON PUBLIC LAND IN MISSOURI.
        Jefferson City: Missouri Dept. of Conservation (Box 180/65101), 1974.
        58 p. Maps. 75-620549.

        All trails are located on federal or state land, and most are in the
        southeast corner of the state. A map, general comments, length, and
        location are given for each of 26 trails. There are no difficulty
        ratings and no index. There's no apparent order in which the trails
        are presented.

MO-2   Marshall, Virginia. WHEELCHAIR SIGHTSEEING IN MISSOURI: A
        WHERE-TO-GO GUIDE FOR PEOPLE WHO CAN'T WALK FAR,
        CAN'T WALK WELL, OR CAN'T WALK AT ALL. Brentwood, MO:
        Oliver Press (2607 Salem Road/63144), 1974. 88 p. Maps. Index.
        76-363270.

        This guide to places in Missouri that the person in a wheelchair can
        manage omits sleeping and eating places.

MO-3   MISSOURI: A GUIDE TO THE "SHOW ME" STATE. Rev. ed.
        American Guide Series. New York: Hastings House, 1954. 654 p.
        Photos., maps.

        This revision of the original WPA guide is in three sections: general
        background, descriptions of 11 principal cities, and 15 statewide high-
        way tours.

MO-4   MISSOURI LIFE: THE MAGAZINE OF MISSOURI. Jefferson City:
        Missouri Life (1209 Elmerine Avenue/65101).

        This bimonthly slick magazine, begun in 1973, is devoted to the
        history, travel, recreation, human interest, business, folklore, etc. of
        Missouri.

MAPS

The OFFICIAL HIGHWAY MAP is available from the Missouri State Highway Commission, Public Information Division, Box 270, Jefferson City, MO 65101 (314/751-2551). The 1978 edition contained a table of facilities at state parks. AAA (US-259), Gousha (US-206), and Rand McNally (US-215) each issue a map of Missouri. See also MO-12.

MAJOR TOURIST ORGANIZATION

MO-5   MISSOURI DIVISION OF TOURISM, Box 1055, Jefferson City, MO 65101 (314/751-4133).

They issue an annual VACATION GUIDE (1979 ed., 43 p.) that describes things to see and do in each of Missouri's 7 regions; has sections on caves, and hunting and fishing; has a list, with facilities, of state parks; a list of historic sites; a center fold-out map on which everything mentioned in the guide is located; information about the state's information centers; and a list of organizations throughout the state that supply information. They also issue a quarterly calendar of events, CAMPING IN MISSOURI (a list, with finding directions and tables of facilities and activities, of all state and federal and selected privately owned campgrounds; a list of hiking and equestrian trails on publicly owned land; and a list of sources of additional information), and MISSOURI FLOAT FISHING AND CANOEING OUTFITTERS (a 16-page list of numerous outfitters arranged by river).

REGIONAL TOURISM ASSOCIATIONS

The state is divided into 7 vacation regions, but there are no specific individual associations to write to. Each is described in the VACATION GUIDE available from the Division of Tourism (MO-5).

OTHER ORGANIZATIONS

MO-6   MISSOURI HOTEL & MOTEL ASSOCIATION, 1800 Southwest Blvd., Jefferson City, MO 65101 (314/636-2107).

INFORMATION CENTERS/INFORMATION PHONES

The Division of Tourism (MO-5) operates 3 Interstate Information Centers: on I-44 west of Joplin, on I-270 in north St. Louis, and on I-55 near Marston in southeast Missouri. The Division may be dialed direct 24 hours a day from Kansas City (861/471-7992) and St. Louis (314/231-4960). A recorded message gives special events, attractions, and gasoline information. The Missouri State

Missouri

Highway Commission, Box 270, Jefferson City, MO 65101 (314/751-2551) issues a folder listing roadside parks and rest areas.

OUTDOOR RECREATION ACTIVITIES

BICYCLING. In 1977 the Missouri Dept. of Natural Resources issued a MIS-SOURI BICYCLE SUITABILITY MAP, a somewhat difficult to read map rating all roads in the state according to use, width, and visibility to motorists. They have also issued a series of bicycle tour maps with each route centered on a specific state park. Both are available from the Missouri Division of Parks and Recreation, Box 176, Jefferson City, MO 65102. The Auto Club of Missouri, Cycling Activities, 201 Progress Parkway, Maryland Heights, MO 63043 also provides information. See also MO-22.

CANOEING AND BOATING. A 55-page booklet, CANOEING IN NORTH-ERN MISSOURI, is available from the Missouri Dept. of Natural Resources, Box 176, Jefferson City, MO 65102. It provides detailed information on 15 of the most floatable streams and rivers north of the Missouri River and includes maps and information on access points. See also MO-5, MO-13, and MO-15.

FISHING AND HUNTING. The Missouri Dept. of Conservation, Division of Fisheries and Wildlife, Box 180, Jefferson City, MO 65101 issues WHERE TO FISH IN MISSOURI and WHERE TO HUNT. See also MO-5 and MO-12.

NATIONAL/STATE PARKS/FORESTS, ETC.

See MO-15.

In 1976 Missouri's 2 national forests, Clark National Forest and Mark Twain National Forest, were designated the Mark Twain National Forest. Maps; floaters' guides; and fishing, trails, and camping information is available by writing to Forest Supervisor, Mark Twain National Forest, 401 Fairgrounds Road, Rolla, MO 65401 (314/364-4621).

The best general source of information on state parks and historic sites is the annual VACATION GUIDE issued by the Division of Tourism (MO-5). The Missouri Dept. of Natural Resources, Division of Parks and Recreation, Box 176, Jefferson City, MO 65102 issues individual map/brochures of each state park and historic site. It also provides information on trails, camping, and lodges in the state parks.

INDIVIDUAL CITIES OR AREAS

Jefferson City—Printed Materials

A map of Jefferson City is available from the Jefferson Bank of Missouri.

Jefferson City—Organizations

MO-7   JEFFERSON CITY AREA CHAMBER OF COMMERCE AND CONVEN-
TION & VISITORS COMMITTEE, Box 776, Jefferson City, MO 65101
(314/634-3616).

They issue a semi-annual VISITOR GUIDE of over 30-pages that has
articles about the city, a map, a walking tour, and descriptions of
other places that may be toured. They also issue lists of accommodations and restaurants. Their walk-in office at 213 Adams Street is
open Monday-Friday, 8A.M.-5P.M.

Kansas City—Printed Materials

MO-8   ACCESSIBILITY DIRECTORY: KANSAS CITY, MISSOURI.   N.p.:
Architectural Barrier Action Committee, 1975.

This guide is available from ACCESS, 3011 Baltimore, Kansas City,
MO 64108.

MO-9   KANSAS CITY VISITOR. Reno, NV: Visitor Publications (4600
Kietzke Lane, Suite 173/89502), 1978. Issued annually. 88 p.

This large, sophisticated guide placed in hotel rooms for the use of
visitors describes the various sections of the city, shopping, antiques,
sports, dining out, museums, galleries, and the performing arts.

MO-10 Parks, Nancy, et al.   GETTING IT TOGETHER IN KANSAS CITY:
A GUIDE TO ENTERTAINMENT, SHOPPING AND RECREATION.
Kansas City: Sheed and Ward, 1975. 128 p. 0-8362-0609-6. 74-
27643.

The authors cover all aspects of visiting and living in Kansas City:
getting entertained, getting fulfilled, getting the kids together, getting
dressed, getting the house together, getting the larder filled, and
getting to know Kansas City better. There is no index.

Maps of Kansas City are available from AAA (US-259); Goushā (US-206);
Hagstrom (US-207); Metro Graphic Arts, 900 40th SE, Grand Rapids, MI
49508; and Rand McNally (US-215).

Kansas City—Organizations

MO-11 CONVENTION & VISITORS BUREAU OF GREATER KANSAS CITY,
City Center Square, 1100 Main Street, Suite 2550, Kansas City, MO
64105 (816/221-7555).

Although the administrative offices are located on the 25th floor, the
bureau operates a Central Ticket Office and a Visitors Information

Center on the Baltimore Street level of City Center Square. They provide a quarterly calendar of events, an industrial tour booklet, restaurant and accommodations guides, a walking/driving scenic tour route and brochure, a visitor's map, and tennis and golf guides. The Vistor Information Center is open Monday-Friday, 9A.M.-6P.M., and on Saturday and Sunday from 10A.M.-4P.M. It also sells tickets to cultural and sports events. There is a Visitor Information Phone (called "VIP") at 474-9600 which is a 24-hour recorded message about the day's entertainment and events.

Ozarks—Printed Materials

MO-12 Carson, George. FISHING-HUNTING GUIDE TO THE OZARK AREA. St. Louis: Geyer Guides (12015 Manchester Road/63131), 1969. 136 p. Maps, photos. 74-9814.

This is an older work, but since good fishing and hunting locations often don't change, it is included here. It should be updated. Maps of 25 lakes and rivers show boat launching sites, camping areas, caves, landing fields, and locations where specific fish species may be caught. The hunting information is very minimal, and this guide is not recommended for this topic.

MO-13 Hawksley, Oz. MISSOURI OZARK WATERWAYS. Jefferson City: Missouri Dept. of Conservation (Box 180/65101), 1976. 114 p. Maps.

This is a "detailed guide to 37 major streams--2200 miles of clear, fast water." Descriptions include a difficulty classification, a map, and milepoint notations.

Ozarks—Organizations

MO-14 LAKE OF THE OZARKS ASSOCIATION, Box 98, Lake Ozark, MO 65049 (314/365-2902).

They issue A COMPLETE VACATION GUIDE TO MISSOURI'S LAKE OF THE OZARKS which is nothing more than 80 pages of advertisements. Their OFFICIAL MAP is more useful; it lists and locates accommodations, restaurants, attractions, campgrounds, marinas, and has a fish and game chart. One of its two large maps gives a decorative, oblique bird's-eye-view of the area.

MO-15 OZARK NATIONAL SCENIC RIVERWAYS, Box 490, Van Buren, MO 63965 (314/364-4621).

This National Park Service area, established in 1964, consists of 134 miles of the Current River and the Jacks Fork, its tributary, as they wind their way through the southeast corner of the state. A map/guide to floating these rivers, information on boat rentals and campgrounds, and a schedule of conducted tours and programs are available from the above address. There are numerous visitor centers and ranger stations in the area, all of which provide information and are closed during the winter months. The park headquarters office at the above address is open year round Monday-Friday, 8A.M.-5P.M.

MO-16 OZARK PLAYGROUNDS ASSOCIATION, Box 187, Joplin, MO 64801 (417/624-4250).

This association provides information on northwest and northcentral Arkansas and southwest Missouri. They issue a calendar of events 3 times a year, but their most comprehensive piece of literature is the large, annual (1978 ed., 93 p.) OZARKS VACATION PLANNING GUIDE. While it is mostly advertisements (which is a directory of sorts), it does have additional information on recreation opportunities, attractions, lodging, restaurants, scenic tours, hunting, fishing, floating, golf courses, and campgrounds.

There is an out-of-state toll-free Ozark-wide motel reservation service at 800/641-4006. In Missouri call 800/492-7092.

St. Louis—Printed Materials

MO-17 COMBINATION ST. LOUIS STREET MAP AND INFORMATION GUIDE. ST. Louis: Geyer Guides (12015 Manchester Road/63131), 1979. Various pagings. Maps, photos. Index.

The 2 component parts of this title are also available as separate books: the ST. LOUIS INFORMATION GUIDE and the ST. LOUIS STREET MAP. The Information Guide section contains descriptions of over 50 points of interest; lists of hotels/motels, restaurants, theaters, etc.; and a general information section (colleges, shopping centers, liquor laws, etc.). The Street Map section covers the metropolitan area, is very detailed, and includes parks, golf clubs, tennis courts, horseback trails, bowling lanes, skating rinks, and campgrounds.

MO-18 COMPLETE RECREATION GUIDE TO EAST CENTRAL MISSOURI. Holts Summit, MO: Recreational Map Co. (32 Perry Drive/65043), 1975. 33 p. Maps, photos., tables. 77-352609.

This is a guide to "outdoor recreational sites within an hour's drive of metropolitan St. Louis open to the general public either on a free or a fee basis." Golf, swimming, overnight camping, picnicking, boating (power, canoe, and sail), water skiing, fishing, hunting, horseback riding, hiking, tennis, and trail bike riding locations are located on tables and keyed to poor, general maps. It is regionally arranged.

MO-19 Dillon, Anne F., and Donnelly, Martha M. THE COMPLETE ST.

LOUIS GUIDE. New ed. St. Louis: the authors, 1976. 144 p. Maps. Index.

The "complete" in the title seems to be very appropriate here. A concise table gives admission and parking information, days and hours open, and phone numbers for all attractions. The main body of the guide covers these attractions on 14 tours with maps. Other sections include activities for children, nightlife, cultural activities, sports, restaurants, hotels and motels, shopping, and transportation and conducted tour information. The book jacket is a useful plastic-coated map on which the attractions are located.

MO-20 ST. LOUIS HAS IT A TO Z FOR THE HANDICAPPED. St. Louis: Easter Seal Society of Missouri, St. Louis Region (4108 Lindell Blvd./63108), 1975. 89 p.

MO-21 Trask, Sandra A., and Majesky, Doris H. ENJOYING ST. LOUIS WITH CHILDREN: A COMPLETE GUIDE TO CHILDREN'S ACTIVITIES--PRESCHOOL THROUGH TEENS--IN GREATER ST. LOUIS. 2d ed. St. Louis: Featherstone Press (Box 12823/63141), 1976. 136 p. Index. 76-9429.

Although of most use to residents, this guide will have to serve visitors, too, because there is nothing better. It is topically arranged with sections on museums and historical sites, birthday parties, the arts, animals, parks, and tours.

Maps of St. Louis are available from AAA (US-259); Champion Map Corp. (US-202); Goushā (US-206); Laclede Gas Co., 720 Olive, St. Louis, MO 63101; and Rand McNally (US-215).

The St. Louis weather information number is 314/936-1212.

St. Louis—Organizations

MO-22 CONVENTION AND VISITORS BUREAU OF GREATER ST. LOUIS, 500 North Broadway, St. Louis, MO 63102 (314/421-1023).

They issue 3 major pieces of literature: a comprehensive, annual (1979 ed., 32 p.) ST. LOUIS VISITORS GUIDE (has a centerfold map and describes places to go, things to do, accommodations, restaurants, shops, parks, theatres, etc.), a detailed road map of the area, and a HIKE, BIKE & SIGHT newspaper that has walking and bike tours of the metropolitan area. They sponsor a Fun Phone at 314/421-2100 which is a recorded message of the day's events. The office above is open Monday-Friday, 9A.M.-5P.M. for walk-in information. They sponsor an airport information center that is open 7 days a week from 8A.M.-8P.M. Foreign language assistance in French, Spanish, German, and Japanese is also available at a telephone display in the airport information center.

MONTANA

BOOKS, ATLASES, MAGAZINES

MT-1   Browning, Bill. A GUEST GUIDE TO MONTANA, THE PROMISED
        LAND. Helena: Montana Travel Hosts Division of the Montana
        Chamber of Commerce, 1975. 131 p. Photos., maps. Bibliography.
        75-322339.

        The first part is not much more than a nicely illustrated state promo-
        tional piece with lots of generalities and no specifics. The second
        section consists of several concise listings: annual events, summer
        theaters, special vacation tours, points of interest, mini-tour routes,
        registered historic places, ghost towns and mines, museums and historic
        centers, parks, forests, monuments, recreation areas, wilderness areas,
        nature trails, wildlife refuges, hunting and fishing information, public
        boating access sites, fish hatcheries, public swimming pools, hot
        springs, power boating waters, campgrounds, Indian reservations, air-
        ports, golf courses, ski trails, snowmobile trails, chambers of com-
        merce, travel agents, travel information agencies, broadcasting stations,
        newspapers, colleges and universities, horse hotels, and livestock
        markets.

MT-2   Konizeski, Dick. THE MONTANANS' FISHING GUIDE. 2 vols.
        Missoula, MT: Mountain Press Publishing Co. (279 West Front Street/
        59801), 1970-75. Photos., maps.

        Volume 1 (3rd ed., 1975, 0-87842-053-5, 75-13141) describes Montana
        waters west of the Continental Divide. Volume 2 (1970, 0-87842-
        016-9, 75-122314) describes Montana waters east of the Continental
        Divide. Many are readily accessible by auto, but most are in primi-
        tive regions inaccessible except by boat or trail. Arranged by large
        river systems or geographic areas (including the national parks), the
        compiler describes the type of fish that can be caught in each of a
        great many creeks, lakes, and ponds that make up the drainage area(s)
        of each river system. A name index would have been helpful.

MT-3   MONTANA: A STATE GUIDE BOOK. American Guide Series. New

York: Viking Press, 1939. 442 p. Photos., maps. Bibliography. Index.

This original WPA guide begins with a general background of Montana, describes 5 cities, 18 highway tours, and 4 park and 10 trail tours in Glacier National Park. There is a Montana western jargon glossary and a chronology of Montana history.

MT-4   MONTANA FARM & RANCH VACATION GUIDE. 4th ed. Bozeman: Montana State University, Cooperative Extension Service, 1976. 12 p. Map.

This guide describes over 50 ranches and/or farms available for a rural life vacation experience.

MAPS

The OFFICIAL HIGHWAY MAP is available from the Travel Promotion Unit (MT-5). The 1978 edition shows locations of points of interest, campsites, winter sports areas, and state parks, monuments, and recreation areas. It contains a list of AM/FM broadcasting stations. Both AAA (US-259) and Rand McNally (US-215) offer a combined Idaho/Montana map. Exxon (US-261) issues a combined Idaho/Montana/Wyoming map. Goushā (US-206) issues a separate Montana map.

MAJOR TOURIST ORGANIZATION

MT-5   MONTANA DEPT. OF HIGHWAYS, TRAVEL PROMOTION UNIT, Helena, MT 59601.

They issue a very comprehensive guide to the state called MONTANA: LAST OF THE BIG TIME SPLENDORS. It contains general information on the state; lists of museums, historic homes, and churches; describes 13 mini-tours; fishing areas; state parks, monuments and recreation areas; historic sites; winter activities; national forests; float trips; Indian reservations; dude ranch vacations; rock hunting; and the state's 2 national parks. It also contains maps and lists of campgrounds, fishing access areas, museums, and points of interest for each of the state's 5 tour regions. In cooperation with Montana Travel Hosts (MT-7) they issue a series of 6 mini-tour brochures and A VISITOR'S ACCOMMODATIONS GUIDE TO MONTANA.

REGIONAL TOURISM ASSOCIATIONS

The state's 5 tour regions are completely described in MONTANA: LAST OF THE BIG TIME SPLENDORS available from either the Travel Promotion Unit (MT-5) or Montana Travel Hosts (MT-7).

OTHER ORGANIZATIONS

MT-6   MONTANA INNKEEPERS ASSOCIATION, 9 Edwards Street, Box 851, Helena, MT 59601 (406/442-5040).

MT-7   MONTANA TRAVEL HOSTS, 110 Neill Avenue, Box 1730, Helena, MT 59601 (406/442-2405).

This is the Tourism Division of the Montana Chamber of Commerce. All of the publications of the Travel Promotion Unit (MT-5) are also available from this group. In addition, they issue a semi-annual calendar of events.

INFORMATION CENTERS/INFORMATION PHONES

Information about the state's 6 Visitor Information Centers and "Port of Entry Cars" is available from Montana Travel Hosts (MT-7). These are also located on the OFFICIAL HIGHWAY MAP. Seven cities (Anaconda, Billings, Butte, Glasgow, Great Falls, Helena, and Kalispell) offer tourist information over CB radio. Break on channel 5 and ask for Montana Travel Hosts.

OUTDOOR RECREATION ACTIVITIES

CANOEING AND BOATING. The Montana Fish and Game Dept., Helena, MT 59601 provides information and brochures on float streams. The May/June 1977 issue of MONTANA OUTDOORS, published by the Fish and Game Dept., 1420 East Sixth Street, Helena, MT 59601, contains a 24-page guide to 27 individual float rivers. Offprints of the article are available from the publisher.

FISHING AND HUNTING. The Montana Fish and Game Dept., 1420 East Sixth Street, Helena, MT 59601 provides much excellent information and detailed maps of where to fish and hunt. They also issue a list of MONTANA LICENSED OUTFITTERS who provide pack animals, guide services, and related services for hunters and fishermen. See also MT-2.

WINTER ACTIVITIES. MONTANA: LAST OF THE BIG TIME SPLENDORS (MT-5) has a brief section that describes winter recreation areas. For snowmobile information, contact the Montana Snowmobile Association, 1843 Dry Gulch Drive, Helena, MT 59601.

NATIONAL/STATE PARKS/FORESTS, ETC.

Glacier National Park

MT-8   Nelson, Dick, and Nelson, Sharon. HIKER'S GUIDE TO GLACIER

NATIONAL PARK. Glenwood, NM: Tecolote Press (Box 217/88039), 1978. 111 p. Maps, photos. 0-915030-24-1.

The authors describe 25 all-day hikes giving the following information for each: length, season to hike, whether or not a vehicle shuttle is necessary, elevation extremes, the names of the topographic quadrangles to use, plus a reproduction of the appropriate topographic map on which the trail has been marked.

MT-9 _____. SHORT HIKES AND STROLLS IN GLACIER NATIONAL PARK. Glenwood, NM: Tecolote Press (Box 217/88039), 1978. 47 p. Maps, photos. 0-915030-23-2.

The authors describe 15 (almost all) of the short trails in the park-- the longest one is 3.8 miles. A complete description, sketch map, and statement of elevation gain is provided for each.

MT-10 1978 WATERTON-GLACIER MOTORIST & HIKER HANDBOOK. Whitefish, MT: Carter Publishing Co. (Box 291/59937), 1978. Issued annually. 54 p. Photos., maps.

This free, somewhat superficial guide contains many advertisements. However, it does describe 7 major road tours, the numerous trails, and has a short section on rafting in the parks. For many visitors this guide may be sufficient.

MT-11 A PHOTOGRAPHIC AND COMPREHENSIVE GUIDE TO GLACIER AND WATERTON LAKES NATIONAL PARKS. Casper, WY: World-Wide Research and Publishing Co., National Parks Division, 1974. 74 p. Photos., maps. 74-176168.

While most of this book is stunning photographs, there are chapters on the human and natural history of the parks and a road guide to the main points of interest. There is also a brief list of recreation and other facilities, including locations of visitor or information centers, within the parks.

MT-12 Ruhle, George C. ROADS AND TRAILS OF WATERTON-GLACIER NATIONAL PARKS. Minneapolis: John W. Forney, 1976. 164 p. Maps, photos. Bibliography. Index. 76-382327.

The first 64 pages are road guides (with odometer readings for points of interest along the way) to 10 major roads in the parks. The next 80 pages describe more than 1,000 miles of trails. There are brief sections on geology, ecology, and camping.

MT-13 Scharff, Robert, ed. GLACIER NATIONAL PARK AND WATERTON LAKES NATIONAL PARK. New York: David McKay Co., 1967. 184 p. Photos., maps. Bibliography. Index. 67-10608.

This guide to seeing Glacier and Waterton Lakes National Parks from both the highway and into the wildernesses on foot and on horse was produced in cooperation with the National Park Service. There are also descriptions of the flora and fauna, of the fishing and boating facilities, and of accommodations and services. Although this book is old, the sections on natural features and roads and trails have not changed that much, and for these, this is still the most thorough guide.

MT-14   GLACIER NATIONAL PARK, West Glacier, MT 59936 (406/888-5441).

The park headquarters is open year-round from 8A.M.-4:30P.M. weekdays. They issue a large map/brochures of the park; DAY HIKES, GLACIER NATIONAL PARK and BACKCOUNTRY, GLACIER NATIONAL PARK, both good map/brochures; plus other information on camping, other accommodations, food service, boat rentals, stores, tours, etc. both within and outside the park; and a fishing map/brochure. There are 3 visitor centers along the "Going-to-the-Sun Road," the main road traversing the park, but none are open year-round. The St. Mary Visitor Center is at the eastern boundary of the park; its phone number is 406/732-5221. The Apgar Information Center is at the western boundary of the park; its phone number is 406/888-5512. The Logan Pass visitor Center is located midway along the road; it does not have a phone number. For a recorded message on current road and trail conditions, campground openings, and visitor services call 406/888-5551. The Glacier Natural History Association, also at the above address, issues several park and trail guides including a MOTORIST'S GUIDE TO GLACIER NATIONAL PARK by Seibel. It was published in 1972 and is now out of print. They also publish THE GLACIER TIMES, a newspapers issued several times a year, that describes visitor services and activities. There are 7 lodges within the park and these are maintained by Glacier Park, Inc. Between May 15 and September 15 contact them at East Glacier, MT 59434 (406/226-9311) for information. For reservations, call 406/226-4841. For information and reservations between September 15 and May 15 contact them at 1735 East Ft. Lowell Road, Suite 7, Tucson, AZ 85719 (602/795-0377). In Montana you can call 800/332-4114 toll-free. A rental auto tape tour (CA-80) of the "Going-to-the-Sun Road" is available at either St. Mary Lodge at the eastern border or West Glacier Cafe at the western border.

There are 10 national forests in Montana and the addresses and phone numbers of each may be obtained from the U.S. Forest Service, Northern Region, Federal Bldg., Missoula, MT 59801. There are 3 National Forest Visitor Centers in the state: Hungry Horse Dam Visitor Center in Flathead National Forest, Madison River Canyon Earthquake Area Visitor Center in Gallatin National Forest, and Aerial Fire Depot Visitor Center, 7 miles west of Missoula, adjacent to the airport.

The Bureau of Land Management, 222 North 32d Street, Box 30157, Billings, MT 59107 issues a BLM RECREATION GUIDE MONTANA which is a map

(1 in. represents about 15 miles) showing all publicly owned lands, state parks, fishing and boating access sites, recreation and camp sites, highway rest areas, and ski areas. They also issue a series, "Public Lands in Montana," of 42 BLM quadrangles (1 in. represents 2.5 miles) covering the entire state which show public land ownership, roads, trails, recreation sites, and other land features. They also supply information on campgrounds located on their land.

The Montana Recreation and Parks Division is part of the Dept. of Fish and Game. The address is 1420 East Sixth Avenue, Helena, MT 59601. An impressive, large fold-out map/brochure (1 in. represents about 17 miles), MONTANA RECREATION GUIDE, showing locations of and giving facilities at state parks, monuments, recreation areas, fishing access areas, wildlife management areas, and fish hatcheries; plus the addresses and phone numbers of the 8 Dept. Regional Offices is available from them. They also issue a brochure on the national and state forests, wilderness and primitive areas, and national parks; plus separate brochures for the individual state parks.

INDIVIDUAL CITIES OR AREAS

Helena—Printed Materials

A map of Helena is available from the Helena Abstract & Title Co., 1 North Last Chance Gulch, Helena, MT 59601.

Helena—Organizations

MT-15   HELENA AREA CHAMBER OF COMMERCE, 201 East Lyndale Avenue, Helena, MT 59601 (406/442-4121).

Their major piece of literature is YOUR PERSONAL GUIDE TO HELENA, MONTANA AND SURROUNDING AREAS INCLUDING MAP AND PERTINENT TIDBITS which includes accommodations; dining guide; shopping centers; sports areas; fishing, hunting, golfing, and skiing; theaters; art galleries; historic areas; points of interest; and a street index.

NEBRASKA

BOOKS, ATLASES, MAGAZINES

NE-1 BREVET'S NEBRASKA HISTORICAL MARKERS & SITES. Sioux Falls,
SD: Brevet Press, 1974. 220 p. Photos., sketches, maps. Indexes.
0-88498-020-0. 74-79979.

The text of each marker is accompanied by a map showing its location
and a sketch or photograph illustrating the event described by the
marker. It is regionally arranged with county, illustration, and general indexes.

NE-2 NEBRASKA: A GUIDE TO THE CORNHUSKER STATE. American
Guide Series. New York: Viking Press, 1939. 424 p. Photos.,
maps. Bibliography. Index.

This original WPA guide begins with a general state review on subjects
from geology to the press, describes tours in 8 cities and towns, and
13 highway tours. There is a chronology of Nebraska history.

MAPS

The HIGHWAY MAP & TRAVEL GUIDE, prepared by the Nebraska Dept. of
Roads, is available from the Division of Travel and Tourism (NE-3). The 1978
edition contains much information on points of interest and lists AM/FM radio
stations. Both AAA (US-259) and Rand McNally (US-215) issue a combined
Kansas/Nebraska map. Exxon (US-261) issues a combined North Dakota/South
Dakota/Nebraska map. Goushā (US-206) issues a separate Nebraska map.

MAJOR TOURIST ORGANIZATION

NE-3 NEBRASKA DEPT. OF ECONOMIC DEVELOPMENT, DIVISION OF
TRAVEL AND TOURISM, Box 94666, 301 Centennial Mall South,
Lincoln, NE 68509 (402/471-3111).

They issue a general brochure, VACATION NEBRASKA, in cooperation with the state Dept. of Roads, the Game and Parks Commission, and the State Historical Society. It is an extensive guide to the recreation, historic, and camping areas of the state plus its parks, lakes, etc. In addition, an annual EVENTS TABLE and a guide to the Oregon Trail are available from them.

OTHER ORGANIZATIONS

NE-4   NEBRASKA LODGING ASSOCIATION, 725 Stuart Bldg., Lincoln, NE 68508 (402/432-8877).

INFORMATION CENTERS/INFORMATION PHONES

There are approximately 20 tourist information/rest areas along Interstate 80 as it passes through Nebraska. During the summer months they are staffed by "Nebraska Vacation Guides" and are open daily from 8A.M.-5P.M. The locations of these may be found on the HIGHWAY MAP & TRAVEL GUIDE.

OUTDOOR RECREATION ACTIVITIES

CANOEING AND BOATING. CANOEING NEBRASKA WATERS, a guide to 9 rivers; and single maps of 22 individual lakes, ponds, and reservoirs showing boat ramps, parking areas, fishing access sites, day use areas, etc. are available from the Nebraska Game and Parks Commission, Box 30370, Lincoln, NE 68503.

FISHING AND HUNTING. Good information on where to both hunt and fish is available from the Nebraska Game and Parks Commission, Box 30370, Lincoln, NE 68503. Also available from them is a monthly magazine NEBRASKA-LAND with articles on state parks, fishing, hunting, wildlife, etc. It is one of the better of the many similiar magazines put out by comparable agencies in many other states. NEBRASKA AFIELD & AFLOAT is a monthly newspaper available from the commission, and it, too, contains much useful information for the user of Nebraska's outdoor areas.

WINTER ACTIVITIES. The Nebraska Game and Parks Commission, Box 30370, Lincoln, NE 68503 issues several guides to cross-country ski trails.

NATIONAL/STATE PARKS/FORESTS, ETC.

Information and maps on Nebraska's only national forest, Nebraska National Forest, may be obtained from the U.S. Forest Service, Rocky Mountain Region, 11177 West 8th Avenue, Box 25127, Lakewood, CO 80225 (303/234-4185).

The Nebraska Game and Parks Commission, Box 30370, Lincoln, NE 68503 may be contacted for information about facilities and use of state parks, recreation areas, wayside areas, and historical parks.

INDIVIDUAL CITIES OR AREAS

Lincoln—Printed Materials

NE-5   A GUIDE BOOK TO LINCOLN FOR THE HANDICAPPED. Lincoln: Mayor's Committee for Employment of the Physically Handicapped, 1967. 28 p.

A new edition planned for June 1978 will be available from the League of Human Dignity, 1118 Sharp Bldg., Lincoln, NE 63508.

Maps of Lincoln are available from the Ashburn Map Co., 4113 Old Denton Road, Fort Worth, TX 76117; Champion Map Corp. (US-202); and Goushā (US-206).

Lincoln—Organizations

NE-6   LINCOLN CHAMBER OF COMMERCE, 1221 N Street, Room 606, Lincoln, NE 68508 (402/432-7511).

They issue a points of interest brochure and map, and a list of hotels and motels in Lincoln. There is a tourist information center at 1435 O Street in downtown Lincoln. For lodging information and reservations call 402/464-2192.

Omaha—Printed Materials

NE-7   AROUND TOWN. Lincoln: Rich Bailey (2000 P Street/68503).

This biweekly entertainment guide to dining, theater, special events, and TV listings in the greater Omaha/Lincoln area contains many advertisements.

NE-8   A GUIDE TO OMAHA FOR THE HANDICAPPED. Omaha: Easter Seal Society for Crippled Children & Adults (Box 14204/68114), 1967.

A new edition was planned for the fall of 1978.

Rand McNally (US-215) puts out a joint Omaha/Council Bluffs map. Other Omaha maps are available from AAA (US-259); Ashburn Map Co., 4113 Old Denton Road, Fort Worth, TX 76117; Champion Map Corp. (US-202); and Metro Graphic Arts, 900 40th SE, Grand Rapids, MI 49508.

Omaha—Organizations

NE-9   GREATER OMAHA CHAMBER OF COMMERCE, 1620 Dodge Street, Suite 2100, Omaha, NE 68102 (402/341-1234).

They issue a city map and listings of points of interest and places with educational tours.

NEVADA

BOOKS, ATLASES, MAGAZINES

NV-1   Dutton, Davis, and Pilgre[e]n, Tedi. WHERE TO TAKE YOUR CHIL-
        DREN IN NEVADA. Los Angles: Ward Ritchie Press, 1973. 88 p.
        Photos., maps. 0-378-03242-9. 73-75099.

        Geographically arranged descriptions of many points of interest to
        children give specific information including hours and costs. There is
        no name index.

NV-2   NEVADA. By the editors of Sunset Books and Sunset Magazine.
        Menlo Park, CA: Lane Books, 1971. 80 p. Photos., maps. Index.
        0-376-06541-9. 70-157176.

        This guide to the major points of interest in Nevada is regionally
        arranged and has a name index. It also has many photographs.

NV-3   NEVADA. Carson City: Nevada Dept. of Economic Development.

        This quarterly magazine, published since 1936, was formerly called
        NEVADA HIGHWAYS AND PARKS. Each issue contains substantial
        information on points of interest; a guide to the state's hotels and
        resorts; and has regular columns listing stars and shows, events, and
        books about the state. There is no index to the magazine.

NV-4   NEVADA: A GUIDE TO THE SILVER STATE. American Guide Series.
        Portland, OR: Binfords & Mort, 1940. 315 p. Photos., maps.
        Bibliography. Index.

        This original WPA guide discusses Nevada's background from natural
        history to sport and recreation, and describes 8 highway tours. There
        is a chronology of Nevada history.

NV-5   Toll, David W. THE COMPLEAT NEVADA TRAVELER: A GUIDE TO
        THE STATE. Reno: University of Nevada Press, 1976. 278 p.

Photos., maps. 0-87417-045-1. 76-22647.

Cities and towns, ghost towns, recreation areas, and developed campgrounds are described concentrating on historic background. Accommodations, restaurants, and other practical information is excluded.

MAPS

The official HIGHWAYS MAP is available from the Dept. of Economic Development (NV-6). The 1978-79 edition includes points of interest, broadcasting
stations, museums, a table of facilities at campgrounds and recreational areas,
and a second map showing early historical trails and ghost towns and mining
camps. Both AAA (US-259) and Rand McNally (US-215) issue a combined
Nevada/Utah map. Exxon (US-261) issues a combined California/Nevada
map. Goushā (US-206) issues a separate Nevada map.

MAJOR TOURIST ORGANIZATION

NV-6   NEVADA DEPT. OF ECONOMIC DEVELOPMENT, Heroes Memorial
        Annex, Carson City, NV 89710 (702/885-4322).

        They issue an informative, general brochure; a monthly list of events;
        a list of local chambers of commerce; a brief rockhound guide/map;
        a brochure on the INDIAN PEOPLE IN NEVADA; and a 48-page
        NEVADA TRAVEL AND CONVENTION GUIDE that describes tour
        packages, attractions, accommodations, and dining in Reno, Lake
        Tahoe, and Las Vegas. They also have an office in Las Vegas at
        2501 East Sahara, Las Vegas, NV 89104 (702/386-5283).

OTHER ORGANIZATIONS

NV-7   UTAH-NEVADA HOTEL & MOTEL ASSOCIATION, 1860 Laurelhurst
        Drive, Salt Lake City, UT 84108 (801/466-6033).

INFORMATION CENTERS/INFORMATION PHONES

There is 1 highway information center in the state, at Jean, NV in the southern tip on Interstate 15 near Las Vegas. It is open year-round and makes
show and room reservations. The phone number is 702/385-2271. There is a
toll-free number, 800/992-0900, ext. 4322, but it is only available within the
state. General information is provided, but no reservations are taken.

OUTDOOR RECREATION ACTIVITIES

CANOEING AND BOATING. See NV-9.

FISHING AND HUNTING. Contact the Nevada Dept. of Fish and Game, Box 10678, Reno, NV 89510. Their AN ANGLER'S MAP OF THE FISHING WATERS OF NEVADA is not as promising as the name implies. It is simply a list of major fishing waters keyed to a grid only; none of them are located or drawn in on the base map prepared by the state Dept. of Highways. However, the 4 area Anglers Guides to (1) northeast Nevada, (2) eastern Nevada, (3) Lake Tahoe, and (4) Lakes Mead and Mohave and the Colorado River, also available from the Dept., provide more detailed maps and information.

WINTER ACTIVITIES. A brief NEVADA SKI DIRECTORY is available from the Dept. of Economic Development (NV-6).

NATIONAL/STATE PARKS/FORESTS, ETC.

Lake Mead National Recreation Area

NV-8   Evans, Douglas B. AUTO TOURGUIDE TO THE LAKE MEAD NA-
        TIONAL RECREATION AREA. Globe, AZ: Southwest Parks &
        Monuments Association, 1971. 39 p. Photos., maps. Bibliography.
        0-911408-22-3. 76-160215.

        This a brief roadguide to 4 tours that can be covered with ease in a
        standard car: Nevada-Lake Mead, Nevada-Lake Mohave, Arizona-
        Lake Mead, and Arizona-Lake Mohave.

NV-9   LAKE MEAD NATIONAL RECREATION AREA, 601 Nevada Highway,
        Boulder City, NV 89005.

        They provide a map/brochure and much literature on the commercial
        marinas and other concessions in the area. A visitor center near
        the west end of Lake Mead is open daily.

There is a KYM'S GUIDE for Lake Mead. It is a detailed map/chart showing locations for fishing, boating, hunting, hiking, and camping. It is available from Triumph Press, Box 75445, Sanford Station, Los Angeles, CA 90075.

Information on the 2 national forests in Nevada, Humboldt and Toiyabe, is available from the U.S. Forest Service, Intermountain Region, Federal Bldg., 324 25th Street, Ogden, UT 84401. The Wheeler Peak Scenic Area is a part of Humboldt National Forest, and Lehman Caves National Monument is located within the Scenic Area. The National Park Service and the Forest Service jointly operate a visitor center at Lehman Caves National Monument.

The Bureau of Land Management, Nevada State Office, Room 3008, Federal Bldg., 300 Booth Street, Reno, NV 89509 issues a GUIDE TO NEVADA CAMPGROUNDS on Bureau of Land Management lands, a statewide map showing publicly owned lands and recreation sites, and hiking brochures to some of their lands. A visitor center for the Red Rock Canyon Recreation Lands near Las Vegas is scheduled to open in 1980. Addresses and phone numbers for their 6 district offices are available from the Reno address.

Information on Nevada's state parks and on campgrounds located on public lands is available from the Nevada State Park System, 201 South Fall Street, Carson City, NV 89701.

INDIVIDUAL CITIES OR AREAS

Carson City—Printed Materials

AAA (US-259) and Arrow Publishing Co. (US-199) each issue a map of Carson City.

Carson City—Organizations

NV-10 CARSON CITY CHAMBER OF COMMERCE, 1191 South Carson Street, Carson City, NV 89701. (702/882-1565).

They issue a street map and a historic tour guide.

Las Vegas—Printed Materials

NV-11 ACCESS LAS VEGAS: A GUIDEBOOK OF LAS VEGAS AND SUR-ROUNDING AREA FOR THE PHYSICALLY HANDICAPPED. Las Vegas: DonRey Media, 1977. 63 p.

NV-12 Anderson, Eddie, et al. LAS VEGAS 1978: AN INSIDER'S GUIDE. Las Vegas: Oracle Publishers, 1977. 144 p. Map. 77-371114.

This is a guide for those who go to Las Vegas for the action. It gives precise information on getting around, accommodations, dress, dining, shows, gambling, sightseeing, kids, weather, sex, divorce, wedding chapels, and churches.

NV-13 Christopher, Gene. ARTHUR FROMMER'S GUIDE TO LAS VEGAS. New York: Frommer/Pasmantier Publishing Co. (distributed by Simon & Schuster), 1977. 200 p. Maps. 0-671-22731-9.

This concise guide for the first-time visitor has chapters on accommodations, dining, gambling, the "strip" and "glitter gulch" areas, other evening activities, sports, and nearby sightseeing attractions. There is no index.

NV-14 Crampton, Charles Gregory. THE COMPLETE LAS VEGAS: INCLUD-

ING HOOVER DAM AND THE DESERT WATER WORLD OF LAKE MEAD AND LAKE MOHAVE TOGETHER WITH A PEEP AT DEATH VALLEY AND A VISIT TO ZION NATIONAL PARK. Salt Lake City: Peregrine Smith, 1976. 151 p. Photos., maps. Bibliography. 0-87905-043-8. 76-45570.

The subtitle tells it all. It is written in a "folksy" style with specific information about addresses, phone numbers, hours, price, etc. Almost half of the book discusses the present-day setting and history of Las Vegas, and a short section tells how to "do the town."

NV-15 Firestone, Eve. UNDERGROUND VEGAS. Las Vegas: GBC Press (Box 4115/89106), 1977. 64 p. Drawings, map. 0-911996-76-1.

Primarily a "survival guide" to Las Vegas with tips on shelter, food, shopping, entertainment, etc., this book, though designed for the resident, can be very useful to the transient tourist as well. Stranded and destitute gamblers will find it quite useful.

NV-16 Sonnett, Robert. GUIDEBOOK TO LAS VEGAS: WHERE TO GO, WHERE TO STAY, WHERE TO EAT, WHERE TO HAVE FUN AND WHAT TO DO IN LAS VEGAS. Los Angeles: Ward Ritchie Press, 1972. 128 p. Photos. 0-378-03642-4. 72-86494.

This book covers a history of Las Vegas, what to wear, transportation, gambling, the big strip hotels, casino center, dining, showrooms, dancing, and tipping.

Maps of Las Vegas are available from AAA (US-259), Arrow Publishing Co. (US-199), Gousha (US-206), Rand McNally (US-215), and the Greater Las Vegas Chamber of Commerce, 2301 East Sahara Avenue, Las Vegas, NV 89105.

Las Vegas—Organizations

NV-17 LAS VEGAS CONVENTION/VISITORS AUTHORITY, Convention Center, Box 14006, Las Vegas, NV 89114 (702/733-2323).

Most of the literature from them has little real information value. It consists largely of their own brochures that are nothing more than pretty pictures (and rather suggestive ones at that) and brochures advertising the individual hotels and casinos. Their more substantial pieces are a general golf and tennis brochure with directory inserts listing specific clubs and courses, a quarterly LAS VEGAS ENTERTAINMENT GUIDE that lists who is appearing at each hotel, and a small map showing locations of hotels and casinos, points of interest, golf courses, and tennis courts. Their walk-in address is 3150 Paradise Road. They have offices in Chicago at One East Wacker Drive, Chicago, IL 60601 (312/329-0310) and in Washington, DC at 1150 Connecticut Avenue NW, Room 201, Washington DC 20036 (202/296-5300).

Reno—Printed Materials

NV-18 Pahner, Stanley W. PONDEROSA COUNTRY: A SCENIC AND HISTORIC GUIDE TO RENO AND VICINITY. Las Vegas: Nevada Publications (Box 15444/89114), 1972. 48 p. Photos., map. 72-87135.

This is a general road guide to 4 tours featuring historical points of interest in 4 directions from Reno plus Reno itself. Many old photographs enhance the historical appreciation.

Maps of Reno are available from Arrow Publishing Co. (US-199), Gousha (US-206), and Rand McNally (US-215).

Reno—Organizations

NV-19 GREATER RENO CHAMBER OF COMMERCE, 133 North Sierra Street, Reno, NV 89505 (702/786-3030).

They issue a general brochure and an annual hotel/motel guide.

NEW HAMPSHIRE

BOOKS, ATLASES, MAGAZINES

NH-1   NEW HAMPSHIRE: A GUIDE TO THE GRANITE STATE. American
Guide Series. Boston: Houghton Mifflin, 1938. 559 p. Photos.,
maps. 0-403-02179-0. 72-84490.

This original WPA guide containing mile-by-mile descriptions and
historical backgrounds of points of interest along the state's highways
is very complete but out of date.

NH-2   NEW HAMPSHIRE PROFILES. Concord, NH: Profiles Publishing Co.
(Two Steam Mill Court/03301).

This is a general magazine of interest to all New Hampshire residents
and friends. Articles range from the specific and informative to
lavish photographic spreads. Some regular sections are: coming events,
real estate directory, dining out listing, and classifieds. It is issued
11 times a year. Indexes are available from Mrs. Helen Ogden,
c/o Manchester City Library, 405 Pine Street, Manchester, NH 03104
and, for issues after 1976, from the Atlantic Indexing Co., Box 262,
Brookline, NH 03033. The publisher also issues a yearly New Hampshire Profiles Calendar, a yearly YANKEE TRAIL GUIDE (it contains
more accommodations listings than historic points of interest), and
other monographs pertaining to the state.

NH-3   NEW HAMPSHIRE RECREATION/VACATION GUIDE. Concord, NH:
Profiles Publishing Co. (Two Steam Mill Court/03301).

This guide to points of interest, with a calendar of events and many
local advertisements, is issued 10 times a year (monthly with combined issues for April/May and February/March). It is free and is
widely available throughout the state and at major out of state information centers in the New England region.

MAPS

The official highway map is available from the Office of Vacation Travel (NH-4). The 1978 edition lists public recreation areas in the state park system and in White Mountain National Forest; radio stations; arts centers and theaters; points of interest; ski areas; hunting, fishing, and boating information; and golf courses. AAA (US-259), Exxon (US-261), Gousha (US-206), and Rand McNally (US-215) each issue a combined Maine/New Hampshire/Vermont map.

PUBLISHERS

See NH-2.

MAJOR TOURIST ORGANIZATION

NH-4 NEW HAMPSHIRE OFFICE OF VACATION TRAVEL, Box 856, Concord, NH 03301 (603/271-2666).

> They issue a calendar of events, an autumn extra recreation calendar, an accommodations and dining directory, a camping guide, a guide to historical markers, an antique dealers directory, and a boys and girls camps directory.

REGIONAL TOURISM ASSOCIATIONS

DARTMOUTH-LAKE SUNAPEE REGION, Box 246, Lebanon, NH 03766 (603/448-3303).

> They issue a guide to events, attractions, and accommodations; a skiing guide; a guide to covered bridges; and a map/directory of the Lake Sunapee area.

LAKES REGION ASSOCIATION, Box 300, Wolfeboro, NH 03894 (603/569-1117).

> They issue an annual comprehensive guide of over 100 pages entitled WHERE TO. . .IN THE LAKES REGION OF NEW HAMPSHIRE: VACATION GUIDE.

MERRIMACK VALLEY REGION, Box 634, Manchester, NH 03105 (603/669-5269).

MONADNOCK REGION ASSOCIATION, Box 269, Peterborough, NH 03458 (603/924-3611).

> They issue MONADNOCK REGIONAIRE and FOUR SEASONS LIST-

ING (both of which list places and events of interest) plus brochures on fall foliage tours and maple sugaring houses.

SEACOAST REGION ASSOCIATION, 121 Water Street, Box 476, Exeter, NH 03833 (603/772-6818).

They issue an annual (1976-77 ed., 61 p.) SEACOST REGION GUIDE which contains local history descriptions of individual communities, plus advertisements of local business establishments.

OTHER ORGANIZATIONS

NH-5   NEW HAMPSHIRE COMMISSION ON THE ARTS, Phenix Hall, 40 North Main Street, Concord, NH 03301 (603/271-2789).

They issue a monthly statewide guide to arts events and A SUMMER-TIME GUIDE TO THE ARTS IN NEW HAMPSHIRE, a regional guide for visitors to theaters, art centers, festivals, and exhibitions.

NH-6   NEW HAMPSHIRE HOTEL & MOTEL ASSOCIATION, R.R. 1, 93 Wentworth Road, Portsmouth, NH 03801 (603/436-8230).

INFORMATION CENTERS/INFORMATION PHONES

The state's 14 highway information centers and rest areas are listed on the official highway map available from the Office of Vacation Travel (NH-4). The office also has a daily taped vacation report available at 603/271-2525 that features events in the summer season, fall foliage reports in autumn, and ski conditions in winter.

OUTDOOR RECREATION ACTIVITIES

BICYCLING.   For information on bike routes contact the Office of Vacation Travel (NH-4).

CANOEING AND BOATING.   SUMMER CANOEING & KAYAKING IN THE WHITE MOUNTAINS OF NEW HAMPSHIRE is available from the White Mountains Region Association (NH-15).   CANOEING ON THE CONNECTICUT RIVER is available from the Office of Vacation Travel (NH-4).   For inland motor boating laws and boat registration information contact the New Hampshire Dept. of Safety, Division of Safety Services, Concord, NH 03301.   For information about salt water boating facilities and regulations contact the New Hampshire State Port Authority, Box 506, 555 Market Street, Portsmouth, NH 03801.

FISHING AND HUNTING.   The New Hampshire Fish and Game Dept., 34

Bridge Street, Concord NH 03301 provides fresh water and saltwater fishing plus hunting information. The Office of Vacation Travel (NH-4) issues a fishing and hunting brochure, and the Seacoast Region Association, listed in the "Regional Tourism Associations" section of this chapter, offers saltwater fishing information.

WINTER ACTIVITIES. Information on ski packages and a lodging guide for the White Mountains may be obtained from: Ski the White Mountains, Box 176, North Woodstock, NH 03262. For reservations on the west side of the Mountains contact: White Mountains 93 Association (Ski 93), Box 517, Lincoln, NH 03251 (603/745-8101). They have a snow phone at 603/745-2409. For reservations on the east side of the Mountains contact the Mt. Washington Valley Chamber of Commerce (NH-12). Also contact the Sunapee Region Ski Area Association, Box 377, Sunapee, NH 03782 (603/763-2301). A snowmobilers guide, available either from the New Hampshire Bureau of Off-Highway Vehicles, State House Annex, Concord, NH 03301 (603/271-2659) or the Office of Vacation Travel (NH-4), describes, with maps, numerous trails throughout the state. The Office of Vacation Travel also issues separate brochures on skiing, ski touring, and winter lodging, and provides information on ski conditions at 603/271-2525.

NATIONAL/STATE PARKS/FORESTS, ETC.

See NH-14.

The Office of Vacation Travel (NH-4) issues a comprehensive guide to state parks. Some state parks have trail guides which may be obtained directly from them; they are not available by mail.

INDIVIDUAL CITIES OR AREAS

Concord—Printed Materials

A map of Concord is available from the New England Map Co., Somerville, MA 02143.

Concord—Organizations

NH-7   GREATER CONCORD CHAMBER OF COMMERCE, 116 North Main Street, Concord, NH 03301 (603/224-2508).

White Mountains—Printed Materials

NH-8   THE AMC WHITE MOUNTAIN GUIDE: A GUIDE TO TRAILS IN

THE MOUNTAINS OF NEW HAMPSHIRE. 21st ed. Boston: Appalachian Mountain Club, 1976. Revised frequently. 491 p. Maps. Index.

First published in 1907, and revised every 2 to 4 years, this guide describes trails and shelters and gives distances.

NH-9   Goff, Howard. AMC GUIDE TO MOUNT WASHINGTON AND THE PRESIDENTIAL RANGE. Boston: Appalachian Mountain Club, 1976. 116 p. Map. 77-353135.

This compact trail guide (excerpted from THE AMC WHITE MOUNTAIN GUIDE [NH-8]) contains much additional material on appreciating the area.

NH-10   Kostecke, Diane M. FRANCONIA NOTCH: AN IN-DEPTH GUIDE. Concord, NH: Society for the Protection of New Hampshire Forests (5 South State Street/03301), 1975. 114 p. Maps, photos.

This is the complete book on Franconia Notch, a model for other areas to emulate. It has natural and human history, descriptions of hikes, ski information, and special sections (rather brief) for the handicapped visitor and for touring with children.

NH-11   Randall, Peter. MOUNT WASHINGTON: A GUIDE AND SHORT HISTORY. Hanover, NH: University Press of New England, 1974. 170 p. Photos., maps. Bibliography. Index. 0-87451-088-0. 73-85237.

This is "a compendium of facts about Mount Washington," providing an overview of its roads, railway, and trails; hotels and buildings; summit; weather, geology, flora and fauna; and scenic areas.

White Mountains—Organizations

NH-12   MT. WASHINGTON VALLEY CHAMBER OF COMMERCE, North Conway, NH 03860 (603/356-3171).

They issue a general guide and a WINTER VACATION GUIDE. They have a toll-free number at 800/258-8980 and a reservations service at the office phone above.

NH-13   WHITE MOUNTAINS ATTRACTIONS ASSOCIATION, Box 176, North Woodstock, NH 03262.

They issue a vacation guide and sponsor a White Mountains Visitor Center in Lincoln, NH.

NH-14   WHITE MOUNTAINS NATIONAL FOREST, Box 638, Laconia, NH 03246.

They issue a map of the forest showing recreation sites, wilderness areas, ski touring trails, off-road vehicle trails, restricted use areas, winter recreation areas, and camping and hiking areas.

NH-15 WHITE MOUNTAINS REGION ASSOCIATION, Box 471, Lancaster, NH 03584 (603/788-2061).

They issue a White Mountains map and guide; SHUNPIKE FALL FOLIAGE TOURS; and information on cross-country ski touring centers, accommodations, canoeing and kayaking, attractions, camping, hiking, and hunting and fishing.

NEW JERSEY

BOOKS, ATLASES, MAGAZINES

NJ-1 Barrett, Pete, and Zicarelli, Mike, eds. THE COMPLETE GUIDE TO
FISHING IN NEW JERSEY. Union City, NJ: Books About New
Jersey (distributed by William H. Wise & Co., 336 Mountain Road/
07087), 1976. 364 p. Photos., drawings, tables, maps. Index.
0-8349-7531-9. 76-21185.

Information on how and where to fish in both fresh and salt water,
lists of charter boats, and a list of useful addresses comprise this
book.

NJ-2 Beil, Preston J., and Beil, Irene A. WHAT TO DO IN NEW JERSEY.
4th ed. What To Do County Publications. Chappaqua, NY: Halliday
Clark, 1976. 160 p. Photos., maps.

Arranged by over 140 categories of organizations, activities, and landmarks, from adult senior citizens to zoos, this listing contains many
names, accompanying addresses, and phone numbers, but there is only
minimal evaluative and descriptive information. The major value of
this title is as an initial finding aid.

NJ-3 Cawley, James, and Cawley, Margaret. EXPLORING THE LITTLE
RIVERS OF NEW JERSEY. 3d ed. New Brunswick, NJ: Rutgers
University Press, 1971. 252 p. Photos., maps. 0-8135-0684-0. 61-
10255.

There are 16 river (and 1 canal) trips described in detail, and 6
"small streams to explore by car" are listed. There is a canoe rental
directory. We think this book is quite good.

NJ-4 Esposito, Frank J. TRAVELLING NEW JERSEY. Union City, NJ:
Books About New Jersey (distributed by William H. Wise & Co., 336
Mountain Road/07087), 1978. 400 p. Photos. Index. 0-8349-
7538-6. 78-70027.

This is a family guide to "historic sites and natural wonders, shopping, and sports, theaters and concerts, restaurants, and hundreds of little-known places and pleasures." Chapters on casinos, boating, bicycling, canoeing, and seafood restaurants have been contributed by experts. The author was both a former travel agent and travel columnist for the NEW BRUNSWICK HOME NEWS.

NJ-5   Gooding, Cynthia. A PRINCETON GUIDE: WALKS, DRIVES & COMMENTARY. Somerset, NJ: The Middle Atlantic Press, 1971. 173 p. Photos., maps. Bibliography. Index. 70-141706.

The author describes 4 walks and 4 drives with commentary providing insights to the legends, anecdotes, architecture, and horticulture of this university community.

NJ-6   Mole, Michaela M., ed. AWAY WE GO! A GUIDEBOOK OF FAMILY TRIPS TO PLACES OF INTEREST IN NEW JERSEY, NEARBY PENNSYLVANIA AND NEW YORK. 4th ed. New Brunswick, NJ: Rutgers University Press, 1976. 237 p. Photos., maps. Index. 0-8135-0817-7. 75-25741.

"One day trips to more than 800 fascinating places in New Jersey. . ." are described in this family field trip guide that is regionally arranged with separate chapters for Philadelphia and New York City. Very thorough coverage with much background and practical information is provided for each place described. It includes where to go to participate in active sports and places to take youth tour groups.

NJ-7   Newberry, Lida, ed. NEW JERSEY: A GUIDE TO ITS PRESENT AND PAST. Rev. ed. American Guide Series. New York: Hastings House, 1977. 756 p. Photos., maps. Index. 0-8038-5048-4. 77-23134.

This is a revised edition of the original 1939 WPA guide. The state is first generally described from history to popular arts, then 27 cities and towns are described. In typical WPA guide format, descriptions for 28 state-wide highway tours follow.

NJ-8   Parnes, Robert. CANOEING THE JERSEY PINE BARRENS. Charlotte, NC: East Woods Press, 1978. 284 p. Maps, photos. Bibliography. 0-914788-03-5. 77-70413.

Sections on general background (historical and natural) of the Pine Barrens in New Jersey and on general canoeing advice precede the detailed descriptions of 13 specific river trips. Campgrounds, canoe rentals, and medical facilities are noted.

NJ-9   Pepper, Adeline. TOURS OF HISTORIC NEW JERSEY. New Brunswick, NJ: Rutgers University Press, 1973. 274 p. Photos. 0-8135-0779-0. 73-6889.

Tours are loosely arranged by region and/or historical motif, and brief information is given for many places off the expressways.

NJ-10   Poor, Harold L. BICYCLING IN NEW JERSEY: 30 TOURS. Short Hills, NJ: Ridley Enslow Publishers (60 Crescent Place, Box 301/ 07078), 1978. 128 p. Maps. 0-89490-013-7. 78-1996.

For each of the 30 trips, detailed directions are given (including a description of the terrain and a running commentary on the places of special interest along the route). The maps (1 for each trip) take a little getting used to.

MAPS

The official highway map and guide is available from the Office of Travel and Tourism (NJ-12). The 1977 edition included information on facilities in state forests, parks, recreation areas, and fish and wildlife management areas; ski areas; and commuter rail services. The office also issues a Newark International Airport Map/Guide. AAA (US-259) issues a joint New Jersey/Pennsylvania map. Goushā (US-206), Exxon (US-261), and Rand McNally (US-215) each issue a separate New Jersey map.

PUBLISHERS

NJ-11   RUTGERS UNIVERSITY PRESS, 30 College Avenue, New Brunswick, NJ 08903.

In addition to publishing several guidebooks to New Jersey, they publish many historical, technical, and general books about the state.

MAJOR TOURIST ORGANIZATION

NJ-12   NEW JERSEY OFFICE OF TRAVEL AND TOURISM. Box 400, Trenton, NJ 08625 (609/292-2470).

They issue a NEW JERSEY VACATION GUIDE (includes information on beach resorts; state forests, parks, and recreation areas; salt water fishing facilities; skiing; summer theatres; public transportation; and historic sites), A LISTING OF NEW JERSEY CAMPSITES (a 44-page booklet arranged by county with maps), SCENIC & HISTORIC TOURS OF NEW JERSEY, and an annual calendar of events.

OTHER ORGANIZATIONS

NJ-13   NEW JERSEY HOTEL-MOTEL ASSOCIATION, 826 West State Street, Trenton, NJ 08618 (609/599-9000).

They issue an annual NEW JERSEY TRAVEL GUIDE which is a regionally arranged listing of member hotels and motels.

INFORMATION CENTERS/INFORMATION PHONES

A map in the general VACATION GUIDE available from the Office of Travel
and Tourism (NJ-12) shows the locations of 4 highway tourist information
centers. The weather information number for northern New Jersey is 201/
936-1212. For southern New Jersey it is 609/936-1212.

OUTDOOR RECREATION ACTIVITIES

BICYCLING. The Greater Cape May Historical Society (NJ-19) issues a SELF-
CONDUCTED BICYCLE TOUR OF CAPE MAY brochure. See also NJ-10 and
PA-41.

CANOEING AND BOATING. Information on canoe trails is available from
the New Jersey Dept. of Environmental Protection, Division of Parks and
Forestry, Box 1420, Trenton, NJ 08625. CANOEING IN NEW JERSEY is
available from the New Jersey Dept. of Community Affairs, 363 West State
Street, Trenton, NJ 08625. BOAT BASINS IN NEW JERSEY, a 56-page listing of marinas, docks, etc., by county, is available from the Office of Travel
and Tourism (NJ-12). See also NJ-3 and NJ-8.

FISHING AND HUNTING. Contact the New Jersey Dept. of Environmental
Protection, Division of Fish, Game & Shellfisheries, Box 1809, Trenton, NJ
08625 for their GUIDE TO WILDLIFE MANAGEMENT AREAS (describes each
of 49 areas, including detailed maps showing best hunting and fishing locations,
roads, and parking areas), their annual DEER GUIDE (a map/brochure showing
hunting locations), NEW JERSEY OUTDOORS (a bimonthly magazine providing
year-round information on hunting, fishing, birdwatching, hiking, canoeing,
etc.), and information on fishing and hunting regulations. They seem to be
weak on fishing information. See also NJ-1.

NATIONAL/STATE PARKS/FORESTS, ETC.

There are no major national parks and no national forests in New Jersey.

The New Jersey Dept. of Environmental Protection, Bureau of Parks, Box
1420, Trenton, NJ 08625 issues a large, thorough, fold-out brochure, NEW
JERSEY INVITES YOU TO ENJOY ITS--STATE FORESTS, PARKS, NATURAL
AREAS, MARINAS, HISTORIC SITES, WILDLIFE MANAGEMENT AREAS, which
locates these on a map and uses several charts and tables to indicate facilities
and activities available at each. Reservations for state forests, parks, and
recreation area campsites are made through them. They provide individual maps

of some state parks and forests that show hiking and canoe trails and campsites. See also A LISTING OF NEW JERSEY CAMPSITES available from the Office of Travel and Tourism (NJ-12).

INDIVIDUAL CITIES OR AREAS

Atlantic City and "The Shore"—Printed Materials

NJ-14   Dunn, G.W. Chip, and Burt, Bernard I. OFFICIAL GUIDE: ATLANTIC CITY: THE OFFICIAL GUIDE OF THE GREATER ATLANTIC CITY CHAMBER OF COMMERCE AND THE CITY OF ATLANTIC CITY. Washington, DC: Acropolis Books, 1977. 84 p. Photos. 0-87491-211-3.

There isn't too much of value in this guide now (at most 20 pages, offering a calendar of events, visitors services telephone numbers, and lists of accommodations and restaurants), and it is largely fleshed-out with pages of old photographs and advertisements. It anticipates the future, however, with sections on a casino preview and gambling instructions, and future editions (if any) will presumably expand in coverage in direct proportion to Atlantic City's economy.

NJ-15   THE GUIDE POST: OCEAN COUNTY, NEW JERSEY VACATION AND BUSINESS DIRECTORY. Toms River, NJ: Dave Johnson (32 Hyers Street/08753), 1976. Issued annually. 80 p. Photos., maps. Indexes.

Ocean County includes all the channel island areas south of Pt. Pleasant to Beach Haven Inlet and includes Island Beach State Park. The GUIDE describes each community and gives information on events, boating, camping, fishing, golf, tennis, yacht clubs, swimming, etc. It has been published since 1945.

Maps of Atlantic City, Cape May County, Ocean County, and all other New Jersey counties are available from Alfred B. Patton, 4143 Swamp Road, Doylestown, PA 18901.

An ATLANTIC CITY LODGINGS GUIDE is available from the Office of Travel and Tourism (NJ-12).

Atlantic City and "The Shore"—Organizations

NJ-16   ATLANTIC CITY VISITOR'S BUREAU, Convention Hall, Atlantic City, NJ 08401 (609/348-7044).

They issue a general guide called ATLANTIC CITY & COUNTY ABC BOOK.

NJ-17   CHAMBER OF COMMERCE OF GREATER CAPE MAY, Box 109, Cape May, NJ 08204 (609/465-7181).

They issue an annual JERSEY CAPE VACATION GUIDE (a booklet of advertisers, mostly motels and campgrounds, in southern New Jersey coastal towns from Ocean County to Cape May), a similar annual guide for just Cape May that includes a calendar of events, and an official tour map which locates points of interest, historical sites, information centers, etc. They operate a year-round information center, open 9A.M.-5P.M., at Crest Haven Road & Garden State Parkway at Mile Post 11 in Cape May Court House, NJ 08210.

NJ-18 GREATER ATLANTIC CITY CHAMBER OF COMMERCE, 10 Central Pier, Atlantic City, NJ 08401 (609/345-2251).

They issue a map of Atlantic City; a hotel/motel/rooming house folder; a restaurant and dining guide; information on fishing and boating, golfing, trailer camps and campgrounds, and scenic and historic tours; and tourist guide maps.

NJ-19 GREATER CAPE MAY HISTORICAL SOCIETY, Box 495, Cape May, NJ 08204

They issue a HISTORIC SITES GUIDE and a SELF-CONDUCTED BICYCLE TOUR OF CAPE MAY brochure.

NJ-20 JERSEY CAPE VACATIONS, Box 365, Cape May Court House, NJ 08210.

They issue an official map of the Jersey Cape, a vacation kit, fishing and camping kits, and a guide book.

NJ-21 OCEAN CITY DEPT. OF PUBLIC RELATIONS, Box 174, Ocean City, NJ 08226.

They distribute a very thorough annual (1976 ed., 80 p.) OCEAN CITY VACATION GUIDE published by Bryan Publishing Co., Box 563, Ocean City, NJ 18226 under the auspices of the Ocean City Hotel, Motel and Restaurant Association. It includes information on accommodations (including guest houses and apartments), events, tide tables, etc. They operate an information center on the Somers Point-Ocean City Blvd. in cooperation with the Ocean City Chamber of Commerce.

Trenton—Printed Materials

A map of Trenton is available from Alfred B. Patton, 4143 Swamp Road, Doylestown, PA 18901.

Trenton—Organizations

NJ-22 MERCER COUNTY CULTURAL & HERITAGE DIVISION, Mercer County Administration Bldg., 640 South Broad Street, Box 8068, Trenton, NJ 08650 (609/939-6701).

Their main efforts go toward initiating, supporting, and maintaining historical and cultural groups. They do issue a map/brochure, HERITAGE TRAILS OF MERCER COUNTY, which describes 3 driving tours of historic sites in Mercer County, the county in which Trenton is located.

NEW MEXICO

BOOKS, ATLASES, MAGAZINES

NM-1   Bodine, John J. TAOS PUEBLO: A WALK THROUGH TIME: A
        VISITOR'S GUIDE TO THE PUEBLO, ITS PEOPLE, AND THEIR CUS-
        TOMS AND THEIR LONG HISTORY. Santa Fe: The Lightning Tree
        (Box 1837/87501), 1977. 48 p. Photos., map. 0-89016-038-4.
        77-73460.

        Part 1 is a walking tour of Taos Pueblo, and part 2 is a general dis-
        cussion of the Pueblo, its history, contemporary lifestyles, dress,
        economics, government, and religion (with a ceremonial calendar).

NM-2   Bryan, Howard. TOURS FOR ALL SEASONS: HOWARD BRYAN'S
        TRIBUNE TRIP OF THE WEEK. Albuquerque: Calvin Horn Publisher
        (Box 4204/87106), 1972. 112 p. Maps. 0-910750-23-8. 72-
        185393.

        This is supposed to be the best of the author's weekly "Let's Tour New
        Mexico" columns that he started doing for the ALBUQUERQUE TRI-
        BUNE in 1967. Forty-nine separate weekend tours are described.

NM-3   Miller, Joseph. NEW MEXICO: A GUIDE TO THE COLORFUL
        STATE. Rev. ed. American Guide Series. New York: Hastings
        House, 1962. 472 p. Photos., maps. Bibliography. Index.

        This revision of the original 1940 WPA guide begins with a general
        description of the state from geology to the arts, and describes 3
        major towns and 18 highway tours. There is a chronology of New
        Mexico history.

NM-4   NEW MEXICO MAGAZINE. Santa Fe: New Mexico Dept. of De-
        velopment.

        This monthly magazine has been published since 1923. It contains
        occasional travel articles, lavish photographic spreads, a restaurant
        article in every issue, and numerous articles about local personalities,

history, and heritage. The magazine also publishes an annual NEW MEXI-
CO CALENDAR, 101 TRIPS IN THE LAND OF ENCHANTMENT (NM-7),
and LISTEN TO THE WIND (a booklet on New Mexico ghost towns). In
addition, they offer their "Southwest Bookshop," a shop-by-mail book
service featuring items of interest to readers of the magazine.

NM-5 Stewart, Ronald L. MONUMENTS OF NEW MEXICO. Boulder, CO:
Pruett Publishing Co., 1974. 134 p. Photos., map. Bibliography.
0-87108-071-0. 73-93253.

Background reading (for better archaeological, historical, and geological appreciation) and a bibliography are provided for each of 10
national monuments, 1 national park, 9 state monuments, and 3 local
monuments.

NM-6 Ungnade, Herbert E. GUIDE TO THE NEW MEXICO MOUNTAINS.
2d ed. Albuquerque: University of New Mexico Press, 1972.
235 p. Maps, diagrams, photos. Bibliography. Indexes. 0-8263-
0241-6. 72-80752.

Ungnade "gives trail and road information into the best known mountain
ranges of New Mexico." It is full of suggestions of where to find
trails in each mountain range and often the information is specific:
e.g., "trail starts 3/4 mile below the picnic ground." The maps in
the book show just the approximate routes for all trails; the author
frequently urges the hiker to use the relevant USGS map, but he
doesn't provide any information about which specific topographic map
or maps to use. Separate chapters are devoted to auto and jeep
trails into the mountains, rock climbing, caves, river boating, and
winter mountaineering.

NM-7 Woods, Betty. 101 TRIPS IN THE LAND OF ENCHANTMENT:
WHERE TO GO, WHAT TO SEE, WHAT TO DO ON 1-DAY TRIPS
IN THE STATE OF NEW MEXICO. 4th ed. Edited by George
Fitzpatrick. A New Mexico Travelguide. Santa Fe: New Mexico
Magazine, 1973. 63 p. Photos., sketch maps, sketches. 74-190381.

The first edition, including 50 trips and published in 1950, was compiled from the "Trip of the Month" column in NEW MEXICO MAGA-
ZINE (NM-4). The individual trip descriptions, which provide mostly
historical and/or natural history information, very brief finding directions, and a map of minimal value, still read like trip columns, but
their number has grown to 101, and, as suggestions for outings, will
keep the user on the road for quite a long time.

MAPS

The official ROAD MAP OF NEW MEXICO is available from the Travel Division
(NM-8). The 1977-78 edition contains information on parks and monuments,

historic churches, Indian reservations, mountain peaks, museums, ski areas, hunting and fishing, AM/FM radio stations, and a small map showing historic trails. AAA (US-259), Exxon (US-261), and Rand McNally (US-215) each issue a combined Arizona/New Mexico map. Gousha (US-206) issues a separate New Mexico map.

PUBLISHERS

See NM-4.

MAJOR TOURIST ORGANIZATION

NM-8 NEW MEXICO TRAVEL DIVISION, Bataan Memorial Bldg., Santa Fe, NM 87503 (505/827-5571).

They issue a large general, photographic booklet; a smaller, but more informative, general guide covering parks and monuments, missions, camping, outdoor recreation activities, ghost towns, Indians, etc. called NEW MEXICO: LAND OF ENCHANTMENT; a very thorough, informative, semiannual calendar of events, ¿QUÉ PASA? which, in addition to the monthly listings of events, contains information on weather, the addresses and phone numbers of all local chambers of commerce, and lists of year-round things to do, including practical information on missions, fishing, Indians, forests, wildernesses, recreation areas, wildlife refuges, parks, camping, backpacking/hiking, bicycling, golf, horseback riding, off-road motoring, and river running; and individual brochures on Indians, ghost towns, guest ranches and resorts, and horseracing.

OTHER ORGANIZATIONS

NM-9 NEW MEXICO HOTEL & MOTEL ASSOCIATION, 2130 San Mateo Blvd., Suite C, Box 3847, Albuquerque, NM 87190.

INFORMATION CENTERS/INFORMATION PHONES

There are 4 permanent (and numerous others that are open in the summer only) Travel Information Centers operated by the Travel Division (NM-8). The Navajo Tribe operates the Navajo Tribal Information Center at Shiprock. Further information on all of these information centers may be obtained from the Travel Division. Their locations are indicated on the ROAD MAP OF NEW MEXICO. The state's toll-free travel information number, 800/545-9876, is available from all states except New Mexico.

OUTDOOR RECREATION ACTIVITIES

CANOEING AND BOATING. Information on canoeing the Rio Grande Wild River in the northcentral part of the state is available from the New Mexico State Office, Bureau of Land Management, Box 1449, Santa Fe, NM 87501 (505/988-6243).

FISHING AND HUNTING. The New Mexico Dept. of Game and Fish, State Capitol, Santa Fe, NM 87503 issues good information on where to hunt and fish, and their NEW MEXICO FISHING WATERS booklet that describes individual areas and locates each on one of six large maps is particularly useful. The July/August 1974 issue of NEW MEXICO WILDLIFE, published bimonthly by the Information and Education Division of the Dept. of Game and Fish, was a special issue devoted exclusively to a guide to the lands and waters administered by the Dept. It contains many maps of individual areas.

WINTER ACTIVITIES. A brochure, WINTER ENCHANTMENT: NEW MEXICO, describes, generally, all the downhill ski areas and other winter activities. It, plus a sheet giving practical information such as phone numbers, rates, elevation for downhill ski areas; and other sheets giving cross-country ski, snowshoe and snowmobile rentals, etc. information are available from the Travel Division (NM-8). Ski New Mexico, Route 4, Tano Point Lane, Santa Fe, NM 87501 arranges ski package trips.

NATIONAL/STATE PARKS/FORESTS, ETC.

Carlsbad Caverns National Park

NM-10 CARLSBAD CAVERNS NATIONAL PARK, 3225 National Parks Highway, Carlsbad, NM 88220 (505/785-2233).

They provide a map/brochure and information on the various cave trips and other activities for visitors. A general guide to the park, with numerous color photographs, CARLSBAD CAVERNS NATIONAL PARK, by John Barnett is published by the Carlsbad Caverns Natural History Association, also at the above address.

Information on the 5 national forests in New Mexico is available from the U.S. Forest Service, Southwestern Region, Federal Bldg., 517 Gold Avenue, SW, Albuquerque, NM 87102. There are 2 National Forest Visitors Centers in the state: Gila Cliff Dwelling Visitor Information Center, Wilderness Ranger District, Rt. 11, Box 100, Silver City, NM 88061 (505/534-9461) and Ghost Ranch Visitor Information Center, Abiquiu, NM 87510 (505/685-4312). Both are open year-round.

Information on 6 recreation sites in New Mexico developed by the Bureau of Land Management, and a large map/brochure, A GUIDE TO PUBLIC LANDS IN NEW MEXICO, is available from the New Mexico State Office, Bureau of Land Management, Box 1449, Santa Fe, NM 87501 (505/988-6243).

New Mexico

A large, informative map/brochure, NEW MEXICO OUTDOORS, containing tabular data on facilities at camping and recreation areas in the national forests in the state, state parks and monuments, national wildlife refuges, Bureau of Land Management areas, national monuments and parks, and tribal areas is available from the Travel Division (NM-8). They, in cooperation with the New Mexico State Park and Recreation Commission, 141 East De Vargas, Santa Fe, NM 87503, produce a more detailed guide to state parks and monuments with more descriptive information than that provided in the tables of the above publication.

INDIVIDUAL CITIES OR AREAS

Albuquerque—Printed Materials

NM-11 ALBUQUERQUE AND NEW MEXICO THIS MONTH. Albuquerque: Albuquerque and New Mexico This Month Magazine (135 Jackson NE/87108).

This monthly guide to dining and entertainment also has some other information on points of interest and events for the Albuquerque area. It has been published since 1963.

Maps of Albuquerque are available from Champion Map Corp. (US-202), Goushā (US-206), and the Albuquerque National Bank, 123 Central Avenue NW, Albuquerque, NM 87102. Rand McNally (US-215) issues a combined Albuquerque/Santa Fe map.

Albuquerque—Organizations

NM-12 GREATER ALBUQUERQUE CHAMBER OF COMMERCE, VISITORS BUREAU, 401 Second Street NW, Albuquerque, NM 87102 (505/842-0220).

They issue a general brochure, a dining guide, a driving guide to major points of interest, and 3 mini-adventure guides to: (1) the Santa Fe Trail, (2) historic churches, and (3) historic sites and the Los Alamos Scientific Laboratory.

Santa Fe—Printed Materials

NM-13 Dutton, Bertha P. LET'S EXPLORE INDIAN VILLAGES PAST AND PRESENT: TOUR GUIDE FOR SANTA FE AREA. Rev ed. Santa Fe: Museum of New Mexico Press, 1970. 65 p. Sketch maps. Bibliographies. 78-136785.

The author describes 4 explorations to all the Pueblos and other Indian-related sites in the greater Santa Fe area. The guide is complete with much historical and ethnic background, plus specific information and instructions for the traveler.

NM-14 Historic Santa Fe Foundation. OLD SANTA FE TODAY. 2d ed. Albuquerque: University of New Mexico Press, 1972. 79 p. Photos., maps. 0-8263-0251-3. 72-86822.

Although we are generally not including detailed historic building guides to specific areas, we've made an exception here. One obvious reason for doing so is that if you've gone to Santa Fe in the first place, you are probably interested in seeing its culturally significant buildings. Two maps in the book locate each structure and will allow you to plan your own walking tour. There is a glossary.

Maps of Santa Fe are available from Arrow Publishing Co. (US-199) and Kasum Communications (DMK City Map Service), 1524 Vista Avenue, Boise, ID 83705. Rand McNally (US-215) issues a combined Albuquerque/Santa Fe map.

Santa Fe—Organizations

NM-15 SANTA FE CHAMBER OF COMMERCE, Box 1928, Santa Fe, NM 87501 (505/983-7317).

They issue a POCKET GUIDE AND CITY STREET GUIDE that is mostly maps, a hotel/motel guide, a restaurant guide, a walking tour guide, a museum guide, and a camping and fishing guide to the area. Two other publications, not issued by them, are usually available from them: a monthly calendar of events and a guide to day trips you can take in the area.

NEW YORK

BOOKS, ATLASES, MAGAZINES

NY-1   FODOR'S NEW YORK 1979. New York: David McKay Co., 1979.
336 p. Index. 0-679-00411-4.

Useful facts are crammed into this rather good guide. General information on planning a trip, weather, general costs, etc., is followed by information on cities, areas, and attractions throughout the state. Over one half of the book is devoted to New York City.

NY-2   A GUIDE TO THE HISTORICAL MARKERS OF NEW YORK STATE.
Albany: University of the State of New York, State Education Dept., Office of State History, 1970. 129 p. Maps.

The title is misleading. This is a guide only to historical area markers which describe significant historical events or trends and not to the more numerous state historical markers which commemorate specific events or individuals. It reproduces the text of each marker and locates it on a regional map.

NY-3   Konski Engineers. Recreational Facilities Division. BICYCLE ROUTES OF CENTRAL NEW YORK. Syracuse, NY: Konski Engineers in cooperation with the Onondaga Cycling Club, 1975. 78 p. Scales vary. 77-355417.

This is a loose-leaf portfolio of 33 detailed bicycle route maps.

NY-4   NEW YORK: A GUIDE TO THE EMPIRE STATE. American Guide Series. New York: Oxford University Press, 1940. 782 p. Photos., maps. Index.

This original WPA guide is arranged in the usual format of the American Guide Series: general background on the state, detailed descriptions of major cities (18 in this New York guide), and mile-by-mile highway tours covering the state. It is comprehensive but out of date.

NY-5 New York-New Jersey Trail Conference & The American Geographical Society. NEW YORK WALK BOOK. 4th ed. American Geographical Society Outing Series. Garden City, NY: Doubleday/Natural History Press, 1971. 326 p. Drawings, maps. Index. 0-385-01724-3. 70-150876.

Over 100 selected hikes within 60 to 70 miles of New York City are described in detail.

NY-6 Rifkind, Carole, and Levine, Carol. MANSIONS, MILLS AND MAIN STREETS. New York: Schocken Books, 1975. 248 p. Photos., maps, drawings. Index. 0-8052-3584-1. 74-26915.

This listing of "buildings and places to explore within 50 miles of New York City" gives brief descriptions, hours, and fees. It has an "Architectural Field Guide and Illustrated Glossary."

NY-7 Sweet, Ellen B. THE 1776 GUIDE FOR NEW YORK. New York: Harper & Row, 1976. 248 p. Maps, photos. 0-06-090437-2. 75-34797.

Concentrating mainly, but not exclusively, on Revolutionary War history, this guide describes nineteen 1- or 2-day excursions from major New York state cities noting sights (with fees and hours) on each.

NY-8 Thurheimer, David C. LANDMARKS OF THE AMERICAN REVOLUTION IN NEW YORK STATE. 4th ed. Albany: New York State American Revolution Bicentennial Commission, 1976. 57 p. Photos., maps.

This is a guide to 40 historic sites related to events or individuals of significance in the Revolutionary War period. All sites are open to the public. Each description includes a map and hours open.

NY-9 YANKEE MAGAZINE'S GUIDE TO THE STATE OF NEW YORK. Dublin, NH: Yankee, 1978. Published annually. 144 p. Photos., map.

This is the first edition of what is expected to be an annual publication. For 10 geographical regions of New York state, plus New York City, this guide, in magazine format, tells what to see plus where to write for further information, has a selected list of lodging and dining places, and a calendar of events.

NY-10 Zook, Nicholas. HOUSES OF NEW YORK OPEN TO THE PUBLIC. Barre, MA: Barre Publishers, 1969. 143 p. Photos. Index. 0-8271-6902-7. 69-12346.

This is a regional guide, in 2 sections, to notable houses throughout New York state. The major section contains rambling discourses on some houses without providing any practical "how to see" information, and another section lists additional houses, giving the practical information but very little appreciative material. There is a name index, but one regional consolidation with equal treatment of all houses would have made this guide more useful.

MAPS

As of this writing, the state does not publish an official highway map. The Division of Tourism (NY-12) issues a tourism map which lists things to see and do, including a list of facilities at state parks and other sources of information for travelers. Points of interests; winter sports areas; campsites; and state parks, recreation areas, historic sites, and roadside parks are keyed to the map. AAA (US-259), Exxon (US-261), Gousha (US-206), and Rand McNally (US-215) each issue a New York state map. See also NY-3 and NY-11.

PUBLISHERS

NY-11   OUTDOOR PUBLICATIONS, Box 355, Ithaca, NY 14850 (607/273-0061).

They publish a large number of guides and "Sportsman's Maps" to the Catskill and Adirondack Mountains. The maps vary in size (average size is about 25 in. x 30 in.) and show locations of hiking trails, campsites, ski areas, lookout towers, fishing areas, etc. For the Catskills, there is an overall SPORTSMAN'S MAP OF THE CATSKILL MOUNTAINS, one for the central Catskill Mountains, 1 for each of the 4 counties (Ulster, Delaware, Sullivan, and Greene) that make up the Catskills, 1 for the Pepacton Reservoir in Delaware County, and 1 for the Ashokan Reservoir in Ulster County. Also for the Catskills there are: FISHING MAP OF THE CATSKILL MOUNTAINS, GUIDE TO TROUT STREAMS IN THE CATSKILL MOUNTAINS, GUIDE TO DEER HUNTING IN THE CATSKILL MOUNTAINS, and NEW YORK CITY RESERVOIRS IN THE CATSKILL MOUNTAINS. For the Adirondacks, there is the SPORTSMAN'S MAP OF THE ADIRONDACK MOUNTAINS, SPORTSMAN'S MAP OF HAMILTON COUNTY, N.Y., and GUIDE TO TROUT WATERS IN THE ADIRONDACK MOUNTAINS.

MAJOR TOURIST ORGANIZATION

NY-12   NEW YORK STATE DEPT. OF COMMERCE, DIVISION OF TOURISM, 99 Washington Avenue, Albany, NY 12245 (518/474-5677).

They issue a very comprehensive 96-page booklet, I LOVE NEW YORK TRAVEL GUIDE, which describes things to see and do, has points of interest listings including a handicapped accessibility key, and gives addresses to write to for further information. They also issue a bimonthly calendar of events, a complete camping guide, and I LOVE NEW YORK OUTDOOR BOOK, a comprehensive guide to outdoor attractions. At this writing, this agency seems to be in the throes of reorganization.

OTHER ORGANIZATIONS

NY-13   NEW YORK–NEW JERSEY TRAIL CONFERENCE, 15 East 40th Street, New York, NY 10016 (212/679-8017).

This nonprofit organization is composed of the major hiking clubs in the southern New York and northern New Jersey area. It marks and maintains 60 individual trails, totaling over 700 miles, in the area. It is a major source of hiking-related information and publishes 3 map sets, 1 guidebook to trails in the area, and a bimonthly journal, TRAIL WALKER, available free to members.

NY-14   NEW YORK STATE HOTEL & MOTEL ASSOCIATION, 141 West 51st Street, New York, NY 10019 (212/247-0800).

They issue an annual directory of NEW YORK STATE HOTELS, MO-TELS, RESORTS.

INFORMATION CENTERS/INFORMATION PHONES

The Division of Tourism (NY-12) operates a street level Travel Center at 6 East 48th Street, just off 5th Avenue in midtown Manhattan (212/758-6820). It is open Monday–Friday, 9A.M.–5P.M. It provides information about vacation attractions in New York state. It also has branch offices in Binghamton, Buffalo, Elmira, Kingston, Jericho (on Long Island), Ogdensburg, Rochester, Syracuse, Utica, and White Plains in the state, and in Washington, DC at 1612 K Street NW, Washington, DC 20006. The division has a toll-free number at 800/833-9840. In New York state, call 800/342-3683. See also the "Adirondack Mountains – Information Centers/Information Phones" section of this chapter.

OUTDOOR RECREATION ACTIVITIES

BICYCLING. See NY-3, NY-36, NY-42, and NY-52.

CANOEING AND BOATING. A DIRECTORY OF BOAT LAUNCHING SITES and CRUISE 'N CHART KITS (the Hudson River and Lake Champlain area, the canal system, and the Lake Erie and St. Lawrence River area) are available from: New York State Parks and Recreation, Marine and Recreation Vehicles, Empire State Plaza, Albany, NY 12238. CANOE TRIPS and ADIRONDACK CANOE ROUTES are available from the New York State Dept. of Environmental Conservation, 50 Wolf Road, Albany, NY 12233. See also NY-20.

FISHING AND HUNTING. FISHING GUIDE, BIG GAME GUIDE, and SMALL GAME GUIDE are detailed maps showing fishing areas and streams, hatcheries, boat launch sites, and campsites (FISHING GUIDE); bear, deer, and special use areas (BIG GAME GUIDE); and small game hunting and boat launch sites (SMALL GAME GUIDE). All 3 guides describe regulations and list Dept. of Environmental Conservation regional offices. These are available from the New York State Dept. of Environmental Conservation, 50 Wolf Road, Albany, NY 12233. The department also issues a guide to FRESHWATER FISHING IN NEW YORK. See also NY-11 and the I LOVE NEW YORK OUTDOOR BOOK issued by the Division of Tourism (NY-12).

WINTER ACTIVITIES. The New York State Dept. of Environmental Conservation, 50 Wolf Road, Albany, NY 12233 issues several guides to winter activities: WINTER HIKING IN THE NEW YORK STATE FOREST PRESERVE, WINTER ACTIVITIES IN NEW YORK STATE PARKS, NORDIC SKIING AND SNOWSHOEING TRAILS IN NEW YORK STATE FOREST PRESERVES (describes, with maps, approximately 30 trails), and SNOWMOBILE TRAILS IN NEW YORK STATE (a compilation of 47 maps on which trials have been indicated). The Division of Tourism (NY-12) issues an annual I LOVE NEW YORK SKIING which contains schedules of facilities, services, and prices for over 150 downhill and ski touring centers. Two state operated 24-hour ski phones are available: 518/474-5677 out of Albany, and 212/755-8100, a recorded message out of New York City. The Central Adirondack Association (NY-25) issues a SNO MOBILE MAP of the area, and they can also be called for a snow conditions report.

NATIONAL/STATE PARKS/FORESTS, ETC.

Fire Island National Seashore

NY-15   FIRE ISLAND NATIONAL SEASHORE, 120 Laurel Street, Patchogue, NY 11772 (516/289-4810).

They issue an official map/brochure and a list of facilities at different regions on the island. Visitor information centers are open from late June to early September at the Watch Hill facility (516/597-6455) and the Sailors Haven facility (516/597-6171) and year-round at the Smith Point West facility (516/281-3010).

Gateway National Recreation Area

NY-16   GATEWAY NATIONAL RECREATION AREA, Headquarters Bldg., #69, Floyd Bennett Field, Brooklyn, NY 11234.

The recreation area was established on October 27, 1972 and consists of 4 separate units around the area where Lower New York Bay and Sandy Hook Bay meet the Atlantic Ocean: Staten Island Unit (212/351-8700), Jamaica Bay Unit (212/252-9286), and Breezy Point Unit

(212/474-4600) in New York, and the Sandy Hook Unit (201/872-0115) in New Jersey. Several good map/guides are available plus a bi-monthly calendar of events.

There are no national forests in New York state.

In addition to the numerous publications mentioned throughout this chapter, the New York State Dept. of Environmental Conservation, 50 Wolf Road, Albany, NY 12233 issues the following: HIKING AREAS OF NEW YORK STATE, and HORSE TRAILS IN NEW YORK STATE.

INDIVIDUAL CITIES OR AREAS

Adirondack Mountains—Printed Materials

NY-17   ADIRONDACK REGION ATLAS. Poughkeepsie, NY: City Street Directory (35 Sandi Drive/12603), 1978. 55 in. x 41 in. sheet. Scales vary. Indexes.

This is not an atlas; it is a large sheet map folded into a stiff cover. The map of the Adirondack region is quite good, but awkward to use in a moving vehicle because of its size. It indicates lakes, streams, parklands, trails (of several sorts), airports, roads, etc. The back of the map has a very good map of the Lake George area. There are inset maps for 21 of the major communities, as well as separate indexes for lakes and streams and localities. The copyright dates on the maps are 1973 and 1974. The profuse advertising in the margins is apparently what is revised with each edition. It also lists radio stations.

NY-18   GUIDE TO ADIRONDACK TRAILS. 9th ed. Glens Falls, NY: Adirondack Mountain Club, 1977. 281 p. Maps.

Detailed text describes trails in the High Peak Region and the 130 mile Northville-Placid Trail.

NY-19   Healy, Trudy. CLIMBER'S GUIDE TO THE ADIRONDACKS: ROCK AND SLIDE CLIMBS IN THE HIGH PEAK REGION. 2d ed. Glens Falls, NY: Adirondack Mountain Club, 1971. 108 p. Maps. Index. 67-22792.

The author includes brief descriptions, with difficulty rating, of 8 rock and 7 slide climbs. There is a glossary.

NY-20   Jamieson, Paul F. ADIRONDACK CANOE WATERS, NORTH FLOW. Rev. ed. Glens Falls, NY: Adirondack Mountain Club, 1977. 299 p. Map. Index. 75-1974.

Jamieson "describes over 700 miles of accessible canoe waters in just two of the five major drainage basins of the Park: the St. Lawrence River Basin and the Lake Champlain Basin." The route information given is very thorough and useful. However, the names of the USGS quadrangles to use for each section, although given, are not designated as such, and the promised river classifications appear only sporadically. The one map provided is useless.

NY-21 Patterson, Barbara M. WALKS AND WATERWAYS: AN INTRODUCTION TO ADVENTURE IN THE EAST CANADA CREEK AND THE WEST BRANCH OF THE SACANDAGA RIVER SECTIONS OF THE SOUTHERN ADIRONDACKS. Glens Falls, NY: Adirondack Mountain Club, 1974. 171 p. Maps (5 in pocket), sketches, photos. Index. 75-317432.

Descriptions of 98 one-day walks, hikes, canoe trips, and bushwhacks in quiet, solitary, natural areas in the southern Adirondacks are regionally arranged with a name index. This same author, under the name Barbara McMartin, has also written OLD ROADS AND OPEN PEAKS published by the Adirondack Mountain Club in 1977. It describes walks and bushwhacks in the southeastern Adirondacks, north of Great Sacandaga Lake.

See also NY-11. The New York State Dept. of Environmental Conservation, 50 Wolf Road, Albany, NY 12233 issues ADIRONDACK CANOE ROUTES, HORSE TRAILS IN THE ADIRONDACK REGION, HIKING LESSER KNOWN ADIRONDACK WILDS, and several regional trail guides.

Adirondack Mountains—Organizations

NY-22 THE ADIRONDACK ASSOCIATION, Box 789, Adirondack, NY 12808

They issue several useful publications. THE ADIRONDACK ADVENTURE is a 23-page guide (rev. ed. published in 1978) describing the area generally and listing other organizations from which information may be obtained. It was published cooperatively by the association; the Adirondack Park Agency, Box 99, Ray Brook, NY 12977; and the Northern New York Tourism Project, Plattsburgh State University College, Plattsburgh, NY 12901. Also available from the association are: ADIRONDACK AREA FISHING WATERS, ADIRONDACK AREA MAP AND INFORMATION GUIDE, CLIMBING THE ADIRONDACK 46, NORTH COUNTRY CRAFT TRAIL MAP, OFF-THE-BEATEN PATH (scenic roads), and THE HISTORIC ADIRONDACKS.

NY-23 ADIRONDACK ATTRACTIONS ASSOCIATION, Box 78, Adirondack, NY 12808.

They issue a JUST FOR FUN MAP on which area attractions are located.

NY-24 ADIRONDACK MOUNTAIN CLUB, 172 Ridge Street, Glens Falls, NY 12801 (518/793-7737).

This is a nonprofit membership corporation supporting conservation and outdoor recreation in the Adirondack region. It assists 24 local chapters, conducts outings, maintains trails and campsites, and collects and publishes information about the Adirondacks. They issue many guidebooks, an ADIRONDACK BIBLIOGRAPHY (basic volume published in 1955 with 1956-65 and 1966-68 supplements; it lists periodical articles and books about the Adirondacks), and ADIRONDAC, the bi-monthly club magazine. The Niagara Frontier Chapter puts out a 54-page WILDERNESS WEEKENDS IN WESTERN NEW YORK published in 1976.

NY-25 CENTRAL ADIRONDACK ASSOCIATION, Old Forge, NY 13420 (315/369-6983 or 315/357-5000).

They issue CENTRAL ADIRONDACK GUIDE (an annual guide to things to do and see with maps and advertisements), VACATIONIST'S TOWN CRIER (an alphabetical listing of area attractions, accommodations, restaurants, and services), a campsite directory, a calendar of events, a winter accommodations directory, a SNO MOBILE MAP, and information about trails.

Adirondack Mountains—Information Centers/Information Phones

The Adirondack Information Center, Route 86, Saranac Lake is operated by the Saranac Lake Chamber of Commerce (518/891-1990). It is open daily from Memorial Day to Labor Day, 9A.M.-8P.M. A Visitor Information Center, Routes 29 and 30, Vail Mills, is operated by the Fulton County Chamber of Commerce (518/883-5995) daily from Memorial Day to Labor Day. The Adirondack Regional Chambers of Commerce, in cooperation with the Warren County Public Information/Tourism Dept., have a toll-free number that provides information on attractions and all kinds of accommodations. Call 800/833-4151. In New York state call 800/342-4132.

Albany—Printed Materials

NY-26 ACCESS TO CAPITALAND. Schenectady, NY: Junior League of Schenectady (Box 857/12301), 1978.

This guide for the handicapped covers Albany, Schenectady, and Troy. A new edition is planned for 1981.

NY-27 GUIDER TO ALBANY. Depew, NY: Guider of Albany (6461 Transit Road/14043).

This is a monthly guide to entertainment, mostly theater, and fine dining for people on the go.

Maps of Albany are available from Arrow Map Co. (US-199) and Champion Map Corp. (US-202).

Albany—Organizations

NY-28 ALBANY AREA CHAMBER OF COMMERCE, 510 Broadway, Albany, NY 12207 (518/434-1214).

Catskills—Printed Materials

NY-29 Adams, Arthur G., et al. GUIDE TO THE CATSKILLS WITH TRAIL GUIDE AND MAPS. New York: Walking News, 1975. 440 p. Maps, photos. Index. 0-915850-02-8. 75-18607.

The 40 detailed trail descriptions are only part of this complete outdoor guide to the Catskills. History, geology, winter sports, museums, historical sites, water sports, and accommodations are noted more briefly.

NY-30 Bennet, John, and Masia, Seth. WALKS IN THE CATSKILLS. New York: East Woods Press, 1974. 203 p. Drawings, maps. Bibliography. 0-914788-00-0. 74-81304.

General information is given for the area with 24 trails described in detail.

NY-31 Mack, Arthur C. ENJOYING THE CATSKILLS. Ithaca, NY: Outdoor Publications, 1972. 104 p. Maps, sketches. 66-28237.

The author presents sections on "getting to the Catskills, Catskill State Park, geology, famous views, forests and wildlife, legends and history, touring the Catskills, wilderness areas, where to hike, major and outlying trails, camping, forest lore, canoeable waters, hunting and fishing, ski touring, and much more. . . ."

See also NY-11. The New York State Dept. of Environmental Conservation, 50 Wolf Road, Albany, NY 12233 issues CATSKILL TRAILS.

Catskills—Organizations

There is no central association providing information on the Catskills. Each of the 4 counties that make up the area must be contacted individually. Each provides information on accommodations and campsites, what to see and do, winter activities, events, hunting and fishing, antique hunting, etc. The offices to contact are: Delaware County Chamber of Commerce, 95 1/2 Main Street, Delhi, NY 13753; Greene County Promotion Dept., Box 467, Catskill, NY 12414; Sullivan County Government Center, Office of Public Information,

Monticello, NY 12701; and Ulster County Public Information Office, Box 3521, Kingston, NY 12401.

Finger Lakes—Organizations

NY-32   FINGER LAKES ASSOCIATION, 309 Lake Street, Penn Yan, NY 14527 (315/536-6621).

They issue a very comprehensive, annual guide of over 200 pages that "contains a wealth of information on the activities in the region as well as facilities that are available to vacationeers" called the FINGER LAKES REGIONAL TRAVEL GUIDE.

The Finger Lakes region had 20 information centers in 1978. They are mostly local chambers of commerce.

Hudson River Valley—Printed Materials

NY-33   Tauber, Gilbert. THE HUDSON RIVER TOURWAY. Garden City, NY: Doubleday, 1977. 203 p. Maps, photos. Index. 0-385-12688-3. 76-42429.

This is a nicely detailed guide to the Hudson River area from Westchester to the Adirondacks. It is divided into 11 tours. Explicit directions are given to all locations, as well as a brief description of sites and sights (with hours, fees, and telephone number). The maps are adequate.

Hudson River Valley—Organizations

NY-34   HUDSON RIVER VALLEY ASSOCIATION, 105 Ferris Lane, Poughkeepsie, NY 12603 (914/452-2850).

They issue WHERE TO GO-STAY-DINE-BUY IN THE HUDSON RIVER VALLEY, HISTORIC/SCENIC HUDSON RIVER VALLEY, and a semi-annual calendar of events.

Long Island—Printed Materials

NY-35   Albright, Rodney, and Albright, Priscilla. SHORT WALKS ON LONG ISLAND. Chester, CT: Pequot Press, 1974. 121 p. Sketch maps. 0-87106-143-0. 74-75075.

The authors give practical suggestions for 41 walks on Long Island. They are arranged by different terrains: beaches, towns, woodlands and bogs, former estates, marshes and creeks, and sand spits and points.

NY-36   Angelillo, Phil. SHORT BIKE RIDES ON LONG ISLAND. Chester,

CT: Pequot Press, 1977. 127 p. Maps. 0-87106-071-X. 76-45045.

Angelillo describes "28 rides that explore the areas of Long Island that best display its essential character and unique historical and geographic features." The rides vary in length from 8 to 24 miles, and each description is accompanied by a map; detailed road instructions; and information on length, duration, terrain, and traffic conditions.

NY-37   LONG ISLAND RECREATION & VISITOR'S GUIDE. Plainview, NY: Long Island Business Review (303 Sunnyside Blvd./11803). Issued annually.

This is a guide to restaurants, accommodations, things to do, and points of interest in Nassau and Suffolk Counties and Queens.

NY-38   Wilensky, Julius M. WHERE TO GO, WHAT TO DO, HOW TO DO IT ON LONG ISLAND SOUND. 5th ed. Stamford, CT: Wescott Cove Publishing Co., [1977?].

This edition was being prepared as we went to press. It will probably be very much like this author's guide for Cape Cod (MA-37), and is recommended on that basis.

Both Exxon (US-261) and Rand McNally (US-215) issue a Long Island/Metropolitan New York City map.

The Long Island weather information number is 516/936-1212.

Long Island—Organizations

NY-39   LONG ISLAND ASSOCIATION OF COMMERCE & INDUSTRY, 425 Broad Hollow Road, Suite 205, Melville, NY 11746 (516/752-9600).

This organization exists mainly to develop business and employment on Long Island, but it does have a tourism arm whose stated goals for 1978 (from the association's 1977 annual report, p. 10) include the publication of a guide to recreation facilities, motels, restaurants, attractions; and the opening of a Long Island Tourist and Business Information Center in New York City. In the meantime, they will send a very thorough 74-page guide to Suffolk County which is the easternmost county. It is thematically arranged, under 30 different activities, from airports to yacht clubs and contains a large pull-out map.

See also FIRE ISLAND NATIONAL SEASHORE (NY-15).

New York City—Printed Materials

NY-40   ACCESS NEW YORK: AN ACCESSIBILITY GUIDE OF SELECTED FA-

CILITIES IN EAST MIDTOWN MANHATTAN. New York: Institute of Rehabilitation Medicine, New York University Medical Center (400 East 34th Street/10016), 1976. 81 p.

NY-41   Britchky, Seymour. SEYMOUR BRITCHKY'S NEW, REVISED GUIDE TO THE RESTAURANTS OF NEW YORK. New York: Random House, 1976. 325 p. Indexes. 0-394-73222-7. 76-15180.

This is "an irreverent appraisal of the best, most interesting, most famous, most underrated or worst restaurants in New York City." Two hundred restaurants are described, located, and rated. There are indexes for type of food served, rating, location, and special features.

NY-42   Carlinsky, Dan, and Heim, David. BICYCLE TOURS IN AND AROUND NEW YORK. New York: Hagstrom Co., 1975. 88 p. Maps. 0-910684-01-4. 75-4036.

After a general discussion of biking and bike safety, bike repair, and a list of bike clubs, 21 bike trips are described in detail with a map for each trip. Distance, terrain, minimum time, and points of interest are noted. Trips in northern New Jersey and southwestern Connecticut are listed, as well as trips in New York City, Long Island, and along the Hudson.

NY-43   CUE: NEW YORK. Philadelphia: North American Publishing Co.

There is a very complete biweekly magazine devoted to listing all sorts of events taking place in the New York City area: art, dance, childrens activities, movies, music, nightlife, places to go, restaurants, sports, theater, things to do, and television.

NY-44   Edmiston, Susan, and Cirino, Linda D. LITERARY NEW YORK: A HISTORY AND GUIDE. Boston: Houghton Mifflin, 1976. 409 p. Photos., maps. Index. 0-395-24349-1. 75-44068.

The authors have chosen 11 tours of Manhattan, plus 1 each in the other boroughs, that show both where individual authors resided and locales used as settings for literary works. Each tour is prefaced by a discursive attempt "to retrace the steps of the city's major writers, and re-create the literary circles and currents in which they moved." There are 27 pages of notes and a 13-page index.

NY-45   Ford, Clebert, and McPherson, Cynthia. A GUIDE TO THE BLACK APPLE. New York: Louis J. Martin & Associates, 1977. 160 p. Maps. Index. 0-916800-12-1. 77-78969.

A guidebook for the Afro-American tourist in New York City, this book has a light touch to its very informative remarks. Churches, museums, historic and scenic sights, shops, restaurants, night spots, theaters, and sources of assistance which are of interest to the black traveler are listed, giving address and telephone number. Each section has its own map.

NY-46 Glaser, Milton, and Snyder, Jerome. THE ALL NEW UNDERGROUND GOURMET. 3d ed. A Fireside Book. New York: Simon & Schuster, 1977. 370 p. Indexes. 0-671-22443-3. 76-46624.

One hundred and thirty inexpensive New York restaurants are described and alphabetically arranged by name with indexes by location and nationality of food served.

NY-47 Hamburg, Joan, and Ketay, Norma. NEW YORK ON $15 AND $20 A DAY. New York: Arthur Frommer (distributed by Simon & Schuster), 1978. Issued biennially. 217 p. Maps.

The main goal of this book is to show how to keep the per day living costs--hotel room and 3 meals--down to $15 to $20 a day. In addition to describing all types of low-cost sleeping arrangements and eating places, there are chapters on sights to see, strolls through ethnic and other neighborhoods, 1-day excursions, bargain nightspots, best shopping buys, New York with children, and for Americans en route to Europe.

NY-48 I LOVE NEW YORK TRAVEL GUIDE: NEW YORK CITY. Albany: New York State Dept. of Commerce, 1978. 36 p. Photos., maps.

This is a joint effort of the New York Magazine Co. and the New York State Dept. of Commerce. It is available from the Division of Tourism (NY-12). It is a brief, but thorough, general guide to getting around, nightlife, hotels and restaurants, theaters, shopping, museums, art galleries, sports, attractions, and points of interest.

NY-49 Lasker, Toy. FLASHMAPS! THE 1978-79 INSTANT GUIDE TO NEW YORK. Chappaqua, NY: Flashmaps (Box 13/10514), 1978. Issued annually. 81 p. Maps. 79-77622.

The 46 maps in this very handy pocket atlas show public transportation, art galleries, museums, major restaurants, theaters, libraries, sports facilities, hotels, hospitals, etc.

NY-50 Levinson, Sandee, and Levinson, Michael. WHERE TO GO AND WHAT TO DO WITH THE KIDS IN NEW YORK. Los Angeles: Price/Stern/Sloan, 1972. 126 p. Index. 0-8431-0172-5. 72-76344.

The chapters in this book are: outdoor activities; restaurants appealing to small-fry; tours and exhibits; concerts, films, TV, and theater; classes and clubs; museums; special places outside the city; and where to take young out-of-towners.

NY-51 McDarrah, Fred W. MUSEUMS IN NEW YORK. 3d ed. New York: Quick Fox, 1978. 349 p. Photos. 0-8256-3112-2. 78-54604.

This is "a descriptive reference guide to 90 fine arts museums, local history museums, specialized museums, natural history and science museums, libraries, botanical and zoological parks, commercial collections, and historic houses and mansions open to the public within the five boroughs of New York City."

NY-52 Macia, Rafael. THE NEW YORK BICYCLER. A Fireside Book. New York: Simon & Schuster, 1972. 123 p. Maps, sketches. 0-671-21176-5. 75-185628.

Most bicycle guide books devote a large number of preliminary pages to bike buying, maintenance, safety, and shops. The real value of this book lies in the 27 tours (from the Central Park area to the Staten Island Bikeway tour) which follow these usual preliminary pages. Each tour includes a map, directions, approximate distance and time, and points of interest. Another guide (pocket size, 48 p.), with less geographical coverage and aimed more at the regular cyclist as opposed to the recreational cyclist, is THE BICYCLIST'S GUIDE FOR MANHATTAN, also published in 1972 by Quadrangle Books for the Fund for the City of New York. Here the preliminaries are followed by lists of bicycle racks and shops in 6 areas of Manhattan and 6 suggested tours, each with a map and directions.

NY-53 MICHELIN GREEN GUIDE TO NEW YORK CITY. 3d ed. Michelin Green Guides. Lake Success, NY: Michelin Tire Corp., 1974. 148 p. Maps, drawings. Index. 2-06-131-500-3. 75-320991.

This is a handy guide to sights to see with detailed sectional maps by a reputable publisher of world-wide guidebooks. It concentrates mostly on Manhattan, with additional small sections covering the other 4 boroughs, the Hudson River Valley, Long Island, and Princeton, NJ.

NY-54 Miller, Stan, et al. NEW YORK'S CHINESE RESTAURANTS. New York: Atheneum, 1977. 217 p. Map. 0-689-60550-6. 76-53403.

This is a rated, alphabetical list of over 80 selected New York City Chinese restaurants, discussing in detail atmosphere, service, food, and the "bar" (i.e., availability of alcohol). Address, telephone number, hours, and credit cards accepted are noted. An index by style of cuisine and a listing of those open after midnight is included. A brief history and description of regional cuisines, a history of Chinatown (with a shopping and walking tour), a glossary of Chinese menu terms, directions for reaching Chinatown, a list of parking facilities, and tips on ordering a Chinese meal are special features of this guidebook.

NY-55 MYRA WALDO'S RESTAURANT GUIDE TO NEW YORK CITY AND VICINITY. 3d ed. New York: Collier Books, a division of Macmillan, 1978. 433 p. Indexes. 73-6484.

The author describes, rates, and gives practical information for about 1,000 restaurants, including those in nearby Connecticut, Long Island, and New Jersey as well as take-out restaurants. There are indexes by rating, geographic area, type of food served, those appropriate for Sunday brunch, after theater, and children.

NY-56 NAGEL'S ENCYCLOPEDIA-GUIDE: NEW YORK CITY. 3d ed. Nagel Encyclopedia Guides. Geneva: Nagel Publishers, 1973. 183 p. Map.

This is a small, convenient foot guide to Manhattan Island as well as the 4 outlying boroughs of Brooklyn, Bronx, Queens, and Staten Island. A small listing (addresses only) of major hotels and restaurants, plus some general practical information on getting around in the city is appended. It is excerpted from the larger Nagel guide to the entire US (US-113).

NY-57 OFFICIAL NEW YORK HACKMEN'S & CHAUFFEURS' GUIDE. 13th ed. New York: Nester's Map & Guide Corp. (244 West 49th Street/ 10019), 1975. 371 p. Maps.

This very practical guide for cab drivers lists, with addresses and telephone numbers, just about every place a cabbie would need to know. In some cases, very specific driving directions are given. A street address guide for Manhattan is included.

NY-58 Reed, Henry H., and Duckworth, Sophia. CENTRAL PARK: A HISTORY AND A GUIDE. Rev. ed. New York: Clarkson N. Potter (distributed by Crown), 1972. 166 p. Photos., maps. 66-22407.

The authors present an extensive history, walking tours of the southern and northern sections, and 8 appendixes on unique aspects of the park, such as recreation and events offered, dates of plant blossomings, birds, monuments and plaques, etc.

NY-59 Routh, Jonathan, with Stewart, Serena. THE BETTER JOHN GUIDE: WHERE TO GO IN NEW YORK. New York: G.P. Putnam's Sons, 1966. 126 p. Drawings. 66-15590.

Toilet facilities in establishments from Bergdorf-Goodman to the Staten Island Ferry to the museums to Coney Island to the airports are described giving hours, numbers, costs, ratings, and atmosphere! Subway, theater, and most park rest rooms are omitted. This book needs to be updated.

NY-60 Sajnani, Daulat N., ed. DISCOVER INDIA IN NEW YORK: AN INDIAN GUIDE TO EVERY PLACE IN TOWN. New York: the author (317 West 100th Street, #4F/10025), 1977. 144 p. 77-151221.

Almost lost among the advertising one finds listings (but no evaluations) of Indian restaurants and shops, movie theaters showing Indian films, and the usual "survival" guide information geared to the Indian resident or traveler.

NY-61 Shaw, Ray. NEW YORK FOR CHILDREN: AN UNUSUAL GUIDE FOR PARENTS, TEACHERS AND TOURISTS. Rev. ed. A Sunrise Book. New York: Dutton, 1974. 167 p. Drawings. 0-87690-117-8. 74-157806.

This is a key to places providing behind-the-scenes tours and unique learning and observing opportunities from acting schools to whaling.

NY-62 Shepard, Richard F. GOING OUT IN NEW YORK: A GUIDE FOR THE CURIOUS. New York: Quadrangle/The New York Times Book Co., 1974. 366 p. Photos., maps. 0-8129-0425-7. 73-79933.

Culled from the "Going Out Guide" columns of the daily NEW YORK TIMES, museums, music, theater, libraries, churches, festivals, lecture circuits, clubs, shopping, and things for free are described, and there is a selective section on available guide services in the city.

NY-63 Simon, Kate. NEW YORK PLACES & PLEASURES: AN UNCOMMON GUIDEBOOK. 4th ed. New York: Harper & Row, 1971. 417 p. Index. 0-06-013881-5. 70-138761.

This is a very complete, but now old, guide to outings, eating, where to take the children, shopping, entertainment, and perennial events in New York City.

NY-64 "Stendahl." BEST RESTAURANTS: NEW YORK. San Francisco: 101 Productions (distributed by Scribners), 1978. 221 p. Sketches. Indexes. 0-89286-137-1. 78-9420.

This is "a critical guide with menus in all price ranges" to 120 restaurants in Manhattan, the Bronx, Brooklyn, Queens, Long Island, Putnam, Westchester and Ulster Counties, and northern New Jersey. It has indexes by area and type of cuisine served. The author writes a restaurant column each Thursday in the New York DAILY NEWS, has a syndicated radio broadcast on wine and food, and engages in many other similiar activities.

NY-65 Stern, Ellen. BEST BETS. New York: Quick Fox, 1977. 144 p. Photos. Index. 0-8256-3074-6. 77-78528.

Over 200 commercial establishments in New York City considered to be the best of their kind are listed by type of commodity or service.

NY-66 STUBS: THE SEATING PLAN GUIDE. New York: Stubs Publication Co., 1978. Issued annually(?). 95 p. Seating diagrams. 0-911458-00-X. 46-22521.

This is a "seating plan guide for New York theaters, music halls, and sports stadia--including box office addresses, telephone numbers, and seating capacities." It includes 6 Washington locations as well as the 79 New York ones.

NY-67 Tauranac, John. SEEING NEW YORK: THE OFFICIAL MTA TRAVEL GUIDE. New York: CBS Publications for Metropolitan Transportation Authority, 1976. 240 p. Maps, photos. 75-18834.

Sponsored by the Metropolitan Transportation Authority, this guide emphasizes getting to places in all the boroughs of New York City by public transportation. Locations of interest to both tourists and residents are listed and briefly described (noting hours and fees and bus and subway routes serving the attraction). The maps of the bus and subway lines in this invaluable book are good.

NY-68 WELCOME TO NEW YORK: VISITORS' GUIDE. New York: Hagstrom Co., 1973. 88 p. Photos., maps. 73-76308.

The value of this work lies in its extensive listings. There are no evaluations and no descriptions for the most part. It ranges from amusement parks to zoos, and includes armories, beaches, houses of worship, consulates, colleges, festivals and parades, libraries, elected officials, historic sites, parking information, racetracks, radio and and television stations, newspapers, stadiums, theaters, transportation, etc. Three general walking tours are included. There is no index, but there is an alphabetical contents page.

NY-69 White, Norval, and Willensky, Elliot, eds. AIA GUIDE TO NEW YORK CITY. Rev. ed. New York: Macmillan, 1978. 653 p. Photos., maps. Index. 0-02-626580-X. 77-21617.

Arranged by the 5 boroughs, the American Institute of Architects, New York Chapter presents these walking tours to "both man-made and natural places and things preserved, or built or restored and recognized as points of enduring interest." There is an architectural glossary. This is a very thorough and pleasing book.

NY-70 Wolfe, Gerard R. NEW YORK: A GUIDE TO THE METROPOLIS: WALKING TOURS OF ARCHITECTURE AND HISTORY. New York: New York University Press, 1975. 434 p. Photos., maps. Bibliography. Index. 0-8147-9160-3. 74-21706.

Twenty walking tours, each 2 to 5 hours in length, and each of a specific section of the metropolis, describe historical and architectural landmarks. Many old photographs are included for greater historical appreciation.

NY-71 Yeadon, David, and Lewis, Roz. THE NEW YORK BOOK OF BARS, PUBS, AND TAVERNS. New York: Hawthorn Books, 1975. 276 p. 0-8015-5372-5. 75-10429.

One hundred and ninety four drinking establishments in Manhattan, arranged into 8 sectional listings, are described in varying detail, noting address, telephone number, hours, dress requirements, credit cards accepted, food (if any) available, and "liveliest times." An alphabetic listing of establishments, "The Pubs At a Glance," lists address, section, page number of the full write-up, and "characteristics" (whether or not clientele is literary, gay, etc.).

There are many maps of New York City. AAA (US-259) and Exxon (US-261) each issue one of New York City and vicinity including Long Island. Others are available from Goushā (US-206), Hagstrom (US-207), and Rand McNally (US-215). A good map titled HELP YOURSELF TO MANHATTAN is published by M.A.P.S., Box 665, New York, NY 10013. It lists and locates points of interest, museums, department stores, several walking tours, and includes a good detailed map of Central Park and a calendar of major free events. See also NY-49, NY-67, NY-74, and NY-76.

The weather information number for New York City is 212/936-1212.

New York City—Organizations

NY-72 THE CITY OF NEW YORK: PARKS, RECREATION AND CULTURAL AFFAIRS ADMINISTRATION, The Arsenal, 830 Fifth Avenue, New York, NY 10021 (212/755-4100 or 212/472-1003).

The above telephone numbers are events information numbers available Monday-Friday, 10A.M.-6P.M.

NY-73 CULTURAL ASSISTANCE CENTER, 1500 Braodway, New York, NY 10036 (212/221-6857).

They issue A GUIDE TO NEW YORK CITY MUSEUMS in cooperation with the Museums Council. The pocket-sized guide describes 115 institutions (museums, zoos, botanical gardens, historic houses) in the 5 boroughs and includes hours and directions on how to get to each by public transportation.

NY-74 NEW YORK CITY TRANSIT AUTHORITY, Public Affairs Dept., 370 Jay Street, Brooklyn, NY 11201 (212/330-1234).

A NEW YORK SUBWAY GUIDE and a MANHATTAN BUS GUIDE are available, as well as SEEING NEW YORK: THE OFFICIAL MTA TRAVEL GUIDE (NY-67). All 3 are excellent publications.

NY-75 NEW YORK CONVENTION & VISITORS BUREAU, 90 East 42d Street, New York: NY 10017 (212/687-1300).

They issue a VISITOR'S GUIDE AND MAP in 7 languages; a quarterly calendar of events; guides to hotels, restaurants, and shopping; and individual what-to-see and do guides to each of the other 4 boroughs of New York City (Bronx, Brooklyn, Queens, and Staten Island). Some Broadway and TV show tickets may be obtained here. They are open daily from 9A.M.-6P.M.

NY-76   PORT AUTHORITY OF NEW YORK AND NEW JERSEY, One World Trade Center, New York, NY 10048.

The Port Promotion Division publishes an annual guide to cruises leaving New York City. The guide also describes restaurants, shopping, and sights-to-see for the person who has a short New York City layover while awaiting a cruise departure. The Aviation Public Services Division (Room 65) publishes a map/guide for Kennedy Airport. The map shows all major automobile access routes to the airport. The guide provides information on public transportation, parking facilities, and the location of airline terminals. They also publish a 23-page guide to FACILITIES AND SERVICES FOR THE HANDICAPPED at Kennedy International, LaGuardia, and Newark International Airports.

NY-77   ROCKEFELLER CENTER GUIDED TOUR AND INFORMATION DESK, 30 Rockefeller Plaza, New York, NY 10020 (212/489-2947).

The center is open daily, except Christmas Day. It offers multilingual guided tours and brochures, one of which is a SHOPS AND SERVICES GUIDE of Rockefeller Center.

NY-78   TIMES SQUARE INFORMATION CENTER, 43d Street between Seventh Avenue and Broadway (212/C15-1234).

This is maintained by the City Dept. of Commerce and is open on weekdays from 10A.M.-8P.M. and on weekends from 10A.M.-6P.M.

See also GATEWAY NATIONAL RECREATION AREA (NY-16).

Niagara Falls/Western New York (Including Buffalo and Rochester)— Printed Materials

NY-79   Arrow Maps. OFFICIAL ARROW MAP ATLAS, METROPOLITAN BUFFALO, INCLUDING NIAGARA FALLS, NEW YORK AND ONTARIO, GRAND ISLAND, AND PART OF ERIE & NIAGARA COUNTIES. Boston: Arrow, 1970. 40 p. Scale: 2 in. represents 1 mile. Index. 77-654561.

NY-80   GEOGRAPHIA'S STREET ATLAS OF ROCHESTER. Rev. ed. New York: Geographia Map Co., 1977. 49 p. Scale: 2 1/2 in. represents 5,000 ft. Index. 77-362431.

NY-81   GREATER NIAGARA VACATIONLAND: YOUR GUIDE TO BUFFALO

AND NIAGARA FALLS. Buffalo, NY: White Directory Publications (605 Grover Cleveland Highway/14226), 1978. Issued annually. 32 p. Photos., maps.

This guide describes shopping; services; places to eat and stay; history, art, and landmarks; and amusements in the Greater Buffalo/Niagara Falls area.

NY-82 GUIDER OF BUFFALO AND THE NIAGARA FRONTIER. Depew, NY: Guider of Buffalo (6461 Transit Road/14043).

This is a monthly guide to entertainment, mostly theater, and fine dining for people on the go.

NY-83 Loker, Donald E. VISITORS GUIDE TO NIAGARA FALLS. Buffalo: Henry Stewart & M. Spitalny & Son, 1969. 64 p. Photos.

Even though somewhat out of date, this is still the most complete guide there is on the area. The photographs, in particular, look dated. The where-to-go, what-to-see, and how-to-get-there information probably hasn't changed too much in 10 years.

NY-84 PEOPLES' GUIDE TO GREATER ROCHESTER AREA. Rochester, NY: Easter Seal Society of Monroe County, 1978.

This is a guide for the handicapped.

NY-85 TODAY IN WESTERN NEW YORK. Buffalo, NY: Sommer & Sons Printing Co. (2210 South Park Avenue/14220).

This guide to live entertainment and the most visited sites in western New York is published every 3 weeks.

NY-86 TRI-CITY DIRECTORY GUIDE FOR THE DISABLED AND ELDERLY. Buffalo, NY: Rehabilitation Association of Western New York, Building Barriers Committee, 1974. 93 p.

This is a guide to the Buffalo and Niagara Falls area.

NY-87 Wilson, Pat, and Wilson, Bruce. SURPRISING ROCHESTER. Rochester: the authors (151 Greystone Lane/14618), 1975. 120 p.

This general guide to services, stores, and entertainments is useful to natives as well as visitors.

Champion Map Corp. (US-202) issues separate maps for Niagara Falls, Buffalo, and Rochester. Rand McNally (US-215) issues a joint Buffalo/Niagara Falls/Rochester map. The local AAA office in Buffalo issues a Buffalo City map with a Niagara Falls inset. AAA (US-259) issues a map of Rochester.

The Buffalo weather information number is (716/643-1212).

Niagara Falls/Western New York (Including Buffalo and Rochester)— Organizations

NY-88 GREATER ROCHESTER AREA CHAMBER OF COMMERCE, 55 St. Paul Street, Rochester, NY 14604 (716/454-2220).

They issue PROFILE ROCHESTER/MONROE COUNTY and lists of hotels, motels, and restaurants.

NY-89 NIAGARA FALLS CONVENTION AND VISITORS BUREAU, 300 Fourth Street, Box 786, Falls Street Station, Niagara Falls, NY 14303 (716/278-8010).

They operate a visitor reception facility in Niagara Falls on the corner of Rainbow Blvd. South and LaSalle Arterial.

NY-90 NIAGARA COUNTY DEPT. OF ECONOMIC DEVELOPMENT & PLAN-NING, Niagara County Court House, Lockport, NY 14094 (716/434-2871).

They issue 4 very useful brochures: a highways brochure with several area maps; a cobblestone map/guide to 50 historic cobblestone structures in the area; a hotel, motel, and campsite listing with map; and a fishing guide with map that also includes boat launch ramp sites. There is a hotline phone (716/433-5606) for information on fishing, hunting, and outdoor recreation.

NY-91 ROCHESTER/MONROE COUNTY CONVENTION AND VISITORS BUREAU, War Memorial, Rochester, NY 14614 (716/546-3070).

They publish WHAT TO SEE. . .WHERE TO SHOP. . .AND DINE. They cosponsor, with the Society for the Genesee and the Lakes, a Thruway Tourist Information Center (Box 45, West Henrietta, NY 14586) at Rochester Exit 46 on the Thruway at West Henrietta. It is open May through October, and the telephone number is 716/334-4420.

Thousand Islands/St. Lawrence Area—Organizations

NY-92 1000 ISLANDS BRIDGE AUTHORITY AND INTERNATIONAL COUNCIL, Box 428, Alexandria Bay, NY 13607 (315/782-4130 and 315/482-2501).

They issue a calendar of events, a fishing guide, and a comprehensive GENERAL INFORMATION BOOK which can be used by either group tour planners or individual travelers. It lists accommodations; restaurants; attractions; camping areas; boat rentals, marinas, and cruises; churches; and transportation services in 9 New York and 3 Ontario communities in the 1000 Islands region. There is a toll-free number for use between March 15 and September 15. New York residents should call 800/962-0001. Out-of-state residents should call 800/448-0193.

NORTH CAROLINA

BOOKS, ATLASES, MAGAZINES

NC-1   Alexandria Drafting Co. FRESH WATER FISHING AND HUNTING IN
NORTH CAROLINA. Alexandria, VA: Alexandria Drafting, 1971.
40 p. Maps, photos., drawings. Scales vary. Index. 75-24469.

There are 19 sectional maps covering the state, and 63 enlargements
showing special areas for the hunter and fisherman. Golf courses,
campgrounds, and hotels/motels are listed. We rate this as very good.

NC-2   _____. SALT WATER SPORT FISHING AND BOATING IN NORTH
CAROLINA. Alexandria, VA: Alexandria Drafting, 1977. 60 p.
Scale: 4 in. represents 5 miles. Index. 77-654529.

In this atlas, 49 colorful charts indicate fishing grounds. There are
also descriptions of marinas.

NC-3   Benner, Bob. CAROLINA WHITEWATER: A CANOEISTS GUIDE TO
WESTERN NORTH CAROLINA. 2d ed. Morganton, NC: Pisgah
Providers (Box 101/28655), 1976. 152 p. Photos.

This is a guide to several dozen rivers including the Chatooga (the
scene of the book and movie "Deliverance") River in South Carolina.

NC-4   Brady, Eric, ed. MOUNTAIN VACATION & TRAVEL GUIDE COVER-
ING WESTERN NORTH CAROLINA. Hendersonville, NC: Carolina
Life, 1978. 64 p. Photos., maps.

The author describes things to see and do, where to shop for mountain
crafts, where to write for further information for 6 regions in the western part of the state, including Great Smoky Mountains National Park
and the Blue Ridge Parkway.

NC-5   Corey, Faris Jane. EXPLORING THE MOUNTAINS OF NORTH
CAROLINA, Raleigh, NC: Provincial Press (2007 Nancy Ann Drive/
27607), 1972. 79 p. Maps, drawings. 73-154256.

With each description accompanied by a map, 20 locales are briefly described noting sights to see.

NC-6 Corey, Jane. EXPLORING THE SEACOAST OF NORTH CAROLINA. Raleigh, NC: Provincial Press (2007 Nancy Ann Drive/27607), 1969. 40 p. Maps, drawings. 77-6837.

Sixteen high spots on the Outer Banks are briefly described and mapped, noting major sights to see.

NC-7 Crow, Jeffrey J., and Moss, Patricia B. A GUIDEBOOK TO REVO-LUTIONARY SITES IN NORTH CAROLINA. Raleigh: North Carolina Dept. of Cultural Resources, Division of Archives & History, 1975. 45 p. Maps. Index. 76-351172.

Nearly 300 sites, each with a brief statement of its historical signifi-cance, are described and located on a map. The guide is arranged by county with a name index.

NC-8 NORTH CAROLINA COASTAL FISHING & VACATION GUIDE. Raleigh, NC: Graphic Press (Box 26808/27611), 1977. Issued an-nually. 144 p. Maps, photos., tables.

Arranged by north, central, and southern sections of the coast, and containing gift coupons, this work has articles on fishing, charts of the coast, tide tables, ferry schedules, and directories of lodgings, fishing piers, boat charters, marinas, and campgrounds.

NC-9 Robinson, Blackwell P. THE NORTH CAROLINA GUIDE. Rev. ed. American Guide Series. Chapel Hill: University of North Carolina Press, 1955. 649 p. Photos., maps.

This revision of the original WPA guide follows the original format: general background, descriptions of 14 cities and towns, and 24 statewide highway tours.

NC-10 Schumann, Marguerite. THE LIVING LAND: AN OUTDOOR GUIDE TO NORTH CAROLINA. Chapel Hill, NC: Dale Press, 1977. 178 p. Photos. Index. 77-150438.

This guide to "parks of significant size, forests, seashores, lakes, recreation rivers, wildlife refuges, and some game lands" is regionally arranged with an index.

NC-11 THE STATE: DOWN HOME IN NORTH CAROLINA. Raleigh, NC: The State (Box 2169/27602).

This monthly magazine, established in 1933, is devoted to subjects of interest to North Carolinians (history, natural history, life styles, lore, etc.). The June issue of each year is devoted to travel and is called the NORTH CAROLINA VACATION GUIDE. It is a county-by-county listing of recreational attractions and information on boating, fishing, golfing, hiking, scenic drives, events, and sources of information. There is a separate, consolidated calendar of events and a full-page listing of free vacation booklets. The magazine publishes an annual scenic engagement calendar. A consolidated index for 1933-63 is available. From 1964 to the present, an annual index has been published in every May issue.

MAPS

The official transportation map and guide to points of interest is available from the Division of Travel and Tourism (NC-13). The 1978-79 edition has very extensive listings of attractions, ski areas, outdoor dramas, historic sites, waterfalls, handicrafts, state and national parks and forests, rock-hounding sites, and ferries. AAA (US-259), Exxon (US-261), Goushā (US-206), and Rand McNally (US-215) each issue a combined North Carolina/South Carolina map. See also NC-1 and NC-12.

PUBLISHERS

NC-12 CAROLINA LIFE. Box 548, Hendersonville, NC 28739.

In addition to the MOUNTAIN VACATION & TRAVEL GUIDE (NC-4) and the GUIDEBOOK TO REVOLUTIONARY SITES (NC-7) this publisher and distributer has an extensive selection of other books reflecting the mountains, history, cooking, Indians, etc. of the Carolinas. Worth mentioning here are the 64-page THE SMOKIES GUIDE by George M. Stephens published in 1978 and the following 5 maps: 100 FAVORITE TRAILS OF THE GREAT SMOKIES AND CAROLINA BLUE RIDGE compiled by the Carolina Mountain Club (Box 68, Asheville, NC 28802) and the Smoky Mountains Hiking Club (5419 Timbercrest Trail, Knoxville, TN 37901) (1978), GREAT SMOKY MOUNTAINS NATIONAL PARK TRAIL MAP (1976), MT. PISGAH AREA MAP (1978), BLUE RIDGE PARKWAY MAP & GUIDEBOOK (1977), and GREAT SMOKIES-BLUE RIDGE VACATION MAP (1978).

MAJOR TOURIST ORGANIZATION

NC-13 NORTH CAROLINA DEPT. OF COMMERCE, DIVISION OF TRAVEL AND TOURISM, 430 North Salisbury Street, Raleigh, NC 27611 (919/733-4171).

They issue an attractions kit of 3 general booklets, NORTH CAROLINA OUTDOORS (a thorough guide to private campsites as well as campsites, facilities, and outdoor recreation opportunities, including hiking, at state parks and national parks and forests), an annual calendar of events, NORTH CAROLINA ONE DAY AT A TIME (describes 10 tours covering the mountain, Piedmont, and coastal areas and the cities of Raleigh, Charlotte, and Winston-Salem), NORTH CAROLINA FISHING, GOLF STATE, U.S.A., and a NORTH CAROLINA DIRECTORY OF ACCOMMODATIONS. Another address may be used: North Carolina Travel, Room 571, Box 77, Raleigh, NC 27611. It is also for the Division of Travel and Tourism and will bring travel literature and information.

OTHER ORGANIZATIONS

NC-14   NORTH CAROLINA INNKEEPERS ASSOCIATION, 709 Raleigh Bldg., Raleigh, NC 27602 (919/821-1435).

NC-15   TRAVEL COUNCIL OF NORTH CAROLINA, Box 1063, Raleigh, NC 27602 (919/834-5079).

This private, non-profit group promotes travel and tourism to North Carolina largely by lobbying for additional operational funds for the Division of Travel and Tourism (NC-13). Any requests they receive for travel information are forwarded to the division.

INFORMATION CENTERS/INFORMATION PHONES

"Welcome Centers" are operated on interstate highways where they cross the border into North Carolina. They are open daily from 8A.M.-5P.M.

OUTDOOR RECREATION ACTIVITIES

BICYCLING. A map packet, BICYCLING HIGHWAYS, is available from the North Carolina Dept. of Transportation, Bicycle Coordinator, Box 25201, Raleigh, NC 27611. In handy pocket size, it describes, with detailed, easy-to-read maps, the hazardous areas, roadway conditions, services, and points of interest along a 700 mile west-east route across the state. Shorter regional routes are planned for the future. The coordinator will also answer individual requests for special routings, places to stay, etc.

CANOEING AND BOATING. A list of boating access areas is available from the North Carolina Wildlife Resources Commission, Archdale Bldg., 512 North Salisbury Street, Raleigh, NC 27611. See also NC-2 and NC-3.

FISHING AND HUNTING. A very extensive (1977-78 ed., 69 p.) compilation of hunting and fishing maps of state game lands, plus hunting and trapping, and an inland fishing regulations digest is available from the North Carolina Wildlife Resources Commission, Archdale Bldg., 512 North Salisbury Street, Raleigh,

NC 27611. FISHING INFORMATION BULLETINS (describing locations, guide services, accommodations, etc. and having good maps) are issued by the Outdoor Editor, North Carolina Travel and Tourism, Box 25249, Raleigh, NC 27611. See also the fishing brochure issued by the Division of Travel and Tourism (NC-13) and NC-1, NC-2, and NC-8.

NATIONAL/STATE PARKS/FORESTS, ETC.

Blue Ridge Parkway

NC-16   Blue Ridge Parkway Association. THE BLUE RIDGE PARKWAY AC-COMMODATIONS & SERVICES. 29th ed. Asheville, NC: Daniels Publications (15 Rankin Avenue/28802), 1978. Issued annually. 23 p. Maps.

This guide to accommodations (including campgrounds), services, and selected attractions is arranged by communities from Shenandoah National Park west to Great Smoky Mountains National Park.

NC-17   Lord, William G. BLUE RIDGE PARKWAY GUIDE. 4 vols. Asheville, NC: Hexagon Co., 1976.

Volume 1 covers Shenandoah Park to Roanoke, volume 2 covers Roanoke to Boone/Blowing Rock, volume 3 covers Boone/Blowing Rock to Asheville, and volume 4 covers Asheville to Great Smokies.

NC-18   Robinson, Donald H. CAMPER'S AND HIKER'S GUIDE TO THE BLUE RIDGE PARKWAY. Riverside, CT: Chatham Press (distributed by Viking Press), 1971. 80 p. Maps, photos. 0-86599-022-1. 72-148579.

The author gives brief descriptions, with maps, of campgrounds, visitor centers, trails, and other facilities and activities at 15 locations along the 469-mile Blue Ridge Parkway.

NC-19   BLUE RIDGE PARKWAY, 700 Northwestern Bank Bldg., Asheville, NC 28801.

They issue a general map/guide to points of interest along the parkway; many trail maps; and brief guides to fishing, blooming periods, and recreational areas along the parkway. There are 6 visitor centers along the parkway, all of which are open from May through October. There is a Cradle of Forestry in America National Forest Visitor Center on Route 276 near Milepost 411 in Pisgah National Forest.

For information about visitor services, accommodations, and reservations along the parkway, contact National Park Concessions, General Offices, Mammoth Cave, KY 42259. AAA (US-259) issues a map/guide to the parkway. See also NC-12.

Cape Hatteras National Seashore

NC-20   CAPE HATTERAS NATIONAL SEASHORE, Route 1, Box 675, Manteo,
NC 27954.

They issue a general map/guide and an information brochure on camping, bicycling, fishing, and swimming.   Information may be obtained
at the National Park Service Headquarters at Fort Raleigh year-round,
and during the summer season at visitor centers near Bodie Island
lighthouse, Cape Hatteras lighthouse, and the village of Ocracoke.

NC-21   THE OUTER BANKS CHAMBER OF COMMERCE, Kitty Hawk, NC
27949 (919/261-2626).

They issue a DIRECTORY OF ACCOMMODATIONS, GOOD FOOD,
SHOPPING, RECREATION, SERVICES and a brief fishing guide.

Alexandria Drafting Co.   (S-16) issues an OUTER BANKS FISHING MAP.   See
also NC-6.

Information and maps about the national forests in North Carolina may be obtained from the U.S. Forest Service, Southern Region, 1720 Peachtree Road
NW, Suite 800, Atlanta, GA 30309.

A good source of information on outdoor facilities and recreation opportunities
will be found in NORTH CAROLINA OUTDOORS available from the Division
of Travel and Tourism (NC-13).   The North Carolina Dept. of Natural &
Economic Resources, Division of State Parks & Recreation, Box 27687, Raleigh,
NC 27611 also supplies information and map/brochures on each of the state
parks.

INDIVIDUAL CITIES OR AREAS

Raleigh—Printed Materials

NC-22   RALEIGH: A GUIDE TO NORTH CAROLINA'S CAPITAL.   Raleigh:
Raleigh Fine Arts Society, 1975.   100 p.   Photos., maps.   Bibliography.   Index.   75-39881.

This is a nicely packaged book, but a table of contents would have
made it more useful.   It describes museums, places of historic and/or
artistic interest, educational and cultural institutions, and sports facilities within easy walking or driving distance of the Capitol building.

NC-23   THE TRIANGLE POINTER: THE "GOOD WORD" ON RALEIGH-
DURHAM-CHAPEL HILL.   Carrboro, NC: The Triangle Pointer (Box
398/27510).

This free, weekly guide to events, sights, dining, lodging, shopping, TV schedules, entertainment, and real estate is found in tourist information centers, car rental offices, and hotels and motels.

Champion Map Corp. (US-202) issues a map of Raleigh.

Raleigh—Organizations

NC-24   RALEIGH CHAMBER OF COMMERCE, Box 2978, Raleigh, NC 27602 (919/833-3005).

They issue a general brochure, but have nothing that is specifically travel oriented. Their walk-in office is located at 411 South Salisbury Street.

NORTH DAKOTA

BOOKS, ATLASES, MAGAZINES

ND-1 BREVET'S NORTH DAKOTA HISTORICAL MARKERS & SITES. Sioux Falls, SD: Brevet Press, 1975. 167 p. Maps, photos. Indexes. 0-88498-024-3. 74-79978.

Geographically arranged, this guide gives the location, a location map, an illustration, and the text of all markers placed by the State Historical Society, the North Dakota Highway Dept., and miscellaneous markers.

ND-2 DAKOTA EDITION. Bismarck, ND: Meyer/Hill Communications (118 North Third Street/58501).

This comprehensive, free guide to North Dakota's "campgrounds, attractions, events, features, and maps" is issued quarterly and contains extensive descriptions of the features and points of interest in all cities and areas of the state.

ND-3 NORTH DAKOTA: A GUIDE TO THE NORTHERN PRAIRIE STATE. 2d ed. American Guide Series. New York: Oxford University Press, 1950. 352 p. Photos. Bibliography. Index.

This revision of the original 1938 WPA guide begins with a survey of the state from natural history to recreation and then goes on to give descriptions of 4 major cities and 10 highway tours. There is a chronology of North Dakota history.

MAPS

The OFFICIAL HIGHWAY MAP is available from the Travel Division (ND-4). The 1978 edition contains a table of facilities at state parks, a list of AM/FM radio stations, and some information about points of interest. AAA (US-259), Goushā (US-206) and Rand McNally (US-215) each issue a combined North Dakota/South Dakota map. Exxon (US-261) issues a combined North Dakota/South Dakota/Nebraska map.

MAJOR TOURIST ORGANIZATION

ND-4   NORTH DAKOTA TRAVEL DIVISION, Highway Dept. Bldg., Capitol
        Grounds, Bismarck, ND 58505 (701/224-2525).

        They issue a large general booklet; several regional brochures, each
        of which contains a map, a campground guide, and describes points
        of interest; an annual calendar of events; and a list of North Dakota
        museums.

REGIONAL TOURISM ASSOCIATIONS

There are several regional associations, but their literature is distributed through
the Travel Division (ND-4) which should be contacted directly.

OTHER ORGANIZATIONS

ND-5   NORTH DAKOTA HOSPITALITY ASSOCIATION, Box 428, Bismarck,
        ND 58501 (701/223-3313).

INFORMATION CENTERS/INFORMATION PHONES

Several Interstate highway information centers are maintained by the Travel
Division (ND-4). They are open from Memorial Day to Labor Day. Their
locations are not indicated on the OFFICIAL HIGHWAY MAP, but a list is
available from the Travel Division. The Travel Division has a toll-free number that can be dialed from anywhere in the continental US: 800/437-2077.
In North Dakota call 800/472-2100.

OUTDOOR RECREATION ACTIVITIES

CANOEING AND BOATING. A brief guide to canoeing 15 different rivers is
found in NORTH DAKOTA CANOEING WATERS available from either the
Travel Division (ND-4) or North Dakota Parks and Recreation, Route 2, Box
139, Mandan, ND 58554 (701/663-9571).

FISHING AND HUNTING. For information and maps on fishing waters and
game management areas contact the North Dakota Game & Fish Dept., 2121
Lovett Avenue, Bismarck, ND 58501 (701/224-2180).

WINTER ACTIVITIES. Brief information on cross-country skiing, snowshoeing,
and snowmobile trails will be found in NORTH DAKOTA RECREATION TRAILS,
available from North Dakota Parks and Recreation, Route 2, Box 139, Mandan,
ND 58554 (701/663-9571).

North Dakota

NATIONAL/STATE PARKS/FORESTS, ETC.

There are no major National Park Service areas and no national forests in North Dakota.

Information on state parks, campgrounds, and a brochure titled NORTH DAKOTA RECREATION TRAILS (lists bicycling, hiking, nature, horseback riding, cross-country skiing and snowshoeing, and snowmobiling trails) are available from North Dakota Parks and Recreation, Route 2, Box 139, Mandan, ND 58554 (701/663-9571).

INDIVIDUAL CITIES OR AREAS

Bismarck—Printed Materials

ND-6   THE GREETER. Bismarck, ND: Meyer-Hill Communications (118 North Third Street/58501).

This is a free, monthly guide to food, lodging, shopping, entertainment, churches, and events in the Bismarck/Mandan area. It also contains several good maps of the area and a list of local transportation services. It is one of the more informative and least visually offensive of this type of city guide.

Bismarck—Organizations

ND-7   BISMARCK AREA CONVENTION AND VISITORS BUREAU, 412 North 6th Street, Bismarck, ND 58501 (701/223-5660).

They provide a general map/guide to Bismarck and other lists of campgrounds, points of interest, motels/hotels, restaurants, and shopping. The above address is open for information queries Monday-Friday, 8A.M.-5P.M. They also sponsor information centers at the Bismarck Municipal Airport and on US Highway 83 outside the city.

OHIO

BOOKS, ATLASES, MAGAZINES

OH-1   Dudas, Jim, ed. THE CLEVELAND PRESS OUTDOOR GUIDE. 11th
ed. Cleveland: The Cleveland Press, 1976. 208 p. Maps, photos.

This is basically a where-to-go fishing guide with brief, highly inadequate sections on canoeing and hiking. There is also a section describing boating areas and a campground directory that are a bit more
informative. In describing each good fishing spot, the editor frequently
gives information on other available outdoor recreation activities plus
campgrounds and cabins. The information could be better organized
and presented.

OH-2   Gerrick, David J. BACK ROADS OF NORTHEAST OHIO. Lorain,
OH: Dayton Labs, 1975. 138 p. Maps. Index.

This is "a guide for those who enjoy biking, camping, climbing, cruising, cycling, dirt biking, driving, exploring, horseback riding, jeeping, jogging, nature studying, photographing, romping, skinny dipping,
spelunking, wading or walking." There is a town and village index
for the maps.

OH-3   THE OHIO GUIDE. American Guide Series. New York: Oxford
University Press, 1940. 634 p. Photos., maps.

This original WPA guide in 3 sections--general background, descriptions
of 19 cities and towns, and 23 statewide highway tours--is comprehensive, but out of date.

OH-4   Osler, Jack M. 50 BEST MINI-TRIPS FOR OHIO. Dayton, OH:
Media Ventures, 1977. 52 p. 0-89645-000-7.

This work was not examined, but is probably very much like the Pennsylvania volume (PA-3) in this series.

OH-5   SEEING OHIO BY WHEELCHAIR. Akron, OH: Fairlawn Junior

Women's Club (Box 5225/44313), 1978. 146 p. Map on cover. Index.

The main body of this extensive guide describes historic, cultural, and scenic points of interest; parks and recreation areas; and restaurants having wheelchair access, rest room grab bars, special parking, elevators, etc. It is arranged by regions with an index by types of points of interest. There are additional lists of highway rest areas and motels/hotels having facilities for the handicapped.

OH-6   UNDISCOVERED OHIO, ECONOMY VACATIONLAND: THE WHERE TO GO, WHAT TO DO, WHERE TO SEE BOOK ABOUT NORTHEAST-ERN OHIO. 4th ed. Garrettsville, OH: The Western Reserve Magazine, 1978. 176 p. 41 p. Maps, photos.

Twelve mapped tours concentrating on history and heritage in the northeastern corner of Ohio make up the main part of this guide. Also included is a brief section on similar points of interest in the rest of Ohio and information on engaging in many outdoor sports and recreations.

MAPS

The official highway map of Ohio is available from either the Ohio Dept. of Transportation, 25 South Front Street, Columbus, OH 43215 or the Office of Travel and Tourism (OH-8). The 1978 edition lists points of interest; forests; lakes, dams, and reservoirs; national parks; colleges and universities; hospitals and institutions; and facilities at state parks. AAA (US-259), Exxon (US-261), Goushā (US-206), and Rand McNally (US-215) each issue a map of Ohio. See also OH-12.

PUBLISHERS

OH-7   THE WESTERN RESERVE MAGAZINE, Box 243, Garrettsville, OH 44231 (216/527-2030).

They publish THE WESTERN RESERVE MAGAZINE which appears bi-monthly and which contains a regular where-to-go, what-to-see column as well as articles on the heritage of Ohio's northeast corner. "The Gadabouts' Go-Go Guides" are an irregularly issued series of mini guides to northeast Ohio. Their most comprehensive guide is UNDIS-COVERED OHIO (OH-6).

MAJOR TOURIST ORGANIZATION

OH-8   OHIO DEPT. OF ECONOMIC & COMMUNITY DEVELOPMENT, OFFICE OF TRAVEL AND TOURISM, Box 1001, 30 East Broad Street, Columbus, OH 43216 (614/466-8844).

They issue a quarterly calendar of events; brochures describing where-to-go and what-to-do in each of the 9 Ohio vacation regions; separate brochures (issued under an overall series title of Travel Ohio) on outdoor dramas, zoos, stagecoach taverns, caves, and the Amish country; and a directory of public and private campgrounds.

REGIONAL TOURISM ASSOCIATIONS

Ohio is divided into 9 regions for tourist promotion purposes. Each has a local council, but the brochures describing points of interest in each region are available from the Office of Travel and Tourism (OH-8).

OTHER ORGANIZATIONS

OH-9   BUCKEYE TRAIL ASSOCIATION, Box 254, Worthington, OH 43085.

The Buckeye Trail encircles the state and is open for use by anyone; neither fees nor membership in the Buckeye Trail Association are required. The association develops and maintains the trail and publishes 22 sectional maps (scale: 1 in. represents 2 miles, each covering approximately 40 miles); 7 guidebooks (each covers about 35 miles of the trail; topographic maps are included); and a 40-page booklet, SHORT HIKES ON THE BUCKEYE TRAIL, that describes, with maps, 18 separate hikes, each about 4 miles in length, along different parts of the trail.

OH-10   THE OHIO HISTORICAL SOCIETY, Interstate 71 and 17th Avenue, Columbus, OH 43211 (614/466-4663).

This nonprofit corporation is located in the Ohio Historical Center which is also a museum devoted to Ohio's natural history, archaeology, and history. Ohio Village, a recreation of early small town life, is adjacent. The Society operates over 50 historic sites throughout the state, and their brochure, OHIO'S YESTERDAY GETAWAYS, describes these. They also issue separate brochures to several of their sites, plus an annual calendar of events taking place either in the center, the village, or other of their sites. They have 2 phone numbers for travel and events information: 614/466-1500, ext. 200 provides information Monday-Friday, 8A.M.-5P.M.; 614/466-1505 provides information Saturday and Sunday, 9A.M.-5P.M., plus a recorded message every day from 5P.M.-8A.M.

OH-11   OHIO HOTEL & MOTEL ASSOCIATION, 611 Beggs Bldg., Columbus, OH 43215 (614/224-9843).

OH-12   OHIO TURNPIKE COMMISSION, 682 Prospect Street, Berea, OH 44017.

They issue an OHIO TURNPIKE MAP (the map of the overall turnpike

is not too easy to read, but the connecting routes inset maps are good
and the list of food and fuel service plazas is valuable), SHELTER
FOR THE NIGHT. . .ALONG THE OHIO TURNPIKE (an exit-by-exit
listing of nearby motels/hotels), CAMPING TONIGHT ALONG THE
OHIO TURNPIKE (an exit-by-exit listing of nearby public and private
campgrounds), and OHIO TURNPIKE TRAVEL TRAILER PARKS (descriptions, with maps, of the 6 service plazas offering overnight travel
trailer facilities).

INFORMATION CENTERS/INFORMATION PHONES

The Office of Travel and Tourism (OH-8) operates 14 travel information centers.
There are 5 open year-round; the other 9 during the summer only. They are
not specifically identified as such on the official highway map, but a list,
with map, is available from the Office of Travel and Tourism. There is a toll-
free INFOHIO phone available in Ohio only. The number is 800/282-0250
and is a 24-hour seven days a week recorded message of statewide events. It
is recorded Mondays during spring, summer, and fall and daily during the ski
season when it is devoted almost entirely to ski conditions. A second toll-free
number, 800/848-1300, will put you in touch with the Office of Travel and
Tourism.

OUTDOOR RECREATION ACTIVITIES

CANOEING AND BOATING. The Ohio Dept. of Natural Resources, Division
of Watercraft, Fountain Square, Columbus, OH 43224 supplies a list of boating
areas and regulations. They also provide OHIO CANOE ADVENTURES, a guide
to several canoe trails. A MAP OF CANOEING STREAMS OF THE UPPER
OHIO BASIN is available from American Youth Hostels, Pittsburgh Council,
6300 Fifth Avenue, Pittsburgh, PA 15232. See also OH-1.

FISHING AND HUNTING. The Ohio Dept. of Natural Resources, Division of
Wildlife, Fountain Square, Columbus, OH 43224 provides a list, with map, of
hunting and fishing areas and regulations. See also OH-1.

WINTER ACTIVITIES. See the toll-free ski conditions phone described in the
"Information Centers/Information Phones" section of this chapter.

NATIONAL/STATE PARKS/FORESTS, ETC.

Information and maps on Ohio's only national forest may be obtained by contacting either Forest Supervisor, Wayne National Forest, Bedford, IN 47421,
or the U.S. Forest Service, Eastern Region, 633 West Wisconsin Avenue, Milwaukee, WI 53203.

The Ohio Dept. of Natural Resources, Division of Parks and Recreation, Fountain Square, Columbus, OH 43224 provides information on facilities and campsites and takes reservations for lodges, cabins, and campsites in state parks. Separate map/guides are available for each state park. The Division of Forests and Preserves, also at the Fountain Square address, provides information on facilities available in state forests.

INDIVIDUAL CITIES OR AREAS

Cincinnati—Printed Materials

OH-13   ATLAS OF CINCINNATI AND VICINITY. Hoboken, NJ: Geographia Map Co., 1972. 70 p. Scale: 2 1/2 in. represents about 1 mile. Index. 73-154442.

OH-14   Junior League of Cincinnati, comp. GREATER CINCINNATI GUIDE-BOOK FOR THE HANDICAPPED. Cincinnati: Hamilton County Easter Seal Society (7505 Reading Road/45237), 1977. 61 p.

Maps of Cincinnati are available from AAA (US-259); Arrow Publishing Co. (US-199); Champion Map Corp. (US-202); Goushā (US-206); George F. Cram, 301 South LaSalle Street, Box 426, Indianapolis, IN 46206; Metro Graphic Arts, 900 40th SE, Grand Rapids, MI 49508; and Rand McNally (US-215). See also OH-13.

Cincinnati—Organizations

OH-15   GREATER CINCINNATI CHAMBER OF COMMERCE, 120 West 5th Street, Cincinnati, OH 45202 (513/721-3300).

They issue a DINING-OUT GUIDE; VISITORS GUIDE TO CINCINNATI; CINCINNATI MAGAZINE; a handbook on entertainment and diversions that includes a city tour, sports, theaters, films, etc.; a lodging list; and a calendar of events.

OH-16   GREATER CINCINNATI CONVENTION & VISITORS BUREAU, 200 West 5th Street, Cincinnati, OH 45202 (513/621-2142).

They are open Monday–Friday, 9A.M.–5P.M. for visitor information. They issue a general booklet, a DOWNTOWN MAP, a LODGING GUIDE, and a RESTAURANT AND SHOPPING GUIDE. They will also provide a brochure describing the city's municipal golf courses.

Cleveland—Printed Materials

OH-17   Hughes, Bill, and Hughes, Betty. RESORTS. Cleveland: The Cleveland Press, 1978(?). 83 p. Photos.

Using Cleveland as the center, the authors describe inns, lodges, and resorts within a 400-mile radius in Ohio, Pennsylvania, West Virginia, Michigan, Canada, New York, Indiana, Kentucky, and Virginia.

OH-18   Professional Group of The Junior League of Cleveland, comp. A GUIDE TO CLEVELAND FOR THE HANDICAPPED. Cleveland: the author, 1967. 44 p.

OH-19   VISITOR'S GUIDE TO CLEVELAND. Cleveland: Cleveland Magazine (1621 Euclid Avenue/44115), 1976. 79 p. Maps, photos.

This guide features a walking tour; brief descriptions of over 101 things to do; family fun ideas; Cleveland after dark; and listings of restaurants, shopping, services, entertainment, and hotels/motels.

Maps of Cleveland are available from AAA (US-259); Arrow Publishing Co. (US-199); Champion Map Corp. (US-202); Metro Graphic Arts, 900 40th SE, Grand Rapids, MI 49508; and Rand McNally (US-215). The Cleveland Metroparks System, 55 Public Square, Cleveland, OH 44113 (216/621-1054) issues a very detailed map/guide to the 13 Metroparks surrounding Cleveland and the recreation opportunities available systemwide. They also issue guides to where to participate in the individual outdoor activities throughout the System and a monthly listing of Metroparks activities called the EMERALD NECKLACE.

The Cleveland weather information number is 216/931-1212.

Cleveland—Organizations

OH-20   CLEVELAND CONVENTION & VISITORS BUREAU, 511 Terminal Tower, Cleveland, OH 44113 (216/621-4110).

They issue THINGS TO DO IN CLEVELAND (a quarterly listing of events, attractions, and points of interest), a hotel/motel listing, a HISTORIC SITE WALKING TOUR, and a restaurant listing. Call 621-9792 for a recording of events.

Columbus—Printed Materials

OH-21   COLUMBUS GUIDE FOR THE HANDICAPPED. Columbus: Goodwill Industries of Central Ohio, 1969. 30 p.

OH-22   Rucker, Marion, and Lapidus, Anne. THE BUCKEYE WAY. Rev. ed. Worthington, OH: The Buckeye Way (Box 732/43085), 1976. 178 p. Maps. Index. 77-358690.

This guide to seeing the sights in Columbus and Franklin County, and

and a few noteworthy sites beyond, stresses the educational over entertainment. There are individual chapters on parks, sports, points of interest for children, eating out with children, shopping, adult activities (mainly educational; no mentions of night life spots), and a calendar of events.

Maps of Columbus are available from Arrow Publishing Co. (US-199), Champion Map Corp. (US-202), and Metro Graphic Arts, 900 40th SE, Grand Rapids, MI 49508.

Columbus—Organizations

OH-23 COLUMBUS CONVENTION & VISITORS BUREAU, 50 West Broad Street, Columbus, OH 43215 (614/221-6623).

They issue a general map/brochure, a THINGS TO DO, THINGS TO SEE brochure, and COLUMBUS HERITAGE TOUR (a walking tour brochure of historic sites in downtown Columbus).

OKLAHOMA

BOOKS, ATLASES, MAGAZINES

OK-1   OKLAHOMA TODAY. Oklahoma City: Oklahoma Tourism & Recreation Dept.

This quarterly magazine, begun in 1956, devotes itself "to the entire state of Oklahoma and its every positive aspect: its scenery; cultural, recreational, and visitor attracting events; its industry; natural and man-made wonders; its achievements; its heritage; its present; and its future."

OK-2   Ruth, Kent, ed. OKLAHOMA: A GUIDE TO THE SOONER STATE. Rev. ed. American Guide Series. Norman: University of Oklahoma Press, 1957. 532 p. Maps, photos. Bibliography. Index. 57-7333.

This revision of the original 1941 WPA guide opens with 14 essays on different aspects of life in Oklahoma. These are followed by descriptions of 12 principal cities and 23 highway tours. There is also a chronology of Oklahoma history.

OK-3   _____. OKLAHOMA TRAVEL HANDBOOK. Norman: University of Oklahoma Press, 1977. 259 p. Photos, maps. 0-8061-1405-3. 76-62517.

Oklahoma place names are presented here in A to Z order. Descriptions for each include location, access by highway, population, derivation of name, date of establishment, historic development, and off-beat details. Concentration is on the latter 2 aspects. There is no practical hours/admission, etc. type information.

OK-4   Wright, Muriel H., et al. MARK OF HERITAGE: AN ILLUSTRATED GUIDE TO MORE THAN 250 HISTORIC SITES IN OKLAHOMA. The Oklahoma Series. Oklahoma City: Oklahoma Historical Society, 1976. 214 p. Photos., map. 75-40255.

This is a comprehensive listing, with explanatory text, of over 250 roadside, granite, and on-site markers placed by the Oklahoma Historical Society.

MAPS

The official state map is published by the Oklahoma Dept. of Transportation, but is also available from the Tourism & Recreation Dept. (OK-5). The 1977 edition lists wildlife areas. See also OKLAHOMA LAKES issued by the Tourism & Recreation Dept. The Oklahoma Turnpike Authority, Box 11357, Oklahoma City, OK 73111 issues an OKLAHOMA TURNPIKES map. In addition to showing major roads, it shows locations of state parks and points of interest, locates and has a diagram of each concession area, locates and gives further information about the visitor information centers, and has a table of tolls. AAA (US-259) issues a combined Oklahoma/Texas map. Exxon (US-261) issues a combined Oklahoma/Kansas map. Both Goushā (US-206) and Rand McNally (US-215) issue a separate Oklahoma map.

MAJOR TOURIST ORGANIZATION

OK-5   OKLAHOMA TOURISM & RECREATION DEPT., 500 Will Rodgers Bldg., Oklahoma City, OK 73105 (405/521-2406).

They issue an annual calendar of events, OKLAHOMA CAMPERS GUIDE (an alphabetical listing of campsites by area), OKLAHOMA STATE PARKS (describes facilities at state parks and lists other state recreation areas), OKLAHOMA STATE RESORTS (describes facilities at 7 state resorts located in state parks), OKLAHOMA LAKES (full descriptions, with maps, of facilities, including campsites, boating, fishing and water sports areas, at each of 29 man-made lakes developed for recreation), OKLAHOMA MUSEUMS AND HISTORIC SITES (arranged by location and includes hours), OKLAHOMA AND THE INDIAN (a map/guide to Indian museums and sites of historical significance plus a calendar of Indian events), and map/guides to points of interest in each of the state's 6 regional areas: Fun Country (southcentral Oklahoma), Frontier Country (central), Great Plains Country (southwest), Green Country (northeast), Kiamichi Country (southeast), and Red Carpet Country (northwest).

REGIONAL TOURISM ASSOCIATIONS

The state is divided into six regions, and information on each region is available from the Tourism & Recreation Dept. (OK-5).

OTHER ORGANIZATIONS

OK-6   OKLAHOMA INNKEEPERS ASSOCIATION, Director, School of Hotel and Restaurant Administration, Oklahoma State University, Stillwater, OK 74074 (405/624-6486).

INFORMATION CENTERS/INFORMATION PHONES

The location of the 10 highway information centers on major highways near the state borders may be found on the official state map and on the OKLAHOMA TURNPIKES map. The toll-free number for reservations at the state resorts is 800/522-3707.

OUTDOOR RECREATION ACTIVITIES

CANOEING AND BOATING. OKLAHOMA LAKES issued by the Tourism & Recreation Dept. (OK-5) gives general locations of boat launching ramps, boat and motor rentals, commercial services, dams, docks, marinas, and sailing areas at 29 Oklahoma lakes.

FISHING AND HUNTING. OKLAHOMA LAKES issued by the Tourism & Recreation Dept. (OK-5) gives general locations where buffalo and deer may be found, and where fishing and hunting may be engaged in near the 29 lakes that are featured in this brochure. For further information contact the Oklahoma Dept. of Wildlife Conservation, 1801 North Lincoln Blvd., Oklahoma City, OK 73105.

NATIONAL/STATE PARKS/FORESTS, ETC.

For information and maps on Ouachita National Forest, which lies in Oklahoma and Arkansas and is Oklahoma's only national forest, contact U.S. Forest Service, Southern Region, 1720 Peachtree Road NW, Suite 800, Atlanta, GA 30309.

For information on state parks, forests, etc. see the OKLAHOMA CAMPERS GUIDE, OKLAHOMA STATE PARKS, and OKLAHOMA STATE RESORTS issued by the Tourism & Recreation Dept. (OK-5).

INDIVIDUAL CITIES OR AREAS

Oklahoma City—Printed Materials

Good maps of Oklahoma City are available from Arrow Publishing Co. (US-199), Champion Map Corp. (US-202), and Rand McNally (US-215).

Oklahoma City—Organizations

OK-7   OKLAHOMA CITY CONVENTION AND TOURISM CENTER, Three Santa Fe Plaza, Oklahoma City, OK 73102 (405/232-2211).

They issue an OKLAHOMA CITY AREA MAP, a general attractions brochure/map, a semiannual calendar of events, and ARTS ALIVE IN OKLAHOMA CITY (a brochure/map describing visual arts, performing arts, and participative arts). This is a walk-in information center.

OREGON

BOOKS, ATLASES, MAGAZINES

OR-1   Bedrick, Ed, and Bedrick, Christina.   177 FREE OREGON CAMP-
        GROUNDS. Lynnwood, WA: Signpost Publications, 1978.

        "Campsite facilities, driving directions, driving hazards for trailers,
        and recreational opportunities are given for each site."

OR-2   Corning, Howard M. OREGON: END OF THE TRAIL. Rev. ed.
        American Guide Series. Portland, OR: Binford & Mort, 1951. 549 p.
        Photos., maps. Bibliography. Index.

        This revision, which is itself in need of updating, of the original
        1940 WPA guide begins with a general discussion of the state from
        natural history to architecture, and then goes on to describe 11
        cities and towns, 10 highway tours, the Mount Hood and Crater Lakes
        areas and the national forests. There is a chronology of Oregon
        history.

OR-3   Feris, Charles M. HIKING THE OREGON SKYLINE: (THE PACIFIC
        CREST NATIONAL SCENIC TRAIL). Beaverton, OR: Touchstone
        Press, 1973. 160 p. Maps, photos. 0-911518-21-5. 73-80048.

        The author describes the 400 mile stretch of the Pacific Crest Trail
        that passes through Oregon where it is known as the Oregon Skyline
        Trail. This guide divides the trail into 22 sections and gives for
        each: road access; altitude; range and season; lodging, meals and
        supplies, campsites, and water information; a detailed trail description;
        and a reproduction of the appropriate USGS topographic map with the
        trail lined in. The book gives trail information going in both north/
        south and south/north directions, but the fullest descriptions occur in
        the former. The latter has many cross references to the fuller north/
        south section.

OR-4   Friedman, Ralph. OREGON FOR THE CURIOUS. 3d ed. Caldwell,
        ID: Caxton Printers, 1972. 246 p. Photos., maps. Index. 0-87004-
        222-X. 75-151057.

This highway guide gives distances from point to point and describes interesting places off the beaten path.

OR-5   Garren, John. OREGON RIVER TOURS. Edited by L.K. Phillips. Portland, OR: Binford & Mort, 1974. 120 p. Maps, photos. Bibliography. 0-8323-0243-0. 74-82937.

A trip narrative, map, and river log giving river miles and time to selected rapids and geographic points is provided for each of 13 river trips.

OR-6   Hawkins, Susan E., and Bleything, Dennis. BACKROADS & TRAILS: THE WILLAMETTE VALLEY. Beaverton, OR: Touchstone Press, 1976. 80 p. Photos., maps. 0-911518-42-8. 76-26309.

Hawkins and Bleything provide ". . .a guide to rural highway routes. . . a guide to forest roads suitable for a family car, and hikes worth driving to for only a day's use." Most of the 16 trips described include hikes as well as drives, and all were chosen as being suitable for a family with young children.

OR-7   Holm, Don. 101 BEST FISHING TRIPS IN OREGON. Caldwell, ID: Caxton Printers, 1970. 207 p. 0-87004-204-1. 79-109542.

This geographically arranged guide provides 101 answers to the question "Where's a good place to go fishin'?"

OR-8   Jankowski, Nick, and Jankowski, Elske. 55 OREGON BICYCLE TRIPS. Beaverton, OR: Touchstone Press, 1973. 127 p. Maps, photos. 0-911518-19-3. 73-80046.

Most of the routes are in the Willamette Valley and along the Oregon coast. A map, distance, riding time, traffic and road conditions, and a graph of elevation gain are included with each trip description.

OR-9   Lampman, Linda, et al. OREGON FOR ALL SEASONS: A MONTH BY MONTH GUIDE TO ACTIVITIES, HAPPENINGS AND EVENTS. Mercer Island, WA: The Writing Works, 1977. 161 p. Photos. Index. 0-916076-17-2. 77-18057.

Things to do and places to visit are briefly listed by season and month.

OR-10   Lowe, Don, and Lowe, Roberta. 100 OREGON HIKING TRAILS. Portland, OR: Touchstone Press, 1969. 240 p. Maps, photos. Index. 75-80014.

Descriptions include a reproduction of the appropriate USGS quadrangle with the trail marked in red, the name of the USGS quad to use, distance, elevation gain, highest elevation, and season to hike. It is geographically arranged with a name index.

OR-11 _____. 70 HIKING TRAILS: NORTHERN OREGON CASCADES. Beaverton, OR: Touchstone Press, 1974. 160 p. Maps, photos. 0-911518-29-0. 74-84378.

This is arranged exactly the same as the authors' other older Oregon hiking book (OR-10). Several of the trails are found in both books, but the descriptions have been rewritten for this book. This one also provides more trails for a smaller geographic area.

OR-12 Mainwaring, William L. EXPLORING THE OREGON COAST. Salem, OR: Westridge Press (distributed by Academic Book Center, Portland), 1977. 63 p. Photos., maps. 0-918832-01-2. 77-77250.

This north to south tour of the Oregon coast, with brief mentions of many points of interest along the way, has many color photographs.

OR-13 MUSEUMS AND SITES OF HISTORICAL INTEREST IN OREGON. 5th ed. Portland: Oregon Historical Society, 1977. 78 p. Bibliography. Index.

This geographically arranged guide with an alphabetical index of towns is revised every 2 years. It gives addresses, phone numbers, hours, admission fees, etc.

OR-14 Newman, Doug, and Sharrard, Sally. OREGON SKI TOURS. Beaverton, OR: Touchstone Press, 1973. 160 p. Maps, photos. 0-911518-18-5. 73-162790.

The authors give a description and a sketch map for each of 65 cross-country ski trails in Oregon.

OR-15 ROGUE RIVER CANYON: RIVER AND TRAIL GUIDE. Eugene, OR: Northwest Cartographics, 1976. Map. 35 in. x 23 in. Scale: 15/16 in. represents 1 mile.

". . .Northwest Cartographics has set a fine example by meeting this need of both 'river rats' and trail hikers. . . . The large-scale folding map. . .from Hog Creek boat landing to Agnes, 53 miles by river, includes all tributaries, rapids, and riffles as well as roads, trails, elevations. . ., campsites, lodges, and boating. . . ."

OR-16 Scofield, W.M. OREGON'S HISTORICAL MARKERS. Portland (?): Touchstone Press, 1966. 103 p. Photos.

OR-17 SUNSET TRAVEL GUIDE TO OREGON. By the editors of Sunset Books and Sunset Magazine. 3d ed. Menlo Park, CA: Lane Publishing Co., 1976. 160 p. Photos., maps. Index. 0-376-06613-X. 74-20020.

This guide to all of the attractions and outdoors of Oregon does not include restaurants and accommodations.

OR-18 Thollander, Earl. BACK ROADS OF OREGON. A Clarkson N. Potter Book. New York: Crown, 1979. Maps, sketches. 0-517-530694.

This is "a charming evocation of rural Oregon, highlighted by 189 black-and-white and color illustrations and 85 useful maps." See also the other books in this author's series listed elsewhere in this information guide.

OR-19 Tuggle, Joyce, and McCarthy, Nancy M. "NOW WHERE?": PLACES IN OREGON TO GO WITH KIDS. 2d ed. Forest Grove, OR: Timber Press (distributed by International Scholarly Book Service), 1977. 132 p. Index. 0-917304-06-3. 77-152539.

Places and activities are described in alphabetical order within geographical areas. Almost half of the book is devoted to the greater Portland area. It includes addresses, phone numbers, costs, and hours. There is a name index, but an index by type of activity would also have been useful.

MAPS

The Oregon official highway map is compiled, published, and distributed by the Dept. of Transportation (OR-20). The 1978 edition contains many insets and an interstate map. Symbols on the map locate state parks, rest areas, and winter sports areas. AAA (US-259), Exxon (US-261), and Rand McNally (US-215) each issue a combined Oregon/Washington map. Gousha (US-206) issues a separate Oregon map.

MAJOR TOURIST ORGANIZATION

OR-20 OREGON DEPT. OF TRANSPORTATION, TRAVEL INFORMATION SECTION, 101 Transportation Bldg., Salem, OR 97310 (503/378-6309).

They issue a large, general booklet that is mostly pretty pictures, a semiannual calendar of events, a directory of guest ranches, a climate brochure, a rockhounding guide, a golf course guide, and a MT. HOOD LOOP SCENIC HIGHWAY DRIVE brochure.

REGIONAL TOURISM ASSOCIATIONS

NORTHEAST OREGON VACATIONLAND, Box 308, La Grande, OR 97850.

They promote tourism and recreation in Baker, Union, and Wallowa Counties in the northeast corner of the state. They issue 2 brochures: the general SWITZERLAND OF AMERICA and SPORTSMEN'S MAP OF NORTHEAST OREGON, a very thorough guide to campgrounds, ski areas, trails, marinas, hunting, fishing, and boating.

OTHER ORGANIZATIONS

OR-21   THE OREGON COAST ASSOCIATION, Box 670, Newport, OR 97365.

They issue a TRAVELGUIDE WITH GUIDE MAPS which lists resorts and motels, restaurants, activities, galleries and crafts, RV and trailer parks, specialty shops, etc. along coastal route 101 going in a north to south direction. There is also a mileage log, and the detailed street maps of communities along the way should be quite useful.

OR-22   OREGON HOSPITALITY & VISITORS ASSOCIATION, 610 SW Broadway, Room 305, Portland, OR 97205 (503/227-1263).

Just about every brochure issued by the Travel Information Section (OR-20) and individual brochures on nearly all individual commercial attractions and establishments are available from this organization. They don't issue any material of their own. They also supply information on tours and tour packages to Oregon.

OR-23   OREGON HOTEL & MOTEL ASSOCIATION, 11933 SE Stark Street, Portland, OR 97216 (503/255-5135).

They issue an annual directory of motels, motor hotels, resorts, and RV parks. It's called the OREGON TRAVELER'S GUIDE.

INFORMATION CENTERS/INFORMATION PHONES

There are 6 staffed visitor information centers at the state borders on major roads. They are only open 6 months out of the year--May to October. There are also numerous Travel InfoCentres at various roadside rest areas throughout the state. They are unmanned, backlighted graphic displays telling where local lodging, restaurants, campgrounds, service stations, recreation, travel services, and scenic attractions may be found. Information on both the manned visitor information centers and the unmanned Travel InfoCentres may be obtained from the Dept. of Transportation (OR-20). Additional information on the Travel InfoCentres may be obtained from Travel InfoCentres, 5201 SW Westgate Drive, Suite 106, Portland, OR 97221 (503/292-2686). The Oregon Hospitality & Visitors Association (OR-22) has a toll-free number at 800/547-4901. It is available Monday-Friday, 8:30A.M.-5P.M.

OUTDOOR RECREATION ACTIVITIES

BICYCLING. OREGON BIKEWAYS is available from the Travel Information Section (OR-20). It lists and locates on a map the general locations of 74 developed bikeways. See also OR-8.

CANOEING AND BOATING. The State Marine Board, 3000 Market Street NE,

Oregon

#505, Salem, OR 97310 supplies several good brochures on boating. The U.S. Forest Service, Pacific Northwest Region, Box 3623, Portland, OR 97208 supplies a good map/brochure on THE ROGUE RIVER: WILD AND SCENIC. The U.S. Army Corps of Engineers, Portland District, Public Information, Box 2946, Portland, OR 97208 provides a good map/guide to 12 OREGON COASTAL HARBORS plus a map/guide, including camping information, to recreation areas they manage in the Willamette Valley and along the Columbia River. See also OR-5 and OR-15.

FISHING AND HUNTING. An OREGON SALMON FISHING brochure is available from the Travel Information Section (OR-20). See also OR-7.

WINTER ACTIVITIES. The Travel Information Section (OR-20) issues a WINTER FUN IN OREGON brochure that includes detailed information on where to go for downhill and cross-country skiing and snowmobiling. See also OR-14.

NATIONAL/STATE PARKS/FORESTS, ETC.

Crater Lake National Park

OR-24   Kirk, Ruth. EXPLORING CRATER LAKE COUNTRY. Seattle: University of Washington Press, 1975. 74 p. Photos., map. Index. 0-295-95393-4. 75-9506.

The geology, flora, fauna, and human history of the area around Crater Lake are presented by Ruth Kirk, one of the best outdoors writers. Sights to see and interesting excursions are described and located.

OR-25   Spring, Bob, et al. CRATER LAKE NATIONAL PARK, KLAMATH BASIN NATIONAL WILDLIFE REFUGES, LAVA BEDS NATIONAL MONUMENT. Seattle: Superior Publishing Co., 1975. 30 p. Photos., map. 75-321539.

This volume has magnificent photographs supplemented by a text which briefly gives history, geology, forests, trails, flowers, auto tours, the park in winter, and information on the Klamath Basin National Wildlife Refuges.

OR-26   CRATER LAKE NATIONAL PARK, Box 7, Crater Lake, OR 97604.

They issue a general map/brochure and information on camping, trails, and fishing. A newspaper called REFLECTIONS, listing activities and visitor services in the park, is published jointly by the Crater Lake Natural History Association and the Crater Lake Lodge Company. The Rim Village Exhibit Bldg. is the information center for the park.

For information on the 13 national forests in Oregon, and a map of the Oregon section of the Pacific Crest National Scenic Trail, write to the U.S. Forest Service, Pacific Northwest Region, Box 3623, Portland, OR 97208. A Cape Perpetua Visitor Center is located in Siuslaw National Forest at about the mid-way point along the Oregon coast.

The Travel Information Section (OR-20) issues OREGON PARKS which presents, in tabular form, data on facilities at almost 600 state parks, wayside or recrea-tion areas, U.S. Forest Service lands, National Park Service areas, Bureau of Land Management lands, county parks, state forests, power or timber company parks, and state safety rest areas. Unfortunately, the map to which each park is keyed isn't the easiest to read. The Travel Information Section also issues map/guides to individual state parks.

INDIVIDUAL CITIES OR AREAS

Portland—Printed Materials

OR-27   Haugen, Michael, and Busch, Richard. PORTLAND AFTER DARK. Portland: H.B. Thumbs, 1977. 224 p. Photos. Index. 77-367557.

OR-28   Hutchins, Nancy, and Meyer, Alice. PORTLAND IN YOUR POCKET. Forest Grove, OR: Timber Press (distributed by International Scholarly Book Service), 1976. 180 p. Maps, photos. Index. 0-917304-01-2.

This is "an essential guidebook for those who visit or live in Portland." The chapters on information; transportation; accommodations; museums and historic buildings; art galleries; parks and gardens; sightseeing; eating and drinking; theater, music, dance; sports and recreation; and shopping will be useful to the visitor.

OR-29   Lampman, Linda, and Sterling, Julie. THE PORTLAND GUIDEBOOK. Mercer Island, WA: The Writing Works, 1976. 216 p. Maps, photos. Index. 0-916076-02-4. 76-21789.

This is a complete guide to the city, including sightseeing; restaurants; entertainment; shopping; transportation; hotels/motels; sports and recrea-tion (broken down by 9 specific activities); parks; art; outlying areas of Mt. Hood, the Willamette Valley, and the coastline; where to take the children; etc.

OR-30   O'Donnell, Terence, and Vaughan, Thomas. PORTLAND: A HISTORI-CAL SKETCH AND GUIDE. Portland: Oregon Historical Society, 1976. 161 p. Photos., maps. Index. 0-87595-051-3. 76-251.

The historical sketch is found in the first 60 pages of this book. The remainder of the book describes 9 tours: 3 walking tours of Portland itself, 3 driving tours of the environs of Portland, and three 1-day tours from Portland. The tours concentrate on buildings of either historical or architectural significance.

OR-31   THE PORTLAND GUIDE. Portland: Richard E. Pulver, Publisher
(256 Westhills Mall, 4475 SW Scholls Ferry Road/97225).

This semimonthly guide to points of interest, restaurants, events, and
shopping has a more pleasing format, with less advertising clutter,
than many other guides of this kind. The maps are of better quality,
too.

OR-32   Russakov, Gloria. GUIDE TO EATING OUT IN PORTLAND. 2d ed.
Portland: New Oregon Publishers, 1975. 220 p. Index. 76-352096.

Address, phone number, hours, extent of bar service, and credit cards
accepted precede the description of each restaurant. The overall
book arrangement is into 3 chapters according to price range with a
fourth chapter headed "Lunch, Brunch & Munch."

Maps of Portland are available from Arrow Publishing Co. (US-199); Gousha
(US-206); Pittmon Maps-Oregon Blue Print Co., 930 SE Sandy Blvd., Portland,
OR 97214; and Rand McNally (US-215).

Portland—Organizations

OR-33   PORTLAND CHAMBER OF COMMERCE, VISITORS INFORMATION
CENTER, 824 SW 5th Avenue, Portland, OR 97204 (503/228-9411).

They issue a Portland tour map and guide, a hotel/motel guide, and
a list of industrial tours.

Salem—Printed Materials

Maps of Salem are available from Arrow Publishing Co. (US-199); Pittmon
Maps-Oregon Blue Print Co., 930 SE Sandy Blvd., Portland, OR 97214; and
The Tourmap Co., East 1104 57th Avenue, Spokane, WA 99203.

Salem—Organizations

OR-34   SALEM AREA CHAMBER OF COMMERCE, CONVENTION & VISITORS
BUREAU, 220 Cottage Street NE, Box 231, Salem, OR 97308 (503/
581-1466).

They issue a street map, general brochure, walking/driving tour guide,
motel guide, and restaurant and entertainment guide.

PENNSYLVANIA

BOOKS, ATLASES, MAGAZINES

PA-1   Burgwyn, Diana. THE 1776 GUIDE FOR PENNSYLVANIA. Harper
        Colophon Books. New York: Harper & Row, 1975. 248 p. 0-06-
        090420-8. 75-27195.

        Fifteen 1- and 2-day excursions are concisely described, noting
        hours and fees for the museums, railroads, mines, and other sights
        encountered. Despite the title, no special emphasis on Revolutionary
        War sites is apparent.

PA-2   GUIDE TO THE HISTORICAL MARKERS OF PENNSYLVANIA. 4th ed.
        Harrisburg: Pennsylvania Historical and Museum Commission, 1975.
        163 p. Photos.

        Arranged by county, this pamphlet reproduces the text of each marker
        erected by the Commission.

PA-3   Osler, Jack M. 50 GREAT MINI-TRIPS FOR PENNSYLVANIA.
        Dayton, OH: Media Ventures, 1978. 52 p. Photos., maps. 0-
        89645-007-4.

        Each page is devoted to describing a destination or area appropriate for
        a family weekend trip. These are arranged in order, beginning in
        Philadelphia and working westward across the state, allowing the trip
        planner to see what's available in larger regions. Severl neighboring-
        state trip suggestions are included at the end. Hours, fees, addresses,
        and phone numbers are provided. Since most of the suggestions are the
        standard ones, this guide is recommended for the first-time or inexperi-
        enced traveler. The author is the travel editor for the Dayton (Ohio)
        DAILY NEWS.

PA-4   PENNSYLVANIA: A GUIDE TO THE KEYSTONE STATE. American
        Guide Series. New York: Oxford University Press, 1940. 660 p.
        Photos., maps. Bibliography. Index.

        This original WPA guide in 3 parts--general background, descriptions of 18 major cities, and 20 mile-by-mile descriptions of the state's highways—is comprehensive but out of date. It concludes with a chronology of state history and a list of population figures for all towns from the 1940 Census.

PA-5   PENNSYLVANIA HIKING TRAILS. 7th ed. N.p.: Keystone Trails Association, 1974. 91 p. Maps.

Thirty-three trails in Pennsylvania and 1 (the Batona) in New Jersey are described. A list of member clubs and sources of general information are also included. An eighth edition was published in 1978.

PA-6   PENNSYLVANIA ILLUSTRATED. Camp Hill, PA: Pennsylvania Illustrated (17 South 19th Street/17011).

All types of articles about living in Pennsylvania are included in this bimonthly magazine: current interests, historical, where-to-go and what-to-do, fine dining, etc. Each issue has an extensive calendar of events. It has been issued since the summer of 1976.

PA-7   PENNSYLVANIA LANDMARKS OF THE REVOLUTION: A BICENTEN-NIAL GUIDEBOOK FOR VISITORS. Harrisburg (?): Bicentennial Commission of Pennsylvania, in cooperation with the Pennsylvania Historical and Museum Commission and the Pennsylvania Dept. of Transportation, 1976(?). 57 p. Photos., maps. Index.

This booklet describes (including name and address of administering agency, hours, charge, special events or activities) 27 Pennsylvania landmarks connected with the Revolutionary War.

PA-8   Puetz, C.J. PENNSYLVANIA: COUNTY MAPS AND RECREATION-AL GUIDE. Harrisburg: Pennsylvania Bureau of Maps, 1977(?). 147 p. Maps, drawings. Indexes.

Essentially this work consists of reproductions (at various scales) of the official transportation maps of each county with an overprinting indicating game lands, parks, and historical sites. Brief histories of the origins of each county, historical tidbits, and a lot of descriptions of wildlife are included. There is a table of facilities for state parks and a gazetteer.

PA-9   Steinmetz, Rollin C. ADVENTURES IN DINING AND INTERESTING PLACES TO VISIT. 2d ed. Lititz, PA: Places, 1975. 181 p. Drawings.

The author gives personal descriptions of 51 dining places throughout Pennsylvania.

MAPS

The official transportation map of Pennsylvania is available from the Pennsylvania Dept. of Transportation, Public Information Office, 109 Transportation and Safety Bldg., Harrisburg, PA 17120. The 1978 edition contains a list of sites and facilities in state parks, forests, historic parks, and national recreation and forest areas (excluding Allegheny National Forest); a list of historic sites and properties; and 18 different inset maps. AAA (US-259) issues a combined New Jersey/Pennsylvania map. Exxon (US-261), Gousha (US-206), and Rand McNally (US-215) each issue a separate Pennsylvania map. See also PA-8 and PA-12.

PUBLISHERS

PA-10 ENTERTAIN, INC., 8 East Lemon Street, Lititz, PA 17543 (717/626-4768).

Known by several names, this organization publishes several monograph guides and several monthly guides to events, shopping, dining, etc. for the central Pennsylvania area. All are individually listed in this chapter with the exception of TODAY magazine, a monthly guide to what to see and do in the Allentown/Bethlehem/Easton, and a similiar guide to the Pottstown/Reading areas.

MAJOR TOURIST ORGANIZATION

PA-11 PENNSYLVANIA DEPT. OF COMMERCE, BUREAU OF TRAVEL DEVELOPMENT, 431 South Office Bldg., Harrisburg, PA 17120 (717/787-5453).

They issue a CAMPGROUND GUIDE (a comprehensive guide to public and privately owned campgrounds), a quarterly calendar of events, and a directory of farm vacations.

OTHER ORGANIZATIONS

PA-12 DALTON RECREATION ASSOCIATION, Box 200, Dalton, PA 18414.

They issue OUTDOOR RECREATION FACILITIES maps, 18 in. x 24 in. sheets with mediocre county maps locating recreational sites on 1 side and facilities tables on the verso. At present, they are available for each of the following counties: Bradford, Carbon, Lackawanna, Luzerne, Monroe, Pike, Schuylkill, Sullivan, Susquehanna, Tioga, Wayne, and Wyoming.

PA-13 PENNSYLVANIA ATTRACTIONS AND TRAVEL ASSOCIATION, Box 801, Harrisburg, PA 17108.

This is an association of privately owned, commercially operated (for the most part) attractions formed to promote tourism in the state. They issue a map/brochure describing the attractions of members.

PA-14   PENNSYLVANIA HOTEL-MOTOR INN ASSOCIATION, 500 North
         Progress Avenue, Harrisburg, PA 17109 (717/657-0703).

PA-15   TRAVEL PENNSYLVANIA ASSOCIATION, Payne Shoemaker Bldg.,
         240 North Third Street, Harrisburg, PA 17107 (717/234-5564 or 717/
         233-8471).

         This is an association of all the county promotion agencies whose pur-
         pose is to lobby for state funds to promote tourism. They issue an
         annual county-by-county visitors guide with 3 supplements: an accom-
         modations guide, a dining guide, and a recreation guide.

INFORMATION CENTERS/INFORMATION PHONES

The Pennsylvania Dept. of Transportation, Public Information Office, 109 Transportation and Safety Bldg., Harrisburg, PA 17120 issues a list and map of highway information centers.

OUTDOOR RECREATION ACTIVITIES

BICYCLING. See PA-21, PA-31, and PA-41.

CANOEING AND BOATING. CANOE COUNTRY, PENNSYLVANIA STYLE,
a map/brochure describing popular waterways, is available from the Pennsyl-
vania Dept. of Environmental Resources, Box 1467, Harrisburg, PA 17120.
CANOEING IN THE DELAWARE AND SUSQUEHANNA RIVER WATERSHEDS
OF PENNSYLVANIA, by Jeff Wilhoyt, is available from American Youth Hostels,
Pittsburgh Council, 6300 Fifth Avenue, Pittsburgh, PA 15232. BOATING
GUIDE TO PENNSYLVANIA WATERS is available from the Pennsylvania Fish
Commission, Bureau of Waterways, Box 1673, Harrisburg, PA 17120. It is a
county directory of access areas, installations, ramps, and facilities. See also
PA-12, PA-34, and PA-48.

FISHING AND HUNTING. The Pennsylvania Game Commission, Public Information Office, Box 1567, Harrisburg, PA 17120 issues 6 regional guides (northeast, southeast, northcentral, southcentral, northwest, southwest) to state game
lands; individual county maps showing lands available for public hunting; and
maps of individual game land tracts showing roads, towns, and prominent natural
land features, as well as descriptions of prevalent game species. The Pennsylvania Fish Commission, Box 1673, Harrisburg, PA 17120 issues a LIST OF
PENNSYLVANIA FISHING WATERS, a regional list (with county index) of all
fishing waters and the types of fish that will be caught at each. See also
PA-8 and PA-12.

WINTER ACTIVITIES. The Bureau of Travel Development (PA-11) issues SKI
PENNSYLVANIA, a directory of ski areas. An annual SNOWMOBILE TRAIL

DIRECTORY and regional snowmobile trail maps are available from the Pennsylvania Dept. of Environmental Resources, Snowmobile Unit, Box 1467, Harrisburg, PA 17120. There is a "Snowmobile Hotline" in operation from December to March; the phone number changes from year to year.

NATIONAL/STATE PARKS/FORESTS, ETC.

Gettysburg National Military Park

PA-16   GETTYSBURG NATIONAL MILITARY PARK, Box 70, Gettysburg, PA 17325.

They issue a general park map/brochure which shows an auto tour, 2 bike tours, a bridle trail, a foot trail, and other visitor services; a brochure outlining a walking tour through the Gettysburg National Cemetery; and a visitor's newspaper, "Four Score & Seven. . .," which describes the various interpretive programs of the park. The visitor center is open daily and has extended evening hours in the summer. In addition to regular information services, they provide (for a fee) licensed battlefield guides that will go with you in your car. There is also a self-guiding auto tour. There is an electric map program housed in the center.

PA-17   GETTYSBURG TRAVEL COUNCIL, Official Information Center, Carlisle & Railroad Streets, Gettysburg, PA 17325 (717/334-6274).

They issue a 31-page information guide describing each day of the battle, attractions, tours, accommodations, campgrounds, restaurants, a downtown Gettysburg walking tour, and various other tour materials and maps. They also operate a walk-in information center at the Carlisle & Railroad Streets address. An auto tape tour (CA-80) is available for rental at the National Civil War Wax Museum, Steinwehr Avenue and Culp Street in Gettysburg.

Independence National Historic Park

PA-18   INDEPENDENCE NATIONAL HISTORICAL PARK, 311 Walnut Street, Philadelphia, PA 19106 (215/597-8974).

They issue a general park map/brochure, and there is a visitor center at Chestnut and Third Streets.

Valley Forge National Historic Park

PA-19   VALLEY FORGE NATIONAL HISTORICAL PARK, Valley Forge, PA 19481 (215/783-7700).

They issue a general map/brochure which includes a bike trail and locations of other visitor facilities; information on foot and horse trails, sledding and cross-country skiing, and fishing; and a calendar of events. There is a visitor center at Route 363 and Outer Line Drive. It is open daily from 8:30A.M.-5P.M.

PA-20 MONTGOMERY COUNTY CONVENTION AND VISITORS BUREAU, One Montgomery Plaza, Suite 207, Norristown, PA 19401 (215/275-0525 or 275-5000).

This association provides good brochures for the Valley Forge area: VISITORS GUIDE, VALLEY FORGE IN A DAY (a tour guide of the Park), a quarterly calendar of events, and a guide to restaurants. It operates an information service, weekends in March and daily in the peak season, in the reception center in Valley Forge Park. The telephone number there is 215/783-0675.

Information and maps on Pennsylvania's only national forest are available from the Forest Supervisor, Allegheny National Forest, Box 847, Warren, PA 16365. A HIKER'S GUIDE TO THE ALLEGHENY NATIONAL FOREST (1977, 96 p.) containing maps and photographs is available from the Sierra Club, Allegheny Group, Box 7404, Pittsburgh, PA 15213.

The Pennsylvania Dept. of Environmental Resources, Bureau of State Parks, Box 1467, Harrisburg, PA 17120 issues PENNSYLVANIA STATE PARKS RECREATION GUIDE, a comprehensive guide to facilities and recreation activities at each state park; and individual maps of the state parks. The Pennsylvania Dept. of Environmental Resources, Division of State Forest Management, Box 1467, Harrisburg, PA 17120 issues a public use map of each state forest on which state forest, park, and game lands; streams and other waters; roads; trails; and vistas are shown. In some cases individual trail maps are available at each state forest. See also the CAMPGROUND GUIDE issued by the Bureau of Travel Development (PA-11).

INDIVIDUAL CITIES OR AREAS

Harrisburg/Pennsylvania Dutch Area/Central Pennsylvania— Printed Materials

PA-21 Barton-Aschman Associates. BIKE TRIPS: SOUTHCENTRAL PENNSYL-VANIA. Harrisburg: Pennsylvania Dept. of Community Affairs, 1976. 17 items. Maps.

This packet describes 14 selected bike tours in detail with accompanying maps noting length, difficulty, points of interest, and road conditions.

PA-22 Carnahan, Peter. THE EARLY AMERICAN SOCIETY GUIDE TO CENTRAL PENNSYLVANIA. Gettysburg, PA: The Early American Society,

1975. 115 p. Photos., maps. Bibliography.

Places to visit, walking and driving tours, places to stay and dine, and information centers are copiously described for Harrisburg, Lancaster (county and city), York, and Gettysburg and, in lesser numbers, for Caledonia, Chambersburg, and Carlisle. It also has brief lists of antique shops and flea markets.

PA-23   KEYNOTE MAGAZINE. Lititz, PA: Entertain, Inc.

This is a monthly information bulletin on where-to-go and what-to-see in the Harrisburg/Hershey/Carlisle areas. It includes dining, theater, art exhibits, shopping, nightly entertainment, and lodgings.

PA-24   Steinmetz, Rollin C., ed. GUIDE TO LANCASTER AND SOUTH-CENTRAL PENNSYLVANIA. Lititz, PA: Lancaster Guide, 1973. 218 p. Photos. Index. 73-166098.

This is a very complete guide to staying in and exploring the Lancaster County area with separate chapters on Hershey, Harrisburg, Gettysburg, York, Carlisle, Lebanon, Berks County, and Chester County.

PA-25   Steinmetz, Ron. RESTAURANT GUIDE. Lititz, PA: Entertain, Inc., 1978. Issued annually. 54 p.

The author describes 36 "fine" restaurants in the central Pennsylvania area.

PA-26   THIS MONTH MAGAZINE. Lititz, PA: Entertain, Inc.

This monthly guide to what to see and do in the Lancaster/York/Hershey area is mainly a calendar of events with theater, art exhibits, nightly entertainment and lodging listings.

Maps of Harrisburg are available from Arrow Publishing Co. (US-199) and Champion Map Corp. (US-202). Champion Map Corp. issues a map of Lancaster.

Harrisburg/Pennsylvania Dutch Area/Central Pennsylvania— Organizations

PA-27   GREATER HARRISBURG AREA CHAMBER OF COMMERCE, 114 Walnut Street, Harrisburg, PA 17101 (717/232-4121).

PA-28   PENNSYLVANIA DUTCH TOURIST BUREAU, 1800 Hempstead Road, Rt. 30 East, Lancaster, PA 17601 (717/393-9705).

There is a walk-in information center at this address. They issue an OFFICIAL DUTCH COUNTRY TOUR GUIDE map and numerous brochures about specific attractions, including information on an auto-tape tour rental (CA-80).

Pennsylvania

See also PA-16 and PA-17.

Philadelphia/Delaware Valley—Printed Materials

PA-29   Alexandria Drafting Co. PHILADELPHIA, PA & VICINITY STREET
MAP. 2d ed. Alexandria, VA: Alexandria Drafting, 1977. 44 p.
Scale: 1 in. represents 2000 ft. Index.

PA-30   Appelbaum, Madelyn, and Goodwin, Patricia, eds. ENJOY PHILA-
DELPHIA: PHILADELPHIA MAGAZINE'S GUIDE. Rev. ed. Philadelphia: Philadelphia Magazine (distributed by Chilton Book Co.),
1976. 368 p. Photos., maps. Index.

The authors describe walking and driving tours of historic sites within
Philadelphia and also in Valley Forge, the Brandywine Valley, and
Bucks County. Present-day points of interest within the city including
the arts, sports, shopping, dining, night life, and those for children
are described. There are chapters on touring the Pennsylvania Dutch
country and on day trips.

PA-31   Bicycle & Pedestrian Transportation Research Center. BIKE TRIPS:
SOUTHEASTERN PENNSYLVANIA. Harrisburg: Pennsylvania Dept. of
Community Affairs, 1976. 16 items. Maps.

This packet of 14 bike tours described in detail with accompanying
maps (at various scales) also notes distance, traffic, terrain, and
points of interest.

PA-32   Carter, Annette. EXPLORING FROM CHESAPEAKE BAY TO THE
POCONOS. Rev. ed. Philadelphia: Lippincott, 1975. 270 p.
Photos., maps. Index. 0-397-01099-0. 75-14092.

This is a compilation of 29 offbeat and uncommercial tours within a
150-mile radius of Philadelphia. Areas outside Philadelphia include
Delaware, southern New Jersey, the Chesapeake Bay, Maryland and
the eastern shore, and Virginia. Numerous sources for further information are also included.

PA-33   Curson, Julie P. A GUIDE'S GUIDE TO PHILADELPHIA. Rev. ed. Philadelphia: Curson House, 1978. 446 p. Maps, drawings. Index.
0-913694-03-7. 76-57914.

One of the very best guidebooks, this covers attractions and sights in
the Philadelphia area, giving for each (where applicable) address,
telephone number, hours, fees, special features and attractions, nearest public transportation, on-site or nearby eating facilities, and
special information for the elderly and handicapped. Unusual and
offbeat attractions as well as the traditional ones are covered, and
there are sections on cultural features, lodgings, restaurants, recreation,
events, transportation, and religious activities.

PA-34 DELAWARE RIVER RECREATIONAL MAPS. Trenton, NJ: Delaware
River Basin Commission, 1966. 10 sheets in folder (11 in. x 28 in.
each sheet). Scale: 5 in. represents about 3 miles.

Ten sectional maps of the Delaware River from Hancock, NY to
Trenton, NJ indicate the location of the stream channel (with depth),
riffles and rapids, private and public access areas, forest cover, and
recreation areas. Streamflow characteristics are noted by a code indicating difficulty. Each sheet has a brief text giving a general description, recreational opportunities, recreational areas, and river access areas. This is very good--we've used it.

PA-35 Gales, Ruth L., and Loewenson, Diane F. BICENTENNIAL PHILA-
DELPHIA: A FAMILY GUIDE TO THE CITY AND COUNTRYSIDE.
Philadelphia: Lippincott, 1974. 424 p. Sketches, maps. Index.
0-397-00898-8. 74-9937.

This is a very thorough guide to the city and surrounding areas, with
emphasis on things to do with the family. It is still very useful despite the passing of the Bicentennial and the use of that word in the
title of this book. Places to visit are arranged by type from historic
sites, to arboretums, to shops and services, and descriptions include
phone number, admission information, and transportation directions.
There are chapters on facilities for the handicapped and one which
gives a monthly calendar of events. The surrounding areas include
the adjacent Pennsylvania counties, Delaware, and the Pennsylvania
Dutch country.

PA-36 GUIDE TO PHILADELPHIA FOR THE HANDICAPPED. Bicentennial ed.
Philadelphia: Mayor's Office for the Handicapped (City Hall Annex,
Room 427/19103), 1976(?). 45 p.

A new edition is expected.

PA-37 Hogarth, Paul. PAUL HOGARTH'S WALKING TOURS OF OLD
PHILADELPHIA: THROUGH INDEPENDENCE SQUARE, SOCIETY
HILL, SOUTHWARK AND WASHINGTON SQUARE. Barre, MA:
Barre Publishing Co. (distributed by Crown), 1976. 154 p. Draw-
ings, maps. Index. 0-517-52384-1. 75-30967.

This book includes 6 walking tours lasting from 2 hours to all day,
describing the historical and architectural points of interest plus
practical visiting information, location on a map, and a watercolor
sketch by the author.

PA-38 Kelly, Patrick. PLACES TO GO AND THINGS TO DO WITH THE
KIDS IN PHILADELPHIA. Philadelphia: LP Productions (6510 Buist
Street/19142), 1978. Photos. Index.

This guide includes participant sports, amusement parks, attractions for
children, industrial tours, historical sights, shopping, entertainment,

instructional classes, clubs, places within a days drive of Philadelphia, and much more. Hours, admission charges, phone numbers, and other practical information is also included.

PA-39   Marion, John F. BICENTENNIAL CITY: WALKING TOURS OF HISTORIC PHILADELPHIA. Princeton, NJ: Pyne Press, 1974. 210 p. Photos., maps. Index. 0-87861-066-9. 73-91977.

The author describes 12 walks around Philadelphia from Independence Square to Germantown pointing out historic houses and buildings and giving consideration to their "history, architecture, myth, legend, folklore, and anecdote."

PA-40   Museum Council of Philadelphia. GUIDE TO MUSEUMS IN THE DELAWARE VALLEY. Edited by Nancy Cramer and Laurie Gearhart. Cranberry, NJ: A.S. Barnes & Co., 1976. 122 p. Photos., maps. 0-498-01952-7. 76-4180.

Descriptions, houts, admission charges, phones, and finding directions are given for 84 museums in northern Delaware, southeastern Pennsylvania, and southwestern New Jersey.

PA-41   Nixdorf, Bert. HIKES AND BIKE RIDES FOR THE DELAWARE VALLEY AND SOUTH JERSEY. Mount Holly, NJ: the author, 1976. 140 p. Maps, photos. Index.

This guide includes exact route descriptions of numerous hikes, suitable for either biking or on foot, in the greater Philadelphia area and southern New Jersey. Other information frequently given for each hike includes: terrain, parking areas, places of interest, eating establishments, and maps to use. It also includes lists of both bike and hiking clubs. It is confusingly arranged, but a locality index helps.

PA-42   AN ORIGINAL GUIDE TO PUBLIC & PRIVATE REST ROOMS PLUS A COMPREHENSIVE LIST OF HISTORIC SITES, PLACES OF INTEREST. Westmont, NJ: W.E. Hoover (08108), 1976. 31 p.

This was prepared for the Bicentennial when the preparer of this guide obtained agreement from numerous establishments (those listed in this guide) to freely offer to the public the use of their rest rooms. Such use may no longer be available, nor may this guide, but if both are, the guide may prove indispensable. It covers Philadelphia, Bucks and Delaware Counties in Pennsylvania, and Camden, Burlington, and Gloucester Counties in New Jersey. The list of points of interest is negligible.

PA-43   Tait, Elaine. BEST RESTAURANTS: PHILADELPHIA & ENVIRONS. San Francisco: 101 Productions, 1979. 225 p. Sketches. Index. 0-89286-150-9.

This work "includes critical reviews of over 100 restaurants in all price ranges with many menus reproduced." The author writes a regular restaurant column for THE PHILADELPHIA INQUIRER.

Good maps of Philadelphia are available from AAA (US-259); Champion Map Corp. (US-202); Exxon (US-261); Franklin Survey, 1201 Race Street, Philadelphia, PA 19107; Gousha (US-206); Hagstrom Co. (US-207); Rand McNally (US-215); and the Southeastern Pennsylvania Transportation Authority, 200 West Wyoming Avenue, Philadelphia, PA 19140. See also PA-29 and PA-34.

The Philadelphia weather information number is 215/936-1212.

Philadelphia/Delaware Valley—Organizations

PA-44   PHILADELPHIA CONVENTION AND TOURIST BUREAU, 1525 John F. Kennedy Blvd., Philadelphia, PA 19102 (215/864-1976).

This is an information center open daily from 9A.M.-5P.M. It issues a VISITORS GUIDE AND HOSPITALITY DIRECTORY, a very thorough quarterly listing of events, a guide to restaurants, a motoring guide to the Liberty Trail, an historic and scenic tour of southeastern Pennsylvania, a guide to hotels and motor inns, and an OFFICIAL MAP OF PHILADELPHIA which has a center city map, a regional map, and an Atlantic City region map. They also sponsor a 24-hour recorded message, "What's Happening in Philadelpia," at 215/864-1990.

See also PA-18, PA-19, and PA-20.

Pittsburgh/Western Pennsylvania—Printed Materials

PA-45   Bruner, Ronald, ed. GILBERT LOVE'S GO GUIDE. Pittsburgh: The Pittsburgh Press, 1976. 119 p. Photos., maps, sketches. Indexes.

This is a regionally arranged guide "to fun and culture within 150 miles of Pittsburgh." There is a chapter on weekend trips and indexes by attraction name and by interest from amusement parks to zoos.

PA-46   A GUIDE TO PITTSBURGH FOR THE HANDICAPPED. Pittsburgh: Open Doors for the Handicapped (1013 Brintell Street/15201), 1962. 84 p.

A new edition is planned.

PA-47   IDEAL ATLAS OF PITTSBURGH AND VICINITY: INCLUDING MAP OF 55 MILES ABOUT PITTSBURGH, COMPLETE STREET INDEX. Rev. ed. New York: Geographia Map Co., 1976. 48 p. Scale: 3 in. represents 4,000 ft. Index. 76-375844.

PA-48   Spindt, Katherine M., and Shaw, Mary. CANOEING GUIDE:

WESTERN PENNSYLVANIA AND NORTHERN WEST VIRGINIA. 6th ed. Pittsburgh: American Youth Hostels, Pittsburgh Council (6300 Fifth Avenue/15232), 1975. 164 p. Photos., maps.

The detailed descriptions of 50 rivers and creeks note especially difficult spots, list relevant maps, note gradient and dry periods, give "scenery/pollution" ratings, and list lakes and reservoirs where canoeing is permitted. The appendixes note associations and groups, information sources, and outfitters.

PA-49 Sundquist, Bruce, and Ham, Clifford C., comps. HIKING GUIDE TO WESTERN PENNSYLVANIA. 3d ed. Pittsburgh: American Youth Hostels, Pittsburgh Council (6300 Fifth Avenue/15232), 1974. 148 p. Maps, photos. Bibliography.

As well as containing general information on hiking in western Pennsylvania (including a list of organizations), this work describes 147 hikes in western Pennsylvania and 29 in adjoining West Virginia, Maryland, Ohio, and New York. A fourth edition was published in 1977.

PA-50 Swetnam, George, and Smith, Helene. A GUIDEBOOK TO HISTORIC WESTERN PENNSYLVANIA. Pittsburgh: University of Pittsburgh Press, 1976. 292 p. Maps, photos. 0-8229-3316-0. 75-33421.

The authors give brief descriptions, hours, admission charges, and locations of approximately 1,300 historic landmarks still standing in 26 western Pennsylvania counties, including the city of Pittsburgh.

Maps of Pittsburgh are available from AAA (US-259), Champion Map Corp. (US-202), Exxon (US-261), Goushā (US-206), and Rand McNally (US-215). See also PA-47.

The Pittsburgh weather information number is 412/936-1212.

Pittsburgh/Western Pennsylvania—Organizations

PA-51 GREATER PITTSBURGH CHAMBER OF COMMERCE, 411 Seventh Avenue, Pittsburgh, PA 15219 (412/391-3400).

They issue A VISITOR'S HANDBOOK TO PITTSBURGH which includes a packet of brochures on things to see and do, maps, and a public transit guide.

PA-52 PITTSBURGH CONVENTION & VISITORS BUREAU, 200 Roosevelt Bldg., Pittsburgh, PA 15222 (412/281-7711).

They issue PITTSBURGH TODAY (a 96-page profile in pictures, an indexed directory, and 5 area maps for visitors), YOU'LL LOVE PITTSBURGH (a visitor's map with guide), a quarterly calendar of events, PITTSBURGH IN YOUR POCKET (self-tours of the Golden Triangle and Mt. Washington), and THE FRENCH AND INDIAN TRAIL. An information center is located at Liberty Avenue and Stanwix Street in Gateway Center. The telephone number there is 412/281-9222.

Pocono Mountains—Printed Materials

PA-53   Knepp, Thomas H. THE POCONOS: A HANDBOOK AND GUIDE TO PENNSYLVANIA'S VACATIONLAND. 6th ed. Stroudsburg, PA: the author (706 Scott Street/18360), 1975. 146 p. Photos., map. Index.

This is a very thorough guide to the Poconos' physical features, history, things to see and do, camps, wildlife, hunting and fishing, and skiing.

A map of the Pocono Mountains Area is available from AAA (US-259).

Pocono Mountains—Organizations

PA-54   POCONO MOUNTAIN VACATION BUREAU, 1004 Main Street, Stroudsburg, PA 18360 (717/421-5791).

They issue POCONO MOUNTAINS OF PENNSYLVANIA: A COMPLETE YEAR 'ROUND TRAVEL GUIDE (the most thorough guide to resorts, golf courses, campgrounds, ski areas, attractions, restaurants, and vacation homesites; the centerfold has a map and brief travel information), PRIVATE CAMPGROUNDS OF THE POCONO MOUNTAINS, SKI THE POCONOS, POCONO ATTRACTIONS, and a monthly calendar of events. They operate 6 tourist information centers. There are 4 open year-round, and 2 are open in the summer only. Their locations and phone numbers will be found in the centefold of the VACATION GUIDE mentioned above.

RHODE ISLAND

BOOKS, ATLASES, MAGAZINES

RI-1   Arrow Publishing Co. OFFICIAL ARROW STREET MAP ATLAS, RHODE
        ISLAND AND SOUTHERN MASSACHUSETTS. Newton Upper Falls,
        MA: Arrow, 1976. 104 p. Scales vary. Index. 77-367467.

RI-2   A GUIDE TO RHODE ISLAND FOR THE HANDICAPPED. East Provi-
        dence: Easter Seal Society of Rhode Island (667 Waterman Avenue/
        02914), 1968.

        A new edition is planned for 1980.

RI-3   RHODE ISLAND: A GUIDE TO THE SMALLEST STATE. American
        Guide Series. Boston: Houghton Mifflin, 1937. 500 p. Photos.,
        maps.

        This original WPA guide in 3 parts--general background, descriptions
        of 7 major cities, and mile-by-mile tour descriptions of the state's
        highways--is comprehensive, but out of date.

RI-4   Steinberg, Sheila, and McGuigan, Cathleen. RHODE ISLAND: AN
        HISTORICAL GUIDE. Providence: Rhode Island Bicentennial Founda-
        tion, 1976. 284 p. Drawings, maps. Index. 0-917012-07-0. 76-
        8800.

        "For tourists. . .the book fills a practical need by providing the most
        up-to-date information about Rhode Island's important historic sites.
        For the Rhode Island citizen, the book presents a fresh look at his
        historical and architectural heritage. . . ." It is regionally arranged
        with an extensive 24-page index and will be of interest mainly to
        architectural buffs.

MAPS

The official map of Rhode Island is available from the Tourist Promotion Division
(RI-5). The 1978-79 edition lists salt water and fresh water beaches; golf and

country clubs; yacht clubs, harbors, and basins; monuments and statues; trout ponds and streams; parks; ski areas; points of interest; and game sanctuaries and preserves. A very good RHODE ISLAND RECREATION MAP, which keys in fresh and salt water beaches; golf and country clubs; yacht clubs, harbors, and basins; boat launching sites and yards; stocked trout ponds and streams; ski areas; camping sites; hiking trails; horseback trails; archery and rifle ranges; canoeing areas; hunting areas; and state park areas and facilities is available from the Rhode Island Dept. of Natural Resources, Division of Parks and Recreation, 83 Park Street, Providence, RI 02903. AAA (US-259), Gousha (US-206), and Rand McNally (US-215) each issue a combined Connecticut/Massachusetts/Rhode Island map. See also RI-1.

MAJOR TOURIST ORGANIZATION

RI-5   RHODE ISLAND DEPT. OF ECONOMIC DEVELOPMENT, TOURIST PROMOTION DIVISION, One Weybosset Hill, Providence, RI 02903 (401/277-2601).

They issue an annual RHODE ISLAND GUIDE (includes a detailed calendar of events by type of activity, points of interest, where to stay, and transportation and tour service information) and an annual camping guide. RHODE ISLAND'S VACATION CLIMATE (prepared by 2 branches of the National Oceanic and Atmospheric Administration-- the Environmental Data Service's Oceanographic Data Center and the Sea Grant Marine Advisory Service of the University of Rhode Island-- in cooperation with the Dept. of Economic Development) provides information on the state's vacation weather, sailing weather, boating, fishing, and other outdoor activities.

OTHER ORGANIZATIONS

RI-6   RHODE ISLAND HOTEL-MOTEL ASSOCIATION, Sheraton Hotel & Motor Inn, 1850 Post Road, US Route 1, Warwick, RI 02886 (401/738-8220).

INFORMATION CENTERS/INFORMATION PHONES

A list of state-wide tourist and visitor information centers and telephone numbers will be found in the RHODE ISLAND GUIDE available from the Tourist Promotion Division (RI-5). The division also has a toll-free telephone number available Monday-Friday from 8:30A.M.-4:30P.M. for residents from Maine to Virginia: 800/556-2484. In Connecticut call 203/566-3977.

OUTDOOR RECREATION ACTIVITIES

CANOEING AND BOATING. BOATING IN RHODE ISLAND lists statewide yachting and boating facilities; boat launching sites; yacht harbors and basins; boating services suppliers; waterside dining spots; yacht clubs; and pleasure, charter, and party boats and is available from the Tourist Promotion Division (RI-5). See also RHODE ISLAND'S VACATION CLIMATE described in RI-5 above.

FISHING AND HUNTING. The Rhode Island Division of Fish and Wildlife, Washington County Government Center, Tower Hill Road, Wakefield, RI 02879 supplies individual maps of each land management area where hunting is allowed. The Tourist Promotion Division (RI-5) issues a brochure on salt water sport fishing. See also the RHODE ISLAND RECREATION MAP described in the "Maps" section of this chapter.

WINTER ACTIVITIES. The Tourist Promotion Division (RI-5) issues a winter recreation brochure.

NATIONAL/STATE PARKS/FORESTS, ETC.

There are no major national parks and no national forests in Rhode Island.

For information on state parks and forests see the RHODE ISLAND RECREA-TION MAP described in the "Maps" section of this chapter and the camping guide available from the Tourist Promotion Division (RI-5).

INDIVIDUAL CITIES OR AREAS

Newport—Printed Materials

RI-7 Formwalt, Elizabeth, and Formwalt, John. A VISITOR'S GUIDE TO AQUIDNECK ISLAND. Middletown, RI: Aquidneck Press (Box 52/ 02840), 1976. 50 p. Photos., maps. 76-150966.

  Although claiming to cover all of Aquidneck Island, four-fifths of this small book is devoted to Newport. Coverage is devoted mostly to places of historic interest, but the person interested specifically in the buildings of Newport will find the Randall (RI-8) guide more thorough. Other areas covered are Middletown, Portsmouth, and the beaches.

RI-8 Randall, Anne. NEWPORT: A TOUR GUIDE. Newport: Catboat Press (Box 673/02840), 1970. 120 p. Photos., maps. Bibliography. Index. 0-912210-01-X. 76-128562.

  This is "a pictorial guide to the architecture of Newport. . .prepared in the form of walking tours." There is a glossary.

Newport—Organizations

RI-9   NEWPORT COUNTY CHAMBER OF COMMERCE, Ten America's Cup
Avenue (Long Wharf Mall), Newport, RI 02840 (401/847-1600).

They issue an annual NEWPORT COUNTY, RHODE ISLAND VISITOR'S
GUIDE (describes points of interest, has a calendar of events, and
lists and has numerous advertisements for local business establishments
and services), a visitor's map, a list of places to stay and eat, and
a brochure describing available tour services. An auto cassette tape
tour, also suitable for bikers, is available for rent here. This address is also a walk-in information center. It is open 7 days a week,
year-round in the summer from 9A.M.-6P.M. and in the winter from
9A.M.-5P.M.

Providence—Printed Materials

Maps of Providence are available from Arrow Publishing Co. (US-199) and
Champion Map Corp. (US-202).

Providence—Organizations

RI-10   GREATER PROVIDENCE CHAMBER OF COMMERCE, 10 Dorrance Street,
Providence, RI 02903 (401/274-1636).

SOUTH CAROLINA

BOOKS, ATLASES, MAGAZINES

SC-1   Arrow Publishing Co. OFFICIAL ARROW STREET MAP ATLAS OF
        OVER 65 SOUTH CAROLINA CITIES AND TOWNS. Newton Upper
        Falls, MA: Arrow, 1976. 99 p. Scales vary. Indexes. 77-367462.

SC-2   SANDLAPPER: THE MAGAZINE OF SOUTH CAROLINA. Columbia,
        SC: Greystone Publisher (305 Greystone Blvd./29202).

        This is a monthly magazine devoted to living in South Carolina.
        Since 1977, the April issue has been devoted to a travel guide.

SC-3   Sloan, Eugene B. SCENIC SOUTH CAROLINA. 2d ed. Columbia,
        SC: Lewis-Sloan Publishing Co., 1971. 228 p. Photos. Index.
        0-911432-00-0. 79-183143.

        This is best used only as an introduction to the scenic attractions of
        South Carolina. Descriptions are very general, and specific informa-
        tion about locations, hours, fees, etc. is lacking. The areas are
        covered in a haphazard order, but there is a name index.

SC-4   SOUTH CAROLINA: A GUIDE TO THE PALMETTO STATE. American
        Guide Series. New York: Oxford University Press, 1941. 514 p.
        Photos., maps.

        This is the original WPA guide in the usual format of this series:
        general background, descriptions of 12 cities and towns, and 21 state-
        wide highway tours. It is comprehensive, but out of date.

SC-5   Spence, Edward L. SPENCE'S GUIDE TO SOUTH CAROLINA. Sulli-
        van's Island, SC: the author, 1976. 146 p. Photos., maps. 76-
        22270.

        The author, an underwater archaeologist, describes the best locations
        in South Carolina to go shipwreck diving, saltwater sport fishing,

shrimping, crabbing, oystering, and clamming. The book includes tables listing facilities at campgrounds and boat landings. Five inset maps show artificial reefs, oyster beds, campgrounds, and best shrimping and crabbing locations.

MAPS

The SOUTH CAROLINA STATE HIGHWAY PRIMARY SYSTEM MAP is available from the South Carolina State Highway Dept., Box 191, Columbia, SC 29202. The 1978 edition lists points of interest, historical sites, and art galleries. AAA (US-259), Exxon (US-261), Gousha (US-206), and Rand McNally (US-215) each issue a combined North Carolina/South Carolina map. See also SC-1.

MAJOR TOURIST ORGANIZATION

SC-6   SOUTH CAROLINA DEPT. OF PARKS, RECREATION AND TOURISM, DIVISION OF TOURISM, Box 71, Room 30, Columbia, SC 29202 (803/758-2279).

They issue SOUTH CAROLINA POINTS OF INTEREST, SOUTH CAROLINA EVENTS (issued annually), SOUTH CAROLINA ACCOMMODATIONS DIRECTORY, SOUTH CAROLINA CAMPING (a list, with map, of state park, privately owned, and federal campgrounds and facilities), SOUTH CAROLINA STATE PARKS (gives descriptions of parks, facilities, and cabin rentals), SOUTH CAROLINA BEACHES, SOUTH CAROLINA GOLF AND TENNIS, JEFFERSON DAVIS TRAIL, and GEORGE WASHINGTON TRAIL (these last 2 publications show the routings of each respective trail and are keyed to highway signs). Many of these publications have been taped for use by the blind and are available to South Carolinians who are registered with the South Carolina State Library, Division for the Blind and Physically Handicapped.

OTHER ORGANIZATIONS

SC-7   SOUTH CAROLINA INNKEEPERS ASSOCIATION, Box 11187, Columbia, SC 29211 (803/252-5646) or Singley Bldg., 1215 Lady Street, Columbia, SC 29201 (803/571-0466).

INFORMATION CENTERS/INFORMATION PHONES

There are 8 highway welcome centers located on major roads at the borders and 1 in the central part of the state at Santee. There are 2 more in the planning stage. All are open 7 days a week 8:30A.M.-6P.M. in the spring, summer, and fall, and 8:30A.M.-5:30P.M. in the winter. Their locations will be found on the SOUTH CAROLINA STATE HIGHWAY PRIMARY SYSTEM MAP.

South Carolina

OUTDOOR RECREATION ACTIVITIES

CANOEING AND BOATING. SOUTH CAROLINA PUBLIC BOAT LANDINGS, available from the South Carolina Wildlife and Marine Resources Dept., Box 167, Columbia, SC 29202, contains many maps showing launch sites.

FISHING AND HUNTING. Contact the South Carolina Wildlife and Marine Resources Dept., Information and Public Affairs, Box 167, Columbia, SC 29202 (803/758-6291). They provide a map/guide to game management (hunting) areas. The Marine Resources Division of the Wildlife and Marine Resources Dept., Box 12559, Charleston, SC 29412 (803/795-6350) is supposed to provide literature and information on fishing in South Carolina; however, repeated letters and calls to them have only gotten us shrimp recipes and a booklet on how to catch crabs! See also SC-5.

NATIONAL/STATE PARKS/FORESTS, ETC.

There are no major national parks in South Carolina. For information and maps on the national forests in South Carolina contact the U.S. Forest Service, Southern Region, 1720 Peachtree Road NW, Suite 800, Atlanta, GA 30309.

For information on state parks and trails within the state parks system contact the South Carolina Dept. of Parks, Recreation and Tourism, Division of Parks, Suite 113, Edgar A. Brown Bldg., 1205 Pendleton Street, Columbia, SC 29201 (803/758-3622). See also the brochure SOUTH CAROLINA STATE PARKS available from the Division of Tourism (SC-6).

INDIVIDUAL CITIES OR AREAS

Charleston—Printed Materials

SC-8   CHARLESTON . . . CITY OF CHARM. Bicentennial ed. Charleston: Wayfarer Publications (Suite 225, First National Bldg., 165 Cannon Street/29403), 1976. Issued annually. 72 p. Photos., maps.

This is a guide to points of interest and outdoor activities with brief sections on dining and shopping.

SC-9   GATEWAY TO HISTORIC CHARLESTON. Charleston: Charleston Gateway (Box 803/29402).

This is a free, monthly guide to sightseeing, dining, and entertainment in the historic area, published since 1956. It also contains a calendar of events, a map, and many advertisements.

SC-10   Junior League of Charleston, comp. HISTORIC CHARLESTON GUIDE-

BOOK. Charleston: Historic Charleston Foundation (51 Meeting Street/29401), 1967. 108 p. Maps, sketches. Bibliography.

This old, but probably still useful, book describes 3 tours within Charleston and 7 out-of-town tours.

SC-11 QUAINT OLD CHARLESTON. Rev. ed. Charleston: John Huguley Co., 1973. 64 p. Photos., map. 76-370210.

This is a guide to Charleston's "homes, gateways, historic landmarks, and distinctive architecture."

Maps of Charleston are available from Arrow Publishing Co. (US-199) and Champion Map Corp. (US-202).

Charleston—Organizations

SC-12 CHARLESTON CONVENTION BUREAU, Charleston County Park, Recreation and Tourist Commission, Box 834, Charleston, SC 29402 (803/723-7641).

They issue a thorough CHARLESTON, S.C. TRIP PLANNER that describes sightseeing, recreational facilities, lodging, dining, shopping, weather, and how to get to Charleston, plus an excellent VISITORS' GUIDE MAP, HISTORIC CHARLESTON, SOUTH CAROLINA, INCLUDING POINTS OF INTEREST AND GENERAL INFORMATION. Their office is at 215 East Bay Street and is open Monday-Friday, 9A.M.-5P.M. They are currently establishing several satellite walk-in information centers throughout the historic area. Their toll-free number, 800/845-7108, can be dialed from any state except South Carolina, Alaska, and Hawaii.

SC-13 CHARLESTON TRIDENT CHAMBER OF COMMERCE, Box 975, Charleston, SC 29402 (803/577-2510).

They issue several good brochures: a general brochure; SIGHTSEEING, ACCOMMODATIONS AND DINING; a schedule of events; and a GUIDE TO ART AND ANTIQUES. They also provide information on the many guide and sightseeing services in the area. They operate a visitor information center at 85 Calhoun Street, Charleston, SC 29401 (803/722-8338). It is open every day except Thanksgiving, Christmas, and New Year's Day from 8:30A.M.-5P.M.

Columbia—Printed Materials

Maps of Columbia are available from Arrow Publishing Co. (US-199) and Champion Map Corp. (US-202).

Columbia—Organizations

SC-14   GREATER COLUMBIA CHAMBER OF COMMERCE, Box 1360, Columbia, SC 29202 (803/779-5350).

They issue a general map (with tours) brochure, an accommodations
list, and a guide for the handicapped and elderly titled ACCESS
COLUMBIA.

Hilton Head Island—Printed Materials

Maps of Hilton Head Island are available from Arrow Publishing Co. (US-199);
Bulls Eye Productions, Hilton Head Island, SC 29928; Plantation Properties,
Hilton Head Island, SC 29928; and Charles Doughtie & Son, Sea Pines, SC
29928.

Hilton Head Island—Organizations

SC-15   HILTON HEAD ISLAND CHAMBER OF COMMERCE, Box 5647, Hilton
Head Island, SC 29928 (803/785-3673 or 785-3613).

They provide information on things to see and do; lists of resorts,
inns, hotels, rental agents; and recreation facilities, including golf
courses and marinas. They publish a monthly magazine about life-styles
on the island called ISLANDER OF HILTON HEAD ISLAND and offprint the restaurant advertisements from this into a separate leaflet
called RESTAURANT GUIDE.

Myrtle Beach—Printed Materials

SC-16   COAST: THE VACATIONER'S GUIDE. Myrtle Beach: Resort Publications (5000 North Kings Highway, Drawer 2448/29577).

This thorough guide (averaging 175 pages) is published weekly from
March 15 to October 30 and monthly in November, December/January,
and February. It covers art, attractions, camping, convention facilities, dining, entertainment, events, lodging, maps, real estate, sports,
tides, tours, transportation schedules, TV listings, weather, and more.
The magazine sponsors a RESERV-EASE phone number which will locate
accommodations for a service charge. Out-of-state call 803/449-7424.
In South Carolina call 803/449-7425.

A map of the area is available from Champion Map Corp. (US-202).

Myrtle Beach—Organizations

SC-17   GREATER MYRTLE BEACH CAMBER OF COMMERCE, 1301 North

Kings Highway, Myrtle Beach, SC 29577 (803/448-5135).

They issue the following materials: THINGS TO SEE & DO ALONG
SOUTH CAROLINA'S GRAND STRAND (a comprehensive guide to
amusements, camping, dining and dancing, fishing, golf and tennis,
shopping, tours and gardens, etc. plus a "yellow pages" of the
Chamber of Commerce's member services), ACCOMMODATIONS
GUIDE (an annual, comprehensive guide, mostly advertisements, to
motels/hotels, campgrounds, mobile home parks, real estate offices,
rentals, guest houses, apartments, and villas), FAMILY CAMPGROUND
GUIDE, FISHING DIRECTORY, and a golf guide.

SOUTH DAKOTA

BOOKS, ATLASES, MAGAZINES

SD-1   BREVET'S SOUTH DAKOTA HISTORICAL MARKERS. Sioux Falls, SD:
         Brevet Press, 1974. 285 p. Photos., maps. Indexes. 0-88498-013-
         8. 73-86007.

         Arranged by 4 regions of South Dakota, the text of each marker is
         reproduced, located on a map, and accompanied by an appropriate
         illustration. There are county, illustration, and marker indexes.

SD-2   Reese, M. Lisle. SOUTH DAKOTA: A GUIDE TO THE STATE.
         2d ed. American Guide Series. New York: Hastings House, 1952.
         421 p. Photos., maps. Bibliography. Index. 52-7601.

         This revision of the original 1938 WPA guide begins with a general
         discussion of "South Dakota Today," describes tours of 9 cities and the
         Black Hills area, and 14 highway tours.

SD-3   WHEELCHAIR VACATIONING IN SOUTH DAKOTA. Pierre: South
         Dakota Division of Tourism, 1976. 35 p. Sketches, sketch maps.

         The original compiler, himself confined to a wheelchair, describes
         those points of interest, motels/hotels, and restaurants in the state
         that are accessible by wheelchair. A new edition is planned for
         1980.

MAPS

The OFFICIAL STATE HIGHWAY MAP is available from the Division of Tour-
ism (SD-4). The 1978-79 edition contains a second map on the reverse
showing locations of points of interest and the areas in which local AM/FM
radio stations may be received. In addition, there is an inset map of the
Black Hills area. The U.S. Forest Service, Forest Service Office Bldg.,
Custer, SD 57730; the U.S. Bureau of Land Management, South Dakota Resource
Area Manager, 310 Round Up Street, Belle Fourche, SD 57717; and the South
Dakota Dept. of Wildlife, Parks & Forestry, Sigurd Anderson Bldg., Pierre,

SD 57501 have cooperatively issued a series of "South Dakota Recreation Guide Maps." So far 9 separate maps have been issued: maps numbered SDI through SD8 cover the the western quarter of the state (1 in. represents about 2 miles) and SD9 covers the Pierre area. Each shows Forest Service lands; Bureau of Land Management lands; national parks or monuments; state parks, fish, or game lands; state school lands; roads; trails; railroads; recreation sites; ranger stations; houses, schools, churches; rivers, lakes, reservoirs, dams; historical spots; boat ramps; mines; caves; and windmills. AAA (US-259), Goushā (US-206), and Rand McNally (US-215) each issue a combined North Dakota/South Dakota map. Exxon (US-261) issues a combined North Dakota/South Dakota/Nebraska map.

MAJOR TOURIST ORGANIZATION

SD-4   SOUTH DAKOTA DIVISION OF TOURISM, 217 Joe Foss Bldg., Pierre, SD 57501 (605/773-3301).

They issue a very comprehensive annual SOUTH DAKOTA VACATION GUIDE of over 70 pages which describes attractions, accommodations, campgrounds, museums, hunting and fishing, skiing and snowmobiling, events, historical markers, etc. Also available from them is an annual calendar of events; a historic homes tourguide; a rockhound guide; and a guide to ranches, campgrounds, and organizations offering trail rides.

OTHER ORGANIZATIONS

SD-5   SOUTH DAKOTA INNKEEPERS ASSOCIATION, Box 1580, Rapid City, SD 57709 (605/343-6917).

INFORMATION CENTERS/INFORMATION PHONES

The Division of Tourism (SD-4) sponsors a toll-free number, 800/843-1930, which can be dialed outside the state.

OUTDOOR RECREATION ACTIVITIES

BICYCLING. A SOUTH DAKOTA BICYCLE RIDING MAP is available from the Division of Tourism (SD-4). It doesn't take you on preselected routes as most guides do. Instead, it shows the average daily traffic and lane width of most roads in the state. Since this map doesn't give route numbers, the user will have to match this map with a highway map to find just exactly which roads are described. Fortunately, this is not too difficult to do in South Dakota since the roads follow a basic grid pattern. National parks and monuments, and state parks and recreation areas are indicated on the map.

FISHING AND HUNTING. The South Dakota Dept. of Wildlife, Parks &

Forestry, Sigurd Anderson Bldg., Pierre, SD 57501 issues 2 comprehensive where-to guides: a 35-page SOUTH DAKOTA ANGLERS ALMANAC and a SOUTH DAKOTA GUIDE TO STATE PUBLIC SHOOTING AREAS AND FEDERAL WATER-FOWL PRODUCTION AREAS. In addition, they make available individual map/guides to fishing, boat ramps, and campsites on the four lakes comprising the "Great Lakes" area of South Dakota which is the dammed up Missouri River as it flows through the state.

WINTER ACTIVITIES. Information on snowmobiling is available from the South Dakota Dept. of Wildlife, Parks & Forestry, Sigurd Anderson Bldg., Pierre, SD 57501. Snow conditions may be obtained from the toll-free number listed in the "Information Centers/Information Phones" section of this chapter. A BLACK HILLS SNOWMOBILE TRAILS map/guide is available from the Division of Tourism (SD-4).

NATIONAL/STATE PARKS/FORESTS, ETC.

Badlands National Monument

SD-6   Badlands Natural History Association. BADLANDS NATIONAL MONU-MENT ROAD GUIDE. Interior, SD: The Association in cooperation with the National Park Service, 1971. 32 p. Maps, sketches. 0-912410-02-7. 72-183761.

Beginning at the eastern boundary, this brief guide describes points of interest along 57 miles of US Route 16A as it passes through the Monument. Brief mentions are made of activities, facilities, and services in and near the Monument.

SD-7   BADLANDS NATIONAL MONUMENT, Box 6, Interior, SD 57750.

They issue a general map/brochure plus information on activities, facilities, backpacking, and backcountry camping. The Cedar Pass Visitor Center is open year-round. The Badlands Natural History Association (also at the above address) operates the bookstore there and issues a quarterly newspaper format guide to activities, trails, wildlife, history, etc. It is called BADLANDS.

Mount Rushmore National Memorial

SD-8   MOUNT RUSHMORE NATIONAL MEMORIAL, Keystone, SD 57751.

They provide a general map/brochure, much information on how the sculpture was created, photography hints, and what to see and do. The visitor center is open year round from 8A.M.-5P.M. and during the summer months from 7A.M.-10P.M. In the summer the sculpture is lighted from 9P.M. to midnight.

Information about state parks, recreation areas, and campsites is available from the South Dakota Dept. of Wildlife, Parks & Forestry, Sigurd Anderson Bldg., Pierre, SD 57501.

INDIVIDUAL CITIES OR AREAS

Black Hills—Printed Materials

SD-9   Fielder, Mildred. HIKING TRAILS IN THE BLACK HILLS. Aberdeen, SD: North Plains Press, 1973. 123 p. Maps, photos. Bibliography. Index. 0-87970-131-5. 73-85969.

This is an exciting book. The information is practical, the maps are easy to read, and the places are Mount Rushmore, Custer State Park, the Black Hills region, the Devils Tower and many, many others.

SD-10   Goodson, Rose M. GUIDE LISTING ATTRACTIONS, PLACES OF INTEREST, BACK ROADS IN THE BLACK HILLS AND BADLANDS. N.p.: 1971. 32 p. Maps, sketches. 74-152428.

Descriptions (brief but giving location, hours, fees, etc.) of everything to see and do in this area are included; easy-to-read maps are included; but the two often are not adjacent on the page. If the reader is willing to page back and forth in the pamphlet's confusing format, it will provide him with at least a good, superficial guide to an area (Badlands, Wounded Knee, Custer State Park, Mount Rushmore, Pierre, Black Hills, and many other areas) that doesn't seem to have any good, general, recent guidebook. There's no index to save the confusing format.

The Forest Supervisor, Black Hills National Forest, Box 792, Custer, SD 57730 (605/ 673-2251) supplies a large map at a scale of 1 in. represents 2 miles. It shows roads, trails, ranger stations and information centers, recreation sites, ski areas, overlooks, points of interest, etc. in Black Hills National Forest. The organization also provides information on hiking and camping. There is a visitor center at the Pactola Reservoir on US 385 west of Rapid City that is open between Memorial Day and Labor Day.

Black Hills—Organizations

SD-11   BLACK HILLS, BADLANDS, AND LAKES ASSOCIATION, Box 539, Sturgis, SD 57785.

See also SD-8.

Pierre—Organizations

SD-12   PIERRE CHAMBER OF COMMERCE, 300 South Highland, Box 548, Pierre, SD 57501 (605/224-7361).

A nice combined map/circle tour route/descriptions of points of interest/ area history brochure, HOWDY PARTNER!, is available from this office.

TENNESSEE

BOOKS, ATLASES, MAGAZINES

TN-1   TENNESSEE: A GUIDE TO THE STATE. American Guide Series.
New York: Viking Press, 1939. 558 p. Photos., maps.

This original WPA guide in 3 sections--general background, descriptions of 7 cities and towns, and 16 state-wide highway tours--is comprehensive, but out of date.

TN-2   TENNESSEE HISTORICAL MARKERS ERECTED BY THE TENNESSEE HISTORICAL COMMISSION. 6th ed. Nashville: Tennessee Historical Commission, 1972. 242 p. Photos. Indexes. 73-169795.

Arranged by highway, north-to-south and east-to-west, this listing gives the text of Tennessee historical markers.

TN-3   TENNESSEE VISITOR GUIDE. Nashville, TN: The Guide Co. (211 Fesslers Lane/37210).

This monthly guide, published since June 1947, describes things to see and do in or near the various cities and towns of Tennessee. It is distributed free by the welcome centers, chambers of commerce, tourist attractions, hotels/motels, and restaurants. It contains many advertisements.

MAPS

The official highway map is available from either the Tennessee Dept. of Transportation, Information Office, 807 Highway Bldg., Nashville, TN 37219 or Tourist Development (TN-4). The 1978 edition lists places of interest and recreation areas. AAA (US-259), Exxon (US-261), Goushā (US-206), and Rand McNally (US-215) each issue a combined Kentucky/Tennessee map.

MAJOR TOURIST ORGANIZATION

TN-4   TENNESSEE TOURIST DEVELOPMENT, 505 Fesslers Lane, Nashville,

TN 37210 (615/741-2158).

They issue a general points of interest booklet (also includes information on outdoor activities, the addresses and phone numbers of the 9
regional tourist offices, a map, a list of facilities at the state parks,
and a calendar of annual events), STATE PARKS IN TENNESSEE (describes, with a list of facilities, each state park), CAMPING IN
TENNESSEE (includes all public and private campsites approved by
the Tennessee Dept. of Public Health), HISTORY IN TENNESSEE
(geographical guide to historical sites giving hours and admission fees),
GOLFING IN TENNESSEE (public and private courses are described
and located on a map), TENNESSEE ACCOMMODATIONS DIRECTORY
(a geographical listing of hotels/motels with facilities available at
each), and CRAFTS IN TENNESSEE (includes a calendar of craft fairs
and events, and lists craft shops and crafts cooperatives).

REGIONAL TOURISM ASSOCIATIONS

EAST TENNESSEE TOURISM ORGANIZATION, Knoxville Tourist Bureau, Box
237, Knoxville, TN 37901 (615/523-2316).

They issue EAST TENNESSEE TOURIST DIRECTORY (a very comprehensive listing of every type of service and facility available arranged
under 80 different headings), FISHING AND CAMPING IN EAST
TENNESSEE (lists fishing docks and campgrounds and resorts), ACCOM-
MODATIONS DIRECTORY AND MAP OF DOWNTOWN KNOXVILLE
and KNOXVILLE AND EAST TENNESSEE (describes things to see and
do plus 4 scenic driving tours in east Tennessee).

FIRST TENNESSEE TOURISM ORGANIZATION, Greater Bristol Area Chamber
of Commerce, Box 1039, Bristol, VA 24201 (703/669-2141).

MEMPHIS DELTA TOURISM ORGANIZATION, Box 224, Memphis, TN 38101
(901/523-2322).

They issue a general map/guide to what to see and do.

MID-CUMBERLAND TOURIST ORGANIZATION
See TN-12.

NORTHWEST TENNESSEE TOURISM ORGANIZATION, Box 63, Martin, TN
38237 (901/587-4215).

They issue a general map/guide to what to see and do.

SOUTH CENTRAL TENNESSEE TOURISM ORGANIZATION, 232 North Military
Avenue, Lawrenceburg, TN 38464 (615/762-6944).

SOUTHEAST TENNESSEE TOURISM ORGANIZATION, Chattanooga Convention & Visitors Bureau, Memorial Auditorium, 399 McCallie Avenue, Chattanooga, TN 37402 (615/266-5716).

> They issue a MAP/GUIDE TO DOWNTOWN CHATTANOOGA; MAP OF LOOKOUT MTN. COUNTRY; WHAT'S HAPPENING IN THE CHATTANOOGA AREA; WHERE TO STAY & DINE IN THE CHATTA- NOOGA AREA; fishing, camping, tennis and golf brochures; and a fall activities brochure.

SOUTHWEST TENNESSEE TOURISM ORGANIZATION, Box 1925, Jackson, TN 38301 (901/423-0772).

UPPER CUMBERLAND TOURISM ORGANIZATION, 28 North Jefferson Avenue, Box 698, Cookeville, TN 38501 (615/526-7100).

OTHER ORGANIZATIONS

TN-5   TENNESSEE HOTEL & MOTEL ASSOCIATION, Home Federal Towers, 5th floor, 230 Fourth Avenue N., Nashville, TN 37219 (615/255-9017).

INFORMATION CENTERS/INFORMATION PHONES

The state sponsors 8 welcome centers along the major interstate routes entering Tennessee. They are open 24 hours a day, 7 days a week.

OUTDOOR RECREATION ACTIVITIES

CANOEING AND BOATING. A brief guide, CANOEING IN TENNESSEE, is available from the Tennessee Wildlife Resources Agency, Box 40747, Elling- ton Agricultural Center, Nashville, TN 37204 (615/741-1431). Large detailed maps of boating areas and launch sites on individual lakes partially administered by the U.S. Corps of Engineers are available either from them (U.S. Army Corps of Engineers, Public Affairs Office, Nashville District, Box 1070, Nash- ville, TN 37203 (615/251-7161)) or from the Tennessee Wildlife Resources Agency.

FISHING AND HUNTING. Contact the Tennessee Wildlife Resources Agency, Box 40747, Ellington Agricultural Center, Nashville, TN 37204 (615/741-1431) for annual hunting and fishing guides and maps of their wildlife management areas. Tourist Development (TN-4) issues FISHING IN TENNESSEE, a where- to guide.

NATIONAL/STATE PARKS/FORESTS, ETC.

Great Smoky Mountains National Park

TN-6   THE MOUNTAIN VISITOR. Gatlinburg, TN: The Mountain Press (Ridge Road, Box 9/37738).

This weekly vacation guide, published in tabloid format since 1964, describes things to see and do in Gatlinburg and the Smokies. It also includes advertisements, accommodations, shops, services, several maps, and a weekly TV section.

TN-7   Murliess, Dick, and Stallings, Constance. HIKER'S GUIDE TO THE SMOKIES. A Sierra Club Totebook. San Francisco: Sierra Club Books, 1973. 375 p. Maps. 0-87156-068-2. 72-83981.

The authors describe 580 miles of backcountry trails in Great Smoky Mountains National Park.

TN-8   GREAT SMOKY MOUNTAINS NATIONAL PARK, Gatlinburg, TN 37738.

They issue a general map/brochure, a backcountry map and camping guide, a camping/fishing guide, and a brochure describing favorite hiking trails.

TN-9   GATLINBURG Chamber of Commerce, Box 527, Gatlinburg, TN 37787 (615/436-4178).

They issue a general map/guide to things to see and do.

AAA (US-259) issues a map of the park. The Carolina Mountain Club, Box 68, Asheville, NC 28802 and the Smoky Mountains Hiking Club, 5419 Timbercrest Trail, Knoxville, TN 37901 issue a 2 ft. x 3 ft. map, 100 FAVORITE TRAILS OF THE GREAT SMOKIES AND CAROLINA BLUE RIDGE, with detailed trail directions on the back. For additional maps of the park see NC-12. An auto tape tour (CA-80) of the park is available for rental from several motels and attractions in Gatlinburg, TN and in Cherokee, NC.

Information about Tennessee's only national forest is available from Forest Supervisor, Cherokee National Forest, Cleveland, TN 37311 (615/476-5528).

The Tennessee Dept. of Conservation, Division of Parks and Recreation, 2611 West End Avenue, Nashville, TN 37203 (615/741-3251) provides information on all outdoor recreation areas and state park resorts and campgrounds, and issues brochures on the individual state parks. They also issue a brief guide, SELECTED TENNESSEE TRAILS, to 36 trails plus maps to some of them. See also STATE PARKS IN TENNESSEE and CAMPING IN TENNESSEE available from Tourist Development (TN-4).

INDIVIDUAL CITIES OR AREAS

Nashville—Printed Materials

TN-10   A GUIDEBOOK TO NASHVILLE FOR THE HANDICAPPED AND
AGING. Nashville: Easter Seal Society for Crippled Children and
Adults of Tennessee, 1968.

TN-11   OFFICIAL NASHVILLE VISITOR'S GUIDE. Nashville: PlusMedia
(Nashville House, One Vantage Way/37228), 1978. Issued annually.
96 p. Photos., maps.

This is a jointly produced guide issued by PlusMedia and the Nashville Area Chamber of Commerce (TN-12). It includes a large section
on where to hear country music, attractions, annual events, accommodations, dining and entertainment, sightseeing and package tours,
transportation, middle Tennessee side trips, recreation, shopping, colleges and universities, and services. It contains many advertisements.

Maps of Nashville are available from Arrow Publishing Co. (US-199); Champion
Map Corp. (US-202); Exxon (US-261); Metro Graphic Arts, 900 40th SE,
Grand Rapids, MI 49508; Rand McNally (US-215); and the local First American
Bank.

Nashville—Organizations

TN-12   NASHVILLE AREA CHAMBER OF COMMERCE, 161 Fourth Avenue
North, Nashville, TN 37219 (615/259-3900).

They represent the Mid-Cumberland Tourist Organization (see the "Regional Tourism Associations" section of this chapter). They issue listings,
with maps, of points of interest, hotels and motels, and dining spots.
They also issue an annual calendar of events. Together with PlusMedia,
they issue the OFFICIAL NASHVILLE VISITOR'S GUIDE (TN-11) and
NASHVILLE!, a slick monthly magazine reporting on city and local
events. They are open at this address Monday-Friday, 8A.M.-4:30P.M.

TEXAS

BOOKS, ATLASES, MAGAZINES

TX-1   BEST RESTAURANTS: TEXAS. By the editors of Texas Critic. San
        Francisco: 101 Productions (distributed by Scribners), 1976. 199 p.
        Indexes. 0-89286-106-1. 76-45456.

        This is a selective guide to restaurants with consistently high standards
        in Austin, Dallas, Fort Worth, Houston, and San Antonio. Included
        with each description are: location, hours, credit cards accepted,
        type of spirits served, food specialty, price category, and a reproduc-
        tion of the menu. Geographical and type of cuisine indexes are in-
        cluded.

TX-2   Bookmap Corp. BOOKMAP OF THE RIO GRANDE VALLEY, WITH
        FISHING-NAVIGATION CHARTS. . . . San Antonio: International
        Aerial Mapping Co., 1973. 128 p. Scales vary. Indexes. 74-
        187219.

        This work also includes fishing tips.

TX-3   Crittenden, Pauline. TEXAS TOURS. Waco, TX: The author, 1975.
        195 p. Photos., maps. 75-32909.

        This book describes 45 tours to "lesser known locales of scenic and/or
        historic interest." The author has written a column featuring short
        trips out of Dallas for over 12 years for THE DALLAS MORNING
        NEWS, and this book is a collection of those columns. Descriptions
        are very brief and focus more on the "wonders" than the practicalities
        of each tour.

TX-4   GUIDE TO OFFICIAL TEXAS HISTORICAL MARKERS. Austin: Texas
        Historical Commission, 1975. 151 p. Index. 76-623201.

        Markers are listed, but with no reproduction of the text of each, under
        the town in which they are located.

TX-5   Howard, Rex Z. TEXAS GUIDEBOOK: AUTHENTIC INFORMATION

ABOUT THE WONDERS OF TEXAS. 5th ed. Edited by F.M. McCarty. Amarillo, TX: F.M. McCarty Co. (Drawer 5248/79107), 1970. 315 p. Photos., maps. Index. 54-1654.

This book suffers primarily from a lack of good layout and professional editing. A Table of Contents is lacking and the first 50 pages of "General Information" are a hodge-podge of little essays of only a few paragraphs about recipes, geology, history, etc. The index helps somewhat by covering these things, but it is confusing in its own way-- the entries are arranged letter by letter so that "Capitals of Texas" appears before "Cap Rock" and all individual page references for the same entry are separated by a hyphen, a method traditionally reserved for showing inclusive pagination, instead of a comma. The bulk of the book is a road guide of the sights to see along the various numbered highways in Texas. The book was originally published in 1948, and while this fifth edition of 1970 appears to be little changed from what one would expect a 1948 guidebook to look like, the suggestions within may still be useful.

TX-6   Little, Mildred J. CAMPER'S GUIDE TO TEXAS PARKS, LAKES, AND FORESTS: WHERE TO GO AND HOW TO GET THERE. Houston: Pacesetter Press (Gulf Publishing Co.), 1978. 140 p. Maps, photos. Index. 0-88415-097-6. 77-73561.

This is a thorough listing of locations, with good detailed maps and lists of facilities and activities. The state is divided into 4 regions with the major parks, lakes, and forests listed alphabetically by region and smaller parks noted briefly at the end of each regional section. There are also brief sections on canoeable rivers and on woodland trails.

TX-7   THE NATIONAL REGISTER OF HISTORIC PLACES IN TEXAS, 1968-1975. Austin: Texas Historical Commission, 1976. 69 p. Photos. 77-622665.

This contains brief descriptions of National Register properties arranged by county. There is no index.

TX-8   Nelson, Dick, and Nelson, Sharon. 50 HIKES IN TEXAS. Tombstone, AZ: Tecolote Press, 1974. 120 p. Photos., maps. Index. 0-915030-02-0. 74-84555.

Descriptions of each hike include a map, distance, time required, and amount of elevation change.

TX-9   Nolen, Ben M. TEXAS RIVERS & RAPIDS. Humble, TX: the author, 1974. 128 p. Maps, photos.

The author gives specific, practical information, including a sketch map, for canoeing 24 Texas rivers, 2 Arkansas rivers, and 1 each in Colorado, Oklahoma, and Mexico.

TX-10   TEXAS: A GUIDE TO THE LONE STAR STATE. Rev. ed. American
         Guide Series. New York: Hastings House, 1969. 717 p. Photos.,
         maps. 0-8038-7055-8. 68-31690.

         This revision of the original 1940 WPA guide is in 3 sections: general
         background, descriptions of 15 Texas cities, and 29 statewide highway
         tours.

TX-11   TEXAS, LAND OF CONTRAST. Austin: State Dept. of Highways
         and Public Transportation, Travel and Information Division, 1978.
         Revised frequently. 160 p. Photos., maps. Index.

         This is a very complete, frequently updated, and free guide to the
         state. The major portion is an alphabetical listing describing individ-
         ual Texas cities and towns with recreational, scenic, and historic
         interests. Accommodations, restaurants, and auto services are omitted.
         It also describes the lakes of Texas; facilities at state parks and
         national and state forests; information on hunting, fishing, and where
         specific rocks and minerals can be found; a list of the 11 tourist
         bureaus (10 on highways and 1 in Austin); a map; information on the
         climate; and entry into Mexico. This is a very impressive and com-
         prehensive guide.

TX-12   TEXAS HIGHWAYS: THE OFFICIAL STATE TRAVEL MAGAZINE.
         Austin: State Dept. of Highways and Public Transportation, Travel and
         Information Division.

         This monthly publication began in 1957. Each issue features several
         tours, descriptions of picturesque towns, a calendar of events, natural
         history articles, and many stunning color photographs. Also included
         is a list of regional chambers of commerce and local convention and
         visitor bureaus.

MAPS

The official highway travel map is available from the State Dept. of Highways
and Public Transportation (TX-14). The 1977-78 edition includes a list of the
state parks. An annual VACATION FUN MAP is issued in English and Spanish
by the Discover Texas Association (TX-16). It describes many attractions and
festivals; has an extensive list of organizations providing tourist information;
and lists several hotels/motels, restaurants, and KOA campgrounds. Although
these are printed on the map in their approximate location, specific information
about addresses and phone numbers is frequently lacking. AAA (US-259) issues
a combined Oklahoma/Texas map. Exxon (US-261), Gousha (US-206), and
Rand McNally (US-215) each issue a separate Texas map. See also TX-2 and
TX-13.

PUBLISHERS

TX-13   INTERNATIONAL AERIAL MAPPING, 8927 International Drive, San

Antonio, TX 78216.

They issue several good atlases of Texas metropolitan areas.

MAJOR TOURIST ORGANIZATIONS

TX-14   STATE DEPT. OF HIGHWAYS AND PUBLIC TRANSPORTATION, TRAVEL AND INFORMATION DIVISION, Austin, TX 78701 (512/475-6338).

This is the major source of travel information even though the Texas Tourist Development Agency (TX-15) is the official tourism agency. They issue TEXAS, LAND OF CONTRAST (TX-11), TEXAS HIGHWAYS (TX-12), a semi-annual calendar of events, a public campgrounds guide (lists only facilities administered by local, state, and federal authorities), a Spanish guide, and a series of 10 trail maps which describe points of interest along 10 regional highways.

TX-15   TEXAS TOURIST DEVELOPMENT AGENCY, Box 12008, Capitol Station, Austin, TX 78711 (512/475-4326).

This is the official state tourist agency, but our letter to them brought no response. Contact the State Dept. of Highways and Public Transportation (TX-14) which provides much good information and maps.

REGIONAL TOURISM ASSOCIATIONS

EAST TEXAS CHAMBER OF COMMERCE, Box 1592, Longview, TX 75601 (214/757-4444).

They issue an annual (1978, 15th ed., 62 p.) EAST TEXAS VACATION GUIDE, a comprehensive guide to what to see and do, including hiking, biking, special events, lodging, restaurants, etc. in or near the major cities and towns of the area. It includes all local chamber of commerce addresses and phone numbers and has many advertisements. The information center of this association is located at 410 North Center Street, Longview and is open Monday-Friday, 8:30A.M.-5P.M. except holidays.

LOWER RIO GRANDE VALLEY CHAMBER OF COMMERCE, Box 975, Weslaco, TX 78956 (512/968-3141).

They publish an annual VACATION GUIDE of over 80 pages to the 4 county (the southernmost in Texas) area served by this association. They also make available maps of the area and of individual cities within the 4 counties. Their information center is located at US 83 Expressway east at FM 1015 in Weslaco.

SOUTH TEXAS CHAMBER OF COMMERCE, 6222 NW Interstate 10, San Antonio, TX 78201 (512/732-8185).

WEST TEXAS CHAMBER OF COMMERCE, Box 1561, Abilene, TX 79604 (915/677-4325).

They issue a general FUN AND ADVENTURE MAP which includes addresses and phone numbers of local chambers of commerce. Their information center is located at 155 Hickory Street in Abilene and is open Monday-Friday, 8A.M.-5P.M.

OTHER ORGANIZATIONS

TX-16   DISCOVER TEXAS ASSOCIATION, 8500 Village Drive, San Antonio, TX 78217.

This organization, formed in 1969, is made up of the leaders of the attractions and resort areas of Texas. They issue an annual VACA-TION FUN MAP (see the "Maps" section of this chapter) in English and Spanish, plus an 8-book series of regional adventures with map and accommodations listings called "Discover Texas."

TX-17   TEXAS HOTEL & MOTEL ASSOCIATION, 8602 Crownhill Blvd., San Antonio, TX 78209 (512/828-3566).

INFORMATION CENTERS/INFORMATION PHONES

The state sponsors 11 tourist bureaus, 10 of which are located on highways and 1 in Austin. A list of these will be found in TEXAS, LAND OF CONTRAST (TX-11), the official highway travel map, and the VACATION FUN MAP (see the "Maps" section of this chapter).

OUTDOOR RECREATION ACTIVITIES

BICYCLING. See TX-23.

CANOEING AND BOATING. For information on Texas waterways contact the Texas Parks and Wildlife Dept., 4200 Smith School Road, Austin, TX 78744. See also TX-2 and TX-9.

FISHING AND HUNTING. Contact the Texas Parks and Wildlife Dept., 4200 Smith School Road, Austin, TX 78744. See also TX-2 and TX-11.

NATIONAL/STATE PARKS/FORESTS, ETC.

Big Ben National Park

TX-18   GUIDE TO THE BACKCOUNTRY ROADS AND THE RIVER: BIG BEND

NATIONAL PARK. Big Bend National Park, TX: Big Bend Natural History Association, 1970. 32 p. Photos., map. 70-289635.

This is a road guide to 3 primitive roads in the park plus a brief guide to running the section of the Rio Grande River which forms the boundary between the park and Mexico.

TX-19   HIKERS GUIDE TO BIG BEND. Big Bend National Park, TX: Big Bend Natural History Association, 1971. 36 p.

This guide includes "descriptions, mileages, and trail conditions of all major trails in the Park, from 1/4 mile strolls to strenuous backpacking routes."

TX-20   ROAD GUIDE TO THE PAVED AND IMPROVED DIRT ROADS: BIG BEND NATIONAL PARK. Big Bend National Park, TX: Big Bend Natural History Association, 1970. 32 p. Photos., map. 70-289637.

Five tours on the major roads of the park are described.

TX-21   BIG BEND NATIONAL PARK, Big Bend National Park, TX 79834.

They supply a general map/brochure plus information on park birds, concessions, explorations, geology, use of personal horses, hunting, history and discovery, motorcycling, naturalist activities, reptiles, river trips, wildflowers, etc.

For information on visitor services and accommodations within the park, contact National Park Concessions, General Offices, Mammoth Cave, KY 42259.

For information and maps on the national forests in Texas contact the U.S. Forest Service, Southern Region, 1720 Peachtree Road NW, Suite 800, Atlanta, GA 30309.

The Texas Parks and Wildlife Dept., 4200 Smith School Road, Austin, TX 78744 provides information on state parks and game lands and issues a monthly magazine, TEXAS PARKS AND WILDLIFE MAGAZINE, containing articles about hunting, fishing, water sports, photography, camping, nature study, etc. TEXAS, LAND OF CONTRAST (TX-11) also contains information on state parks, lakes, and national and state forests.

INDIVIDUAL CITIES OR AREAS

Austin—Printed Materials

TX-22   Bookmap Corp. BOOKMAP OF AUSTIN AND ADJACENT AREAS. . . .

San Antonio: International Aerial Mapping Co., 1972. 115 p.
Scale: 1 in. represents 2,300 ft. Index. 74-187217.

TX-23   Pratt, Kevin. THIRTY BIKE RIDES IN THE AUSTIN AREA. Austin:
Jenkins Publishing Co., 1973. 76 p. Maps, drawings. 0-8363-
0127-7.

The general biking information includes the usual safety tips and a
list of Austin bike shops. Each ride has its own map, and the description notes terrain, road conditions, distance, and offers brief
comments, usually including a list of sites/sights/attractions keyed to
the map.   .

Maps of Austin are available from Champion Map Corp. (US-202), Exxon
(US-261), and Goushā (US-206). See also TX-22.

Austin—Organizations

TX-24   AUSTIN CHAMBER OF COMMERCE, Box 1967, Austin, TX 78767
(512/478-9383).

They distribute a brochure of their own describing points of interest
and containing a list of hotels and motels. Also available from them
is a detailed city map put out by the American National Bank of
Austin and a map/guide to the adjacent lakes and other attractions
issued by the Highland Lakes Tourist Association also at the above
address. The address of the Chamber of Commerce is 901 West Riverside Drive.

Dallas/Fort Worth—Printed Materials

TX-25   ACCESS DALLAS '77. Prepared by the Committee for the Removal of
Architectural Barriers. Dallas: Easter Seal Society (4429 North
Central Expressway/75205), 1977. 128 p.

TX-26   Trim, Laura. NORTH TEXAS, EVERY NOOK AND CRANNY:
OUTINGS AND ADVENTURES WITHIN A ONE-HUNDRED MILE
RADIUS OF DALLAS. Dallas: the author, 1975. 240 p. Sketches,
sketch maps. Bibliography. Index. 76-351371.

What to see and do in Dallas and Forth Worth are covered in detail
from historic sites to annual events. From there the author goes north,
east, south, and west to describe other localities offering similiar
points of interest.

Maps of Dallas are available from American Geographic, 3109 West Thompson
Road, Fenton, MI 48430; Arrow Publishing Co. (US-199); Champion Map Corp.
(US-202); Dallas Chamber of Commerce, 1507 Pacific Avenue, Dallas, TX

75201; Exxon (US-261); Gousha (US-206); and Rand McNally (US-215). Maps of Fort Worth are available from Exxon (US-261), Gousha (US-206), and Rand McNally (US-215).

Dallas/Fort Worth—Organizations

TX-27   DALLAS CONVENTION AND TOURISM BUREAU, 1507 Pacific Avenue, Dallas, TX 75201 (214/651-1020).

They issue a points of interest map and listing, an airline service map, a restaurant guide, a lodging map and directory, and a quarterly calendar of events.

TX-28   FORT WORTH AREA CONVENTION & VISITORS BUREAU, 700 Throckmorton Street, Fort Worth, TX 76102 (817/336-2491).

They issue TOURING FORT WORTH AND THE TARRANT COUNTY AREA (also available in Spanish and Japanese), a hotel/motel guide, and A GUIDE TO DINING & ENTERTAINMENT.

Houston—Printed Materials

TX-29   Coates, Felicia, and Howle, Harriet. TEXAS MONTHLY'S GUIDE TO HOUSTON. Rev. ed. Austin: Texas Monthly, 1976. 377 p. Index. 76-41135.

While two thirds of this book contains "survival" information on where to shop, how to get help, and includes a list of clubs, there is a large section describing restaurants with a cuisine index, smaller sections on museums, parks, the performing arts, sports, and a calendar of annual events.

TX-30   A GUIDE TO HOUSTON FOR THE HANDICAPPED. Houston: The Coalition for Barrier Free Living (Box 20803/77025), 1977.

A new edition was planned for 1979.

TX-31   HOUSTON/HARRIS COUNTY ATLAS. 17th ed. Houston: Key Maps, 1976. 666 p. Scale: 1 in. represents 1/2 mile. Index.

TX-32   Shelton, William, and Kennedy, Ann. HOUSTON: SUPERCITY OF THE SOUTHWEST. A McDonald City Guide. Garden City, NY: Dolphin/Doubleday, 1978. 148 p. Maps. Index. 0-385-11405-2. 76-57516.

This good, general guide to Houston has sections on several driving tours, children's activities, shopping (including antique shops), museums/galleries, walking tours, night life, restaurants, sports, and places to stay. The final chapter is on "Galveston and the Gulf of Mexico" and notes briefly, activities, sights, and restaurants in the Galveston area. Like the other titles in this series (which are in no way related to the fast food chain of the same name), this is a handy, pocket-sized volume and easy to use.

TX-33   THIS IS HOUSTON. Chicago: Rand McNally, 1974. 49 p. Maps, photos. 75-310174.

Preliminary pages describe transportation systems, points of interest, selected hotels and motels, selected restaurants, and cultural and sporting events. The remaining pages are a city atlas with a street directory.

TX-34   Zal, Eli, and Milburn, Doug. THE INTREPID WALKER'S GUIDE TO HOUSTON: EXPLORING THE CITY ON FOOT AND BIKE. Houston: Texas Chapbook Press, 1975. 64 p. Maps, photos. 75-328040.

This guide "for the most part avoids the cliche tourist attractions and instead concentrates on the hidden, forgotten, out-of-the-way sights." Each of 7 tours includes a map, descriptions of points of interest, exact directions, and requires about 2 hours if on foot.

Maps of Houston are available from AAA (US-259); Arrow Publishing Co. (US-199); Exxon (US-261); Goushā (US-206); Houston Chamber of Commerce, 1100 Milam, 25th floor, Houstin, TX 77002; and Rand McNally (US-215). See also TX-31 and TX-33.

Houston—Organizations

TX-35   GREATER HOUSTON CONVENTION AND VISITORS COUNCIL, 1522 Main Street, Houston, TX 77002 (713/658-9201).

They issue a brochure describing points of interest, attractions and tour services, a monthly calendar of events, an accommodations directory, and a restaurant directory.

San Antonio—Printed Materials

TX-36   ACCESS SAN ANTONIO. San Antonio: Easter Seal Society of Bexar County (2203 Babcock Road/78229), 1977. 69 p.

TX-37   Blackmon, Peggy P. SCENIC GUIDE TO SAN ANTONIO. San Antonio: the author, 1963. 58 p. Photos., map.

This guide, with descriptions of major landmarks in San Antonio with a fold-out tour guide map, should be updated.

TX-38   Bookmap Corp. BOOKMAP OF SAN ANTONIO AND ADJACENT AREAS. . . . San Antonio: International Aerial Mapping Co., 1972. 128 p. Scale: 1 in. represents 2,750 ft. Index. 74-187218.

TX-39   Ramsdell, Charles. SAN ANTONIO: A HISTORICAL AND PICTO-
RIAL GUIDE. Revised by Carmen Perry. Austin: University of Texas
Press, 1976. 291 p. Photos., maps. Index. 0-292-77525-3. 75-
45323.

This is the guide to San Antonio, which "recounts early Texas history
in considerable detail. . . . It also provides helpful information on
the missions, museums, parks, the zoo--everything the visitor to San
Antonio might wish to see."

Maps of San Antonio are available from Exxon (US-261); Ferguson Map Co.,
1518 North St. Marys, San Antonio, TX 78215; Goushā (US-206); and Rand
McNally (US-215). See also TX-38.

San Antonio—Organizations

TX-40   GREATER SAN ANTONIO CHAMBER OF COMMERCE, 602 East Commerce, Box 1628, San Antonio, TX 78296 (512/227-8181).

They issue a SAN ANTONIO MINI-GUIDE, a historical information
guide, and a city map. There is a walk-in information center at the
corner of Commerce and South Alamo Streets.

TX-41   SAN ANTONIO CONVENTION & VISITORS BUREAU, Box 2277,
San Antonio, TX 78298 (512/223-9133).

They issue a VISITOR AND CONVENTION GUIDE; a VISITORS
MAP; a lodging guide; a hotels, motels, and campground guide; and
PASEO DEL RIO SHOWBOAT (a monthly events newspaper). There is
an information center at 321 Alamo Plaza (across from the Alamo).
There is a toll-free number available at 800/531-5700.

UTAH

BOOKS, ATLASES, MAGAZINES

UT-1   Barnes, Francis A. CANYON COUNTRY CAMPING: A COMPLETE
GUIDE TO ALL KINDS OF CAMPING WITHIN THE CANYON COUN-
TRY OF SOUTHEASTERN UTAH. Canyon Country Guide Book Series,
no. 10. Salt Lake City: Wasatch Publishers, 1978. 96 p. Photos.,
maps. 0-915272-16-4. 77-95041.

This guide covers 4 types of camping: off-highway overnight parking,
commercial campgrounds, public campgrounds, and primitive camping.
Only the public campgrounds (those administered by either the state of
Utah, the National Park Service, the U.S. Forest Service, or the
Bureau of Land Management) are identified and described, although
no mailing addresses are provided. However, the general locations
of where any of the 4 types of camping may be found are provided
through a series of charts to 19 different individual highways and to
16 specific areas.

UT-2   _____. CANYON COUNTRY EXPLORING: AN INTRODUCTION
TO THE INCOMPARABLE CANYON COUNTRY OF SOUTHEASTERN
UTAH, AND THE VARIOUS MEANS BY WHICH IT CAN BE EXPLORED.
Canyon Country Guide Book Series, no. 2. Salt Lake City: Wasatch
Publishers, 1978. 64 p. Photos., maps. Bibliography. 0-915272-
12-1.

The arrangement of this book is good, but the information presented is
quite unsatisfactory except, perhaps, to the first-time traveler sitting
in an armchair planning a possible trip. The 3 main sections describe
different ways to explore by land, by water, and by air. In the
water section, for example, 4 methods are discussed: by powerboat,
by rubber raft, by canoe or kayak, and by commercial tour. All
these sections, however, are very superficial, and no specific information of any kind is provided. If the traveler wants to know the names
of outfitters who provide pack trips, commercial land tours, rafting
trips, commercial air tours, etc., he is told to contact a park visitor
center or a local chamber of commerce. The names and addresses of

these are not given, however. There is a brief bibliography, but half of it is devoted to other books issued by Wasatch Publishers.

UT-3   _____. CANYON COUNTRY HIKING AND NATURAL HISTORY: A HIKING GUIDE TO SOUTHEASTERN UTAH WITH A DESCRIPTION OF THE NATURAL HISTORY OF THE AREA. Canyon Country Guide Book Series, no. 3. Salt Lake City: Wasatch Publishers, 1977. 176 p. Maps, photos. Bibliography. 0-915272-07-5. 76-58119.

This guide is geographically arranged into 9 areas in southeast Utah. Information given for each area includes: a general map, names of the USGS maps covering the area, suggested base camps, access routes, and general topography and area notes. Several hikes in each area are described, including mileage, USGS map to use, season to hike, and access.

UT-4   _____. CANYON COUNTRY OFF-ROAD VEHICLE TRAIL MAP: ARCHES & LA SALS AREAS. Canyon Country Guide Book Series, no. 7. Salt Lake City: Wasatch Publishers, 1978. Map.

UT-5   _____. CANYON COUNTRY OFF-ROAD VEHICLE TRAIL MAP: CANYON RIMS & NEEDLES AREAS. Canyon Country Guide Book Series, no. 9. Salt Lake City: Wasatch Publishers, 1978. Map.

UT-6   _____. CANYON COUNTRY OFF-ROAD VEHICLE TRAIL MAP: ISLAND AREA. Canyon Country Guide Book Series, no. 5. Salt Lake City: Wasatch Publishers, 1978. Map.

UT-7   _____. CANYON COUNTRY OFF-ROAD VEHICLE TRAILS: ARCHES & LA SALS AREAS. Canyon Country Guide Book Series, no. 6. Salt Lake City: Wasatch Publishers, 1978. 96 p. Photos., maps, 0-915272-13-X.

UT-8   _____. CANYON COUNTRY OFF-ROAD VEHICLE TRAILS: CANYON RIMS & NEEDLES AREAS. Canyon Country Guide Book Series, no. 8. Salt Lake City: Wasatch Publishers, 1978. 96 p. Photos., maps. 0-915272-14-8.

UT-9   _____. CANYON COUNTRY OFF-ROAD VEHICLE TRAILS: ISLAND AREA. Canyon Country Guide Book Series, no. 4. Salt Lake City: Wasatch Publishers, 1978. 96 p. Photos., maps. 0-915272-15-6.

Each of the 3 areas covered by this series (UT-4 through UT-9) has 2 printed pieces: a guidebook describing numerous off-road vehicle trails and an accompanying map, based on the USGS 1:62,500 (1 in. represents approximately 1 mile) quadrangles, on which each trail is located. The Arches & La Sals areas are located to the north and east of Moab and include all of Arches National Park. The Canyon Rims & Needles areas are located to the south and west of Moab and include all of the Bureau of Land Management's Canyon Rims Recreation Area. The island area is located west of Moab and includes the Island in the Sky district of Canyonlands National Park.

UT-10 _____. CANYON COUNTRY SCENIC ROADS: AN AUTOMOBILE TOURING GUIDE TO THE COLORFUL HIGHWAYS AND ROADS IN SLICKROCK COUNTRY IN SOUTHEASTERN UTAH. Canyon Country Guide Book Series, no. 1. Salt Lake City: Wasatch Publishers, 1977. 80 p. Photos., maps. 0-915272-08-3.

This is a brief, but thorough, beginning guide to 7 scenic roads, 3 national Parks (Arches, Canyonlands, Natural Bridges), 4 state parks in the canyon area of southeast Utah accessible by the family car. There is also a brief section on facilities, services, and supplies in the area.

UT-11 Evans, Laura, and Belknap, Buzz. DESOLATION RIVER GUIDE. Boulder City, NV: Westwater Books, 1974. 55 p. Maps, photos. 74-80877.

This is a graphic, mile-by-mile guide to 200 miles of the Green River from Dinosaur National Monument south through Desolation and Gray Canyons to the town of Green River (CANYONLANDS RIVER GUIDE (UT-23) follows the Green River south). The scale is approximately 1 in. represents 1/2 mile and features bordering the river shore (contours, roads, etc.) are drawn in. There is very little text.

UT-12 Huser, Verne. CANYON COUNTRY PADDLES: A PRACTICAL, INFORMATIVE, AND ENTERTAINING GUIDE TO RIVER RUNNING USING THE KAYAK, CANOE, OR RUBBER RAFT IN SOUTHEASTERN UTAH. Canyon Country Guide Book Series, no. 12. Salt Lake City: Wasatch Publishers, 1978. 96 p. Photos., map. Bibliography. 0-915272-18-0.

Half of this book is devoted to how-to information on equipment, logistics, health and safety, and natural history. Only general suggestions are given for running the Colorado, Green, and San Juan Rivers and for 4 other seasonal rivers negotiable only during spring run-off.

UT-13 SUNSET TRAVEL GUIDE TO UTAH. Menlo Park, CA: Lane Books, 1971. 80 p. Photos., maps. Index. 73-140163.

This is a good guide for the first-time traveler who wants to know a little something about the major points of interest in the state. It is arranged by regions with a name index.

UT-14 UTAH: A GUIDE TO THE STATE. American Guide Series. New York: Hastings House, 1941. 595 p. Photos., maps. Bibliography. Index.

This original WPA guide begins with a general state background from natural history to the arts, and then describes 4 cities, 10 highway tours, and 12 national parks and monuments. There is a chronology of Utah history.

UT-15   UTAH HOLIDAY. Salt Lake City: Utah Holiday Publishing Co. (246 West First South/84101).

UTAH HOLIDAY is published monthly in 2 editions: 1 for residents using the above title, and 1 for visitors called the VISITORS GUIDE TO UTAH. The latter edition contains complete information on events, each of the travel regions, outdoor activities, restaurants, golf courses, etc. The edition for residents includes only the events information from the other edition, but with the addition of numerous articles, fiction/poetry, advertisements, etc. reflecting a sophisticated Utah lifestyle, it becomes the slicker and fatter edition of the two.

UT-16   UTAH TRAVEL GUIDE. Salt Lake City: Utah Travel Council in co-operation with the Utah Innkeepers Association, 1978. Issued annually. 110 p. Maps. Index.

The guide begins with general information on climate, national parks, hunting, fishing, campgrounds, and rockhounding. The bulk of the guide gives detailed information on the following for each of the 9 travel regions: points of interest, lists of services available in the major communities, visitor information centers, tours, seasonal events, and accommodations. It contains many advertisements.

MAPS

The UTAH HIGHWAY MAP is available from the Travel Council (UT-18). The 1977-78 edition provides little other than what is usually found on an official state map. It does contain a small map showing the locations of national forests, parks, monuments, recreation areas, and Indian reservations; and a list of AM/FM radio stations. For detailed recreation and topographic information the Travel Council issues a set of 8 "Multipurpose Maps." Using the USGS 1:250,000 (1 in. represents approximately 4 miles) topographic maps as a base, each shows recreational sites and federal agency land ownership on one side, and on the other side lists campgrounds and gives travel information. They are available for the following 8 geographic regions: southeastern Utah, southeastern central Utah, northeastern central Utah, northeastern Utah, southwestern Utah, southwestern central Utah, northwestern central Utah, and northwestern Utah. The Bureau of Land Management, Moab District, 125 West 2d Street, Moab, UT 84532 (801/259-6111) issues a guide to INTERSTATE 70 POINTS OF INTEREST. It describes "lands nobody wants" lying between the Colorado/Utah border and Fremont Junction, east of Salina, UT. Both AAA (US-259) and Rand McNally (US-215) issue a combined Nevada/Utah map. Exxon (US-261) issues a combined Colorado/Utah map. Goushā (US-206) issues a separate Utah map. See also UT-4, UT-5, and UT-6.

PUBLISHERS

UT-17   WASATCH PUBLISHERS, 4647 Idlewood Road, Salt Lake City, UT
84117 (801/278-3174).

They publish numerous guidebooks to hiking, ski touring, trails
throughout the state, and have an extensive series of "Canyon Country Guide Books" (12 as of this writing) which covers exploring,
hiking, scenic roads, camping, canoeing, and off-road vehicle trails
in the canyon country of southeastern Utah.

MAJOR TOURIST ORGANIZATION

UT-18   UTAH TRAVEL COUNCIL, Council Hall/Capitol Hill, Salt Lake City,
UT 84114 (801/533-5681).

They issue 2 general pieces of literature that are mostly pretty
pictures--a brochure and a large booklet. Their annual UTAH TRAV-
EL GUIDE (UT-16) is their most informative piece of literature. They
also issue both an annual and monthly calendar of events, a fall color
tours brochure, and an annual booklet describing package tours and
other touring information, such as transportation services, accommodations, events, and a list of package tour operators. They also issue
a directory of both public and privately owned campgrounds.

REGIONAL TOURISM ASSOCIATIONS

BRIDGERLAND TOURIST COUNCIL, Cache Chamber of Commerce, 52 West
2d North, Logan, UT 84321 (801/752-2161).

They cover Cache and Rich Counties in the northcentral section of
the state. They issue a general brochure and a list of motels.

CANYONLANDS, Moab Chamber of Commerce, Box 550, Moab, UT 84532
(801/259-7531).

They cover Grand and San Juan Counties in the southeastern section
of the state. They issue a general brochure, GREAT CIRCLE OF THE
SOUTH WEST TOUR (describes a self-guided tour covering 7 national
parks and 6 national monuments), UTAH CANYONLANDS SEE & DO
GUIDE (map/brochure of parks/monuments, points of interest, historic
sites, camping and boating areas, 4-wheel drive trails, and airstrips),
UTAH'S TRAIL OF THE ANCIENTS MAP & GUIDE (map/guide to prehistoric and modern Indian cultures and geological areas and including
information on trails, campgrounds, and picnic areas), and UTAH'S
CAMPGROUNDS, ACCOMMODATIONS AND SERVICES (guide to
motels, campgrounds/trailer parks, tour/expedition outfitters, restaurants, and transportation services). The walk-in address for the above
office is 805 North Main Street in Moab. This regional association

has an additional office at the San Juan Tourist Council, Box 668, Monticello, UT 84535 (801/587-2833). Their walk-in address is at 88 North Main Street In Monticello.

CASTLE COUNTRY, Box 1037, Price, UT 84501 (801/637-0459).

They cover Carbon and Emery Counties in central southeastern Utah. They issue a general map/brochure describing points of interest and including a list of annual events.

COLOR COUNTRY, Cedar City Chamber of Commerce & Information Center, Box 220, Cedar City, UT 84720 (801/586-4022).

They cover Beaver, Iron, Garfield, Washington, and Kane Counties in the southwest and southcentral sections of the state. They issue an overall map/brochure describing national parks and monuments, fishing lakes, state parks, ghost towns, boating, hunting, camping, and skiing areas as well as individual similiar brochures for each of the 5 counties comprising the area. They have a walk-in address at 286 North Main Street in Cedar City.

DINOSAURLAND, Vernal Area Chamber of Commerce, 120 East Main, Vernal, UT 84078 (801/789-1352).

They cover Daggett, Duchesne, and Uintah Counties in the northeast corner of the state. They issue a general map/brochure describing points of interest and locating campgrounds, a list of hotels/motels, and a brochure describing eight 1-day self-guided tours. They sponsor a walk-in visitor center: Dinosaurland Information Center, Natural History State Museum, 235 East Main, Vernal, UT 84078 (801/789-4002).

GOLDEN SPIKE EMPIRE, Box 1601, Ogden, UT 84401 (801/399-8288).

They cover Box, Elder, Davis, Morgan, and Weber Counties in the northwest corner of the state. They issue a general map/brochure showing points of interest, and locations of airports, boating areas, camping areas, historic sites, picnicking, skiing, and snowmobiling areas. They have a walk-in address at 25th Street and Wall Avenue in Ogden. It is open Monday-Friday, 8:30A.M.-5P.M.

GREAT SALT LAKE COUNTRY, Salt Lake Visitor's Bureau, Suite 200, The Salt Palace, Salt Lake City, UT 84101 (801/521-2882).

They cover Salt Lake and Tooele Counties. See UT-35 for a full description.

MOUNTAINLAND, Mountainland Association of Government, 160 East Center Street, Provo, UT 84601 (801/377-2262).

They cover Utah, Wasatch, and Summit Counties in the north central section of the state. They issue 2 major pieces of literature: a general map/brochure describing activities and 3 tours of the area and a general all-purpose listing of events, attractions, restaurants, lodging, campgrounds, transportation and tour services, museums, theaters, and golf courses in each of the communities in the area as well as state parks and national forest information.

PANORAMALAND'S VISITORS BUREAU, Monroe, UT 84754 (801/527-4239 or 801/527-3575).

They cover Juab, Sanpete, Millard, Sevier, Piute, and Wayne Counties in the west central section of the state. They issue a general map/brochure describing points of interest and outdoor activities.

OTHER ORGANIZATIONS

UT-19   UTAH-NEVADA HOTEL & MOTEL ASSOCIATION, 1860 Laurelhurst Drive, Salt Lake City, UT 84108 (801/466-6033).

UT-20   UTAH STATE HISTORICAL SOCIETY, 307 West Second South, Salt Lake City, UT 84101 (801/533-5755).

This is a temporary address. The society will move into the Denver & Rio Grande Railroad Depot when renovations are completed. They issue a brief guide to UTAH HIGHWAY HISTORICAL MARKERS and an extensive list, with descriptions, of historic sites arranged by county. Neither publication is indexed, and their usefulness is therefore limited.

INFORMATION CENTERS/INFORMATION PHONES

There are 4 information centers located at major entrances to the state, but they are not indicated on the UTAH HIGHWAY MAP. They are: (1) on US 40 at the Natural History State Museum in Vernal, UT 84078 (801/789-4002); (2) on I-15 4 miles south of St. George (801/673-4542); (3) east of I-80 at Echo Junction (801/336-2588); and (4) on I-70 just east of US 163 near Thompson (801/285-2234). Call 801/521-8102 for a summer recreation/winter ski report recorded message. For highway conditions call 801/532-6000.

OUTDOOR RECREATION ACTIVITIES

CANOEING AND BOATING. For information on boating contact the Utah State Division of Parks and Recreation, 1596 West North Temple, Salt Lake City, UT 84116 (801/533-6012). See also UT-11, UT-12, UT-23, and UT-26.

FISHING AND HUNTING. For information, contact the Utah State Division of

Wildlife Resources, 1596 West North Temple, Salt Lake City, UT 84116 (801/533-9333). Their UTAH FISHING AND HUNTING GUIDE contains mostly general information, but it does include a selected list, with map, of good fishing waters plus a selected list, with map, of waterfowl areas. Their annual UTAH DEER HUNTING PROCLAMATION has a large map showing deer hunting areas. Another 44-page booklet from them, POPULAR UTAH FISHING WATERS by Arnold Bangerter (revised edition published in 1972), describes, with maps, 14 lakes, reservoirs, and rivers.

WINTER ACTIVITIES. A very detailed annual directory of downhill ski areas in Utah is available from either the Travel Council (UT-18) or the Utah Ski Association, 19 East Second South, Salt Lake City, UT 84111 (801/534-1779). A brief guide, with maps, of snowmobile trails, called UTAH SNOWMOBIL-ING, is available from the Utah State Division of Parks and Recreation, 1596 West North Temple, Salt Lake City, UT 84116 (801/533-6012).

NATIONAL/STATE PARKS/FORESTS, ETC.

Arches National Park

US-21   ARCHES NATIONAL PARK, 446 South Main Street, Moab, UT 84532 (801/259-7166).

This area was proclaimed as a national monument in 1929 and established as a national park in 1971. A general map/brochure is available. The visitor center, located at the southern entrance, is open all year. The number there is 801/259-5267.

See also UT-24.

Bryce Canyon National Park

UT-22   BRYCE CANYON NATIONAL PARK, Bryce Canyon, UT 84717 (801/834-5322).

They issue a general map/brochure, plus information on campgrounds, trails, visitor services, and winter activities. The visitor center is open all year, 7 days a week, except Christmas and New Year's Day.

See also UT-29.

Canyonlands National Park

UT-23   Belknap, Bill, and Belknap, Buzz. CANYONLANDS RIVER GUIDE. Boulder City, NV: Westwater Books, 1974. 63 p. Maps, photos. 0-916370-08-9. 74-80876.

This volume in the Westwater river guides series picks up the Green River at the town of Green River, UT (where the DESOLATION RIVER GUIDE [UT-11] leaves off) and follows it 120 miles south to the Confluence in Canyonlands National Park where it meets the Colorado River (126 miles of this River north from the Confluence to Westwater, UT are also included). From the Confluence, it follows the Colorado south through Lake Powell and to the Glen Canyon National Recreation Area (the Colorado is continued in GRAND CANYON RIVER [AZ-18]). Like the other volumes in this series, this book is mainly a graphic mile-by-mile representation (1 in. represents approximately 1/2 mile) of the rivers and the shorelines with very little text.

UT-24   Price, Raye C. GUIDEBOOK TO CANYONLANDS COUNTRY. Pasadena, CA: Ward Ritchie Press, 1974. 96 p. Photos., map. Index. 0-378-03772-2. 73-77046.

History, personal reminiscence, and tips for travelers are all interwoven in chapters about Arches and Canyonlands National Parks, the town of Moab, and the Colorado River which winds through the entire area.

UT-25   CANYONLANDS NATIONAL PARK, 446 South Main Street, Moab, UT 84532 (801/259-7166).

Much of this park is accessible only through off-road means: dirt roads suitable to any vehicle, easy and hazardous 4-wheel drive routes, foot trails, and raft trips on the Green or Colorado Rivers and through Cataract Canyon. Information on all these types of trails and means of exploration, plus a general map/brochure, is available from the above address. There are no information centers, but there are ranger stations at the northern and eastern road entrances to the park.

Glen Canyon National Recreation Area

UT-26   Dowler, Louise B., and Dowler, Warren L. DOWLER'S LAKE POWELL BOAT & TOUR GUIDE. 3d ed. Sierra Madre, CA: the authors (526 Camillo Street/91024), 1977. 57 p. Maps, photos. Bibliography. Index. 0-930188-07-1. 77-80564.

Basically, this is a collection of 15 colored and sometimes difficult to read maps (at a scale of 1 in. represents 1 and 2/5 miles) covering 170 miles of the Lake Powell waterway from Glen Canyon Dam to Cataract Canyon. The maps are basically USGS topographic reproductions which have added symbols indicating where facilities, points of interest, depth and type of water, and channel markers will be found. Brief written notes offering similar information accompany the maps. It stresses fishing and water sports.

UT-27   GLEN CANYON NATIONAL RECREATION AREA, Box 1507, Page, AZ 86040.

Although the National Recreation Area Headquarters of this popular boating and water sports area, as well as the visitor center at Glen Canyon Dam, are both located in the Page, AZ area, approximately five miles from the Arizona/Utah border, most of the land area is located in Utah. The general map/brochure available from the above office leaves a lot to be desired and, at best, provides a quick reference to facilities at the 7 marinas in the Recreation Area. The large map is somewhat hard to read, doesn't contain much information, and is not recommended for actual navigation. This major information piece for such a popular area needs to be redone.

A better source of information for this area is the Page-Lake Powell Chamber of Commerce, Box 727, Page, AZ 86040 (602/645-2741) which will provide information on accommodations, rentals, excursions, services, etc. There is a KYM'S GUIDE for Lake Powell. It is a detailed map/chart showing locations for fishing, boating, hunting, hiking, and camping. It is available from Triumph Press, Box 75445, Sanford Station, Los Angeles, CA 90075. A STAN JONES' BOATING AND EXPLORING MAP OF LAKE POWELL AND ITS CANYONS, at a scale of 3/8 in. represents about 1 mile, and now in a fifth edition, is available from Sun Country Publications, Box 955, Page, AZ 86040. It includes a general waterway guide to all the canyons in the area, plus information about the navigational buoys, marinas, points of interest, fishing, trails, wildlife, etc. A LAKE POWELL MAP/GUIDE is available from the American Adventures Association, 1865 South Main, Suite 27, Salt Lake City, UT 84115. The map indicates the topography of the Glen Canyon area noting facilities and points of interest while the guide part lists marinas (noting facilities) and a rating for each canyon (giving location, general description, photogenic features, etc.)

Zion National Park

UT-28   Blake, Reid. ZION TRAILS: A HIKING GUIDE TO THE BEST TRAILS IN ZION NATIONAL PARK. Salt Lake City: Wasatch Publishers, 1977. 48 p. Maps, photos. 0-915272-09-1.

This is a guide to 7 trails, including the famous Zion Narrows trail. Descriptions include hiking time, distance, availability of water, elevation gain, the name of the USGS map to use, access, and trail highlights.

UT-29   A PHOTOGRAPHIC AND COMPREHENSIVE GUIDE TO ZION & BRYCE CANYON NATIONAL PARKS. Casper, WY: World-Wide Research & Publishing Co., National Parks Division, 1972. 64 p. Photos., maps. 72-194460.

While mostly stunning photographs, this guide also contains the following for each park: a motorist's guide, brief mentions of hikes, visitor facilities (including visitor centers), and recreation opportunities.

UT-30   ZION NATIONAL PARK, Springdale, UT 84767 (801/772-3256).

They issue a general map/brochure that includes some information on trails and visitor services, plus leaflets on campgrounds, backcountry camping, geology, and flora and fauna. The visitor center, located near the South Entrance to the park, is open all year. The Zion Natural History Association, also at the above address, sells several publications on the park, including their own 24-page GUIDE TO THE TRAILS--ZION NATIONAL PARK. A revised edition was published in 1975.

A brochure describing each of the 14 NATIONAL PARK AREAS IN UTAH (with an address and phone number for each) is available from the National Park Service, Rocky Mountain Regional Office, Public Affairs Office, Box 25287, Denver, CO 80225 (303/234-3095). A brochure describing the 5 major national parks and 2 national recreation areas in Utah is available from the Travel Council (UT-18).

Information on each of the 8 national forests in Utah is available from the U.S. Forest Service, Intermountain Region, Federal Bldg., 324 25th Street, Ogden, UT 84401.

BLM DEVELOPED RECREATION SITES IN UTAH and information on the Bonneville Salt Flats and the Pony Express Trail in western Utah are available from the Bureau of Land Management, Utah State Office, 136 East South Temple, Salt Lake City, UT 84111.

A map/brochure, THE STATE PARKS OF UTAH, WITH A TRAVELER'S GUIDE TO HISTORIC, SCENIC AND WATER RECREATION AREAS, is available from the Utah State Division of Parks and Recreation, 1596 West North Temple, Salt Lake City, UT 84116 (801/533-6012). It also lists the 11 state parks providing visitor information facilities.

INDIVIDUAL CITIES OR AREAS

Salt Lake City—Printed Materials

UT-31   ACCESS SALT LAKE. Salt Lake City: Utah State Board for Vocational Education, Division of Rehabilitation Services (250 East 500 South Street/84111), 1978.

UT-32   Czerny, Peter G. THE GREAT SALT LAKE. Provo, UT: Brigham Young University Press, 1976. 121 p. Photos., map. Bibliography. 0-8425-1073-7. 76-4080.

Although this is primarily a book of colored photographs, the text does include a few suggestions for visitors, and because nothing better could be found for the Great Salt Lake, this book is included.

UT-33   Kuehl, Barbara, and Uhlenberg, Beverly. DISCOVER SALT LAKE
         CITY. Salt Lake City: the authors, 1975. 103 p. Maps, photos.
         75-319615.

         This is a concise, clearly organized, regional guide which includes
         maps, touring time, parking and bus information, points of interest,
         and area restaurants. In addition, there is a chapter on entertain-
         ment--which includes nightlife, sports, and culture--plus one brief
         chapter on some things to see and do away from the city.

UT-34   SALT LAKE COUNTY STREET DIRECTORY ATLAS: 66 SECTION
         MAPS. Salt Lake City: Salt Lake Street Directory (Box 1201/84101),
         1974. 176 p. Scales vary. Index. 76-361659.

Maps of Salt Lake City are available from AAA (US-259), Goushā (US-206),
Rand McNally (US-215), and the Salt Lake City Area Chamber of Commerce,
19 East 2d South, Salt Lake City, UT 84116. See also UT-34.

Salt Lake City—Organizations

UT-35   SALT LAKE VALLEY CONVENTION AND VISITORS BUREAU, Suite
         200, The Salt Palace, Salt Lake City, UT 84101 (801/521-2822).

         They issue 2 pieces of literature: a general brochure describing,
         with a good map, all the things to see and do in the area; and a
         combination "picture map" and guide to restaurants, transportation
         services, hotels/motels, campsites, theaters, museums, golf courses,
         and picnic areas.

VERMONT

BOOKS, ATLASES, MAGAZINES

VT-1   Bearse, Ray, ed. VERMONT: A GUIDE TO THE GREEN MOUN-
TAIN STATE. 3d ed. New American Guide Series. Boston:
Houghton Mifflin Co., 1968. 452 p. Photos., maps. 68-14344.

This revision of the original WPA guide includes a general background
on the history, natural resources, and recreation of the state plus a
detailed gazetteer section.

VT-2   Colter, Janet, and Colter, Rudyard. FAVORITE VERMONT SKI INNS
AND LODGING GUIDE. New York: McGraw-Hill, 1977. 221 p.
Maps, drawings. Index. 0-07-012085-4. 77-12542.

"Detailed information on 238 inns, motels, dorms, condominiums, and
chalets" is given in this guide. It also lists "222 recommended restaurants, 116 preferred night spots, all as reported by alpine and
nordic skiers." Arranged geographically by skiing area, the brief
descriptions (including location, type, plan, rooms, facilities, etc.)
and comments (ranging from short mention of AAA rating to rather full
and penetrating analyses of the establishment) are supplemented by an
appendix of "special facilities."

VT-3   GAZETTEER OF VERMONT HERITAGE. Chester, VT: The National
Survey, 1974. 95 p. Photos., maps.

The general historical section and the biographical section are minor
parts of this volume. The bulk of the volume is devoted to an alphabetical listing of towns and cities, with notes on historical events. A
list of museums in the state, giving location, hours, and fees, is included.

VT-4   GUIDE BOOK OF THE LONG TRAIL. 20th ed. Rutland, VT: Green
Mountain Club, 1971. 152 p. Maps, tables. Index.

This is a detailed description of the Long Trail, "a footpath in the
wilderness over the Green Mountains of Vermont from Massachusetts

to Canada," giving hiking time and distance tables. A 21st edition was published in 1977.

VT-5   Kunin, Madeline, and Stout, Marilyn. THE BIG GREEN BOOK: A FOUR-SEASON GUIDE TO VERMONT. Barre, MA: Barre Publishing Co. (distributed by Crown), 1976. 344 p. Drawings, maps. Index. 0-517-52092-3. 75-44340.

Overwhelmingly complete, this is the one book to buy if you're buying only one. The state is divided into 4 sections and information on recreation, "exploring nature" sites, villages, architecture, arts, crafts, foods and inns, shopping, antiquing, and things to do with children is given for each. Sources for further information are noted. Appendixes note the location of official information centers, historical tours, factory tours, and give 7 "wonderful Vermont recipes."

VT-6   Schweiker, Roioli. CANOE CAMPING: VERMONT AND NEW HAMPSHIRE RIVERS. A GUIDE TO 600 MILES OF RIVERS FOR A DAY, WEEKEND, OR WEEK OF CANOEING. Edited by Catherine J. Baker. Somersworth: New Hampshire Publishing Co., 1977. 91 p. Maps, photos. 0-912274-71-9. 76-52884.

The author describes, with maps, tables, general water details, and information on riverside campsites, fishing areas, hikes, etc., 14 rivers or river segments. The book doesn't tell you about specific trips for a day, a weekend, or a week. You pick your own river segments from the river tables which give mileages between good break points on the rivers.

MAPS

The official state map is available from the Information and Travel Division (VT-7). The 1978-79 edition lists radio stations; hospital emergency rooms; public golf courses; fish and game information; historic places; museums; privately owned campgrounds; state liquor stores and agencies; and parks, forests, and public recreation areas. AAA (US-259), Goushā (US-206), and Rand McNally (US-215) each issue a combined Maine/New Hampshire/Vermont map.

MAJOR TOURIST ORGANIZATION

VT-7   VERMONT AGENCY OF DEVELOPMENT AND COMMUNITY AFFAIRS, INFORMATION AND TRAVEL DIVISION, 61 Elm Street, Montpelier, VT 05602 (802/828-3236).

They issue an annual THE VERMONT GUIDE (giving brief descriptions of the history and attractions in every town in the state); an extensive annual VISITORS HANDBOOK (consisting mainly of a listing of accommodations, shops, and other visitor services); SHORT WALKS ON THE TRAIL; a calendar of events (issued 3 times a year); a list of housekeeping cottages, chalets, camps, and private homes available for rent; a guide to historic sites; a crafts directory; a directory of boys and girls camps; an antiquing directory; and individual brochures providing information on each of the following: maple sugar houses open to the public, private campgrounds, state forests and parks, craft/treasure trails, riding stables and riding events, and tennis resorts and facilities.

OTHER ORGANIZATIONS

VT-8   THE GREEN MOUNTAIN CLUB, Box 889, 43 State Street, Montpelier, VT 05602 (802/223-3463).

This is a private, nonprofit corporation which maintains hiking trails in Vermont and which is a member of the Appalachian Trail Conference (N-55). They publish a GUIDE BOOK OF THE LONG TRAIL (VT-4) and a brochure, DAY HIKING IN VERMONT (descriptions of 19 day hikes). A VERMONT HIKER'S GUIDE was to have been published in 1978.

VT-9   VERMONT HOTEL-MOTEL-RESTAURANT ASSOCIATION, 148 State Street, Montpelier, VT 05602 (802/229-0062).

VT-10   VERMONT STATE CHAMBER OF COMMERCE, Box 37, Montpelier, VT 05602 (802/223-3443 or 802/229-0154).

They issue VERMONT'S GAZETTEER (an extensive regional listing of restaurants, lodging, camping, shops, attractions, etc.); an extensive annual map and guide to eating, lodging, and attractions; and a map and guide to covered bridges, craft and gift shops, antique shops, and country stores.

INFORMATION CENTERS/INFORMATION PHONES

Vermont is one of the few states making a comprehensive effort to provide systematic on-the-road travel information. It was the first to have a highway information center. Through its Travel Information Council, a citizen policy-making board in the state government, it is replacing all highway advertising with "Official Business Directional Signs" which advise the traveler of such services available at road junctions and the number of miles to each. At major intersections and locations, "Travel Information Plazas" are found from which are dispensed "Travelers Service Guides" which provide directions to businesses in each respective area of Vermont. These information plazas are quite numerous and are located on the official state map by the symbol "T." The state map also contains a list of local chambers of commerce.

OUTDOOR RECREATION ACTIVITIES

BICYCLING.   BICYCLE TOURING IN VERMONT is available from the Ver-

mont Recreation and Park Society, c/o Recreation Section, Agency of Environmental Conservation, Dept. of Forests, Parks and Recreation, Montpelier, VT
05602. This 35-page booklet describes 19 different tours varying in length
from 25 to 461 miles.

CANOEING AND BOATING. Information on summer canoe trips and a bro-
chure, CANOEING ON THE CONNECTICUT RIVER, are available from the
Vermont Agency of Environmental Conservation, Dept. of Forests, Parks and
Recreation, Montpelier, VT 05602. They also supply information on boating.
The Information and Travel Division (VT-7) issues a brochure describing boat-
ing and water sports facilities. See also VT-6.

FISHING AND HUNTING. For a VERMONT FISHING GUIDE, a VERMONT
HUNTING GUIDE, and full information on laws and regulations, contact the
Vermont Agency of Environmental Conservation, Dept. of Fish and Game,
Court Street Office Bldg., Montpelier, VT 05602. The official state map
contains a brief summary of regulations and license requirements and informa-
tion on 43 wildlife management areas.

WINTER ACTIVITIES. The Information and Travel Division (VT-7) issues an
annual ski guide that includes information on both downhill skiing and ski
touring areas. The Vermont State Chamber of Commerce (VT-10) issues a
guide/map and maintains a 24-hour number for ski reports (802/223-2957).
Information on ski touring trails and snowmobile trails is available from the
Vermont Agency of Environmental Conservation, Dept. of Forests, Parks and
Recreation, Montpelier, VT 05602 (802/828-3375). Information on snowmobile laws, rules, and regulations is available from the Vermont Dept. of Public Safety, Montpelier, VT 05602. See also VT-2.

NATIONAL/STATE PARKS/FORESTS, ETC.

There are no National Park Service areas in Vermont. For information and
maps on Green Mountain National Forest, Vermont's only national forest,
contact the Forest Supervisor, Green Mountain National Forest, Federal Bldg.,
151 West Street, Rutland, VT 05701 (802/775-2579).

For a guide (which includes a campsite reservation application) to state parks
and forest recreation areas plus information on hiking in Vermont, contact the
Vermont Agency of Environmental Conservation, Dept. of Forests, Parks and
Recreation, Montpelier, VT 05602 (802/828-3375).

INDIVIDUAL CITIES OR AREAS

Montpelier—Organizations

See Vermont State Chamber of Commerce (VT-10).

VIRGINIA

BOOKS, ATLASES, MAGAZINES

VA-1   Corbett, H. Roger. VIRGINIA WHITE WATER: A CANOEING GUIDE TO THE RIVERS OF THE OLD DOMINION. Springfield, VA: Seneca Press, 1977. 289 p. Maps. 77-375692.

This canoeing guide is "a compilation of technical data, trip descriptions, maps, and historical facts for 87 rivers, creeks, or runs in Virginia. It is the first volume of a two volume series. . . ." We rate this as very good.

VA-2   Dohme, Alvin. SHENANDOAH: THE VALLEY STORY. Washington, DC: Potomac Books, 1972. 248 p. Photos., maps. Index. 0-87107-014-6. 78-85812.

This is both an "informative history and a sightseeing guidebook." The last 150 pages include 14 tours of the region, plus where-to-go information on 21 different vacationing activities from historic homes to sports to eating in unusual places. Sources of further information are included.

VA-3   FRESH WATER FISHING AND HUNTING IN VIRGINIA. Alexandria, VA: Alexandria Drafting Co., 1976. 88 p. Scales vary. Indexes. 77-359016.

We rate this an excellent publication for the sportsman with its lists of fishing waters by county, its detailed maps of hunting areas, and its indexes to towns and recreational facilities.

VA-4   SALT WATER SPORT FISHING AND BOATING IN VIRGINIA. Alexandria, VA: Alexandria Drafting Co., 1977. 116 p. Scale: 4 in. represents 5 miles. Index. 77-350576.

This publication has 33 colorful charts indicating fishing grounds. These are supplemented by descriptions of marinas.

VA-5   VIRGINIA: A GUIDE TO THE OLD DOMINION. American Guide
        Series. New York: Oxford University Press, 1940. 710 p.
        Photos., maps.

        This original WPA guide begins with a section of essays covering
        "Virginia's Background," describes 15 major cities, and concludes
        with itineraries for 24 state-wide road tours. It is comprehensive,
        but out of date.

VA-6   Voges, Nettie A. OLD ALEXANDRIA, WHERE AMERICA'S PAST
        IS PRESENT. McLean, VA: EPM Publications, 1975. 208 p.
        Photos., map. 0-914440-10-1. 75-23343.

        This book contains "four walking tours through the lively Virginia
        port, past its architecturally beautiful 18th century houses, into
        churches and public buildings, plus visits to archeological digs and
        the old ramparts."

VA-7   Wuertz-Schaefer, Karin. HIKING VIRGINIA'S NATIONAL FORESTS.
        New York: East Woods Press, 1977. 201 p. Maps, photos. Bib-
        liography. 0-914788-05-1. 77-70414.

        Fifty-two hikes are described in good detail, listing length, difficulty,
        elevations, markings, and the USGS quadrangle which show the
        trails. General hiking advice is also included.

MAPS

The official state highway map is available from the Virginia Dept. of Highways and Transportation, Public Relations Office, 1221 East Broad Street,
Richmond, VA 23219. The 1978 edition lists selected points of interest; facilities in national and state parks and forests; waysides for picnicking; and
has another map on the reverse side which locates recreational sites, historical
and cultural points of interest, rest areas, official information stations, and
other travel information centers. AAA (US-259), Exxon (US-262), Goushā
(US-206), and Rand McNally (US-215) each issue a combined Delaware/
Maryland/Virginia/West Virginia map.

MAJOR TOURIST ORGANIZATION

VA-8   VIRGINIA STATE TRAVEL SERVICE, 6 North Sixth Street, Richmond,
        VA 23219 (804/786-2051).

        They issue a general geographical points of interest booklet, CHOOSE
        YOUR VIRGINIA, CIVIL WAR BATTLEFIELD PARKS, a golf brochure,
        and a catalog describing 26 16mm full-color travel films on vacation-
        oriented attractions, cities, and regions in the state. They sponsor
        2 out-of-state branch offices at the following addresses: (1) Virginia
        State Travel Service, 11 Rockefeller Plaza, New York, NY 10020

(212/245-3080) and (2) Virginia State Travel Service, 906 17th Street NW, Washington, DC 20006 (202/293-5350).

REGIONAL TOURISM ASSOCIATIONS

EASTERN SHORE OF VIRGINIA CHAMBER OF COMMERCE, Box 147, Accomac, VA 23301 (804/787-2460).

They issue a general brochure describing points of interest on Virginia's Eastern Shore, a directory of member services, VIRGINIA'S EASTERN SHORE TOUR (this is not too good--the sketch map is vague and the points of interest are listed but have no descriptions), and DELMARVA'S NATIONAL HERITAGE CHURCH TOUR (map and descriptions of 45 churches) prepared by the Delmarva Advisory Council. They also supply information on the mail boat to Tangier Island.

OTHER ORGANIZATIONS

VA-9   VIRGINIA HOTEL & MOTEL ASSOCIATION, 300 West Franklin Street, Richmond, VA 23220.

INFORMATION CENTERS/INFORMATION PHONES

A list and locations of the highway travel information stations will be found on the official highway map.

OUTDOOR RECREATION ACTIVITIES

CANOEING AND BOATING. BOATING ACCESS TO VIRGINIA WATERS is a detailed map/guide to over 200 launch sites and adjacent services and is available from the Virginia Commission of Game & Inland Fisheries, 4010 West Broad Street, Richmond, VA 23230 (804/257-1000). See also VA-1 and VA-4.

FISHING AND HUNTING. Guides on where to go hunting and fishing are available from the Virginia Commission of Game & Inland Fisheries, 4010 West Broad Street, Richmond, VA 23230 (804/257-1000). The State Travel Service (VA-8) issues a brochure on saltwater and freshwater fishing. See also VA-3 and VA-4.

NATIONAL/STATE PARKS/FORESTS, ETC.

Chincoteague National Wildlife Refuge

VA-10   Firestone, Linda, and Morse, Whit. A GUIDEBOOK TO VIRGINIA'S

FAVORITE ISLANDS: CHINCOTEAGUE AND ASSATEAGUE. Richmond, VA: Good Life Publishers, 1976. 71 p. Photos., map. 0-917374-00-2. 76-22264.

Full of information on what to see and do, where it's located, and when it's happening, but organized in a vague and rambling manner, this is a less useful book than it might be. Restaurants and accommodations are also noted.

VA-11 CHINCOTEAGUE NATIONAL WILDLIFE REFUGE, Box 62, Chincoteague, VA 23336 (804/336-6122).

They issue a general map/brochure, a calendar of events, and information about the ponies, fishing areas, birds and other wildlife, and wildlife tours. The visitor information center is open 1–4P.M., December–March and 9A.M.–4P.M. all the other months.

VA-12 CHINCOTEAGUE CHAMBER OF COMMERCE, Box 258, Chincoteague, VA 23336 (804/336-6161).

They supply a list of accommodations, recreations, restaurants, churches, shops, and services. Write to them for information about the annual pony penning held the last Wednesday and Thursday in July.

Alexandria Drafting Co. (S-16) issues a CHINCOTEAGUE-ASSATEAGUE FISHING AND RECREATION MAP that indicates fishing grounds, campgrounds, marinas and launching sites, wrecks, and the locations of businesses which advertise in the margins. The back of the sheet has a detailed street map of Chincoteague noting the location of commercial concerns which advertise.

Colonial National Historic Park

VA-13 COLONIAL NATIONAL HISTORICAL PARK, Box 210, Yorktown, VA 23690.

"This Park encompasses most of Jamestown Island, site of the first permanent English settlement; Yorktown, scene of the culminating battle of the American Revolution in 1781; a 23 mile parkway connecting these and other colonial sites with Williamsburg; and Cape Henry Memorial, which marks the approximate site of the first landing of Jamestown's colonists in 1607." There are visitor centers in Jamestown and Yorktown.

Shenandoah National Park

VA-14 Denton, James W. CIRCUIT HIKES IN SHENANDOAH NATIONAL PARK. 10th ed. Washington, DC: Potomac Appalachian Trail Club, 1976. 86 p. Maps, photos. 0-915746-08-5. 76-21937.

Twenty-two hikes, each with its own good map, are described in detail. A circuit hike is one which returns the hiker to his/her starting point.

VA-15 SHENANDOAH NATIONAL PARK, Rt. 4, Box 292, Luray, VA 22835 (703/999-2241).

They issue a general map/brochure, a calendar of events, and information on camping, hiking, backcountry exploration, and bicycling. There are 2 visitor centers, both open daily from 9A.M.-5P.M. The Shenandoah Natural History Association, also at the above address, provides and sells hiking and trail guides and maps and general books dealing with the history, folklore, and natural history of the area.

Within the park, lodging (including reservations) and other services are provided by ARA Virginia Sky-Line Co., Box 727, Luray, VA 22835 (703/999-2211). In the winter months call 703/743-5108. An annual SHENANDOAH VALLEY ACCOMMODATIONS, RESTAURANTS AND CAMPGROUND GUIDE to the Shenandoah region as a whole is available from the Shenandoah Valley Travel Association, Box 488, New Market, VA 22844 (703/740-3132).

INDIVIDUAL CITIES OR AREAS

Norfolk/Newport News/Virginia Beach—Printed Materials

VA-16 Alexandria Drafting Co. HAMPTON & NEWPORT NEWS STREET MAP. Alexandria, VA: Alexandria Drafting, 1974. 28 p. Scale: 1 in. represents 2,000 ft. Index. 75-328796.

VA-17 _____. NORFOLK & VICINITY STREET MAP. Alexandria, VA: Alexandria Drafting, 1974. 39 p. Scale: 1 in. represents 2,000 ft. Index. 75-328800.

Virginia Beach, Portsmouth, Chesapeake, and Suffolk are included, along with Norfolk.

VA-18 A GUIDEBOOK TO NORFOLK FOR THE HANDICAPPED AND AGING. Norfolk: Health Information Center, 1967.

A map of the Norfolk/Hampton Roads/Newport News area is available from Rand McNally (US-215). Maps of Norfolk are available from AAA (US-259); American Map Co., 1926 Broadway, New York, NY 10023; Champion Map Corp. (US-202); Exxon (US-261); and Gousha (US-206). Separate maps of Newport News and Virginia Beach are available from Champion Map Corp. See also VA-16 and VA-17.

Virginia

Norfolk/Newport News/Virginia Beach—Organizations

VA-19   NORFOLK VISITORS BUREAU, Box 238, Norfolk, VA 23501 (804/441-5166).

They issue NORFOLK TOUR and GUIDE TO NORFOLK'S LODGING (also includes restaurants). Information centers are available at the Norfolk International Airport (Monday-Friday, 9:30A.M.-6P.M.), at Ocean View Beach (9A.M.-5:30P.M., 7 days a week, May through Labor Day), and a dowtown office in the "Scope" complex (Monday-Friday, 8:30A.M.-5P.M.). The phone number above is to the downtown office and is the only available information number.

VA-20   VIRGINIA BEACH CHAMBER OF COMMERCE, Box 390, Virginia Beach, VA 23458.

They supply many brochures on what to see and do, including an area driving tour and an accommodations directory.

Richmond—Printed Materials

VA-21   Beach, Marie, ed. GUIDE TO RICHMOND. Midlothian, VA: Prides Crossing (Box 242/23113), 1976. 200 p. Photos., maps. 76-150519.

This is "a handbook on what the city offers to residents, newcomers, and tourists. It includes detailed information on shopping and restaurants, museums and historic landmarks, restored and interesting neighborhoods, antique and flea markets, sports, the arts, recreation and tours plus a day trip directory to tourist spots in Virginia from Mount Vernon to Monticello, Williamsburg to Virginia Beach."

VA-22   RICHMOND GUIDE FOR THE HANDICAPPED AND AGING. Richmond: Easter Seal Society for Crippled Children and Adults, 1969.

Maps of Richmond are available from Champion Map Corp. (US-202), Exxon (US-261), Goushā (US-206), and Rand McNally (US-215).

The Richmond weather information number is 804/936-1212.

Richmond—Organizations

VA-23   METROPOLITAN RICHMOND CONVENTION AND VISITORS BUREAU, 201 East Franklin Street, Richmond, VA 23219 (804/649-0373).

They issue a map/guide, a hotel/motel guide, a dining guide, 50 THINGS TO SEE AND DO IN RICHMOND WITHOUT GETTING WET, WALKING TOUR, and CERTIFIED TOUR GUIDE SERVICE. There is a visitor information center at 1700 Robin Hood Road, at the intersection of I-95 and I-64, exit 14. The phone number there is 804/358-5511.

Williamsburg—Printed Materials

VA-24 COLONIAL WILLIAMSBURG: OFFICIAL GUIDEBOOK & MAP. 7th
ed. Williamsburg: Colonial Williamsburg, 1972. 110 p. Separate
map in back. Index. 0-910412-32-4. 56-402.

This is a guide "containing a brief history of the old city, and of
its renewing, with remarks on the 6 chief appeals thereof; and descriptions of near one hundred and fifty dwellings--houses, shops
& publick buildings." The easy-to-read guide-map shows all buildings (with a name index), locations of rest rooms, and insets showing
road approaches and the "Gateway to Colonial Williamsburg" area
where the information center is located. The guidebook has been
recorded for the blind, and a braille map of the historic area is
included with it.

A detailed map of Williamsburg will be found in VA-16.

Williamsburg—Organizations

VA-25 THE COLONIAL WILLIAMSBURG FOUNDATION, DEPT. OF TRAVEL,
Drawer C, Williamsburg, VA 23185 (804/229-1000, ext. 2751).

They publish the OFFICIAL GUIDEBOOK & MAP (VA-24) and the
following brochures: a calendar of events issued in the spring,
autumn, and at Christmas; accommodations; dining; A GUIDE FOR
THE HANDICAPPED (contains suggestions for blind and deaf visitors
and descriptions of access to the various buildings for visitors with
limited mobility); and group tours. The information center's hours
of operation are April to November, 8:30A.M.-10P.M. and November to March, 8:30A.M.-9P.M. There is a toll-free reservations
number for accommodations, dining, conferences, and group tours:
800/446-8956; in Virginia call 800/582-8976.

VA-26 WILLIAMSBURG AREA CHAMBER OF COMMERCE, Box HQ, Williamsburg, VA 23185 (804/229-6511).

They issue a complete and concise guide on to where to stay, where
to eat, what to do, and what to see in Williamsburg, Jamestown,
Yorktown, and Busch Gardens.

WASHINGTON

BOOKS, ATLASES, MAGAZINES

WA-1   ACCOMMODATIONS DIRECTORY FOR THE HANDICAPPED TRAV-
ELLER: STATE OF WASHINGTON. Olympia: Washington Dept. of
Social and Health Services, Division of Vocational Rehabilitation,
EMBER Project, 1976. 396 p.

WA-2   Bedrick, Ed, and Bedrick, Christina. 121 FREE CAMP GROUNDS
IN WASHINGTON STATE. Seattle: Superior Publishing Co., 1977.
103 p. Photos., maps. 0-87564-625-5. 77-3215.

For each listed campground, a snapshot accompanies the brief notation of location and facilities.

WA-3   Crain, Jim, and Milne, Terry. CAMPING AROUND WASHINGTON.
New York: Random House, 1974. 94 p. Maps. Indexes. 0-394-
70683-8. 73-20590.

Twenty-three "trip maps" covering the entire state show trails, campsites, roads, park and forest areas, ranger stations or visitor centers,
places of interest, and cities or towns. Accompanying text briefly
describes the points of interest and campsites in each of the 23 areas.
Indexes by type of activity (birdwatching, etc.) and features (volcanic
activity, etc.) are keyed to specific campgrounds to aid in trip
planning.

WA-4   Darvill, Fred T., Jr. NORTH CASCADES HIGHWAY GUIDE.
Mount Vernon, WA: Darvill Outdoor Publications (Box 636/98273),
1973. 47 p. Maps. 0-915740-03-6. 73-162011.

This is a detailed road guide to State Route 20 which is the major
west/east road through the area. Points of interest, campsites, other
visitor facilities (gas stations, etc.), trails, etc. are located by odometer readings. There are 28 trails described.

WA-5   Darvill, Fred T., Jr., and Marshall, Louise B. WINTER WALKS
        AND SUMMER STROLLS, I AND II. Rev. ed. 2 vols. Lynnwood,
        WA: Signpost Publications, 1977. Maps.

        These small volumes describe, with individual maps for each, easy,
        snowfree, year-round, walks at low elevations, most of which are
        suitable for families with young children. Volume I describes 56
        walks in Whatcom, Skagit, San Juan, and Island Counties in the
        northwest corner. Volume II has the same format and covers trails
        near Seattle and Everett.

WA-6   Faber, Jim. AN IRREVERENT GUIDE TO WASHINGTON STATE.
        Garden City, NY: Doubleday, 1974. 178 p. 0-385-06692-9. 73-
        22798.

        This rambling, opinionated guide is best used for suggestions. It must
        be perused and cannot be opened to a specific place for specific in-
        formation. There is no index, and there are no maps. It is, how-
        ever, chuck full of useful facts about where and how to go. Orga-
        nizations providing visitor information are listed as well as the phone
        numbers of all local chambers of commerce.

WA-7   Furrer, Werner. KAYAK AND CANOE TRIPS IN WASHINGTON.
        Rev. ed. Lynnwood, WA: Signpost Publications, 1978. Maps.

        This is a guide to 36 flatwater and whitewater trips in the state of
        Washington.

WA-8   Jones, Stan. WASHINGTON STATE FISHING GUIDE. Seattle:
        the author, 1970. 288 p. Maps, photos. Index. 72-14194.

        Arranged by county, this is a guide to rivers, lakes, creeks, etc.,
        giving the type of fish found, best season, etc. for each. Individual
        county maps are included, but the specific water areas described are
        not located on them. A list of "resorts" is also provided for each
        county. Principal streams and lakes in Olympic and Mount Rainier
        National Parks are listed as are guides and packers who will arrange
        trips. This guide should be updated.

WA-9   Kirk, Ruth. EXPLORING THE OLYMPIC PENINSULA. 2d ed.
        Seattle: University of Washington Press, 1976. 118 p. Photos.,
        maps. Bibliography. Index. 0-295-95528-7. 77-358219.

        This book begins with the history, cultural, human, and natural, of the
        peninsula. A road guide section includes maps with scenic drives
        indicated, suggestions on what to do, main supply centers, camp-
        grounds, special events, and a directory of communities. The trail
        guide section is brief but full of suggestions. There is a directory
        of picnic areas, campgrounds, fishing areas, etc. and a list of orga-
        nizations supplying information.

WA-10 _____. WASHINGTON STATE NATIONAL PARKS, HISTORIC
SITES, RECREATION AREAS AND NATURAL LANDMARKS. Seattle:
University of Washington Press, 1974. 63 p. Photos., maps.
0-295-95323-3. 74-6020.

This is a nice introduction to North Cascades, Mount Rainier, and
Olympic National Parks; Fort Vancouver, Whitman Mission, and San
Juan Island National Historic Sites; Coulee Dam National Recreation
Area; and 24 other natural landmarks and historic places in Washington. Stunning color photographs; historical and natural history descriptions; and practical information, such as road directions, trails,
fishing, camping, addresses to write to for further information, etc.
are also provided.

WA-11 Majors, Harry M. EXPLORING WASHINGTON. Holland, MI:
Van Winkle Publishing Co. (84 West 20th Street/49423), 1975.
176 p. Maps, photos. Index. 77-356600.

This is a large book (16 in. x 12 in.) reproducing 27 maps of the state
at about 1 in. representing 4 miles with main features (geographical,
cultural, etc.) keyed to an excellent, if brief, text on the pages
following each map. The text ranges from short notes to rather full
histories. Nice black-and-white photographs are included. We rate
this a very good book.

WA-12 Majors, Harry M., and McCollum, Richard C. MONTE CRISTO
AREA: A COMPLETE OUTDOOR GUIDE. Seattle: Northwest Press,
1977. 212 p. Maps, photos., diagrams. Bibliography. Index.
77-79115.

The subtitle is definitely right, and although the Monte Cristo region
is just one part of the North Cascades, we include the book here
because it is so thorough. There are separate chapters on (1) history;
(2) geology; (3) road log (with USGS quadrangle reproductions);
(4) campgrounds (each is described with a sketch showing individual
sites); (5) trails (detailed descriptions of 20 trails including length,
elevation gain, highest elevation, and USGS quadrangle reproduction);
(6) scrambles (suggestions for 12 cross-country traverses with accompanying USGS quadrangle); (7) peaks (a historical register of what
peaks have been scaled is given rather than detailed climbing instructions); and (8) botany (with identification sketches of each species
described). The many photographs serve a purpose too. They either
enhance historical appreciation or facilitate identification of terrain
features.

WA-13 Manning, Harvey. FOOTSORE 1: WALKS & HIKES AROUND
PUGET SOUND. Seattle: The Mountaineers, 1977. 214 p. Photos.,
maps. Index. 0-916890-53-8. 77-23727.

_____. FOOTSORE 2: WALKS & HIKES AROUND PUGET SOUND.
Seattle: The Mountaineers, 1978. 214 p. Photos., maps. Index.
0-916890-54-6. 77-23727.

_____. FOOTSORE 3: WALKS & HIKES AROUND PUGET SOUND. Seattle: The Mountaineers, 1978. 232 p. Photos., maps. Index. 0-916890-65-1. 77-23727.

The easy walks of usually no more than 1 day's duration described in these volumes seem almost inexhaustible. FOOTSORE 1 covers Seattle, the Puget Sound Trail from Tacoma to Everett, Overlake Highlands and Sammamish Valley, Issaquah Alps, Cedar and Green Rivers, and White River. FOOTSORE 2 covers Snoqualmie River, Great Big Western Tree Farm (Tolt River), and Skykomish River. FOOTSORE 3 covers Stillaguamish River, Skagit River, the Puget Sound Trail from Everett to Bellingham, the Northern Isles, and North Kitsap and Olympic Peninsulas. A forthcoming FOOTSORE 4 will cover the Carbon River, Puyallup River, Nisqually River, Deschutes River, the Puget Sound Trail from Tacoma to Olympia, South Kitsap Peninsula, South Olympic Peninsula, and the Islands of Vashon and Blake in the Sound.

WA-14   Marshall, Louise B. HIGH TRAILS: GUIDE TO THE PACIFIC CREST TRAIL IN WASHINGTON. 4th ed. Lynnwood, WA: Signpost Publications, 1973. 154 p. Maps, photos. Index. 0-913140-08-2. 73-178306.

This is a north/south mile-by-mile hiking guide to the 80 miles of the Pacific Crest Trail that lie in Washington. It contains elevation charts, and reproductions of USGS survey maps on which the trail is marked.

WA-15   Mueller, Marge. THE SAN JUAN ISLANDS: AFOOT AND AFLOAT. Seattle: The Mountaineers, 1978. 200 p. (approximately). Photos., maps. 0-916890-63-5.

This is "a guide to everything you can do and see in the San Juan Islands, whether you come by boat, car or on foot from the ferry. . . a winning combination of trip details, maps, photos, and history."

WA-16   Satterfield, Archie. WASHINGTON FOR ALL SEASONS. Mercer Island, WA: The Writing Works, [1978?]. 160 p. 0-916076-23-7.

This is "a month-by-month guide to Washington activities and events that is similiar to OREGON FOR ALL SEASONS" (OR-9).

WA-17   Scofield, W.M. WASHINGTON'S HISTORICAL MARKERS. A Souvenir Book. Portland, OR: Touchstone Press, 1967. 79 p. Photos., map. Index. 0-911518-15-0. 67-8968.

Photographs of 49 highway markers are enlarged so the user of this book can read the text on each. It is regionally arranged with a name index.

WA-18   Speidel, William C. THE WET SIDE OF THE MOUNTAINS (OR

PROWLING WESTERN WASHINGTON). Seattle: Nettle Creek Publishing Co., 1974. 452 p. Maps. Bibliography. Index. 0-914890-01-8. 74-83445.

This is a chatty, informal guide to Washington west of the Cascades. It is regionally arranged by cities or towns. If the user can make it past all the anecdotes, he/she will find brief mentions of many points of interest. There are regular sections on where to shop, eat, and sleep, plus information about annual events and the addresses and phone numbers of local chambers of commerce.

WA-19 Spring, Ira, and Manning, Harvey. 101 HIKES IN THE NORTH CASCADES. Seattle: The Mountaineers, 1970. 231 p. Maps, photos. Index. 77-133504.

WA-20 _____. 102 HIKES IN THE ALPINE LAKES, SOUTH CASCADES, AND OLYMPICS. Seattle: The Mountaineers, 1971. 240 p. Maps, photos. Index. 79-166974.

These 2 books are identical in format, the only difference being the geographical area covered. Each hike description includes a general map, distance and hiking time, elevation gain and highest elevation, best season, and the name of the USGS map to use. A second edition of the South Cascades volume was planned for 1978.

WA-21 Sterling, E.M. TRIPS AND TRAILS: FAMILY CAMPS, SHORT HIKES AND VIEW ROADS. 2d ed. 2 vols. Seattle: The Mountaineers, 1977-78. Photos., maps. Bibliography. Index. 67-26501.

Lack of outdoor experience is no barrier to enjoying these trips and trails. Volume 1 describes 67 trips on the east and west slopes of the North Cascades. Volume 2 describes 80 trips in the Olympics, Mount Rainier, and South Cascades.

WA-22 SUNSET TRAVEL GUIDE TO WASHINGTON. By the editors of Sunset Books and Sunset Magazine. Menlo Park, CA: Lane Publishing Co., 1973. 160 p. Photos., maps. Index. 0-376-06843-4. 73-75757.

This is a guide to attractions and the outdoors of Washington which should include more practical how-to-get-around information. It is best used as an introduction to the state. It does not include restaurants and accommodations information. A revised 1978 edition has been published.

WA-23 WASHINGTON: A GUIDE TO THE EVERGREEN STATE. American Guide Series. Portland, OR: Binford & Mort, 1941. 687 p. Photos., maps. Bibliography. Index.

This original WPA guide begins with a general discussion of Washington past and present and then goes on to describe 11 cities, 9 highway tours, 4 park and 2 trail tours in Mount Rainier National Park, Olympic National Park, and 6 tours of Puget Sound and nearby islands. There is a chronology of Washington state history.

WA-24 WASHINGTON STATE OUTDOOR RECREATION GUIDE. Moscow, ID: Northwest Experience Publishing Co. (Box 8187/83843), 1978. Issued annually(?). 18 p. Maps. Index.

This guide lists state parks and the facilities at each in 6 geographic regions of the state. Each is located on a map. Also included is general information on the use of the parks, including campsite reservations, and a list of sources of additional information.

WA-25 Woods, Erin, and Woods, Bill. BICYCLING THE BACKROADS AROUND PUGET SOUND. Seattle: The Mountaineers, 1972. 200 p. Maps. Index. 0-916890-31-7. 72-92589.

The authors give terrain, a large clear map, and a mileage log for each of 54 tours ranging in length from 2 hours to 2 or 3 days duration. There is a name index and a list of tours by length.

WA-26 _____. BICYCLING THE BACKROADS OF NORTHWEST WASHING-TON. Seattle: The Mountaineers, 1976. 208 p. Maps, sketches. Index. 0-916890-44-9. 76-19258.

This book begins where the authors' other bicycling book (WA-25) leaves off in providing an expanded choice of day, weekend, and longer rides in the greater Puget Sound area. Detailed mileage logs and clear maps are given for each of the 39 trips described.

MAPS

The official HIGHWAY MAP AND GUIDE is available from the Public Affairs Office, Washington State Dept. of Transportation, Transportation Bldg., Olympia, WA 98504. The 1978 edition contains many inset maps showing ferry routes, airports, roadside rest areas, and parks and recreation sites. It also contains many interstate strip maps. A small section lists other sources for transportation and travel information. AAA (US-259), Exxon (US-261), and Rand McNally (US-215) each issue a combined Oregon/Washington map. Goushā (US-206) issues a separate Washington map. See also WA-11 and WA-29.

PUBLISHERS

WA-27 THE MOUNTAINEERS, 719 Pike Street, Seattle, WA 98101 (206/682-4636).

This outdoors organization publishes many excellent where-to guides to Washington for a wide range of activities: short hikes, expedition hikes, rock climbing, mountaineering, bicycle trips, canoeing and kayaking, and skiing and snowshoeing.

MAJOR TOURIST ORGANIZATION

WA-28   WASHINGTON DEPT. OF COMMERCE AND ECONOMIC DEVELOPMENT, TRAVEL DIVISION, Room 101 General Administration Bldg., Olympia, WA 98504 (206/753-5610).

They issue a general brochure that lists sources of additional information, a special events calendar issued several times a year, "Discover Washington Driving Series" (gives mileage logs for 18 separate tours, some of which are the same as the Automobile Club of Washington's (WA-29) "Explore and Enjoy" series), a directory of golf courses in the state, a directory of state chambers of commerce and convention and visitors bureaus, and information on industrial tours.

REGIONAL TOURISM ASSOCIATIONS

OLYMPIC PENINSULA TRAVEL ASSOCIATION, Box 625, Port Angeles, WA 98362.

They issue an annual DIRECTORY (1978, 46th ed., 34 p.) of accommodations, shops, restaurants, and other services. For a copy write to Washington State Ferries (WA-30).

OTHER ORGANIZATIONS

WA-29   AUTOMOBILE CLUB OF WASHINGTON, 330 Sixth Avenue North, Seattle, WA 98109 (206/292-5353).

They publish many good local maps and guides, but these are available only to AAA Auto Club members. They issue 4 TRAVEL-RECREATION MAPS, one each for Mount Rainier, Mt. Baker, Olympic Peninsula, and Okanogan. The maps are good and contain information on parks and campgrounds, trails, ranger stations, boat launch sites, ski areas, etc. They issue maps to all of the major areas in the state plus a map of the San Juan Islands and a ferry system map of Puget Sound and the Strait of Georgia. They also issue 2 series of driving guides to individual popular areas in the western part of the state. The "Explore and Enjoy" series consists of 9 separate tour brochures to such places as Grand Coulee, north and central Cascades, and Yakima Valley. The "Mini Tour" series consists of 6 separate tour brochures to such places as Port Townsend and Snoqualmie.

WA-30   WASHINGTON STATE FERRIES, Seattle Ferry Terminal, Seattle, WA 98104 (206/464-6400).

Their 26-page FERRY GUIDE is a complete guide to using the ferry system that runs between Seattle, the towns of Puget Sound, and the San Juan Islands. It describes 6 tours and lists other sources of travel information. They have an information booth in the Pier 52 terminal and a toll-free (available in the state only) information number at 800/542-0810. Both are available daily from 8A.M.-8P.M.

WA-31 WASHINGTON STATE LODGING ASSOCIATION, 9103 33d West, Tacoma, WA 98466 (206/565-1147).

INFORMATION CENTERS/INFORMATION PHONES

The official HIGHWAY MAP AND GUIDE shows locations of visitor information centers at interstate and other major highway border crossings into the state.

OUTDOOR RECREATION ACTIVITIES

BICYCLING. The Washington Dept. of Transportation, Highway Administration Bldg., Olympia, WA 98504 has identified bike routes on its state highway system. A BIKE BOOK available from them contains a map identifying these routes. Once you have chosen a route, and send them that information marked to the special attention of "Bike Routes," they will send a personalized routing guide with detailed strip maps showing the route, describing wayside road conditions, and showing all roadside features such as scenic sites, campgrounds, parks, information centers, etc. A WHATCOM COUNTY BIKE BOOK of 48 pages by Patrick Vala and published by Signpost Publications (W-50) has not been examined by us. See also WA-25 and WA-26.

CANOEING AND BOATING. The Washington State Parks and Recreation Commission, Box 1128, Olympia, WA 98504 issues a brief guide to salt water marine facilities. The Washington Public Ports Association, Box 1518, Olympia, WA 98507 issues a guide to recreational boating facilities on public port property. The Travel Division (WA-28) issues a guide to tour packages involving water (houseboat vacations, river float trips, excursions, etc.) called WASHINGTON STATE WATER ADVENTURES. See also WA-7.

FISHING AND HUNTING. The Washington Game Dept., Attention: Information Team, 600 North Capitol Way, Olympia, WA 98504 (206/753-5707) supplies much useful information and maps on freshwater fishing, hunting, bird watching, etc. The Game Dept., in cooperation with the U.S. Dept. of Interior, Bureau of Reclamation, Box 815, Ephrata, WA 98823, has issued a COLUMBIA BASIN RECREATION AREAS map (scale: 1 in. represents about 5 1/2 miles). It shows public land ownership and locations of 12 wildlife recreation areas. Numerous booklets on where to and how to catch different types of saltwater fish are available from the Washington Dept. of Fisheries, Information and Education Office, 115 General Administration Bldg., Olympia, WA 98504 (206/753-6552 or 6583). Their best where-to publication is PUGET SOUND PUBLIC SHELLFISH SITES, a series of 28 large, detailed maps which indicate sites where clams, oysters, crabs, and shrimp may be taken, as well as boat access information. The Travel Division (WA-28) issues a guide to both saltwater and freshwater fishing vacation tour packages called FISHING WASHINGTON STATE and a brief guide to SALMON FISHING IN WASHINGTON STATE. See also WA-8.

WINTER ACTIVITIES. The Travel Division (WA-28) issues a brochure on ski packages called SKI WASHINGTON STATE.

NATIONAL/STATE PARKS/FORESTS, ETC.

Mount Rainier National Park

WA-32   Kirk, Ruth. EXPLORING MOUNT RAINIER. Seattle: University of Washington Press, 1968. 104 p. Photos., maps. Bibliography. Index. 0-295-73850-2. 68-11047.

The first half is devoted to the natural and human history of Mount Rainier National Park. The "Enjoying the Park" section describes, with maps, 5 trips by car; brief mentions of numerous hiking and climbing trails; and includes a directory, now out of date, of visitor services, campgrounds, picnic areas, sources of information, etc. This title needs to be updated.

WA-33   Spring, Ira, and Manning, Harvey. 50 HIKES IN MOUNT RAINIER NATIONAL PARK. Seattle: Mount Rainier Natural History Association and The Mountaineers, 1969. 120 p. Maps, photos. Bibliography. Index. 0-916890-19-8. 78-84752.

Each hike description includes a general sketch map, distance, hiking time, and elevation gain.

WA-34   MOUNT RAINIER NATIONAL PARK, Tahoma Woods, Star Route, Ashford, WA 98304 (206/569-2211).

They provide a large, general map/brochure and information on campgrounds, other types of accommodations outside the park, hiking trails, backcountry use, winter activities, horse use, fishing, flora and fauna, etc. For summit climbs contact Rainier Mountaineering, Inc., 201 St. Helens, Tacoma, WA 98402 (206/627-6242 or 206/569-2227). Their summer address is Mount Rainier National Park, Paradise, WA 98397 (206/569-2227). There are 4 visitor centers in the park. Those at Longmire and Paradise are open all year. Those at Ohanapecosh and Sunrise are open in the summer only. The Mount Rainier National Park Hospitality Service operates several facilities and lodges in the Park. For information and reservations contact them at 4820 South Washington, Tacoma, WA 98409. In the winter call 206/475-6260; in the summer call 206/569-2706.

North Cascades National Park

WA-35   Darvill, Fred T., Jr.   DARVILL'S GUIDE TO THE NORTH CASCADES NATIONAL PARK & ASSOCIATED AREAS.   2 vols.   Mt. Vernon, WA: Darvill Outdoor Publications (Box 636/98273), 1972.   Maps, photo.

Volume 1 describes 89 trails in the western section, including Ross Lake National Recreation Area, Glacier Peak Wilderness, and Mt. Baker National Forest.   Volume II describes 50 trails in the eastern section, including Okanogan National Forest, Pasayten Wilderness, Manning Provincial Park, Glacier Peak Wilderness, Wenatchee National Forest, and Lake Chelan National Recreation Area.   The hikes are given a difficulty rating on a 5-point scale of easy to strenuous. Most of the trail descriptions date from approximately 1966 to 1971, but each volume has a section of additions and corrections updating the trail notes to 1975.

WA-36   May, Allan.   UP AND DOWN THE NORTH CASCADES NATIONAL PARK.   Longmire, WA: Mount Rainier Natural History Association, 1973.   96 p.   73-76467.

This is a very complete guide to the history, geology, flora and fauna, roads, lakes, visitor services, and trails.   It includes Ross Lake and Lake Chelan National Recreation Area.

WA-37   NORTH CASCADES NATIONAL PARK, 800 State Street, Sedro Woolley, WA 98284.

They provide a map/brochure and information on campgrounds; accommodations and services; hiking, trails, and backcountry areas; weather; and streams and boating.   Information on the adjacent Ross Lake and Lake Chelan National Recreation Areas is also available from this address.   Information may also be obtained at the ranger stations in Marblemount (206/873-4590) and Stehekin.   The latter is located in Lake Chelan National Recreation Area.

Olympic National Park

WA-38   Leissler, Frederick.   ROADS AND TRAILS OF OLYMPIC NATIONAL PARK.   3d ed.   Seattle: University of Washington Press, 1976. 84 p.   Photos.   16 maps in back.   Index.   0-295-95143-5.   57-3575.

Sixteen areas within the park are described.   The sometimes difficult to read maps show roads, campgrounds, ranger stations, trails, mountains, streams, and lakes.   The text, geared toward each map, describes points of interest and mileage points along each road and trail to be found on each of the maps.

WA-39   Wood, Robert L.   TRAIL COUNTRY: OLYMPIC NATIONAL PARK.

Seattle: The Mountaineers, 1968. 298 p. Photos., maps. Index. 68-16316.

The author, who knows this area extensively, first describes its historic and natural history and follows this with a complete hiking guide (giving maps, mileages, and terrain) to 17 trails.

WA-40 _____. WILDERNESS TRAILS OF OLYMPIC NATIONAL PARK. Seattle: The Mountaineers, 1970. 219 p. Maps, photos. Index. 79-125995.

The trail and beach sections of the author's large comprehensive volume (WA-39) covering all aspects of the park have been repackaged here into a handy, portable size. The descriptions are detailed and easy-to-read maps are included.

WA-41 OLYMPIC NATIONAL PARK, 600 East Park Avenue, Port Angeles, WA 98362.

They issue a general map/brochure and information about points of interest, facilities and services, camping, trails and backcountry use, climate, boating and fishing regulations, glaciers, rain forests, and THE OLYMPIC NATIONAL PARK BUGLER, a newspaper issued several times a year that describes times and places for naturalist activities. There are 3 visitor centers in the park: the main one, the Pioneer Memorial Museum, near Port Angeles at Mount Angeles Road (Highway 111) and Park Avenue, is open year-round; the Storm King Visitor Center at Lake Crescent is open only in the summer; and the Hoh Rain Forest Visitor Center is open all year. Several lodges and resorts in the park are managed by an outside concessioner. For information and reservations contact National Park Concessions, Inc. at either Star Route 1, Port Angles, WA 98362 (206/928-3211) or General Offices, Mammoth Cave, KY 42259.

The National Park Service and the U.S. Forest Service operate a joint information office, called the Outdoor Recreation Center, at 915 Second Avenue, Seattle, WA 98174 (206/442-0170). It is open Monday-Friday, 8A.M.-4:30 P.M. They can supply brochures, maps, and information on areas under their administration in the states of Alaska, Washington, Oregon, and Idaho. This is a separate office from the Pacific Northwest Regional Office of the National Park Service also located in Seattle (US-239).

Information on the 7 national forests in Washington, plus a detailed map of the Washington section of the Pacific Crest National Scenic Trail, is available from the U.S. Forest Service, Pacific Northwest Region, Box 3623, Portland, OR 97208.

Information on state parks and historic sites is available from the Washington State Parks and Recreation Commission, Box 1128, Olympia, WA 98504.

INDIVIDUAL CITIES OR AREAS

Olympia—Printed Materials

AAA (US-259) offers a Bremerton/Olympia/Aberdeen/Hoquiam City map. Arrow Publishing Co. (US-199) issues a map of Olympia.

Olympia—Organizations

WA-42 OLYMPIA AREA VISITOR/CONVENTION BUREAU, Box 1427, Olympia, WA 98507 (206/357-3362).

They issue a general guide, a sketch map, and a list of motor inns. Their walk-in center is located at 1000 Plum Street.

Seattle—Printed Materials

WA-43 ACCESS SEATTLE: A GUIDEBOOK FOR THE DISABLED. Seattle: Easter Seal Society for Crippled Children and Adults of Washington (521 Second Avenue West/98119), 1977.

WA-44 Atkinson, Allegra, and Arkley, Rose. IN AND AROUND SEATTLE WITH CHILDREN. Seattle: Ariel Press, 1972. 213 p. Map. Index. 72-85250.

For annotation, see WA-45.

WA-45 Cohn, Rosanne, and Ranicke, Maxine. DISCOVER SEATTLE WITH KIDS: WHERE TO GO AND WHAT TO SEE IN AND AROUND SEATTLE. Mercer Island, WA: The Writing Works, 1977. 133 p. Sketches. Index. 0-916076-19-9. 77-26062.

A spot check of places in these 2 guides to Seattle for children showed little variation. Both are arranged thematically. The 1977 book projects a "neat things to do" style, while the 1972 book is more reserved in approach and a bit fuller in coverage. The "where to explore outside of Seattle" suggestions vary widely between the two. The restaurant, hours, and other timely information will, of course, be more current in the 1977 book. The map in the 1972 book is practically unreadable.

WA-46 OUR TOWN SEATTLE: THE RESIDENT & TOURIST COMPANION. 4th ed. Mercer Island, WA: Our Town Publications (Box 641/98040), summer-fall 1978. 48 p.

This is mostly a guide to restaurants and shops, but it does include brief sections on points of interest, entertainment, museums, parks, and sports.

WA-47 Satterfield, Archie, and Dowd, Merle E. THE SEATTLE GUIDEBOOK.

3d ed. Mercer Island, WA: The Writing Works, 1977. 212 p.
Maps, drawings. Index. 0-916076-18-0. 77-93061.

The thorough, practical coverage of this book includes sightseeing, walking tours, entertainment, sports and recreation, shopping, restaurants, places to stay, parks, galleries and museums, transportation, "bits and oddments" (includes where to take the children), and telephone numbers. A fourth edition was to be published in 1979.

WA-48 SEATTLE GUIDE. Seattle: Seattle Guide (600 First Avenue, Pioneer Bldg., Suite 310/98104).

This weekly guide to what to see and do has been published since 1922. It contains several good maps, capsule restaurant descriptions, a list of sources of information, "half" emergency (minor crises) telephone numbers, and hints for automobile drivers. Compared to many other guides of this type, this one has a very appealing and uncluttered format.

WA-49 Thomas Brothers Maps. KING-PIERCE-SNOHOMISH COUNTIES POPULAR STREET ATLAS. Los Angeles: Thomas Bros., 1976. Various pagings. Scales vary. Index.

Maps of Seattle are available from the Automobile Club of Washington (WA-29); Goushā (US-206); Kroll Map Co., 2700 Third, Seattle, WA 98121; Rand McNally (US-215); and The Tourmap Co., East 1104 57th Avenue, Spokane, WA 99203. See also WA-49.

The Seattle Weather information number is 206/662-1212.

Seattle—Organizations

WA-50 SEATTLE-KING COUNTY CONVENTION & VISITORS BUREAU, 1815 Seventh Avenue, Seattle, WA 98101 (206/447-7273).

They issue a VISITORS' GUIDE, an accommodations guide, a calendar of events, a restaurant guide, and a very detailed King County street map. In addition to this office, which is open 7 days a week in the summer, they operate information booths at the Sea-Tac International Airport and at the Seattle Center. The latter is open only during the summer.

WEST VIRGINIA

BOOKS, ATLASES, MAGAZINES

WV-1   Burrell, Bob, and Davidson, Paul. WILD WATER WEST VIRGINIA: A
        PADDLER'S GUIDE TO THE WHITE WATER RIVERS OF THE MOUN-
        TAIN STATE. 2ed. Parsons, WV: McClain Printing Co. (available
        from: West Virginia Wildwater Association, 1412 Western Avenue,
        Morgantown, WV 26505), 1975. 162 p. Maps. Bibliographies.
        Index. 0-87012-123-5. 72-77291.

        "This book is aimed at the intermediate to advanced paddler who
        possesses the basic skills and judgement to paddle moving water."
        Each trip description includes a water difficulty rating, gradient,
        water volume, scenery rating, paddling time, water level, USGS
        map(s) to use, and shuttle information. The general introductory
        chapter gives phone numbers for obtaining water level information.
        The bibliographies at the end of each of the 9 river systems covered
        in this volume include mostly local histories.

WV-2   WEST VIRGINIA: A GUIDE TO THE MOUNTAIN STATE. American
        Guide Series. New York: Oxford University Press, 1941. 559 p.
        Photos., maps.

        This is the original WPA guide in the usual format for this series:
        general state background, descriptions of 11 major cities, and 23
        highway tour itineraries. It is comprehensive, but out of date.

WV-3   WEST VIRGINIA HIGHWAY MARKERS: HISTORIC, PREHISTORIC,
        SCENIC, GEOLOGIC. Rev. ed. N.p.: West Virginia Historic
        Commission, 1967. 263 p. Photos. Index.

        Arranged alphabetically by the subject matter of the marker, the text
        of each marker, along with its location, is given. There are addi-
        tional lists of markers by county and by highway.

WV-4   WEST VIRGINIA TRAVEL GUIDE FOR THE HANDICAPPED. Charles-
        ton: National Rehabilitation Association, West Virginia Chapter,
        1974. 42 p.

A new edition is planned. This guide is also available from the Travel Development Division (WV-5).

MAPS

The official West Virginia highway map is available from either the West Virginia Dept. of Highways, Public Information Division, Charleston, WV 25305 or the Travel Development Division (WV-5). The 1978 edition contains a list of points of interest and historic sites; parks, forests, and natural areas; and the addresses of the 7 regional travel councils. AAA (US-259), Exxon, (US-261), Goushā (US-206), and Rand McNally (US-215) each issue a combined Delaware/Maryland/Virginia/West Virginia map.

MAJOR TOURIST ORGANIZATION

WV-5   WEST VIRGINIA DEPT. OF COMMERCE, TRAVEL DEVELOPMENT DIVISION, 1900 Washington Street East, Charleston, WV 25305 (304/ 348-2286).

They issue a semi-annual calendar of events; a campground directory; COUNTRY INNS OF WEST VIRGINIA; a hotel/motel directory; SCENIC TOUR GUIDE (road guides, with maps, of 8 tours); WILD WONDERFUL WEST VIRGINIA A TO Z (describes the state from archaeological mounds to zithers); individual brochures on covered bridges, golfing, and farm vacations; and the brochures from the 7 regional travel councils and from the Dept. of Natural Resources described elsewhere in this chapter.

REGIONAL TOURISM ASSOCIATIONS

COUNTRY ROADS TRAVEL COUNCIL, Box 744, Parkersburg, WV 26101 (304/428-8117).

They issue a general map/guide with points of interest and HUNTING & FISHING ALONG THE LITTLE KANAWHA.

EASTERN GATEWAY TRAVEL COUNCIL, 110 West Burke Street, Martinsburg, WV 25401 (304/267-8287).

They issue a general map/guide with points of interest plus individual brochures on parks and recreation areas, historic areas, scenic spots, radio stations, and annual events and activities.

MOUNTAINAIRE TRAVEL COUNCIL, Box 1119, Princeton, WV 24740 (304/ 425-4237).

They issue a general map/guide with outlines for 6 road tours; a list of special events; a list of golf courses; and a list, with facilities, of parks, forests, and recreation areas.

MOUNTAINEER COUNTRY TRAVEL COUNCIL, 321 Morgantown Avenue, Morgantown, WV 26505 (304/296-9500).

They issue a general map/guide with points of interest and a brochure describing parks, forests, and camping facilities.

NINE VALLEY TRAVEL COUNCIL, 900 MacCorkle Avenue, St. Albans, WV 25177 (304/727-9976).

They issue 9 VALLEY REGIONAL TOUR GUIDE, 9 VALLEY ACCOM-MODATIONS & SERVICE DIRECTORY, 9 VALLEY CALENDAR OF EVENTS, 9 VALLEY TRADITIONAL HANDCRAFTS, and 9 VALLEY GLASS FACTORIES.

POTOMAC HIGHLAND TRAVEL COUNCIL, Burlington, WV 26710 (304/289-3636).

They issue a general map/guide with points of interest, a service directory, a park and forest facilities chart, and a brochure on natural areas.

UPPER OHIO VALLEY TRAVEL COUNCIL, 1012 Main Street, Wheeling, WV 26003 (304/233-2575 or 233-1320).

They issue a general map/guide with points of interest; a calendar of fairs, festivals, and events; and individual brochures describing golf courses, parks and recreation, and historic spots.

OTHER ORGANIZATIONS

WV-6   WEST VIRGINIA HOTEL & MOTEL ASSOCIATION, 2843 MacCorkle Avenue, St. Albans, WV 25177 (304/727-2201).

INFORMATION CENTERS/INFORMATION PHONES

A list of the highway information centers may be found on the official highway map. A list of them may also be obtained from the Travel Development Division (WV-5). The division sponsors a toll-free travel information number at 800/624-9110. It may be called from all states east of the Rocky Mountains. See the "National/State Parks/Forests, etc." section of this chapter for the toll-free number for state parks information and reservations. The state also provides "Operation Latch-String," an informal travel information network in which trained participating CB operators, identified by special bumper stickers on their vehicles, will provide tourist information to those travelers who request "Operation Latch-String" on channel 19.

OUTDOOR RECREATION ACTIVITIES

CANOEING AND BOATING. The Travel Development Division (WV-5) supplies numerous brochures of organizations offering white water adventures plus its own guide to whitewater trips. The West Virginia Dept. of Natural Resources, State Office Bldg. 3, 1800 Washington Street East, Charleston, WV 25305 issues miscellaneous canoeing brochures. See also WV-1.

FISHING AND HUNTING. Hunting and trapping maps and regulations plus map/guides to individual public hunting and fishing areas are available from the West Virginia Dept. of Natural Resources, State Office Bldg. 3, 1800 Washington Street East, Charleston, WV 25305.

WINTER ACTIVITIES. A SKI WEST VIRGINIA brochure is available from the Travel Development Division (WV-5).

NATIONAL/STATE PARKS/FORESTS, ETC.

Harpers Ferry National Historic Park

WV-7   HARPERS FERRY NATIONAL HISTORICAL PARK, Harpers Ferry, WV 25425.

They issue a map/brochure on the park, brochures on some of the individual houses, and information on nearby trails. Their visitor center is open 8A.M.-5P.M. every day except Christmas and New Year's Day.

The Harpers Ferry-Bolivar Merchant's Association, The Towne House, Harpers Ferry, WV 25425 (304/535-6610) issues a guide to shops, campgrounds, outfitters, etc.

Monongahela National Forest

WV-8   HIKING GUIDE TO MONOGAHELA NATIONAL FOREST AND VICINITY. 3d ed. Webster Springs, WV: West Virginia Highlands Conservancy (Box 711/26288), 1977. 178 p. Maps, photos. Bibliography. 77-155649.

Good detailed descriptions are given for about 150 trails. There are also comparative tables.

WV-9   Weiss, Raymond B. A SCENIC GUIDE TO THE MONONGAHELA NATIONAL FOREST. Rev. ed. Parsons, WV: McClain Printing Co., 1973. 89 p. Photos., map in pocket. 0-87012-067-0. 77-81636.

This guide covers all the major and many minor places of interest in

the forest, giving "where possible, background information of historical significance, natural history, geography, etc. . . ." Sites are
described regionally, locations are keyed onto the accompanying map,
but there is no alphabetical name index.

WV-10 MONONGAHELA NATIONAL FOREST, Box 1231, Elkins, WV 26241

Maps of the entire forest are available at scales of 1/2 in. represents
6 miles and 1/4 in. represents 1 mile. A map of the Spruce Knob-
Seneca Rocks National Recreation Area (within the forest) is available
at a scale of 1/2 in. represents 1 mile. There is a Cranberry Mountain National Forest Visitor Center within the forest.

Information on facilities and phone numbers at various state vacation parks,
day-use parks, natural areas, historic sites, and state forests will be found in
the brochure WEST VIRGINIA STATE PARKS & FORESTS. It may be obtained
from the West Virginia Dept. of Natural Resources, State Office Bldg., 3,
1800 Washington Street East, Charleston, WV 25305 (304/348-2766). West
Virginia residents may use a toll-free number, 800/642-9058, for state parks
information and reservations. Residents from Indiana, Ohio, Kentucky, Pennsylvania, western New York, Maryland, Virginia, Delaware, North Carolina,
South Carolina, and Washington, DC should call 800/624-8632.

INDIVIDUAL CITIES OR AREAS

Charleston—Printed Materials

Maps of Charleston are available from Champion Map Corp. (US-202) and
Metro Graphic Arts, 900 40th SE, Grand Rapids, MI 49508.

Charleston—Organizations

WV-11 CHARLESTON REGIONAL CHAMBER OF COMMERCE & DEVELOP-
MENT, 818 Virginia Street East, Charleston, WV 25301 (304/345-
0770).

They issue a large booklet describing present-day industry, culture,
life-styles, etc. and separate brochures and flyers on points of interest,
cultural facilities, parks and recreation, and sports activities.

WISCONSIN

BOOKS, ATLASES, MAGAZINES

WI-1   BREVET'S WISCONSIN HISTORICAL MARKERS AND SITES. Sioux
        Falls, SD: Brevet Press, 1974. 254 p. Photos., maps. Indexes.
        0-88498-015-4. 74-79980.

        Location, map, illustration, and text are given for 204 official
        markers in Wisconsin. In the back there is a numerical listing of
        Registered Landmarks (these are placed by a program separate from
        the Historical Marker and Sites Program), a county index, a historical
        marker numerical index, an illustration index, and a general index.

WI-2   Brody, Polly. DISCOVERING WISCONSIN. Madison: Wisconsin
        House, 1973. 396 p. Photos., maps. Index. 0-88361-003-5. 73-
        76675.

        Dividing the state into 9 regions, the author, in a rambling and dis-
        cursive (the publisher calls it "charming and anecdotal") manner, very
        thoroughly describes the major attractions (much of the practical in-
        formation is now out of date) and gives a historical background for
        each. Many minor attractions are listed. There is a county-by-
        county listing of recreational (hunting, fishing, camping, skiing, etc.)
        facilities.

WI-3   CANOE TRAILS OF NORTH-CENTRAL WISCONSIN. Rev. ed. Lady-
        smith, WI: North Central Canoe Trails (Box 9/54848), 1978. 64 p.
        Maps.

        This guide contains detailed maps and directions for canoeing 10 rivers
        and creeks in the north central section of Wisconsin. There is a
        title variation: WISCONSIN'S NORTH CENTRAL CANOE TRAILS. The
        book is also available from Wisconsin Tales & Trails (WI-20).

WI-4   CANOE TRAILS OF NORTHEASTERN WISCONSIN. By the editors
        of Wisconsin Trails Magazine. Madison: Wisconsin Tales & Trails,
        1972. 72 p. Maps, photos. 72-85448.

River maps (showing access points, campsites, landmarks, and river details) are given for each trail, most of which can be canoed in 1 day. Accompanying descriptions include put-ins and take-outs as well as landmarks of the terrain.

WI-5   CANOE TRAILS OF SOUTHERN WISCONSIN. By Michael E. Duncanson. Madison: Wisconsin Tales & Trails, 1974. 64 p. Maps, photos. 74-77134.

This title is similar to the two above canoeing books, but it covers the southern section of the state.

WI-6   Church, Charles F. EASY GOING: A COMPREHENSIVE GUIDE TO DOOR COUNTY, INCLUDING GREEN BAY, ALGOMA AND KE-WAUNEE. Easy Going Series, no. 3. Madison: Tamarack Press, 1977. 154 p. Maps, photos. Index. 0-915024-12-8. 76-54994.

WI-7   _____. EASY GOING: A COMPREHENSIVE GUIDE TO SAUK AND COLUMBIA COUNTIES. Easy Going Series, no. 1. Madison: Tamarack Press, 1976. 141 p. Maps, photos. Index. 0-915024-03-9. 75-11855.

WI-8   Dunn, Michael J. EASY GOING: WISCONSIN'S NORTHWOODS, INCLUDING VILAS AND ONEIDA COUNTIES. Easy Going Series, no. 5. Madison: Tamarack Press, 1978. Maps, photos. Index. 0-915024-16-0. 78-908.

WI-9   Rath, Sara. EASY GOING: MADISON AND DANE COUNTY. Easy Going Series, no. 4. Madison: Tamarack Press, 1977. 199 p. Maps, photos. Index. 0-915024-13-6. 77-8058.

WI-10   Stewart, James C., and Stewart, Shirley L. EASY GOING: A COMPREHENSIVE GUIDE TO GRANT, IOWA, AND LAFAYETTE COUNTIES. Easy Going Series, no. 2. Madison: Tamarack Press, 1976. 143 p. Maps, photos. Index. 0-915024-05-5.

This is a very thorough series (WI-6 through WI-10). It is arranged geographically by individual locales within counties. Information is always given in a standardized order: general history and description, map, historic sites, natural areas, recreational facilities (everything from scuba diving to snowmobiling), businesses (everything from antique shops to movie houses), events, and a directory of emergency telephone numbers, churches, restaurants, lodging, and campgrounds.

WI-11   Puetz, C.J. GUIDE TO FUN IN WISCONSIN. Kaukauna, WI: Clarkson Map Co., n.d. 113 p. Maps, drawings. Index.

County road maps are reproduced (at various scales) with an overprinting indicating various recreational activities. There are some fairly detailed maps of selected parks and forests. Tour suggestions and information on wildlife are included as are tables of campsites noting facilities, tables of lakes listing fish that may be caught at each, a list of public hunting grounds, and a list of ski areas. There is a gazetteer of communities.

WI-12   Purinton, James. WISCONSIN COASTAL HISTORY TRAILS. 2 vols. Madison: Wisconsin Coastal Zone Management Development Program, 1976. Maps, photos. 76-623716.

Each volume covers trails along each of the 2 Great Lakes bordering the state: Lake Superior (42 pages) and Lake Michigan (70 pages). Descriptions of historical points of interest along Wisconsin's coastal boundary are included with the hiker, biker, and boater in mind. Information is presented as a tour and there are many maps (including large ones in pockets) to help the user find his/her way.

WI-13   Schweitzer, John, and Schweitzer, Midge. CROSS COUNTRY SKEE: AN EXCLUSIVE GUIDE TO WISCONSIN AND UPPER MICHIGAN SKI TOURING AREAS. Appleton, WI: Acme Press, 1977. 242 p. Maps. Bibliography. Index. 77-153994.

A detailed map, facilities, and finding instructions are given for a large number of ski trails. It is arranged alphabetically by county.

WI-14   Shidell, Doug, and Van Valkenberg, Philip. BICYCLE ESCAPE ROUTES: A TOURING GUIDE TO WISCONSIN. Madison: Wisconsin Tales & Trails, 1975. 80 p. Maps in book plus 3 unattached sheets of 6 maps. 0-915024-04-7. 74-22866.

Six areas in the southern half of Wisconsin have been mapped showing numerous small circle tours all of which are connected to provide several continuous bike routes through this part of the state. The text describes points of interest and campsites, all of which are keyed to all of the maps. The unattached maps show overall routes. The maps in the text are enlargements of selected smaller areas. Although the text does not give road directions, and the sheet maps are a bit difficult to read, the avid cyclist will make much use of the suggested routes.

WI-15   Van Valkenberg, Philip. WISCONSIN BIKE TRIPS. Madison: Wisconsin Tales & Trails, 1974. 48 p. Maps, photos. 0-915024-01-2. 74-77230.

Good maps and extensive descriptions outline 20 circle tours in 18 counties that can be biked by beginners as well as experts. The time required for each tour is not given, but they average about 15 miles in length and are, therefore, suitable for 1-day trips.

WI-16   WISCONSIN: A GUIDE TO THE BADGER STATE. Rev. ed. American Guide Series. New York: Hastings House, 1964. 651 p. Photos., map.

This is a partial revision of the original WPA guide. The general background and the descriptions of the 9 cities are unchanged, but the maps and 24 statewide highway tours have been updated. Even with the revisions, this work, though comprehensive, is still basically out of date.

WI-17　WISCONSIN STATE ATLAS. Rev. ed. Rockford, IL: Rockford Map Publishers, 1973. 246 p. Scales very. 76-362828.

This atlas contains descriptions, maps, and tables of hunting lands, campgrounds, fishing lakes and trout streams, 47 canoe trails, several 1-day tours, bike routes, accommodations, restaurants, and golf courses. In the middle will be found readable, but small, reproductions of each official county map.

WI-18　WISCONSIN TRAILS. Madison: Wisconsin Tales & Trails.

This large, glossy, quarterly magazine nearly always devotes several article in each issue to enjoying outdoors Wisconsin and usually spotlights a historical site and/or major point of interest. There is a regular "Where to Go, What to Do" column.

WI-19　WONDERFUL WISCONSIN: 4 SEASONS VACATION GUIDE. Williams Bay, WI: Wisconsin Vacationland (Box 779/53191), 1979. Issued annually. 432 p. Photos., maps, tables. Index.

Although containing mostly advertisements for motels/resorts and other establishments providing visitor services, this guide contains 2 other types of information. First, there are suggestions of things to do and points of interest in each of 7 regions of the state. Second, scattered throughout the guide are the sections that really make this title worthwhile: a 3-page canoe trails section, a 12-page listing of fairs and events, an 8-page listing of cross-country ski areas, a 5-page list of downhill ski areas, a 10-page list of historical markers, and a 35-page campground directory.

MAPS

The OFFICIAL STATE HIGHWAY MAP is available from the Division of Tourism (WI-21). The 1978-79 edition has a table of state parks and forests (indicating which have facilities for handicapped persons) and lists sources of information for travel in Wisconsin. AAA (US-259), Goushā (US-206), and Rand McNally (US-215) each issue a separate map of Wisconsin. Exxon (US-261) issues a combined Illinois/Wisconsin map. See also WI-11 and WI-17.

PUBLISHERS

WI-20　WISCONSIN TALES & TRAILS and TAMARACK PRESS, Box 5650, Madison, WI 53705.

In addition to publishing the numerous titles mentioned throughout this chapter, they provide a book-buying service selling their own books plus several natural history, historical, and "treasury" volumes; a Wisconsin calendar; a Wisconsin puzzle; and a Wisconsin heritage map. The books bearing the Tamarack Press imprint are copyrighted by Wisconsin Tales & Trails.

MAJOR TOURIST ORGANIZATION

WI-21   WISCONSIN DIVISION OF TOURISM, Box 7606, Madison, WI 53707 (608/266-2161).

A lot of good materials are available from this office. GUIDE TO WISCONSIN ATTRACTIONS is an alphabetical listing, with the briefest of descriptions, of all points of interest in the state. There is no attempt to show locations. WISCONSIN AUTO TOURS MAP AND GUIDE gives a map and mileage log descriptions of points of interest for each of 25 different tours. TRAVELERS GUIDE TO HISTORIC WISCONSIN lists museums, historic sites, and historic markers and locates each on a map. They also issue a calendar of annual events (this is not a day-by-day listing of events), and leaflets on autumn tours, barn art, and cheese factory tours. The annual WISCONSIN CAMPGROUND DIRECTORY, issued by the Wisconsin Association of Campground Owners, is a very thorough listing of privately owned campgrounds arranged by city. It is available from this office.

REGIONAL TOURISM ASSOCIATIONS

WISCONSIN DELLS REGIONAL CHAMBER OF COMMERCE, Box 175, Wisconsin Dells, WI 53965.

They issue an annual (1978 ed., 39 p.) TRAVEL GUIDE to the Dells territory that lists attractions, events, accommodations, campgrounds, restaurants, services, radio and TV stations, churches, and several good maps. They sponsor 2 information centers open in the summer months only: Wisconsin Dells Information Center, 115 Wisconsin Avenue, Wisconsin Dells, WI 53965 (608/254-8088); and Lake Delton Information Center, Lake Delton, WI 53940 (608/254-2662).

OTHER ORGANIZATIONS

WI-22   WISCONSIN INNKEEPERS ASSOCIATION, 509 West Wisconsin Avenue, Room 612, Milwaukee, WI 53203 (414/271-2851).

WI-23   WISCONSIN RECREATION INDUSTRIES, Route 2, Box 42-1, Woodruff, WI 54568.

They issue an annual (1978 ed., 23 p.) GUIDE TO FOUR SEASONS VACATION FUN listing accommodations, restaurants, services (attractions, shops, real estate companies, chambers of commerce, etc.), and supporting members in 7 regions of the state.

INFORMATION CENTERS/INFORMATION PHONES

There is a Wisconsin Vacation Center at 205 North Michigan Avenue, Chicago, IL 60601 (312/332-7274). The Division of Tourism (WI-21) has a walk-in center in Madison at 123 West Washington Avenue. It is open Monday-Friday, 8:30A.M.-5P.M. There are 7 tourist information centers on the major highways at the state borders. Some centers are open year-round; others are open only from May to October. Their locations and season will be found on the OFFICIAL STATE HIGHWAY MAP.

OUTDOOR RECREATION ACTIVITIES

BICYCLING. WISCONSIN BIKEWAY MAP AND GUIDE shows a general map and sectional maps for the 300 mile Wisconsin Bikeway that stretches across the southern half of the state from Kenosha to La Crosse. It also includes written directions, general weather conditions, and a list of selected bike shops. WISCONSIN BICENTENNIAL BIKE MAP describes bike routes in 12 counties, 9 cities, 4 state bike trails, and includes additional information on public camping areas, bike shops, local attractions, and sources of information for the same 12 counties that the bike routes cover. Both publications are available from the Division of Tourism (WI-21). See also WI-14, and WI-15.

CANOEING AND BOATING. A 72-page CANOEING GUIDE TO THE INDIAN HEAD RIVERS OF WEST CENTRAL WISCONSIN by Michael E. Duncanson describes 50 different trips on 11 different rivers with portages, campsites, and historic attractions. This and CANOEING THE WILD RIVERS OF NORTHWEST WISCONSIN are available from Wisconsin Indian Head Country, 3015 East Clairemont Avenue, Eau Claire, WI 54701. The Division of Tourism (WI-21) issues a pamphlet, WISCONSIN CANOEING, that describes briefly the major canoeing rivers of the state. See also WI-3, WI-4, and WI-5.

FISHING AND HUNTING. Contact the Wisconsin Dept. of Natural Resources, Box 7921, Madison, WI 53707. They issue a guide and map of PUBLIC LANDS OPEN TO HUNTING. See also WI-11.

WINTER ACTIVITIES. The Division of Tourism (WI-21) issues separate brochures on downhill skiing, cross-country skiing, and snowmobile trails. All provide excellent, detailed, practical information on where to engage in each of these activities. See also WI-13.

Wisconsin

NATIONAL/STATE PARKS/FORESTS, ETC.

There are no major National Park Service areas in Wisconsin. Information on the 2 national forests in Wisconsin may be obtained from the U.S. Forest Service, Eastern Regional Office, 633 West Wisconsin Avenue, Milwaukee, WI 53203.

A VISITOR'S GUIDE TO WISCONSIN'S STATE PARKS, FORESTS AND OTHER RECREATION LANDS is available from the Wisconsin Dept. of Natural Resources, Box 7921, Madison, WI 53707. It includes addresses, phone numbers, and information on campgrounds and reservation of campsites, trails, and other available facilities each state park, forest, and trail.

INDIVIDUAL CITIES OR AREAS

Madison—Printed Materials

WI-24 WISCONSIN'S CAPITAL WITH EASE. Madison: Easter Seal Society of Wisconsin (2702 Monroe Street/53711), 1973.

See also WI-9.

Maps of Madison are available from Arrow Publishing Co. (US-199) and Champion Map Corp. (US-202).

Madison—Organizations

WI-25 GREATER MADISON CONVENTION AND VISITORS BUREAU, 152 West Johnson Street, Madison, WI 53703 (608/255-0701).

They issue a general brochure, a detailed map with street index, and separate brochures on things to see and do, motels/hotels, and restaurants. There is a visitor hotline for emergency medical services at 608/262-2398. They will be moving soon from the Johnson street address, but their new address was not known at the time of this writing.

Milwaukee—Printed Materials

WI-26 Bednarz, Wilma, and Miniace, Dorothy. WHERE TO GO AND WHAT TO DO WITH THE KIDS IN MILWAUKEE. Los Angeles: Price/Stern/Sloan, 1974. 159 p. Index. 0-8431-0273-X.

This guide "covers everything of possible interest to children--and their parents--in the greater Milwaukee area--amusement parks, beaches, bicycling, camping, classes, clubs, concerts, exhibits, festivals, films, museums, parades, parks, picnicking, tours, etc.-- most of it free!" Addresses, phone numbers, fees, hours, and exact directions are given for each place, event, etc. described.

WI-27   Junior League of Milwaukee, in cooperation with the Easter Seal Society for Crippled Children and Adults of Milwaukee County, comps. A GUIDEBOOK TO MILWAUKEE FOR THE HANDICAPPED AND AGING. Milwaukee: the Society (5225 West Burleigh Street/ 53210), 1970.

Maps of Milwaukee are available from AAA (US-259); Arrow Publishing Co. (US-199); Exxon (US-261); Gousha (US-206); Metro Graphic Arts, 900 40th SE, Grand Rapids, MI 49508; Milwaukee Map Service, 4519 West North Avenue, Milwaukee, WI 53208; and Rand McNally (US-215).

The Milwaukee weather information number is 414/936-1212.

Milwaukee—Organizations

WI-28   GREATER MILWAUKEE CONVENTION & VISITORS BUREAU, 828 North Broadway, Milwaukee, WI 53202 (414/273-3950).

They issue a general brochure that includes a map and briefly de-scribes points of interest, museums, sports, performing arts, theaters, annual events, and parks and recreation. Their FUNTOURS brochure gives practical information for over 65 places to visit and/or tour. A calendar of events is issued every 2 months, and there are separate guides for hotels/motels and dining/entertainment. The address above is the main information center and all inquiries should be directed there. They are open Monday-Friday, 8:30A.M.-5P.M. They also operate an information center at General Mitchell Field (the airport), 5300 South Howell Avenue, Milwaukee, WI 53207 (414/747-4808). It is open daily from 7:30A.M.-9:30P.M. The bureau also provides a 24-hour recording of daily events, the FUN LINE, at 414/799-1177.

WYOMING

BOOKS, ATLASES, MAGAZINES

WY-1   Bonney, Orrin H., and Bonney, Lorraine G. GUIDE TO THE
        WYOMING MOUNTAINS AND WILDERNESS AREAS. 3d ed. Chi-
        cago: Swallow Press, 1977. 701 p. Photos., maps. Index. 0-
        8040-0578. 77-154538.

        This extremely thorough guide gives background (geology, history) and
        general advice (which maps to use, safety rules, hunting and fishing
        laws, etc.) before discussing, in detail, 466 climbs in 11 ranges in
        Wyoming. There is a small section on winter sports and rockhound-
        ing. This is an overpowering book, so complete that 4 separate
        field guides have been excerpted from it: (1) THE TETON RANGE
        AND GROS VENTRE RANGE, 2d ed., 1977; (2) YELLOWSTONE
        PARK AND THE ABSAROKA RANGE, 2d ed., 1977; (3) WIND RIVER
        RANGE, 2d ed., 1968; and (4) BIG HORN RANGE, 1977.

WY-2   WYOMING: A GUIDE TO ITS HISTORY, HIGHWAYS AND PEOPLE.
        American Guide Series. New York: Oxford University Press, 1941.
        490 p. Photos., maps. Bibliography. Index.

        This original WPA guide begins with a general discussion of the state,
        past and present, and follows with tours of 4 major cities, 13 high-
        way tours, and the loop tour of Yellowstone National Park. There is
        a chronology of Wyoming history and a cowboy lingo glossary.

WY-3   Wyoming Recreation Commission. WYOMING: A GUIDE TO HIS-
        TORIC SITES. Basin, WY: Big Horn Book Co., 1976. 327 p.
        Photos., drawings, maps. Index. 0-89100-000-3. 76-47109.

        This listing, alphabetically arranged by county, of the major historic
        sites in Wyoming gives location, concise description, background, and
        whatever else seems appropriate for any given site. The list of mu-
        seums, by county, notes address, hours, and if admission is charged.
        The list of illustrations includes credit lines.

MAPS

The OFFICIAL HIGHWAY MAP is available from the Wyoming Travel Commission (WY-4). The 1978 edition includes information on historic trails, sites, events, ski areas, and radio stations. Both AAA (US-259) and Rand McNally (US-215) issue a combined Colorado/Wyoming map. Exxon (US-261) issues a combined Idaho/Montana/Wyoming map. Goushā (US-206) issues a separate Wyoming map.

MAJOR TOURIST ORGANIZATION

WY-4   WYOMING TRAVEL COMMISSION, I-25 & Etchepare Circle, Cheyenne, WY 82002 (307/777-7777).

Wyoming issues a wealth of informative literature for the traveler: a large general booklet; a quarterly calendar of events; a map/guide to dude ranches, lodges and resorts; a hotel/motel directory; 4 extensive regional (northern, central, southern, western) self-guiding tour guides which include information on events and recreation opportunities; a brief backpacking/climbing guide; and a DIRECTORY OF WYOMING that lists national and state parks, travel-related associations, major events, radio stations, and local chambers of commerce.

OTHER ORGANIZATIONS

WY-5   COLORADO-WYOMING HOTEL & MOTEL ASSOCIATION, Radisson Denver Hotel/Penthouse #4, 1790 Grant Street, Denver, CO 80203 (303/839-1151).

INFORMATION CENTERS/INFORMATION PHONES

There are no border highway information centers. The major walk-in sources of information throughout the state are the Wyoming Travel Commission (WY-4); the Sheridan Chamber of Commerce, I-90 at Fifth Street, Sheridan, WY 82801; the Jackson Hole Chamber of Commerce (WY-12); and the Casper Chamber of Commerce, 500 North Center Street, Casper, WY 82602 (307/234-5311).

OUTDOOR RECREATION ACTIVITIES

CANOEING AND BOATING. The FAMILY WATER SPORTS guide available from the Wyoming Travel Commission (WY-4) contains information on where to go for canoeing, kayaking, rafting, floating, commercial float trips, water skiing, and swimming, plus locations of boat ramps and marinas. See also WY-7.

FISHING AND HUNTING. A map and table showing types of fish to be found in 62 fishing areas will be found in the FAMILY WATER SPORTS guide available from the Wyoming Travel Commission (WY-4). PUBLIC HUNTING AND FISHING ON WYOMING GAME AND FISH DEPARTMENT AREAS, a 76-page guide describing and including a map of 48 separate areas, is available from the Wyoming Game and Fish Dept., Cheyenne, WY 82002 (307/777-7728). Rising Trout Publishing Co., Box 2201C, Jackson, WY 83001 (307/733-5607) publishes a 200-page WYOMING FISHING GUIDE by Ken Knapp. It is arranged county-by-county and contains 25 county maps.

WINTER ACTIVITIES. The Wyoming Travel Commission (WY-4) issues an annual brochure on where to go for downhill and cross-country skiing, and snowmobiling.

NATIONAL/STATE PARKS/FORESTS, ETC.

Grand Teton National Park

WY-6   Bonney, Orrin H., and Bonney, Lorraine G. BONNEY'S GUIDE: GRAND TETON NATIONAL PARK AND JACKSON'S HOLE. Houston, TX: the authors, 1972. 144 p. Photos., maps. Index. 72-197454.

Historical lore and practical information are combined in this road guide to 23 tours in this area. Trail descriptions, cafes, campgrounds, garages, boating places, ranches, stores, etc. are mentioned as they appear along the road. In addition, the reader wanting to know, for example, where there are campgrounds, can do so through a detailed index.

WY-7   Huser, Verne, and Belknap, Buzz. GRAND TETON NATIONAL PARK SNAKE RIVER GUIDE. Boulder City, NV: Westwater Books, 1972. 72 p. Maps, photos. 72-86478.

This graphic guide shows mileages, river characteristics and rapids, and roads and contours of the river banks of that portion of the Snake River in Wyoming from the South Entrance Station of Yellowstone National Park south to the Palisades Reservoir at the Wyoming/Idaho border. The scale of the maps is 1 in. represents approximately 1/2 mile. There's very little descriptive text accompanying the river guide, but there are sections in the back giving fishing information, brief essays on the animals and geology of the area, and a list of concessioner-guides available for Snake River float trips.

WY-8   Lawrence, Paul. HIKING THE TETON BACKCOUNTRY. A Sierra Club Totebook. San Francisco: Sierra Club, 1973. 159 p. Maps, photo. 0-87156-092-5. 73-79896.

An introductory section discussing geology, flora and fauna, weather, hiking, equipment and clothing, and park regulations is followed by descriptions of 46 area trails. Appendixes give campground and fishing information.

WY-9   Petzoldt, Paul. PETZOLDT'S TETON TRAILS: A HIKING GUIDE TO THE TETON RANGE WITH STORIES, HISTORY AND PERSONAL EXPERIENCES. Salt Lake City: Wasatch Publishers, 1976. 160 p. Photos., maps. 0-915272-05-9. 76-16302.

Seventeen trails in Grand Teton National Park, 2 in Bridger-Teton National Forest, and 16 in Targhee National Forest are covered. Specific route information is given, as well as the USGS maps to use, and hiking distances. The author is the senior advisor for the National Outdoor Leadership School and is a professional mountaineer.

WY-10 A PHOTOGRAPHIC AND COMPREHENSIVE GUIDE TO GRAND TETON NATIONAL PARK. Rev. ed. Casper, WY: World-Wide Research and Publishing Co., National Parks Division, 1976. 68 p. Photos., maps. 76-150295.

While most of this book consists of stunning photographs, there are also general descriptions of major roads and hiking trails. A brief list of recreation and other facilities, as well as visitor centers, is included.

See also WY-17.

739-7349

WY-11 GRAND TETON NATIONAL PARK, Box 67, Moose, WY 83012 (307/733-2880).

They issue a very large, informative map/guide providing information on trails, viewing areas, campgrounds, marinas, swimming areas, and such visitor services as lodging, stores, gas stations, etc. There are 2 visitor centers: Moose Visitor Center is open daily all year except December 25, and Colter Bay Visitor Center is open daily from May to October. A 24-hour recorded message about weather, activities, and available facilities may be dialed at 307/733-2220. TEEWINOT is the quarterly Park newspaper issued by the Grand Teton Natural History Association, and it contains full information on events and visitor services. An auto-tape tour (CA-80) of the Park may be rented at either visitor center.

WY-12 JACKSON HOLE CHAMBER OF COMMERCE, 532 North Cache, Jackson, WY 83001 (307/733-3316).

The mailing address is Box E. They are open year-round with evening hours in the summer. Their own publications include a general brochure; an annual guide to where to go, stay, and eat; a large annual street map and area guide; and numerous mimeographed leaflets listing accommodations, restaurants, entertainment, transportation services, and outdoor recreation opportunities. In addition, they stock countless brochures describing individual outfitters and guide services, winter activities, resorts, ranch camps, etc.

Yellowstone National Park

WY-13   Bach, Orville E., Jr. HIKING THE YELLOWSTONE BACKCOUNTRY. A Sierra Club Totebook. San Francisco: Sierra Club, 1973. 228 p. Maps, photos. 0-87156-078-X. 72-96121.

If you are going to Yellowstone to see more than just Old Faithful and to take the popular 142 mile all-day circular road tour, this is the book for you. It briefly describes all the trails in the park area. The serious hiker will want to obtain more detailed maps, information, and backcountry permits. These are appendixes on boating and fishing regulations.

WY-14   Kirk, Ruth. EXPLORING YELLOWSTONE. Seattle: University of Washington Press in cooperation with the Yellowstone Library and Museum Association, 1972. 120 p. Photos., maps. Index. 0-295-95174-5. 78-178702.

The author begins with the early exploration and the founding of the park; describes the geology, plant and wildlife; and concludes with a guide to seeing the park by car, trails, and boat.

WY-15   Lystrup, Herbert T. HAMILTON'S GUIDE: YELLOWSTONE NATIONAL PARK. West Yellowstone, MT: Hamilton Stores, 1976. 160 p. Photos., folded map in back. Index.

This guide, by a former park ranger naturalist, is very complete. It describes the Grand Loop Road tour, flora and fauna, campgrounds, some trails, services and concessions, etc. It is extensively indexed.

WY-16   A PHOTOGRAPHIC AND COMPREHENSIVE GUIDE TO YELLOWSTONE NATIONAL PARK. Casper, WY: World-Wide Research & Publishing Co., National Parks Division, 1975. 48 p. Photos., maps. 76-350302.

This guide is mostly stunning photographs. Most of the text consists of a road guide to the Grand Loop Road within the park. There is brief mention of recreation opportunities, a table of geyser activity, and a table of other facilities, including visitor centers.

WY-17   Scharff, Robert, ed. YELLOWSTONE AND GRAND TETON NATIONAL PARKS. New York: David McKay Co., 1966. 209 p. Photos., maps. Bibliography. Index. 66-17872.

This is a guide to seeing both national parks from the highway, on foot, or on horseback. There are descriptions of the plants and wildlife, fishing and boating facilities, seeing the parks in winter, and accommodations and services (this part will be out of date). The book was produced in cooperation with the National Park Service.

WY-18   YELLOWSTONE NATIONAL PARK, Box 168, Yellowstone National Park, WY 82190 (307/344-7381).

They issue a large, informative map/guide with details about trails, campgrounds, lodging, boat ramps, and other visitor services; information on camping; fishing and boating regulations; and the park in the winter. There are 5 visitor centers in the park: Grant Village Visitor Center (307/242-7537), Canyon Visitor Center (307/242-7593), and Fishing Bridge Visitor Center (307/242-7291) are open only from May 1 to October 31; Old Faithful Visitor Center (307/545-7201) is open also during these months plus from mid-December to mid-March; and Mammoth Visitor Center (307/344-7381, ext. 357) is open all year. For current park information call 307/646-7398. For information as you drive through the park tune your radio to 1606. THE YELLOWSTONE EXPLORER is a newspaper published by the Yellowstone Library and Museum Association and Yellowstone National Park concessioners. It lists all events and services available to visitors. An auto-tape tour (CA-80) may be rented at any of the 5 entrances to the park. The Yellowstone Park Co., Box 414, Yellowstone National Park, WY 82190 (307/344-7311) operates most of the lodgings and expeditions within the park.

A MAP & GUIDE, YELLOWSTONE PARK in 2 sheets is available from the American Adventures Association, 1865 South Main, Suite 27, Salt Lake City, UT 84115. The map part indicates topography and notes falls, geysers, campgrounds, launch sites, ranger stations, etc. The guide part lists campgrounds (noting facilities), ranger and fire lookout stations, wildlife, trails, and rivers, creeks, and lakes (with fishing information).

Information on Bighorn National Forest, Medicine Bow National Forest, and Shoshone National Forest may be obtained from the U.S. Forest Service, Rocky Mountain Region, Box 25127, Lakewood, CO 80225. Information on Bridger-Teton National Forest may be obtained from the U.S. Forest Service, Intermountain Region, Federal Bldg., 324 25th Street, Ogden, UT 84401.

The Bureau of Land Management, Wyoming State Office, Box 1828, Cheyenne, WY 82001 (307/778-2220, ext. 2334) provides land ownership maps at various scales. At this writing they did not publish anything specifically showing recreation sites or opportunities.

A general brochure on state parks, historic sites, and trails is available from the Wyoming Recreation Commission, 604 East 25th Street, Cheyenne, WY 82002 (307/777-7695). A guide to both public and private campgrounds is available from the Wyoming Travel Commission (WY-4).

INDIVIDUAL CITIES OR AREAS

Cheyenne—Printed Materials

A map of Cheyenne is available from Frontier Printing, 313 West 16th Street, Cheyenne, WY 82001.

Cheyenne—Organizations

WY-19 GREATER CHEYENNE CHAMBER OF COMMERCE, Box 1147, Cheyenne, WY 82001 (307/638-3388).

They issue a general brochure and another giving a map and specific information on points of interest, recreation opportunities, events, historical sites, parks, and area tours. Their walk-in office is located at 122 East 17th Street.

THE UNITED STATES TRAVEL INDUSTRY

SOURCE MATERIALS

TI-1   FORECASTING TRAVEL AND TOURISM: AN ANNOTATED BIBLIOG-
RAPHY. Special Studies in Travel Economics and Marketing. Washington, DC: U.S. Travel Data Center, 1979. 53 p.

This annotated bibliography "provides brief descriptions of more than
100 forecasting studies issued by government, industry, and academic
organizations, both foreign and domestic."

TI-2   Goeldner, Charles R., and Dicke, Karen. BIBLIOGRAPHY OF
TOURISM AND TRAVEL RESEARCH STUDIES, REPORTS, AND AR-
TICLES. 3 vols. Boulder: University of Colorado, Graduate School
of Business Administration, Business Research Division in cooperation
with The Travel Research Association, 1971. Indexes. 73-635333.

This is an annotated listing of "studies, surveys, statistical abstracts,
articles, and similar publications with facts and figures related to the
travel industry of the world" published on or after January 1, 1960.
Volume 1 contains publications dealing with the US as a whole and
its regions, volume 2 covers the 50 individual states, and volume 3
contains foreign publications. There is considerable overlap between
the listings in these volumes and the authors' TRAVEL RESEARCH
BIBLIOGRAPHY (TI-3), but the 2 are not mutually exclusive. The advantage of this bibliography is that it is annotated. The advantage of
the other is that it includes more recent citations.

TI-3   _____. TRAVEL RESEARCH BIBLIOGRAPHY: A BIBLIOGRAPHY OF
THE HOLDINGS OF THE TRAVEL REFERENCE CENTER. Boulder:
University of Colorado, Graduate School of Business Administration,
Business Research Division in cooperation with The Travel Research
Association, 1976. 213 p. Index.

This bibliography lists travel research reports and other information on
hand as of June 30, 1975 in the Travel Reference Center, a joint
venture of The Travel Research Association (TI-30) and the University

of Colorado, Graduate School of Business Administration, Business Research Division. The 2,371 listings (there are no annotations) are arranged in 5 sections: (1) periodicals and reports, (2) bibliographies, (3) national, (4) state, and (5) international.

TI-4 _____. TRAVEL TRENDS IN THE UNITED STATES AND CANADA. 5th ed. Boulder: University of Colorado, Graduate School of Business Administration, Business Research Division in cooperation with The Travel Research Association, 1978. 216 p. 0-89478-038-7.

This guide contains 83 statistical tables and accompanying text devoted to numbers and types of visitors, length of stay, expenditures, and type of transportation used in visits to recreational areas and states. The tables have been compiled from data from numerous agencies and organizations. The final 50 pages contain Goeldner's "Where to Find Travel Research Facts" described in the "Source Materials" chapter of this information guide (SM-8).

TI-5 IMPACT OF TRAVEL ON STATE ECONOMIES. Washington, DC: U.S. Travel Data Center, 1976. 63 p.

This study provides detailed estimates of expenditures, business receipts, employment, payroll and tax receipts attributable to travel in each of the 50 states and the District of Columbia. Also included are estimates of the economic impact of travel in Puerto Rico and the Virgin Islands and the impact of foreign visitor spending on US employment, payroll, and tax revenue. The estimates are based on a Travel Economic Impact Model developed by the Data Center for the U.S. Dept. of the Interior.

TI-6 Lehmann, Armin D. TRAVEL AND TOURISM: AN INTRODUCTION TO TRAVEL AGENCY OPERATIONS. Indianapolis: Bobbs-Merrill, 1978. 358 p. Photos., maps, diagrams. 0-672-97090-2. 77-12589.

This is the most recent and comprehensive overview of the work and opportunities of a travel agency career by an expert in the field. It was written primarily as a textbook for those studying travel agency careers. Reference guides, tariff regulations, ticketing, group bookings, and package tours are all generally explained in the section describing "The Business of Travel." The largest portion of the book is devoted to describing the major tourist attractions, document requirements, currency, and major airports for each of the major world travel areas and countries. There are 8 appendixes: (1) an extensive glossary of travel industry terms including the many acronyms used, (2) a list of the major international airlines, (3) city and airport codes, (4) government and state tourist offices, (5) trade journals and periodicals, (6) overseas hotels of major US hotel chains, (7) profiles of major cruise ships, and (8) a list of the major charter operators.

TI-7   National Tourism Resources Review Commission. DESTINATION
        USA. 6 vols. Washington, DC: U.S. Government Printing Office,
        1973. Photos., charts, maps.

        Public Law 91-477, Section 6, of October 21, 1970 (84 Stat 1071)
        established the National Tourism Resources Review Commission which
        was to investigate the "domestic travel needs of the people of the
        United States and of visitors from other countries at the present time
        and to the year 1980." This is the report of that investigation.
        Volume 2, "Domestic Tourism," reports on such things as economic
        characteristics of domestic tourism, the organization and management
        problems of the tourism industry, urban and rural tourism resources,
        and chapter 9 (pp. 103-124) deals with "Tourism Information Facili-
        ties." This is an in-depth look at local, state, regional, federal,
        and business travel promotion efforts in the form of travel offices,
        advertising campaigns, literature, sales packages, travel exhibits,
        state magazines, highway information centers, highway signs, and
        telephone and radio facilities. There are also sections on sources of
        information used by travelers for trip planning, a discussion of what
        should be incorporated into a total travel information system, and the
        weaknesses of various types of information facilities. The chapter is
        documented with 29 references.

TI-8   NATIONAL TRAVEL EXPENDITURE STUDY: SUMMARY REPORT.
        Washington, DC: U.S. Travel Data Center. Issued annually.

        The data presented is derived from a National Travel Expenditure
        Model, designed by the Data Center to simulate traveler spending.
        Estimates of American travel expenditures for transportation, lodging,
        food, entertainment/recreation, and incidentals are broken down by
        trip purpose, means of transportation, and numerous other trip and
        traveler variables. The study has been issued since 1975, and it
        analyzes data for the year preceeding the date of each report.

TI-9   NATIONAL TRAVEL NEWS DIRECTORY. Washington, DC: Discover
        America Travel Organizations, 1977. Issued annually. 54 p.

        This listing of all news media outlets and other public relations con-
        tacts interested in the US travel industry is probably the most com-
        plete directory of this kind available. It lists travel industry maga-
        zines; newspapers having travel features; in-house publications; news
        services and syndicates; consumer magazines; syndicated travel columns;
        official state magazines promoting travel; television network and state
        radio and television broadcasting associations; national travel and
        tourism associations; the airlines; auto rental firms; bus, cruise, and
        rail lines; selected sightseeing companies; travel show producers; na-
        tional accommodations and restaurant chains; selected attractions;
        selected outdoor recreation groups; selected advertising and public
        relations firms; city and metropolitan promotion agencies; regional
        promotion organizations; firms and organizations cooperating in travel
        development; federal travel promotion agencies; congressional tourism

committees; official state and territorial travel offices; travel research associations; and universities with travel business/travel research
curricula.

TI-10   NATIONAL TRAVEL SURVEY. Washington, DC: U.S. Travel Data
Center.

The Center's annual travel survey (not to be confused with the U.S.
Census Bureau's quinquennial NATIONAL TRAVEL SURVEY [TI-15]) has
been published since 1974 in quarterly and full year printed reports
and on computer tapes for the same reporting periods. Comparisons
are made of numerous trip and traveler characteristics. Data is
gathered through quarterly household surveys using the same basic
questionnaire as the Census Bureau. The Data Center adds a few
more questions, uses a smaller sample, and, of course, collects data,
4 times a year, instead of once every 5 years.

TI-11   SURVEY OF STATE TRAVEL OFFICES. Washington, DC: U.S. Travel
Data Center. Issued annually.

This was first issued for the period 1973/74. It is based on a Data
Center questionnaire survey of government travel offices in each of
the states, the District of Columbia, and the 3 US Territories.
Tables are used to present data on the organization and activities of
each travel office. Among the activities analyzed are general promotion activities (out-of-state cities in which information centers are
maintained, addresses of nonofficial statewide tourism associations,
and toll-free telephone numbers), press and public relations activities
(names of travel-related publications and their frequency), and welcome centers activities (in 1977/78 there were a total of 355 such
centers and they were maintained by 47 states; an average state
operates 7 permanent and 1 mobile welcome center).

TI-12   TRAVEL DATA LOCATOR INDEX: A REFERENCE GUIDE TO CUR-
RENT DATA ON TRAVEL AND RECREATION. 2d ed. Washington,
DC: U.S. Travel Data Center, 1978. 222 p.

This is a cross-indexed list of statistical information that will be
found in numerous publications, most of them officially issued. It is
arranged by broad subjects, with many subheadings reflecting various
aspects of the travel and recreation field and tells where data on
each subject may be found.

TI-13   TRAVEL MARKET YEARBOOK. Stamford, CT: Travel Marketing
(31 Wallacks Lane/06902), 1978. Issued annually. 96 p. Index.

This annual "brings together statistics on many facets of the travel
industry gathered from government and industry sources. . .subjects
covered include air carriers, travel agents, car rentals, automobile
travel, international travel, hotels and motels, and sports."

TI-14   TRAVEL OUTLOOK FORUM PROCEEDINGS. 3d ed. Washington,
         DC: U.S. Travel Data Center, 1978. Issued annually. 171 p.

         This includes all the papers presented at this annual symposium where
         travel experts examine developments, problems, and prospects in the
         industry. It is jointly sponsored by the Travel Data Center (TI-31)
         and The Travel Research Association (TI-30).

TI-15   U.S. Dept. of Commerce. Bureau of the Census. CENSUS OF
         TRANSPORTATION. Vol. 1: NATIONAL TRAVEL SURVEY. Wash-
         ington, DC: U.S. Government Printing Office, 1963 to date (every
         5 years).

         The Census of Transportation was undertaken for the first time on a
         national basis in 1963. In that year it consisted of 4 separate sur-
         veys and part 1 of the Passenger Transportation Survey (Volume 1) is
         the National Travel Survey. Beginning in 1967, the Census of Trans-
         portation has been undertaken every 5 years. Since that time, it
         consists of 3 separate surveys: the National Travel Survey, the
         Truck Inventory and Use Survey, and the Commodity Transportation
         Survey. The National Travel Survey is presented as volume I of
         each of the quinquennial Censuses of Transportation. It is based
         on information obtained from a nationwide probability sample (6,000
         households in 1963; 24,000 in 1977) and attempts to "provide a mea-
         sure of the volume and characteristics of nonlocal travel by the
         civilian noninstitutional population of the United States." Numerous
         trip variables are compared with selected socioeconomic characteristics
         of the travelers in increasingly detailed statistical tables each time
         the survey is undertaken.

TI-16   WORLD TRAVEL DIRECTORY: OFFICIAL GUIDE TO THE WORLD-
         WIDE TRAVEL INDUSTRY. New York: Ziff-Davis Publishing Co.
         Issued annually(?).

         This sourcebook lists 25,000 worldwide retail and wholesale travel
         agents and 500 North American wholesalers. It includes destination
         descriptions for each state and 100 countries; passport, visa, and
         inoculation regulations; currency exchange information; and month-by-
         month weather charts for 200 cities.

MAGAZINES

TI-17   TRAVELAGE EAST. New York: Reuben H. Donnelley Corp. (888
         Seventh Avenue/10019). Issued weekly. Began publication in 1967.

TI-18   TRAVELAGE MIDAMERICA. Chicago: Reuben H. Donnelley Corp.
         (2416 Prudential Plaza/60601). Issued bimonthly. Began publication
         in 1975.

TI-19   TRAVELAGE SOUTHEAST. New York: Reuben H. Donnelley Corp.

(888 Seventh Avenue/10019). Issued monthly. Began publication in 1976.

TI-20   TRAVELAGE WEST. San Francisco: Reuben H. Donnelley Corp. (582 Market Street/94104). Issued weekly. Began publication in 1969.

This series of regional news magazines (TI-17 to TI-20) for the travel industry covers industry-wide happenings, news of local agencies, and many advertisements to advise agents of new sales packages and products. Regular features in each edition include listings of area seminars, sales sessions, and social events; listings of employment opportunities; and "The Sales Rack," descriptions of new brochures and travel promotion materials.

TI-21   THE TRAVEL AGENT. New York: The American Traveler (2 West 46th Street/10036). Subscriptions may be ordered through the following toll-free number: 800/223-0535.

This newsmagazine for the travel industry was established in 1929 and is now published twice a week. It regularly features articles about industry developments and extensive write-ups about sales opportunities in individual travel market areas. There are several regular features. "Tariff Alert" alternates in every other issue with "Travel Agent Proficiency Tests." The former is a tabular summary of significant rate changes and proposals by the different airlines mostly, but also sometimes by hotels and tour operators. The latter is a test (with answers) designed to improve the technical knowledge of travel agency staff. "Rating Hotels Around the World" appears irregularly and is a continuing country-by-country listing of individual hotels giving number of beds, rates, commission paid to agents, and a brief statement of its latest rating by 3 rating services (Fielding, Fodor, STAR). "Familiarization Trip Schedules" also appears irregularly and lists reduced rate trip offers for agents to take in order to aid them in selling those same trips and countries to their clients. Each November there is an additional issue called the "Travel Blue Book and ASTA Convention Issue." It contains a state-by-state analysis of travel agent sales, the most comprehensive listing anywhere of travel films (arranged by country with a state-by-state breakdown for the US), US and Canadian market profiles, and a list of those agencies having one million dollars or more in annual travel sales.

TI-22   TRAVEL TRADE. New York: Travel Trade Publications (605 Fifth Avenue/10017) (212/752-3233).

This weekly newspaper is devoted to news coverage and analysis of travel industry happenings. Each issue also contains several "Showcases" in which travel selling opportunities in different areas of the world are highlighted. Seven other separate sections are published as part of the newspaper package. BUSINESS TRAVEL MAGAZINE contains marketing features and in-depth news analyses to help travel agents improve and expand their operations toward the traveling businessperson. It is issued the first Monday of every month. DISCOVER AMERICA MAGAZINE is the official publication of Discover America Travel Organizations (TI-28) and is the voice of the domestic travel industry. It has a regular feature describing new publications both of the official state travel agencies and other agencies and publishers. It is issued the third Monday of every month. The TOUR CALIFORNIA GUIDE, issued the fourth Monday of every month, is designed to increase the effectiveness of selling California by agents. Two sections appear at frequent, but irregular, intervals: the SALES GUIDES provide complete sales and marketing information for specific areas around the world (each is devoted to one area, country, or state), and the SALES PACKAGES provide a unique means for mailing actual sales promotion brochures of tour packages, attractions, etc. designed to be distributed by the industry. The PERSONNEL SALES GUIDE is issued semiannually in May and November and is a directory of hotels and hotel representatives, tour operators, carriers, tourist boards, etc. The DISCOVER AMERICA ANNUAL SALES GUIDE appears each May and is a state-by-state directory of tourist offices, attractions, and sales packages. TRAVEL TRADE celebrated its fiftieth anniversary with a mammoth 209-page January 31, 1979 issue that featured (1) an extensive report, with tables, by futurologist Herman Kahn on the future of travel in the next 50 years, and (2) a year-by-year account of the growth of travel and the travel industry from 1929-1978.

TI-23   TRAVEL WEEKLY: THE NATIONAL NEWSPAPER OF THE TRAVEL INDUSTRY. New York: Ziff-Davis Publishing Co. (One Park Avenue/10016).

This magazine (the world "newspaper" in the subtitle is misleading) began publication in 1958 and is issued twice a week. Of interest to travel agents, it regularly covers news items on developments in the travel industry or those of interest to the travel trade, and numerous articles and advertisements describing sales information, opportunities, and packages to aid the agent in selling his/her products. A regular feature is "The Rate Desk" which lists major new airline passenger fares on file with the Civil Aeronautics Board.

PUBLISHERS

TI-24   THE REUBEN H. DONNELLEY CORP., 2000 Clearwater Drive, Oak Brook, IL 60521 (312/654-6000 for office). For subscription information call 800/323-3537 in the US except Illinois, Alaska, and Hawaii. In Illinois call 800/942-1888. In Alaska and Hawaii call 312/654-6162.

They are a major publisher of source materials for the travel industry. These include: (1) the 4 regional editions of TRAVELAGE (TI-17 to

TI-20); (2) the OFFICIAL AIRLINE GUIDE (US-121); (3) POCKET FLIGHT GUIDE, a monthly pocket-sized listing of the most frequently traveled air routes published for the frequent flyer and available in both a North American and a European edition; (4) the OAG TRAVEL PLANNER & HOTEL/MOTEL GUIDE (US-120); (5) OAG WORLDWIDE TOUR GUIDE, a catalogue of tours by destination areas and special interest categories with an air charter section and a list of tour operators (issued 3 times a year); (6) OAG WORLDWIDE CRUISE & SHIPLINE GUIDE, contains information on shipline companies, ship profiles, maps of individual port terminals, cruise listings, and port-to-port and ferry schedules (issued bimonthly); (7) OAG AIR CARGO GUIDE, a monthly guide in 2 parts listing cargo flight schedules (part 1) and describing packaging requirements (part 2); and (8) AIR-CARGO MAGAZINE, a monthly publication for the industry. This company is not to be confused with R.R. Donnelley and Sons, Co., which produces maps used by the travel industry in directories, atlases, and give-away literature.

TI-25   ZIFF-DAVIS PUBLISHING CO., PUBLIC TRANSPORTATION AND TRAVEL DIVISION, One Park Avenue, Room 618, New York, NY 10016.

This major publisher of directories and aids for the travel industry issues the HOTEL AND TRAVEL INDEX (US-90), WORLD TRAVEL DIRECTORY (TI-16), TRAVEL WEEKLY (TI-23), THE OFFICIAL HOTEL & RESORT GUIDE (US-122), and OFFICIAL MEETING FACILITIES GUIDE, issued twice a year and giving vital statistics on over 800 worldwide meeting facilities and convention centers.

ORGANIZATIONS

TI-26   AMERICAN SOCIETY OF TRAVEL AGENTS (ASTA), 711 Fifth Avenue, New York, NY 10022 (212/486-0700).

"The trade association of travel agents, tour operators, and suppliers to the industry with world-wide membership exceeding 15,000. ASTA's purpose is to promote and advance the interests of the travel agency industry and safeguard the travelling public against unethical practices." The society was founded in 1931. They issue a monthly newsletter called ASTA TRAVEL NEWS.

TI-27   ASSOCIATION OF RETAIL TRAVEL AGENTS (ARTA), 8 Maple Street, Croton-on-Hudson, NY 10520 (914/271-9000 or 212/299-5151).

They promote the interests of retail travel agents and agencies in the US through representation on industry councils, testimony before Congress, and participation in the Civil Aeronautics Board, Dept. of Transportation, and Federal Maritime Commission proceedings. They were founded in 1962. Their newsletter is the monthly ARTAFACTS.

TI-28   DISCOVER AMERICA TRAVEL ORGANIZATIONS (DATO), 1899 L
Street NW, Washington, DC 20036 (202/293-1433).

This organization came into being in 1969 when the National Association of Travel Organizations, an industry-wide association founded in
1941 principally by state government travel directors, merged with
Discover America, an organization formed in 1965 following a Presidential proclamation and Congressional resolution.   DATO is a nonprofit organization composed of paying members who are active in
the US travel industry.   In addition to its main purpose of promoting
and facilitating travel to and within the US, DATO deeps a watch-
dog eye on governmental actions that might affect the industry and is
frequently involved in lobbying activities.   To capitalize on the
diversity of travel opportunities in the US, and to foster cooperative
promotion efforts, DATO has set up 9 US travel regions: (1) New
England Region, (2) Eastern Gateway Region, (3) George Washington
Country, (4) Travel South Region, (5) Great Lakes Country, (6)
Mountain West Region, (7) Frontier West Region, (8) Islands, East
and West, and (9) Far West Region.   These regions, and, in fact,
most of the operations of DATO, are probably not directly visible to
the average traveling American, but their logo, a red arrow with a
blue tail inclosing 2 stars, bisected by a weather vane and inclosed
in a box with the words "Discover America" probably is.   They issue
3 major publications, mostly for use within the industry, but each
containing much valuable factual information.   Two of these are
issued in cooperation with TRAVEL TRADE (TI-22).   DISCOVER
AMERICA MAGAZINE is published the third Monday of every month
and is devoted to domestic travel news, features, and sales.   DIS-
COVER AMERICA SALES GUIDE is issued annually in May and is a
comprehensive reference guide to the travel offices, attractions, and
package tours in each state.   It is arranged by the above mentioned
9 DATO regions.   The third publication is the NATIONAL TRAVEL
NEWS DIRECTORY (TI-9).   The DATO Board of Directors defines
"travel industry" as follows: an interrelated amalgamation of those
businesses and agencies which totally or in part provide the means of
transport, goods, services, accommodations and other facilities for
travel out of the home community for any purpose not related to local
day-to-day activity.

TI-29   SOCIETY OF AMERICAN TRAVEL WRITERS, 1120 Connecticut Avenue
NW, Suite 940, Washington, DC 20036 (202/785-5567).

The society, begun in 1956, is a professional association of writers,
photographers, editors, broadcasters, and public relations representatives whose aim is to serve the traveling public.   Members receive
a monthly newsletter, THE TRAVEL WRITER.   An annual ROSTER OF
MEMBERS (1978 ed., 103 p.) and an annual TRAVEL MARKET GUIDE
(1978, 12th ed., 24 p.), a guide to the media that accept travel
articles and photographs, are also issued by the society.

TI-30   THE TRAVEL RESEARCH ASSOCIATION, Box 8066, Foothill Station,
Salt Lake City, UT 84108 (801/581-3351).

This organization (TTRA) was formed in 1970 to improve the quality, scope, and acceptability of travel research. Members include government agencies; accommodations, attractions, and resorts; recreation enterprises; public relations firms; travel agencies; research and consulting firms; etc. There are several local chapters and an annual conference, the proceedings of which are available to members. In addition TTRA cosponsors the annual Travel Outlook Forum (TI-14) with the U.S. Travel Data Center (TI-31). Members receive the quarterly JOURNAL OF TRAVEL RESEARCH which contains articles about current travel research plus a regular "Travel Research Bookshelf." TTRA has established a Travel Reference Center at the University of Colorado, Graduate School of Business Administration, Business Research Division, Boulder, CO 80309 (303/492-8227) to assist the travel industry in finding information sources. The person to contact there is Karen Dicke. The center will loan books, make photocopies, answer reference questions, and conduct literature searches. The holdings of the center will be found in the TRAVEL RESEARCH BIBLIOGRAPHY (TI-3). The Business Research Division conducts and publishes its own studies of various segments of the travel industry, including TRAVEL TRENDS IN THE UNITED STATES AND CANADA (TI-4).

TI-31   U.S. TRAVEL DATA CENTER, 1899 L Street NW, Washington, DC 20036 (202/293-1040).

The center was organized in 1973 as an independent, nonprofit corporation dedicated to collecting and disseminating statistical data on the travel activities of Americans and of foreign visitors to this country. Until that time, the only regularly collected travel data in the US were the domestic travel surveys (TI-15) conducted every 5 years by the U.S. Bureau of the Census and the U.S. Travel Service's (US-241) data which focused only on international travel trends. The center's research efforts in gathering and analyzing travel data result in a number of publications designed to provide economic and market research information on various sectors of the travel industry. Most of them are described individually in the "Source Materials" section of this chapter. TRAVEL PRINTOUT is the Data Center's monthly newsletter reporting on current travel trends, results of Data Center studies, and other projects involving travel research and marketing. Regular features are "Current Travel Indicators," which presents recent monthly data on receipts and volume in various sectors of the travel industry, and a statistical table on visitors to areas administered by the National Park Service. They also publish an annual (1st ed., 1979) PROGRAM AND MEMBERSHIP GUIDE which includes statements of purpose and policy, program objectives, current membership, the annual research program, custom research available, and comprehensive membership information. Numerous other monographs have been prepared by the Data Center, all of which are described in its annual free PUBLICATIONS CATALOG. Nine levels of memberships are available, and they include free copies of all reports and opportunities to engage in additional data gathering activities.

INDEXES

There are six different indexes to this information guide: author, title, subject, geographic, organization, and publisher. They are alphabetized letter by letter. The references are to item numbers or to a page or pages (number(s) preceded by a "p.") when the information is not found within an annotation. The user is referred to the preliminary section, "How To Use This Information Guide" (p. ix), for an explanation of the item number code.

In some cases, the item number does not always reflect the contents of the item. For example, a hiking guide covering both Massachusetts and Rhode Island has the item number "MA-1" and has entries under both Massachusetts and Rhode Island in the geographic index. But in the subject index, under hiking, the item number "MA-1" will appear, which may erroneously suggest to the user that the work is only about hiking in Massachusetts. The reader using the two letter state code and looking for hiking in Rhode Island will miss this title unless he or she also checks the geographic index.

Some titles appearing in upper case throughout the text have not been indexed. They are either considered too ephemeral, or they are not essentially travel materials. Short titles are used in the index, except in instances where one short title duplicates another. Underlined numbers following some index headings refer to the most informative entry when several items or pages are noted.

The contents of monographic works have been selectively indexed but this has not been done for the main general promotion pieces issued by the major travel organizations. However, their separate specialized publications have been selectively indexed. Most publications of local convention and visitors bureaus and chambers of commerce are not usually indexed because nearly all of these organizations issue the same type of literature.

The index gives only inclusive pagination for the entire US section, the four regional sections, and each of the individual states. Separate item numbers appearing within these sections are not indexed under these large geographic headings. However, many regional guides cover just three or four states. In such cases the item will be indexed under each of the states in its coverage. The same is true with major specific geographic areas or cities included in the state guides. Obviously, though, each area or city mentioned in every guide has not been indexed.

Many state agencies mentioned in the text, especially those appearing in the "Outdoor Recreation Activities" sections, have not been indexed by name. They are not primarily travel organizations and have been included in the text only as a source for information that is basically of a subject nature. There are general references to these sections in the subject index. Regional tourism associations are not indexed. Some national parks and forests are listed in the index of organizations. The reference is to the item where the mailing address and the telephone number of the park or forest supervisor is given.

AUTHOR INDEX

A

Abeloe, William N. CA-1
Adams, Arthur G. NY-29
Aero Surveys of Georgia GA-9
Agnew, Jeremy CO-1
Aiello, Roger FL-33
Airport Operators Council International
US-2
Aitchison, Stewart W. AZ-25
Akey, Denise SM-6
Alaska Travel Publications, editors
of AK-27
Albright, Priscilla NY-35
Albright, Rodney NY-35
Alegre, Mitchell R. US-4
Alexandria Drafting Co. DC-1,
GA-10, MD-16, NC-1 to NC-2,
PA-29, VA-16 to VA-17
Allen, Gene P. SM-14
Alper, M. Victor N-1, S-1
Alvord, David N-52
American Geographical Society NY-5
American Geological Institute p. xx
American Heritage, editors of US-88
Anderson, Eddie NV-12
Angelillo, Phil NY-36
Angelo, Joseph A., Jr. US-8
Annand, Douglass R. US-9
Anthrop, Donald F. CA-90
Appelbaum, Madelyn PA-30
Apte, Stu FL-29
Arkley, Rose WA-44
Arnot, Phil CA-87
Arrow Maps NY-79

Arrow Publishing Co. CT-13,
FL-41, MA-11, MD-17, RI-1,
SC-1
Asa, Warren US-12
Asher, Spring GA-2
Association for Living Historical
Farms and Agricultural Museums
US-13
Atkinson, Allegra WA-44
Atwater, Maxine H. US-14

B

Babb, Laura L. DC-2
Bach, Ira J. IL-12
Bach, Orville E., Jr. WY-13
Badlands Natural History Association
SD-6
Bagg, Alan C-1
Baker, Catherine J. VT-6
Baker, Cozy US-17
Barish, Jane US-18
Barish, Mort US-18
Barnes, Francis A. UT-1 to UT-10
Barnes, Richard DC-17
Barnett, John NM-10
Baron, Andrea IL-13
Barrett, Pete NJ-1
Barton-Aschman Associates PA-21
Baxter, Robert US-19
Beach, Marie VA-21
Bearse, Ray MA-2, ME-2, VT-1
Beck, David CA-2
Bednarz, Wilma WI-26
Bedrick, Christina OR-1, WA-2

511

Author Index

Bedrick, Ed OR-1, WA-2
Beil, Irene A. NJ-2
Beil, Preston J. NJ-2
Beiser, Karl N-52
Belknap, Bill UT-23
Belknap, Buzz AZ-18, HI-1, UT-11, UT-23, W-5, WY-7
Belknap, Jodi HI-1
Benner, Bob NC-3
Bennet, John NY-30
Benton, Chris IL-14
Benton, Christine M. N-4
Beram, Sandy N-5
Berkowitz, Alan DC-3
Berman, Steve N-6, N-7
Berssen, William W-19
Beymer, Robert MN-1
Bicycle & Pedestrian Transportation Research Center PA-31
Birnbaum, Stephen US-20
Bixby, William CT-1
Blackmon, Peggy P. TX-37
Blaisdell, Paul H. N-52
Blake, Reid UT-28
Blanchard, Fessenden S. MD-8
Blankenship, Samuel M. S-2
Bledsoe, Harriett L. FL-24
Bleything, Dennis CA-32, OR-6
Bloemendaal, Dirk C. MI-1
Blue Ridge Parkway Association NC-16
Boatner, Mark M. US-21
Bodine, John J. NM-1
Bogert, Joan AZ-27
Bogert, John AZ-27
Bone, Robert W. HI-2
Bonney, Lorraine G. WY-1, WY-6
Bonney, Orrin H. WY-1, WY-6
Bookmap Corp. AZ-33, TX-2, TX-22, TX-38
Boston Society of Architects MA-14
Brady, Eric NC-4
Brandon, Jim US-22
Brant, Michelle CA-140
Brant, Warren E. C-2 to C-4
Brein, Michael HI-28
Brennan, Jimmy LA-11
Brewster, David W-1
Bridge, Raymond W-2
Britchky, Seymour NY-41

Brody, Polly WI-2
Brookins, Jean A. MN-3
Brosnahan, Tom N-9
Browder, Sue US-23
Brown, Dale C. MS-7
Brown, Leslie US-60
Brown, Robert L. W-46
Brown, Sheldon S. US-24
Browning, Bill MT-1
Bruner, Ronald PA-45
Bryan, Edwin H., Jr. HI-3
Bryan, Howard NM-2
Bryant, Beth DC-5
Bryfonski, Dedria N-10
Buchanan, James W. MN-2
Budd, Barbara MN-5, MN-17
Bulkin, Rena CA-3
Bunker, Gerald AZ-2
Burgwyn, Diana PA-1
Burmeister, Walter F. S-3
Burnham, Linda US-97
Burrell, Bob WV-1
Burroughs, Polly MA-27 to MA-28
Burt, Bernard I. NJ-14
Busch, Richard OR-27
Bush, Hal AK-5
Bushnell, Oswald A. HI-29
Butchart, Harvey AZ-19
Butcher, Devereux US-25
Byers, Jane C. CT-20

C

Calder, Jean US-26
Calhoun, James LA-1
Calhoun, Nancy H. LA-1
California Critic, editors of CA-31, CA-46
Camaro Eating Teams CA-15
Camphouse, Marjorie V. CA-7
Cantor, George C-5
Carlinsky, Dan NY-42
Carlson, Raymond SM-1, US-27 to US-28
Carnahan, Peter PA-22
Carson, George MO-12
Carter, Annette PA-32
Carter, Randy S-4
Cary, Norman M., Jr. US-29
Casewit, Curtis W. CO-2, US-30, W-3

Author Index

Nienhueser, Helen AK-13
Nixdorf, Bert PA-41
Nolen, Ben M. TX-9
Norback, Craig US-118
Norback, Peter US-118
Norton, Barbara CO-11
Norton, Boyd CO-11
Nueckel, Susan SM-17

O

O'Donnell, Terence OR-30
Oglesby, Claire C. US-125
O'Keefe, M. Timothy US-126
Olmsted, Nancy CA-154
Onosko, Tim US-127
O'Reilly, John FL-31
Ormes, Robert CO-12
Osler, Jack M. FL-11, IL-8,
    IN-5, KY-7, MI-10, OH-4,
    PA-3

P

Paananen, Wayne US-128
Pahner, Stanley W. NV-18
Palzer, Bob C-10
Palzer, Judy C-10
Papenfuse, Edward C. MD-5
Papy, Frank FL-32
Parks, Nancy MO-10
Parnes, Robert NJ-8
Pashdag, John CA-109
Patterson, Barbara M. NY-21
Patterson, Jerry KS-3
Paulsen, Reinhart US-128
Pepper, Adeline NJ-9
Perdue, Lewis S-10
Perrero, Laurie FL-46
Perrero, Louis FL-46
Perrin, Alwyn T. US-130
Perrin, Rosemarie D. US-131
Peters, Robert E. MN-8
Petzoldt, Paul WY-9
Phillips, L.K. OR-5
Piggott, Margaret H. AK-14
Pilgreen, Tedi NV-1
Pilgren, Tedi AZ-5
Polk, Nicki MA-20
Pollak, Rita MA-17

Pomada, Elizabeth CA-42
Poor, Harold L. NJ-10
Postal, Bernard US-132
Powell, Ron DC-15
Powers, Edward US-133
Pratt, Kevin TX-23
Pratt, LeRoy G. IA-2
President's Committee on Employ-
    ment of the Handicapped SM-18
Price, Raye C. UT-24
Price, Steven D. US-134
Professional Group of The Junior
    League of Cleveland OH-18
Puetz, C.J. FL-12, MI-11,
    PA-8, WI-11
Purinton, James WI-12
Pyle, Sara US-135

R

Ramsdell, Charles TX-39
Randall, Anne RI-8
Randall, Charles E. US-136
Randall, Peter NH-11
Ranicke, Maxine WA-45
Rath, Sara WI-9
Rathbun, Linda M. HI-13
Read, R.B. CA-155 to CA-156
Reamy, Lois US-141
Reed, Henry H. NY-58
Reese, M. Lisle SD-2
Reichert, Arthur CA-21
Rice, William US-143
Rifkind, Carole NY-6
Riley, Frank W. CA-22
Riley, Laura US-144
Riley, William US-144
Ripley, Sheldon N. MA-3
Rivkin, Dyann IL-13
Robinson, Blackwell P. NC-9
Robinson, Donald H. NC-18
Robinson, John CA-23
Robinson, William F. N-34
Robinson, William M., Jr. MD-6
Rohde, Jill IL-21
Rohde, Ron IL-21
Roth, Claire Jarett US-10
Rothafel, Roxy N-35
Routh, Jonathan NY-59
Rubenstein, Robert W-21

Author Index

TITLE INDEX

A

Abandoned New England   N-34
Access Amtrak   US-291
Access Atlanta   GA-8
Access Chicago   IL-11
Access Dallas   TX-25
Accessibility Directory: Kansas City, Missouri   MO-8
Access Lansing   MI-22
Access Las Vegas   NV-11
Access National Parks   US-1
Access New York   NY-40
Access Salt Lake   UT-31
Access San Antonio   TX-36
Access Seattle   WA-43
Access to Boston in '76   MA-10
Access to Capitaland   NY-26
Access Travel: Airports   US-2
Access Washington   DC-12
Accommodations Directory for the Handicapped Traveller   WA-1
Adirondack Canoe Waters, North Flow   NY-20
Adirondack Region Atlas   NY-17
Adventures in California   CA-8
Adventures in Dining and Interesting Places to Visit   PA-9
Adventures in the Wine Country   CA-123
Adventure Travel   US-47, US-93
Adventure Travel (magazine)   US-190
Adventure Travel Newsletter   US-218
AIA Guide to New York City   NY-69
Airguide Traveler, The   W-18

Air Taxi Charter and Rental Directory of North America   US-3
Alabama   AL-2
Alabama Canoe Rides and Float Trips   AL-1
ALA Sights to See Book   US-257
Alaska   AK-7
Alaska: The Complete Travel Book   AK-15
Alaska: The Magazine of Life on the Last Frontier   AK-1
Alaskafest   AK-23
Alaska Fishing Guide   AK-2
Alaska Geographic   AK-20
Alaska Hunting Guide   AK-3
Alaska Journal, The   AK-20
Alaska Sportsman   AK-1
Alaska Travel Guide   AK-4
Alaska Travel Handbook   AK-5
ALA Top Tours   US-257
ALA Where to Stay Book   US-257
ALA Where to Take the Kids Book   US-257
Albuquerque and New Mexico This Month   NM-11
All about Camping in Alaska and the Yukon   AK-10
All about the Boston Harbor Islands   MA-18
All New Underground Gourmet, The   NY-46
All Night L.A.   CA-109
All the Best in Hawaii   HI-21
All the Southwest   W-16
Aloft   US-250

Title Index

Title Index

Title Index

F

Fabulous Florida FL-9
Facts about Alaska AK-20
Family Guide to Amusement Centers, A US-92
Family Guide to Cape Cod, The MA-31
Family Guide to Honolulu and the Island of Oahu HI-30
Famous and Historic Trees US-136
Famous Guide to Boston MA-20
Farm, Ranch & Countryside Guide US-48
Favorite Vermont Ski Inns and Lodging Guide VT-2
Feet First CA-113
Festivals Sourcebook US-183
50 Best Mini-Trips for Kentucky KY-7
50 Best Mini-Trips for Ohio OH-4
50 Biking Holidays CA-36
55 Oregon Bicycle Trips OR-8
55 Ways to the Wilderness in South Central Alaska AK-13
50 Great Mini-Trips for Illinois IL-8
50 Great Mini-Trips for Indiana IN-5
50 Great Mini-Trips for Michigan MI-10
50 Great Mini-Trips for Pennsylvania PA-3
50 Great Mini-Trips in Florida FL-11
50 Hikes in Arizona AZ-9
Fifty Hikes in Central Pennsylvania N-52
Fifty Hikes in Connecticut N-52
Fifty Hikes in Maine N-52
Fifty Hikes in Massachusetts N-52
50 Hikes in Mount Rainier National Park WA-33
Fifty Hikes in New Hampshire N-52
Fifty Hikes in New Hampshire's White Mountains N-52
50 Hikes in Texas TX-8
Fifty Hikes in Vermont N-52
Fifty More Hikes in New Hampshire N-52
50 Northern California Bicycle Trips CA-40

50 Short Climbs in the Midwest C-1
50 Southern California Bicycle Trips CA-47, CA-58
50 West Central Colorado Hiking Trails CO-10
Find Your Own Way in Downtown Atlanta GA-12
Firestone/Morse Guide to Florida's Enchanting Islands, The FL-1
Fishing and Hunting in Maine ME-9
Fishing-Hunting Guide to the Ozark Area MO-12
Flashmaps! The 1978-79 Instant Guide to Chicago IL-19
Flashmaps! The 1978-79 Instant Guide to New York NY-49
Flashmaps! The 1977-78 Instant Guide to Washington DC-13
Flightime US-243
Florida FL-2
Florida Bicentennial Trail, The FL-3
Florida Golf Guide FL-4
Florida 1976 FL-5
Fodor's Budget Travel in America 1979 US-59
Fodor's California 1979 CA-14
Fodor's Far West US-61
Fodor's Florida 1979 FL-6
Fodor's Hawaii 1978 HI-6
Fodor's Indian America US-85
Fodor's Mid-Atlantic US-62
Fodor's Mid-West US-63
Fodor's New England US-64
Fodor's New York & New Jersey US-65
Fodor's New York 1979 NY-1
Fodor's Old West W-7
Fodor's Old South S-8
Fodor's Only-in-America Vacation Guide US-60
Fodor's Rockies & Plains US-66
Fodor's Seaside America US-153
Fodor's South-West US-67
Fodor's the South US-68
Fodor's U.S.A. US-69
Footsore WA-13
Forecasting Travel and Tourism TI-1

42 More Short Walks in Connecticut CT-9
Franconia Notch NH-10
Freedom by the Bay MA-22
Fresh Water Fishing and Hunting in North Carolina NC-1
Fresh Water Fishing and Hunting in Virginia VA-3
Frontier US-248
Fun Land U.S.A. US-127

G

Gateway to Historic Charleston SC-9
Gay Insider, The US-91
Gazetteer of Vermont Heritage VT-3
Geographia's Street Atlas of Rochester NY-80
Georgia GA-4
Georgia Life GA-3
Getting It Together in Kansas City MO-10
Getting Off on 96 & Other Less Traveled Roads CA-32
Ghost Towns of the Colorado Rockies W-46
Ghost Towns of the Northwest W-46
Gilbert Love's Go Guide PA-45
Glacier National Park and Waterton Lakes National Park MT-13
"Go . . . Don't Go" Guide to Delaware and Nearby Pennsylvania, The DE-2
Going Out in New York NY-62
Going Places US-192
Gold Diggers Atlas W-12
Golden Gate Park at Your Feet CA-142
Gomer's Budget Travel Directory US-102
Go Straight on Peachtree GA-11
Grand Canyon National Park AZ-21
Grand Canyon River Guide AZ-18
Grand Canyon Treks (and) Grand Canyon Treks II AZ-19
Grand Teton National Park Snake River Guide WY-7
Graphic Street Guide of Northern Kentucky KY-1

Great Diving-I US-109
Greater Cincinnati Guidebook for the Handicapped OH-14
Greater Hartford Handbook for the Handicapped CT-14
Greater Niagara Vacationland NY-81
Greater Washington Area Bicycle Atlas with Maps, Descriptions and Resources for Cycling in the Mid-Atlantic States DC-3
Great Family Fun Guide to Arizona, The AZ-5
Great Family Fun Guide to San Francisco, The CA-149
Great Lakes Guidebook, The C-5
Great Restaurants of California, The CA-15
Great Salt Lake, The UT-32
Green Acres School's Going Places with Children in Washington DC-9
Greeter, The ND-6
Guest Guide to Montana, the Promised Land, A MT-1
Guia de la Florida en Español FL-5
Guide Book of the Long Trail VT-4
Guidebook to Canyonlands Country UT-24
Guidebook to Denver for the Handicapped, A CO-30
Guidebook to Des Moines for the Handicapped, A IA-7
Guidebook to Historic Western Pennsylvania, A PA-50
Guidebook to Las Vegas NV-16
Guide Book to Lincoln for the Handicapped, A NE-5
Guidebook to Milwaukee for the Handicapped and Aging, A WI-27
Guidebook to Nashville for the Handicapped and Aging, A TN-10
Guidebook to Norfolk for the Handicapped and Aging, A VA-18
Guidebook to Revolutionary Sites in North Carolina, A NC-7

Title Index

Title Index

Title Index

Title Index

SUBJECT INDEX

A

Access guides. See Handicapped and special traveler

Accommodations MI-7, MT-5, N-58, NC-8, NC-13, NC-16, NH-4, NH-15, NY-29, PA-15, SC-6, US-97, US-234, US-257, US-259, VA-25, VT-7, WI-17. See also Camping; Hotels and motels; House exchange services; Housekeeping cottages; Inns and taverns; Resorts; Tourist homes

low cost US-18, US-27, US-34, US-277 to US-279, US-284, US-287, US-289. See also Budget travel

Adventure travel US-47, US-93, US-130, US-190, US-218, W-38. See also Outdoor recreation; specific types of activities

Agricultural travel MI-13, US-13. See also Farm vacations

Airlines AK-23, HI-23 to HI-24, US-3, US-120 to US-121, US-243 to US-256. See also Airports; Air travel

Airports DC-21, IL-2, NY-76, US-2, US-11, US-120, US-200, W-18. See also Airlines; Air travel

Air travel US-3, W-18. See also Airlines; Airports

American Guide Series p. xxi

American Indians. See Indians, American

American Revolution. See Revolutionary War

Amusement parks US-92, US-127

Animals. See Birdwatching; Pets; Zoos

Antiques N-23, NH-4, US-10, VT-7

Arboretums. See Gardens

Archaeology N-34, US-70

Architecture DC-11, DC-20, IL-12, MA-14, MA-19, NY-6, NY-69, NY-70, OR-30, PA-37, RI-4, RI-8, S-18, SC-11, US-24, US-105, p. xix. See also Historic houses

Art. See Museums

Arts events NH-5. See also Theaters

Atlases. See Maps

Automobile travel C-12, CA-32, CA-76, CA-79 to CA-80, CO-5, CO-23, FL-20, IL-20, IN-6, MA-5, MD-11, ME-9, MN-5, MT-10, MT-12, N-4, N-36, NC-11, NJ-5, NM-6, NV-8, NV-18, OH-12, OR-4, S-19, SD-6, TX-5, TX-14, TX-20, US-71, US-83, US-138 to US-139, US-172, US-257 to US-265, UT-10, W-20, W-34, WA-4, WA-21, WA-28 to WA-29, WA-38,

OR-1, PA-8, PA-11, PA-54,
RI-5, S-6, SC-5 to SC-6,
SD-4, TN-4, TX-6, TX-14,
US-117, US-137, US-150,
US-187, US-200, US-227,
US-259, US-269 to US-271,
UT-1, UT-18, VT-7, W-2,
W-9, W-17, W-34, W-37,
W-50, WA-2 to WA-3, WA-21,
WI-11, WI-17, WI-21, WV-5,
pp. 153, 187(2), 222, 250,
254. See also "National/
State Parks/Forests, etc."
section in each state chapter
recreational vehicles US-167,
US-184
Canoeing and kayaking AK-14,
AK-18, AL-1, AZ-18, C-8,
C-10, CT-6, GA-7, ID-3,
IL-4, IL-7, IN-1 to IN-2,
KY-9, MD-6, MD-20, ME-12,
MI-1 to MI-2, MI-7, MN-1,
MN-14, MO-13, MO-15,
MO-18, N-2, N-17, NC-3,
NH-15, NJ-3, NJ-8, NY-20
to NY-21, NY-29, OR-5,
OR-15, PA-34, PA-48, S-3
to S-5, S-17, SM-21, SM-29,
TX-9, TX-18, US-38, US-47,
US-55, US-93, US-100,
US-106, US-130, US-135,
US-162, US-186, US-220,
US-226, UT-11 to UT-12,
UT-23, VA-1, VT-6, W-5,
W-9, W-23 to W-24, W-26,
W-50, W-53 to W-54, WA-7,
WA-27, WI-3 to WI-5, WI-17,
WV-1, WY-7. See also
"Outdoor Recreation Activities"
section in each state chapter
Car rentals HI-22, US-121, US-272
to US-275. See also Automo-
bile travel
Chambers of Commerce SM-28. See
also "Individual Cities or Areas"
section in each state chapter
Charts SM-27, US-224. See also
Maps
Children CA-42, CA-106, CA-114,
CA-133, CA-145, CA-151,

CA-153, CO-31, DC-9, GA-2,
IL-13, LA-14, MA-15, MI-20,
MN-16, MO-21, MS-5, N-5,
N-15, NH-10, NV-1, NY-50,
NY-61, OR-19, PA-38, US-82,
US-257, WA-44 to WA-45,
WI-26. See also Family travel
Civil War PA-16, US-40, VA-8,
WV-7
Climate US-133
Climbing AK-28, C-1, CA-164,
CO-21, NM-6, NY-19,
NY-22, US-47, US-93,
US-130, W-9, W-31, W-50,
W-53, WA-27, WY-4. See
also Hiking
Coastal areas AK-8, C-5, CA-13,
CA-35, CA-37, CA-57,
CA-74, FL-1, HI-5, MA-18,
N-10, NC-6, NC-8, OR-12,
OR-21, SC-6, SC-16,
US-153, VA-10, W-36, WI-12.
See also Surfing
College and university vacations
US-18, US-53
Commercial tours. See Industrial
tours
Country travel. See Back roads and
country travel
Cross-country skiing. See Ski touring
Cruises AK-9, C-16, NY-76,
US-73. See also Ferries
Cruising. See Boating

D

Diabetic traveler US-225
Dining. See Restaurants
Diving CA-57, FL-13, SC-5,
US-47, US-93, US-109,
US-126, US-130, W-9
Dude ranch vacations. See Ranch
vacations

E

Educational vacations US-18, US-53
Elevation guides US-96
Ethnic traveler. See Black-American
traveler; Jewish traveler

Subject Index

Subject Index

WA-1, WA-43, WI-24, WI-27,
WV-4, p. 233
Health foods restaurants. See Restaurants, health foods and
vegetarian
Highway markers. See Historic sites
Highways. See Elevation guides;
Maps; Mileage guides
Highway tours. See Automobile
travel; Back roads and country
travel; Short trips
Hiking AK-13 to AK-14, AK-28,
AR-3, AZ-2, AZ-9, AZ-19,
AZ-22, C-13 to C-14, CA-25
to CA-26, CA-32, CA-38,
CA-54, CA-71, CA-76,
CA-81, CA-87, CA-94 to
CA-95, CA-97, CA-154,
CA-164, CO-9 to CO-10,
CO-12, CO-18, CO-21,
CO-26, CT-4, FL-19, HI-4,
HI-16 to HI-18, IN-6, IN-9,
KY-9, MA-1, MA-9, MA-35,
MD-4, MD-20, ME-1, ME-13,
MI-1, MI-9, MI-16, MN-2,
MO-1, MO-5, MO-18, MT-8
to MT-10, MT-12, N-6,
N-18, N-22, N-40, N-52,
N-54 to N-55, N-59, NC-11
to NC-12, NC-18, NH-8 to
NH-10, NH-15, NM-6, NY-5,
NY-11, NY-13, NY-18,
NY-21, NY-24, NY-29,
OH-9, OR-3, OR-6, OR-10
to OR-11, OR-15, PA-5,
PA-41, PA-49, S-2, S-11,
S-13, S-20, SD-9, SM-21,
TN-7, TX-8, TX-19, US-46
to US-47, US-93, US-100,
US-130, US-145, UT-3, UT-17,
UT-28, VA-7, VA-14, VT-4,
VT-8, W-2, W-9, W-25,
W-31, W-34, W-41 to W-42,
W-50, W-53, WA-14, WA-19
to WA-21, WA-27, WA-33,
WA-35, WA-38 to WA-40,
WI-12, WV-8, WY-1, WY-8
to WY-9, WY-13, pp. 153,
163, 222. See also Backpacking; Climbing; Walking

Historical markers. See Historic sites
Historic houses DE-2, GA-5, LA-1,
MA-4, MA-6, MS-1, N-21,
N-49, NY-6, NY-10, NY-51,
NY-73, NY-90, RI-8, S-18,
SD-4, US-81, US-88. See
also Architecture; Restored areas
Historic sites CA-1, CA-6, CA-140,
CA-162, CO-5, DC-20, FL-3,
FL-8, HI-29, IA-2, ID-1,
IL-1, IL-9, IN-3, KS-1,
KY-3, KY-8 to KY-9, KY-13,
LA-4, MA-6, MA-22, MI-7,
MI-14, MN-3 to MN-4,
MN-12, MO-5, MS-4 to MS-5,
N-21, N-25, N-34, ND-1,
NE-1, NE-3, NH-2, NH-4,
NJ-9, NJ-12, NM-5, NM-14,
NV-18, NY-2, NY-7, NY-22,
NY-29, NY-70, OH-10, OK-4
to OK-5, OR-13, OR-16,
OR-30, PA-2, PA-8, PA-37,
PA-39, PA-50, RI-4, RI-7,
S-1, S-8, SC-10 to SC-11,
SD-1, SM-5, TN-2, TN-4,
TX-4, TX-7, US-29, US-87,
US-105, US-114 to US-115,
US-178, US-201, UT-20,
VA-6, VT-3, VT-7, W-4,
W-7, WA-10, WA-17, WI-1,
WI-12, WI-21, WV-3, WY-3,
pp. xix, 223. See also Archaeology; Civil War; Ghost towns;
Living history exhibits; Restored
areas; Revolutionary War
Homosexual traveler US-91
Horseback riding MI-16, MO-5,
MO-18, VT-7
Horse vacations US-47, US-93,
US-134. See also Pack trips
Hosteling US-12, US-222
Hotels and motels AK-24, AL-4,
AR-4, AZ-16, CA-78, CO-22,
CT-12, DC-27, DE-7, FL-18,
GA-6, HI-22, HI-25, IA-6,
ID-7, IL-2, IL-7, IL-10,
IN-2, IN-7, KS-5, KY-4,
KY-10, LA-5, MA-7, MD-12,
ME-11, MI-15, MN-13,
MO-6, MS-6, MT-6, NC-1,

N

National forests GA-5, ID-3, ID-6,
N-37, US-86, US-100,
US-238, VA-7, WV-8 to WV-9,
p. 164. See also "National/
State Parks/Forests, etc." section
in each state chapter
National monuments. See National
parks
National parks C-15, DC-29, ID-3,
N-37, N-57, N-61, SM-15,
US-1, US-15, US-25, US-74,
US-150, US-173 to US-174,
US-179, US-239, W-10,
W-27, W-30, W-34, W-47,
W-58 to W-59, W-61, WA-10.
See also "National/State Parks/
Forests, etc." section in each
state chapter
Natural areas CT-3, IA-2, IL-14,
MI-11, N-27, N-37, NC-10,
TX-6, US-230, W-34, W-39,
WA-10. See also Wildlife
sanctuaries and refuges
Negro traveler. See Black-American
traveler
Nudist traveler US-119

O

Observatories US-98
Older traveler ME-6, TN-10,
US-219, VA-18, VA-22,
WI-27
One-day trips. See Short trips
Outdoor areas. See National forests;
National parks; Natural areas
Outdoor recreation AZ-6, C-15,
CA-69, CO-3, CO-18 to
CO-19, CT-3, ID-3, ID-6,
IL-7, IN-6, KY-5, LA-4,
ME-12, MS-3, N-26, NC-11,
NC-13, NE-3, NY-12, OH-1
to OH-2, PA-12, PA-15,
PA-34, SM-19, SM-24, US-51,
US-100, US-204, US-216,
W-9, WA-10, WA-24, WA-29.
See also Adventure travel;
specific types of activities;

"Outdoor Recreation Activities,"
"State Parks/Forests, etc."
section in each state chapter

P

Pack trips SD-4, US-47, US-93.
See also Horse vacations
Parks. See National parks; Natural
areas; State parks
Pets US-166
Planning. See Travel planning
Plant tours. See Industrial tours
Presidents and their homes US-81
Primitive areas. See Natural areas
Public facilities. See Restrooms

R

Races and marathons. See Running
Radio assistance S-19, p. xxii
Radio stations US-128
Rafting. See Canoeing and kayaking
Railroads. See Train travel
Ranch vacations AZ-15, CO-20,
MT-4, OR-20, SD-4, US-48,
W-43, W-56, WY-4
Recreation. See Outdoor recreation
Recreational vehicle camping. See
Camping, recreational vehicles
Refuges, wildlife. See Wildlife
sanctuaries and refuges
Religious landmarks US-105, US-181
Rentals. See Car rentals; House-
keeping cottages
Resorts OH-17, US-97, US-148,
W-3, W-43, WY-4
Restaurants AZ-27, AZ-30, CA-15
to CA-16, CA-31, CA-44 to
CA-46, CA-63 to CA-65,
CA-104, CA-107, CA-152 to
CA-153, CA-155 to CA-156,
DC-8, DC-17, DC-25, FL-14,
FL-37, GA-6, HI-33, ID-7,
IL-17 to IL-18, IL-21, KY-4,
LA-9 to LA-11, MA-23 to
MA-24, MI-7, MN-9, NH-4,
NY-41, NY-46, NY-54 to
NY-55, NY-64, OR-32, PA-9,
PA-15, PA-25, PA-43, TX-1,

Subject Index

US-143, US-159, US-172, US-213, US-227, VT-9, W-1, W-21, WI-17
health foods and vegetarian US-45
Restored areas   CT-16 to CT-17, US-4, US-13, US-39, US-79, US-142, VA-24 to VA-25. See also Historic houses; Historic sites
Restrooms NY-59, PA-42
Revolutionary War MA-3, MD-3, N-1, N-21, NC-7, NY-7 to NY-8, PA-7, PA-18 to PA-19, S-1, US-21, US-157, US-239. See also Historic sites
River running. See Canoeing and kayaking
Roads. See Automobile travel; Back roads and country travel; Elevation guides; Maps; Mileage guides
Rockhounding AZ-15, CA-76, CO-3, CO-5, ID-6, MS-3, NV-6, OR-20, SD-4
Ruins. See Archaeology; Ghost towns
Running US-43, US-149
RV camping. See Camping, recreational vehicles

S

Sailing. See Boating
Sanctuaries, wildlife. See Wildlife sanctuaries and refuges
Scuba diving. See Diving
Seacoasts. See Coastal areas; Diving; Surfing
Senior citizens. See Older traveler
Servicemen US-29, US-160
Ships, historic US-78
Short trips C-12, CA-19, CA-39, CA-55, DC-16, FL-11, IA-3, IL-8, IN-5 to IN-6, KY-7, KY-9, MI-10, MN-11, MT-5, N-5, N-32, N-36, N-38, NC-13, NM-2, NM-7, NY-7, OH-4, PA-1, PA-3, TX-3, US-41, WI-17
Skiing C-17, CA-100, CO-2 to CO-5, CO-23, IA-3, ID-3, ID-6, ID-11, IL-7, KY-5, ME-9, MI-9, N-26, N-35, NH-10, NY-11, PA-54, US-54, US-57, US-94, US-240, VT-2, W-9, W-28, W-53, WA-27, WI-11, p. 187. See also Ski touring; "Outdoor Recreation Activities" section in each state chapter
Skin diving. See Diving
Ski touring AK-30, CA-2, CA-111, CO-15 to CO-16, CO-21, ME-9, MI-3, N-47, N-52, NH-15, OR-14, US-36, US-47, US-93, US-130, US-152, US-231, UT-17, W-28, WI-13. See also Skiing; "Outdoor Recreation Activities" section in each state chapter
Snowmobiling C-9, IL-7, ME-9, MI-9, NY-25, US-47. See also "Outdoor Recreation Activities" section in each state chapter
Snowshoeing WA-27
Spas CA-10, ID-6
State parks C-15, CA-23, IL-7, IN-2 to IN-3, KY-9, LA-4, MA-1, MI-1, MI-6 to MI-7, MI-11, MO-5, MS-5, N-37, NC-13, OK-5, SC-6, TN-4, TX-6, UT-10, VT-7, W-34, WA-24. See also "National/ State Parks/Forests, etc." section in each state chapter
Student traveler US-5, US-180
Surfing CA-29, HI-20

T

Taverns. See Bars; Inns and taverns
Telephone directories. See Toll-free telephone directories
Tennis HI-22, MO-18, MS-5, N-26, NV-17, SC-6, US-30, US-170, US-175, VT-7, W-3
Theaters DC-10, KY-4, N-19, NY-66
Theme parks. See Amusement parks
Toll-free telephone directories US-165, US-171

GEOGRAPHIC INDEX

Geographic Index

Cape Hatteras and Outer Banks NC-6, NC-20 to NC-21

Cape May NJ-17, NJ-19 to NJ-20

Captiva Island FL-1

Carlsbad Caverns National Park NM-10

Carmel CA-31, CA-40, CA-121, CA-159, US-193

Carson City NV-10

Cascades area CA-75, OR-11, WA-12, WA-19 to WA-21, WA-29. See also North Cascades National Park

Catskills NY-29 to NY-31

Central region (US) pp. 94-97, US-56, US-63, US-112, US-251, W-33

Champaign/Urbana IL-2

Charleston (SC) SC-8 to SC-13

Charleston (WV) WV-11

Chesapeake and Ohio Canal National Historical Park MD-1, MD-4

Chesapeake Bay MD-8 to MD-10, PA-32

Cheyenne WY-19

Chicago IL-2, IL-11 to IL-24, US-193, US-196, US-198, US-259

Chincoteague National Wildlife Refuge MD-13, VA-10 to VA-12

Cincinnati KY-1, OH-13 to OH-16, US-193, US-198

Cleveland OH-17 to OH-20, US-198

Colonial National Historical Park VA-13

Colorado pp. 181-90, TX-9, W-2, W-5, W-11, W-16, W-17, W-24, W-27, W-46, W-49, W-53, W-57, p. 158

Colorado River AZ-10, AZ-18

Columbia SC-14

Columbus OH-21 to OH-23, US-193

Concord NH-7

Connecticut pp. 191-95, N-5, N-7, N-15, N-31 to N-32, N-52, N-55, NY-5 to NY-6, NY-42, NY-55

Continental Divide Trail W-41

Crater Lake National Park OR-24 to OR-26, W-30

Craters of the Moon National Monument W-30

D

Dallas TX-3, TX-25 to TX-27, US-193, US-196, US-198

Death Valley National Monument CA-49, CA-81 to CA-83, NV-14, W-49

Delaware pp. 196-98, N-4, N-16, N-18, N-31, N-38, N-46, PA-32, PA-35, PA-40

Delaware River PA-34

Denver CO-30 to CO-33, US-196, US-198

Des Moines IA-7 to IA-8

Detroit MI-4, MI-18 to MI-21, US-193, US-198

Dinosaur National Monument CO-24, UT-11, W-5

Disneyland. See Anaheim/Orange County/Disneyland

Disney World. See Walt Disney World

District of Columbia pp. 199-206, MD-1, MD-4, N-29, N-61, NY-66, S-11, US-196, US-198, US-259

Dover DE-9

E

Estes Park CO-29

Everglades National Park FL-22 to FL-23

F

Fairbanks AK-26, AK-33 to AK-34

Finger Lakes area N-52, NY-32

Fire Island National Seashore NY-15

Florida pp. 207-19, S-19

Florida Keys. See Keys/Key West

Fort Worth TX-26, TX-28, US-193, US-196, US-198

Frankfort KY-12

Fresno p. 153

G

Gateway National Recreation Area NY-16

Georgetown DC-20

Georgia pp. 220-24, N-55, S-19

Geographic Index

Lake Michigan. See Great Lakes
Lake Ontario. See Great Lakes
Lake Powell AZ-10, UT-23, UT-26, p. 452
Lake Superior. See Great Lakes
Lake Tahoe CA-31, CA-38 to CA-39, CA-67, CA-99 to CA-101 CA-159, NV-6, p. 153
Lancaster County PA-22, PA-24, PA-26, PA-28, PA-30, PA-35
Land between the Lakes S-21
Lansing MI-4, MI-22, MI-23
Lassen Volcanic National Park CA-38, CA-67, CA-75, CA-86
Las Vegas CA-3, NV-6, NV-11 to NV-17, US-196, W-49
Lava Beds National Monument OR-25, W-30
Lewis and Clark Trail W-22
Lincoln NE-5 to NE-7
Little Rock AR-8
Long Island N-32, NY-35 to NY-39, NY-42, NY-53, NY-55, NY-64
Long Trail VT-4
Los Angeles CA-46 to CA-47, CA-102 to CA-117, US-193, US-196, US-198, US-259
Louisiana pp. 263-68, S-18
Louisville KY-13 to KY-15

M

Mackinac Island MI-24
McKinley, Mount. See Mount McKinley National Park
Madison US-196, WI-9, WI-24 to WI-25
Maine pp. 269-73, N-13, N-52, N-55
Mammoth Cave National Park KY-11
Marin County CA-162, p. 179
Martha's Vineyard MA-27, MA-33, MA-36, MA-40
Maryland pp. 274-79, DC-3, DC-6, DE-5, N-4, N-16, N-18, N-38, N-46, N-55, PA-32, PA-49, S-5, S-10 to S-11, S-16
Massachusetts pp. 280-90, N-1, N-7, N-13, N-52, N-55, NY-5, RI-1

Maui HI-18
Mendocino CA-67
Mesa Verde National Park CO-25, CO-27
Miami/Miami Beach FL-35 to FL-40, US-193, US-196, US-198, US-259
Michigan pp. 291-98, C-1, C-8 to C-10, C-13, IN-10, WI-13
Milwaukee US-196, WI-26 to WI-28
Minneapolis C-6, MN-15 to MN-19, US-196, US-198
Minnesota pp. 299-305, C-1, C-8 to C-10, C-13, CA-71
Mississippi pp. 306-9, S-18
Mississippi River C-2, C-4, C-6, C-11, C-16, LA-12, p. 253
Missouri pp. 310-16, C-13
Mojave Desert CA-49, CA-59
Monongahela National Forest WV-8 to WV-10
Montana pp. 317-22, C-18, W-2, W-9, W-13, W-24, W-31, W-60
Monterey CA-31, CA-40, CA-121 to CA-122, CA-159, US-193, US-196
Montgomery AL-6 to AL-7
Montpelier p. 458
Mother Lode country CA-31, CA-33 to CA-34, CA-39 to CA-40, CA-73
Mount McKinley National Park AK-26 to AK-29
Mount Rainier National Park W-30, WA-8, WA-10, WA-21, WA-29, WA-32 to WA-34
Mount Rushmore National Memorial SD-8 to SD-10
Myrtle Beach SC-16 to SC-17
Mystic CT-16 to CT-18

N

Nantucket MA-28, MA-33 to MA-34, MA-41
Napa Valley CA-31, CA-39, CA-41, CA-123 to CA-127, CA-146, CA-159
Nashville TN-10 to TN-12, US-193
Natchez MS-7 to MS-9
Nebraska pp. 323-26, C-18, W-13

Geographic Index

ORGANIZATION INDEX

A

Acadia National Park ME-14
Adirondack Association, The NY-22
Adirondack Attractions Association NY-23
Adirondack Mountain Club NY-24
ALA Auto and Travel Club US-257
Alabama Bureau of Publicity and Information AL-3, pp. 111, 113
Alabama Hotel and Motel Association AL-4
Alabama Power Co. p. 111
Alabama Travel Council AL-5
Alaska Airlines AK-23
Alaska Hotel/Motel Association AK-24
Alaska Magazine Travel Service AK-1
Alaska Marine Highway System AK-25
Alaska Railroad AK-26
Alaska State Division of Tourism AK-22
Albany Area Chamber of Commerce NY-28
Allegheny Airlines US-243
Allstate Motor Club US-258
Aloha Airlines HI-23
Amana Colonies Travel Council IA-4
American Adventurers Association, The US-93, US-190, US-218
American Airlines US-244
American Association of Retired Persons US-219

American Automobile Association US-259
American Canoe Association US-220
American Indian Travel Commission US-221
American Society of Travel Agents TI-26
American Youth Hostels US-222
Amtrak Travel Center US-291
Anaheim Area Visitor & Convention Bureau CA-118
Anchorage Chamber of Commerce AK-31
Anchorage Convention/Visitors Bureau AK-32
Appalachian Mountain Club N-54
Appalachian Trail Conference, The N-55
Arches National Park UT-21
Arizona Hotel & Motel Association AZ-16
Arizona Office of Tourism AZ-15, AZ-22, p. 127
Arkansas Dept. of Parks and Tourism AR-3, pp. 136, 138, 139
Arkansas Innkeepers Association AR-4
Assateague Island National Seashore MD-13
Association of Retail Travel Agents TI-27
Atlanta Chamber of Commerce GA-13
Atlanta Convention & Visitors Bureau GA-14
Atlantic City Visitors Bureau NJ-16

Hot Springs National Park AR-6
Hot Springs Visitor & Convention
  Bureau AR-7
Howard Johnson's US-282
Hudson River Valley Association
  NY-34
Hughes Airwest US-249
Hyatt International Hotels US-283

I

Idaho Division of Tourism &
  Industrial Development ID-6,
  pp. 235, 236(2), 237
Idaho Innkeepers Association ID-7
Idaho Outfitters and Guides Associa-
  tion ID-8
Illinois Adventure Center IL-9
Illinois Hotel & Motel Association
  IL-10
Illinois Office of Tourism IL-9,
  pp. 240, 241, 242(3),
Imperial "400" Motels US-284
Independence National Historical
  Park PA-18
Indiana Dunes National Lakeshore
  IN-11
Indiana Hotel & Motel Association
  IN-7
Indianapolis Chamber of Commerce
  IN-14
Indianapolis Convention and Visitors
  Bureau p. 251
Indiana Tourism Development Division
  IN-6, p. 248
International Visitors Service Council
  of Greater Washington Organiza-
  tions DC-28
Iowa Hotel & Motel Association IA-6
Iowa Travel Development Division
  IA-3, pp. 252, 253(2)
Isle Royale National Park MI-17

J

Jackson Chamber of Commerce MS-11
Jackson Hole Chamber of Commerce
  WY-12
Jacksonville Beaches Area Chamber
  of Commerce FL-28

Jefferson City Area Chamber of Com-
  merce and Convention and Visitors
  Committee MO-7
Jellystone Campgrounds US-269
Jersey Cape Vacations NJ-20
Juneau Chamber of Commerce AK-35

K

Kampgrounds of America US-270
Kansas Hotel & Motel Association
  KS-5
Kansas Tourist & Tourism Division
  KS-4, pp. 255, 256
Kennebec Valley Chamber of
  Commerce ME-16
Kentucky Division of Travel and
  Tourism KY-9, pp. 259, 260-61
Kentucky Hotel & Motel Association
  KY-10
Ketchum-Sun Valley Chamber of Com-
  merce ID-10

L

Lake Mead National Recreation Area
  NV-9
Lake of the Ozarks Association
  MO-14
Lansing Regional Chamber of Commerce
  MI-23
Lassen Volcanic National Park CA-86
Las Vegas Convention/Visitors
  Authority NV-17
Lincoln Chamber of Commerce NE-6
Little Rock Bureau for Conventions
  and Visitors AR-8
Long Island Association of Commerce
  & Industry NY-39
Louisiana Hotel-Motel Association
  LA-5
Louisiana Tourist Development
  Commission LA-4, p. 266
Louisiana Travel Promotion Association
  LA-6
Louisville Visitors Bureau KY-15

M

Mackinac Island Chamber of Commerce
  MI-24

571

PUBLISHER INDEX

Publisher Index

Ref.   Post, Joyce A.
E   Travel in the United States : a
169.02Z   guide to information sources / Joyce
Z99   Post, Jeremiah Post. -- Detroit, MI :
P85   Gale Research Co., c1981.
                xxii, 578 p. ; 22 cm. -- (Geography
            and travel information guide series ;
            v. 3) (Gale information guide
            library.)

                Includes indexes.
                ISBN 0-8103-1423-1

1. United States--Description and travel--1960-
--Bibliography.   2. Tourist trade--United
States--Bibliography.   I. Post, Jeremiah
Benjamin, 1937-   II. Title.

MUNION ME   821116   821112 CStoC
C000512   KW /JW   A*   82-B9909
                                 81-4375